Conflict, Identity, and Reform in the Muslim World

Conflict, Identity, and Reform in the Muslim World

Challenges for U.S. Engagement

Daniel Brumberg *and*
Dina Shehata, *editors*

UNITED STATES INSTITUTE OF PEACE PRESS
WASHINGTON, D.C.

The views expressed in this book are those of the authors alone. They do not necessarily reflect views of the United States Institute of Peace.

UNITED STATES INSTITUTE OF PEACE
1200 17th Street NW, Suite 200
Washington, DC 20036-3011
www.usip.org

First published 2009

Printed in the United States of America

The paper used in this publication meets the minimum requirements of American National Standards for Information Science—Permanence of Paper for Printed Library Materials, ANSI Z39.48-1984.

Library of Congress Cataloging-in-Publication Data

Conflict, identity, and reform in the Muslim world : challenges for U.S. engagement / Daniel Brumberg and Dina Shehata, editors.
p. cm.
ISBN 978-1-60127-020-7 (pbk. : alk. paper)
1. Islamic countries—Politics and government—21st century. 2. Social conflict—Islamic countries. 3. Social change—Islamic countries. 4. Group identity—Islamic countries. 5. Islam and politics—Islamic countries. 6. United States—Foreign relations—Islamic countries. 7. Islamic countries—Foreign relations—United States. I. Brumberg, Daniel. II. Shehata, Dina.
JQ1852.A58C66 2009
320.917'67—dc22

2009012839

Contents

Part III: Fixing Politics? Power Sharing and Political Reform

Letter from the President of the United States Institute of Peace

In the aftermath of the September 11 terrorist attacks, the Institute launched the Muslim World Initiative to address the vital foreign policy and national security challenges associated with the many and diverse Islamic societies around the globe. Over the years we have focused on three cross-cutting themes: how to mobilize moderate leaders and publics, how to marginalize militants and extremist elements, and how to bridge the divide between the United States and the Muslim world. Through our education, training, and centers of innovation, which include programs on religion and peacemaking and promotion of the rule of law, we are building networks of moderate leaders and countering extremism by creating programs that foster civil society. One of the fruits of this initiative is this volume, *Conflict, Identity, and Reform in the Muslim World: Challenges for U.S. Engagement.*

I want to recognize the editors of this book, Daniel Brumberg and Dina Shehata, for their efforts in compiling the writings of a talented international group of authors, for the astute judgment they have brought to this project, and for their work in framing the analysis presented here. The events of recent years underscore the need for sound scholarship and analysis to inform policymakers and identify best practices in the field. I also want to express my appreciation to Abiodun Williams, vice president for our Center for Conflict Analysis and Prevention, for overseeing this project.

The United States needs to muster all of its natural talent as we seek a deeper appreciation of the diverse countries, cultures, and peoples that make up the Muslim world. We need detailed comprehension of the roles of media, religion, justice systems, and education in advancing tolerance and nonviolent approaches to dealing with sources of conflict. The United States Institute of Peace is committed to playing an active role in diminishing the sources of mistrust and misunderstanding that lead to political violence. I believe this volume will enhance understanding and inform better policymaking.

Richard H. Solomon

Preface

This volume, *Conflict, Identity, and Reform in the Muslim World: Challenges for U.S. Engagement*, echoes all of the Muslim World Initiative's themes but approaches them in a unique manner. It evaluates the evolution of U.S.-Muslim relations in the context of conflicts within the Muslim world over identity, society, ideology, and politics. These conflicts escalated after the attacks of September 11, 2001, and especially after the invasion of Iraq. U.S.-Muslim relations became entangled in them, as did efforts to promote political reform and democracy.

Although this volume was not specifically designed as a policy blueprint, it offers important lessons and insights for the U.S. administration, elucidating the complex interplay of U.S.-Muslim relations and conflicts within the Muslim world. These insights apply not only to Iraq, but more broadly to the Middle East, South Asia, and Southeast Asia.

First, the West in general and the United States in particular seek engagement with the Muslim world to enhance peacemaking within states and to advance regional peacemaking between states. But one cannot engage a single country's peoples, movements, parties, or governments without affecting its neighbors. As the Obama administration pledges new resources to enhance security and peacemaking in the Middle East and South Asia, it will have to grapple with overlapping domestic and regional conflicts.

Second, the United States' plans to advance reform, human rights, and governance in three countries of particular interest—Iraq, Afghanistan, and Pakistan—will affect the broader region for years to come.

Third, it is not the case, as the conventional wisdom would have it, that the key issue in the U.S.-Muslim world relationship is Islam, or the Islamic faith. The book focuses on a multitude of identities—Islamic, secular, ethnic, ideological—that frame political action and conflict in the "Muslim world." This elucidation of the multiplicity and elasticity of identities offers an important cautionary tale for the current administration as it tries to chart a new course.

Conflict, Identity, and Reform in the Muslim World: Challenges for U.S. Engagement is the most recent title in a growing list of important and influential publications on peace and conflict in the Muslim world produced by the U.S. Institute of Peace. The Institute's experts, grantees, and fellows have published more than ninety books, reports, and articles on this important subject, and a small percentage of these reports are included in this volume. Among recent books are three in the Pivotal States series—*Iran's Long Reach* by Suzanne Maloney, *Faith and Politics in Nigeria* by

John N. Paden, and *The New Turkish Republic* by Graham E. Fuller—as well as *Negotiating with Iran: Wrestling the Ghosts of History* by John W. Limbert and *The Future of Afghanistan*, edited by J Alexander Thier.

Abiodun Williams

Introduction

Daniel Brumberg and *Dina Shehata*

The United States Institute of Peace (USIP) is an unusual organization in many ways. A research institute that promotes scholarship on peacemaking and conflict resolution, it also has an activist and advocacy mission to advance local, regional and global solutions to a vast range of conflicts, and where possible, to create mechanisms to prevent such disputes from exploding in the first place. Created by Congress in 1984 and publicly funded, it is nevertheless an independent institution that provides analyses and recommendations that often challenge the premises or direction of U.S. foreign policy. Academics, policy makers within and outside the U.S. government, and non-governmental organization (NGO) activists on a global level look to USIP for a distinctive combination of analytical objectivity and passionate commitment to the principle that conflicts ultimately must be resolved on the terrain of social and political action.[1]

With the attacks of September 11, 2001, and the 2003 invasion of Iraq, USIP faced the task of pursuing its mission in a global context of escalating security threats. With the U.S.-led struggle against terrorism and insurgency often overshadowing diplomacy, dialogue, or negotiation, many Muslims concluded that U.S. efforts to reach out to the Muslim world were a smokescreen for the use of force. However exaggerated or unwarranted, such suspicions complicated efforts to advance a vision that spoke credibly to the two conflict arenas that USIP sought to address after September 11: conflicts within and between Muslim states and societies, and conflicts between the United States and that diverse range of states and societies that, for want of a better term, we call the Muslim world.

Seeking to illuminate the two arenas of conflict, USIP supported dialogue and track-two meetings that brought American academics, policymakers, and NGO activists together with their counterparts from Iraq, Iran, Egypt, Morocco, Yemen, Jordan, Sudan, Nigeria, and elsewhere. At the same time, it promoted innovative research on religious and political

1. For an overview of USIP's history and programs, see Corine Hegland, "Foreign Affairs: Peace Work," *National Journal Magazine*, April 26, 2008, pp. 33–44, available at http://www.nationaljournal.com/njmagazine/fa_20080426_5541.php.

conflicts in the Middle East and beyond. USIP's fieldwork in Iraq, Yemen, Afghanistan, the Balkans, Indonesia, and Nigeria demonstrates its grassroots commitment to peacemaking[2] while USIP's support of high-profile, bipartisan analyses, such as the *Iraq Study Group Report,* has helped to redefine some of the contours of U.S. Middle East policy.[3] In the past seven years, these and other efforts have produced a wealth of books, reports, and studies. As their full depth and scope cannot be conveyed in a single volume, this book highlights a complex issue that has received scant attention in policy and academic circles: the analytical and policy challenges that escalating identity conflicts within Muslim-majority states pose both the Muslim world and the West.

This focus on Muslim-world conflicts is not meant to downplay the vital task of addressing the breach between the United States and the Muslim world. U.S.–Muslim-world relations continue to suffer, though less from an existential clash of civilizations[4] and far more from basic disagreements over daunting foreign policy questions, such as the Israeli-Palestinian conflict, the legitimacy of using violence for political ends, or conflicting perceptions of the credibility and ultimate purpose behind the U.S. push for democratic reforms.[5] In the years after September 11, these and other issues created a shared antipathy toward the United States; magnified by globalized communications, this resentment dominated policy debates in the capitals of the West and the Muslim world. But the 2003 toppling of Saddam Hussein took the lid off simmering sectarian, religious, and ideological tensions between Christian and Muslims, Muslims and ethnics Kurds, and most of all, between Shi'ites and Sunnis. Though rooted in Iraq's historical experience, these tensions echoed in many quarters of the Muslim world. Across the Middle East, sectarian conflicts between Shi'ites and Sunnis in Kuwait, Bahrain, and Saudi Arabia; ethnic tensions between Berbers and

---

2. Seven USIP centers or programs have supported or organized conflict resolution studies or grassroots initiatives in the Muslim world. The Center for Mediation and Conflict Resolution (http://www.usip.org/mediation/index.html) has been active in Kashmir, Darfur, Nigeria, and Israel/Palestine. The Religion and Peacemaking Program (http://www.usip.org/religionpeace/index.html) has been active in Iran, Pakistan, Afghanistan, and Iraq. The Center for Conflict Analysis's Muslim World Initiative (http://www.usip.org/muslimworld/index.html) has focused its energies on the Arab world. The Education and Training Center (http://www.usip.org/training/onsite) has been active in Iraq, Sudan, Pakistan, Afghanistan, Palestine-Israel, and the Balkans. The Center for Post-Conflict, Peace, and Stability Operations (http://www.usip.org/peaceops/index.html) has an extensive Iraq program as well as projects in Afghanistan and Sudan. USIP's Rule of Law program (http://www.usip.org/ruleoflaw/index.html) has been active in Afghanistan and Iraq. Finally, the Grants and Fellowship Program (http://www.usip.org/gf.html) has supported a wide variety of research on political and social change in the Muslim world and on U.S.-Muslim relations.

3. The *Iraq Study Group Report* can be found at http://www.usip.org/isg/index.html.

4. See Samuel P. Huntington, "The Clash of Civilizations?" *Foreign Affairs*, vol. 72, no. 3 (Summer 1993), pp. 22–49.

5. See Shibley Telhami, *Reflections of Hearts And Minds: Media, Opinion, and Identity in the Arab World* (Washington, DC: Brookings Institution, 2007).

Sunni Arabs in Algeria and Morocco and between Kurds and Turkish nationals; and ideological tensions between Islamists and non-Islamists all intensified.[6] In South Asia, tensions mounted among Pashtuns, Tajiks, and Hazaras, particularly after the 2002 downfall of the Taliban and the ensuing bid to build a democratic polity in Afghanistan. In neighboring Pakistan, ethnic conflicts between Pashtuns on one side and Sindhis, Balochs, Pathans, and Hazaras on the other worsened in tandem with ideological disputes between Islamists and non-Islamists and sectarian conflicts between Sunnis and Shi'ites.[7]

As such tensions grew, the problem of dissension, or *fitna,* sometimes seemed to eclipse the issue of Muslim-U.S. relations.[8] Yet rather than disappearing, Muslim-U.S. disputes became entangled in the prevailing identity conflicts. The Iraq gambit placed the United States at the center of a violent internal power struggle; Washington's subsequent efforts to promote power sharing in Afghanistan and to prod Middle East leaders to democratize drew the United States into a wider maze of religious, ethnic, and ideological disputes. Thus policy makers and activists in the United States, Europe, and the Muslim world today face a growing challenge: how to prevent disputes that are now woven into the fabric of Western-Muslim relations from splintering entire political communities. Can Western governments and NGOs help rival parties in the Muslim world forge democratic, power-sharing solutions that promote domestic peace and reconciliation? Or will such efforts only exacerbate identity conflicts in ways that widen the U.S.-Muslim or Western-Muslim divide?

This book addresses these and other related questions by highlighting insights from a talented group of international scholar-activists. Many are independent analysts who bring a diverse range of normative, analytical, and disciplinary interests to their work. But this diversity of perspective is equally true of contributors from USIP: Far from articulating some impos-

---

6. See Ellen Knickmeyer, "Sectarian Strife in Iraq Imperils Entire Region, Analysts Warn," *Washington Post,* November 16, 2006, p. A1. For a broader view of the Islamic World's chief sectarian schism, see Vali Nasr, *The Shia Revival: How Conflicts within Islam Will Shape the Future* (New York: Norton, 2006). While recognizing the importance of ethnoreligious conflict in the Middle East, we join Eric Davis in warning against the "conclusion that the region's instability and violence are a function of a defective political culture." Sectarian conflicts are rooted in many factors, including the dynamics of state and nation building as well as the instrumentalization of confessional identifies by regimes, oppositions, and foreign powers. The use and abuse of identity cleavages is a major theme in this book. On this critical topic, also see Eric Davis, "A Sectarian Middle East?" *International Journal of Middle East Studies,* vol. 40, no. 4 (November 2009), pp. 555–558.

7. For a critical view of the argument that Pakistani society is fractured along ethnoreligious lines, see Arif Rafiq, "Like a Broken Record: Selig Harrison on Ethnic Discord in Pakistan," The Pakistan Policy Blog, available at http://pakistanpolicy.com/2008/02/01/like-a-broken-record-selig-harrison-on-ethnic-discord-in-pakistan/.

8. See Gilles Kepel, *The War for Muslim Minds: Islam and the West* (Cambridge, MA: Harvard University Press, 2004).

sible or unwelcome consensus, their essays reflect the contending analyses and views that are central to the institute's work. Our goal is to reflect this pluralism while identifying points of convergence and difference that together suggest innovative ways to address the interwoven arenas of U.S.-Muslim relations and Muslim-world democratic conflict resolution.

This book is divided into six parts. Part one introduces a question that once had largely concerned scholars but now preoccupies policy makers as well: Does the future of the diverse societies that constitute the Muslim world hinge on an elemental reinterpretation of Islamic ideals—in effect, a renewal or reformation of Islamic thought? Or does it largely depend on the pragmatic exigencies of political and institutional reform? Because the debate between renewal and reform frames many of the issues explored in the subsequent chapters of this book, we carefully delineate its main contours while also highlighting the grand debate's policy implications for scholars and activists seeking to promote more democratic conflict resolution in the Muslim world.

Part two and part three use the renewal-reform debate to explore the complex link between identity conflicts and political reform in Muslim majority polities. When Washington proclaimed its Freedom Agenda in 2003, more than a few U.S. policy makers and media pundits argued that political reform might very well alleviate such identity conflicts.[9] However, such expectations suggested a lack of a familiarity with a fundamental paradox of democratic reform in societies deeply divided by ethnic and religious cleavages: as Arend Lijphart and other scholars have long argued, because elections raise the prospect that one group might use the ballot to impose its religious or ideological agenda on others, political reform can sometimes heighten tensions among competing identity groups.[10] While this democratic paradox is dramatically manifest in the conflicts between Shiites and Sunnis in Iraq, it has emerged in less dramatic but equally important forms in corners of the Middle East and South Asia, particularly when Islamist electoral gains have provoked the fears of their non-Islamist rivals.[11]

---

9. *New York Times* columnist Thomas Friedman was perhaps the most vocal pundit making the democratic case for Iraq. See his "Four Reasons to Invade Iraq," in *Slate's* forum, "Liberal Hawks Reconsider the Iraq War," http://www.slate.com/id/2093620/entry/2093763/. The optimistic case for Iraq was made most cogently by Adeed I. Dawisha and Karin Dawisha in "How to Build a Democratic Iraq," *Foreign Affairs*, vol. 82, no. 3 (May–June 2003), pp. 36–50.

10. Arend Lijphart, *Democracy in Plural Societies* (New Haven, CT: Yale University Press, 1977). See also Larry Diamond and Marc Plattner, eds., *Nationalism, Ethnic Conflict, and Democracy* (Baltimore and London: Johns Hopkins University Press, 1994).

11. The term *non-Islamist* is preferred to *secular*, as the latter term is far too narrow for this reader's purposes. The term *non-Islamists* includes secularists, but it also refers to traditional or even orthodox Muslims who favor distancing mosque and state, as well as to Sufi Muslims, who seek to protect their mystical practices by opposing efforts to politicize Islam. That said, when the identity divide pivots around an Islamist-secular cleavage, we use the terms *Islamist* and *secular* to capture it.

This book's contributors analyze the prospects for mitigating identity conflicts through two different though potentially complementary analytical angles. Part two employs a culturalist lens to highlight the interpretive struggle among Muslim intellectuals to reshape Islamic ideas. Part three employs a political-institutional lens to explore efforts to forge political accommodations that cut across sectarian or Islamist–non-Islamist divides.

The next two parts of the volume explore prospects for narrowing the U.S.-Muslim divide in ways that facilitate democratic conflict resolution in the Middle East and the wider Muslim world. Part four highlights efforts to narrow the cultural and religious chasms between the United States and the Muslim world. The contributors—some of whom have worked on the problem directly as conflict mediators—emphasize the positive role that religious leaders have played in tackling this difficult challenge. Part five explores U.S. and European efforts to engage mainstream Islamist activists and, more ambitiously, to help Islamists and their non-Islamist rivals forge a common vision of political reform.

The conclusion argues that conflict resolution in the Muslim world is unlikely to succeed without a concerted effort to strengthen the architecture of peacemaking and security in the Middle East and South Asia. This architecture must include—and yet move far beyond—the challenge of actively advancing a comprehensive Arab-Israeli peace. As the United States and its Western allies look ahead to the second decade of the millennium, their wider task is to forge a multifaceted Muslim-world diplomatic strategy that advances dialogue with friends of the United States, such as Turkey, as well as with rivals, such as the Islamic Republic of Iran and even Afghanistan's Taliban. A bold strategy of engagement, pursued by a new administration in Washington in concert with European allies, might reinforce the political leverage of moderates, enhancing the prospects for genuine and sustainable political reform in the Middle East and the wider Muslim world.

The Grand Debate: Islamic Renewal or Political Reform?

What are the obstacles to and opportunities for creating new avenues of U.S.-Muslim world engagement and cooperation? Are the barriers and openings rooted in a long enduring cultural or religious divide? Or are they of more recent ideological and political vintage and thus susceptible to a dynamic of political, legal, or institutional engineering, a dynamic that might eventually navigate beyond—or even transform—the supposed impediments of culture or religion?

In the wake of the violence and fears generated by the terrorist attacks of September 11, 2001, the above questions were hotly debated in Washington and beyond, first by scholars and eventually by policymakers, political activists, journalists, and media pundits. The shift to a wider public policy debate occurred in tandem with, and in response to, the Bush administration's bold decision to make Middle East democracy promotion a top U.S. foreign policy. Henceforth, at stake was not simply an issue of academic analysis; more fundamentally at play were the contrasting policy prescriptions that flowed from what we call the Grand Debate over Islam, democracy, and U.S. foreign policy.[12] Complex, multifaceted, and often contentious, two camps—the Islamic renewalists and the institutional reformists—defined the main contours of this debate.

Abdeslam Maghraoui articulates the Islamic renewalist position. A Moroccan-American scholar and former director of USIP's Muslim World Initiative, his article is informed by an implicit and crucial assumption, namely that the Muslim world and the West are not separated by a static cultural divide, but rather by their very different developmental paths. The West benefited from the separation or distancing of church and state, while the Muslim world suffered from the reinvigoration of the bonds between politics and religion. Yet, Maghraoui suggests, the failure of the Muslim world to experience its own Reformation was a product of social and political conditions rather than a consequence of any logic intrinsic to the Islamic faith itself. There is no reason why Islamic values cannot be worked to legitimate a modern or pluralistic vision of politics; inasmuch as an *ijtihad,* or independent interpretation, provides a method for advancing such a project while still remaining authentic to Islam, hopes for political reform in the Middle East hinge—first and foremost—on a transformation of Islamic thought.

Maghraoui acknowledges that the "battle . . . over the soul of Islam" faces many obstacles. He warns against the simplistic idea that Muslim thinkers can or should emulate the historically unique experience of the Protestant Reformation. Yet in a strong echo of the modernist Islamic tradition—to which he clearly subscribes—Maghraoui suggests that within Islam there is a wide symbolic field for a reinterpretive enterprise that could produce a de facto Muslim Reformation. The question is who should pursue this mission and how it should be achieved.

The complexity of the author's answers lies in a strand of his argument that is easily missed, but vital to his policy prescriptions: While Islamic values may be flexible, Maghraoui argues that their interpretation is dominated by traditional leaders and institutions that have legitimacy within conservative sectors of Muslim societies. Thus the modernist project can

---

12. For an instructive look at how this debate unfolded in official circles of the U.S. policy making community, see United States Department of State, "Islam and Democracy: Possibilities, Challenges, and Risks of Bringing Democracy to Islamic Nations, Government, and People," presentation at the secretary's open forum, Washington, DC, June 16, 2003, available at http://www.state.gov/s/p/of/proc/22190.htm.

only advance through, rather than against, the will of the "religious councils, tribal chiefs, charismatic leaders, local assemblies, and similar informal bodies." What is more, it must be pursued prudently, lest it fall into the hands of extremists. Because even the most "moderate Islamic parties" are likely to "fall back on conservative, populist ideologies to harness votes," Maghraoui suggests a certain tension between the modernist project and democratic politics.

If Maghraoui's argument is not in favor of autocracy or against U.S. support for democratic reform, it certainly amounts to an implicit call for restraint. The author seems to envision a process of political liberalization that creates sufficient space for independent Muslim intellectuals to argue for an Islamic renewal, while insuring that traditional leaders and institutions play a stabilizing role in advancing a modernist project. Mincing few words, Maghraoui invokes the "lesson of Iraq" to warn against the polarizing effects of a system of "majority rule" and argue in favor of a consensual system for "negotiating divisive, substantive issues."

How can the United States promote this tricky balancing act—promoting modernist ideas while sustaining traditional and even autocratic institutions and elites, without playing into the hands of either ruling despots or radical Islamists, both of whom have asserted that their autocratic agendas will defend Islamic values? Maghraoui's answer is for the United States to pursue a policy of "normative engagement" with mainstream Islamist activists while helping modernist intellectuals to unify their ranks. In this way, "American policy could tip the balance between extremist and modernist interpretations of Islam." Some analysts might question this last and decidedly bold assertion, but arguments in favor of engaging Islamists have provided powerful rationales for U.S. official and non-governmental support of mainstream Muslim groups in Morocco, Egypt, Yemen, Algeria, Jordan, Nigeria, Pakistan, Indonesia, and Malaysia.

David Smock endorses such efforts, but makes the case that they should not be limited to Islam itself. The larger challenge is for the U.S. government to "devise a better strategy to effectively and respectfully engage" with a "religious realm" that includes representatives who speak for all the major faiths of the Muslim world. Such an initiative, he argues, must contend with the failure of U.S. policy makers to appreciate the positive role that Jewish, Christian, and Muslim leaders have played in mediating a vast array of conflicts. But how can policymakers and activists enhance the authority of such religious leaders while avoiding the pitfall of privileging the role of religion in conflicts that are not necessarily born purely and simply of religion? After all, as Smock observes, disputes that appear to be religious often pivot around social and political struggles dressed up in the claimed moral certainties of religious symbols. Moreover—as Iraq, Somalia, Afghanistan, Sudan, and Nigeria all clearly show—ethnicity, clan, and regional identities rather than religion frequently define the actual cleavages of political conflict or civil war. If domestic and regional conflicts have such multiple roots and identities, how can religious leaders credibly and effectively mediate such disputes?

The answer, Smock suggests, lies in interfaith dialogue and mediation, the immediate purpose of which is not to resolve all the diverse issues that divide contending groups, but to use the moral authority of religious leaders to create a safe umbrella under which rivals can begin to "diffuse interfaith tensions," creating the elemental trust required for more comprehensive efforts at conflict resolution. Highlighting experiments in interfaith dialogue and mediation in Sudan, Iran, Iraq, and Israel-Palestine—several of which USIP supported or organized—Smock's analysis suggests that efforts to mitigate Muslim-world identity conflicts should include, but not rely on, a transformation of Islam. What counts is a wider sociopsychological dynamic that must engage and also transcend the boundaries of competing faiths, so that Islam is only part of the solution.

Daniel Brumberg echoes some of the themes raised in Smock's analysis but directs them in a very different direction. A keen proponent of the institutional-reform wing of the Grand Debate, Brumberg warns against the "erroneous assumption that Islam itself provides the foundation of political identity." While the Islamic faith will always shape public life, he argues that identity conflicts pivot around a complex array of disputes, some of which are ideological or even cultural. The author points to Morocco to illustrate this point. There, Islamists and non-Islamists not only disagree about the extent to which Islamic law should shape politics; on a more basic level, they articulate conflicting definitions of Moroccan identity. Given the virtually existential nature of this divide, Brumberg raises doubts about the capacity of any modernist Islamic project to bridge it. Moreover, he analyzes a range of social, political, and ideological conditions that, in the Arab world in particular, have hampered efforts to mobilize mass constituencies behind the modernist project that the Islamic renewalists advocate.

If a reinterpreted Islam is not the solution, what is to be done? The answer, Brumberg argues, is not to fix Islam, but rather to repair the political and institutional context in which Islamists and their many rivals compete. Taking a conceptual page out of the literature on regime transitions and political pact making,[13] the author advocates negotiating institutional and constitutional guarantees to ensure that democratic reforms produce governments that incorporate all groups—including those who have the most to lose as a result of a free and open ballot. Absent such power-sharing

---

13. Guillermo O'Donnell, Philippe Schmitter, and Lawrence Whitehead, *Transitions from Authoritarian Rule: Tentative Conclusions about Uncertain Democracies* (Baltimore: Johns Hopkins University Press, 1986).

provisions, many non-Islamist political actors who might otherwise favor democracy will continue to rely on autocratic regimes for protection.

The problem is that strongly institutionalized autocracies have little reason to change the political game in ways that might undermine the state-managed protection racket. Brumberg argues that, instead of promoting constitutional, legal, and institutional reforms that could give non-Islamists the means to compete with Islamists, autocrats have chosen to limit the playing field to a two-player—and highly polarized—standoff between themselves and Islamists. In this way they have effectively heightened the risks of democratic reform, not merely for non-Islamists, but also for Western democracy promoters seeking to ensure that elections strengthen political pluralism.

What is the solution to the dilemmas of democratic reform if autocracies have set the traps that await political reformers? The answer is far from obvious, not only because regimes have little interest in changing the status quo, but also because most Islamist parties want to sustain the populist mystique that comes from being—or appearing to be—the only viable alternative to existing regimes. What incentive do Islamists have to challenge a two-way political contest that makes their slogan of "Islam is the solution" (*al islam hu il hal*) sound so compelling? Islamic renewalists argue that this incentive can only come from a long-term intellectual struggle that could easily be undermined by a premature rush to elections. Institutional reformists acknowledge these risks but hold that the hazards are outweighed by sustaining a status quo that is widening the breach between regimes and youthful societies. The challenge, Brumberg and other reformists argue, is to advance reforms that give non-Islamists a chance to compete with Islamists, reducing the uncertainties of free elections.

The tricky bit is getting the timing right. Institutional reformists and Islamic renewalists are motivated by a common desire: to ensure that democracy does not compromise freedom. Renewalists look to a long-term process of dialogue and *ijtihad* to realign politics, while reformists hope for such a transformation, but hold that Muslim-world identity conflicts necessitate more timely institutional and political reforms.

Islamic Renewal: Fixing Islam?

The cultural challenges of reforming the Muslim world are daunting; they include technical problems associated with the practice of independent interpretation, or *ijtihad,* as well as political, practical, and philosophical questions, not least of which are the practical and moral purposes of the interpretive enterprise itself. The political and institutional challenges are equally complex, but they are not bounded by any particular cultural or religious logic. On the contrary, reformists argue that there comes a point where the costs of a "mutually harmful stalemate" convince protagonists to accept a mutually beneficial agreement or political pact—an agreement rooted in a pragmatic ethos that all political leaders can grasp, regardless of cultural differences. Yet as the essays included in this volume also show, when it comes to the concrete dynamics of conflict resolution, the specific and universal logics of culture and institutions are bound together. Institutional changes may be vital to creating the legal and organizational umbrella under which the dynamics of cultural dialogue, reinterpretation, and transformation unfold.

"*Ijtihad*: Reinterpreting Islamic Principles for the Twenty-first Century," written by David Smock, highlights a USIP-hosted debate between a distinguished group of leading Muslim scholars. While offering a range of views, the scholars agree on these points. First, if Islam is a total way of life in theory, in practice the rules of conduct collectively known as *sharia* have been deduced from a range of sources, creating a flexible process of legal reasoning that Muslim scholars have used to imbibe insights from many cultures and civilizations. Second, the flexibility has limits, one of which is that the practice of *ijtihad* is restricted to jurists who have the requisite legal training and expertise. Third, in Sunni Islam—the dominant branch of the religion—the scope for independent interpretation was theoretically closed during the Abbasid Dynasty (750–1258), thus limiting *ijtihad* to the four existing schools of Islamic jurisprudence. Fourth, there is a pressing need to reopen, or at least expand, the space for and by which *ijtihad* is pursued.

Who then has the right to lead the reinterpretive enterprise, and what are its proper vehicles, subjects, and scope? While all the participants in the debate affirm that democratic reforms are essential for *ijtihad,* they emphasize the need for greater political freedoms, leaving the reader to ponder what role elections should play. If only Muslim jurists can engage in *ijtihad,* elected assemblies may not be the proper vehicles for Islamic renewal. That said, given the very unhappy experience of countries that have created clerical councils to supervise legislation, such as the Islamic Republic of Iran, there are clear dangers in making conservative jurists the arbiters of any reinterpretive enterprise. Viewing this catch-22, one Muslim scholar calls for entirely removing the interpretive process from any one elite orinstitution, be it an elected assembly, high court, or even university. As Ingrid Mattson puts it: "Our problems are not going to be solved by having scholars think more deeply. If we limit . . . innovation to . . . those who have the qualifications to reason from the text, we are not going to get anywhere." Thus, she concludes, *ijtihad* must be left to the creative domain of individual imagination.

Mattson's position may seem radical and even unpractical: If everyone can contribute to the Islamic renewalist project, the end-product may be a chaotic multitude of ideas that has no authoritative spokesperson or arbiter. Yet, though it is perhaps a little unruly, Mattson's proposal is in keeping with the pluralistic ethos of Islamic modernists, most of whom believe that Islamic jurists and their semiofficial institutions are major obstacles to Islamic renewal. Paradoxically, the conservative wing of the renewalist project—sometimes referred to by the imperfect term *fundamentalist*—shares this critical view of Muslim jurists. Fundamentalists and modernists both seek to bypass the four major schools of Sunni Islamic jurisprudence in favor of an interpretive enterprise rooted in the founding ideals of Islam itself. Yet beyond this shared impulse, modernists and fundamentalists differ as to how to identify these values, and moreover, who should do the identifying.

Ahmad Moussali's essay, "Two Discourses on Modern Islamic Political Thought: Fundamentalism and Modernism," probes the divergent paths of fundamentalist and modernist thought. Although complex for the uninitiated, his analysis helps to explain why it is that conservative Islamic thinkers have often proven far more influential than their modernist rivals, a point of great consequence for conflict resolution in the Muslim world.

The appeal of fundamentalist thought, Moussali argues, cannot be attributed exclusively to the strong psychological attraction it exerts during periods of great social, political, and cultural change. It is far more than a salve for alienation that exercises its healing magic through a language of religious fanaticism. Instead, Muslim fundamentalism, the author argues, is informed by a deeper worldview—a vision with philosophical and practical complexities, contradictions, and nuances that must be grasped, particularly by those most eager to provide credible Islamic alternatives. Central to this worldview, Moussali suggests, is the notion of a "morality that is beyond the scope of human reason." God has given man the intuition, or *fitra,* to grasp God's revelations, but the truths that Prophet Mohammad revealed—eventually written down in the Quran—are natural, objective facts or laws that society must obey without "logical proofs." Moreover, because God's laws cannot be authenticated, challenged, or recast by dint of man's reason, it follows that any political or social order that upholds and defends God's divine laws is acceptable and even legitimate. Yet if in theory this position allows for a highly pragmatic approach to politics, such pragmatism has its limits. As Moussali notes, from a fundamentalist perspective, "any social order that is incapable of fulfilling human *fitra* is unnatural, unjust, and unsuitable." In their quest for a political order that manifests the spiritual and worldly unity (*tawhid*) of God's divine message, fundamentalists came to champion a vision of community that ties together "politics, economics, ethics, theology, and all aspects of life." If not totalitarian, this understanding of *tawhid* is totalistic and illiberal, and thus profoundly suspicious of the Enlightenment ideals that guide so much of Western political thought.

However, Moussali does not attribute the hostility to Western ideals to Islam itself. Although influenced by and partly derived from Islamic ideas, fundamentalists and modernists both advance *ideological* constructions, the precise contents of which differ from thinker to thinker and from era to historical era. Moussali argues that the contemporary construction of *tawhid* was loaded with meanings that were never present in its original, traditional form. More important for our purposes, Moussali's analysis demonstrates that while struggling to forge a culturally or religiously authentic worldview, fundamentalists and their modernist cousins borrowed selectively from Western political thought. This paradox was harder for the former than the latter to tolerate, as fundamentalists made a fetish of their anti-Westernism, whereas modernists openly embraced Western ideas. Such openness gave the latter's ideas a tolerant, flexible, and pluralistic hue. But their acceptance of the West also plays into the hands of fundamentalists, who often accuse their modernist rivals of advancing Western ideals in a superficially Islamic cloth.

The fundamentalist accusation has some merit. As Moussali himself notes, "the nature" of modernist thought "was oriented for immediate political goals but not fully grounded in theoretical advancements." In their quest to advance a more tolerant political vision that brought West and East together, the modernists focused their critique on the rigidity—rather than the content or consistency—of fundamentalist or traditionalist ideas. Similarly, while they advanced a case for democracy by linking Western notions of political participation to Quranic concepts such as *shura* (consultation) and *ijma* (consensus), modernists did not provide an intellectually coherent theory that they could defend adequately on religious grounds: "The fact they did not write a theory," the author argues, "allowed the fundamentalists to use the adopted modernist notions" to construct their own interpretations of *shura* and *ijma*. Embedded in a traditionalist framework, the masses often viewed fundamentalist constructions of democracy as more authentic than the pro-Western vision that the modernists advanced.

This perception of inauthenticity has had serious implications for efforts to advance democratic conflict resolution in the Arab and wider Muslim world. It not only goes a long way toward explaining why fundamentalists have been more successful than modernists in mobilizing a mass base; it also helps to account for the difficulties that Islamists and non-Islamists have had in forging political alliances. Non-Islamists often suspect that the Islamists are committed to notions of political participation that are only superficially democratic, if not autocratic. Fearing that Islamists use ideological camouflage to mollify non-Islamists—while ultimately, and successfully, directing their real message to a mass base of angry youth—non-Islamists have not only spurned offers from Islamists to join forces, but they have often relied on the protection that autocratic regimes offer. As a result, the breach between society and state has widened.

Keenly aware of this unhappy trend, in recent years modernists from Morocco to Jakarta have striven to direct their ideas to a wider and more youthful public. USIP has supported some of these efforts, as the two remaining contributions in part two demonstrate. Mohammad Abu-Nimer's "Islamic Principles of Nonviolence and Peace Building: A Framework" is both an academic analysis that echoes some points made by Moussali and a modernist tract that makes a powerful case that, in the author's words, "the ultimate purpose of the Qura'nic revelation for Muslims is to create a peaceful and just social order." Like other modernists, Abu-Nimer relies on the Quran to argue that Islamic values such as *qist* (fair play), *ihsan* (kindness), and *salam* (peace) require an "uncompromising militancy of nonviolent techniques." Focusing on these techniques, his analysis includes but moves beyond well-known Quranic admonitions on the questions of justice ("bear witness for justice and let not hatred of a people seduce you," 5:8), the sacredness of human life ("if any one saved a life, it would be as if he saved the life of the whole people," 5:32), or the need to tolerate differences ("so that you may know one another," 49:13). Abu-Nimer's essay advocates a comprehensive Islamic vision of conflict resolution, as relevant to disputes between Muslims and non-Muslims as it is to conflicts among Muslims. In both cases, he argues, the Quran highlights the critical role that third-party arbitration plays in facilitating reconciliation. What is more, in his discussion of Islamic community, or *ummah,* and in the ensuing analysis of pluralism and diversity, Abu-Nimer makes a strong case for respecting ideological and religious diversity within the Muslim community itself. "Muslims," he writes, "have freedom of choice and decision . . . after the message of Islam has been delivered."

David Smock's "Applying Islamic Principles in the Twenty-first Century" moves the discussion from the realm of theory to that of action and policy. Surveying efforts in Nigeria, Iran, and Indonesia to resolve internal religious, ideological, and ethnic conflicts, he reminds us that the interpretive enterprise pursued by Muslim peace advocates has scored some modest but still important successes. These include a USIP-supported peace education project in Indonesia's conflict-ridden Aceh province.[14] Invoking Quranic as well as traditional Acehnese values, the project produced a 385-page teaching manual that was distributed and actually taught in local religious primary schools. In short, the modernist message was not only directed to a grassroots audience; it was placed in the hands of traditional

14. For more on this, see U.S. Institute of Peace, "Religious Education in Indonesia: Implications for Interreligious and Interethnic Relations Public Event," public event at USIP, Washington, DC, November 21, 2006, available at http://www.usip.org/events/2006/1121_religious_education.html.

religious teachers, or *ulema,* who were then given the challenge of making its message accessible to their students.

This program illustrates the enduring challenges that the modernist enterprise faces: how to render a complex vision meaningful to new generations in contexts of domestic, regional, and global strife. In Indonesia, where many primary religious schools, or *pesantran,* are run independently of the state, some teachers have tried to advance a more tolerant vision of Islam. Their efforts have been reinforced at the university level by think tanks and government-supported Islamic centers of education. By contrast, in the Arab world, governmental and educational institutions are under the thumb of autocratic governments or clerical institutions, neither of which favor a modernist project. Such differences illustrate one of the Islamic renewalists' most important points, namely that a transformation of Islamic thought requires support from the highest institutions of the state. Yet precisely because most autocratic rulers and their clerical establishments not only spurn modernist ideas but sometimes echo fundamentalist notions, the struggle to promote a more pluralistic Islamism will take many years. This sobering reality points to the institutional challenges of political reform and to the key role that such reform could play in promoting, rather than exacerbating, identity conflicts.

Fixing Politics? Power Sharing and Political Reform

There are two related reasons why institutional solutions to identity conflicts make sense. First, the intellectual transformation that the Islamic renewalist camp advocates is unlikely to take root in the near or medium term. In the interim, other methods must be found to address the identity conflicts that are tearing at the fabric of the political community in the Middle East and South Asia. Second, the identity disputes cannot be reduced to questions of Islamic identity or to some all-encompassing, binary conflict between Islamists and secularists. Equally and sometimes more important are religious conflicts between Muslim majorities and non-Muslim (Christian) minorities, sectarian disputes between Shi'ites and Sunnis, and ethnonational disputes between Arabs and Berbers or Kurds, or in Afghanistan, ethnoreligious conflicts among Pashtuns, Tajiks, and Hazaras. Exacerbated by myriad socioeconomic conflicts, these disputes can-not be resolved by relying on the long-term and often irrelevant dynamics of Islamic renewal. Instead, they must be addressed through a process of negotiation over the institutional and legal parameters of a new politi-cal system that guarantees power sharing and inclusion for all relevant groups.

Such power-sharing arrangements are hard to forge and even harder to sustain. In highly institutionalized autocracies, such as Egypt, Tunisia, Syria, or Algeria, rulers have few incentives to negotiate with opponents.

Moreover, as noted above, where autocratic states protect key groups, there is little incentive for the latter to join in a common campaign for dramatic political change. By contrast, in weak or collapsed states, such as Somalia, Afghanistan, and post-2003 Iraq, oppositions might have an opportunity to replace the existing regime.[15] But absent an indigenous third party to legitimately enforce that order, power sharing often depends on a security blanket from outside military forces. Welcomed by some and hated by others, foreign forces may not be well placed to advance domestic reconciliation, but they cannot exit prematurely without inviting renewed or even intensified domestic political conflict.

Afghanistan and Iraq illustrate the challenges and dilemmas spawned by foreign intervention and the subsequent effort to promote democratic conflict resolution in weak or toppled states. Encouraged by a very partial victory over the Taliban, in 2002 the United States and its Western allies supported a national reconciliation process that inadvertently exacerbated identity conflicts. A similar story began unfolding a year later in Iraq. But in contrast to previous cases of U.S. or European intervention in the Muslim world, such as Kosovo and Afghanistan, the Iraq case was distinguished by the scale and centrality (if not quasi-unilateralism) of U.S. intervention, as well as by the depth of ethnoreligious conflict—a challenge for which Washington was ill-prepared. Yet if subsequent U.S. missteps grew out of such exceptional circumstances, Iraq's sad story nevertheless suggests wider lessons about the complex dynamics of democratic power sharing that apply beyond the country's borders.

Power Sharing in Weak States: Afghanistan and Iraq

Thomas Johnson's "Afghanistan's Post-Taliban Transition" illuminates a tale of what political scientists call path dependency, or the long-term (and in this case, negative) cumulative consequences of the initial decisions made in building a new political system.[16] The story begins with the 2001 defeat of the Taliban and is followed by the signing of the Bonn Agreement in December of that same year, the creation of an interim power-sharing cabinet under President Hamid Karzai, the selection of the Grand Assembly, or *loya jirga*, in 2002, the naming of a constitutional review commission (CRC) in 2003, and the holding of presidential elections in 2004 and legislative elections in 2005. At each stage of the story, the actions and choices

---

15. Weak state means a state that has limited control over the means of coercion and exercises minimal legal, constitutional, and administrative authority over substantial degrees of its national territory. Power-sharing arrangements are usually closely concerned with efforts to forge interim governments, to negotiate a political and constitutional exit from a period of internal conflict. On this issue, see Karen Guttieri and Jessica Piombo, eds., *Interim Governments: Institutional Bridges to Peace and Democracy?* (Washington, DC: USIP Press, 2008).

16. See S.J. Liebowitz and Stephen E. Margolis, "Path Dependence, Lock-In, and History," unpublished paper, available at http://www.pub.utdallas.edu/~liebowit/paths.html.

of Afghanistan's leaders mirrored what the author sees as a basic, long-standing social reality:

> Not only do Afghans lack a sense of national identity . . . they . . . do not agree on what form of state Afghanistan should have. . . . Pashtuns would like a strong, Pashtun-run central state. Tajiks focus on power sharing in the central state, and Uzbeks and Hazaras desire recognition . . . and . . . local government. . . . Pashtuns emphasize tribal structures and codes at the expense of the state.

From the outset, the internationally blessed Bonn Agreement promised to exacerbate the above tensions. After all, rather than setting the stage for a process of international reconciliation and peacemaking, it provided a platform by which the "winners of the U.S.-led Operation Enduring Freedom" shut out their major rivals, that is, the Taliban and their allies in the Pashtun community. Yet, the author notes, as even the winners were "historically opposed," sectarian conflict emerged in the heart of the government. Karzai's efforts to balance the primacy of power and place given to Panjshiri Tajiks in the cabinet by appointing more Pashtuns may have mollified the latter. But his decisions also provoked the Tajiks, undercutting the authority of the new government. While subsequent drafting of the constitution provided an opportunity to create a genuine and more inclusive domestic peace process, in an interesting foretelling of what happened in Iraq two years later, the truncating of the period set out for drafting the new constitution cut out nonsectarian leaders. This opened the door to a Pashtun *jihadi*-dominated commission, which proceeded to draft a constitution favoring the ideological and institutional interests of tribal warlords and religious figures. The October 2004 presidential elections further institutionalized sectarian politics, as did the 2005 legislative elections. Indeed, the single nontransferable vote system (SNTV) weakened political parties as it reinforced confessional politics. Three years after waging war against the Taliban, Washington found itself allied with an Afghani government in which half of the elected parliament was made up of Islamist or religious leaders. Without intending it, the United States and its allies blessed a political dynamic that may have facilitated the 2005–06 revival of the Taliban.

Jonathan Morrow's "Iraq Constitutional Process II: An Opportunity Lost" offers a similar story of missteps and unintended disasters. Morrow and other USIP colleagues participated in efforts to bring Sunni leaders into Iraq's constitution-making process, and his frustration with the results is not hard to miss.[17] Nevertheless, his coolheaded conclusions are echoed

17. For examples of the activities and initiatives undertaken by USIP's Rule of Law Program in Iraq, see http://www.usip.org/ruleoflaw/projects/countries/iraq.html.

in many other accounts of the events and decisions that provoked Sunni Arab opposition to Iraq's first democratic constitution.[18]

Morrow's assessment rests on a premise that all advocates of institutional analyses hold dear, namely that in societies deeply divided by ethnoreligious conflicts, the process of constitution making itself determines, and thus is in some ways more important than, the substantive outcome of the process. In divided societies, constitution making is inextricably intertwined with peacemaking.[19] As the author observes, from the outset many Iraqis viewed a permanent constitution

> as a kind of intercommunal peace treaty. This constitution-as-treaty would not be a principled discussion leading to the consolidation of Iraqi political identity, it would, more modestly, represent a modus vivendi to settle competing interests surrounding religious law, local self-governance, and resource management.

In their efforts to shape the modus vivendi, political leaders representing Kurds, Shi'ites, and Sunnis competed to define the negotiating agenda and the terms of the final bargain. Throughout the process, Kurds and Shi'ites—who together account for some 75 percent of the Iraqi population—joined forces to outmaneuver Sunnis. The latter's boycott of the January 2005 parliamentary elections put Sunnis at a disadvantage from the start. But in Morrow's view, the root cause of Sunni alienation lay in the decision to limit constitution making to only one month. This truncated schedule did not allow for integrating Sunni leaders into negotiations, even when Shi'ite and Kurdish leaders made a tactical retreat by adopting mechanisms that gave Sunnis a somewhat greater voice in the discussions. Given their history of persecution under Sunni-minority rule, it is possible that no reworking of the process could have blunted Shi'ite and Kurdish determination to advance positions that the Sunnis rejected. As Morrow notes, the Sunnis adamantly opposed the Shi'ite position on federalism, so much so that "the gap . . . may not have been reconcilable."

The really big question, which applies especially well to Iraq but has wider resonance, is if historical legacies are so deeply embedded as to preclude democratic pacts in countries deeply divided by identity conflicts. To this question Morrow offers a well argued if modest no. Although Sunnis understandably feared that federalism amounted to little more than a Kurdish and Shi'ite codeword "for partition," a rebalancing of powers between the center and the provinces might have enhanced Sunni interests. As the author observes, "Conventional wisdom presented Iraq as a centralized

---

18. See, e.g., Larry Diamond, *Squandered Victory: The American Occupation and the Bungled Effort to Bring Democracy to Iraq* (New York: Henry Holt, 2005).

19. For a discussion of power sharing and constitutional reform in Africa, see Francis M. Deng, *Identity, Diversity, and Constitutionalism in Africa* (Washington, DC: USIP Press, 2008).

state undergoing . . . decentralization, when the reality was almost diametrically opposite. Regional powers were . . . negotiating the terms of a possible delegation of powers to the center." That Sunni leaders failed to recognize and act on this opportunity was not a consequence of some historical fate. Rather, it was at least partly the result of contextual factors, not least of which was the Sunnis' inability to "rally constituents . . . around a coherent constitutional strategy," as well as the Sunnis' lack of experience, talent, and resources in the art of negotiations by comparison to their Shi'ite and Kurdish rivals. Under such trying circumstances, the one-month timeline to negotiate a constitution precluded a basic shift in Sunni perceptions or strategy, even when some Sunni leaders began to recognize that certain federal arrangements might benefit them. In Morrow's view, if Iraq's story may have elements of a Greek tragedy, it played more like a sad farce, with the cumulative consequences of misperceptions, missteps, and mistakes producing a disaster that might have been avoided. Mincing no words, the author assigns primary responsibility for this unhappy outcome to the United States. If "Iraq's constitutional process was seen, with some justification, as an insult to Sunni Arab Iraqis," this resulted from the "pressure-cooker approach" that Washington used to push Kurds, Shi'ites, and Sunnis toward an agreement.

Readers must judge for themselves whether Morrow's analysis supports his sharp judgment. More important is his wider analytical point—which all institutional reformists embrace—that while historical legacies matter, through a combination of political will and imaginative thinking, leaders can overcome the great structures of an inherited past. If leadership is important, the problem is that much time and some pain is often required before protagonists grasp the logic of compromise. While one can never know whether the particular story that Morrow tells might have turned out differently, one must ask whether Iraqi and U.S. leaders have learned something from the two years of conflict that followed the disaster of 2005. If they have, can Iraq's leaders, with U.S. support, snatch victory from the jaws of defeat?

The odds are not great. As Rend Al-Rahim Francke's "Political Progress in Iraq During the Surge" demonstrates, despite the costs of violence that all groups shouldered as a result of the failure to compromise, the heavy weight of history continues to shape the attitudes of Shi'ites and Sunnis. The former believe that, after "centuries of oppression," they have an absolute right to rule. For Shi'ites, "demography *is* democracy" (Rahim's emphasis). Sunnis, by contrast, "have an existential fear of Shia domination and cannot accept the reality that they are no longer the ruling elite." These attitudes notwithstanding, the author argues that in 2007 more moderate leaders began to emerge. Their voices were raised in tandem with the U.S.-led military surge in the Sunni tribal areas (Anbar, Diyala, and south of

Baghdad). By backing tribal groups willing to battle the Iraqi branch of al-Qaeda, the United States enhanced the leverage of Sunnis in the struggle to renegotiate the parameters of power sharing. While this was an important development, the introduction of another sectarian player into a fractionalized political arena complicated matters, as it antagonized Shi'ites while exacerbating personal, ideological, and resource-based disputes within the Shi'ite and Sunni camps. More violent than intercommunal disputes, these intracommunal tensions undercut the leverage of leaders who had the courage to push for a more inclusive system.

Prime Minister Nuri al-Maliki's spring 2008 campaign against Shi'ite militias took aim at the threat of intracommunal tension. But if the already fragmented ranks of radical Shi'ite Sadr militia were further weakened, and if the surge restored a measure of peace and safety on the ground—thus discouraging Iraqi civilians from turning to militias for protection—Iraq's long-term political prognosis remains guarded. The problem is not merely the persistence of communal tensions; the essential problem lies in the double-edged nature of power sharing itself. Although communal pacts move ethnoreligious conflict from the battlefield to the political arena, they are negotiated by the sectarian rivals whose conflicts created the impetus for power sharing in the first place. Invariably, many of these leaders develop an interest in resisting demands for change made by insiders who want a larger piece of the confessional pie or, even more so, by outsiders seeking a nonconfessional or fully democratic system. Moreover, because demands for change cannot be easily negotiated, they quickly invite renewed violence. In short, by institutionalizing sectarian conflicts under the umbrella of elite cartels, power-sharing systems can freeze or even exacerbate communal tensions, blocking a transition to a competitive, nonsectarian democracy.[20]

How can leaders assure that the long-term costs of power sharing do not exceed its short-term benefits, particularly when sectarian leaders can rarely see beyond their noses? For better or worse, the job of getting leaders to see the bigger picture often falls in the lap of a foreign power or powers, who in the absence of a strong state, must act as third-party enforcers of the original power-sharing deal. Yet as the North Atlantic Treaty Organization (NATO) learned in the Balkans and as the United States has experienced bitterly in Iraq, because sectarian leaders invariably—and often correctly—believe that such third-party enforcers are not neutral, outside forces face huge hurdles in their efforts to redesign the power-sharing system.

The Iraqi story amply illustrates the overlapping problems. As Morrow notes, by privileging sectarian leaders and their institutions, the confessional

20. See Donald Rothchild, "Executive Power-Sharing Systems: Conflict Management or Conflict Escalation," in Guttieri and Piombo, eds., *Interim Governments*, pp. 73–93.

system adopted in 2005 virtually froze all forces that advocated a nonsectarian or secular agenda. Three years later, the barriers to entrance are huge, giving women's groups, civil society activists, and middle-class professionals few if any opportunities to espouse a national Iraqi agenda. Certainly, the parliament seems to be the least likely candidate to embrace this nonsectarian mission. As Rahim observes, "parliament . . . has little power" because all legislation ultimately must be blessed by groups who not only stand outside parliament, but whose armed militias resist the efforts of the fledgling Iraqi army to defend the integrity of a weak state.

Power Sharing (and Hoarding) in Strong States: Morocco, Egypt, and Yemen

Advocates of democratic conflict resolution face numerous challenges in strong states, two of which merit emphasis.[21] First, they must forge an accommodation between state and society under conditions that favor states or regimes. With robust security establishments and a vast range of economic and political resources to buy off potential opponents, strong states have little incentive to compromise their powers. Second, proponents of power sharing must unite the opposition.[22] In societies suffering from ethnoreligious and ideological conflict, this task is formidable, and well aware of this, autocrats have skillfully manipulated opposition divisions. As noted above, in the Arab world, authoritarianism is sustained by a protection racket that regimes use to coopt groups that feel most threatened by the uncertainties of a democratic process. Unless these vulnerable groups can be convinced that they have more to gain than to lose by withdrawing their tacit consent for authoritarianism, they are unlikely to support demands for any basic political reform. Such change thus requires pacts or political alliances between rival opposition groups. Without a shared vision of power sharing, autocrats will continue to coopt key elements of the opposition, forestalling demands for a power-sharing arrangement that realigns the relationship between state and society.

If cross-cutting ideological alliances are a necessary condition for democratic change, the record suggests that a certain degree of political reform can nevertheless be sustained without opposition pacts. As Brumberg has argued, the "liberalized autocracies" of the Arab world are especially adept

---

21. Strong state means a state that enjoys a significant degree of control, ranging from substantial to monopolistic, over the means of coercion and a significant degree, ranging from substantial to complete, of judicial-bureaucratic control over territorial boundaries. Thus state strength must be viewed in terms of a low to high continuum, with Morocco and Egypt at the high end and Yemen at the lower end.

22. See Marc Howard Morjé and Philip G. Roessler, "Liberalizing Electoral Outcomes in Competitive Authoritarian Regimes," *American Journal of Political Science*, vol. 50, no. 2 (April 2006), pp. 365–381.

at using state-controlled political openings in the press, parliaments, electoral, and NGO arenas to selectively win over or coopt potential opponents.[23] Because they feel threatened by Islamists, some secular elites readily accept the seductive offer of state-controlled political liberalization. This offer usually comes in the form of opportunities to build "civil society organizations," not a few of which are discreetly or even openly funded by the state. These quasi-autonomous, quasi-official organizations give non-Islamists a chance to advance agendas that secularists would otherwise not be able to secure through democratic political contests, which in the Arab world invariably favor the better-organized and more popular Islamist forces.

That said, state-managed liberalization is not designed to favor secularists exclusively. On the contrary, Arab regimes use selective political liberalization to channel political, institutional, and economic favors to both secular and mainstream Islamist groups. By allowing the latter room for maneuver, the state creates space for the threat that induces secular groups to seek state protection in the first place. Thus state-managed political liberalization is a highly effective strategy for both containing and dividing oppositions.

State-managed liberalization can be found throughout the Muslim world. At various times, the rulers of Turkey, Indonesia, and Pakistan have tolerated or even supported Islamist forces to deflect internal and external pressures for substantive political change.[24] Yet, however effective, the use of such survival strategies has lacked the institutional coherence and durability that has animated the Arab world's liberalized autocracies, which have not only endured, but prospered: In the past ten years, Yemen, Algeria, Qatar, and Bahrain have joined the liberalized autocracy club. Even Saudi Arabia has seemed ready to apply—very cautiously and slowly—for membership.

That the liberalized autocracy club has expanded can be attributed partly to U.S. pressures for political reform after the 2003 invasion of Iraq and the initiation of the Freedom Agenda. As Mona Yacoubian's "Promoting Middle East Democracy II: Arab Initiatives" shows, most of the reform projects proposed during the 2003–05 period hewed closely to the logic of state-controlled liberalization. The only project that defied this logic was the June 2004 Doha Declaration. Issued after a two-day conference organized by the Egyptian reformer Sa'ad Ed-Din Ibrahim, the declaration called for "'national pacts' that would delineate the principles of political participation" for both oppositions and the regimes. In sharp contrast, the

23. Daniel Brumberg, "The Trap of Liberalized Autocracy," *Journal of Democracy*, vol. 13, no. 4 (October 2002), pp. 56–68.

24. The strategic use of political liberalization is a survival strategy widely used in developing states. See Marina Ottaway, *Democracy Challenged: The Rise of Semi-Authoritarianism* (Washington, DC: Carnegie Endowment for International Peace, 2003).

2004 Alexandria Charter promised no such pact; largely orchestrated by the Egyptian government, it was an implicit effort to coopt liberal reformers and appease international demands for reform. This cooptation pattern emerged throughout the Arab world, as government after government effectively reshaped the reform agenda to avoid the challenges of substantive democratization.

While the governments' efforts left the basic institutions of autocracy intact, in a few instances, they allowed for a measure of genuine—if highly circumscribed—political reform. The most notable example of such hobbled progress is Morocco. After assuming the throne in 1999, King Mohammed seemed to open the door to a genuine process of negotiation and reconciliation between the regime and the opposition. In 2004 the king did what no ruler of any Muslim-majority state had ever done: He established a truth and reconciliation commission (TRC) to publicly expose human rights abuses that had occurred under the previous monarch—his own father. This bold move seemed to signal a new political era in Morocco. After all, where such commissions have been established, such as South Africa, the public ritual by which the victims of human rights abuses exposed their wounds and their abusers acknowledged their guilt (and asked for forgiveness) facilitated the transition to democracy.[25]

But as Pierre Hazan illustrates in "Morocco: Betting on a Truth and Reconciliation Commission," Morocco's TRC was never intended as a necessary, if clearly insufficient, step along the path to a renegotiated vision of state-society relations. On the contrary, by selecting prominent leftists and liberals to head up the commission, King Mohammed sought to display his reformist credentials while soliciting the support of secular elites during a period of rising challenges from Islamist radicals, including terrorist attacks. In this way he divided the opposition while enhancing his authority as the ultimate arbiter of the political field, a role the constitution bestows upon the Moroccan king as Commander of the Faithful.

Why did honorable men and women accept appointment to a commission with a mission that was skewed to serve the regime's purposes? This very legitimate question points to a wider dilemma facing all oppositions in liberalized autocracies: whether to play a regime-controlled game in the hope that its rules can be tweaked to favor opposition interests, or to boycott the game and lose any chance to shape regime policies? As Hazan notes, in Morocco, the president of the TRC, the late Driss Benzekri, wagered "that the work of the truth commission" would "create a dynamic of . . . reform, leading to a parliamentary monarchy." But this was not to be the case. As Hazan further notes, the monarch and his appointed commis-

25. See Susan Collins Marks, *Watching the Wind: Conflict Resolution during South Africa's Transition to Democracy* (Washington, DC: USIP Press, 2000).

sioners used different language to describe the TRC's mission. Invoking the Islamic concept of forgiveness, the king emphasized his supreme authority to speak on behalf of a community of Muslim believers united by a supposed common religious ethos. By contrast, the commissioners spoke in familiar legal terms of amnesty to "keep the process in the realm of politics." In short, the king sought to depoliticize the entire process while the opposition sought to enhance the TRC's role as a key element in a wider architecture of political reforms.

The Moroccan story reminds us that so long as oppositions remain divided by conflicting visions of reform, hopes for a negotiated pact or accommodation between regimes and oppositions remain slim. A minimal level of societal and ideological unity is a necessary though insufficient condition for substantive democratic reforms. Is such unity possible in the Muslim and particularly Arab world, where the divide between Islamists and non-Islamists remains ideologically and politically salient? How can civil society organizations and political parties create common ground? Finally, does political participation itself encourage political learning or ideological moderation, without which there is little hope for cross-ideological alliances?

USIP has both funded and organized a number of studies that address the above questions. Judy Barsalou's contribution to this volume, "Islamists at the Ballot Box," summarizes the findings of three USIP-funded studies of elections involving Islamist groups in Egypt, Jordan, Kuwait, and Turkey. The authors of these studies offer a variety of insights, but all of them cast doubt on the conventional wisdom that political participation provides an enduring, powerful incentive for ideological moderation. Carrie Rosefsky Wickham argues that in Egypt, Kuwait, and Jordan, mainstream Islamist parties "reject the liberal ethos which informs the secular legal codes of the West." Janine Clark argues that in Jordan, "cross-ideological interactions per se cannot be said to lead to the increased . . . moderation of Islamist parties." Perhaps most revealing, reflecting on his study of Turkey's Justice and Development Party (JDP), Tepe Sultan suggests that there is good reason to wonder if this democratically elected, post-Islamist party is ready to "translate its commitment to the procedures and ideals of democracy to the actual practice of liberal democracy."

USIP's Muslim World Initiative casts further light on the complex question of ideological moderation in its Arab Political Oppositions Project. Supported by the United States Agency for International Development's Office of Democracy and Governance, this project focused on efforts to forge Islamist–non-Islamist alliances in Egypt, Morocco, Jordan, and

Yemen.[26] All four studies demonstrate that fundamental—even existential—ideological differences continue to undermine alliance building in the Arab world. Yet if these differences loom large, the four studies also suggest that regimes have successfully manipulated ideological tensions to divide oppositions. This manipulative strategy has proven most effective in regimes that tolerate political pluralism, whereas they have been somewhat less successful in more closed regimes.

The studies' seemingly counterintuitive conclusion actually makes sense. In more open systems, especially monarchies, rulers stand—or appear to stand—above the partisan political fray, arbitrating political, social, and economic conflicts in ways that promote myriad client-like relationships between regimes and their divided oppositions. In more closed systems—especially presidential regimes that rule via a dominant ruling party—oppositions have fewer incentives and channels to lobby regime patrons and thus are more likely to cooperate. More autocracy can be a unifying force, whereas more pluralism can be a source of disunity.

Dina Shehata's contribution to this volume, "Islamists and Non-Islamists in the Egyptian Opposition," illustrates just how successfully Egypt's leaders have deployed repressive laws and informal client networks to fragment or coopt oppositions.[27] But Shehata also suggests that opposition leaders bear some responsibility for their fate. Contradicting the prevailing wisdom about the presumed moderating effect of political participation on mainstream Islamists parties, she argues that Islamists are most likely to form alliances when they are weak and most likely to spurn cooperation with secularists when they feel emboldened or closer to power. Her study suggests that, absent a change in the balance of power between Islamists and secularists, or a shift in the doctrines that Islamists and secularists espouse, the prospect for sustainable alliance making remains slim. For this reason, the author places her hopes on a new generation of actors who might find common ground because they are not beholden to long-standing political parties or organizations, such as Egypt's Muslim Brotherhood. Egypt's 2004–06 Kifaya movement may have signaled the rise of such new leaders, although the movement's travails suggests that advocates of Islamist-secular reconciliation have a difficult road to travel.

Yemen offers the Arab world's only case of a sustained Islamist-secular opposition alliance that has partly transcended narrow tactical considerations. The shift to a solidly strategic vision of alliance may be far from complete, but the progress so far can be attributed partly to the origins of

---

26. See Muslim World Initiative, "Oppositions, Liberalization, and Democracy: A New Dynamic?" available at http://www.usip.org/muslimworld/projects/liberalization_democracy.html.

27. This essay summarizes the main findings of Dr. Shehata's contribution to USIP's Arab Political Oppositions Project.

the Joint Meeting Parties (JMP) alliance. In their essay "The JMP Alliance: New Political Pragmatism in Yemen?" Iris Glosemeyer and Hesham Sallam show that, during the brief 1994 civil war, the Islamist-oriented Islah backed the efforts of the northern-based GPC to bring the southern-based, secular-oriented Yemen Socialist Party (YSP) to heel. Given this bitter legacy, it took a formidable incentive for YSP and Islah to even imagine a coalition. The impetus emerged when the ruling GPC turned against Islah. Threatened, Islah leaders initiated talks with the YSP; as in Egypt, a perception of weakness—rather than a transformation of ideological commitments—was the original motivating force behind an Islamist opening to secular opposition groups.

So far this story is by no means unique. As any good student of conflict resolution and political reform knows, a change of doctrine rarely brings rivals to the negotiating table. On the contrary, democratic transitions are often launched by rivals who view democratic reform not as an intrinsically worthy end, but rather as a means to shift conflicts to a nonviolent arena of politics. But for democratic peacemaking to succeed, at some point rivals must forge a common vision of reform.[28] In Yemen, the proverbial hatchet may be buried, but wounds are still fresh. Moreover, Islah is hardly united. Its urban political wing backs the JMP, but many of its tribal leaders continue to accept the patronage of President Salih and his allies in the ruling party.[29] Such splits might help to account for the absence of any reference in the JMP's founding documents to matters of first principle, such as the role of Islamic law. For the moment, the alliance agrees on the mechanics rather than the ultimate purpose of democratic reform.

The Challenges of Engagement

Yemen's JMP was not created in a regional or global vacuum. On the contrary, the National Democratic Institute (NDI), a foreign-policy wing of the U.S. Democratic Party, helped bring together the leaders who created the alliance.[30] That NDI did so during a period of growing estrangement between the United States and the Muslim world suggests that Arab political activists

28. John Waterbury casts doubt on the notion that ideological rivals—particularly religious actors—have the will or capacity to forge and sustain a common strategic commitment to democracy. See his "Democracy Without Democrats? The Potential for Political Liberalization in the Middle East," in Ghassan Salame, ed., *Democracy Without Democrats? The Renewal of Politics in the Muslim World* (London: I.B. Tauris, 1994), pp. 24–37. For a broader critique of the means or process-oriented theory of democratic transitions, see Thomas Carothers, "The End of the Transitions Paradigm," *Journal of Democracy,* vol. 13, no. 1 (January 2002), pp. 5–21.

29. See April Longley, *Shifting Light in the Qamariyya: The Reinvention of Patronage Networks in Contemporary Yemen*, Georgetown University, Department of Government, PhD Dissertation, April 2008.

30. For NDI's programs in Yemen, see "NDI: Yemen," available at http://www.ndi.org/yemen#PoliticalContext.

can and sometimes do distinguish between the overall foreign policies of the U.S. government and the particular motivations and goals of American democracy promoters, including those working for or supported by the U.S. government.

The U.S. work in Yemen is just one example of Western efforts to assist governments and oppositions in finding common political ground. As noted at the outset of this essay, in the wake of September 11, and even more so following the 2003 U.S.-led campaign in Iraq, these efforts multiplied in a context of escalating identity conflicts in the Middle East. This unprecedented intertwining of U.S. foreign policy and Muslim-world identity disputes posed a difficult challenge for the United States. After all, in many quarters of the Muslim world, Washington was viewed as both an instigator of conflict and as a partisan ally of one group or another. As a result, the U.S. effort to support democratic conflict resolution ran headlong into a widespread perception that the Freedom Agenda would endure as long as political reforms did not strengthen exponents of terrorism or, more generally, political forces opposed to U.S. foreign policy.[31]

Events in late 2005 and early 2006 seemed to bear out the prediction. Islamist electoral successes in Egypt and then Palestine were followed by a backlash against democracy promotion in some arenas of the U.S. foreign policy establishment. Whether justified or not, the developments became intertwined in a broader debate regarding the proper role that Western governments and civil society organizations should play in engaging social, religious, and political forces in the Muslim world.[32]

Part four highlights the importance of people-to-people diplomacy—especially between religious leaders—in advancing Muslim-Muslim and Muslim-U.S. relations since September 11. The American Muslim community emerged as an increasingly important player in a range of bridge-building initiatives. These civil society–focused programs not only tackled the challenge of promoting understanding between the Muslim world and the United States; they also addressed the complex task of building bridges within regions of the Muslim world suffering identity conflicts. Part five moves beyond people-to-people diplomacy to explore the wider issue of Muslim-U.S. relations and the challenges of democratic conflict resolution. These topics encompass but surpass the role of Islamists. In a context of escalating identity conflicts throughout the Middle East, a democracy promotion strategy that privileges religious domains could exacerbate disputes

---

31. On the corrosive effect of Washington's credibility problem in the Muslim and especially Arab world, see Thomas Carothers, *U.S. Democracy Promotion during and after Bush* (Washington, DC: Carnegie Endowment for International Peace, 2007).

32. See Susan B. Epstein, Nina M. Serafino, and Francis T. Miko, "Democracy Promotion: Cornerstone of U.S. Foreign Policy?" CRS Report for Congress, December 28, 2007, available at http://ftp.fas.org/sgp/crs/row/RL34296.pdf.

between Islamists and non-Islamists in ways that reinforce the leverage of ruling autocrats. The trick is to recognize Islam's importance while promoting institutional solutions that provide for the inclusion of all relevant groups in efforts to promote democratic conflict resolution.

Engaging Peoples and Politics

People-to-people dialogues, particularly those undertaken by non-governmental religious organizations, occupy an important place in the recent history of Western-Muslim relations. During the 1970s and 1980s, the Arab-Israeli conflict provided the most compelling impetus for such efforts, as Muslim, Christian, and Jewish leaders began meeting in myriad interfaith dialogues. During the 1990s the rise of Islamist activism helped to expand the scope of such initiatives. The idea of an essential clash of civilizations—advanced by conservative American scholars such as Samuel Huntington, but paradoxically supported by many of his Islamist critics—created the impetus for a new dialogue between civilizations. Seizing the moment, Iran's former president, Mohammed Khatami, advocated a new era of people-to-people exchanges between the Muslim world and the West.[33] The tragedy of September 11 at first seemed to work against such initiatives. Yet ensuing events—including the U.S.-led war in Afghanistan, the toppling of Saddam Hussein, and the onset of civil conflict in Iraq, as well as the specter of radical Islamist terrorism in the heart of Western Europe—all combined to create an even greater impetus for religious leaders to seek common ground.

David Smock's "Building Interreligious Trust in a Climate of Fear: An Abrahamic Trialogue" summarizes two such dialogues, the first of which occurred less than a year after September 11. Organized by USIP's Religion and Peacemaking Initiative, the two meetings brought together twenty-one religious leaders from Europe, the Middle East, and the United States. Not surprisingly, the Arab-Israeli dispute loomed large throughout the discussions. Addressing this key issue, religious leaders argued that any hopes for a productive dialogue requires, at the very least, a readiness to empathize with the pain and suffering of both Israelis and Palestinians. This very important message rings true to this day; after September 11, it served as a point of departure for a much wider and fundamental debate. As Smock notes, the debate included but extended far beyond the usual suspects of cultural and religious misunderstandings among Christians, Jews, and Muslims. The conference participants tackled the more pressing issue of confronting the efforts of extremists on both sides of the Western-Muslim divide "to see a clash of religiously defined civilizations."

33. See Address by Mohammed Khatami, "Round Table: Dialogue among Civilizations: United Nations, New York, September 5, 2000," available at http://www.unesco.org/dialogue/en/khatami.htm.

To counteract extremism, religious moderates must challenge and discredit the efforts of religious extremists to define Muslim, Christian, or Jewish civilization for everyone. Interfaith dialogues may provide a useful framework for coordinating such efforts. But, as the author notes, insofar as the "participants . . . tend to be like-minded moderates," they may not "reflect the majority view of their coreligionists." In a context of escalating domestic, regional, and global conflict, the need for dialogue can expand in tandem with approaches that can become increasingly irrelevant or ineffective by bringing together seemingly politically acceptable religious leaders only. Yet if interfaith dialogues include radical leaders who have the ear of their restive or alienated publics, this more inclusive approach could work against compromise and interfaith understanding. As David Smock notes, the effort to make religion part of the solution rather than part of the problem "carries liabilities," not least of which is the tendency of many coreligionists to grasp their faith in exclusivist terms. After September 11, the challenge for moderates was not merely to advance a pluralist vision; the greater task was to demonstrate that the religious, cultural, and ethical walls that religious extremists build to define the boundaries of their respective civilizations are not immutable. Turning the proverbial apple cart over, one prominent Muslim thinker, Dr. Abdul Aziz Said, put it this way:

> The shared cultural roots joining Islam with the West are forgotten far too often. . . . Classical Islamic civilization was constructed out of Arab, Biblicist, and Hellenic cultures, but cast a wider net by integrating Persian, Central Asian, and Indian components within its cultural synthesis. Historically, Islam is the true bridge between East and West.

Said's spirited defense of religious eclecticism subverts the very notion of a culturally or religiously coherent civilization and implies that Muslims should embrace a pluralistic vision that requires dialogue and compromise, not merely between but within civilizations. Such a vision is bound to encounter resistance from radical Islamists, for whom the dualistic concept of a conflict between Islamic and Western civilizations constitutes the essential point of departure. Following September 11, that radical Islamist resistance exploded in a wave of terrorist bombings carried out by European affiliates (or sympathizers) of al-Qaeda.[34] Although one of the attacks' strategic goals may have been to punish Spain and Britain for supporting

34. From 2002 to 2005, a series of terrorist bombings occurred in Europe, the Middle East, Africa, and Southeast Asia, carried out by local affiliates or followers of al-Qaeda: on April 11, 2002, a Tunisian synagogue bombing; on October 12, 2002, a bombing in Bali, Indonesia; on November 28, 2002, attacks on Israeli tourists in Mombasa, Kenya; on May 16, 2003, suicide bombing attacks in Casablanca; on November 15, 2003, car bombs at two Jewish synagogues in Istanbul; on November 20, 2003, a second pair of bombings at the British consulate and the offices of the London-based HSBC bank in Istanbul; on March 11, 2004, ten bombs exploded within minutes of each other on four crowded commuter trains in the center of Madrid; and on July 7, 2005, the London tube bombings.

the U.S.-led campaign in Iraq, the bombings were probably also designed to widen the already considerable gap between a new generation of alienated Muslim immigrants and their host populations. But if these campaigns failed to unleash a new conflict between civilizations in the heart of Western Europe, they vastly complicated efforts to enlist Muslim diasporas in the quest for Muslim-Western engagement. By 2006, the intriguing idea that the leaders of these communities might create a new East-West synthesis—a notion championed by Arab-European writers such as Tariq Ramadan—had fallen on very hard times indeed.[35]

The unhappy trend was not replicated in the United States. On the contrary, as Qamar ul-Huda explains in "The Diversity of Muslims in the United States: Views as Americans," American Muslim interest groups, professional associations, and advocacy organizations have come to occupy increasingly important positions in the associational landscape of American political life. These groups advocate a moderate Islamic vision that calls for interfaith dialogue and an active respect for ideological diversity within Muslim communities.

What explains the dynamic of integration and moderation? Paradoxically, part of the answer lies in September 11. In its wake, American Muslim leaders sought to disassociate their organizations and religion from terrorist acts. Moreover, with the passing of the USA Patriot Act, they felt a pressing duty to create new organizations that could defend the civil rights of Muslim organizations and individuals. Yet, in retrospect, September 11 only accelerated a process that had started well before that fateful day. The creation of the Muslim Public Affairs Council in 1998 and the Council on American Islamic Relations in 1994 set important precedents for a quintessentially American tale of diaspora awakening, organization, and integration into a pluralistic arena of interest-group representation. American Muslim organizations, Huda writes, reflect and reinforce an ethos of being "included in the larger spectrum of American society and liberal democracy."

The developments in the American Muslim community have global implications. American Muslim organizations such as the Center for the Study of Islam and Democracy, KARAMAH, and the Cordoba Initiative have taken their efforts to promote interfaith dialogue and pluralist approaches to Islam to the Muslim world itself. These and other groups, Huda argues, are not only creating a "distinct position and identity from the global Muslim community"; they are building multiple bridges of understanding, between the West and the Muslim world and between and within Muslim communities.

35. For an overview of the thinking of Tariq Ramadan, a Swiss national and grandson of Hasan al-Banna, the founder of Egypt's Muslim Brotherhood, see his Web site at http://www.tariqramadan.com/spip.php?lang=en.

Engaging Parties and Movements: Beyond Islam

People-to-people exchanges, particularly between religious leaders, can sometimes create crucial terrain for rebuilding trust between the United States and the wider Muslim world. Yet if such efforts have expanded since September 11, they have done so in tandem with, and partly as a consequence of, the increasing efforts of Western governments and NGOs to advance democratic forms of conflict resolution in the Middle East. These efforts, as noted above, have survived the growing estrangement between the United States and the Muslim world, but their future remains unclear. Islamist electoral successes in Palestine and Egypt in 2005–06, as well as the reassertion of the Taliban in Afghanistan and Pakistan, have raised basic questions about whether the United States and its Western allies can promote democratic reforms in the Muslim world, or whether they should remain committed to the work.

Complicating the picture, from the outset some European leaders harbored doubts about the ultimate motives behind Washington's Freedom Agenda. They not only wondered whether the Iraq gambit had irrevocably discredited that agenda, but also feared that political reforms would destabilize Arab states in ways that undermined the domestic stability of Britain, France, Germany, Spain, Belgium, and Holland, all of which were contending with rising Islamist militancy and the specter of instability in Muslim communities.[36] Stoked by a new generation of disaffected Muslim immigrants, this militancy seemed to escalate in tandem with a U.S. democracy agenda that largely ignored an issue of paramount concern to many Muslims: the Palestinian-Israeli conflict. Most Western European leaders considered it folly to promote democracy without an equal or even more robust bid to resolve this long-standing dispute.

If the suspicions and fears that the Iraq gambit provoked still lingered in 2006, in the ensuing two years, escalating security challenges in Lebanon, Iran, Israel, Palestine, Afghanistan, and Pakistan provoked a policy shift in Washington that was welcome news in many Western European capitals. Tracing this shift in "Between Realism and Wilsonianism: The U.S. and the Muslim World after Iraq," Daniel Brumberg argues that a sudden embrace by U.S. policy of a more realpolitik approach to the Muslim world promises

36. Gilles Kepel argues that Islamist militancy in Western Europe was most pronounced—and violent—in those countries that, in the name of pluralism or multiculturalism, had tolerated the emergence of Islamist subcultures, as occurred in the United Kingdom. By contrast, in countries that tried to assimilate Muslims, such as France, outbreaks of violence in the Muslim community had more to do with social disadvantage than cultural or religious alienation. While Kepel makes a strong case, it is likely that France would have witnessed an outbreak of Islamist violence had it backed Washington's Iraq gambit, or had its press been involved in media controversies similar to those that broke out in Holland in 2004–05. See Kepel's *Beyond Terror and Martyrdom: The Future of the Middle East* (Cambridge, MA: Harvard University Press, 2008).

to be as unrealistic and unproductive as was the previous period of neo-Wilsonianism.[37] Rather than abandoning the quest for democracy, the United States and its Western allies must forge new policies that carefully balance the quest for security and reform in ways that speak to the complexities, contradictions, and tensions that animate politics in the Muslim world.[38]

Using and Abusing Islam in Weak States: Sudan, Somalia, and Pakistan

Will the new administration in Washington be up to the task of balancing security and reform and will it find like-minded allies in Western Europe? Steven Heydemann's "The Challenge of Political Islam: Understanding the U.S. Debate" points to the basic conundrum that policy makers will have to address. On the one hand, he notes that "more than six years" after September 11, "no overarching architecture for managing U.S. responses to political Islam has taken hold." On the other hand, policy coherence may be "neither feasible nor desirable." Total coherence involves imposing overly rigid and even ideological solutions on complex realities; a more pragmatic approach allows greater flexibility. Such an approach must apply strategies of engagement, accommodation, negotiation, containment, and confrontation, depending on the different mix of challenges that Islamist groups present. The trick is to make sure that such "flexibility and responsiveness" constitutes a "policy asset rather than a source of confusion, mixed signals, and flawed implementation."

If Islamist movements and ideologies present formidable challenges, the quest to forge a more coherent engagement strategy must also acknowledge that, in the Muslim world, Islam (or political Islam, i.e., Islamism) itself is not always the source of the problem or the solution to it. As argued above, the Muslim world is split by myriad identity conflicts that are religious, ethnic, sectarian, and ideological. Islamists might welcome policies that reduce the challenges of U.S.-Muslim world engagement to questions of religion, but left to its own devices, such a policy could easily exacerbate wider identity disputes, working against democratic conflict resolution.

The dangers of reducing politics in Muslim-majority countries to matters of faith—or the political construction of faith—are especially evident

37. Brumberg's paper, as well as those of Steven Heydemann, Annette Weber, Dorina Bekoe, and Steven Cook that follow, was originally prepared for the USIP-German Institute for International and Security Affairs (SWP) 2007 Berlin conference, "The Challenge of Islamists for EU and U.S. Policies: Conflict, Stability and Reform." See http://www.usip.org/muslimworld/events/0927_berlin_conference.html for the conference and USIP-SWP monograph that was published after the Berlin meeting.

38. USIP's Muslim World Initiative has organized the Study Group on Reform and Security in the Muslim World to help define a more coherent and sustainable strategy for balancing security and political reform. See http://www.usip.org/muslimworld/projects/reform_security.html.

in weak or failed states. No strategy to promote conflict resolution can hope to succeed in such states if it focuses purely on the issue of political Islam: State weakness or collapse often has occurred precisely because ethnic or tribal groups successfully resisted the unitary ideologies and programs of modern Islamist groups. Annette Weber's "Islam and Symbolic Politics in Somalia" amply demonstrates this lesson. The country's repeated slide into civil war and state collapse, Weber argues, can be partly attributed to a "massive influx of Wahhabi charities" and to the rise of radical Islamist movements, which in 2006 became active in the Islamic courts. While these movements "used and abused" Islam, regional and international actors also aggravated the situation. Rather than recognizing the heterogeneous nature of the Islamic courts, the United States backed an alliance of warlords against Islamist radicals, magnifying the latter's appeal. Although the U.S.-backed Ethiopian invasion of Somalia in December 2006 provoked Islamists into a tactical retreat, Weber argues that U.S. policies backfired by creating a "mobilization factor for jihadists not yet seen in Somalia."

Sudan offers a second cautionary tale. As Dorina Bekoe notes in "The Conflicts in Sudan: American and European Policies," U.S. and EU efforts to address violent conflict between Khartoum and its regional challengers in Southern Sudan, Darfur, and Eastern Sudan are of recent vintage, poorly informed, and thus, marked by a tendency to frame conflicts in terms of simplistic dichotomies such as Muslim versus Christian, Arab versus non-Arab, or north versus south. Such binary categorizing reflects and distorts a complex reality. Khartoum has tried to impose versions of Islamist rule on the animist or Christian south for decades. Yet this policy—which, during the 1970s and early 1980s, the United States effectively abetted in a bid to counter Marxist Ethiopia—misses the underlying economic and resource conflicts that in recent years have pitted Khartoum against the regions. These conflicts were supposed to be addressed through a power- and wealth-sharing arrangement envisioned in the 2006 Eastern Sudan Peace Agreement. But the international community has failed to give the agreement sustained financial and diplomatic support. Thus Sudan languishes, in part because the West no longer attributes decisive strategic importance to that hapless country.

The same cannot be said for Pakistan, which in the coming decade will pose some of the most vexing problems for the United States and its Western allies. The great paradox of Pakistan is that while Islamists have rarely scored major electoral successes, and identity cleavages pivot largely around ethnicity and region, radical Islamists are making steady political and military inroads. This development can be attributed partly to the shifting in 2002–03 of the war on terrorism to Iraq and, three years later, to Washington's counterinsurgency strategy in Iraq, which has induced al-

Qaeda's allies to direct their terrorist campaign back to Afghanistan and Pakistan. But radical Islamist gains in Pakistan also stem from the conditional support that Washington gave President Parviz Musharraf in the years after September 11. This policy did little to help Pakistan's leaders collectively remedy the problems of an endemically weak and fragmented state. On the contrary, Washington's policy came at the expense of promoting a democratically elected government that could tackle the threat of radical Islam with a modicum of popular support.

USIP Pakistan Policy Working Group's recent report, *The Next Chapter: The United States and Pakistan,* points to the challenges ahead.[39] Going to the heart of the matter, the report notes that Musharraf's own government—particularly its security services—allowed "extremism to fester in tribal areas" while promoting "a strategic doctrine on Afghanistan that tolerated, if not assisted, the Taliban." Such policies, combined with deep personal divisions within the non-Islamist opposition parties, set the stage for the resumption in 2007 of democratic politics in a context of growing security threats and political fragmentation within and between the main political parties. Looking to the immediate future, the report urges the United States to adopt a policy of aggressively supporting economic development and political institution building. For this purpose, Washington should press "Pakistan political parties to achieve . . . reconciliation," transparency, and accountability. Without such a policy, the report warns that "political parties may be doomed to repeat the familiar cycle of delegitimization, incomplete terms of office, and prolonged military intervention" that has haunted Pakistan for decades.

Engaging Islamists and Non-Islamists in Strong States

Given Pakistan's geostrategic importance to Washington, it is hardly surprising that the United States tolerated General Pervez Musharraf's authoritarian policies. Autocrats exploit whatever leverage they can from "partnering" with the United States in the struggle against Islamist radicalism—a strategy that, by hook or by crook, Washington has sometimes abetted. But as the case of Pakistan also demonstrates, such a policy can backfire when it effectively discredits regimes in ways that encourage support for Islamist extremists. That autocrats from Cairo to Islamabad are not eager to promote democratic alternatives to these extremists is a problem discussed several times in this volume. Whether the United States and its Western allies can undermine such a cynical protection racket is one of the most crucial and complex challenges Washington must confront.

---

39. See Pakistan Policy Working Group, *The Next Chapter: The United States and Pakistan* (Washington, DC: USIP Press, 2008), available at http://www.usip.org/pubs/ppwg_report.html.

That said, in some corners of the Arab world, the United States has scored a few modest successes in its efforts to undermine the allure and logic of the autocratic protection racket. These gains come not merely from a strategy of engaging mainstream Islamist parties, but from pushing a process of political mobilization that enhances non-Islamist voices to promote alliance making across the Islamist-non-Islamist divide. Mona Yacoubian's "Engaging Islamist and Promoting Democracy" analyzes the efforts of U.S. democracy promoters to advance Islamist-non-Islamist cooperation in Jordan, Morocco, and Yemen. Her analysis demonstrates that these effects are rarely decisive; they are constrained by myriad domestic political factors, such as regime type, the nature of opposition-regime relations, and the relative balance of power between Islamists and non-Islamists.

Generally speaking, all strong regimes pay a price for imposing a system that makes non-Islamist groups depend on their protection. Having weakened non-Islamists, rulers find themselves confronted by a rising tide of Islamism that strengthens the leverage of regime hard-liners, thus widening the gulf between states and societies. However, regime type can matter in ways briefly discussed above. U.S. efforts to promote more moderate Islamist forces, and in particular, to encourage such forces to work with their secular rivals, have been least effective in the two monarchies that Yacoubian analyzes. In Morocco and Jordan, the arbitrating role of monarch has encouraged a patron-client relationship with both mainstream Islamist and non-Islamist forces. Under these conditions, there have been few if any opportunities for the United States and the West to push an existing process of intraopposition cooperation forward.[40] By contrast, in the one case of presidential rule that Yacoubian analyzes, the efforts of President Ali Abdul Salih to consolidate and extend his power created an impetus for cooperation between Islah and the Yemen Socialist Party. This development created an opportunity for U.S. democracy promoters, who in 2006 skillfully assisted in creating the Joint Meeting Parties, or JMP.

Reflecting this alliance, one Islamist leader acknowledges that Islah and the YSP have "subordinated" their "ideological agendas to the one thing we all have in common . . . which was the realization that political reform was a necessity if we were to save democracy." Such pragmatism can jump start democratic conflict resolution. But as previously argued, without a deeper vision of democracy as an end rather than a means, Islamist–non-Islamist cooperation will remain an insufficient condition for sustained and peaceful political reform.

---

40. Building on Yacoubian's research, the Muslim World Initiative has a grassroots project directed at encouraging Islamist–non-Islamist dialogue. See "Wasat Generation Dialogues: Easing Sectarian and Ideological Conflicts in the Middle East," available at http://www.usip.org/muslimworld/projects/wasat_generation.html.

Reform, Security, and Diplomacy: Challenges Ahead

Mounting instability in Lebanon, Iraq, Palestine, Pakistan, and Afghanistan has fostered a new consensus in Washington and European capitals that democratic conflict resolution in the Muslim world requires a sustained effort to reinvigorate the architecture of security and peacemaking in the Middle East and South Asia. Autocrats would surely welcome this realist shift, hoping that they could brandish their security credentials to deflect demands for political change. Successful regional peacemaking could counter such regime survival tactics by enhancing the leverage of moderate actors, facilitating democratic peacemaking at the national level. If handled intelligently and carefully, regional security and domestic reform can be mutually reinforcing.

The failure to address and ultimately resolve the Palestinian-Israeli conflict highlights the complex synergies between reform and security. Although Hamas is opposed to any two-state solution to the conflict, its rise as a political force in the West Bank and Gaza came about partly because of a failed peace process. Had progress toward an economically and politically sustainable Palestinian state living in peace alongside Israel been achieved early on, it is likely that elections would have strengthened Palestinian advocates of peace, creating a more stable environment for domestic reconciliation in the Palestinian community itself. Moreover, as Daniel Kurtzer and Scott Lasensky argue in *Negotiating Arab-Israeli Peace: American Leadership in the Middle East,* the multiplier effect of Arab-Israeli peace would be considerable. A vibrant peace process might in the short run mobilize the suppliers of Islamist radicalism, but in the longer run, Israeli-Palestinian peace would also reduce the demand or support for militant ideology and action within the wider Muslim community. Thus, the authors conclude, without a sustained U.S. commitment to push all parties toward a just and comprehensive settlement of the Arab-Israeli dispute, Washington has little chance of achieving its wider strategic and political goals—including democracy—in the Middle East.[41]

Any push for Arab-Israeli peace must unfold alongside a wider bid by the United States and its Western allies to advance peacemaking and regional cooperation in other arenas of the Middle East and South Asia. As in the Israel-Palestine area, such efforts could enhance prospects for domestic political reform in Muslim-majority states suffering from destabilizing identity conflicts.

The essays on Turkey, Afghanistan, and Iran included in the final section of this volume highlight the complex and sometimes corrosive synergies

---

41. Daniel C. Kurtzer and Scott B. Lasensky, *Negotiating Arab-Israeli Peace: American Leadership in the Middle East* (Washington, DC: USIP Press, 2008).

between regional and domestic political reform. As Steven Cook notes in "Islamist Political Power in Turkey," the electoral successes of the Islamist-oriented Justice and Development Party (AKP) poses local, regional, and national challenges. Although the AKP's leaders claim that the party is post-Islamist and adheres to a secularist agenda, many Turkish secularists harbor strong concerns about the party's ultimate aims. This divide looms over Turkey's political horizon, threatening to undo the country's rocky transition to full, competitive democracy.[42] Membership in the European Union could go a long way in encouraging all parties to forge common ground. Yet, as Cook writes, inasmuch as "most people within the EU believe that there is no place for an overwhelmingly Muslim country in Europe," a key structural incentive for advancing democratic consensus building in Turkey may go missing.

There is little doubt that the United States has advocated Turkish EU membership in the hope that it would moderate the AKP's policies and thus enhance political reconciliation between Islamists and secularists. Given Europe's unease, one may never have the opportunity to test the theory that EU membership would strengthen the leverage of AKP moderates. However, Cook's essay suggests a different regional path to promoting democratic peace building in Turkey. Paradoxically, that path is rooted in escalating security challenges, not least of which is the U.S. invasion of Iraq: In responding to these events, Turkey's leaders are fashioning a realpolitik strategy that, far from expressing an Islamist agenda, seeks good relations with all neighbors. Such pragmatism, Cook argues, could be marshaled to promote Middle East stability and peacemaking, provided that Ankara is allowed to "come into its own" as a major economic, political, and diplomatic player. This process could also facilitate democratic consensus building in Turkey, particularly if Ankara effectively helps to mediate conflicts between Israel and its Arab neighbors and, more globally, between the United States and Iran.

Turkey's ability to mediate disputes between the Muslim world and the West is a function of the coherence and strength of the Turkish state. Although identity conflicts between Islamists and secularists, or Turkish nationals and the Kurdish minority, continue to rattle Turkey's political system, the state is sufficiently robust to absorb such shocks. Despite—or perhaps due to—periodic threats from the military, the political elites on both sides of the Islamist-secular divide have stepped back repeatedly from the brink,

---

42. See Gallup, "Role of Sharia: A Fault Line in Turkish Society," available at http://www.gallup.com/poll/109318/Role-Sharia-Fault-Line-Turkish-Society.aspx. On the political implications of this fault line for the evolution of Turkey's democracy, see Cemal Karakas, *Turkey: Islam and Laicism between the Interests of State, Politics, and Society,* report no. 78 (Frankfurt: Peace Research Institute Frankfurt, 2007), available at http://www.hsfk.de/downloads/prif78.pdf.

enhancing efforts to square the quest for political stability with the equally important drive for democratic reform.

By contrast, the great challenge in Afghanistan is to advance domestic peacemaking and reform in a weak and fragmented state that is suffering from a growing Islamist insurgency, led by a revived Taliban and al-Qaeda forces. Mohammad Masoom Stanekzai's "Thwarting Afghanistan's Insurgency" sets out a comprehensive national reconciliation strategy, designed to deflate the Taliban's sails. In contrast to the gloomy analysis of Afghanistan that appears earlier in this book, Stanekzai argues that after long years of conflict, the "majority" of Afghans are "willing to support a peace process" that includes elements of the Taliban. President Hamid Karzai foreshadowed this policy in April 2003, when he declared that "a clear line has to be drawn between the ordinary Taliban who are real and honest . . . and those who still use the Taliban cover to disturb peace and security." This promise went unfulfilled, but Stanekzai argues that declining popular support for the Taliban, the growing strength of the Afghan military, and a much-improved annual economic growth rate have created a window of opportunity to advance national reconciliation.

Such domestic conditions, if they can even hold, will be at best a necessary but insufficient condition for progress. Success in Afghanistan, the author argues, will require nothing less than a surge of NATO and International Security Assistance Force (ISAF) troops, without which the "cost of security over the long term will be intolerably high." What is more, he suggests that the United States must coax Pakistan, India, and Afghanistan into a direct dialogue aimed at ending the "use of Afghanistan soil as a proxy Indo-Pakistani battleground." Without such a regional initiative, Pakistan's notorious security services will probably continue to support the Taliban, undercutting the leverage of the Afghanistan government in ways that work against domestic reconciliation.

Stanekzai may be asking a lot, particularly given that the *mujahideen* and Taliban occupy positions in the elected national assembly, or Wolesi Jirga, and that warlords aligned with the Taliban are unlikely to support reconciliation if it requires giving up opium cultivation, upon which the economy depends. These and other challenges are formidable. Still, to set the stage for talks with the Taliban, the United States and its Western allies will probably have to increase military, economic, and humanitarian support for Afghanistan, where, of course, the post-September 11 struggle against al-Qaeda began.

An enhanced engagement strategy in Afghanistan will attract Iran's attention. Hard-liners will not welcome the prospect of more U.S. troops on the Islamic Republic's southeast flank; that said, in 2002, Tehran supported the U.S. effort to crush the Taliban.[43] From Iran's perspective, a revived Taliban could invite a return to civil war, a prospect that would hardly serve Tehran's interests. Thus it is not inconceivable that U.S.-Western efforts to rescue Afghanistan from total chaos might facilitate talks between Washington and Tehran. Moreover, as the United States struggles to define and implement a feasible exit strategy from Iraq—one that enhances rather than undermines domestic political reconciliation—there may be further incentive to engage Iran. Given that the long-term prospects for sustaining democratic power sharing in Iraq are not encouraging, it is likely that at some point, Washington and Tehran will have to find ways to talk to one another about Iraq's future.

Any engagement strategy faces enormous obstacles, not least of which is Iran's enhanced influence in the Middle East and its associated quest to build a nuclear power complex that serves military ends. Paradoxically, U.S. policy opened the door to this development: By suggesting that the effort to promote democracy in Iraq was a prelude to regime change in Damascus or Tehran, U.S. officials and their allies in some Washington think tanks encouraged Iran's bid to shape the Iraqi political arena to serve its own interests. Closely aligned with Iraq's two main Shi'ite parties, Tehran's leverage has increased in tandem with its worrisome drive for nuclear energy.[44]

A second crucial factor hindering U.S.-Iranian engagement is the complex and potentially explosive interplay of Iranian domestic politics and foreign policy. Iran's current regime was founded partly on an ideology of hostility toward Israel and the United States; its leaders cannot completely shed this ideological inheritance without antagonizing powerful domestic forces. President Khatami learned this lesson the hard way: When he promoted a "dialogue of civilizations" that sought to create a new foundation for U.S.-Iranian reconciliation, his domestic opponents saw in this campaign a bid to increase the domestic political leverage of the reform movement. Matters only worsened in 2002 when Iran was included in the Axis of Evil, an action that seemed to help seal the fate of Iran's reformists.[45] By 2005, the hard-liners, led by newly elected president Mahmoud Ahmadenejad, reasserted control over the political system.

43. There is evidence that Iran's Revolutionary Guard has given tactical support to the Taliban. While this cynical policy amply reflects the enduring influence of Iran's hard-liners, under different circumstances—particularly in the context of a wider U.S.-Iranian dialogue on the nuclear question—Washington and Tehran might once again find common ground in Afghanistan.

44. See Geoffrey Kemp, "Iran and Iraq: The Shia Connection, Soft Power, and the Nuclear Factor," Special Report 156 (Washington, DC: USIP Press, 2005), available at http://www.usip.org/pubs/specialreports/sr156.html.

45. See Daniel Brumberg, *End of a Brief Affair? The United States and Iran,* Carnegie Policy Brief no. 14 (Washington, DC: Carnegie Endowment for International Peace, 2002), available at http://www.carnegieendowment.org/publications/index.cfm?fa=view&id=922&prog=zgp&proj=zdrl.

Ahmadenejad has had some success with the messianic, populist, and anti-American and anti-Israeli ideology that the late Ayatollah Khomeini had championed.[46] Yet Iran's Islamic Revolution was constructed around the conjoining of an array of contending and even contradictory ideological traditions, some of which Khatami and his allies in the reformist movement tried to recast in their effort to advance a pluralistic vision of reform at home and engagement abroad.[47] If they did not succeed, there are still powerful forces in Iran that want to resuscitate the engagement agenda. These forces include pragmatic conservatives within the regime, who favor a more normal relationship with Washington.

The last essay, "Negotiating with the Islamic Republic of Iran: Raising the Chances for Success," highlights the opportunities for and impediments to forging an effective engagement strategy with Iran.[48] The author, John Limbert, a distinguished American diplomat and scholar of Iran, was also one of the hostages held in the U.S. Embassy by Iranian students from November 1979 to January 1981. Thus he brings a unique combination of personal and professional experience to bear on this most complex of subjects.

Limbert begins his analysis by noting that in May and July 2007, Tehran and Washington held the "first official bilateral . . . contacts since relations were formally broken in . . . April 1980." That these talks were held in Baghdad should come as little surprise, as with the possible exception of Afghanistan, there is no other country in the Muslim world where the United States and Iran might find a greater measure of diplomatic (and actual) common ground than in Iraq. However, though the rationale for dialogue grew in the wake of the Iraq gambit, U.S.-Iranian relations are weighed down by a thirty-year cold war, the legacies of which—as Limbert shows—have repeatedly made any effort to substantially redefine the relationship politically risky for leaders in both Washington and Tehran.

The risk is not equally shared. Because "many in power in Iran today have gained their positions by riding waves of anti-American sentiment," and because the country's leaders "see the power of American popular culture as a direct threat . . . to the dominant ideology," Iranian advocates of engagement have to navigate a sea of obstacles far more daunting than those that their analogues in Washington face. American diplomats must surely be sensitive to the many wounds that the United States suffered in

46. See Suzanne Maloney, *Iran's Long Reach: Iran as a Pivotal State in the Muslim World* (Washington, DC: USIP Press, 2008).

47. Daniel Brumberg, *Reinventing Khomeini: The Struggle for Reform in Iran* (Chicago: University of Chicago Press, 2000).

48. Given Iran's enhanced strategic position in the Middle East, any opening to Iran would require efforts to shape a regional environment that would reduce Iranian leverage and thus provide a more productive incentive for Tehran to engage Washington. For this purpose, U.S. engagement of Syria and a strong push for Israeli-Syrian peace may be a prerequisite for effective U.S.-Iranian engagement.

its contentious relations with Iran. But their primary challenge is to forge a strategy that anticipates the cultural, ideological, psychological, and institutional landscape of Iranian politics in ways that advance rather than undermine the cause of U.S.-Iranian engagement.

Limbert offers fifteen points that he argues should facilitate, but by no means guarantee, successful diplomacy with Tehran. While many of his points are relevant for all negotiators in all negotiations, he highlights two potentially countervailing challenges specific to the Iranian arena. First, he warns against treating the Iranian side as irrational. Such an approach, he argues, creates a "self-fulfilling prophecy" by effectively inviting Iran to comply with the "time-honored view of Iranians as emotional or incomprehensible." Instead, the United States should focus on potential areas of converging U.S.-Iranian geostrategic interest, paying careful attention to talking to the "right people," even if this means negotiating with hard-liners. Second, Limbert suggests that U.S. negotiators with Iran must attend to the many cultural and symbolic minefields that await them. The Iranian quest for dignity is a psychological challenge that clashes with the pragmatic, problem-solving bent of U.S. diplomats. How to address the important symbolic aspect of discussions is a tricky question, particularly when U.S. diplomats often suspect that their Iranian counterparts play the respect card to avoid making the hard choices involved in genuinely normalizing U.S.-Iranian relations.

Scholars of conflict resolution argue that the most effective way to tackle such emotive issues is through "symbolic incentives and concessions." Using culturally relevant gestures and statements that show empathy for a rival's deepest grievances, negotiators can reinforce the political leverage of moderates, opening up the possibility for material concessions that otherwise could not be imagined.[49]

Limbert's analysis points toward the logic of symbolic incentives, but also argues that ultimately, the first priority for Iran's leaders is very concrete: "regime survival." Do American leaders have the political will and domestic support to, in the author's words, "reassure the Iranian side" that an agreement "will not destabilize the Islamic Republic?" And even if conditions emerge for formal U.S. recognition of the legitimacy and sovereignty of the Islamic Republic, would Iran's leaders reciprocate, knowing that normalizing relations with the United States entails relinquishing one of the last remaining ideological props of the Islamic Revolution? Because a genuine opening to the United States could eventually strengthen Iranian moderates and even tilt the balance of power back to the reformists, would

49. See Jeremy Ginges, Scott Atran, Douglas Medin, and Khalil Shikaki, "Sacred Bounds on Rational Resolution of Violent Political Conflict," *Proceedings of the National Academy of Sciences*, vol. 4, no. 19 (May 2007), pp. 7357–7360.

the Islamic Republic's supreme leader ever countenance a real burying of the hatchet with Washington?

There are no easy answers to these difficult questions. Engagement and normalization with rivals always entails daunting and complex tradeoffs. But one thing is clear: Without a bold effort to test the waters, the U.S.-Iranian cold war will continue, a prospect that surely warms the hearts of radicals throughout the Middle East and beyond. As the United States and its Western allies look beyond a decade of estrangement with a Muslim world increasingly fragmented by its own domestic and regional conflicts, the impetus for dialogue with both friends and foes will grow in concert with the benefits and risks associated with a sustained strategy of engagement.

Part I

The Grand Debate:
Islamic Renewal or Political Reform?

1

American Foreign Policy and Islamic Renewal

Abdeslam M. Maghraoui

Nearly five years after 9/11, the United States still lacks an integrated and sustainable strategy to confront religious extremism in the Muslim world. The challenges in Iraq and uncertainties in Afghanistan are raising doubts about the current thrust of the "Global War on Terrorism." The prospect of electoral victories by hard-line Islamists is dimming the hope that promoting democracy will produce moderate regimes and good relations with the United States. And attempts to win "hearts and minds" through public diplomacy have not yielded significant results. A June 2006 Pew Global Attitudes survey shows that unfavorable opinions of the United States are still widespread in five traditionally moderate Muslim countries (Indonesia, Jordan, Lebanon, Pakistan, and Turkey).

Missing from U.S. policies is the recognition that the challenge comes not only from conflict with western modernity but also ideological conflicts inside the Muslim world. A simmering, historically rooted battle *within Islam* pits modernists against radical Islamists. Following the 1979 Islamic revolution in Iran, conservative Sunni regimes unleashed their own brand of puritanical Islam to counter the growing ideological influence and political dynamism of the Shi'ite revolution. Saudi financial largesse and Wahabism, a doctrine that advocates a literal, legalistic, and purist interpretation of the Qur'an, have influenced the Sunni response to the Shi'ite challenge.

Sunni extremists have gained ground during the past three decades as a result of the poor social and economic performance and repressive nature of Muslim political regimes. The three Arab Human Development Reports published by the United Nations between 2002 and 2004 show the Arab part of the Muslim world lagging behind other regions in social opportu-

Abdeslam M. Maghraoui, "American Foreign Policy and Islamic Renewal," Special Report 164 (Washington, DC: USIP, 2006).

nity, knowledge, and good governance.[1] Fragmentation of religious authority in Sunni Islam and official religious scholars' reluctance or failure to reinterpret Islamic laws also are serious problems. With no institutionalized authority comparable to the Catholic papacy and the Shi'ite *velayat-e faqih* (rule of the jurist), an independent legal scholar, a respected preacher, or even a fanatic can issue a *fatwa* (a religious edict or opinion). Although the vast majority of fatwas issued on any given day are about mundane matters and have nothing to do with politics or violence, they undermine the authority of official religious institutions, who in turn use the prevailing "anarchy of fatwas" to monopolize and limit the scope of *ijtihad*, or reasoned interpretation.

Standard economic and political reform policies, often touted as the solution to the Muslim world's problems, are necessary but no longer sufficient to address a crisis of this magnitude. Perhaps a freer political environment and social and economic incentives could have reinforced ideological moderation if they had been implemented decades ago.

Today, however, the major battle is over the soul of Islam and will require substantive, normative, and institutional reforms. The outcome of this religious and ideological contest will be determined by the balance of power and influence between radical Islamists, bent on imposing a puritanical form of Islam through intimidation and violence, and moderate Muslims who aim to renew Islam from within.

The single most important step the United States can take to combat Islamist extremism is to support "Islamic renewal," a recent, diffuse but growing social, political, and intellectual movement that aims to cultivate modern norms and address modern needs by drawing on Islamic traditions. Its objective is profound reform of Muslim societies and polities. Although they do not comprise an ideologically homogenous and uniformly committed movement, various actors with similar agendas and significant social backing are involved. The movement may include women's groups such as the Sisters in Islam networks in Indonesia and Malaysia, AISHA Arab Women Forum, Karamah: Muslim Women Lawyers for Human Rights, or the anonymous group of progressive Muslim women that published "Claiming our Rights: A Manual for Women's Human Rights Education in Muslim Societies." It includes moderate Islamist parties, such as Egypt and Jordan's *wasat* parties, that call for "self-reform," and Turkey's and Morocco's Justice and Development parties, which define themselves as modern political actors taking progressive Islamic positions. And it includes hundreds of active democracy networks (such as the Philippine Council for Islam Democracy, the U.S.-based Center for the Study of Islam

1. Arab Human Development Report 2002, *Creating Opportunities for Future Generations*; 2003, *Building a Knowledge Society*; 2004, *Freedom and Good Governance* (New York: United Nations Development Program).

and Democracy, or the International Center for Islam and Pluralism in Jakarta), and lively Web sites that foster international communication and transmission of progressive Islamic ideas (Liberal Islam Network, Liberal Islam.net, IslamOnline.net, ProgressiveIslam.org).

In general, the Islamic renewal movement comprises four broad groups. Proponents of "civic Islam" include civil society organizations that advocate women's equality, human rights, social responsibility, environmental protection, and similar social issues but make no overt claim to political power. Referring to the progressive teachings of Islam, they call on regimes to enact reforms and respect basic rights. Proponents of "Islam and democracy" include parties and movements that see no incompatibility between Islamic values and teachings and modern democratic principles. This group advocates participation in the political process with the goal of achieving power and applying political reforms on the basis of Islamic principles. Proponents of "reforms within Islam" include leading religious figures, scholars, and academic institutions that call for reinterpretation of Islamic laws, a historical reading of Islam and the Qur'an, and the modernization of Islamic knowledge. "Culturally modern Islam" developed mainly among Muslim communities living in the West. These diaspora groups and organizations, which try to articulate a "western Islamic identity," see no tension between being a Muslim and a citizen of a western democracy. Tying these diverse actors together is their commitment to modernize Islamic institutions, traditions, and practices.

In some instances the Islamic renewal movement also includes governments. In Malaysia, for example, Prime Minister Abdullah Badawi uses his country's broad and entrenched tradition of democratic Islam as a model to call for religious moderation throughout the Muslim world. In Morocco, the monarchy applied progressive interpretations of specific clauses in Islamic law to reform the family code and grant women equal civil rights in 2004. In a parallel effort, the government opened one of Morocco's most prestigious seminaries to women, and some fifty women imams and preachers (*murshidat*) graduated in 2006; sixty more enrolled that year. This is a first in Islamic history and a major breakthrough for a conservative society in which women have been excluded from the public sphere. Thanks to the education ministry's revision of school curricula and textbooks, Moroccan children learn about religious freedom and tolerance, universal principles of human rights, minority rights, and gender equality. The revisions draw on both international agreements and Islamic principles. To carry out these reforms, the monarchy carefully chose the language to explain the changes and involved civil society, religious scholars, political parties, the government, and the parliament.

The United States is well positioned to support this movement and engage "moderate" Islam. Contrary to common perceptions in the West, the word "moderate" accurately describes the vast majority of Muslims, who reject violence, yearn for justice and accountable governance, and value Muslim traditions of family, knowledge, and prosperity. An oft-cited saying of the Prophet Muhammad honors any Muslim who bequeaths "good offspring, useful knowledge, or honestly earned wealth." Emphasizing these aspects of Islam will discredit the extremists' message of hate, despair, and destruction. Moreover, these aspects of Islam have an enormous potential for religious moderation that the United States is better placed to understand and appreciate than secular Europe, communist China, nationalist Russia, or the region's repressive governments. Among all liberal democracies, the United States shows the broadest social and political support for religious compassion, religious figures and institutions, religiously based charities, and even virtuous politics. Yet many U.S. policymakers and strategists have overlooked Islam's ethical appeal.[2]

The United States can support reforms in the Muslim world by refocusing its already existing USAID programs, its democratization projects, and its public diplomacy initiatives to pay more attention to ongoing ideological conflicts. These reforms are more likely than forced regime change, democratic elections, or skilled marketing of U.S. foreign policies to build open and peaceful Muslim societies and good U.S.-Muslim relations.

This report discusses the inadequacy of current policies toward the Muslim world in light of its internal ideological conflict. We then develop the idea of "Islamic renewal." The third section outlines specific recommendations for the U.S. government and other international actors.

A definitional note: "Islamist" political parties and movements seek to legitimate or overturn a political order on the basis of their interpretation of Islamic principles. "Extremist" groups eschew nonviolence in the name of the principles of the pious ancestors (*al-salaf al-salih*) and literal interpretation of the Qur'an. "Moderate" parties and movements accept and apply human reason to Islamic principles, law or precedents. They see no incompatibility between participation in the modern political process and Islamic values. Within these camps, theological variations and differing degrees of "extremism" and "moderation" are the products of local power relations.

Current U.S. Policies

Since September 11, 2001, there has been no lack of ideas and initiatives to confront challenges from the Muslim world. Three efforts have received special attention from the Bush administration and in public discourse: the Global War on Terrorism (GWOT), the Middle East Partnership Initiative

2. Roxanne Euben, *The Enemy in the Mirror: Islamic Fundamentalism and the Limits of Western Rationalism* (Princeton: Princeton University Press, 1999).

(MEPI) to promote democratic reform, and the public diplomacy campaign to improve America's image in the Muslim world.

The components and declared objectives of these efforts often conflict with one another. For example, the global war on terrorism requires the cooperation of security services that form the backbone of authoritarian regimes in Muslim countries. Such cooperation undermines both democratic ambitions and the effort to change negative attitudes about the United States in the Muslim world. This initiative conflicts with one of MEPI's major objectives: to push for political reforms and free elections. But free elections in some states are likely to bring to power Islamic fundamentalists. Such an outcome seems to conflict with the anti-terrorism strategy that conflates various Islamist groups into a monolithic threat, regardless of political, ideological, or strategic motivations. Furthermore, one of the major tasks of public diplomacy is to discredit the extremists' message by promoting credible moderate voices. Yet these come from moderate Islamist parties or organizations that are often under the scrutiny of local governments and may never be granted a U.S. visa or entry into the United States.

The U.S. strategy toward the Muslim world also shows misunderstanding of its political cultures. The war on terrorism is a primary example. Because the ideological and political differences among Islamic groups are still misunderstood or too subtle to warrant attention, the tendency has been to use terms such as "jihadists," "Salafists," or "extremists," regardless of context. Yet empirical evidence from various countries points to a discernable pattern of ideological radicalization and a parallel shift to violence every time Islamist parties with a reformist agenda are weakened. Being aware of these patterns and shifts is important to understanding ideological extremism and combating terrorism.

For example, the first violent radical group in the twentieth-century Muslim world emerged as the result of a split among Egypt's Muslim Brothers in the 1970s. Members of *Al-Takfir wal-Hijra* (Excommunication and Exodus) broke with the Muslim Brotherhood after successive Egyptian governments rejected its reformist agenda and killed its leaders or sent them to jail. In addition to fighting the regime, the group's objective was to "cleanse" Egyptian society through *takfir*, or excommunication, a violent doctrine that targets alleged Muslim apostates. This major ideological break with traditional Islamist reformist movements paved the way for a potent alliance with the Salafists and their global agenda. The Egyptians Ayman al-Zawahiri, al-Qaeda's second in command, and Sheikh Omar Abdel Rahman, the blind cleric convicted of planning the World Trade Center bombing in 1993, emerged from this ideological rupture. They led *al-Jihad al-Islami* and *Jama'at al-Jihad*, which also split from the Muslim Brotherhood in the 1970s.

The pattern of political exclusion, ideological radicalization, and ensuing links between groups fighting local "infidels" and Salafists fighting external "infidels" can be seen in other situations. The banning of the Islamic Salvation Front in Algeria after it won local and national elections in 1990 and 1991 led to the emergence of two violent organizations, the Armed Islamic Groups and the Salafist Preaching and Combat Group. Both embraced a *takfiri* ideology that was behind many of the killings of civilians during the 1990s. At least one of these groups has been linked to international terrorist networks.

The same split explains the emergence and links of two Moroccan groups, the Straight Path and the Salafist Group for Preaching and Combat, to global terrorism; their members were convicted in the Madrid and Casablanca terrorist attacks. When the reformist *al-Adl wal-Ihssan* and the Justice and Development Party made no headway during the monarchy's guided political opening of the 1990s, various *takfiri* groups emerged in Fez, Sale, Tangiers, and Casablanca. In 2002, for example, extremists assassinated more than 166 civilians during illegally organized "apostasy trials" in Morocco. These examples show that to understand religious extremism in the Muslim world, it is critical to take ideological shifts and conflicts into account. However, because the global war on terrorism is not sharply focused, analysts could reinforce the dominance of the Salafi jihadist camp by lumping together diverse groups under the same rubric.

Democracy promotion policies in the region also reflect a lack of understanding. The equation of democratic reforms with free parliamentary elections assumes the intrinsic legitimacy of formal political institutions as an arena in which national actors can negotiate interests and resolve conflicts facing the community. Yet every survey conducted in Muslim societies, including Arab, non-Arab, African, and Asian countries, suggests that they harbor deep and widespread suspicion of formal political authority.[3] This suspicion is unlikely to disappear with the democratization of the political process. Throughout Islamic history, political leaders have not enjoyed the esteem granted to religious scholars, tribal chiefs, or mystics who kept a distance from state power.

One lesson to be drawn from Iraq, for example, is that the formal political process, which privileges majority rule over traditional consensus, might not be the best mechanism for negotiating divisive substantive issues. Religious councils, tribal chiefs, charismatic leaders, local assemblies, and similar informal bodies can be more effective in reinforcing political legitimacy through popular consultation, negotiation, and concessions.

Finally, efforts to improve America's image in the Muslim world must go beyond influencing Muslim public opinion through better communication.

---

3. Ronald Inglehart, "The World Views of Islamic Publics in Global Perspective," *World Values Survey Research Papers* 06-02, May 20, 2006 (Center for the Study of Democracy, http://repositories.cdlib.org/csd/wvsrp/06-02).

We cannot assume that Muslims would change their attitudes if the United States simply changed the packaging of its policies and values.

There is a need for a new vision and a grand strategy to serve the mutual interests of the United States and the Muslim world. At the core of that vision and strategy should be the idea of *tajdid*, or renewal of Islam by modernist Muslim scholars and thinkers for the benefit of Muslim societies. This is not a zero-sum game; the United States *can* help itself by helping the Muslim world.

What Is Tajdid or Islamic Renewal?

The term "Islamic renewal" describes the systematic reconsideration and rationalization of Islamic doctrines, institutions, beliefs, and practices. Many individuals and institutions are involved. Although not formally connected, their efforts coalesce around research centers, individual scholars, modernist religious figures, moderate religious organizations, political parties, and activist Web sites scattered throughout the Muslim world and the Muslim diaspora in the West. While geographically diffuse and lacking a coherent agenda, these efforts have two overarching purposes. The first is to reclaim the Islamic heritage from traditional clerics (associated with autocratic states), extremist Islamist groups (bent on waging holy war against the West and their own "adulterated" societies), and fundamentalist movements (whose goal is to apply strict Sharia law once they gain power through democratic elections or through informal da'wa—a religious call to fellow Muslims to abide by Islamic principles). The major fault lines between modernist Muslim reformers and radical Islamists include the sources of law in the country, the role of religion in public life, gender equality, the foundations of government, the balance between individual and collective rights, and relations with other religions.

The reformists' second goal is to adapt Islamic principles, values, and institutions to the modern world while recognizing the importance of Islam as a cultural frame of reference.

In the western context, the idea of "Islamic renewal" recalls the Christian Reformation. This frequently used analogy requires a word of caution, however. First, Islam does not have a church to be reformed and separated from the state, and it does not have a single religious leader such as the pope from whom religious scholars can dissent. Furthermore, the history of the Christian Reformation is not linear and coherent, as is conventionally assumed. Any analogy would have to specify the geographical location, historical context, and sociological strand of various Christian Reformations at different times and places. Finally, while the Christian Reformation analogy might render intelligible what the Muslim world is going through, it could create false political expectations and posit erroneous evolutionary stages.[4]

At the same time, the idea of "Islamic renewal" may evoke in western popular understanding the specter of Islamic fundamentalism wrapped in legal garb. So we must distinguish the renewal movement from both the conservative Islamist parties that seek to establish Sharia through democratic elections and the more moderate Islamist parties that advocate a modern social and political agenda. Conservative Islamist parties use the modern political process as a peaceful means to establish and legitimate the Islamic state, economy, and society. Although moderate Islamic parties are forward-looking and do not advocate strict application of Sharia, their main objective is still to achieve political power. That may involve building alliances with religious conservatives and curtailing basic democratic rights if necessary. Hence, without a broad modernist worldview, even moderates may fall back on conservative, populist ideologies to harness votes during severe domestic or external crises (such as Bangladesh in 1991, Indonesia in 2004, Malaysia in 1999, Pakistan in 1990 and 1993, and Turkey in 1995 and 1999).

As a strategy, "Islamic renewal" can bring coherence to a significant but scattered cluster of Muslim reformist ideas and tie them to a social and political agenda that includes reform of family codes to give women equal rights; revisions of textbooks to teach human rights and religious pluralism; and modernization of Islamic charities, schools, and consultative traditions. The movement is already a fact on the ground. Various influential Arab and Muslim reformists, including secular human rights and women's groups, consider modernist Islamic values as a means to advocate broad-based social and political change.[5] This is a promising development that also holds great potential for U.S. engagement in the region.

A Culturally Viable Movement

Reformers in the Muslim world always have drawn on Islamic traditions. The concepts of renewal (*tajdid*), reform (*islah*), and renaissance (*nahda*) are firmly rooted in Islamic history. Efforts to renew and reform Islam thus continue a long tradition. The modernizing movement can draw on many historical precedents.

---

4. The example of Reform Judaism is particularly relevant to Muslim diasporas in Europe and America. See, for example, Dana Evan Kaplan, ed., *The Cambridge Companion to American Judaism* (New York: Cambridge University Press, 2005).

5. See Mona Yacoubian, *Promoting Middle East Democracy II: Arab Initiatives*, USIP Special Report 136, May 2005.

In the early period of Islam, the Prophet Muhammad saw himself primarily as a religious reformer with an egalitarian social agenda. Muhammad's attention to the need for reform and renewal is recorded in a prophetic saying (*hadith*) that explicitly calls upon Muslims to renew their faith at the beginning of each century.

During the medieval period, the expansion of Islam from seventh-century Arabia to twelfth-century Asia, Europe, and Africa brought Muslims into contact with diverse peoples and cultures. The Islamic expansions unleashed a profound, and in many ways continuing, debate about the Muslim capacity to adapt to changing needs, cultures, and societies. An important legacy of this process is *ijtihad*, or reinterpretation of the Qur'an and the Sunna (the two main canons of Islam). The existence of four Sunni schools of jurisprudence (*Hanafi*, *Hanbali*, *Maliki*, and *Shafi'i*), alongside the *Shi'i Jafari* school and various mystical orders, attests to the fluidity of Islam and its historic adaptability to worldly considerations and diverse spiritual needs.

In the modern period, Muslims have had to revise or bypass Islamic law to adapt their states and societies to changing realities. The collapse of the Ottoman Empire and the rise of modern nation states following European colonization forced Muslim religious scholars and jurists to rethink the classical Islamic theory of international relations (*siyar*) and adapt it to secular international law.[6] Although many states in the Muslim world still considered themselves part of the *umma* (Muslim community) and formed various Islamic intergovernmental organizations, they fully embraced the notion of national sovereignty and interacted with one another on the basis of international law and norms, even when these contradicted international Islamic legal arguments.[7]

Another significant precedent is the adaptation of Muslim legal traditions to modern public law. With the exception of Saudi Arabia, most Muslim states borrow from modern European penal codes. The aspect of Islamic law that has resisted change is the body of laws regulating personal issues such as marriage, divorce, inheritance, and custody of children. But even here, significant departures from the Sharia have taken place in countries like Tunisia, Morocco, Turkey, and Indonesia.[8]

A third area where Islamic law and institutions have adapted to international standards is human rights. Numerous studies have shown that lack of tangible progress in this area has more to do more with politics than

---

6. See, for example, Abd al-Hamid Abu Sulayman, *The Islamic Theory of International Relations: New Directions for Islamic Methodology and Thought* (Herndon, VA: International Institute of Islamic Thought, 1987).

7. Abdeslam Maghraoui, "Ambiguities of Sovereignty: Morocco, The Hague and the Western Sahara Dispute," *Mediterranean Politics* 8, no. 1 (spring 2003), 113–126.

8. Mahnaz Afkhami and Erika Friedl, *Muslim Women and the Politics of Participation: Implementing the Beijing Platform* (Syracuse: Syracuse University Press, 1997).

theology.[9] In the end, for the Islamic renewal project to succeed, Muslim modernist thinkers from different countries need to share their experiences and strategies. Equally important is "cross-topical" fertilization, through which methods to accommodate secular international law and national sovereignty can be applied to women's rights, freedom of belief, and human rights.

A Strong Philosophical Legacy

The Islamic renewal movement can also draw on a progressive Muslim political philosophy. Many important social concepts in Islam, such as *maslaha 'amma* (common good), *masali'h al-'ibad* (the welfare of the people), *'adl* (social justice), *rahma* (compassion in social interactions), *ahl al-dhima* (religious minority rights), and *fard 'ayn* (human beings' capacity to act responsibly), are clearly applicable to modern society. Notions of *ijma'* (consensus), *shura* (consultation), *'aqd* (contract), *haqq* (right), *naskh* (change or abrogation of existing laws or Qur'anic injunctions), *talfiq* (invention), *kiyas* (reasoning by analogy beyond scriptural evidence), and *ijtihad* provide a formidable politico-conceptual apparatus to revise anachronistic rulings and legitimize modern, accountable governance. Last, religiously prescribed values, such as the protection of human life, personal property, moral and intellectual integrity, and the natural environment, provide ample means for molding a modern ethical outlook.

Implications for U.S. Foreign Policy

The importance of supporting "Islamic renewal" to counter religious extremism and enhance relations between the Muslim world and the West cannot be overstated. The fundamental question is whether the U.S. government can play a role without compromising the nascent renewal movement. Skeptics point to two major problems: Faith-based initiatives are unlikely to muster American political support because they raise thorny constitutional issues. The other challenge is that the U.S. government is not trusted in the region. Any overt American role could undermine the modernists' agenda and position. These are valid concerns.

However, the United States is already implicitly involved in reforms with religious connotations. USAID and State Department programs that aim to revise textbooks, upgrade primary and secondary education, empower women, engage with moderate Islamists, modernize the legal systems, or encourage interfaith dialogue already involve normative issues and taking sides in religious conflicts.

9. Abdullahi An-Naim, *Toward an Islamic Reformation: Civil Liberties, Human Rights, and International Law* (Syracuse: Syracuse University Press, 1990).

As for the U.S. standing in the region, Islamic renewal provides a great healing opportunity, perhaps the only realistic one. Calling on Muslims to reform their societies on the basis of their own humanistic traditions and cultural heritage is surely less controversial for the United States than supporting regime change, cooperating with local security agencies, or pushing for reforms in the name of an abstract, secular notion of western democracy.

Current efforts by various government programs involving implicit religious reforms are insufficient and do not have a major impact because they lack clarity of purpose and coordination. They do not adequately involve independent American institutions, international agencies, and transnational civil society. They lack an explicit commitment and a concerted effort to engage with broad Muslim constituencies through trusted local charities, civic groups, and moderate religious movements. The involvement of the Islamic renewal movement would reinforce U.S. engagement, international backing, and Muslim support for meaningful, forward-looking reforms in the Muslim world. Outside the Islamic framework, there is no real chance for substantive, progressive, and sustainable reform in the Muslim world.

Democratic reforms in the Muslim world during the coming decade are likely to bring to power Islamist political parties. "Islamic politics" has emerged as the most likely choice among a constituency of hundreds of millions of people stretching from the Atlantic Ocean to Southeast Asia. Religious values and beliefs continue to inform social interactions at the community level; influential social groups throughout the Muslim world, including social, political, and economic elites, adhere to such a vision; and the formal political process has been shifting to accommodate "Islamic politics." Religion in politics is a reality in the Muslim world.

But what brand of "Islamic politics" will triumph? The radical, extremist version certainly has gained ground during the past decade, but a modernist, humanistic form of Islam should not be dismissed. U.S. policies could help tip the balance.

Before us is a historic opportunity for positive change in the Muslim world and for constructive American engagement. The most realistic and sustainable strategy for the United States today is to support a broad-based Islamic renewal movement by modernist Muslim thinkers for the explicit benefit of Muslim societies. Only a modern, reformed Islam can provide the normative appeal to mobilize broad Muslim constituencies against religious extremism, for modern accountable governance, and for better understanding with the West. The development of such movements in the Muslim world is the terrorists' biggest fear and vulnerability. A renewal movement that addresses the Muslim world's major problems, using familiar language, historical references, and religious values, and providing a hopeful alternative to al-Qaeda's message of violence and self-destruction, will discredit not only bin Laden and his associates but the Salafi jihadist ideology as a whole.

America's most obvious allies in this effort are independent, moderate Muslim thinkers, scholars, and community leaders who may question the moral superiority of "secular reason" but are willing to confront violence, oppression, and intolerance in the name of Islam. Moderate Islamist parties throughout the region, charitable groups with a social agenda in Morocco, Egypt, or Indonesia, international Islamic feminist networks, religious literary circles in Turkey, or prominent Islamic universities such as Malaysia's, are all potential partners. The other religious actors are either ideologically opposed to a modernist project or do not have the political will to carry it out. The Salafists, who seek a society patterned exclusively on the Qur'an and Sunna, radically oppose modernity—which for them includes Islam's ninth-century, classical, golden age. Salafists include violent groups like al-Qaeda and its affiliates and nonviolent groups associated with schools, sects, and doctrines that reject *ijtihad* and call for a return to an unmediated, original Islam.

Proponents of traditional Islam, including official religious scholars, state-run religious institutions, and chief muftis of prominent religious universities such as al-Azhar, are generally not hostile to the West. But they often are too closed-minded or dependent on authoritarian governments to provide a credible alternative to the Salafi onslaught. And radical Islamist parties—who compete for votes with the moderate Islamists—can be tempted by ideological extremism if they participate in the political process.

Despite growing efforts and networks, the prospects for an Islamic renewal across countries and regions remains slim, unless these scattered efforts and networks coalesce in a coherent movement that can articulate a common modernist vision and propose concrete reforms to achieve it.

Conclusion

Current U.S. efforts to fight terrorism, promote democratic change, and improve America's image in the Muslim world are insufficient because they do not pay attention to the religious debate in the Muslim world. The United States could address these challenges by using the enormous, yet neglected, normative capital of Islamic reformist traditions in partnership with viable and credible Muslim partners. Obviously, the mechanisms, specific policies, and programmatic priorities of these concepts must be developed, refined, and synchronized to maximize impact and ensure cumulative success.

Policymakers should take into consideration differences among Muslim states and societies, as well as the varying degrees of religious sensitivity.

For example, it would be ill-advised to make Saudi Arabia the test case of religious reforms in the Muslim world or to assert the human origin of the Qur'an as the starting point of the Islamic renewal project. Nonetheless, the principles of reforms outlined in this essay are realistic and grounded in historical precedents. U.S. policymakers are beginning to see the importance of engaging not just states and opposition groups, but Islam itself. Indeed, as the ideological fault lines become more apparent, several U.S. government agencies already are implicitly taking sides by supporting "moderate" Islamic leaders, groups, or parties. In this situation, American detachment is not a realistic option.

Recommendations

1. The United States should support the establishment of a "Muslim World Foundation" to foster the development of peaceful, prosperous, and open Muslim societies and polities. Modeled after the Asia Foundation and funded by an Act of Congress, such a body would focus on the major crosscutting challenges, including religious reforms, facing the Muslim world. But a Muslim World Foundation need not be an exclusively U.S. body. The United States could adopt a centuries-old Islamic endowment tradition called *wakf*, used by leaders, states, and wealthy individuals to provide for charities, schools, and universities. The Muslim World Foundation would draw on local and international experts, donors, and partners. And it would collaborate with government and non-governmental associates across the Muslim world to pursue its agenda. As a nonprofit and independent organization, the Muslim World Foundation would retain its intellectual credibility and ability to act as a convener and peacemaker, regardless of international tensions or U.S. policies.

2. The United States should provide special grants to American universities to promote Muslim modernist works and ideas and translate them into concrete policies. Muslim modernist thinkers are scattered throughout the world, and when they meet—on rare occasions—their debates and conference proceedings are not translated into practical reform policies. It is essential to establish regional forums where Muslim modernist thinkers meet regularly to sort out political, philosophical, and ideological differences and identify common denominators and goals. It is not sufficient to mobilize modernists to express themselves. It is also important to identify specific reform policies to be addressed to people and governments in the Muslim world, as well as to the international community—including western powers, the United Nations, the Organization of the Islamic Conference, the International Court of Justice, and the World Bank.

The Arab Human Development Reports provide a very useful model. A similar series, exposing in stark terms the decay of Islamic cultures and civilizations and written by respected, diverse, and sympathetic Muslim scholars, would get the Muslim world's attention.

3. The United States should engage Islamist parties on normative grounds. Throughout the region, Islamist parties have emerged as major actors and likely winners when allowed to compete without constraint. Some of these parties run on conservative agendas and promise to apply strict Sharia; others are more liberal and advocate a modern social agenda. Yet most are pragmatic and willing to compromise on how much of Islamic law should be applied. This raises the issue of how to integrate Islamists into the democratic process without compromising the spirit of democracy or the rules and procedures that sustain it.

In other words, the rationale of organizing free elections to promote democracy is questionable if the likely winners might subvert democratic norms and procedures. Yet too many procedural constraints and pre-negotiated arrangements could delegitimize the democratic process. When incentives are offered to moderate Islamists, the conservative rank-and-file and constituencies may rebel. Hence, institutional constraints to limit the power of Islamists, or incentives that look like cooptation measures, may actually backfire.

Instead of coercion and cooptation, "normative engagement" is a more constructive strategy. That is, debate with Islamists must take place about substantive issues such as civil liberties, freedom of worship, individual autonomy, women's rights, the rights of minorities, political pluralism, limitations on the powers of the state, and similar issues. For example: How would verbal commitment to the full range of civil and political rights play out in the real world? If Islamist leaders qualify the relevance of "divine sovereignty" and emphasize the role of elected rulers, that does not guarantee they will respect modern democratic rights. Anti-democratic norms and restrictions can be imposed in the name of a conservative majority that believes ultimate sovereignty rests with God. Islamist leaders are not clear about whom they represent. Some Islamic principles may well be compatible with modern democratic norms, but the challenge is how Muslims choose to apply them. The possibility exists that different, even contradictory, interpretations of Islamic principles can arise and, in the absence of institutionalized religious authority accepted by all, lead to the subversion of democratic norms.

4. The United States should put more emphasis on substantive social, educational, and religious reforms. National elections are essential to democratic legislative and executive authority. But if abstracted from substantive issues, the exercise will result in a superficial formal process manipulated by semi-authoritarian rulers and radical Islamists. Concern with normative, substantive issues does not preclude other crucial institutional reforms. The development of a robust civil society, an independent judiciary, a transparent government, a depoliticized military, and accountable security forces is just as important for creating hospitable conditions for democratic representation. Moreover, combining limited elections with serious institutional reforms to enhance the state's performance and accountability can easily be justified according to Islamic discursive conventions. Equally important, however, is the need for the U.S. government to encourage religious reforms to modernize Islamic principles, teachings, institutions, practices, and jurisprudence. The cornerstone of these reforms is the effort to expand the conceptual boundaries and foundations of Sharia beyond the Qur'an and Sunna, or what Muslims consider the fundamental basis of Islam. In other words, it is important to establish publicly that *ijtihad* has been a major source in the formulation of Islamic law. This point is important in justifying modern advances in women's rights, civil rights, human rights, and the accommodation of cultural and religious differences on Islamic grounds.

5. The United States should refocus and coordinate public diplomacy, democracy promotion, and aid programs to reinforce Islamic religious reforms and renewal. Public diplomacy should link American values and Islam's humanist traditions. Muslims are proud of a golden-age heritage they associate with openness, tolerance, and scientific achievements. Islamic traditions are entirely compatible with American values such as tolerance and entrepreneurship. Emphasizing these aspects of Islam and similar American values will help discredit Islamic extremists.

Democracy initiatives should include religious reform. If permissible, organizations such as the National Democratic Institute and the National Endowment for Democracy should expand their programs beyond elections, political parties, and parliaments. Nothing in their mandate would prevent them from supporting the modern training of religious scholars, judges, and imams; providing special scholarships to women studying religious topics; and reprinting and disseminating writings by modernist Muslim scholars. The United States should support local groups at the forefront of these reforms.

6. The United States should consider supporting religious charities. Because many Muslim governments' social safety nets are weak or nonexistent, religious organizations provide many services to the needy, including clinics, childcare, and disaster relief. Concerns that these networks are linked to terrorism are often misplaced. Extremists with a global jihadist agenda do not open local "soup kitchens" to build electoral support. They pursue different strategies. USAID should work with Islamic social networks and give impetus to moderate Islam by funding small charities and training programs for youth and women.

2

Religion in World Affairs: Its Role in Conflict and Peace

David R. Smock

In recent decades, religion has assumed unusual prominence in international affairs. A recent article in *The Economist*[1] asserts that, if there ever was a global drift toward secularism, it has been halted and probably reversed. In the article, Philip Jenkins, a noted scholar from Pennsylvania State University, predicts that when historians look back at this century they will see religion as "the prime animating and destructive force in human affairs, guiding attitudes to political liberty and obligation, concepts of nationhood and, of course, conflicts and wars." The article then cites statistics from a public opinion survey in Nigeria demonstrating that Nigerians believe religion to be more central to their identity than nationality. Nigerians are thus more likely to identify themselves first and foremost as Christians or Muslims rather than as Nigerians. The horrendous events of September 11, the conflagration in Iraq, and the aggressive assertiveness of the quasi-theocratic Iran only confirm in the popular mind that religion lies behind much of contemporary international conflict.

Religion and Conflict

Throughout the world, no major religion is exempt from complicity in violent conflict. Religious conviction certainly was one of the motivations for the September 11 attacks and other violent actions by Muslim extremists in Pakistan and Afghanistan. Some Buddhist monks assert an exclusively Buddhist identity for Sri Lanka, fanning the flames of conflict there. Some Christian and Muslim leaders from former Yugoslavia saw themselves as protecting their faiths when they defended violence against the opposing faith communities in the Balkan wars.

1. "In God's Name," The Economist, November 1, 2007.

David R. Smock, "Religion in World Affairs: Its Role in Conflict and Peace," Special Report 201 (Washington, DC: USIP, 2008).

Yet we need to beware of an almost universal propensity to oversimplify the role that religion plays in international affairs. Iran's international assertiveness is as much due to Iranian-Persian nationalism as it is to the dictates of Shiite clerics. The international policies that Iran's clerics adopt are rarely driven by theological precepts or religious doctrine, but rather political power calculations and a desire to preserve the quasi-theocratic status quo. Similarly, in Iraq, conflict between Sunnis and Shiites rarely stems from differences over religious doctrine and practice, but rather from historical and contemporary competition for state power. Sunni and Shiite identities are as much ethnic as religious, and intergroup relations between the two are very similar, though more violent, than relations between Walloons and Flemish in Belgium or between English and French in Canada, where language and culture rather than religious beliefs constitute the primary sources of division. Meanwhile, the Kurds—the third principal constituent community in Iraq—is ethnically based. Most Kurds are also Sunni Muslims. This is not to suggest that religious identity is synonymous with ethnic identity, as in many circumstances religious identity implies explicitly religious behavior and belief. But in many circumstances the lines between ethnic and religious identities become so blurred that parsing them to assign blame for violence is difficult if not impossible. Religious identity has often been used to mobilize one side against the other, as has happened in Iraq, Sudan, and elsewhere; populations have responded to calls to defend one's faith community. But to describe many such conflicts as rooted in religious differences or to imply that theological or doctrinal differences are the principal causes of conflict is to seriously oversimplify and misrepresent a complex situation.

The decades-long civil war in Sudan is often described as a religious conflict between Muslims and Christians, with the north being predominantly Muslim and the south predominantly Christian or animist. There is some truth to this characterization, particularly after 1989, when an Islamic fundamentalist government came to power in Khartoum with an agenda to Islamicize all of Sudan. But the differences between north and south go well beyond religion and rarely are the disagreements religious or theological in character. Northerners speak Arabic and want Arabic to be Sudan's national language. Southerners generally speak Arabic only as a second or third language, if at all, and prefer English as the lingua franca. Northerners are more likely to identify with the Arab world, whereas southerners tend to identify themselves as Africans. Racial identity is thus fundamental to the division between north and south. The religious division between Christian and Muslim happens to overlap with these racial, ethnic, and geographical divisions, but the conflict's divide has not been not confined to or even dominated by religion. British colonial policy also reinforced the divisions between north and south, and over the past twenty years Christians have fought Christians in the south and Muslims have fought Muslims in Darfur.

In Nigeria, religion is divisive and a factor in conflict, but it is often exaggerated as the cause of conflict. The popular press asserts that tens of thousands of Nigerians have died in religious warfare over the last decade. True, many died, both Christians and Muslims, in riots over Danish cartoons depicting Mohammed. Others were killed when Christians opposed extending the authority of *sharia* courts in several northern states. But the causes of many of the killings have not been exclusively religious. In places like Kaduna and Plateau State, conflicts described as religious have been more complicated than that; the causes also include the placing of markets, economic competition, occupational differences, the ethnic identity of government officials, respect for traditional leaders, and competition between migrants and indigenous populations.[2]

In both Somalia and Afghanistan, one source of the conflicts there is over which brand of Islam will prevail. But in both cases clan and ethnic differences define the composition of the forces in conflict as much as religious differences do. In the Arab-Israeli conflict, the management of and access to religious sites are sources of serious disagreement and extreme religious groups—both Jewish and Muslim—exacerbate the problem. But religion is not the principal factor underlying the conflict; rather, conflict is principally over control of land and state sovereignty.

All of these cases demonstrate that while religion is an important factor in conflict, often marking identity differences, motivating conflict, and justifying violence, religion is not usually the sole or primary cause of conflict. The reality is that religion becomes intertwined with a range of causal factors—economic, political, and social—that define, propel, and sustain conflict. Certainly, religious disagreements must be addressed alongside these economic, political, and social sources to build lasting reconciliation. Fortunately, many of the avenues to ameliorate religious violence lie within the religious realm itself.

Religious Activism to Promote Peace with Justice

The public perception prevails that religion is a principal source of international conflict, but the role of religion as a force in peacemaking is usually overlooked. The United States became heavily engaged in trying to bring peace to Sudan because evangelical Christians pressured the Bush administration to deepen its engagement. Evangelical concern was based initially

2. David R. Smock, ed., *Religious Contributions to Peacemaking: When Religion Brings Peace, Not War,* USIP Peaceworks no. 55 (Washington, DC: United States Institute of Peace, 2006), p. 17.

on an oversimplified view of the conflict, that an Islamic fundamentalist government was forcing Christians and animists in southern Sudan to convert to Islam. As evangelicals mobilized, they developed a more nuanced and authentic understanding of the conflict. Jews have joined Christians and others in bringing public attention to the crisis in Darfur because widespread slaughter there has been viewed as genocide, provoking memories of the Holocaust.

Religious communities have also directly opposed repression and promoted peace and reconciliation. Churches in Eastern Europe mobilized opposition to Soviet occupation. More famously, clergymen Desmond Tutu, Frank Chikane, and Beyers Naude in South Africa worked to break the bonds of apartheid. This effort entailed not only civil disobedience and advocacy for international sanctions against South Africa, but also shaming white South African Christians into recognizing that their effort to justify apartheid biblically contradicted biblical teachings. The Dutch Reformed Church—sometimes described as "the Nationalist Party at prayer"—did not fully accept that argument until after the government abandoned apartheid, but many whites did become uncomfortable with the structures they had devised and imposed.

More recently, the civil disobedience of Buddhist monks in Burma (Myanmar) dramatically illustrated how religion could motivate the promotion of human rights and peace. In addition to the street demonstrations that garnered so much national and international attention, the monks' refusal to accept alms from members of the military was a particularly poignant declaration that the regime's policies and actions violated Buddhism's fundamental precepts. The regime recognized that the demonstrations generated much greater international attention and domestic pressure than would have been the case if they had been exclusively secular. The monks' moral authority and respect that others had for them, the symbolic resources they drew upon, their chants for compassion, and their nonviolent approach all contributed to a deeply persuasive message and image. The largely religious leadership of the U.S. civil rights movement in the 1960s carried similar moral weight and authority.

According to Douglas Johnston, in promoting peace and reconciliation, religious leaders and organizations offer credibility as trusted institutions; a respected set of values; moral warrants to oppose injustice; unique leverage for promoting reconciliation among conflicting parties; capability to mobilize community, nation, and international support for a peace process; and a sense of calling that often inspires perseverance in the face of major and otherwise debilitating obstacles.[3]

---

3. Douglas Johnston, "The Religious Dimension," unpublished paper, n.d., p. 3, based upon Johnston, ed., *Trumping Realpolitik: Faith-Based Diplomacy* (New York: Oxford University Press, 2003).

Religious Mediation and Facilitation

Religious leaders and institutions can be mediators in conflict situations, serve as a communication link between opposing sides, and provide training in peacemaking methodologies. In the summer of 2001, Rabbi Menachem Froman, chief rabbi of the Tekoa settlement in the West Bank, approached the United States Institute of Peace and indicated that one of the two chief rabbis of Israel, Bakshi Doron, and the chief Palestinian sheikh, Talal Sidr, wanted to come to the Institute to sign a joint declaration for religious peace between Israel and Palestine. While the Institute welcomed this initiative, it did not turn out to be feasible, largely because of visa problems that Sidr encountered. But then Archbishop of Canterbury George Carey became involved and in January 2002 helped organize a large conference in Alexandria, Egypt for many of the most highly placed Jewish, Muslim, and Christian leaders from Israel and Palestine. The participants signed a declaration of religious peace that became known as the Alexandria Declaration. The Alexandria process has continued since then, with regular interfaith meetings of religious leaders held in Jerusalem, guided by Canon Andrew White of the Foundation for Relief and Reconciliation in the Middle East (FRRME), Rabbi Michael Melchior, and, until his death, Sheikh Talal Sidr. The Institute has been the principal financial backer of the Alexandria process since it began. With financial support from the Institute and other sources, Rabbi Melchior has also established centers in Israel and Gaza to promote interfaith dialogue more broadly in Israel and Palestine.

Recently, under the leadership of Rabbi David Rosen and Muslim and Christian leaders in Israel and Palestine, a new interfaith organization has been launched with a similar mission to that the Alexandria process, namely, to provide a religious track to what hopefully will be a political track to promote peace in the Middle East. Before the Annapolis peace conference in November 2007, this Council of Religious Institutions in the Holy Land sent a delegation to Washington consisting of the highest-ranking Jewish, Muslim, and Christian leaders in the Holy Land to reinforce the message that religious leaders in Israel and Palestine are committed to a serious peace process. They agreed upon a six-point plan to use their positions of leadership "to prevent religion being used as a source of conflict, and to serve the goals of a just and comprehensive peace and reconciliation."

Rabbi Froman has reached across the typical lines of religious and ethnic division to communicate with Hamas. When Hamas leader Sheikh Ahmed Yassin (who was killed in 2004) was incarcerated in an Israeli prison, Froman visited him frequently, and the two men formed a bond due to their shared religiosity despite their adherence to different traditions. Before Yasser Arafat's death, Froman regularly visited his offices in Ramallah carrying messages between him and the Israeli government. With Hamas's rise to power in Gaza, Froman has contacted the new leadership and offered to establish lines of communication between Hamas and the Israelis, an offer that the Israelis have not yet taken up.

For the past five years the Institute also has partnered with a remarkable pair of religious peacemakers in Nigeria, the Reverend James Wuye and Imam Mohammed Ashafa of the Inter Faith Mediation Center. Remarkably, roughly simultaneous epiphanies transformed the pastor and imam from religious warriors to religious peacemakers. They had been engaged in the violent struggle between Christians and Muslims in Kaduna, Nigeria before they committed their lives to turning religious conflict into peace and reconciliation. Joint activities between the Institute and the Inter Faith Mediation Center have included training for young Nigerian religious leaders in peacemaking techniques; sponsoring a religious summit for top Muslim and Christian leaders in Nigeria to combat violence during Nigeria's 2007 elections; and efforts to establish a strong interfaith council in Nigeria that includes Christian and Muslim leaders. Their work brought peace mediations to two different parts of Plateau State, where thousands have died in fighting between Christians and Muslims. In Yelwa-Nshar, where over 1,000 villagers were slaughtered in May 2004, the pastor, imam, and author of this paper successfully mediated a peace agreement that ended violence and resulted in a compact to promote reconciliation and the resolution of contentious issues between Christians and Muslims. The peacemaking methodology drew from Western conflict-resolution techniques as well as traditional Nigerian approaches, but religious components were also central. These included using scripture, with both pastor and imam quoting both the Bible and the Qur'an, along with exhortation based on religious principles. In 2008 the Institute will assist the pastor and imam to travel to other African countries to share their peacemaking methodologies with religious peacemakers in those countries. In addition the Institute will finance the production of a DVD illustrating these methodologies so that prospective peacemakers in Africa and beyond can benefit from the successes that the pastor and imam have achieved.

In Sudan, Christian-Muslim relations remain tense despite the Comprehensive Peace Agreement signed in 2005 to end the north-south war. With assistance from the Institute, the Sudan Inter Religious Council (SIRC), our partner organization in Sudan, has organized high-level meetings between Muslim and Christian leaders. It has also established local interfaith peace committees where Sudan faces its most volatile intergroup relations. In 2008 SIRC will focus on strengthening interfaith peace committees in Darfur, where the tensions are most acute.

In 2005, the Institute, along with Catholic University and the International Center for Religion and Diplomacy, cohosted a visit by a delegation of nine religious leaders from Iran, including seven Muslims, one Christian, and one Jew. A week of meetings with U.S. religious and secular leaders opened up deeper understanding between the Iranians and Americans. As the week progressed, it became evident that the Iranians were much more comfortable discussing sensitive issues with Americans when the discussions took place in a religious context. The Iranian delegation refused to visit congressional offices to meet with members of Congress, but when a meeting was relocated to a townhouse owned by the National Prayer Breakfast, the Iranians did not hesitate to meet with several members of the House and the Senate, where they discussed some of the most divisive issues that make U.S.-Iran relations so conflicted.

Building on this insight, the Institute decided to send a delegation of American Muslim specialists on Islamic peacemaking to Iran to meet with their Iranian counterparts. This trip, organized by the Salaam Institute, took place in October 2007. Members of the delegation gained valuable insights into Iranian society and Iran's intellectual and religious life. Doors were opened to them because they were Muslims and their Iranian counterparts were enormously grateful for the visit. They were fascinated to be able to relate to religious brethren and to learn that Islam thrives in the United States. The Institute and the Salaam Institute plan to invite a return delegation of Iranian specialists on Islamic peacemaking to the United States in 2008.

The Institute's partner working in the religious realm in Iraq is Canon Andrew White of FRRME. After helping to found the interfaith Iraqi Institute of Peace in Baghdad with Institute support and partnership, White helped organize the Iraqi Inter-Religious Congress (IIRC). In 2007 the IIRC brought together a cross section of high-level Sunni, Shiite, and Christian leaders who committed themselves to promoting peace in Iraq. After meetings held between Sunni clerics and advisers to Grand Ayatollah Ali Sistani, a delegation of Sunni clerics met with the ayatollah in November 2007. Following that meeting Sistani issued a *fatwa* condemning violence against all Iraqis and urged Shiites to make special effort to protect Sunnis. This breakthrough occurred because the approach was religious and despite the fact that an Anglican priest was the initiator.

Interfaith Dialogue

Interfaith dialogue is another form of religious peacemaking. Rather than seeking to resolve a particular conflict, it aims to defuse interfaith tensions that may cause future conflict or derive from previous conflict. Shortly after September 11, when tensions worldwide were particularly high between Muslims on one side and Christians and Jews on the other, the Institute, focusing on the United States and Europe, organized a series of interfaith dialogues to generate lessons about how to defuse interfaith tensions. These lessons are summarized in *Building Interreligious Trust in a*

Climate of Fear: An Abrahamic Trialogue.[4] This was followed by an edited volume, *Interfaith Dialogue and Peacebuilding,*[5] which drew on cases from the Balkans, Northern Ireland, the Middle East, and elsewhere to extract lessons about how to conduct effective interfaith dialogue. The Institute will soon offer an online course about interfaith dialogue on its website. Other Institute publications have provided guidance about how to evaluate the success of interfaith dialogue[6] and how a religious community can learn about the faiths of other religious communities in educational institutions.[7]

The Union for Reform Judaism and the Islamic Society of North American recently cooperated to produce curriculum material for Jewish-Muslim dialogue. The program, entitled *The Children of Abraham: Jews and Muslims in Conversation,* addresses scripture, theology, ethical principles, and diversity within the two traditions. The material also addresses sensitive issues at the heart of disputes between the global Jewish and Muslim communities, including the status of Jerusalem, Islamophobia, and anti-Semitism.[8]

In 2007, 138 Muslim scholars, clerics, and intellectuals gathered in Amman, Jordan and issued "A Common Word Between Us and You," a statement that declared common ground between Christianity and Islam. The signatories to this message came from every denomination and school of thought in Islam. Every major Islamic country or region in the world was also represented in this message. The declaration cites scriptural parallels between the two faiths and the many similarities in their core teachings. A large group of Christian scholars and clergy signed a response prepared at Yale Divinity School expressing appreciation for the Muslim declaration and concurring with its central assertions. The Vatican also issued a positive response and invited some of the Muslim signatories to meet with the Pope.[9] This exchange underscored what is so often forgotten in these times of Christian-Muslim tension, namely, the similarities between the two faiths.

Interfaith Dialogue in the Middle East, published recently by the Institute's press,[10] demonstrates that interfaith dialogue is an expanding enterprise even where interreligious tensions are the greatest, as in Israel-Palestine,

---

4. USIP Special Report 99 (Washington: United States Institute of Peace Press, 2003).

5. David Smock, ed. *Interfaith Dialogue and Peacebuilding* (Washington: United States Institute of Peace Press, 2007).

6. Renee Garfinkel, *What Works? Evaluating Interfaith Dialogue Programs,* Special Report 123 (Washington: United States Institute of Peace Press, 2004).

7. David Smock, *Teaching about the Religious Other,* Special Report 143 (Washington: United States Institute of Peace Press, 2005).

8. Union for Reform Judaism, URJ–Muslim Dialogue, available at http://urj.org/muslim dialogue/ (accessed January 15, 2008).

9. The original letter and the responses can be read at A Common Word, available at www.acommonword.com (accessed January 15, 2008).

10. Mohammed Abu-Nimer, Emily Welty, and Amal I. Khoury, *Unity in Diversity: Interfaith Dialogue in the Middle East* (Washington: United States Institute of Peace Press, 2007).

Lebanon, and Egypt. The research findings also demonstrate the extent to which interfaith dialogue needs to be tailored to the particular religious and political context in which it is occurring. One particularly sensitive issue in the Israeli-Palestinian context is the asymmetry of power among the Jewish, Muslim, and Christian communities and the need to ensure that Palestinian participants play an equal role to Jews in the conception, organization, and implementation of an interfaith dialogue process.

Not infrequently the most contentious interfaith relationships can turn out to have the most meaningful and productive exchanges. In 2005 the embassy of Saudi Arabia asked the Institute to host five Muslim scholars from Saudi Arabia for a week of religious discussions in Washington. The Institute accepted on the condition that it fully controlled whom the Saudis would meet and what the agendas for the discussions would be. One day was devoted to meeting with Muslim counterparts, another day to meeting with Christian clergy and theologians, and a third day to meeting with Jewish leaders, primarily orthodox rabbis. By far the most productive meeting was that held between the Saudis and the Jewish leaders. Unlike the Christians and the Muslims, who principally sought to establish their common humanity with the Saudis, the Jewish leaders and Saudi scholars addressed the tough issues. The Jewish leaders asked the Saudis if they could accept the existence of a Jewish state in the Middle East. The Saudis in return wanted to know if they could be critical of the policies of Israel without being accused of anti-Semitism. Each side spoke to the other with firmness and respect, and an atmosphere of civility prevailed, enabling the participants to address the issues honestly and forthrightly.

U.S. Government Neglect of the Religious Dimension

Given the importance of religion as both a source of international conflict and a resource for peacemaking, it is regrettable that the U.S. government is so ill equipped to handle religious issues and relate to religious actors. An act of Congress in 1998 authorized the establishment of both the Office of Religious Freedom in the State Department and the U.S. Commission on International Religious Freedom. As a result, religious freedom is a significant issue on the U.S. foreign policy agenda. But religious conflict and religious peacemaking are too frequently neglected. Former Secretary of State Madeleine Albright addresses this issue in her recent book,[11] noting the shortcomings of the Clinton administration along with all other U.S. administrations in understanding and addressing religious factors. She recommends that all foreign-service officers be trained in relevant religious subjects and that specialists on religion be posted to U.S. embassies abroad.

---

11. Madeleine Albright, *The Mighty and the Almighty* (New York: HarperCollins, 2006).

A report published in 2007 by the Center for Strategic and International Studies picks up Albright's points.[12] The report concludes that

> U.S. government officials are often reluctant to address the issue of religion, whether in response to a secular U.S. legal and political tradition, in the context of America's Judeo-Christian image overseas, or simply because religion is perceived as too complicated or sensitive. . . . Current U.S. government frameworks for approaching religion are narrow, often because they approach religions as problematic or monolithic forces, overemphasize a terrorism-focused analysis of Islam, or marginalize religion as a peripheral humanitarian or cultural issue. . . . Institutional capacity to understand and approach religion is limited due to legal limitations, lack of religious expertise or training, minimal influence for religion-related initiatives, and a government primarily structured to engage with other official state actors.[13]

These and other analysts argue that if the U.S. government is to insert itself into international conflicts or build deeper and more productive relationships with countries around the world, it needs a better strategy to engage effectively and respectfully with the religious realm. As September 11 and the current situation in Iraq attest, failure to understand religious motivations and interpretations of political situations is ultimately to our nation's detriment. As has increasingly been learned in Iraq, however, engaging religious leaders can create tangible and positive results that contribute to peace and global security.

Conclusion

In June 2007, reflecting a growing international awareness of the past neglect of religion, Sheikha Haya Rashed Al Khalifa, the president of the United Nations General Assembly, stated that "promoting a true dialogue among civilizations and religions is perhaps the most important political instrument that we can use to reach out across borders and build bridges of peace and hope."[14]

This report has sought to demonstrate the nature of the religious dimension of international conflict, which is sometimes neglected, often misunderstood, and frequently exaggerated. It has also illustrated how religious leaders have addressed conflict and injustices confronting their societies. In addition, religious leaders have employed a variety of peacemaking techniques, ranging from mediation and facilitation to interfaith dialogue, to address conflict around the globe and make the world a more peaceful place.

---

12. Liora Danan and Alice Hunt, *Mixed Blessings: U.S. Government Engagement with Religion in Conflict-Prone Settings* (Washington, DC: Center for Strategic and International Studies, 2007). Available at www.csis.org/media/csis/pubs/070820_religion.pdf (accessed January 19, 2008).

13. Danan and Hunt, *Mixed Blessings*, p. 3.

14. United Nations press release, June 13, 2007.

3

Islam Is Not *the* Solution (or *the* Problem)

Daniel Brumberg

The quest to repair, reinterpret, reform, or otherwise fix Islam can be seen in a range of official and nongovernmental initiatives, the likes of which were hardly imaginable before Al Qaeda's emergence. Colloquia on *ijtihad* (the interpretation of Islam), conferences promoting liberal Islamic networks, and the funding of liberal Muslim thinkers and their writings are but a few examples of recent efforts to support Muslim voices that have been drowned out by the din of Islamist populism. This development should warm many hearts in the Arab world. After all, Islamists themselves have long argued that democratic reform requires a transformation of Muslim consciousness, asserting that the evolution of Islamic identity is the source of the problem and thus the core of the solution.[1]

That an expanding circle of academics, journalists, and policymakers in the United States has adopted some version of this argument is a trend that holds both promise and concern. Because, with few exceptions, Islamists remain the best organized and most influential opposition forces in the Arab world, any policy that does not engage mainstream Islamists, particularly advocates of a more pluralistic Islam, will fail to be credible or effective. Yet, without understanding the intricacies of Islamist politics, U.S. efforts to enlist Islamists and their ideas in the cause of democracy will do little good and might do considerable harm. The problem is not merely that an uncritical engagement might strengthen illiberal Islamist forces.[2] The more fundamental problem is the erroneous assumption that Islam itself provides the foundation of political identity.

1. See Raymond William Baker, *Islam Without Fear: Egypt and the New Islamists* (Cambridge, MA: Harvard University Press, 2003). See also *Muslim Democrat* 7, no. 1 (April 2005), http://www.islam-democracy.org/.

2. See Gregory Gause, "Can Democracy Stop Terrorism," *Foreign Affairs* 84, no. 5 (September/October 2005): 62–76.

Daniel Brumberg, "Islam Is Not *the* Solution (or *the* Problem)," *The Washington Quarterly* 29, no. 1 (2006): 97–116. Reprinted with permission.

Challenging this assumption and the misleading policies that have emerged from it is tricky. Who today would assail a policy that, to its credit, has broken with the "soft bigotry of low expectations"[3] that long guided Washington's approach to the Middle East? As President George W. Bush has repeatedly stated, it is wrong to assume that "millions of men and women are condemned by history or culture to live in despotism."[4] Yet, even if bigoted notions about an intrinsically "authoritarian" Islam are dangerous, so too is the facile conviction that, with the proper formula and a dose of wise clerical leadership, Islam and democracy will join forces. One should be wary of replacing an outdated ethnocentrism with an equally simplistic universalism. To jump from one to the other conflates a vaguely messianic impulse to bridge the divide between the Islamic world and the West with the more prosaic task of grasping how the thorny question of identity, and not merely Islam itself, fits into the complex puzzle of democratic transformation.

On this score, the "Islam is the solution" approach—a policy that seeks to promote democracy through supporting new Islamic thinking and new Islamic parties—suffers from three shortcomings. For one, it greatly underestimates the political, social, and ideological obstacles to disseminating a liberal Islamic ethos. These barriers are so formidable that, for the foreseeable future, any effective engagement with Islamists will require dealing with activists, many of whom espouse ideas profoundly at odds with U.S. notions of democracy and freedom.

Second, naming Islam as the solution exaggerates the extent to which Islam shapes Muslims' political identity. Not only do ethnicity and tribal affiliation often trump religion, but many Muslims, both practicing and nonpracticing, believe that their version of Islam should be separated or at least distanced from politics. Indeed, little consensus exists in the Arab world about the proper relationship between mosque and state. On the contrary, that world is rent by profound divisions over the very question of national identity—what it means to be Egyptian, Moroccan, Algerian, Bahraini, or Iraqi.

Finally, the idea of Islamic democracy fails to recognize that there is no Islamic solution to such identity conflicts. As the drama in Iraq demonstrates, absent consensus over national identity, this solution requires power-sharing arrangements that offer as many groups and voices as possible a seat at the table of multiparty government. This kind of consensus-building approach cannot succeed unless all groups check their religions at the door. Indeed, they must agree to constitutional and legal protections

---

3. Fouad Ajami, "Bush Country," *Wall Street Journal*, May 16, 2005, p. A16.

4. The White House, "Remarks by the President at the 20th Anniversary of the National Endowment for Democracy," November 6, 2003, http://www.whitehouse.gov/news/releases/2003/11/20031106-3.html.

that guarantee Muslims—Shi'a and Sunni—as well as non-Muslims the right to believe or not to believe as they please.

How then to secure this institutional compromise, particularly when it flies in the face of what it means to be an Islamist in today's Arab world? The idea that such an agreement must await an "Islamic Reformation" is unrealistic. Although advocates of liberal Islam deserve U.S. support, it will take decades for them to secure a politically significant foothold in the Arab world. Democratic reform cannot be postponed, however, and the focus of U.S. policy should therefore be less on ideas and far more on promoting the institutional and procedural reforms that will prod mainstream Islamist politicians and parties to forge a democratic power-sharing accommodation both with regimes and with non-Islamist political parties (all groups—secular, Muslim, and/or ethnic—that do not support an Islamist agenda, such as the "Islamization" of education or, more ambitiously, the creation of an Islamic state). In practical terms, this means helping non-Islamists build constituencies and effective political parties, because it is only through the carrots and sticks of real political competition that Islamists will see the logic behind shelving their ideological priorities in favor of a system of compromise and multiparty coalition government. The examples of Turkey and Indonesia amply demonstrate just how critical such institutional incentives and constraints are to promoting democracy. Although their democracies are far from consolidated and the Islamic parties that participate or lead their governments are not as united or as ideologically coherent as some suggest, Turkey and Indonesia nevertheless illustrate that, for democracy to have any hope in the Arab world, it is not Islam that must be fixed, but politics itself.

The Allure and Limits of Islamic Modernism

The fact that democracy promoters in the United States and their allies in print and television media have embraced those Muslim intellectuals who have boldly asserted that Islam demands democracy is a positive development. It required courage to defy the myriad Arab nationalists and Islamists who argued that any Arab who took up the Bush administration's call for democracy was a mere lackey of the United States or, worse yet, of Israel. Although those accusations intimidated some, other Muslim liberals have welcomed the warm hug of prominent foreign policy commentators, despite their giddy naïveté or occasional ignorance about the origins and evolution of what goes under the broad heading of "Islamic modernism."[5]

That phenomenon was hardly as novel as some of these commentators imply. Egypt's grand mufti, Muhammad Abduh, and his student, Ali Abdul

5. See Thomas Friedman, "Brave, Young and Muslim," *New York Times*, March 3, 2005, p. A31.

Raziq, pioneered an innovative way of thinking about the relationship between Islam and politics some 120 years ago. Since that time, the underlying assumptions of what we now call Islamic modernism have remained the same, even though successive generations of intellectuals have pushed this approach in attempts to address its repeated failure to galvanize Arab imaginations beyond a thin stratum of Western-oriented Muslims. The Islamic modernists' approach pivots around the basic idea that it is both possible and vital to distinguish between the timeless, core values of Islam and the way such norms are interpreted to address the evolving political, legal, social, and economic needs of each generation. Values such as tolerance, justice, equality, and moderation are identified from a comprehensive or holistic reading of the Koran, rather than from any particular line or paragraph. Islamic modernists argue that a literalist reading of any injunction in the Koran can be deeply antagonistic to Islam because that interpretation conflates the Koran's ageless ideals with the time-specific tasks that Muhammad faced. Without a grasp of how the evolution of human intellect and reason effectively re-reveals "revealed truth," thereby creating what some modernists call a "living *shari'a*," or modern Islamic law, Islam cannot realize its full potential.[6]

It is from this point of view that modernists argue for democracy because it is said to be consonant with notions of participation and justice, manifested, they argue, in the Prophet Muhammad's call for *shura* (consultation). They claim that democracy is the most efficient system for nurturing a modern and yet culturally authentic Islam. By linking the quest for democracy and freedom with the need to protect society's religious heritage, the modernist project has inspired many Muslim intellectuals to call not merely for democracy, but also for a kind of Islamic Reformation. For example, Morocco's Abdou Filali-Ansary and Iran's Abdul Karim Soroush, among others, have pushed the Islamic modernist project down a distinctly liberal path by arguing that Islam's spiritual influence would be enhanced by making the individual, rather than governments or states, the focal point for interpreting or experiencing faith.

Unfortunately, in the Arab world the very features that have drawn such thinkers to Islamic liberalism have sometimes alienated a far larger group of Muslim intellectuals and activists. The problem with the Islamic modernists' arguments is that their project hinges on a complex and often opaque interpretive schema difficult for lay people to grasp. More crucially, many

---

6. For a useful introduction to Islamic liberals, see Charles Kurzman, *Liberal Islam: A Sourcebook* (New York and Oxford: Oxford University Press, 1998). See also Larry Diamond, Marc F. Plattner, and Daniel Brumberg, eds., *Islam and Democracy in the Middle East* (Baltimore and London: Johns Hopkins University Press, 2003). For a classic example of the conceptually challenging nature of Islamic Modernism, see Fazlur Rahman, *Islam* (Chicago: University of Chicago Press, 1979).

find it difficult to avoid concluding that the core values that modernists attribute to Islam come from Western political thought, and the validity of this claim is far less politically relevant than the perception that Islamic modernism is a Western project dressed in a thin Islamic garb. Why sweat through a complicated series of interpretations to conclude that Islam demands, for example, equal rights for women or equality of citizenship for Muslims and non-Muslims when it is far easier and perhaps more honest to embrace Western ideas?

Islamic fundamentalists insist that a literalist reading of the Koran is the only defense against a slippery slope that will eviscerate Islamic laws of whatever distinct message God meant them to have. The efforts of Islamic modernists to advance an Islamic Reformation have been especially susceptible to such fundamentalist critiques. Because Sunni Islam does not provide for a clerical establishment but nevertheless calls for a linkage between religion and politics, it is unclear how to justify a Protestant-like movement to challenge a "church" whose very existence Islam does not clearly mandate. Islamic modernists' audacious bid to liberate the interpretation of Islam from the control of the quasi-official clerical establishments in Egypt, Turkey, Morocco, and Tunisia collides with this paradox by raising the awkward question of how any construction of Islam, including a liberal one, will take root, absent an authoritative political body to legitimate and disseminate it. The modernists' response to this conundrum is that democratic politics itself will eventually provide the vehicle for the triumph of a pluralist Islam. Yet, this retort not only places undue faith in the capacity of democracy to produce a rational or liberal thinking but also sidesteps the concern of many orthodox Muslims that, once the state no longer controls Islam, any amateur can step in, thus setting the stage for ideological, legal, and social chaos, or *fitna*. This is why most mainstream Islamists, the majority of whom are lay activists, do not so much question the right of the state's clerics to interpret Islam as assail those clerics for not defending the "correct" form of Islam. This allegation is obviously self-serving. The bid to legitimate an Islamic Reformation has actually often strengthened fundamentalists, who plausibly argue that Islam is nothing without the state's control. The inopportune conditions in which Islamic modernism has struggled have magnified the allure of this counterargument. Islamic modernism has often emerged in the crucible of a great crisis, when the ostentatious corruption and economic inequality that accompany rapid development have nurtured fears of a new cultural and economic Western invasion.

Globalization has reinforced such paranoia by expanding the gap between the haves and have-nots. Globalization's losers fill the urban slums of Rabat, Algiers, Cairo, and Amman, creating an enormous pool of potential recruits for illiberal Islamism, whereas the winners are found among the Westernized intelligentsia and small-business community. Is it any wonder then that, when Islamic modernists raise their pens, they often provoke a counterattack from illiberal Islamists? Not only does the latter group have the advantage of numbers and organization, but it also benefits from the belief that its adherents are defending the identity of the Islamic *umma* (community) and not their lily-livered modernist opponents. These perceptions have proven disastrous for Islamic modernists.

Caught between illiberal Islamists and autocratic regimes, some of which have actually tolerated or even assisted the former in an effort to silence liberal thinkers, the modernists have faced two unfavorable options: retreat or exile. Those who have chosen retreat include thinkers such as Egypt's Khaled Muhammad Khaled, who defected to a fundamentalist vision after spending years advocating democracy. The rather long list of prominent Islamic liberals who have gone into exile includes Egypt's Khaled Abou El-Fadl, who now teaches at the University of California at Los Angeles, and Nasr Abu Zeid, who currently resides in Amsterdam; Sudan's Abdullahi an-Naim, now a professor of law at Emory University; and Pakistan's late Fazlur Rahman, who taught at the University of Chicago. The fact that many leading Muslim liberals have found a safer home in U.S. universities speaks volumes about the enduring crisis of Islamic modernism.

Given the dilemmas facing Islamic liberals, might their cause be best served by making Arab states the principal advocates of a pluralist Islam? The idea is popular in Washington, but applying it to the Middle East is a tricky matter. Arab rulers are reluctant to offend clerical establishments that have grown increasingly reactionary and influential. Responding to this trend, the rulers of Egypt and Kuwait have at times indulged the religious authorities by encouraging, or at least not opposing, the efforts of conservative judges to persecute liberals for "un-Islamic" views. However loathsome such ideological concessions may appear, it is unrealistic and possibly counterproductive to demand that Arab regimes purge advocates of illiberal Islam from powerful institutions such as Egypt's Al-Azhar University or that they compel their religious institutions to rewrite religious textbooks to meet the standards of Islamic modernism. The problem is not merely that institutions such as Al-Azhar command a level of authority that is easier to inflame than it is to undermine; the fundamental obstacle is rooted in the Islamic liberal approach itself. Most clerics are hesitant to adopt interpretations of Islam that their traditional followers question or do not comprehend, and many clerics fear that they would lose power by demanding the separation of mosque and state. It is not clear how or why clerics should use their authority to legitimate a reformationist logic that rejects that very authority! Hard-line Sunni clerics regularly hurl this contradiction at reformist clerics. These turncoats, the Sunnis assert, are undermining the very edifice of Islam.

Paradoxically, more autocracy might be the most effective way to overcome state-supported clerics' resistance to advancing a modernist agenda. For example, the government of Tunisia has disseminated a pluralistic vision of Islam through the state's public schools, a policy whose legitimacy is suspect because it has been implemented by a police state that has repressed Islamists. Morocco has taken a more pluralistic approach through consultative councils whose mission is to create a consensus on controversial policies such as reforming the personal status laws and, more recently, revising religious textbooks. The very legitimacy of Morocco's endeavor, however, rests on the shoulders of the monarch, who as *amir al-mumineen* (commander of the faithful) has the constitutional right to interpret what is Islamic. Many Islamists have decried this power as undemocratic, arbitrary, and thus un-Islamic. Still, given the conservatism of the clerical establishment and secular groups' fears that any reformist agenda would be captured either by clerics or Islamists, it is difficult to imagine a way forward other than making reform dependent on the supreme power of Morocco's young king. Whether this gambit succeeds or is undercut by a change of heart on the part of the monarch, it is worth emphasizing that no other Arab state has a commander of the faithful, which is a unique office in the Arab world whose very existence illustrates the challenges of promoting a state-based reform of Islam that has both religious authority and democratic credentials.[7]

Is Islam the Foundation of Political Identity?

Washington's fascination with modernist Islam is animated by a very old idea, namely, that Islam defines the political identity of the Arab world. This view is naturally the party line of Islamists, which is reason enough to avoid accepting the proposal at face value. Even "objective" evidence, however, such as election results, that is often cited to support this thesis must also be viewed skeptically. Although Islamists have emerged as one of the strongest, if not the strongest, opposition force wherever reasonably competitive elections have been held, these "facts" do not support the seductive conclusion that, given a free choice among alternative ideologies, most Muslims will always embrace an Islamist agenda. The real problem is that, in the Arab world, the fundamentalist agenda has an organized constituency while the non-Islamist agenda is either controlled by a discredited authoritarian regime and/or has little organized basis in society itself. As a result, the multiplicity of cultural, religious, ethnic, and linguistic cleavages that are an everyday reality throughout the Arab world do not find a direct or democratic expression in formal political life.

---

7. See Abdeslam Maghraoui, "Depoliticization in Morocco," *Journal of Democracy* 13, no. 4 (October 2002): 24–32.

There are, of course, partial exceptions to this rule. The first is Lebanon, whose "confessional democracy" has been both praised and damned for institutionalizing (some say magnifying) divisions among Sunnis, Shi'ites, Druze, Orthodox Christians, and Roman Catholics. The second exception is Iraq, where Shi'ites, Kurds, and Sunnis are pursuing a bitter struggle to define a democratic power-sharing system. In fact, however, the identity conflicts that have beguiled Iraq and Lebanon are echoed from Rabat to Kuwait City. Some of these conflicts run along ethnic-national fault lines, as in Morocco and Algeria, where Berber minorities have tended to reject collectivist notions of political identity based on Arabism or Islamism. Elsewhere in the Arab world, the cleavage is religious or sectarian, as in Bahrain, where a Sunni minority has dominated the Shi'ite majority through its control of the monarchy. By contrast, in Jordan a nationalist-traditionalist cleavage between Palestinians and Bedouin tribal groups has loomed large and has sometimes become violent, a pattern that has been repeated in Yemen, where the effort of the tribal-Islamist North to impose itself on the South, many of whose elites inherited the modernizing, secular influence of the former Soviet Union, has bedeviled the country's "unification" since 1991.

Yet, the sharpest divide, which is not so much religious or ethnic as it is ideological and even existential, pits those Muslims who want to align politics with religion against those who wish to keep these spheres apart. The latter are by no means only Western-oriented secularists; they include Sufi Muslims, whose mystical practices most Islamists reject, and traditional or even pious Muslims, who believe that faith is a personal matter. Thus, the key divide of concern here is not between Islamists and secularists; it is between Islamists and non-Islamists. The most salient expression of this fissure is found in North Africa, where Muslims who identify with French language and culture have become separated from those who regard the Arab-Islamic world as their wider home. Even though Arab rulers have tried to deflect this trend by fostering a sense of nationalism, in recent years globalization has widened the gulf between French and Arab Muslims by creating cultural and economic networks that bind the former to western Europe and the latter to the ideological and religious world of pan-Islamism. This polarizing dynamic has also destabilized countries that do not suffer the kind of cultural or linguistic bifurcation typical of the Maghreb. In Egypt, which is often touted as the most culturally unified Arab country, globalization has taken the metropolis of Cairo by storm, vastly expanding the cultural and socioeconomic gap between those who live in privileged neighborhoods such as Ma'adi and Heliopolis and those who suffer, sometimes just a few blocks away, in the slums of Imbaba and Boulak al-Dakrour. Satellite television networks such as Al Jazeera have obscured this divide by fostering a shared sense of grievance against the United States and Israel.

This consensus of resentment cannot create a common vision of politics, however, much less a new formula for democratizing the region.

This absence of a consensus over national identity, rather than any particular brand of Islamism, be it moderate, radical, illiberal, or modernist, is one of the primary roots of autocracy in the Arab world. Even if the most restrained of Islamists reject violence and promise to adhere to the rules of democracy, this pledge alone cannot ease the fears of ethnic, secular, or even some traditionalist Muslims that democracy will give Islamists a mandate to impose their agenda. Consequently, despite growing dismay over the costs of autocracy, thousands of would-be democrats in Morocco, Algeria, Egypt, Jordan, Kuwait, and Yemen are still not ready to risk their lives to openly challenge the status quo. Such worries are matched by the perception among Islamists that the very purpose of the Arab world's autocracies is to give ethnic, religious, or ideological minorities a vehicle for thwarting the majority. The tragedy of the Middle East is that the fears of both sides are justified, and as a result, it has been difficult to negotiate an exit from the authoritarianism that has haunted the region for decades.

It's about Institutions, Not Islam

How then can democracy be made a winning proposition for all concerned? Regime change, either from below or from above, will not achieve this goal. On the contrary, as the experience in Iraq shows, even in the wake of toppling a despotic regime, democratization is more likely to produce civil war than to bring about stable and inclusive political change unless a political process is established that reduces citizens' fear that free elections will lead to their subjugation at the hands of the winners. That democratization could become part of the problem rather than the solution is not a popular statement to make these days. On the contrary, many a Middle East watcher has been rendered light-headed by the recent "Arab Spring," with its rousing images of thousands of Iraqi citizens defying the insurgents to vote, of a million Lebanese protesting Syria's occupation, or of hundreds of Egyptians defying President Husni Mubarak with their Kifaya movement, which is led by a group of largely secular intellectuals and professionals who have had "enough" (*kifaya* in Arabic) with the status quo. Yet, despite such good news, Arab regimes and their opponents must still devise a democratic solution to the identity conflicts that have kept the pot of autocracy boiling.

Power Sharing Is (Part of) the Solution

Such a solution will be found less in the ethereal realm of ideas than in the quintessentially political process of creating procedures, laws, and institutions that ensure the inclusion of all significant groups in democratically elected, multiparty, power-sharing governments. The purpose of such consensual democracy is not to bridge the identity gap between Islamists and non-Islamists or the gap between Berbers and Arabs. On the contrary, precisely because the very *raison d'être* of democratic power-sharing is to include all voices that accept the rules of the game and reject violence, the price for a seat at the table of government must include accepting the premise that the government will not impose any one group's cultural or religious agenda on the rest of society. In short, some kind of explicit or implicit distancing of mosque and state is vital. This is a prerequisite not because people come to believe in it as a matter of first-order principles, but rather because, as a pragmatic matter, only a constitutional order that defends everyone's right to practice or not practice his or her religion freely can secure a polity that is democratic, inclusive, and reasonably peaceful.

Unfortunately, the prospects for a move toward substantive, democratic power-sharing remain modest. There are a host of reasons, including the support that relatively friendly Arab autocracies, such as Egypt and Tunisia, still receive from the United States. Yet, the more elementary domestic obstacle lies in the surprisingly durable nature of Arab autocracies. Over the last decade, many of these regimes have survived by enforcing a system of autocratic power-sharing and state-managed pluralism that gave secular, Islamist, and ethnic groups room to express their views in the press and even in elected, state-controlled assemblies but that provided no basis for translating these voices into a unified movement capable of threatening regimes.

Although opposition groups complained endlessly about such limitations, their members were reluctant to defy this system of liberalized autocracy, in part because, despite its flaws, it offered two advantages. First, it gave opposition groups space to criticize regimes and mobilize public support, something that Islamists were especially good at because, in contrast to their secular rivals, they controlled mosques and other religious institutions through which they could attract a mass following. Second, the power-sharing arrangement enforced a measure of peaceful coexistence by providing state-controlled legislatures under whose roofs competing groups could raise their respective political and cultural agendas without fearing that they would be dominated by the other. In short, precisely because such legislatures and the state-managed system that created them allowed no group real power, many opposition groups came to prefer, or at least tolerate, liberalized autocracy. They feared that democratization would create real winners and losers and thus invite political conflict or even civil war. Although manipulated by autocratic regimes, such apprehensions were sustained by the civil conflict that engulfed Algeria during the 1990s, by the civil war that erupted in Yemen in 1993, and by the memory of Lebanon's civil war, the termination of which was marked by the 1989 Taif Accords.

In the course of the last year, this tacit political consensus has frayed in several Arab countries, including Yemen and Egypt, as secularists and Islamists have concluded that the costs of liberalized autocracy are too high. Islamists have sunk deeper ideological roots in Egypt, Morocco, Yemen, and Kuwait, in part by expanding their direct or indirect control over professional associations, publishing houses, and even educational institutions, such as Egypt's Al-Azhar University, that are in theory controlled by the state. Yet, increasing ideological influence rarely offers a chance for actual political power—a point that has encouraged Islamists to explore cooperating with secular forces. For their part, some non-Islamists have concluded that the only way to escape the snare of state-managed liberalization is to roll the dice and demand real democratic reforms.

These intersecting calculations have produced new efforts at forging alliances and cooperation, as reflected in the Doha Declaration signed by Islamist, liberal, and Arab nationalist intellectuals and political activists in June 2004.[8] The key feature of this agreement is a call for national pacts that would define the rules and procedures for a new era of democratic government. Such pacts can play two critical roles in helping regimes and oppositions define an exit from a legacy of autocratic government. First, pacts within oppositions can enhance the political leverage of oppositions by deflecting the divide-and-rule strategies that autocrats have long used to sustain their power. Second, by providing a set of mutual guarantees that protect the basic political interests of all groups, pacts can enhance the political leverage of regime reformers, thus effectively creating a pro-democracy alliance between regime actors and opposition forces. Absent such an alliance, it is difficult to imagine how Arab regimes can move beyond the state-managed liberalizations that endure despite increasing dissatisfaction with the status quo of liberalized autocracy.[9]

Promoting Competition

The Doha Declaration represents a small but potentially important step forward. Its significance lies in the fact that it demonstrates the capacity of opposition groups with conflicting cultural and ideological agendas to find some kind of common ground. The prospects for pacts will remain limited, however, and even ephemeral as long as non-Islamist forces are so

8. See Mona Yacoubian, "Promoting Middle East Democracy II: Arab Initiatives," Special Report 136 (Washington, DC: May 2005).

9. For this classic work on regime-opposition pacts, see Guillermo O'Donnell and Philippe C. Schmitter, eds., *Transitions From Authoritarian Rule, Tentative Conclusions About Uncertain Democracies* (Baltimore and London: Johns Hopkins University Press, 1986).

outnumbered and, more importantly, so out-organized that they can have little hope of competing with Islamists. This problem is evident in Iraq and is bound to surface if and when the venue for pact-making shifts from the artificial arena of a pan-Arab conference of opposition forces in Qatar to the critical arena of national politics in Algeria, Bahrain, Jordan, Morocco, Egypt, Yemen, or Kuwait. Each of these countries has experienced regime-controlled attempts to promote national dialogues and even formal pacts. For the most part, however, such pacts have helped to redefine the rules of liberalized autocracy rather than set out a new agenda for genuine democratization. Yet, despite all the good news arising from the Arab Spring, support for negotiating such an agenda will remain limited as long as regimes and their tacit allies in non-Islamist opposition movements continue to fear that any genuine democratic pacts would be a Trojan horse for Islamist domination.

Given this complex situation, the initial focus of democracy promoters within and outside the Arab world should not be on pact-making per se. Rather, their efforts should be directed at promoting institutional and legal reforms that boost the mobilizing capacity of non-Islamist forces. The latter will never have any hope of competing with Islamists as long as the playing field remains tilted in Islamists' favor. Paradoxically, this tilting is a direct consequence of the very controls that liberalized autocracies maintain over the nature and scope of political participation. Because only Islamist parties, by virtue of their access to mosques, religious charities, and other bodies, have the means to challenge or partly circumvent such regime controls, non-Islamists have been left with the unenviable choice of supporting regimes or allying with opposition forces whose ideological agendas they reject but cannot deflect, given the overwhelming advantages enjoyed by Islamist parties. For this reason, non-Islamists are unlikely to take the risk of forging opposition alliances until a more competitive playing field emerges.

Turkey and Indonesia: Difficult Lessons for the Arab World

How then can a more competitive playing field be promoted? Some experts have looked to the recent experiences of Turkey and Indonesia for answers because, in both countries, Islamist parties have endorsed and enforced pluralistic and democratic arrangements that respect the political and cultural interests of non-Islamists. This development has prompted talk of a new, alternative "Muslim democracy" that might eventually take root in the Arab world, even though neither of these cases is an Arab country.

The good news is that the experiences of Turkey and Indonesia demonstrate that democratization and accommodation between Islamists and non-Islamists does not require a magical transformation of Islamic consciousness. Modernist ideas have found a more responsive chord in both countries than they have in the Arab world. What has counted most, however, is the fact that in Indonesia and Turkey secularists and traditional non-Islamic Muslim parties have retained organized political support in society, a situation that has compelled Islamists to shelve religious agendas, such as the imposition of Islamic law or, more ambitiously, the quest to establish an Islamic state, in favor of the politics of accommodation. The stick of military establishments that serve as de jure or, in Indonesia's case, de facto enforcers of the state's secular identity, coupled with the carrot that comes from the links between the export-oriented business sector in each country and the international business community, have also combined to create a web of incentives and opportunities encouraging Islamist parties to respect the rules of democratic, pluralistic politics.

The bad news is that the pragmatic calculus that has helped advance democracy in Indonesia and Turkey is not written in stone. Rather, it is the product of a particular balance of domestic, regional, and global forces that could shift dramatically, undermining the evolving balance of power that has encouraged Islamist parties in those countries to subordinate their Islamist policies to democratic governance. Moreover, even if the constraints and incentives that have thus far helped to secure a pragmatic consensus in favor of democratic secular politics endure in Indonesia and Turkey, the systems in place in these countries will be extremely difficult to replicate in the Arab world. With the possible exception of Morocco, most Arab states do not boast a pro-democratic, export-oriented business class. Moreover, although the militaries or security establishments in the Arab world are very powerful, there is no legal or cultural tradition that would support their formal intervention in politics. The most crucial point is that, with the possible exception of Morocco, not one of the Arab world's liberalized autocracies boasts a political arena in which non-Islamist parties can mobilize a significant following. Consequently, talk of importing the Turkish model or of bringing "L'Islam des Tropiques" to the Arab world is, as they say in Arabic, *kilam fadi* (empty words).[10]

Leveling the Playing Field: Organizing Non-Islamists

Even though talk of importing this or that non-Arab model may be considered grandiose, naïve, or simply silly, it is useful to consider the kinds of reforms that might promote a level of competition sufficient to make pact-making and democratization a more viable and winning proposition not only for Islamists but also, and more importantly, for non-Islamists. It is

10. For a related but slightly different perspective, see Vali Nasr, "The Rise of 'Muslim' Democracy," *Journal of Democracy* 16, no. 2 (April 2005): 11–27.

non-Islamists who need the most help, not their Islamist rivals. This point is not easily advanced in Washington, where the quest to find politically acceptable Islamist interlocutors or, more ambitiously, to fix Islam itself has often obscured the need to engage non-Islamists.

Some might argue that focusing on non-Islamist parties is a waste of time because they tend to represent a miniscule part of the population while their Islamist competitors speak for an overwhelming majority. Yet, this thinking is misguided. Islamists are powerful not because they represent the majority, but rather because they speak for an organized plurality that can usually deliver 30–40 percent of a relatively free vote. This may not seem like a very large number, but its political significance has been greatly magnified and distorted by the striking capacity of Arab regimes to use the tools of financial and political patronage, not to mention their control of the media, to mobilize their own constituencies and/or to intimidate would-be voters who are not regime loyalists into abstaining or to voting for regime candidates. These political facts of life have left a fragmented array of secularists, business people, Muslim traditionalists, and ethnic groups with the unenviable choice of staying home, voting for corrupt regimes, or sending a protest vote by pulling the lever for Islamists, despite the former's qualms about the latter.

To change this calculus of apathy, cynicism, or anger, democracy promoters in the United States must encourage reforms that give non-Islamists an organizational alternative to the regimes as well as to their Islamist opponents. The "damned if you do, damned if you don't" choices that non-Islamist voters face when political systems are dominated by a lose-lose, two-way contest between regimes and Islamist oppositions cannot be remedied through elections themselves. Rather, more dramatic, long-term reforms must be enacted to eventually produce a political field that features at least three, if not four or five, main contenders.

Adapting U.S. Policy to Focus on Institutions, Not Islam

The Bush administration is hardly oblivious to the need for a reform strategy that helps galvanize underorganized, non-Islamist constituencies. Therefore, with the notable exceptions of Iraq and Afghanistan, it has focused this strategy far less on elections and far more on medium- and long-term structural changes aimed at strengthening civil societies, promoting women's political participation, and advancing market-oriented economic reforms. The problem with this largely bottom-up, "demand-side" approach is that it does not sufficiently address the supply side of the problem, which is nothing less than overly centralized states that provide no truly effective outlets for political leaders other than regime cronies to freely mobilize and then formally and effectively represent competing constituencies. Although there are signs that the Bush administration's Middle East Partnership Initiative (MEPI) is adding more supply-side, state-focused programs to its agenda, the emphasis remains on civil society.[11] The fact of the matter is that independent parties with the legal right and organizational capacity to mobilize freely barely exist in the Arab world. Indeed, in Bahrain, Qatar, and Kuwait, they are forbidden, and elsewhere they are emasculated by an array of laws and complicated bureaucratic procedures. Because non-Islamists are the primary victims of these obstacles, the Bush administration must press Arab leaders to drop these laws and procedures and to enact constitutional and legal reforms, without which legislatures will remain little more than debating societies, a situation that only reinforces the resignation and apathy of Arab youth.

Moreover, Washington must expand its grassroots, political party programs and target them at constituencies that have little or no effective representation. Such constituencies are not limited to women, even though U.S.-sponsored democracy assistance programs tend to make women a top priority. Because many women are, in fact, often sympathetic to Islamists and are even Islamists themselves, particularly women who live in urban areas and are literate, a policy designed to level the political playing field must reach out to ethnic groups such as Berbers and Kurds, traditional Muslims in urban and especially rural areas, middle-class professionals, and independent business people.

This last group could be an especially significant target. Many Arab economies' direct or indirect dependence on oil exports or other external rents has limited the capacity of the business sector to act as an independent political force, but there are ways to nudge this group from its tacit or active support of autocracy and toward support for democratic reforms. The January 2004 Arab Business Council Declaration, which states that "economic reform necessitates the development of governance systems in the Arab world," is a tepid but potentially significant step that suggests that some business people might welcome more initiatives to link economic and political reforms.[12] Therefore, U.S. nongovernmental organizations (NGOs) that have focused on promoting private-sector initiatives, such as the Center for International Private Enterprise, must now begin to design programs that will help the business sector forge organizational and financial ties with political parties. Absent such initiatives, it is difficult to see how the Arab world's silent pluralities will secure the economic resources to stand on their own.

---

11. For an overview of official U.S. efforts to promote democracy in the Arab world, see the Middle East Partnership Initiative's Web site, which can be found at http://mepi.state.gov/mepi/.

12. See Arab Business Council of the World Economic Forum, "Economic Reform Priorities in the Arab World: A Private Sector Perspective," January 20, 2004, http://www.weforum.org/pdf/ABC/ABC_R1.pdf.

Such fundamental political restructuring of the institutions of political representation does not mean abandoning Washington's traditional focus on grassroots civil society programs. To be effective, however, the United States must not shy away from promoting civil society organizations that have an explicitly political role, namely, to enhance the credibility and organizational effectiveness of political parties, elections, and legislative bodies. The promotion of local, provincial, and national election-monitoring associations or of citizens' groups that work to improve local and national legislatures would make political participation a credible and attractive option for the thousands of young people who do not currently participate. Toward this end, rather than becoming directly involved in such initiatives, an approach that would rob them of credibility and thus undermine their effectiveness, official and nonofficial U.S. organizations such as the National Endowment for Democracy, MEPI, and the U.S. Agency for International Development should promote partnerships between indigenous Arab NGOs and their Western counterparts, with the former take a leading role in project design and implementation wherever possible.

In concert with the above, it is vital that the U.S. government support the efforts of Arab political activists to create forums through which Islamists and non-Islamists can pursue dialogues about the purposes of political reform. Such bridge-building activities could occur via citizens' groups or professional associations, but to be most effective, the effort should be based in secondary schools and public universities. Some Arab regimes will resist this idea, fearing that any independent political activities would benefit only Islamists. Even though that concern is understandable, until universities make room for extracurricular programs, for example, open student elections, party formation, and organized discussions of politics, either Islamists or regime cronies will control whatever politics that exist in the lecture halls and classrooms. As always, the losers will be the silent plurality of young people who scorn participating in formal political life.

Over time, structural political reforms that enhance competition and participation, combined with new initiatives to promote dialogues between Islamists and non-Islamists, will help level the playing field in ways that could facilitate the negotiation of new national pacts. In Egypt, Jordan, Kuwait, Bahrain, and Yemen, regimes have implicitly acknowledged the transforming and thus threatening potential of such pacts by sponsoring national dialogues or covenants designed to preempt reforms that transcend the limits of liberalized autocracy. Yet, these orchestrated initiatives have run out of steam. Washington should encourage the efforts of ruling elites and their mainstream opponents to pursue dialogue about the fundamentals of constitutional and legal reform.

Iraq and Beyond

It is in the context of such dialogues that the United States needs to continue its engagement with Islamists. The word "continue" is emphasized, because democracy promoters in the United States such as the National Democratic Institute and the National Republican Institute have for several years regularly included Islamist parties and leaders in their programming. Yet, the nature and focus of U.S. engagement must shift. In addition to the technical assistance provided in areas such as campaign management and legislative procedures, the emphasis must now turn to helping Islamists appreciate that an implicitly secular logic of democratic accommodation with non-Islamists can bring concrete benefits, not least of which is the possibility of actually representing elected constituencies in multiparty governments that wield real political authority and power.

This sensitive subject has occasionally been tackled in international meetings that bring activists from post-conflict regions such as the Balkans together with Arab activists who have experienced civil conflicts in Yemen, Lebanon, and Algeria. Outside of Iraq, however, this type of dialogue is not a central feature of U.S. aid programs. It needs to be, not because Islamists should be versed in de Tocqueville, Madison, or Dahl, but rather because it is important for them to grasp the practical returns that come from achieving a democratic peace with their rivals. At the same time, Washington must not shy away from publicly or privately calling to task Islamic parties or organizations, such as Jordan's Islamic Action Party, that profess support for democracy while tolerating and occasionally promoting intolerant ideas and programs.

On this score, NGOs such as Human Rights Watch or Amnesty International could play an especially helpful role by monitoring the programs and rhetoric of Islamist parties that have become politically active fairly recently, such as Morocco's Justice and Development Party, or that are now aspiring to gain legal certification and join the political fray, such as Egypt's Wasat Party. This new generation deserves a chance, but they must also know that the international community will play a vital role in monitoring the efforts of the Arab world's diverse communities to share power peacefully and democratically.

That said, no one should minimize the challenges and even dangers that attend any effort to promote genuine accommodation. Indeed, democratic power-sharing arrangements have downsides. Rather than diminish, they can solidify and even intensify identity divisions between Islamists and non-Islamists or between Shi'a and Sunni Muslims. Moreover, to endure, power-sharing rules and procedures often require enforcement by a legitimate and most of all powerful third party. Precisely because societies that suffer from deep religious, ethnic, or ideological cleavages often lack such a third party, however, they often must depend on external forces, such as the various NATO stabilization forces in the Balkans, the United States in Iraq, or even Syria in Lebanon, to provide the military and policy backbone that weak states lack.

Unfortunately, there may be no way around this weak-state problem or any of the other liabilities that arise from democratic power-sharing if only because the Arab world does not have better democratic alternatives. It is in this context that both the promises and dangers of the Bush administration's gambit in Iraq become clear. Although the escalating challenges that the United States faces in Iraq can be partly attributed to misguided policies, Iraq was always one of the least likely candidates to succeed at building a power-sharing government. A country that endured decades of a neo-totalitarian, minority regime that persecuted and terrorized a narrow majority faced, from the start, an uphill battle in fostering the trust and institutional guarantees essential to pact-making.

This thought is sobering because, for many years to come, the United States will have to remain the military guarantor of a tenuous power government in Baghdad (a role many Iraqis reject) and also because Iraq has become the Arab world's litmus test for democratic power-sharing. Although it is too early to predict failure or to dismiss the possibility of success, one thing is clear: if the democratization of identity conflict in Iraq produces civil war, Arab autocrats might very well point to Iraq's fate to enforce a new "Winter of Autocracy," one that will make the brief Arab Spring seem like a passing dream. That is why it is imperative for the United States to look beyond Iraq and to prod Arab leaders and their oppositions to initiate substantive democratic reforms and power-sharing initiatives. This will certainly not be easy, but we can take encouragement from the fact that efforts to produce some level of political and ideological accommodation has already taken place in Morocco, Yemen, Kuwait, Bahrain, and Jordan, albeit under the increasingly shaky roofs of liberalized autocracies. The challenge now will be to rebuild and transform this mixed legacy so that democratic power-sharing becomes a viable option.

None of these initiatives can substitute for the struggles of Muslim thinkers to renew Islam in a more pluralistic light. Those who have done so have risked the wrath of autocratic regimes and illiberal Islamists, thus earning the respect and support of the United States as well as its European friends. It is important, though, to be realistic about the practical impact that these efforts to promote Islamic liberalism will have in the short and even medium term. Democratization in the Arab world is a pressing need. Therefore, the United States, in concert with the European community, must foster the incentives and constraints that make accommodation a logical priority. Absent these efforts, Islamists and their rivals will never reconcile, a prospect that can only encourage Arab autocrats everywhere.

Part II

Islamic Renewal:
Fixing Islam?

4

Ijtihad: Reinterpreting Islamic Principles for the Twenty-first Century[1]

David R. Smock

Muslims all over the world believe that the Qur'an is the literal word of God as revealed to Prophet Muhammad through the Angel Gabriel at the beginning of the seventh century. The Qur'an was revealed over the course of twenty-three years. Most of its verses came in response to and as guidance for emerging situations or conditions faced by the Prophet and his community of believers. Because any verse, when taken out of context, could be misunderstood or misapplied, a science known as asbab an-nouzoul ("the causes for the revelation") was developed to understand the specific reasons for and conditions related to any particular verse, thus enabling interpreters to better determine its meaning.

According to Radwan Masmoudi, president of the Center for the Study of Islam and Democracy, while there has been no disagreement among Muslims that the Qur'an is the literal word of God, there has been and continues to be substantial disagreement about the meanings of certain verses and their application to different situations. That is why, following

1. On March 19, 2004, the United States Institute of Peace and the Center for the Study of Islam and Democracy cosponsored a workshop entitled "Ijtihad: Reinterpreting Islamic Principles for the Twenty-first Century." The discussion focused on how the sacred texts of the Qur'an and the sunna could be reinterpreted to take account of contemporary realities and to promote greater peace, justice, and progress within the Muslim world and in its relations with the non-Muslim world. The four presenters, all experts on Islamic law and interpretation, were Muzammil H. Siddiqi, a member of the Fiqh (Islamic Law) Council of North America who teaches at California State University and Chapman University; Imam Hassan Qazwini, director of the Islamic Center of America, based in Detroit; Muneer Fareed, associate professor of Islamic studies at Wayne State University; and Ingrid Mattson, professor of Islamic studies and director of Islamic Chaplaincy at Hartford Seminary. The workshop was cochaired by Radwan Masmoudi, president of the Center for the Study of Islam and Democracy, and David Smock, director of the Religion and Peacemaking Initiative of the United States Institute of Peace (http://www.usip.org/religionpeace/).

David R. Smock, "Ijtihad: Reinterpreting Islamic Principles for the Twenty-first Century," Special Report 125 (Washington, DC: USIP, 2004).

the death of Prophet Muhammad in 632 CE and for at least the first eight or nine centuries of Islam, there were a wide variety of opinions and schools of thought on almost every issue and question. Another science known as ijtihad (or reasoning and interpretation) was developed by Muslim scholars in order to understand and apply the message of the Qur'an to varying societal needs and conditions.

Sharia (Islamic law) is also subject to interpretation and to the ever-changing needs of society. Its guiding principles were designed to protect the individual and the society, but it was not established as a set of fixed rules. To respond to the changing needs of Muslim societies, Muslim jurists and scholars have relied on the well-established process of innovation, ijtihad. This process is based not only on the Qur'an and religious tradition (sunna), but also on reason, deduction, and prioritization.

The following examples illustrate the use of ijtihad. Fifteen years after the death of Prophet Muhammad, Caliph Omar ibn-al-Khattab stopped cutting off the hands of thieves because most of them were stealing out of necessity due to hunger, poverty, and drought. While this contradicted a verse from the Qur'an, he justified his decision by stating that the principles of justice and fairness were supreme. Similarly, in 2000, councils of Muslim ulamas (scholars) in Europe and the United States decreed that it was permissible for Muslims residing in the West to buy houses with mortgages and to pay interest on these loans. This contradicted a Qur'anic teaching against charging and paying interest, but respected Muslim scholars justified the ruling, arguing that such permission was necessary for Muslims to meet their financial and social needs in the West. Another example is a case in which Imam Muhammad Ibn Idris al-Shafi'i, one of the founders of Islamic jurisprudence, gave a certain legal opinion in Baghdad. One year later he moved to Cairo, and in response to the same question he gave a very different opinion. Someone questioned him, "Oh Imam, last year in Baghdad you gave a different answer," and he replied, "That was in Baghdad and this is in Cairo. That was last year and this is now." When employing ijtihad, scholars considered the time, place, norms, and prevailing conditions when they rendered their religious advice and opinions.

According to Masmoudi, the process of ijtihad has enabled Muslims to be flexible and to learn from other cultures and civilizations. Islam teaches that no one owns the truth and that the true believer is always in search of the truth and wisdom; wherever he finds them, he follows. This ongoing search for truth and for the overarching Islamic principle of justice has led Muslims and Muslim scholars to respect one another's opinions, making them willing to change their own opinions if proven wrong. Muslim religious scholars used to say, "This is my opinion and I could be wrong. And this is someone else's opinion and they could be right." No one had a monopoly on the truth.

Until about 1500 CE, this process allowed Muslims and Muslim societies to continually adapt in the face of changing societal conditions and new advances in knowledge. Unfortunately, as Muslim civilization began to weaken about four or five centuries ago in the face of Western advances, Muslims began to adopt a more conservative stance in an attempt to preserve traditional values and institutions. As a result, many scholars became inclined to view innovation and adaptation negatively.

According to Masmoudi, this was the beginning of the decline of Muslim civilization. Since then, Islamic law has become increasingly detached from reality and modernity. Old interpretations no longer provide suitable answers to the difficult questions facing the Muslim world.

Many Muslims believe that they must choose between Islam and modernity, or Islam and democracy. According to Masmoudi, this is a false choice. When faced with this decision, most Muslims would choose Islam and reject anything that they regarded as alien or contrary to the principles of their faith. For this reason there is a crisis in the Muslim world today. There is no way out of this predicament without renewing the concept of ijtihad and using the process to develop modern interpretations of Islamic principles compatible with both the word of God and the situations, ideas, and values that have emerged over the past several centuries.

To explore these issues, the United States Institute of Peace and the Center for the Study of Islam and Democracy invited four highly respected scholars of Islam to discuss ijtihad and its role in addressing the contemporary needs of Muslims and Muslim societies. The panelists were asked to consider the following questions:

- How does ijtihad work, and how can it be used to address the needs of Muslim societies in the twenty-first century?
- Who has the right to perform ijtihad, and how can the door of ijtihad be reopened?
- What are the main problems, challenges, and handicaps facing the Muslim world today, and how can they be addressed?
- What is the role of American Muslim leaders and organizations in promoting a more tolerant, modern, and moderate interpretation of Islam?
- How should Islam adapt to changing societal conditions, needs, and priorities in its quest for social justice and equality?

The rest of this report summarizes the panel discussion.

How Does Ijtihad Work?

According to Muzammil H. Siddiqi, a member of the Fiqh (Islamic Law) Council of North America who teaches at California State University and

Chapman University, Islam is a total way of life. Muslims are obliged to abide by the rules of Allah in every aspect of their lives, always and wherever they live. However, the actual rules of Allah as given in the Qur'an and the sunna are limited. The Qur'an contains only six hundred verses directly related to laws, and there are approximately two thousand hadiths (sayings of the Prophet that were not published in the Qur'an) that deal with laws. Muslims believe that the entire Qur'an is from God. The hadiths, however, contain some statements that definitely come directly from Prophet Muhammad and others that are of only probable or even questionable authenticity. Additionally, in both the Qur'an and hadiths, some statements have definite meanings, while others have probable meanings. Thus all statements in the Qur'an and hadiths can be divided into four categories, those with

- definite source, definite meaning;
- definite source, probable meaning;
- probable source, definite meaning; and
- probable source, probable meaning.

The work of the interpreter of the text (the mujtahid) is to ascertain the authenticity of the source(s) and then

- discover the laws through the interpretation of the sources;
- extend the laws to new cases that may be similar to the cases mentioned in the sources for which the laws cannot be discovered through literal interpretation (this is called the method of analogy, or qiyas); and
- extend the laws to new cases that have not been covered by the previous two methods by looking at the general principles and objectives of the sharia (this method is known as istihsan or istislah—general interests of the community).

The basic role of the mujtahid is to explain and articulate the law of God in a particular situation. The mujtahid takes on the considerable responsibility of explaining the will of God to individuals and communities.

Who Can Perform Ijtihad?

The right to engage in ijtihad, according to Imam Hassan Qazwini, director of the Islamic Center of America, belongs to an individual who is a recognized expert in jurisprudence and who is qualified to derive Islamic law from original sources. This requires wide expertise and many years of studying jurisprudence, the fundamentals of jurisprudence, hadiths, the biographies of hadith narrators, commentary on the Qur'an, Arabic grammar and eloquence, and logic. Additionally, in this era, knowledge of philosophy, economics, and sociology is increasingly necessary. A mujtahid should also display qualities such as piety and moral integrity.

There are currently some roadblocks to increasing the numbers and power of the mujtahids. For instance, Siddiqi noted that while most Muslim jurists are well versed in the classical sources, many of them do not use the tools of linguistics, logic, and semantics in their interpretations. Moreover, Muslim societies tend to lack the freedom required for scholars to locate information resources and to freely debate issues, with constraints imposed not only by political authorities but also by religious establishments. In addition, Islamic educational systems are usually outdated and thus do not provide adequate preparation for the tasks that mujtahids must perform.

How Might Ijtihad Be Revived?

One of the gravest mistakes Muslims have committed, according to Qazwini, is closing the doors of ijtihad. They have limited legal interpretation to only four prominent scholars: Malik Ibn Anas, Abu Hanifa al-No'man, Muhammad Ibn Idris al-Shafi'i, and Ahmad Ibn Hambal—the heads of the Maliki, Hanafi, Shafi'i, and Hambali schools of thought. The motivation for this was political. During the Abbasid Dynasty (750–1258 CE), the Abbasids decided to outlaw all other sects in order to strictly control religion and worship, as well as political matters.

Closing the doors of ijtihad has had extremely detrimental ramifications for the Muslim world. According to Qazwini, this decision has resulted in chronic intellectual stagnation, as thousands of potential mujtahids and scholars have been prohibited from offering workable solutions to newly emerging problems. Muslim thinkers have become captive to rules that were made long ago, leaving little scope for liberal or innovative thought.

Governments in Muslim countries today, many of which are corrupt, greatly benefit from the absence of ijtihad. Moreover, these governments help keep the doors of ijtihad closed in order to control the religious establishment. Since religious bodies in Muslim countries rely on government financing, this makes them captive to government policies. The domination of the religious establishments by secular governments has been so powerful that it has often made religious authorities look inept. The first step toward opening the door of ijtihad, according to Qazwini, should be the liberation of religious establishments from the influence of political regimes. Religious authorities should dissociate themselves from political regimes so that they can independently issue and interpret religious law.

There cannot be true ijtihad, Siddiqi pointed out, unless scholars are free to express their opinions and other scholars are free to criticize them if they make errors. Freedom of expression is inherent in the concept and practice of ijtihad. This means that the democratization of Muslim societies and basic freedom for scholars is sine qua non for this process to work.

Reforming Muslim educational systems is also essential, including revising the curricula of religious schools and seminaries. Instead of learning about only a single school of interpretation, which is common practice, students should be exposed to all such schools. Instead of studying only the rulings and interpretations of the schools, students should also learn about the evidence used to arrive at these interpretations, as well as other methods of interpretation. Students should also study comparative religion, modern logic, philosophy, psychology, and history, as well as economics and political theory as background for improved interpretation. Islamic schools and seminaries should also pay more attention to the great Islamic literature on the objectives of sharia.

Siddiqi also asserted that ijtihad should be a collective endeavor. There are currently several national and international fiqh councils (councils of jurisprudence and interpretation of sharia), but they need to be better organized and they should work together collaboratively. Sharia experts, both men and women, should be members of these councils. Membership should not be limited to sharia scholars; experts from the fields of medicine, astronomy, economics, social and political sciences, and law should also be included as consultants and advisers. Even non-Muslim scholars who are sympathetic and objective should be invited to contribute. These councils should not only issue rulings but also provide the evidence and methodologies behind their rulings. They should also strive to build consensus as much as possible.

As Masmoudi pointed out, all four panelists mentioned the lack of freedom and democracy as serious impediments to ijtihad. Without freedom and democracy, which are sharply limited in the Muslim world and particularly in Arab countries, ijtihad cannot be performed. Democracy is the key to opening up ijtihad, and ijtihad is the key to solving the principal problems confronting the Muslim world today.

What Issues Should Be Subjected to Ijtihad?

Many issues facing Muslims today require ijtihad, and the following ones, according to Siddiqi, require urgent attention:

- The role of women. The role of women in Islam needs to be reviewed by carefully examining the original texts.
- Sunnis and Shiites. The gap in doctrine between various Islamic madhahib (schools and sectarian positions) should be narrowed.
- The spirit of globalization. Using modern ijtihad, Muslims should reinterpret the classical division of the world into darul Islam (the

world of Islam) and darul Harb (the world of non-Muslims). Emphasis should be placed on a one-world view and responsible citizenship in our global village. Ijtihad should also be used to foster better relations between people of diverse faiths and cultures by promoting dialogue among various groups rather than encouraging the notion of a clash of cultures and civilizations.

- Economics. There is a need to radically rethink Islamic economic theories, in the process incorporating elements of modern economic theories. Why is the Muslim world impoverished and how can this be changed? What kind of collaboration is possible between Muslims and world economic bodies without compromising authentic Islamic values and principles of justice, equity, and fairness?
- Unity among Muslim states. Islamic political thinking and statecraft should also be reviewed. How can Muslim states be brought together to collaborate more closely, and what new structures are needed to promote unity among Muslim states? Ethical and moral standards of the Islamic state need to be examined, as does the promotion of individual freedom, especially that of religious minorities.
- Muslims in non-Muslim countries. Ijtihad should be used to guide the almost one-third of the umma (the worldwide Muslim community) that is living as minorities in non-Muslim countries. What Islamic rules and guidelines should these Muslims follow to be good citizens of their native or adopted land? How can they become active and responsible participants in the life of these countries while not neglecting their Islamic beliefs and values?

According to Qazwini, other major obstacles facing Muslims and the practice of ijtihad today include prejudice, intellectual stagnation, political dictatorship, rejection of others, lack of democracy and freedom, factionalism, and extremism. Regrettably, these illnesses pervasive in Muslim societies are worsening, reaching a point where they may spiral out of control.

Noting that the panelists involved in the discussion on March 19, 2004, represented the entire Muslim spectrum—men and women, Shiites and Sunnis, religious scholars and academic scholars—Qazwini proposed that the panel could present the Muslim world with an ideal image of Islam's tolerance and openness. There is no doubt that living in the United States gives one a sense of appreciation for pluralism. Muslims in the United States also enjoy more freedom, even religious freedom, than exists in most Muslim countries. Muslim Americans could project this positive perspective, including their openness with one another, mutual tolerance, and participation in interfaith dialogue, to the greater Muslim world, becoming a model for millions of Muslims around the globe.

An Alternative Approach: Creative Impulse and Imagination

Muneer Fareed, associate professor of Islamic studies at Wayne State University, and Ingrid Mattson, professor of Islamic studies and director of Islamic Chaplaincy at Hartford Seminary, held a somewhat different view than the other panelists of the role of ijtihad. Fareed suggested that ijtihad can be viewed in three different ways: as a legal tool, as a form of legal reasoning, and as a creative impulse. Muslim scholars, however, remain unclear as to the precise nature of ijtihad. Generally when the term is used, it implies analogical reasoning, a legal tool.

The increasing attention paid to ijtihad by Muslim scholars can be attributed to the fact that it remains the only means of legitimate rational reasoning within the house of Islam. Islam is a religion of revelation, in which God spoke to the Prophet Muhammad, who, in turn, transmitted this speech of God, fleshing out its details and providing commentary on its application. In Islam, truth is both divine and divinely absolute, and so there is little room for rational inquiry.

Ijtihad flourished in two periods of Muslim history, the ninth and the nineteenth centuries. During the first period, ijtihad functioned as legal reasoning. During the second period, however, some scholars looked to ijtihad as the "creative impulse" necessary to unleash Muslim potential and create a new world, one that would allow Islamic civilization to thrive. But this movement was thwarted by the ulama. These custodians of the tradition were disinclined to accept ijtihad as creative impulse. In addition, the movement itself was a threat to their status and even to their livelihood.

In the twentieth century, Islam suffered humiliation on many fronts, because of colonialism, the dismemberment of the Caliphate, and the abolition of Islamic law by Mustafa Kemal Ataturk in Turkey. As a result, many enlightened, Western-educated Muslims began to search for something within Islam that would allow Muslims to think freely and to engage and embrace the positive elements of their civilization. Ijtihad thus presented itself, but this time as a creative impulse rather than as legal reasoning. When the Prophet spoke of ijtihad or when he approved of its application, he seemed to have done so in terms of ijtihad qua creative reasoning.

The challenge for Muslims going forward is to determine whether this creative reasoning should be complementary and therefore parallel to divine text, or whether it should remain as it has been in the past, subordinate to the text. That today is the great question. It is also a challenge to all who consider Islam to be not just a religion, but also a civilization with much to offer the world at large.

Islamic legal expert Mattson remarked that although she is passionate about legal reasoning and the scholarly aspects of the law, she would not want to live in a land in which the law was simply created by scholars such as herself. As it turns out, Muslim civilization was not built by a set of scholars sitting in a room writing down rules about what was and was not permissible who then instructed people to follow the law. Islamic civilization was built by people with initiative, imagination, and creativity who were interested in constructing creative lives and forging good relationships with others. It was only when these leaders encountered difficulties that they consulted religious scholars.

So what was it that drove them? What created civilization? What allowed people to have an optimistic outlook? Creativity built on the belief that there were always new possibilities available and that God gave us this earth and this life with permission to use them creatively.

According to Mattson, "legal reasoning—even the best legal reasoning—is not the solution to our problems. Why are we Muslims still in the situation in which we find ourselves? Our problems are not going to be solved by having scholars think more deeply. If we limit change and innovation to only those who have qualifications to reason from the text, we are not going to get anywhere."

A verse in the Qur'an reads, "Perhaps your Lord will put love between you and those whom you now consider enemies." Mattson proposed that this verse calls us to imagine a different future, rather than reason our way out of things. "We must first have a vision of a different tomorrow and know that there is the possibility of the world being different. Even when we are so mired in our own emotions, our own day-to-day struggles, our own difficulties that we cannot imagine a way out, faith and creativity help us know it is possible for God to create a different future. It is possible for God to put love between you and your enemies." So imagination is key to a better future. It is the key to a good society. It must work hand in hand with but not be superseded by legal reasoning. Reason by itself, when misused, can lead to disastrous conclusions and actions. It can lead to the most terrible yet very rational projects. Without inputs from ethics and from imagination, reason can lead us seriously astray. Mattson argued that the frequently employed legal principle in ijtihad that "necessity dictates exception" is a valuable but limited tool. A Muslim might find himself or herself in a situation in which, because of the limits of his or her job, he or she cannot go to the Friday prayers. So necessity dictates exception. But scholars cannot keep making laws on the basis of exceptions for Muslims living in so-called non-Muslim countries. The world is pluralistic and is becoming increasingly so. More creative approaches to ijtihad must be developed and employed.

According to Mattson, one of the principal problems facing Muslims is that "because of our very narrow vision, our legalistic vision, and our authoritarian models of decision making, we are excluding those people who can offer us a different vision of the future." She suggested that comedians, poets, and musicians should come forward to articulate a different view of reality. "We will have arguments about the limits that should be imposed on these new visions. When have we gone too far and violated something fundamental to our being Muslim? We need to have that discussion, but we should not be afraid to allow creativity to flourish, because without it we won't have a promising future."

Another challenge: the Muslim world is often mired in nostalgia for past glories, and traditional approaches to ijtihad often lock Muslims into the past. An example of this is the difficulty that Muslim scholars had in the nineteenth century in condemning slavery and advocating its abolition. Traditional scholars at that time held the view that slavery had always existed and that their laws regulating it allowed for the good treatment of slaves. These scholars could not imagine a world without slavery, and this lack of imagination prevented them from moving forward. "I am a scholar and I engage in scholarship all the time," said Mattson. "But to put everything in the hands of scholars will limit and cripple us and will mean that we will end up in a situation not much better than we are in today. I believe there is another door open, a theological door, which places more emphasis on the natural law tradition in Islam. Reason is not the only complement to revelation. In Islam there is something called fitra, an innate, God-given sense of right and wrong. It can be squelched or cultivated. With the right support it can make us moral people."

Conclusion

One of the principal reasons for the failure of Muslims to reconcile Islam and modernity is that the process of ijtihad was closed several centuries ago. However, the sacred texts of Islam need to be interpreted in the light of contemporary realities and modern knowledge. For ijtihad to be performed successfully in a society, democracy and freedom of expression must prevail. While scholars of Islamic law clearly have very important roles to play in the revived practice of ijtihad, they should not have exclusive responsibility over this practice. Faithfulness to the text needs to be combined with creative imagination to produce the most enlightened reinterpretations, suitable for the twenty-first century. Muslim scholars and leaders in the United States and other Western societies have particular opportunities as well as a responsibility to lead a revival of ijtihad. Muslim scholars in the West have the freedom to think creatively while still being faithful to the texts, and their new interpretations could stimulate new thinking among the more traditional religious establishments in Muslim countries.

5

Two Discourses on Modern Islamic Political Thought: Fundamentalism and Modernism

Ahmad S. Moussalli

Most modern Western political thinkers have demystified the state and related its legitimacy to serving worldly concerns, such as satisfying the needs of its citizens and society at large. The vast majority of classical, medieval, and modern Muslim thinkers have not, however, removed the aura of mysticism from the state. Though they accept that a main task of the state is to order worldly concerns of its members, this in itself is not seen as a sufficient moral or political ground for citizens' submission to a specific ruling power and system. While organizing human affairs, resolving conflicts, conducting relations among states, and even promoting survival are valid occupations of the state, they do not legitimize one political system or another, unless linked to supranational Islamic orientation.

Muslim thinkers have offered more specific grounds for justifying the necessity of attaining an Islamic state. These grounds include establishing a moral society on the basis of God's *shari'a* (law) for the service of the oneness of God. Good politics, then, aims at the attainment of an Islamic system grounded in both a philosophy of normative principles and a method of applying a set of prescriptive remedies to social and political problems. Put differently, the legitimacy of an Islamic state is rooted in a general philosophy of life and a particular moral and political philosophy. In modern times, two major dominant Islamic discourses, fundamentalism and modernism, have been developed as modern interpretations of Islam aimed at remedying the ills and reviving Muslim societies.

Set forth below is the ideological and political discourses of both Islamic modernism—referred to, sometimes, as reformism—as advocated by Jamal

---

Ahmad S. Moussalli, *Moderate and Radical Islamic Fundamentalism: The Quest for Modernity, Legitimacy, and the Islamic State* (Gainesville: University Press of Florida, 1999), 19–45. Reprinted with permission of the University Press of Florida.

al-Din al-Afghani (1839–1897), Muhammad 'Abduh (1849–1905), Muhammad Iqbal (1875–1938), and 'Ali Shari'ati (1933–1977), and Islamic fundamentalism, as advocated by Abu al-A'la al-Mawdudi (1903–1980), Hasan al-Banna (1906–1949), Sayyid Qutb (1906–1966), and Ayatollah al-Khumayni (1903–1989). This examination will present the theoretical roots of Islamic fundamentalism set out by these authors.

They have been selected not only because they represent the two trends but also because of their formative role in their creation. Al-Afghani, for instance, the most outstanding Muslim modernist and activist, set the agenda for modern Islamic thought throughout the Muslim world. He was thus known as the sage and awakener of the East. He called for a reworking of Islamic thought to include Western science, democracy, and constitutional government. Rulers and opposition alike tried to tempt him to join their camps, and he vascillated among them before ultimately dying in Turkey after suffering from jaw cancer. 'Abduh, a disciple and friend of al-Afghani who joined him in exile in Paris in 1879 after they were expelled from Cairo, attempted to interpret Islam in terms of modernity and developed the doctrines of *al-maslaha* (interest) as utility, *shura* (consultation) as parliamentary democracy, and *ijma'* as public opinion. Al-Afghani and 'Abduh published *al-'Urwa al-Wuthqa* (the tightest bond), which became very influential throughout the Muslim world. 'Abduh became the mufti of Egypt in 1899 and tried to reform Al-Azhar by introducing modern sciences into its curriculum. Rashid Rida joined 'Abduh in 1897 and became very close to him. Rida published the very influential magazine *al-Manar* until 1935, and many credit him with the development of the modern view of an Islamic state. Iqbal, who received his Ph.D. from Trinity College in England in 1905, was the most well-known Pakistani reformer. He is probably the most philosophic among the modernist reformers who tried to blend the culture of the East with that of the West. He became very influential throughout the Islamic world, especially on the Indian subcontinent, and was elected to the Indian parliament in 1936. He was also a member of the All-India Muslim League. In Iran, Ali Shari'ati, who held a doctorate from the Sorbonne, spent his life lecturing and established a strong organization, Husayniyah-yi Irshad, that focused on developing intellectual activities and spreading the message for social justice. The organization became one of the centers for opposition to the Sha, and Shari'ati was repeatedly imprisoned by the regime. He was found dead, apparently from a heart attack, in England, but rumors suggested that he had been assassinated by Iranian agents. His main contribution is his interpretation of Islam in terms of modernity and as a social, economic, and political philosophy.

In the fundamentalist camps, the political thought of al-Mawdudi, the most renowned Pakistani fundamentalist and the founder of the fundamentalist Jamat'ati-I Islami, exerted tremendous influence on Muslims throughout the world. His idea of Islam as a system and method, and his doctrines of paganism of the world and governance, became central issues that distinguish fundamentalism from other trends. In Egypt in 1927, Hasan al-Banna founded the first full-fledged Islamic fundamentalist movement, the Muslim Brotherhood, in the Arab world; it spread throughout the Muslim world and became the prototype that most Islamic movements tried to imitate. While working as a teacher after receiving a bachelor of arts degree from Dar al-Ulum, he strove to link political and economic issues to religion and argued that Islam was a complete moral, economic, social, political, and philosophical system. Al-Banna called for active commitment to Islam through political actions that seek the establishment of the Islamic state. The assassination of al-Banna in 1949 led to splits within the movement. It was Qutb, however, who developed the ideological basis of Islamic activism that later manifested itself in radical and violent groups. Qutb, who was imprisoned for over a decade and finally hanged in 1966, viewed societies as being responsible for the "un-Islamic" actions of their government and, therefore, as paganist as their rulers. He called for a total revolution against all human systems.

Unlike Qutb, in 1979 al-Khumayni achieved an Islamic revolution in Iran and established an Islamic state, the Islamic Republic of Iran. He based the legitimacy of the government on the guardianship of the jurist and called for almost total adherence to the Imam's representative: Khumayni, himself. Finally, Abul Hasan al-Nadawi, whose numerous writings have spread all over the Muslim world, is still probably the most important fundamentalist writer on the need for Islam as a civilizational force in world politics. He influenced many Muslim audiences in different countries, including Sayyid Qutb while on a visit to Egypt in 1951. Because of his influence in rearguing the modern world's need for Islam, he was granted the Saudi King Faysal Award in 1979 for the service of Islam. Al-Nadwat al-'Ulama' and al-Jama'a al-Islamiyya currently live in England.

This essay consists of three parts. Part one deals with the ideological and philosophical foundations of both modernism and fundamentalism; part two focuses on modernist and fundamentalist normative political principles. Part three delineates some of the major conclusions about knowledge, politics, and ideology. The objective of this essay is to show the philosophic level of both fundamentalism and modernism and to dispel many erroneous and imprecise notions concerning fundamentalist and modern discursive thinking.

Fundamentalist Islamic thought has generally been treated as a reaction to passing political, social, and economic phenomena—a treatment that carries some truth and includes, in fact, Western philosophies. However, it does not follow that fundamentalism lacks deep-rooted principles and should be dismissed as religious fanaticism.[1] For instance, depicting the Muslim Brotherhood, the most distinguished and powerful fundamentalist organization, as a militant group believing in the "literal interpretation of the Koran and the Sunna," working for "the revival of the principle of *jihad*, holy war," without attempting to arrive at "a restatement of Islamic doctrines"[2] misses essential points concerning fundamentalism.

However, the negative propaganda that fundamentalism has received from both Arab and foreign media, scholars, and governments has precluded understanding the theoretical and practical contributions of fundamentalism. Consequently, this has prevented serious thinking concerning fundamentalism's basic assumptions and doctrines as well as its intellectual prospects. Substantial academic works have been produced on the philosophy of contemporary modernist Muslim reformers such as Jamal al-Din al-Afghani, Muhammad 'Abduh, and Muhammad Iqbal. At the same time, in-depth theoretical studies of fundamentalism lag behind studies on fundamentalist terrorism or militancy. Superficial readings of fundamentalism do not reflect precisely the complexity of fundamentalism and do not account for a variety of fundamentalist discourses developed by major theoreticians such as Sayyid Qutb, Abu al-A'la al-Mawdudi, the founder of the Islamic movement in Pakistan, and Hasan al-Banna, the founder of the Muslim Brethren, who neither advocate a literal interpretation of the Holy Qur'an nor think that Islamic doctrines are in need of restatement.

Islamic fundamentalism could not be studied only as a set of political movements; it must also be viewed as a set of intellectual discourses and critiques of philosophy, political ideology, and science. Its philosophical tradition includes both a belief in the existence of objective and ultimate truth and a claim of limited human subjective understanding of that truth. Further, fundamentalism attempts to offer a way of life and thought based on its understanding of both God's law (*shari'a*) and nature. Its political ideology refutes the notions of both an ultimate human authority and man's possessive nature. Thus, fundamentalism upholds the need for setting up virtuous, just, and equal societies. In this sense, fundamentalist calls for an immediate political project, the Islamic state, are linked to achieving these

---

1. Halpern, Manfred. *The Politics of Change in the Middle East and North Africa*. 4th ed. (Princeton, N.J.: Princeton University Press, 1970); Sharabi, Hisham. "Islam and Modernism in the Arab World." In *Modernization and the Arab World*, eds. J.H. Thompson and R.J. Reischauer (Princeton, N.J.: Van Nostrand, 1966), 26–36; and Khadduri, Majid. "From Religious to National Law." In *Modernization and the Arab World*, eds. J.H. Thompson and R.J. Reischauer (Princeton, N.J.: Van Nostrand, 1966), 37–51. See also Dessouki. Ali E. Hillal, ed. *Islamic Resurgence in the Arab World*. New York: Praeger, 1982; Curtis, Michael, ed. *Religion and Politics in the Middle East*. Boulder, Colo.: Westview Press, 1981.

2. Armajani, Yahya. *Middle East: Past and Present*. (Englewood Cliffs, N.J.: Prentice Hall, 1970), 287–88.

societies. Whether such a philosophy is well-grounded or properly developed, and whether one accepts or rejects fundamentalism, should not make it a passing phenomenon.

Philosophical Foundations

The principles of reason and religion and of philosophy and science are the underpinning of the intellectual foundations of both Islamic fundamentalism and Islamic modernism. The comparison and contrast of the different views on these principles reveal the different conceptual understanding of both movements; in fact, that understanding distinguishes one movement from the other.

Reason and Religion

While fundamentalists look primarily at reason, they make the existence of morality a natural, objective reality that is beyond the scope of human reason. Living in harmony with this universal moral system thus requires revelation. For al-Mawdudi and Qutb, God has created in the human being a *fitra* (intuition), which acts as the recipient of revelation and assures obedience to God, who created the universal laws in both their physical and moral forms. Universal natural laws are not value-free but aim at the well-being of this universe. Both universal moral and natural laws are created by God to serve human beings.

According to Qutb, Islam conforms to *fitra* and to the universe, since all are parts of a divine creation. This is why our happiness hinges on correspondence among the parts, themselves, and between the parts and the whole. Conversely, unhappiness is the consequence of disunity: mind against body, humans against humans, humans against society, and, ultimately, humans against nature, as in the case of adopting a nondivine *nizam* (system). While knowledge and happiness are based on their correspondence to *fitra*, Qutb makes happiness equal to fulfilling human *fitra* in nature, which is nothing less than total obedience to God's laws.[3] Thus, it is apparent that, for Qutb as well as for other fundamentalists, nature plays an essential role in laying the foundation of knowledge. Hence, a correct definition of any doctrine must be developed according to an accurate understanding of nature. The nature of Islamic social justice, for instance, cannot be realized comprehensively without being grounded in an Islamic worldview. Social justice is a derivative of *tawhid* (oneness of God).[4]

To the fundamentalists, religion functions as philosophy. Ancient and medieval philosophers argued that the good city, knowledge, and happiness

3. Qutb, Sayyid. *Hadha al-Din*. 4th ed. Cairo: Maktabat Wahba, n.d.

4. Qutb, Sayyid. *Al-'Adala al-Ijtima'iyya fi al-Islam*. 10th ed. Cairo: Dar al-Shuruq, 1980.

depend on correct metaphysics attained by reason.[5] However, Qutb views the good state, knowledge, and happiness as derivatives of correct doctrines. This kind of linkage—that is, making the validity of any political system dependent on its ability to promote happiness—shows that good politics is the art of seeking the fulfillment of the divine purpose in creating humans. Such a fulfillment requires a correct understanding of nature. It follows, then, that any social order that is incapable of fulfilling human *fitra* is unnatural, unjust, and unsuitable to human beings and to the divine design.[6]

While *fitra* directs humans to the good, fundamentalists still view humans as having diverted their natural drive and forgotten *fitra*, and as having replaced them with thought and desire. Humans have involved themselves in philosophy, and this has led mankind to wrong conclusions, as symbolized in worshiping ungodly things and abstract ideas. Nonetheless, humans look for God as naturally as they seek water and shelter. Put simply, moral laws, residing in *fitra*, are intuitive and natural. Al-Mawdudi, for instance, contends that humans agree that a well-administered society enjoys cooperation, mutuality, advice, social justice, and equality; humans also agree that theft, adultery, murder, spying, jealousy, and so forth are evil.[7]

Conversely, while modernism agrees that moral laws are natural, it argues that they are so because they can be authenticated and demonstrated by reason. 'Ali Shari'ati, for instance, argues that Islam—as opposed to Marxism, which equates moral laws with social customs and economic materialism—attributes moral laws to the primordial nature of humans.[8] Reason, however, is the instrument that locates them. While Jamal al-Din al-Afghani insists on the existence in humans of an urge to rise above bestiality and to improve their lives, he tells us that following the *fitra* without reason cannot be the primary instrument for the pursuit of knowledge and the cultivation of civilization. In particular, progress requires the study of science, itself necessary for knowledge. Solid moral and religious grounds require solid knowledge.[9]

---

5. On the *fitra* and its importance, see Qutb, *Khasa'is al-Tasawwur al-Islami wa Muqawwimatuh*. Vol. 1. (Cairo: Issa al-Halabi, n.d.), 4, 51, 83, 114, 127, 133, 134, 135, 137, 146–47, 166–67, 206, 207, 210; and idem, *Hadha al-Din*, 11. In *Khasa'is* (116–18, 140, 164–65), Qutb uses numerous Qur'anic verses to support his position—for instance, 2:164; 3:2–6, 191; 4:82; 6:12–19; 13:8–16; 33:62; 55:82; and, especially, 30:30. See also idem, *Al-Mustaqbal li-Hadha al-din*. 2nd ed. (Cairo: Maktabat Wahba, 1965), 11–13, 57–61.

6. Qutb, *Al-Mustaqbal*, 17–18.

7. Al-Mawdudi, Abul al-A'la. *Mafahim Islamiyya*. (Kuwait: Dar al-Qalam, 1977), 10–12, 28–29; and idem, *Nizam al-Hayat fi al-Islam*. (Beirut: Mu'assasat al-Risala, 1983), 6–7.

8. Shari'ati, Ali. *Marxism and Other Western Fallacies*. Translated by R. Campbell. Berkeley, Calif.: Mizan Press, 1980, 80.

9. Al-Afghani, Jamal al-Din. *Al-'Urwa al-Wuthqa*. (Cairo: Dar al-'Arab, 1957), 60–61; and Amara, Muhammad. *Al-A'mal al-Kamilah: Jamal al-Din al-Afghani*. (Beirut: Al-Mu'assasa al-'Arabiyya li al-Dirasat wa al-Nashr, 1980), 9–13, 16–17.

The first major difference that emerges, then, between the two discourses is that, whereas Qutb and al-Mawdudi locate the secrets of human nature in intuition and make them known only to God, al-Afghani, 'Abduh, Iqbal, and Shari'ati view humans as potential knowers, though they may not attain the ultimate knowledge. The difference arises from divergent functions of reason: *fitra* manifests itself to al-Mawdudi, Qutb, and other fundamentalists in obedience to God but to al-Afghani, 'Abduh, and others in the pursuit of knowledge.

This is why Qutb, al-Mawdudi, and al-Nadawi divide systems of thought, life, and action into two cardinal categories relevant to their proximity to divine laws: the divine and the humanly created. Those individuals who regulate their lives and behavior according to the system derived from a divine creed are followers of divine religion. However, those individuals who derive their system from anything else are the followers not of divine religion but of human religion.[10] This division is due to the fundamentalists' identification of religion with any system of life based on a metaphysical concept and accompanied by a social and political order. Every system of life is then a religion, and the religion of a group is the system that regulates the life of that group. Put differently, religion is not only an abstraction, a metaphysical doctrine, an emotion, or a belief; it is, equally, the culture or the system that regulates behavior. Communism is thus presented not only as a social system but also as a metaphysical doctrine based on material contradiction and ultimately as a religion."[11]

This is the reason, for fundamentalists, requiring proofs before submitting to God is unbelief. They view Islam as total submission with or without logical proofs. Belief in the day of judgment, for instance, should be adhered to whether a logical proof can be found or not. Although Islam is not opposed to reason, it requires that a logical proof should follow belief and not vice versa.[12] For Hasan al-Banna, logical proofs and syllogisms are accepted because the mind is spoken to in the Holy Qur'an. However, their service is to defend religion against myth and distortion. More important, God's existence needs no proof; rather, belief in it is intuitive. And the question "who created God?" is a misguided question, as humans are incapable of understanding even themselves.[13]

---

10. Qutb, *Al-Mustaqbal*, 12–14; and idem, *Khasa'is*, 212–215. The Qur'anic verses that Qutb quotes in *Khasa'is*, 212–15. The Qur'anic verses that Qutb quotes in *Khasa'is* (36–39, 230) include 12:40; 42:21; 5:47; 4:65; 9; 10:18; and 39:3–4.

11. Qutb, *Al-Mustaqbal*, 15–17.

12. Al-Mawdudi, Abul al-A'la. *Nahnu wa al-Hadara al-Gharbiyya*. (Beirut: Mu'assasat al-risala, 1983), 146–48, 150, 174.

13. Al-Banna, Hasan. *Majmu'at Rasa'il al-Imam al-Shahid Hasan al-Banna*. (Cairo: Dar al-Qalam, n.d.), 429–31, 471–74.

The modernists agree that religion is intuitive rather than volitional, but they postulate the harmony of reason and religion. To Muhammad 'Abduh, there is a general agreement among Muslims that some issues in religion cannot be believed in except through reason—as in knowing, for instance, God's ability to send messengers. If God is good, then He must send messengers to teach and warn humans, or else His punishment does not seem to be warranted. 'Abduh also argues that most Muslims have agreed that religion advances principles that transcend human understanding. Religion does not, however, advance principles that are opposite to reason. For instance, human reason can prove logically that God exists but cannot show His essence because the finite cannot understand the infinite.[14]

According to 'Abduh, religion remains the main element in morality and one of the greatest human forces, for it influences the majority more than reason does. More important, reason is the source for knowing and using religion; however, once belief is attained, the Prophet should be followed.[15] Similarly, to Iqbal, while religion starts with feeling, it has never taken itself as a matter of feeling, alone, and has constantly striven after metaphysics. Religion is not a partial issue, mere feeling or mere action; rather, it is an expression of complete humanity. In Islam, the ideal and the real are not two separate or opposite forces, and Islam bridges the gap between the two. The ideal must eventually absorb the real.[16] Shari'ati further defines Islam as a profound spiritual, idealistic, intelligible, and logical interpretation of the universe that is fully attuned to earthly realities and divinity.

Philosophy and Science

The difference between modernism and fundamentalism thus lies in the fundamentalist perception of Islam as an intuitive and self-evident truth as opposed to the modernist acceptance of philosophy in principle and the consequent need for proof. 'Abduh's acceptance of individual pursuit of knowledge falls within this difference. For him, finding rational proofs strengthen religion and facilitates submission to Prophetic teachings. Again, while the fundamentalist denial of the ability of human reason to arrive at truth without revelation hampers developing rational discourses, the modernist call for the cultivation of reason strengthens the development of Islamic rational discourses.

This difference, however, goes beyond just the employment of reason, to include the nature of reason, which itself hinges on understanding the worldview of Islam (*tawhid*). Al-Mawdudi and Qutb define Islam as both

---

14. 'Abduh, Muhammad. *Risalat al-Tawhid*. 2nd ed. (Beirut: Al-Mu'assasa al-'Arabiyya li al-Dirasat wa al-Nashr), 1981, 19–20, 31, 36–51.

15. Ibid., 111–13.

16. Iqbal, Muhammad. *The Reconstruction of Religious Thought in Islam*. (Lahore: Ashraf, 1960), 2, 9, 22.

an active program for a life and a discourse aimed at constructing a world-wide framework based on *hakimiyya* (divine governance). *Tawhid*, as the fundamental component of Islam, is not only a religious principle; more important, it requires eliminating independent earthly human systems opposed to *hakimiyya* and human transformation. An act like this indicates that God's governance of the universe negates the legitimacy of independent human governments.[17] An essential part of the fundamentalists' conception of *tawhid* is then turned into a process of negation of, and opposition to, any human-made system that is not grounded in *hakimiyya*. Any meaningful search for ultimate truths in this universe is, therefore, denied if it is unrelated to God.

The modernists, in contrast, view *tawhid* constructively. They posit it as a starting point that seeks development and understanding. Because not everything is given, human beings have to exert themselves. *Tawhid* is not an instrument of negation and opposition but is, to paraphrase Iqbal, a working force for the establishment of equality, solidarity, and freedom. In Iqbal's view, the state becomes nothing more than an attempt to transform these principles into a definite organization.[18] For Shari'ati *tawhid* views the whole universe as a single living and conscious organism that possesses intelligence, will, purpose, and feeling.[19]

Like 'Abduh, al-Afghani makes science the ultimate interpreter, both when Qur'anic verses are obscure or when they are contradictory to science. The Qur'an provides very general principles that must not contradict "the stipulation of reason and the achievement of science." And al-Afghani employs *ta'wil* (interpretation) as the method to resolve any possible contradiction between scientific facts and *shari'a* postulates, as in the case of the story of creation versus the theory of evolution.[20]

However, fundamentalism conceptualizes the function of science differently. Al-Mawdudi asserts that Islam encourages beneficial scientific experiments. However, the bias of experimental science, which is essentially developed in the West, makes it lacking in universality and places it in the service of nationalism, immorality, and unbelief.[21] While agreeing with al-Mawdudi on his opinion about the materialistic direction of science, nonetheless al-Banna and Qutb view science as a historical part of Islamic contribution to civilization and, consequently, as universal.

---

17. Al-Mawdudi, Abul al-A'la. *Minha al-Inqilab al-Islami*. 3rd ed. (Beirut: Mu'assasat al-risala, 1981), 28–34; idem, *Nahnu*, 267–70; and idem, *Nizam*, 21–22.

18. Iqbal, *Reconstruction*, 145–55.

19. Shari'ati, Ali. *On the Sociology of Islam*. Translated by Hamid Algar. (Berkeley, Calif.: Mizan Press, 1979), 83.

20. Al-Afghani, *A'mal*, 440–41.

21. Al-Mawdudi, *Nahnu*, 13–18.

Notwithstanding occasional negative remarks about science, the modernists generally look to Western scientific thought, as well as to the newly discovered scientific knowledge, as the core needed for a new and modern interpretive discourse of the traditions of both Islam and the Qur'an. Thus, the modernists' rejection of medieval thought, medieval theology, and ancient philosophy is due to their unscientific nature. For the modernists, science replaced the speculative philosophy that medieval thinkers had extensively employed in the exposition of Islam and the development of science. This is why Iqbal calls for a scientific writing of a new Islamic theology. An important instance that he provides is the interpretation of the Qur'anic verses that describe God as light. Muslim *'ulama'* (religious scholars) have interpreted these verses as metaphors for omnipresence. Iqbal's interpretation takes from modern physics the idea that the velocity of light cannot be exceeded and is the same for all observers. Since light approaches most nearly the absolute, the metaphor of light as applied to God must be viewed as a suggestion of the absoluteness of God and not of His omnipresence.[22]

Such an emphasis on the interpretive power of science compelled the modernists to devalue the importance of revelation and to provide very important but shaky new interpretations while critiquing tradition and philosophical methods of religious interpretation. To an extent, moral philosophy and religious precepts became dependent on the authority of science and, consequently, weakened. The modernists are not aware that, even if one assumes the absolute truth of scientific knowledge, science is still incapable of finding moral and metaphysical laws. If God cannot be located in spatiotemporal parameters, as Muslim theologians and others believe, then it does not matter much if one interprets the metaphor of God as light to mean absoluteness or omnipresence. The moral obligation to obey God's teachings does not change or affect the theory of light, which has nothing to do with the metaphysical understanding of God. Whether the light travels in particles or in straight lines has no bearing on God's essence and attributes or even on moral laws.

Despite these limitations, science constitutes a quintessential part of the modernist new theology employed to reinterpret and redirect modern Islamic discourses on philosophy, theology, and political thought, whereas fundamentalists disclaim the validity of science as a theological, exegetical, or interpretative power over scripture. Although more attentive to the possible negative effects of science in interpreting scripture, the fundamentalist alternative denies the role not only of science in the interpretation of scripture but also of philosophy, theology, and even history. Fundamentalists disregard the substantive and instrumental importance of history in

---

22. Iqbal, *Reconstruction*, 8, 63–64, 70.

interpreting the Qur'an, as the real Qur'anic writing and its transmission, as well as their accuracy, are validated by historical processes. Moreover, discrediting historical processes leads to enfeebling the Prophet's *sunna* (traditions), since the *sunna's* efficacy also relies on historical transmission. The fundamentalists concur on the accuracy of both the Qur'an and the *sunna*—an assumption that underscores the problem of dismissing historical processes and their significance on various developments of knowledge.[23]

However, the fundamentalists validate borrowing from only the generations of the Prophet Muhammad and the first two caliphs to Qutb or from the first four caliphs to al-Mawdudi and the majority of fundamentalists. The reason for the exemption of these caliphs from the frailties of human existence is that they paid due attention to the real meaning of Islam. As opposed to the modernists, the fundamentalists demystify normative developments in history as well as history itself—with the exception noted above. While they do not deny the existence of some occasional good guidelines, they nonetheless view history as being essentially corrupt and falling short of an ideal Islamic worldview. Demystifying history is, by and large, a profound threat to the orthodox establishment of Sunnism as well as to Shi'ism, whose authorities lie in historical developments of both doctrines and sects. Traditional imperatives, such as the doctrines of great founders of theological and jurisprudential schools like Abu Hanifa, al-Shafi'I, Ibn Hanbal, and Malik or al-Ghazali and al-Baqillani, have been turned into reasonable historical interpretations, but they are not the only ones. Such imperatives lack the quintessential meanings that have been attached to and are turned into nothing more than an *ijtihad* (reasoning) that could easily be changed by another *ijtihad*.

While producing new interpretations, the modernists have not challenged the normative status of Islamic theological and jurisprudential schools. 'Abduh's rejection of the human being's complete understanding of divine things is traditional, both in substance and method. His *Risalat al-Tawhid* (Treatise on oneness) is mainly a layman's reinterpretation of major works on medieval theology without the hairsplitting argumentation and discussion about divine attributes. That science is congruent with religion, or that they are not contradictory, is an argument also put forward by the great scholar al-Ghazali in his *Tahafut al-Falasifah* (Incoherence of the philosophers), similar to the argument put forth against the futility of discussing divine attributes. Again, al-Kindi, Ibn Sina, and Ibn Rushd introduced the sciences of the day into intellectual circles. In other words, the modernists have been instrumental in opening up the closed intellectual

23. On the role of history for the authenticity of the Holy Qur'an, see as-Said, Labib. *The Recited Koran*. Translated by Bernard Weiss, M.A. Rauf, and Morroe Berger. (Princeton, NJ: Darwin Press, 1975), 19–60, 121–25. Also, on the importance of historical accuracy for understanding the *shari'a*, see Hodgson, Marshall. *Venture of Islam*. Vol. 1. (Chicago: University of Chicago Press, 1961), 315–58.

circles to the need for rearguing traditions and modernizing Islamic interpretations by using all possible tools at hand.[24]

In a pointed dissension to this, the fundamentalists, in general, see the Islamic and Western past and present disciplines of philosophy, jurisprudence, and theology as superannuated. These disciplines are historically developed and as such have no universal values. Although not aware of it, the fundamentalists are indirect historicists; they view almost all old, medieval, and even modern interpretations as nothing more than temporary readings of—or the imposition of different meanings by different readers into—the religious text. However, the real meaning of the text is reserved only to the author, and no reader can make a claim to its universal reading. Fundamentalists look at the divergent readings as the outcomes of a complex set of conditions that make a reader read or interpret a text in one way or another. Divergence of theological, jurisprudential, philosophical, and political tools and sects is the product of specific ways of living that may not necessarily fit contemporary societies and problems. Put differently, what is more important than the logic of a reading itself and its pragmatic aftermath? Qutb and other fundamentalists transmute their rejection of historical readings into the possible legitimacy of new readings that are relevant to the problems of this age.

Political Principles

Tawhid has been developed by the fundamentalists to a point where it is used as the cord that ties together politics, economics, ethics, theology, and all other aspects of life. Because God, as the Creator, is the fountain of every material and spiritual thing, He is viewed as the ultimate authority in political life, as well. To the fundamentalists, humans' theoretical, theological, and political submission should be directed only to God. By this, they go beyond the traditional theological submission as understood in the old, medieval, and modern history of Islam. In this sense, they could not but load this doctrine of *tawhid* with ultimate political importance by insisting on subordinating politics and political philosophy to the highest kind of religious doctrine, *tawhid*. This is why they confuse religiosity with proper

24. See 'Abduh, *Risalat*, 17–51. The traditional structure of his arguments, like his description of God's actions, is noticeable. For a brief essay on, and references to, al-Ghazali's understanding of science and logic as not being contrary to religion, see Marmura, Michael. "Ghazali's Attitude to the Secular Sciences and Logic." In *Essays on Islamic Philosophy and Science*, ed. George Hourani (Albany: State University of New York Press, 1975). Also, for more details, see al-Ghazali, *Tahafut al-Falasifah*. (Cairo: Dar al-Ma'arif, 1957) 74, 77–78, 83–87, 89–124; and on the division of philosophy, idem, *Al-Munqidh min al-Dalal*. (Cairo: Maktabat al-Jundi, 1973), 47–57. On 'Abduh's reluctance to involve himself in controversies, see his treatment of the Muslim philosophers, wherein he explains their differences from the main orthodoxy without commending or censuring them (*Risalat*, 28–32).

political behavior. Thus, establishing the state on the basis of divine governance becomes a must for the legitimacy of any political regime.

However, the fundamentalists' rejection of modernity does not make their thought traditional as a matter of necessity. In fact, part of fundamentalists' criticism centers on traditional establishments and their religious and political roles. Traditional religious *'ulama'* do not, according to Qutb, comprehend the true Qur'anic spirit. Their imitation of a defunct jurisprudence that is irrelevant to modern living and their complacency toward political power lead to the alienation of Islam from the populace. The secular elites do not fare better, for they have marginalized Islam from the administration of government. Thus, the rejection of both secular and religious elites makes the fundamentalists advocates of a new model for Muslims who properly comprehend both religion and modernity. While underscoring the fragility of Muslim civilization, al-Mawdudi, Qutb, and other thinkers believe that only an Islamic revival, not traditionalism, can be instrumental in motivating an Islamic renaissance. Muslims must aim at inventing a new science and philosophy that must be developed from the essence of Islam, or else there is no opportunity to recapture scientific and political supremacy.[25]

Such a notion is very significant in the explication of the fundamentalist political project, at both the theoretical and practical levels. While the modernists' acceptance of the West led to their adoption of Western political theories, it precluded developing an original political theory or a few underpinnings for theory building. Their attempts introduced some Western political doctrines, like democracy and republicanism, and some practical recommendations to rulers. The nature of their political thought was oriented for immediate political goals but not fully grounded in theoretical advancements. Even the modernist criticism of traditionalism was not directed at traditions, per se, but at its rigid interpretation, which prevented making traditions suitable to Western notions, especially on the harmonious nature of religion and science. History again was not discredited as such but used to show how the Muslims, through various stages of development, dealt with foreigners and their compendium of knowledge.

We must keep in mind that the modernists, themselves, had no claim to any sort of theory building but were very keen on the need to bring together the West and the East, both scientifically and religiously. This is why the modernists did not shy away from adopting ideas from the West. The fact that they did not write a theory allowed the fundamentalists to use the adopted modernist notions to build their theory, such as when they introduced *shura* (consultation) as democracy. The modernists should, however, be credited for open-mindedness and for Islamicizing essential concepts,

25. Al-Mawdudi, *Nahnu*, 23–25, 47–51.

such as democracy and pluralism. The revival of an intellectual atmosphere in the Muslim world is due to the modernists, as is the belief in the possible congruence between Islam and the West.

However, the fundamentalists have taken over and produced a multitude of readings in which the essential discourse converges on intellectual and political transformation that could be either moderate or radical. The essence of the fundamentalist political discourse consists of three basic doctrines.

Legislation

Dismissing traditional readings and developing new ones have moved the fundamentalists from being just a political movement with specific ideological orientations to being a religious and intellectual movement seeking alternative religious, political, and intellectual readings that replace traditional and modernist Islamic and Western readings. Their alternative readings have centered on the discourse on *tawhid* and divine *hakimiyya* (governance). Al-Banna, Qutb, and al-Mawdudi, for instance, make God not only the source of legislation but also the focus of the new society that should aim at obedience to Him. Emphasizing the need to link even civic ethics to obedience follows suit. To Qutb, *tawhid* is not only human liberation from authority, but it forms the basis of any ethical, moral, and political system. Because Qutb believes that the basis of moral and ethical systems is divine, humans should not impose their systems. The Muslim society must follow the intuitive moral system, as revealed in the universal divine Qur'anic norms. These norms are not humanly derived, and their application is not an imposition on human nature. The divine system, as presented by the *shari'a* is, therefore, necessary for human well-being and for avoiding misery. To Qutb, Islamic *shari'a* is not a social but an eternal phenomenon, postulating the duties and rights of individuals and the state. Thus, legislating the basic principles of government, morality, and legality is sealed off from human calculation. However, these comprehensive, yet flexible, Qur'anic principles are designed to suit all ages and societies. The task of humans is to codify from—or read into—these general principles what is appropriate to society.[26]

Consequently, any deviation from *tawhid*, whether legal, political, or even personal, is a vitiation of true Islam, the fundamentalists argue. Sovereignty, both in a strict sense and in a general sense, belongs only to God, not to the individual, Qutb contends. Radical fundamentalism considers any kind of submission to human, social, political, or individual pressures as *shirk*, or unbelief. However, accepting the weakness of humans and the existence of uncontrollable events and difficult conditions, moderate

26. Qutb, Sayyid. *Mar'rakat al-Islam wa al-Ra'simaliyya*. 4th ed. (Beirut: Dar al-Shuruq, 1975), 60; also see 49.

fundamentalism gives more leeway to interpret the issue of sovereignty. For both trends, however, human programs and systems must not contradict divine ordinances. While divine sovereignty covers the mundane and the sublime, its implication is mostly related to politics that orders human life. The law of God is meaningful in terms not only of the beyond but also of the here and now. It penetrates both human conscience and, more significantly, humans' political identity. Although the concern for the next life is part of religion, earthly living is as important, since it is the bridge between the profane and the sacred. Thus, the goal of *shari'a* is to sanctify what is profane so that the duality between the other life and this life is, at least, softened and, at best, terminated. Consequently, human will must be consumed in the divine will—an act that makes human will an expression of the divine and, consequently, humans' political actions and systems, divine actions and systems. Only in this way can an individual evaluate others' behavior and thought. It is only in this way that a fundamentalist, especially a radical, considers himself as a representation of what God wanted humans to be like, the ideal human type, his task then goes beyond normal self-understanding. The *shari'a* becomes to a fundamentalist the only meaningful law and an Islamic system the only acceptable system.[27] This argument is used to vindicate the fundamentalists' call for nonreconciliation with Western thought because of a perceived basic incongruence between Islamic ideals and non-Islamic ones.

It is in this context that one can understand al-Mawdudi's argument that it is only through the sublimation of lower instincts, and not through their scientification or rationalization, that humans honor themselves. Will must be used even to turn instinctual worship of God to an intentional one. Any detraction from such worship dishonors the human being and leads him to fall again to the animalistic, instinctual state—al-Mawdudi gives the West as an example.[28]

Thus far, the fundamentalists' argument, especially the radical, has been to underline the need for modern and new foundations of an Islamic civilization. Their deliberate dismissal of Western civilization and past Islamic civilization leads them to uphold the need for "Islamic authenticity" as a ground for developing new theories. This applies also to the formal aspect of government, such as proper forms of an Islamic state. While the moderate trend uses some Western doctrines, like democracy, such doctrines are always underpinned by Islamic doctrines, like *shura*.

---

27. Qutb, *Hadha al-Din*, 16–19; idem, *Ma'alim fi al-Tariq*. 7th ed. (Beirut: Dar al-Shuruq, 1980), 49–114 *passim*; idem, *Fi Zilal al-Qur'an*. (Beirut: Dar al-Shuruq, n.d.), 34; idem, *Fiqh al-Da'wa*, (Beirut: Mu'assasat al-Risala, 1970) 60–61; idem, *Al-'Adala al-Ijtima'iyya fi al-Islam*. 10th ed. (Cairo: Dar al-Shuruq, 1980), 105; and idem, *Tafsir Surat al-Shura*. (Beirut: Dar al-Shuruq, n.d.), 51.

28. Al-Mawdudi, *Mafahim Islamiyya*, 24–25.

Revolution

While the modernists reject numerous medieval Islamic theories of Islam, they are not theoretically antagonistic to Western principles and theories and do not pinpoint any basic, inherent animosity between Islam and the West. This is why they have had no hesitation in adopting Western political and scientific theories; Al-Afghani, 'Abduh, and Iqbal have no theoretical problem, for instance, in accepting republican forms of government.[29]

To many fundamentalists, however, and the radicals in particular, *tawhid* denies the theoretical and practical possibility of dialogue and compromise. Qutb argues that *tawhid* is a revolution against all formal or informal institutions that claim any authoritative or normative role—an act that is considered to be an infringement on the divinity of God. For instance, a legislature that legislates in its own name is seizing God's divine authority to legislate.[30] A massive infringement on this level must lead to eradicating the institution that committed it. According to Qutb, a change like this is no less than a revolution aimed ultimately at conscious transformation of social and political institutions. This notwithstanding, individuals are not forced to become Muslims, though they must not create obstacles to developing a Muslim society and an Islamic state, as these two entities shoulder the responsibility of ending human enslavement to human beings and to material things. This responsibility is not limited to Muslim countries but includes all the countries of the world. Therefore, no compromise on this issue is entertained. According to Qutb and al-Mawdudi, compromise denies the possibility of reconstructing the world and leads Muslims to give up some principles and to accommodate others. Thus, radical fundamentalists theoretically link radical change to creativity, assuming that the old cannot be renovated but must be destroyed.[31]

For radical fundamentalists, such a change or revolution necessitates transforming the positive force of *tawhid* to a position of realistic activism. Revolution must be ready to challenge—nationally, regionally, and internationally—all sorts of powers, systems, ideologies, and philosophies.[32] This transformation cannot take place without first owning the necessary philosophical and political knowledge of the others, because ideas must be confronted by ideas and material objects with their like. An ideology cannot fight a gun; fighting a gun requires a stronger gun. The foremost

29. See Iqbal, *Reconstruction*, 157. Al-Afghani, for instance, accepted the rule of the Ottoman Caliph 'Abd al-Hamid and argued for the modernization of the Muslim *umma* through a spiritual and political regeneration of Muslims and by adopting Western institutions.

30. Qutb, *Ma'alim*, 26; see also 101; idem, *Al-Ra'simaliyya*, 70. See also idem, *Al-'Adala*, 250. In *Al'Adala* (249–50 and 258), Qutb quotes the following verses: 3:139–140; 4:59, 65, 74, 144; and 8:60.

31. Qutb, Sayyid. *Fi al-Tarikh: Fikra wa-Minhaj*. (Cairo: Dar al-Shuruq, 1974), 24–25.

32. Qutb, *Ma'alim*, 68.

material obstacle is the governments and societies of the world, as Islam's field of operation is the world, not only the Muslim countries. Therefore, an Islamic revolution must be set up where the objective is the total abolition of the regimes that are essentially based on the government of humans over humans, or simply *al-jahiliyya* (paganism). Individuals must be liberated from the shackles of the present and the past and given the choice of a new life. Such a new life, however, cannot be achieved without providing a new Islamic context in which the individual has a real choice to follow Islam or not.[33]

Another principle illustrating the untraditional political behavior of Islamic fundamentalism is its call for revolution. Muslims have traditionally accepted more or less unjust rulers who nominally adhered to Islamic law. Great jurists and theologians such as Ibn Taymiyya, al-Ghazali, and Ibn Jama'a demanded yielding to unjust rulers because the scourges of revolutions outweighed their possible benefits.[34] The fundamentalists now view revolting against unjust and unelected rulers not only as a political doctrine but also as an ethical obligation. In particular, the view of Islam as a revolution, disseminated by Sayyid Qutb in the second half of the twentieth century, represents a radical development within the history of Islamic political thought. Revolution is now loaded with political, ethical, theological, and metaphysical connotations. Its fulfillment becomes a synonym for the righteous application of Islamic teachings. Thus, Qutb and al-Mawdudi postulate Islam as a total revolution against ungodly human conditions, the rectification of which requires nothing less than total annihilation of human delusions about knowledge and power. Again, al-Mawdudi makes God's messengers advocates of radical, comprehensive transformation of all existing institutions. For Qutb, al-Banna, al-Mawdudi, and Khumayni, revolution became a quest for universal change to bring about justice and happiness, which must not be hindered by any authority.[35] In the view of the fundamentalists, the revolutionary aspects of Islam are not contingent upon the nature of Islam.

The rise of fundamentalism is not invited only by a particular environment "produced of a crisis situation characterized by economic difficulties, moral and ideological confusion, and political instability."[36] It is the other way around. The absence of revolution for the fundamentalists indicates

---

33. Ibid., 67–71. Also, Qutb quotes in *Al-'Adala* (67) the following verses to support his argument: 3:64; 12:40; and 43:84.

34. Amara, Muhammad. *Muslimun Thuwwar*. (Beirut: Al-Mu'assasa al-'Arabiyya li al-Dirasat wa al-Nashr, 1981), 154; also, the whole chapter on al-Afghani. See also idem, *Al-Islam*, 234–38; and idem, *A'mal*, 333.

35. Al-Mawdudi, Abul al-A'la. *Al-Jihad fi-Sabilillah*. (Beirut: Mu'assasat al-risala, 1983), 25–28.

36. Dessouki. Ali E. Hillal. "Islamic Organization" In *Islam and Power*, ed. A. Dessouki. (Baltimore: Johns Hopkins University Press, 1981), 113.

the depth of corruption and injustice in the conscience of Muslims, the intensity of crisis, and the loss of true Islam, a religion that is neither submissive nor stagnant. Thus, the fundamentalists' emphasis on the religious nature of activism is indicative of the superiority of praxis over theory and the importance of good action over good theory. For the fundamentalists, then, the actual formation of a good Muslim society takes precedence over the development of a seemingly coherent theory. In fact, such a formation is *tawhid* in action. Indeed, the collective formation of ideas for fundamentalism cannot be described in traditional terms, except when one means the text. But traditionalism is not the text; it is, rather, the interpretations that have been necessarily linked to the text. In a Christian context, one might make a comparison to Martin Luther, whose call to return to the scripture contradicted traditionalism.

For the fundamentalists *tawhid* must revolutionize the conscience and must be expressed in a popular movement. It must also transform the secular into the religious and go beyond the narrow limits of human existence to the unity of humankind. Revolution aims, then, at translating *tawhid* and *wahda* (unity) into a social and political movement against the universal state of moral and political bankruptcy which justifies itself by materialistic progress. However, the fundamentalists view such progress and its moral bankruptcy as a state that is not conducive to the general objective of humankind—that is, happiness. Instead, it is a source of misery that has plunged people into lust, selfishness, infidelity, and disunity. This state of affairs cannot be alleviated by taking a step here or there; its change requires a total mental, social, political, and intellectual revolution that sweeps away materialism along with its manifestations.[37]

Revolution is not, however, a synonym for a coup d'ètat or a forceful seizure of power; it is an attempt at a total transformation that changes the way people think and live. The fundamentalists view this change to be within the natural development of humankind. It is, according to the fundamentalists, a natural right for people to revolt, and force is justified when obstacles are imposed on this development. In particular, the fundamentalists are concerned with the state's denial of their activities to propagate their understanding of Islam. Freedom to propagate is basic to the fundamentalists who want to call people to their ideas. Any obstruction of propagation is, thus, identified with standing against Islam itself, since Islam is essentially a call for change.

This situation leads to the necessity of setting up a vanguard whose raison d'être is struggle, or *jihad*, against the institutions resisting the

37. Al-Afghani, Jamal al-Din. "Political Writings." Pt. 2 of *Al-A'mal al-Kamilah* Edited and introduced by Amara, Muhammad (Beirut: Al-Mu'assasa al-'Arabiyya li al-Dirasat wa al-Nashr, 1980), 9, 10, 11–13. On the fundamentalists, see, for instance, Asad, Muhammad. *Islam at a Crossroad.* (Lahore: Arafat Publications, 1963), 3; the quotation is from al-Mawdudi, *Nahnu*, 79.

propagation of Islam. A vanguard, in the view of al-Banna, al-Mawdudi, and Qutb, must be responsible for making people aware of existing inhuman conditions and the need to reorganize human institutions on the principles of *tawhid* and justice. Assuming power ideally should be the result of popular approval.[38] The fundamentalists presume that making the truths of Islam known is sufficient to induce people to follow Islamic teachings. Their insistence on people's freedom to adopt any philosophy of life springs from their confidence in Islam's natural appeal.

Part of the difference between the fundamentalist view and the modernist view can be attributed to the historical conditions of the two groups. Al-Afghani and 'Abduh, for instance, were writing while the Islamic caliphate was still an international empire; Qutb and al-Banna were writing under either an oppressive national state or British colonialism. However, this might help us understand only part of their motivations. Viewing Islam as a moderate or radical revolution may be the outcome of the political inability of the modernists to revive Islam in the realm of politics. The fundamentalist rejection of the present and the past reflects the modernist inability to produce real reform because of deep-rooted corruption and injustice. Thus, nothing but uprooting an un-Islamic society can be satisfactory to radical fundamentalists; there is no possibility of a Muslim society or an Islamic state without universal changes.[39]

Foremost among the required changes is the denial of historical normativeness, which becomes the basis for renewing religion. Thus, the fundamentalists postulate reworking religious principles in terms of Muslim modern experience. What was good in the past was good not because of its normative status but because of its derivative nature from Islam. The first two caliphs in Islam were good, according to Qutb, not because they had special status but because they were able to exemplify Islam teachings in their society. They did not force themselves on the people but were elected and were good examples of Islamic political behavior. To apply this to today's circumstances means that only those individuals who are elected by *shura* are good examples of Islamic political behavior. The fundamentalists are not attempting to relive the life of early Muslims but simply to derive certain examples in order to show the possibility of applying the *shari'a*. This thinking should not mean, however, that Muslims ought to imitate that period. The fundamentalist view is that Islam is capable of setting up in every age a new society that should be morally and materially more progressive. Material and moral progress is a preoccupation of Islamic fundamentalism, as it does not call for setting up a new Islamic state in order to reestablish the state of *al-Madina*. A new Islamic state does not

38. For example, al-Mawdudi Abul al-A'la. *Minhaj al-Inqilab al-Islami*. 3rd edition. (Beirut: Mu'assasat al-risala, 1981), 5–6; idem, *Nahnu*, 193–94.

39. Qutb, Sayyid. *Ma'alim fi al-Tariq*. 7th ed. (Beirut: Dar al-Shuruq, 1980), 22.

necessarily look like the first Islamic state. However, what is common between the first and the new are the moral, political, and religious grounds that created the community and justified the state.

Consequently, statements that give the impression of history brought to a standstill do not reflect precisely the fundamentalist project. The writings that deny the new fundamentalist project and link the present and the future to a lost golden past[40] miss basic differences between the ideals postulated by the traditionalists and those of the fundamentalists. While Qutb, for instance, views the first community as the best example of an Islamic nation, this is so only because the first community upheld *tawhid* and justice. Again, the first caliphate amplified the legitimate exercise and transition of power by communal consent. Thus, though the interpretations of *tawhid*, justice, *shura*, and *ijma'* (consensus) may differ from one time to another, they are potentially applicable to all ages. Their linkage to the Qur'an forms both the religious and political bases of the Muslim community. The death of the Prophet does deny the possibility of setting up a new ideal Muslim community. Fundamentalist arguments are based on the assumed possibility of an ideal Islamic state whose attainability hinges on an ongoing process of rereading the text and its principles in terms of current conditions. If fundamentalists believe in the futility of establishing an Islamic state, what then are they doing? In fact, the opposite is true; their notion of Islamic revival hinges on the rise or fall of the anticipated Islamic state and society. The perfection of government and society is not linked in fundamentalist thought to the existence of a superhuman institution but, instead, to the application of the Qur'an. The superhuman bond is nothing but the Qur'an, and its perfection is the measure of human behavior. That the Prophet Muhammad represented a flashing instance of that perfection is, for the fundamentalists, the outcome of applying the Qur'an. Again, political freedom, morality, and justice are theoretical possibilities that are applicable today.

However, some scholars acknowledge that, while fundamentalists are working in a radically changed environment, they still entertain traditional modes of understanding and behavior. Some scholars argue that fundamentalism assumes that "things can and should go as much as they have for generations past." Again, while it speaks to a changed milieu and is not a blind opponent of social change, it still stresses that "change must be governed by traditional values and modes of understanding."[41]

As we have seen, the fundamentalists reject both elite and public modes. Traditional modes should not mean, however, the Qur'an and the *sunna*,

---

40. Naff, Thomas. "Towards a Muslim Theory of History." In *Islam and Power*, ed. A. Dessouki. (Baltimore: Johns Hopkins University Press, 1981), 28.

41. Humphreys, Richard "Islam and Political Values in Saudi Arabia, Egypt, and Syria." In *Islam and Power*, ed. A. Dessouki. (Baltimore: Johns Hopkins University Press, 1981), 108.

for they are source material for understanding. The fundamentalist modes are, indeed, untraditional both in reading the text and in political behavior. For instance, they reject theology, philosophy, and history. Again, while the political behavior of Muslims traditionally has been acquiescent, the fundamentalists are, by and large, revolutionary.

Fundamentalists like Qutb and al-Banna do propose a new, comprehensive reading of Islam. Simply, this reading is the individual's interpretation of the Qur'an without any authoritative human guide. Although it is difficult in practice, since reading the Qur'an requires the mastery of many disciplines like linguistics and grammar, it only underlines the importance of individual freedom—an act that abolishes the authority of tradition. It opens the door wide for the ideologization of Islam through a political reading or a new political Qur'anic exegesis as a source for Islamic revival.

Thus, an activist political behavior, in the fundamentalist view, takes precedence over submission to social and political traditions. Authoritative exegeses and authoritarian governments were both dropped as proper means of reading the text and dealing with reality, respectively. Of course, certain values, especially the moral, are shared between the fundamentalist Muslims and ordinary Muslims. However, their justification for the fundamentalists lies only in the Qur'anic text, not in society or history.

Consensus

The untraditional and revolutionary interpretations employed by the fundamentalists are more apparent when studying their understanding of two essential political concepts—namely, consensus (*ijma'*) and revolution. Consensus, whose employment was theoretical in matters of jurisprudence and theology, is viewed as the source of political transformation. It has been used traditionally to arrive at one Qur'anic reading or another and has been relegated to the scholarly elites in order to convince the community to follow one interpretation or another. Now, the fundamentalists view it as a source for freeing the community—not only from conservative, traditional readings of scholars but, more important, from the tyranny of both rulers and political traditions. Thus, all fields of Islamic sciences and other aspects of life become the proper interest of ordinary Muslims and subject to their approval. No legitimate legal or political principles can be imposed on the community without its consent. The historically derived, normative status of the scholars and of political authority is denied and replaced by a need for a continuous process of ratification and agreement by the community. No political leader or religious scholar has the right to impose his will on the people.[42]

---

42. On traditional understanding of the Qur'an and the *sunna*, see Peters, F.E. *Allah's Commonwealth*. (New York: Simon and Schuster, 1973) 41–134; Gibb, Hamilton A.R. *Mohammadanism*. (Oxford: Oxford University Press, 1976), 24–35, 36–48; and Gibb, *Studies on the Civilization of Islam*. (Princeton, N.J.: Princeton University Press, 1982), 186–207.

In the view of the fundamentalists, consensus is a political tool used to check the Islamicity of the state rather than to control heretical views in the community. By freeing consensus from its historical limitations, the door is now open to the fundamentalists to use it as a device to measure political behavior. This also leads to the need for communal involvement in political matters regarding the forms and the content of politics. Now it is only the community that can speak with an authoritative voice; individuals have only opinions. The right to create political institutions, to evaluate political behavior, or to interpret the scripture is communal. Equality of rights and duties is postulated as a necessary condition for proper political behavior. This is why most fundamentalists make popular consensus a necessary condition for electing a legitimate Muslim ruler. Any ruler who comes to power without popular approval, even though he upholds Islamic law, is not legitimate. This view contrasts with medieval thinkers' acceptance of seizure of power, which the fundamentalists see as yielding to political power and betraying God's trust. God's delegation of authority is to all humankind as His vicegerent and is not bestowed on particular scholars, classes, or rulers. Consequently, no seizure of power can be legitimately justified.

This idea of legitimacy is also extended to include both the intellectual and the political realms. While historically the elites looked upon themselves as ipso facto communal representatives, the fundamentalists turn down any suggestion of particular privileges to any elite, be it political or religious. While most fundamentalists acknowledge differences among individuals, they are nonetheless against the institutionalization of intellectual and political elitism. No group of people can rightfully claim to have more rights or to enjoy special prerogatives.

Most fundamentalists play down the importance of consensus in theology, which was the main goal of traditional theology. As noted previously, people should be capable of reading and interpreting the text without an authoritative human intercessor. Legitimate interpretations must not contradict the text, on the one hand, but must be grounded in *tawhid*, on the other. Divine governance, representing the practical embodiment of *tawhid*, must appear in Muslims' unity and must be the principle of revival. Any revival that lacks this governance is indistinguishable from un-Islamic ones, since the moral grounds for an Islamic revival must always be present and embodied in the setting up of a Muslim society and an Islamic state.[43]

Needless to say, such an understanding of *tawhid* leads, in the long run, to some difficulty in understanding the text itself. Opposing textual interpretations can be provided by different groups to support various political

---

43. On the reason for modern Islamic revival and its beginning, see Gibb, *Mohammadanism*, 111–31. On modern concepts of the Islamic state, see Enayat, Hamid. *Modern Islamic Political Thought*. (Austin: University of Texas Press, 1982), 69–110. On the lack of leadership and existence of absolutism, see Cragg, Kenneth. *Contemporary Counsels in Islam*. (Edinburgh: Edinburgh University Press, 1956), 181–93.

views. Again, while the fundamentalist understanding may seem more liberal than the traditional, it carries within it the possibility of more authoritarianism, since some groups or individuals may claim to be representing the true meaning of Islam at a specific historical epoch—a claim upheld by many radical fundamentalist groups nowadays. This is the reason some other criterion, besides the text, must be employed to prevent incoherent or circular interpretations of the text.

Nevertheless, the rule of Islam is by no means the rule of theocracy; it is the rule of Islamic law, however vaguely defined. Qutb and al-Banna argue against the legitimate existence of an Islamic clergy, who are no more than scholars. A proper Islamic rule is no more than the systematic rule of Islamic law where Islamic ideas spread and where Islamic regulations define the forms of government and society. Thus, the inherent authority of the clergy is denied by all Sunni fundamentalists. To describe the proper Islamic government as a theocracy is, therefore, a misnomer, since it gives the wrong impression about Islam. Neither theory nor practice lends credibility to theocracy in Islam.[44]

The Shi'ite brand of Islamic fundamentalism, as advocated by Ayatollah Khumayni, may more appropriately be called theocratic. Khumayni advocates in his *Al-Hukuma al Islamiyya* (The Islamic government) the legitimate rule of only jurists, because a proper Islamic government must be based on jurisprudence.[45] However, the majority of the fundamentalists rule out the need for a clergy to bestow legitimacy on Islamic government. Its legitimacy springs from adhering to divine governance and from the execution of the *shari'a*. While for Khumayni and Qutb, the *shari'a* forms the basis of government, Qutb views the right to rule as a matter of delegation from the people, but Khumayni views it, directly and indirectly, as issuing from the *Imam*.[46]

While the fundamentalists converge ideologically on many issues, there are still many differences that are basic and essential. It is noteworthy that, while al-Mawdudi, for instance, suspects the serenity of the majority because of their deficient analytical skills, he feels that an elite must lead the way. He makes the goodness, as well as the corruption, of the people dependent on their elite. However, this does not mean that the elite has any intrinsic status; its role is social and political.[47] It is preferable that an elite starts the process of reformation, or else a popular movement may lead to the termination of the benefits of revolution. Revolutions may lead to more dislocations than corrections. However, Qutb, al-Banna, and others are

44. Qutb, 58, 63–69, 72.

45. On differences between the Shi'ite and Sunnite attitudes toward governments, see Lambton, Ann. *State and Government in Medieval Islam.* (Oxford: Oxford University Press, 1981), 246–63; Peters, *Allah's Commonwealth*, 544–634; and Enayat, *Modern Islamic Political Thought*, 18–51.

46. Enayat, *Modern Islamic Political Thought*, 207–9, 230–32.

47. Al-Mawdudi, *Nizam*, 54; also see 50–53.

more trusting of the people, for true reformation cannot take place except by grassroots changes brought about by the people.

Conclusion

The basic objective of both modernism and fundamentalism is to raise Muslim consciousness and to induce a social and political movement aimed at attaining material, political, and spiritual progress. A new reading of Islam becomes, for both the modernists and the fundamentalists, the basic condition for starting a modern process of reformulating Islamic history and reforming Islamic civilization. However, the process, itself, reformulates the tenets of political Islam and reforms the principles of political rule. The need for serious reexamination and reinterpretation of Islamic literature and, of course, the long-standing interpretations of Islam is postulated in order to accommodate modernity and modern human needs.

While modernism advocates Islam as the avenue for salvation, the modernization of Islam is to be conducted in line with the philosophy and politics of the West. However, Islamic morality is the distinguishing mark between Islam and other systems. No total or unending confrontation is postulated as a prelude to progress and development. On yet another level, religion's most important function is the calculation of morality. Although *tawhid* is the fundamental, comprehensive, and metaphysical doctrine, it becomes the linchpin in the process of unifying and liberating humankind. However, fundamentalism, especially its radical interpretation, looks at *tawhid* as essentially an instrument of political government.

For radical fundamentalism, *tawhid* becomes a justification for dominating others, while in the moderate fundamentalist view, it is justification for not being dominated by others. Fundamental doctrines such as sovereignty are grounded in the Qur'anic discourse, itself used to produce a legitimate popular discourse that makes legitimacy a matter of popular consent. Charged with interpreting the divine word, the *umma* (community) enjoys the only legitimate power; other powers are only derivative and hinge on Muslims' approval. Both modernist and fundamentalist discourses demystify history and call on humans to shoulder their responsibilities in charting their present lives and futures as well as in reviving religion. The essence of development lies in human nature: humans should not wait for salvation; they should achieve it. Spiritual, intellectual, political, and economic regeneration is the proper domain of humans, who must first purify themselves and then move to unite themselves with fellow human beings. However, the fundamentalists insist on complete purification and solid unification before any real process of regeneration can take place.

Fundamentalists' textual analysis of the scripture has a lot to do with their indifference to the possibility of other valid, but opposing, opinions. The modernists, however, whose textual analysis of the scripture relates to nontextual criteria, are more capable, in principle, of absorbing differences. Purification becomes an individual—not necessarily collective—act. Unity becomes, as well, more accommodating of diversity, since scientific discoveries reflect the possibility of reinterpretation or rediscovery of the truth. Thus, the process of regeneration for the modernists is always tentative, because it depends on a relative science, whereas the process of regeneration for the fundamentalists, especially the radicals, is ultimately absolute, because it depends on an absolute text. Not only is the difference between the two discourses methodological, but it leads also to the development of different normative systems.

While to a modernist, knowledge precedes belief, for a fundamentalist, it is otherwise. Knowledge to a fundamentalist becomes an act of belief, while to a modernist, belief is an act of knowledge. However, both view belief and knowledge as the basic two underpinnings for a sound revival. The absence of either leads to imbalance and to derailing any process of regeneration.

The two discourses are much concerned with regeneration and authenticity. While the modernist entertains and judges the authentic in terms of the new (science), the fundamentalist subjects the new to the authentic (revelation). The fundamentalist uses authenticity as the yardstick to measure all things, while the modernist uses the new as the yardstick. Again, the modernist makes the authentic yield to the new; the fundamentalist makes the new conform to the authentic.

6

Islamic Principles of Nonviolence and Peace Building: A Framework

Mohammed Abu-Nimer

There is solid agreement among scholars, in the second and third groups (studies of just war and peace and studies of peace building and nonviolence), that Islam as a religion is built upon a foundation of peaceful values and principles. In order for practitioners and advocates of peace building to utilize an Islamic framework in the settlement of various disputes, it is necessary to address such questions as: What are the values and principles that facilitate peace-building and nonviolent strategies? To what extent are those values and strategies supported by and based in Islamic religion and tradition? How, and in what context, are those values expressed? This chapter identifies a set of Islamic principles and beliefs that support the application of nonviolent and peace-building strategies. The chapter is not a comprehensive analysis of the Islamic laws or Shari'ah on peace building, nor is it an attempt to fully account for all possible sources in the Qur'an or Hadith that relate to peace in Islam. Rather, it aims to capture the basic religious and traditional peace-building principles and beliefs and their day-to-day practices on social and political levels. Discussing these values and principles would contribute to the building of a larger analytical and theoretical framework for peace building derived from Islamic religion and tradition.

The Pursuit of Justice

While this is not a theological study of Islam, whose purpose is to explore the foundational Islamic values of peace building and nonviolence, I must nevertheless rely mainly on the Qur'an and Hadith as the two most reliable and accepted religious sources in Islam. How does Islam view the relationship

---

Mohammed Abu-Nimer, *Nonviolence and Peacebuilding in Islam: Theory and Practice* (Gainesville: University Press of Florida, 2003), 48–84. Reprinted with permission of the University Press of Florida.

between peace and social justice? This question has been ignored by Western writers, in part because they tend to focus on the political relationship between Muslim and non-Muslim nations. Social justice is just one of a number of values that relate Islam to peace. Many Muslim and non-Muslim scholars have pointed to Islamic principles and values such as unity, supreme love of the creator, mercy, subjection of passion, and accountability for all actions, all of which are supported by innumerable verses in the Qur'an that command believers to be righteous and above passion in their dealings with their fellow human beings. Love, kindness, affection, forgiveness, and mercy are recommended as virtues of the true faithful (Ahmad 1993, 40). Other Islamic values directly related to peace building are *'adl* (justice), *ihsan* (beneficence), *rahmah* (compassion),[1] and *hikmah* (wisdom). Still others, discussed by Abdul Ghaffar Khan, are *'amal*, *yakeen*, and *muhabat* (service, faith, and love). Moreover, Islam emphasizes social justice, brotherhood, equality of mankind (abolition of slavery, and racial and ethnic barriers), tolerance, submission to God, and recognition of the rights of others. These values are repeatedly affirmed both in the Qur'an and in the Prophet's tradition.

George Hourani (1985) lists the main virtues taught by the Qur'an: "Piety, i.e., humble obedience and fear of God; honesty in dealings; justice and avoidance of all wrongdoing; and chastity. Love of God and fellow is rarely mentioned explicitly, but is really implied by the other virtues." This essay discusses seventeen such values and principles found in the Qur'an and Hadith, values that clearly demonstrate an affinity between Islam and peace building.

A major call of Islamic religion is to establish a just social reality. Thus, any act or statement from Muslims should be evaluated in terms of its potential contribution to that end. In Islam acting for the cause of God is synonymous with pursuing *'adl*, justice. Islam calls for such action by the strong and weak alike. It is the Muslim's duty to work for justice and reject oppression on both interpersonal and structural levels. The following Qur'anic verses forcefully convey this outlook: "Allah commands justice, the doing of good, and liberality to kith and kin, and He forbids all shameful deeds, and injustice and rebellion: He instructs you, that ye may receive admonition" (16:90). "Ye who believe! Stand out firmly for justice, as witnesses to Allah, even as against yourselves, or your parents, or your kin, and whether it be [against] rich or poor: for Allah can best protect both. Follow not the lusts [of your hearts], lest ye swerve, and if ye distort [justice] or decline to do justice, verily Allah is well-acquainted with all that ye do" (4:135).

---

1. Several Qur'anic verses (e.g., 90:17) emphasize the value of compassion among people. The same value is stressed in: "He who does not show compassion to his fellow men is undeserving of God's compassion" (Muhammad ibn Isma'il al-Bukhari, *Al-adab al-mufrad* [Cairo: n.p., 1959], book 34, ch. 53, 47–48).

"O ye who believe! Stand out firmly for Allah, as witnesses to fair dealing, and let not the hatred of others to you make you swerve to wrong and depart from justice. Be just: that is next to Piety: and fear Allah. For Allah is well-acquainted with all that ye do" (5:8). Among the words most commonly associated with the noun *'adl*, Khadduri (1984, 6) lists *qist, qasd, istiqamah, wasat, nisab, hissah,* and *mizan*. Based on such dictionaries as Ibn Manzur, *Lisan al-Arab*, and al-Fayruzabadi, *al-Qamus al-Muhit*, the verb *'adala* (in its various forms) means (1) to straighten or fix; (2) to straighten up or sit straight; (3) to amend or modify; (4) to run away, depart, or deflect from one (wrong) path to the other (right) one; (5) to be equal or equivalent, to match, or to equalize; (6) to balance or counterbalance, to weigh, or to be in a state of equilibrium.

In Islam, divine justice is enshrined in the revelation and divine wisdom that was communicated by the Prophet Muhammad. Justice rooted in divine wisdom is applicable to all times and all people. However, public rulings, laws, and the opinion of scholars arrived at through human reasoning (*ijtihad*) necessitates adaptation and refinement to address the changing world (Khadduri 1984, 3). Thus, scholars agree on the divine nature of justice but disagree on how it should be implemented on earth.

Muslims therefore maintain the core belief that a higher standard of justice must be found, consisting of a higher set of values, norms, and virtues to be realized on earth. This belief motivated scholars to seek the criteria and expressions of justice for human life. As Ibn Khaldun argues, individuals are innately driven to seek justice and are, by their nature, just—whether this "just nature" is guided by reason, revelation, or social habit (Khadduri 1984, 227).

All the diverse schools of jurisprudence agree that divine justice is ideally realized Islam. Such belief indicates the following assumptions:

1. Justice is known to man through available evidence (both revelation and reason). However, knowing justice through revelation is the more dominant belief.
2. Whether justice is the embodiment of the highest human virtues or a direct emanation from God (perfection), it is an ideal notion that Muslims are obliged to pursue.
3. Those who believe in a single, just God are the subjects of divine justice, and all others are the objects of that justice. Divine justice is conceived as divine laws, eternal, perfect, and existing irrespective of time and place, as a design for universal application to all men. Even men who do not believe in one God can seek refuge in it.
4. The standards of justice, whether determined by revelation or reason, indicate for men the path for right and wrong, so that all, each according to his "light," would pursue the right and reject the wrong

in order to achieve the good in this life and salvation in the next (Khadduri 1984, 192).

This ideal and comprehensive notion of justice can facilitate the development of Islamic peace-building strategies because of an overarching emphasis on individual responsibility and the primary moral obligation to fight against injustice. The early caliphate was known for its emphatic pursuit of justice, particularly the rule of 'Umar Ibn al-Khatab, a period widely revered by Muslims that also provides models for the pursuit of justice in society.

In tracing the Islamic notion of justice from its inception as a religion into the modern age, Khadduri identifies two main approaches: the modernist (rationalist or reformist) and the revivalist (revelationist). The debate between them has not necessarily been negative, or mutually exclusive, but functional and complementary in achieving progress in Islamic societies. If the modernists leap too far ahead of the mainstream in their reforms, the revivalists force them to step back and allow time for the new ideas to be assimilated.

In underscoring the centrality of justice in Islamic tradition, scholars have pointed to the number of times that the term *justice* (or *injustice*) has been mentioned in the Qur'an. For example, Khadduri states, "In the Qur'an there are over two hundred admonitions against injustice expressed in such words as *zulm, ithm, dalal*, and others, and no less than almost a hundred expressions embodying the notion of justice, either directly in such words as *'adl, qist, mizan*, and others as noted before, or in a variety of indirect expressions." Except for the existence of one God, no other religious moral principles are more emphasized in the Qur'an and the traditions than the principles of justice, uprightness, equity, and temperance (1984, 10).

In spite of this major emphasis on justice, however, there are no specific measures in the Qur'an or traditions that spell out how to establish justice on earth. Such responsibility was undertaken by Islamic scholars who have attempted to derive from authoritative texts the specific elements necessary to guide Muslims in their pursuit of justice. As a result justice is one of the most studied concepts in Islam. Some scholars have conceptualized categories of Islamic justice, while others have approached it chronologically or thematically. For example, in his comprehensive treatment of the term *justice*, Khadduri (1984) includes thematic categorical analysis of the political, theological, philosophical, ethical, legal, international, and social forms of justice. Indeed the search for specific theological understanding and application of justice in Islam is one of the most important contributions of Muslim scholars throughout the Islamic history. The most important theological approaches to justice to emerge from this effort are identified by Khadduri: the Jabarites or those who follow strict interpretation of predestination; all humans and their acts are created by God and man's life on earth is the unfolding of divine will; the Qadarites, who maintain that all humans are created by God, but man alone is responsible for his action, or simply that man has choice; exponents of rational justice, who like Mu'atazila argued that the individuals are capable of deciding and carrying the responsibility of their actions; and that there are two levels of justice—human and divine (Khadduri 1984, 41); and Sufis (mystics), who articulate a notion of justice as defined through spirituality and meditation. Sufis believe that *haq* (truth) is the highest value that can be derived from "a spiritual experience gained directly from union with God and not from ordinary human action." *Haq* embodies all other values. It is expressed as the kingdom of God, within every person, which can be experienced and communicated through the heart (*qalb*), spirit (*ruh*), or "inward secret" (*sirr*) (71). Divine justice is not to be gained in the hereafter, but in the present through contemplation of light, beauty, and love of God. In possession of these qualities, a person attains inward satisfaction and knows implicitly the practice and laws of divine justice.

The Qur'an repeatedly reminds Muslims of the value of justice, which it presents not merely as an option but as a divine command (see esp. verses 4:58, 5:8, 16:90, 42:15, and 57:25). Justice is an absolute and not a relative value, a duty to be pursued among the believers and with the enemies, too.[2] On this point, the Qur'an is clear: "Serve Allah, and join not any partners with Him; and do good—to parents, kinsfolk, orphans, those in need, neighbours who are near, neighbours who are strangers, the companion by your side, the wayfarer (ye meet), and what your right hands possess: for Allah loveth not the arrogant, the vainglorious" (4:36). "God does command you to render back your trust to those to whom they are due. And when you judge between people, that you judge with justice. Indeed, how excellent is the teaching that He gives you. For verily God hears and sees all things" (4:58). "O, Ye who believe, be steadfast in service of God's truth and bear witness for justice and let not hatred of a people seduce you so that you deal with them unjustly. Act justly for that is what piety demands" (5:8). "God loves those who are just" (60:8).

The Islamic tradition calls for resistance to injustice through activism, third-party intervention, and divine intervention. The interconnection and interdependence of peace building and justice are thus never far from the surface in Islam. Peace is the product of order *and* justice. The notion that

2. Howeidy cites al-Zamakshari: "And in this—pursuing justice with enemies—there is a great warning that justice is a duty to be applied when dealing with the infidels (*Kuffar*), who are the enemy of God. If it had such a powerful characteristic with enemies, then what duty and impact will it have among the believers, who are God's supportive favorites!" Fahmi Howeidy, *Al-Islam wa al-Demugratiah* (*Islam and Democracy*) (Cairo: Cairo Center for Translation and Publication, 1993), 121.

peace cannot be achieved without justice is echoed in the works of numerous peace-building researchers and activists (see Lederach 1997; Burgess and Burgess 1994). The imperative to strive for peace through justice falls equally on ruler and subject and is a natural obligation for all humanity (Kelsay 1993). Muslims are thereby expected to mobilize steadfastly against injustice. Mahmoud Ayoub (1996, 43) draws on the following verse to describe the special obligation that the Muslim community has in relation to justice: "Thus have We made of you an *Ummah* justly balanced [*wasat*, on middle ground] that ye might be witnesses over the nations, and the Messenger a witness over yourselves" (2:143). Based on this and other verses (55:9, 60:8), *qist* (the notion of dealing fairly with others, equity, fair play) is social justice in its broadest sense—first in our relationship to God and second in our relationship to society. From these perspectives, Muslims find a sacred obligation to treat one another with *qist*.

Mahmoud Ayoub (1996) also emphasizes the notion of *wasat* (middle ground) and *al-nasf* (sharing the equity, to do or demand justice; *al-nasf* and *insaf* mean justice) as representing the characteristic of fairness in Islam by drawing on such verses as: "There is no god but He: that is the witness of Allah, His angels, and those endued with knowledge, standing firm on justice [*qist*]. There is no God but He the Exalted in Power, the Wise" (3:18). There is also an important distinction between *'adli* and *qist* (justice, equity, fair play). Justice also has a legal meaning in terms of just laws. Shari'ah is the norm by which Muslims seek to administer and supervise a just order. The lack of codified law in the Shari'ah is not seen as a weakness but rather as a stronger method of procedural justice, since Islamic social and ethical codes were intended to remain flexible to allow for changes in space, time, circumstances, and variations (Ayoub 1996, 43). Scholars agree that such injunctions as *al-zakah*, the levy to purify wealth for the welfare of the poor, and *al-awqaf*, the estates in mortmain and their usage to assist the poor, are central to ensure the realization of justice.[3]

Isamic principles and teachings are clearly compatible with contemporary notions of nonviolent activism that mobilize communities to resist social injustice. Contrary to the popular misperceptions among the opponents of this method of resolving conflicts, this approach does not mean submission or passivity in the face of aggression and injustice, as has been

3. Based on Nimat Barazangi, M. Raquibuz Zaman, and Omar Afzal, eds., *Islamic Identity and the Struggle for Justice* (Gainesville: University Press of Florida, 1996). The prophetic tradition supports such a notion of moderation and fairness: "You should act in moderation." Sahih al-Bukhari, vol. 7, book 70, no. 577; vol. 8, book 76, no. 470. (Except where indicated, all Sahih al-Bukhari Hadith citations in this study are based on the translations in Muhammad Muhsin Khan, *The Translation of the Meaning of* Sahih al-Bukhari: *Arabic-English*, 6th rev. ed. Jami' al-sahih, English and Arabic, 9 vols., (Lahore: Kazi Publications, 1983). These were verified with the Arabic edition of Muhammad ibn Isma'il al-Bukhari, *Sahih al-Bukhari*, 8 vols., (Beirut: Dar al-Kutub al-I'lmiya, 1998), Arabic.

argued by militants in struggles in areas such as Palestine, Northern Ireland, and South Africa. Instead, the practices of Gandhi and Martin Luther King, among others, clearly demonstrate the uncompromising militancy of nonviolent techniques. Nonviolent strategies can dissolve the structural violence embedded in certain social conflicts, thus going beyond superficial tinkering or temporary solutions, which may defuse tensions while preserving an unjust system. The primary goal of theories and concepts of conflict transformation and nonviolence is to overcome the underlying bases of structurally violent systems (Galtung 1969), on both the micro and macro level, as a prerequisite for the realization of a just society.[4]

The Universality and Dignity of Humanity

The universality of humanity is a central precept in Islam, amply affirmed throughout the Qur'an and Hadith and conveyed through the belief in the equality of origins and rights and the essential solidarity of all people. Humans are regarded as the most dignified and exalted of all creatures, with the potential for knowledge and moral action. All humans are born with knowledge of God, and the Qur'an is intended to be a way for humans to remember their origin and cultivate their connection with God. Humanity is God's vicegerent on earth. The Qur'an states, "Behold, thy Lord said to the angels: 'I will create a vicegerent [khalifah] on earth.' [The angels] said: 'Wilt Thou place therein one who will make mischief therein and shed blood?—Whilst we do celebrate Thy praises and glorify Thy holy [name]?' He said: 'I Know what ye know not' " (2:30). Human beings are a manifestation of God's will on earth and part of a larger, divine plan. Thus, protecting human life and respecting human dignity is sacred in Islam. The Qur'an also stresses the honor bestowed on humans: "We have honoured the sons of Adam; provided them with transport on land and sea; given them for sustenance things good and pure; and conferred on them special favours, above a great part of Our Creation" (17:70). Thus, the life of a person should be aimed at preserving human dignity and pride. Islamic scholars have cited several Qur'anic verses to establish the importance of human dignity and pride: "We have indeed created man in the best of moulds" (95:4). "It is We Who created you and gave you shape; then We bade the angels bow down to Adam, and they bowed down; not so Iblis [Satan]; he refused to be of those who bow down" (7:11).

It is considered a good deed to intervene or act to protect the basic dignity and pride of the person, as a divinely created being deserving of respect and protection. "In Islam, every person has human sacredness and

4. In peace studies there is an emphasis on all aspects of justice (distributive, procedural, and restorative components).

he is under a protection [that is] sacrosanct until he violates his own sanctuary. By committing a crime, the person with his own hands removes such blanket of protection and immunity. Due to this human dignity, Islam protects its enemies, as well as its children and elders. God blessed humans with such dignity, as the base for all human relationships" (Daraz n.d., 164, cited in Howeidy 1993, 27). Thus, when addressing conflicts based on Islamic values, promoting and preserving the dignity of the parties involved becomes an important motivation in resolving the conflict.

The foundational idea in the Qur'an is that people are one community. It reflects the universality and inclusivity of Islam in dealing with all mankind. Accounting for the diversity of cultures and faiths in the world, the Qur'an notes that human differenes are also intended as God's will so that "you may know one another" (49:13). Thus Muslims repeat: God is the creator of all people.

Equality

Islamic teachings point beyond the settlement of short-term disputes; they aspire to unite humanity in a single family based on the equality of all members. This precept is based on the idea of the oneness and common origin of all people: "O mankind! We created you from a single [pair] of a male and a female, and made you into nations and tribes, that ye may know each other [not that ye may despise each other]. Verily the most honoured of you in the sight of Allah is [he who is] the most righteous of you. And Allah has full knowledge and is well acquainted [with all things]" (49:13).

In Islam there is no privilege granted based on race, ethnicity, or tribal association. The only two criteria for judging human worth are faith (*iman*) and good deeds (*'aml al-salih*). The Qur'an emphasizes repeatedly that there are no differences whatsoever between people except in their devotion to Allah, the creator of all humans. A well-known Hadith confirms this principle of equality: "All people are equal, as equal as the teeth of a comb. There is no claim of merit of an Arab over a Persian (non-Arab), or of a white over a black person, or of a male over a female. Only God-fearing people merit a preference with God" (M. Ali, 1944).

The Prophet acknowledges the common origin and universal equality of humans: Ibn Taymiyya, a well-known Muslim scholar (1263–1328), argued in these terms: "The desire to be above other people is injustice because all people are of the same species. A man's desire to put himself higher and reduce the others lower is unjust" (al-Sharif al-Radi 1978, 1:77; also, see Kishtainy 1990, 12). Islam underscores that all people are the children of Adam and Eve, a point often cited by traditional mediators and arbitrators as a reminder of the brotherhood of the contending parties.

The Sacredness of Human Life

Peace-building approaches assume that human life is valuable and must be protected and that resources should be used to preserve life and prevent violence. The Qur'an clearly affirms the sacredness of human life: "And if any one saved a life, it would be as if he saved the life of the whole people" (5:32). "Not for [idle] sport did We create the heavens and the earth and all that is between!" (21:16; see also 44:38). "Nor take life—which Allah has made sacred—except for just cause" (17:33). Human actions have consequences, and life is an integral part of the great cosmic purpose (Saiyidain 1994, 29).

Islam also prohibits the destruction or waste of resources that serve human life. Even when Muslims launched an armed conflict in the early period, their rulers instructed them to avoid gratuitous destruction. When the first caliph, Abu Bakr, dispatched his army on an expedition to the Syrian borders, he declared: "Stop, O people, that I may give you ten rules for your guidance on the battlefield. Do not commit treachery or deviate from the right path. You must not mutilate dead bodies. Neither kill a child, nor a woman or an aged man. Bring no harm to the trees, nor burn them with fire, especially those which are fruitful. Slay not any of the enemy's flock, save for your food. You are likely to pass by people who have devoted their lives to monastic services; leave them alone" (Sahih Muslim, vol. 3, bk. 19, no. 4456; also in al-Tabari 1969, 3:226–27).

Under pressure from his followers to go to war, Caliph Imam Ali uttered the following words: "If I order you to march on them [the enemy] on warm days, you say, 'This is the fire of summer. Give us time until the heat is over.' If I ask you to march on them in winter, you say, 'This is the bite of the frost. Give us time until the cold is over.' All this and you fleeing from the heat and the cold, but, by God, you are more in flight from the sword" (al-Sharif al-Radi 1978, 1:77; Kishtainy 1990, 12). Saving lives, exhibiting patience, and avoiding violence are values that are implicit in the Imam's remarks.

Peace-building initiatives in Islam enhance the protection of human rights and dignity and promote equality among all people, regardless of their race, ethnicity, or religious affiliation.

A Quest for Peace

Peace in Islam is understood as a state of physical, mental, spiritual, and social harmony, living at peace with God through submission, and living at peace with one's fellow human beings by avoiding wrongdoing. Islam obligates its believers to seek peace in all life's domains. The ultimate purpose of Qur'anic revelation for Muslims is to create a peaceful and just social order. But, as mentioned earlier, there are certain conditions in which

Muslims are allowed to use limited defensive force. "There are circumstances in which Islam contemplates the possibility of war—for instance, to avert worse disasters like the denial of freedom to human conscience—but the essential thing in life is peace. It is towards the achievement of peace that all human efforts must be sincerely diverted" (Saiyidain 1994, 164). Peace is viewed as an outcome to be achieved only after full submission to the will of God. Thus, peace has internal, personal, and social applications, and God is the source and sustainer of such peace. Accordingly, Muslims trust that the best way to ensure peace is by total submission to God's will and to Islam (Kelsay 1993).

Shunning violence and aggression in all its forms has been another primary focus of Islamic values and tradition. Many Qur'anic verses stress this principle, among them: "Whenever they kindle the fire of war, God extinguishes it. They strive to create disorder on earth and God loves not those who create disorder" (5:64). "God commands you to treat [everyone] justly, generously, and with kindness" (16:90). "Repel evil with that which is best [not with evil]: We are well acquainted with the things they say" (23:96). Thus when evil is done to you, it is better not to reply with evil, "but to do what best repels the evil. Two evils do not make a good" (A. Ali 1991, 859, comm. 2934). (It is best to use forgiveness and amnesty.) Even in conflict, Islamic doctrine prefers peace to war or violence: "But if the enemy inclines towards peace, do though [also] incline towards peace, and trust in Allah: for He is the One that heareth and knoweth [all things]" (8:61).

The quest for peace is also clear in the Prophet's tradition and life. The Prophet's tradition also supports the shunning of violence and calls for restraint. Such teaching is clear in the Hadith: "The Jews came to the Prophet and said, 'Death overtake you!' 'Aishah said, 'And you, may Allah curse you and may Allah's wrath descend on you.' He [the Prophet] said: 'Gently, O 'Aishah! Be courteous, and keep yourself away from roughness'" (Sahih al-ukhari 1998, vol. 8, bk. 73, no. 57). Forgiveness and amnesty are also viewed as the best reaction to anger and conflict.[5] The use of violence as a means to address conflict was discouraged in the Prophet's life and Qur'an and always framed in terms of a means of last resort. During the Meccan period of the Prophet's life (610–622 C.E.) he showed no inclination to use force in any form, even for self-defense. Instead, he waged nonviolent campaigns of resistance, through all his teachings in that period, during which Muslims were a minority. The Prophet's teachings at this time in particular were focused on the value of patience and steadfastness in facing oppression. For thirteen years the Prophet fully adopted nonviolent methods, relying on his spiritual preaching in dealing with aggression and confron-

5. In support of such an interpretation, see verses such as 41:34, 7:56, 7:199, and 28:54, in which Muslims are expected to exercise self-restraint and to control their anger and their reaction to evildoing.

tation. During this time, though he was tortured, accused of blasphemy, and humiliated, and his family and supporters were ostracized, he neither cursed his enemies nor encouraged violence. On the contrary, his teachings were centered around prayer and the hope for enlightenment and peace. Ibn Umar relates that someone asked the Prophet, "Who is the best Muslim?" He replied, "The one whose hand and tongue leave other Muslims in peace" (Sahih al-Bukhari 1998, vol. 1, bk. 2, no. 10).[6]

In Islam the quest for peace extends to both interpersonal and community quarrels and disagreements. Muslims should not use violence to settle their differences but rely on arbitration or other forms of intervention; several Qur'anic verses instruct believers to refer disputes to God and to His Prophet (see 40:12, 5:95, 40:47–48, 2:13, 3:55). "And obey Allah and His Messenger; and fall into no disputes, lest ye lose heart and your power depart; and be patient and persevering: for Allah is with those who patiently persevere" (8:46).

The various Islamic principles and values of peace cannot be fully identified without revisiting the concept and understanding the value of jihad. Esposito (1988, 40) has noted that the concept of jihad is commonly seized upon by Westerners in characterizing Islam as a religion spread by the sword, or through holy war, whereas modern Muslim scholars are more apt to explain jihad as simply defensive in nature.

Scholars agree that there are conditions that permit the use of force, but they have remained sharply divided on the nature of jihad. Many studies conclude that jihad does not mean the constant use of the sword to resolve problems with a non-Muslim enemy or among Muslims. In addition to the Qur'anic verses that indicate the possibility of peaceful and nonviolent jihad, various Islamic sects have argued that there are several levels of jihad and that the jihad against self-desires, temptations, and selfishness is the most difficult to achieve.[7]

Peacemaking

In the peace-building field, in general, open, face-to-face communication about problems and conflicts is deemed more productive than avoidance or violence, reducing the cost of conflict by addressing all the grievances of

6. The complete saying of the Prophet is translated by Mohammad Muhsin Khan: "A Muslim is the one who avoids harming Muslims with his tongue and hands. And a *Muhajir* [emigrant] is the one who gives up [abandons] all that Allah has forbidden."

7. There are Muslim groups (e.g., Sufism, Ahmadiyyah) that emphasize the spiritual rather than the physical jihad. The Sufi teachings explain that "The warrior [*mujahid*] is one who battles with his own self [*nafs*] and is thus on the path of God." Javad Nurbakhsh, *Tradition of the Prophet*, 2 vols. (New York: Khaniqahi-Ni'matullahi Publications, 1983), 2:76. Other groups suggest that *da'wah* (the call to spread Islam through preaching and persuasion) is the major form of jihad for Muslims.

the conflicting parties. A third party plays an integral part in peace-building intervention by facilitating communication, reducing tension, and assisting in rebuilding relationships. Islam encourages such active intervention, particularly among Muslims themselves. "If two parties among the Believers fall into a quarrel, make ye peace between them: but if one of them transgresses beyond bounds against the other, then fight ye [all] against the one that transgresses until it complies with the command of Allah; but if it complies then make peace between them with justice, and be fair: for Allah loves those who are fair [and just]. The Believers are but a single Brotherhood: so make peace and reconciliation between your two [contending] brothers; and fear Allah, that ye may receive Mercy" (49:9–10).

These verses have been cited by scholars searching for a legitimate basis for the use of violence in Islam and thus to refute the pacifist hypothesis. Nevertheless, the passage clearly supports the concept of mediation and fair and just third-party intervention. In addition, it reflects as a core Islamic value the shunning of aggression, exemplified in the following passage: "[A]nd let not the hatred of some people in [once] shutting you out of the Sacred Mosque lead you to transgression [and hostility on your part]. Help ye one another in righteousness and piety, but help ye not one another in sin and rancour" (5:2). In other words, hatred and lack of tolerance should not lead you to become an aggressor or be hostile to the other disputant, even if you have been shut out of the house of God, which is considered an act of violence. According to both the Qur'an and the Prophet's tradition, Muslims have to settle their conflicts peacefully. "[S]hould they [two] reconcile with each other . . . [this] reconciliation is best" (4:128). Another clear call for peacemaking and reconciliation is: "In most of their secret talks, save [in] him who orders charity or kindness, or conciliation between mankind and he who does this seeking the good pleasure of Allah, we shall give him great reward" (4:114).

Peacemaking and reconciliation of differences and conflict are preferred and highlighted by the Prophet's tradition. He instructed his followers: "He who makes peace between the people is not a liar" (Sahih al-Bukhari 1992, vol. 3, bk. 49, no. 857). The Prophet's intervention in resolving the problem of the Black Stone in Mecca is based on a well-known Hadith—as a classic example of peace building (Ibn Hisham 1992, 192–99). It illustrates the creativity of a peaceful problem-solving approach conducted by a third party (in this case, the Prophet himself). The clans of Mecca had a dispute over the Ka'bah's building and the lifting of the Black Stone to its higher location. The clans asked for the Prophet's advice and intervention, due to his reputation as a trustworthy and faithful person. The Prophet proposed a simple yet creative method to resolve the dispute. He placed the stone on a cloak and asked each clan to hold one side of the cloak and jointly lift the stone to the desired height. Then he placed the Black Stone in its new location.[8]

This type of arbitration in Islam was also explored by other researchers (e.g., Khadduri 1955). He identified several occasions in which the Prophet acted as arbitrator before and after prophethood. For example, in the incident of the Aws and Khazraj tribes of Medina, the Prophet acted as mediator according to the Arab tradition and ended their enmity; in arbitration between the Prophet and the Banu Qurayza (a Jewish tribe), both agreed to submit their dispute to a person chosen by the tribes. Khadduri concludes that third-party intervention was an acceptable option to end fighting. The decision of the third-party member is binding if their decision is not affected by their relatives. Khadduri also mentions the arbitration case between Ali and Mu'awiya, which was initiated to end their fighting.

In short, Islamic values shun aggression, violent confrontation, and bigotry and favor the methods of peace building and nonviolence for resolving conflicts. Such values correspond to those identified by contemporary practitioners and scholars in peace building (conflict resolution and peace studies) as foundational strategies in the field of conflict resolution (see, e.g., Laue 1978; Burgess and Burgess 1994).

Knowledge and Reason

Rationality, reason, and cost-benefit calculations are presumed to be prerequisites for successful dialogue and most conflict resolution processes. Conflict resolution and peace-building methods tend to assume that a rational approach to problems is more effective in reaching peaceful agreements and reducing the potential damage ensuing from conflicts. *Hikma* (wisdom) and *'aql* (rationality) are two major Islamic virtues, repeatedly cited in the Qur'an and Hadith. "Invite [all] to the Way of thy Lord with wisdom and beautiful preaching; and argue with them in ways that are best and most gracious" (16:25). This verse clearly encourages the faith-based use of reason, dialogue, and courtesy in dealing with others.[9]

Like Khadduri, George Hourani (1985) traces the history and centrality of rationalism within the Mu'atazilite [path of unity and justice] school of the ethics of reason.[10] Sachedina (2000, 21) also conceptualizes the relationship

8. For full details of these events in the life of the Prophet, see 'Abd al-Malik Ibn Hisham, *Al-sirah al-nabawiyah* (Beirut: Dar el-Fikr, 1992).

9. See Khadduri's discussion of philosophical justice and its roots in Islamic tradition by analyzing the work of the great Islamic philosophers al-Farabi, al-Kindi, Ibn Rushd, and Ibn Sina. Majid Khadduri, *The Islamic Conception of Justice* (New York: Johns Hopkins University Press, 1984).

10. In his discussion of the debate between traditionalist *naql* (transmitted knowledge) or *'aql* (reason), George Hourani identifies four major approaches to interpretation of the Islamic sources on ethics: (1) revelation and independent reason, which includes revelation supple-

between God and humanity from a rationalist perspective dependent on revelation that connects divine justice with human interaction. However, God grants humans free choice over, and responsibility for, their actions. This stream in Islamic philosophical and theological thought is most associated with the Mu'atazilite and different Shi'ite schools. The Mu'atazilite rationalists believed in natural human reason, which allows them to discover and decide on the ethical choices available to them. From this perspective, humans are autonomous sources of ethical knowledge. God created humans to be capable of knowing good and evil objectively. God's justice then depends on the objective knowledge of good and evil as determined by reason. The Ash'ari, or revelationists, believed that discovering the God-human relationship and scope of divine justice is beyond human logic. Thus, without justification or explanation, and strictly on the basis of trust and faith, Muslims should accept divine will and its creation of everything around them, including human knowledge. In this view, God alone is the source of all actions and provides humans with some voluntary choice. Values have no guidance; it is the will of God that reveals and imposes upon actions. As Sachedina explains, "God-Human relations are founded on individual autonomy as regulated by divine jurisdiction; interhuman relations are within the jurisdiction of human institutions founded on political consensus with the purpose of furthering social justice and equity" (2000, 5).

Thinking and pursuing knowledge are two central virtues in Islamic tradition and scripture. Many traditional sayings support these virtues: "The acquisition of knowledge is compulsory for every Muslim, whether male or female." "The best form of worship is the pursuit of knowledge" (Sunan Ibn Majah n.d., bk. 19, no. 108, 22–23). "Worship without knowledge has no goodness in it, and knowledge without understanding has no goodness in it, and the recitation of the Qur'an which is not thoughtful has no goodness in it" (Abu Dawud 1998, bk. 20, ch. 1; al-Tirmidhi 1965, bk. 19). "Thinking deep for one hour [with sincerity] is better than seventy years of [mechanical] worship" (Ibn Majah cited by al-Albani 1988).

A number of Qur'anic verses encourage the use of the mind: "And He hath constrained the night and the day and the sun and the moon to be of service to you and the stars are made subservient to you by His command. Lo! Herein are portents for people who use their mind" (16:12). Reason and

---

mented by independent reason (itjihad), and independent reason supplemented by revelation (Mu'atazilite); (2) revelation supplemented by dependent reason, which called for the return to tradition; (3) revelation alone; and (4) revelation extended by imams. (George Hourani, *Reason and Tradition in Islamic Ethics* [London: Oxford University Press, 1985], 227–73). That reason preceded revelation was mainly supported by Muslim philosophers such as al-Farabi (870–950), Ibn Sina (980–1037), and Ibn Rushd (1126–1198), who was more forthcoming on the role of religion and faith in the individual's life. Al-Ghazali (1058–1111) attacked all the previous philosophers for their perceived departure from religion and revelation.

reflection are viewed as paths to spiritual wisdom: "Do not be like those who say we hear and they hear not. Lo! The worst of beasts in God's sight are the deaf and dumb, who understand not" (8:21–22).

The story of creation in the Qur'an teaches us that when the angels claimed that Adam was going to do evil things on the earth, God told them: "I know what you do not know" (2:30). However, God granted Adam knowledge of the names of things, a power the angels did not possess. Thus, humans are endowed with a creative power for knowledge.

Several nineteenth-century Islamic reformists emphasized the elements of knowledge and reason in Islam. For instance, Jamal al-Din al-Qasimi and Taher al-Jaza'iri elaborated on reformist Islamic views similar to those being spread by Abduh, Rida, and Kwakibi in Egypt. Like Abduh, Qasimi endeavored to reconcile reason and revelation in Islam. He argued that "Islam is a rational religion: Islam calls on man to use reason; and whoever employs reason to study the natural world will grow stronger in faith" (Commins 1986, 406). Similarly, Hussein Nasr (1998) has argued that knowledge is one of the most important principles characterizing Islam.

The above appreciation of reason and pursuit of new information and knowledge in Islam can be a central theme in resolving conflicts and reducing enmity and misperceptions between enemies. For example, the various approaches of problem solving in the field of conflict resolution are based on the control of emotions and rational thinking. Such an approach of rational problem solving can be easily developed utilizing Islamic teachings of knowledge and rational thinking.

Creativity and Innovation

Nonviolent strategies encourage creativity and innovation in dealing with conflicts and relationships be generating new options that do not compromise the sense of justice. *Ijtihad* (independent judgment) is a notion that has been advanced not only among the *'ulama* (religious scholars) but also among other Muslims as a powerful tool of nonviolent conflict resolution for Muslims. In the 1930s, Muhammed Iqbal (1875–1938), one of the major figures in modern and modernist Islam, called for "the transfer of the power if *ijtihad* from individual representatives of schools to a Muslim legislative assembly" (Iqbal 1930). *Ijtihad* is the intellectual effort to interpret divine will for human implementation, the basic outlines for which were considered fully defined and codified in the eleventh and twelfth centuries, when the "door of *itjihad*" was proclaimed closed. Iqbal called for the reopening of *ijtihad* for Muslims. He argued that the closing of the door of *ijtihad* is pure fiction, prompted partly by the crystallization of legal thought in Islam and partly by an intellectual laziness that turns great thinkers into idols, especially in a period of spiritual decay. He predicted that "modern Islam is not bound by this voluntary surrender of intellectual independence" (Iqbal 1930).

According to Khurshid Ahmad, vice president of the Jami'at al-Islami (Islamic association) in Pakistan, "God has revealed only broad principles and has endowed man with the freedom to apply them in every age in the way suited to the spirit and conditions of that age. It is through *ijtihad* that people of every age try to implement and apply divine guidance to the problem of their age" (Voll and Esposito 1994, 12).

The notion that there are multiple interpretations for Islamic religious sources is also acknowledged by Sachedina (2000), who argues that there are various and subtle possibilities for interpretation. He echoes the repeated claim by Muslim reformists that individual *ijtihad* is a duty that can be practiced by any Muslim as long as the methods and the weighing of the argument are vigorous and drawn from authoritative texts. But the fact that such scholars offer an interpretation of Qur'anic passages immediately places them in conflict with traditionalists, who have closed the doors of *ijtihad*.

Closing the door of *ijtihad* has been viewed as a great obstacle in the revival of virtually every aspect of Islamic civilization. Thus when exploring the Islamic roots of pluralism, Sachedina (2000, 133–34) calls for opening the process of reasoning and inferring the decisions from the revelation, and encourages scholars not to regard existing historical interpretation as sacrosanct. Most of the judicial decisions regarding the autonomy and treatment of non-Muslims have become irrelevant in the pluralist, increasingly interdependent reality of the modern days.[11] Muslim jurists issued their teachings either under circumstances of domination or in efforts to curry favor with leaders, conveniently overlooking the essential Islamic premises of inclusivity and pluralism, in addition to the basic principle that being "the community sent by God" means the preservation of the rights of the other and creating socially and politically just societies rather than looking for political expansion or consolidation (138).

Having said that, it is important to point out that *ijtihad* requires creativity, flexibility, and the ability to abandon old perceptions and meet new challenges. These traits are also core requirements for many peace-building efforts (dialogue, mediation, nonviolent mobilization, and protest movements). Farid Esack (1998) maintains that Muslims cannot stop thinking and rethinking their environment or accept the notion that the door of creative juristic thinking (*ijtihad*) is closed. He asks, "How does one fast from dawn to dusk when you end up in a place where the sun does not set

11. Saiyidain went even further in encouraging scholars to engage in interpretation: "Even if my competence to undertake an authentic interpretation of the message of Islam would be in doubt, I strongly affirm the right of any serious, honest and intelligent person to do so. Such reinterpretation becomes necessary in every age for a variety of reasons" (Khwaga Ghulam Saiyidain, *Islam, the Religion of Peace*, 2nd ed. [New Delhi: Har-Anand, 1994], 3).

for six months?" (10). Muslims will always be confronted with new dilemmas and challenges based on new knowledge and deeper awareness.[12]

In the case of the Black Stone, the Prophet proposed a simple yet creative means of resolving the dispute: He had the quarreling clans join together to lift the stone to the desired height. The resolution of this problem implies a repudiation of violence and competition, and an appreciation of the creative possibilities of joint problem solving. In fact, there are many accounts of interventions by the Prophet in which he utilized such skills and principles in arbitrating or mediating disputes; these examples serve as powerful referents and resources for conflict resolution efforts.

Forgiveness

The forgiveness that vanquishes hatred and anger is a prized virtue in Islam, greater even than justice (24:43, 42:40). In fact, believers are urged to forgive even when they are angry. The Prophet said, "God fills with peace and faith the heart of one who swallows his anger, even though he is in a position to give vent to it" (42:37, see also verse 42:37 on forgiveness and control of anger). The Prophet himself, when he entered Mecca with the first Muslim followers, set an example of great forgiveness toward the Meccans, who had fought him by declaring the whole place as a sanctuary (Sahih al-Bukhari 1992, vol. 5, bk. 59, no. 603).[13] The Prophet always prayed when he was persecuted during the Mecca period, saying, "Forgive them, Lord, for they know not what they do."[14]

Forgiveness also figures prominently in the Qur'an as the way people should interact with each other: "Keep to forgiveness [O Muhammad] and enjoin kindness, and turn away from the ignorant" (7:199). An interpretive text says, "The most gracious act of forgiving an enemy is his who has the power to take revenge" (Saiyidain 1994, 93).

Mercy is another quality or behavior expected from a Muslim and is one of the most frequently cited and revered attributes of God. God has mercy upon those who are merciful to others (7:151). Mercy is an important step in the process of forgiveness and reconciliation. The value of forgiveness

---

12. Shari'ah is the divine will for human behavior interpreted by Muslim scholars and is presented through specific legal codes (*fiqh*), the science of Islamic law. For more on the much debated "closing of the doors of itjihad" and the present need for reform and dynamism, see Muhammad Iqbal, *Six Lectures on the Reconstruction of Religious Thought in Islam* (Lahome: Kapur Art, 1930); also see Tamara Sonn, *Islam and the Question of Minorities* (Atlanta: Scholars Press, 1996).

13. Another saying supports such a forgiving attitude when the Prophet entered Mecca: "There is no censure from me today on you [for what has happened is done with], may God, who is the greatest amongst forgivers, forgive you" (Muhammad Ibn Sa'd, *Al-Tabaqat al-kubra*, 9 vols. (Beirut: n.p., 1957), 2:142.

14. Muhammad Ibn Is'haq, *Kitab al-siyar wa-al-maghazi* (Beirut: Dar al-Fikr, 1978), 184; *Life of Mohammed* (English trans. Of Sirat Ibn Is'haq 1955, 193).

and its relationship to mercy is similarly supported by a story about some of the Prophet's followers who asked him to invoke the wrath of God upon the Meccans because of their persecution of Muslims. His reply to them was: "I have not been sent to curse anyone but to be a source of *rahmah* [compassion and mercy] to all" (al-Bukhari, 4:175, 9:141; cited in Nurbakhsh 1983, 2:81). When applying these principles of forgiveness to current realities, it is clear that instead of vengeance, there is a need to rediscover the processes and values of restoration through forgiveness and compassion in Muslim political society.

Individuals' responsibility for their actions and the process of gaining forgiveness is clearly prescribed in the following verses: "When those come to thee who believe in Our Signs, say: 'peace be on you;' Your Lord hath inscribed for Himself [the rule of] Mercy: verily, if any of you did evil in ignorance, and thereafter repented, and amended [his conduct], lo! He is Oft-Forgiving, Most Merciful. Thus do We explain the signs in detail: that the way of the sinners may be shown up" (6:54–55). To "service of the divine" is the way to implement repentance (*tawbah*), through which the "arrogant and jealous self, melted in the furnace of self-reproach, reforms in remorse and turning toward God by seeking the forgiveness of one's fellow humans" (Sachedina 2000, 111). The cycle of revenge must be broken by Muslims because "restoration is a source of life" (see Qur'an, 2:179) not revenge or vengeance (112). In this context—the use of jihad in the Qur'an as a means for restoration rather than retribution—individuals can use jihad to demonstrate a moral resolve to work for peace and justice. Thus, humans are expected to initiate a process of restoring their relationships as part of their nature and their place in God's order, and must act responsibly toward each other to gain God's forgiveness.

Retribution is usually attached to the principle of forgiveness in Islamic tradition. In general, retribution tempered with pardon leads to restoration in Muslim culture and community. Acknowledgment is considered the first step, as a "turn to God," an act of asking forgiveness (*ghufran*). Acknowledgment means quickly humbling oneself and then asking for forgiveness (Sachedina 2000, 103). In pre-Islamic society, primarily retributive measures were used to resolve conflicts, which caused tremendous fratricidal suffering, division, and destruction. The excessive nature of these retributions and the continuing reach of the conflicts over generations needed to be curbed. The Qur'an provided clear guidance for the Arab tribes on how exactly they should implement the law of fair retribution (2:178).[15]

15. Abdulaziz Sachedina, *The Islamic Roots of Democratic Pluralism* (New York: Oxford University Press, 2000), 105. Sachedina identifies two social goals as underlined in the Holy Book: to place moral and legal restrictions on the process of retribution, and to offer an alternative way to restore relations through forgiveness, blood money, and other compensation.

Deeds and Actions

In Islam the real test is in action. Lip service is not enough. God judges kindly those who have faith and have done good deeds: "On those who believe and work deeds of righteousness, will [Allah] Most Gracious bestow Love" (19:96). "If you do good, it will be for your own self; if you do evil, it will react on you" (17:7). An individual is responsible for his or her deeds; no one else can guide him or bear the responsibility of others' actions: "He that doeth good shall have ten times as much to his credit: He that doeth evil shall only be recompensed according to his evil: no wrong shall be done unto [any of] them" (6:160). "It was not We that wronged them: they wronged their own souls: the deities, other than Allah, whom they invoked, profited them no whit when there issued the decree of thy Lord: nor did they add aught [to their lot] but perdition!" (11:101). "Whoever works righteousness, man or woman, and has Faith, verily, to him will We give a new Life, and life that is good and pure, and We will bestow on such their reward according to the best of their actions" (16:97).

According to Islam, a person bears three major types of responsibilities in the execution or avoidance of which he or she will be judged by God: (1) responsibility toward Allah, to be fulfilled through the performance of religious duties faithfully; (2) responsibility toward oneself, by living in harmony with oneself; (3) responsibility toward other humans, by living in harmony and peace with them.[16]

Involvement through Individual Responsibility and Choice

Moral choice and rational persuasion are important Islamic principles that emphasize responsibility for one's own actions. Even the Prophet himself was not responsible for the decisions of others: "But if they turn away, Say: 'Allah sufficeth me: there is no god but He: on Him is my trust—He the Lord of the Throne [of Glory] Supreme!' " (9:129). If others do not accept God's message, it is their choice, their responsibility. Allah is the sole arbiter of humans' choices. Individual responsibility, choice, and God's arbitration on Judgment Day are also reflected in verses 18:29, 34:28, 88:21–22, and 109:6.

"Now then, for that [reason], call [them to the Faith], and stand steadfast as thou art commanded, nor follow thou their vain desires, but say: 'I believe in the Book which Allah has sent down; and I am commanded to judge justly between you. Allah is our Lord and your Lord: For us [is the responsibility for] our deeds, and for you for your deeds. There is no contention between us and you' " (42:15).

16. Interview with Sheik Arimiyawo Shaibu, an Islamic scholar in Pakistan, March 1998. See Catholic Relief Services, *Report on Islam, Peace, and Justice* (Baltimore: n.p., 1999).

The sense of individual choice and the call for involvement extends to the political system, in which the ruler expects his followers to take full responsibility for fighting injustice.[17] Abu Bakr told his people, "I am no better than you . . . I am just like any one of you. If you see that I am pursuing a proper course, then follow me; and if you see me err, then set me straight" (al-Tirmidhi 1959, ch. 53). Persuasion thus not only puts humans in charge of their own fate, it also supports individual actions.

Persuasion is a major strategy in the Qur'an, underscoring the privileged position of reason and intellect, and reflected in the numerous verses that present the arguments of those who opposed the Prophet, as well as the systematic refutations of those arguments through rational proof and evidence (Howeidy 1993).

Syed Nawab Naqvi (1994) establishes the importance of "free will" and choice in Islam by deducing basic axioms supporting these precepts: "in the Islamic ethical scheme, man is the best of God's creation"[18] (cited by al-Bukhari, ch. 53; also cited by Muhammad Ali 1944). Man is God's vicegerent [*khalifah*] on earth: "It is He Who hath made you [His] agents, inheritors of the earth: He hath raised you in ranks, some above others: that He may try you in the gifts He hath given you: for thy Lord is quick in punishment: yet he is indeed Oft-Forgiving, most Merciful" (6:165). Hence, the purpose of human life is to realize one's status as a moral agent invested with free will and able to make choices between good and evil, right and wrong. By virtue of his or her freedom, a person can either realize the truth of being God's vicegerent on earth or deny him- or herself this exalted role by making wrong choices. In other words, humans will be held accountable for the choices they make (Naqvi 1994, 25). Thus according to Islam, every human is endowed by creation with a natural ability (*fitrah*) for knowledge and justice. Thus it is up to individuals to discover their role in life and how they are going to serve humanity. *Fitrah* provides moral direction. There are certain responsibilities and actions which will guide this *fitrah* to be achieved or revealed. *Fitrah* does not judge the wrong or right of human faith but rather evaluates the moral righteousness of the actions. *Fitrah* has

---

17. See other verses emphasizing the same principle of individual choice and responsibility: 5:8, 9:6, 16:125, and 42:48.

18. The ethical axioms in Islam are: (1) unity (*tawhid*); (2) equilibrium (*al-'adl wa al-ihsan*): the desirability of an equitable distribution of income and wealth, the need for helping the poor and the needy, the necessity for making adjustment in the entire spectrum of consumption, production and distribution relations, and others. This is all to prevent or correct *zulm*; (3) free will (*ikhtiyar*): man is capable of choosing the right choice if he follows the correct path of God. But man is also capable of making the wrong choice. Man is free to make the choice, but his freedom is not absolute; and (4) responsibility (*fard*): responsibility toward himself, God, and others. By doing good things and observing his faith, man can ensure his correct path. The person is thus an integral participant of society. Man will not be responsible for what others have done and will not be questioned about others' deeds. Syed Nawab Haider Naqvi, *Islam, Economics, and Society* (New York: Kegan Paul International, 1994).

the capacity to relate and integrate individual responsibility with spiritual and moral awareness (as described by *taqwah*—a keen spiritual and moral perception and motivation) (Sachedina 2000, 82–86). Thus, it is the individual responsibility for human choice that leads to going astray (away from the straight path) and not utilizing the innate universal gift of divine justice given by the Creator to every human. Everyone has the autonomy and capacity to discover divine justice (3:86, 3:90).

Since deeds and individual responsibility are so central to Islam, involvement in community life becomes the most visible channel for meaningful deeds. Therefore, Muslims are urged to improve their communal life, to support one other, and to combat poverty. Such goals can be attained only through actions, the doing or shirking of which is the criterion by which God judges humans. Peace building in Islam is thus based on a framework of deeply embedded religious beliefs regarding individuals' responsibility for their actions and their active participation in a larger social context.

Patience (*Sabr*)

Muslims are encouraged to be patient and to suspend their judgment of others, whether Muslim or non-Muslim. *Sabr* (patience) is a virtue of believers, who are expected to endure enormous difficulties and still maintain a strong belief in God. It should be pointed out that in Arabic, "*Sabr* implies many shades of meaning, which it is impossible to express in one English word. It implies (1) patience in the sense of being thorough, not hasty; (2) patient perseverance, constancy, steadfastness, firmness of purpose; (3) systematic as opposed to spasmodic or chance action; (4) a cheerful attitude of resignation and understanding in sorrow, defeat, or suffering, as opposed to murmuring or rebellion, but saved from mere passivity or listlessness, by the element of constancy or steadfastness."[19]

The Qur'an elaborates on this idea in the following passages: "Nay, seek [Allah's] help with patient perseverance and prayers: it is indeed hard, except to those who bring a lowly spirit" (2:45). "O ye who believe! Seek help with patient Perseverance and Prayer: for Allah is with those who patiently persevere" (2:153). "But if ye persevere patiently, and guard against evil—then that will be a determining factor in all affairs" (3:186). "O ye who believe! Persevere in patience and constancy; vie in such perseverance; strengthen each other; and fear Allah; that ye may prosper" (3:200).

There are at least fifteen additional Qur'anic verses that encourage Muslims to be patient and steadfast in their daily lives and in their pursuit of a

19. Based on the Abdullah Yusuf Ali interpretations, *The Meaning of the Holy Qur'an* (Brentwood, MD: Amana Corporation, 1991), 28, comm. 61 of sabr in the Qur'an.

just life.[20] Patience is a key virtue in peace-building and socioeconomic development projects, whose benefits are often more apparent in the long term than in the short term.

Patience is also associated with making a personal and individual sacrifice. "Be sure we shall test you with something of fear and hunger, some loss in goods or lives or the fruits [of your toil], but give glad tidings to those who patiently persevere" (2:155). Patience and perseverance, as interpreted by Yusuf Ali, are not mere passivity (A. Ali 1991, 62, comm. 158). "It is active striving in the way of truth, which is the way of Allah." Thus, oppression and persecution can be resisted and overcome with praying and active patience (a believer continues to fulfill his/her duties as a Muslim and practices patience as a form of resistance). Patience and restraint are better than revenge. The Prophet said, "Power resides not in being able to strike another, but in being able to keep the self under control when anger arises" (Sahih al-Bukhari 1998, vol. 8, bk. 73, no. 135). Even when arguing or engaging in a conflict, the Prophet said: "Whoever has (these) four qualities is a hypocrite, and whoever has any one of them has one quality of hypocrisy until he gives it up. These are: whenever he talks, he tells a lie; whenever he makes a promise, he breaks it; whenever he makes a covenant, he proves treacherous; and whenever he quarrels, he behaves impudently in an evil-insulting manner" (vol. 3, bk. 43:18). "And if ye do catch them out, catch them out no worse than they catch you out: but if ye show patience, that is indeed the best [course] for those who are patient. And do though be patient, for thy patience is but from Allah; nor grieve over them: and distress not thyself because of their plots. For Allah is with those who restrain themselves. And those who do good" (16:126–28).

In commenting on these verses, Yusuf Ali says:

> In the context this passage refers to controversies and discussions, but the words are wide enough to cover all human struggles, disputes, and fights. In strictest equity you are not entitled to give a worse blow than is given to you. But those who have reached a higher spiritual standard do not even do that . . . Lest you should think that such patience only gives an advantage to the adversary, you are told that the contrary is the case: the advantage is with the patient, the self-possessed, those who do not lose their temper or forget their own principles of conduct (A. Ali 1991, 670, comm. 2163).

This strong command instructs Muslims on how to use patience and self-restraint in reacting to conflicts, a type of patience that will give them the advantage. Sabr is an important quality of believers as agents of change in Islam. The same characteristic is required of peace builders and those engaged in sustainable development. Assisting people and promoting

20. Some of those verses are: 10:109; 11:115; 16:126–27; 20:130–32; 40:55, 77; 46:35; 50:39; 70:5; 73:10–11.

peaceful coexistence in conflict areas requires patience among both the interveners and the beneficiaries.

Collaborative Actions and Solidarity

Peace-building approaches assume that collaborative efforts to resolve a problem are more productive than competitive efforts by individuals. A well-known saying in the Islamic tradition is "God's hand is with the group [*jama'ah*]," which is often cited to motivate disputants to reach an agreement and gain strength by working together. It also contains the pragmatic idea of reducing costs and damages that might be incurred in a conflict. This idea is also used to forge unified support against an outside enemy and to motivate people to avoid political and social rivalries (*fitnah*). In general, the saying encourages the collaborative approach to life's challenges, including, potentially, collective undertakings for social or economic development or peace building.

In Islam the basis for solidarity is wider than the Muslim community alone; all humans have a common origin in God, who created them all equal. Therefore, they should assist one another and not neglect one another's needs. "O mankind! Reverence your Guardian-Lord, Who created you from a single Person, created, of like nature, his mate, and from them twain scattered [like seeds] countless men and women—fear Allah, through Whom ye demand your mutual [rights] and [reverence] the wombs [that bore you]: for Allah ever watches over you" (4:1).

Solidarity among Muslims is a central value too, reflected in another well-known traditional Hadith: "Help your brother, whether he is an oppressor or he is an oppressed one. People asked: 'O, Allah's Apostle! It is all right to help him if he is oppressed, but how should we help him if he is an oppressor?' The prophet said: 'By preventing him from oppressing others'" (Sahih al-Bukhari 1992, vol. 3, bk. 43, no. 623). The Prophet also declared: "None among you has faith until you desire for your fellow Muslims what he/she desires for him/herself" (Sahih al-Bukhari 1992, vol. 1, bk. 2, no. 12).

This is a clear summons to avoid the use of violence and prevent aggression by Muslims against other Muslims and non-Muslims. Solidarity in this context is different from mere tribal solidarity, or *'asabiyah*—assisting members of the same tribe, clan, or family against outsiders regardless of the conditions.[21] Nonviolent strategies in Islam are most effective if they are based on collective approaches and political and social solidarity.

21. Islam attempted to abolish the dependence on tribal solidarity by emphasizing a higher order of unity among individuals; however, it remains a strong norm among many Arab and non-Arab Muslims.

The Ummah

The concept of the Ummah has been a foundation for collective action since the time of the Prophet. During the early period of Islam in Mecca, the Prophet propagated such values of collaboration and collectivism to mobilize his followers and to respond nonviolently to the accusations and attacks of his opponents. Brotherhood and equality are the founding principles of the concept of the Ummah (Khadduri 1984, 143).

Some argue that the concept of Ummah has vanished because of the contending political regimes in the Muslim world, that it applied only when Muslims were all under the same political authority. But Farid Esack argues that "the notion of Ummah has not only survived but continues to give Muslims a deep sense of belonging." The Ummah has even expanded to include non-Muslims. All those who believe in God are members of this community too. Esack adds, "The universal community under God has always been a significant element in Muslim discourse against tribalism and racism" (Esack 1998, 10).[22] In supporting this argument, other scholars stress that the People of the Book (i.e., Christians, Jews, and Muslims), as recipients of the divine revelation, were recognized as part of the Ummah, based on the following Qur'anic verse: "And surely this, your community (Ummah), is a single community" (23:52). The charter of the Medina—the first constitution created by the Prophet—is another proof of such an inclusive and religiously diverse community.[23]

The Prophet instructed his followers on many occasions on the importance of solidarity between the believers and Muslims. He compared their relationship to the organs of the body, which communicate pain if one part is ill, or to a building, which is strengthened by the coherence of its parts. "The believer to another believer is like a building whose different parts enforce each other. The Prophet then clasped his hands with fingers interlaced [while saying that]" (Sahih al-Bukhari 1992, vol. 3, bk. 43, no. 626).

Islam has been considered a religion of structural transformation and change, particularly in its impact on pre-Islamic civilizations. In this context, the principle of Ummah, in both its specific and general meanings, has

---

22. Farid Esack has completed a pioneer study on the Islamic theology of liberation based on the experience of Muslims in South Africa in fighting apartheid. He describes the use of Islamic beliefs and values in mobilizing Muslims to resist the South African system, particularly by building community coalitions with non-Muslims. Such experience affirms the great potential to construct coalitions across religious boundaries and identities in resisting war, violence, and injustice. Farid Esack, "Religion and Cultural Diversity: For What and with Whom?" Paper presented at the Islam and Cultural Diversity Conference, Center for Global Peace, American University, Washington, DC, 1998.

23. Akbar Ahmed supports this notion of the Ummah being a diverse religious and individual community, particularly in the Medinan period, in which the Qur'an mentions the concept of community forty-seven times, as compared to only nine times in the Meccan period. Akbar Ahmed, *Discovering Islam: Making Sense of Muslim History and Society* (London: Routledge and Kegan Paul, 1988).

emerged in Muslim history as a powerful mechanism of social and political transformation (Wahid 1993).

Peace-building initiatives can preserve a community's structure and identity throughout the planning, implementation, and follow-up stages of social change. Communal solidarity can thus contribute to the success of the overall process. The idea of Muslim community has proved a powerful tool of social mobilization and selflessness and thus has enormous potential for contributing to peaceful conflict resolution.

Nonviolence and peace building are based on collective and collaborative approaches that aim to respond to the needs and interests of the parties; they seek to create future bonds, relationships, and agreements between disputing parties. Collective approaches allow victims of injustice to exert influence and power over the other side. The purpose of the collective mobilization of power is to create a change in the behavior and perception of the other side. Such methods have been used by many leaders of nonviolent movements on various political and social levels. Practitioners of conflict resolution use this method to assist a party in realizing its power base. It is clear that the Ummah offers a powerful mobilizing tool for various Muslim communities to pursue justice and assert themselves nonviolently to redress structural injustices.

Pluralism and Diversity

Pluralism and diversity are among the core values of the Islamic religious and cultural tradition. The Qur'an recognizes diversity and the tolerance of differences based on gender (49:13; 53:45), skin color, language (30:23), belief, and rank (64:2, 6:165). Harmony between the different social groupings and communities is praised, and competition and control of one by the other is condemned (2:213, 10:19, 7:38, 13:30, 16:63, 29:18, 35:42, 41:42, 64:18). The Qur'an asserts that differences are inherent in human life and part of God's plan for humanity. Thus, ethnic, tribal, and national differences have no real bearing on closeness to God. The extent and degree of faith is the sole criterion by which different groups will be judged. The existence of difference among people is a basic assumption in Islam. Scholars cite the Prophet's saying, "My Ummah's differences are a mercy" (Howeidy 1993, 23).[24]

To protect such diversity among people, the Qur'an repeatedly emphasizes the respect and protection of People of the Book, and the Prophet stressed that "on the day of Judgment I myself will act as the accuser of any person who oppresses a person under protection [*dhimma*] of Islam, and lays excessive [financial or other social] burdens on him" (al-Baladhuri

24. The authenticity of this Hadith is in doubt; nevertheless it is widely used among Muslims.

1866, 162; cited in Sachedina 2000). The Prophet also supported the unity and harmony of Islam with other religions: "We the prophets are brothers and our religions are one and the same" (Ibn Hisham 1992, 501–4).[25]

Thus, differences among people are an inevitable and integral feature of humanity. "If thy Lord had so willed, He could have made mankind one People: But thy will not cease to dispute" (11:118). These differences are integrally related to the free will that God has bestowed on humanity, for people should be expected to be diverse not only in nationality and affiliation, but also in the expression of their faith and the path that they choose to follow (also see Qur'an, 10:99). Such a principle of free will and an individual's responsibility for all his or her actions is reflected in the Qur'an: "If Allah so willed, He could make you all one People: but He leaves straying whom He pleases, and He guides whom He pleases: but ye shall certainly be called to account for all your actions" (16:93).

Tolerance of the "other," or non-Muslim, believers (People of the Book) is repeatedly accepted and emphasized in Islam. The equality of the followers of different religions is reiterated in both the Qur'an and Hadith. Muslims are asked to remember that there is no difference in the treatment of people of different religions except in their faith and deeds (3:113–14, 2:62, 5:68). The Qur'an calls on Muslims to abandon fighting and to coexist peacefully with people of other religions. It reaffirms the validity of the traditions of other faiths and requires its followers to respect their scriptures. In fact, the expansion of Islam through *al-da'awah* in Asia and Africa or the Pacific region took place mainly among non-Muslims. Under such circumstances Islam could not have survived or prospered without having been strongly pluralistic and tolerant of diversity (Esack 1998).

There are many Qur'anic verses supporting this strong notion of pluralism in Islam. Some of these verses follow:

> Say, "O People of the Book! come to common terms as between us and you: that we worship none but Allah; that we associate no partners with Him; that we erect not, from among ourselves, lords and patrons other than Allah." If then they turn their back, say ye: "Bear witness that we [at least] are Muslims [bowing to Allah's Will]" (3:64)
>
> Say, "O People of the Book, you have no ground to stand upon unless you stand fast by the Torah and the Bible and all that has been revealed to you from your Lord. . . . Those who believe (in the Qur'an), those who follow the Jewish scriptures and Sabians and the Christians—any people who believe in God, the Day of Judgment, and do good deeds, on them shall be no fear nor shall they grieve." (5:68–69)

Pluralism prevailed in the early Muslim community. There was no single Islamic law or constitution, no standardization of the Islamic law. The Sunni tradition yielded four legitimate schools of thought, none of which were

25. Abi al-Fida 'Ismail Ibn Kathir, *Mukhtasar Tasfir Ibn Kathir* (Beirut: Dar al-Ma'rifah [Muhammad Kurayyim Rajih], 1983), 2:588.

limited to purely legal precepts (Esack 1998). In fact, the Qur'an is used to legitimize the validity of difference (*ikhtilaf*). Several interpretations of the Qur'an coexisted simultaneously in several areas. On the other hand, Islam has been intolerant of unbelievers, or infidels (*kafir*; pl. *kuffar*). Throughout history those who were cast as infidels were persecuted and punished by rulers and other followers.

The Medina charter, which was contracted between the Prophet and the various tribes, is an example of the high level of tolerance and respect of diversity assumed by Islam. Under the charter, all Muslims and Jewish tribes (apparently, no Christians were involved at that time, but it was used as a guiding principle in dealing with Christian tribes later) are considered one community, but each tribe retains its identity, customs, and internal relations. The charter was supplemented by a set of rules derived from the Qur'an and Sunnah to protect the rights of each group. Freedom of religion and the right not to be guilty because of the deed of an ally were among the protected rights.

Pluralism in Islam is reflected in the belief that the people are one community (Ummah), bound by a moral and spiritual identity and not by any other categories (such as race, birth, or gender). Sachedina even goes further, rejecting a narrow interpretation of the Qur'an verses that suggest salvation to Muslims only. He refutes the notion that the principle of "only my religion is genuine" exists in the Qur'an or the belief that only Islam rests on truths received in revelation, only Islam possesses the intrinsic values necessary for attaining religious perfection. In refuting these three principles of antipluralism he reinterprets the Qur'an verses that historically have been used to support such principles (2000, 37–40). For example, he explains that when commentators and interpreters explain the term Islam they restrict it to the Muslim community instead of explaining it as an act of surrender and submission to God, usually including all the *mu'ahidin* (people who believe in one God and are in peaceful relations with Muslims). Another example of change in interpretation is the use of the term *unbeliever*. Historically it referred to the pagan Arabs, whom the Muslim attempted to convert. However, with time, interpreters began expanding the term to include Christians and Jews. This tendency contradicts both the Prophet's teachings and the Quran's equal recognition of the People of the Book.

The Qur'an emphasizes repeatedly that "humankind is one community." Among the principles Sachedina (2000, 23–25) identifies as the basis for religious pluralism in Islam are: (1) the unity of humankind under one God; (2) the particularity of religions brought by the prophets; and (3) the role of revelation (the Qur'an). As Sachedina asserts, these principles do not deny the contradictions that might exist among religions, and they recognize the oneness of humanity and the need to work for better understanding among people of faith. The notion of freedom of conscience in matters of faith is the cornerstone of the Qur'an's notion of religious pluralism, both at the interreligious and intrareligious levels. Such principles constitute a strong base for Islamic approaches to interfaith dialogue and understanding.

Of critical importance to peace-building strategies and conflict resolution practices are seven main principles (*usul*) derived from the Qur'an that support coexistence and tolerance (Howeidy 1993, 202):

1. Human dignity deserves absolute recognition, regardless of a person's religion, ethnicity, or creed (see verse 17:70). This dignity is an immunity for the individual given by God.
2. All humans are related and spring from a common origin (4:1, 5:32, 6:98).
3. The differences among people are designated by God and are part of his plan for humanity. Differences in ethnicity, race, culture, and so on, are a factual and integral part of life (10:99, 11:188, 199, 30:22).
4. Islam acknowledges other religions and asserts their unified origin (2:135, 42:13).
5. Muslims have the freedom of choice and decision after the calling for submission or the message of Islam has been delivered (see verses 2:256, 17:107, 18:29, 109:46).
6. Judgment belongs to God alone and only on Judgment Day (16:124, 31:23, 42:48, 88:25–26).
7. Muslims should practice good deeds, justice, and equity in their dealings with all human beings (4:135, 5:8, 60:8).

Differences are a given in Islam. Therefore there is no justification for violating people's rights to existential or identity rights based on their religious affiliation (42:15). This outlook explains why Islam was not consumed or corrupted by the many cultures it confronted as it spread across civilizations. Instead, it created a new civilization. Islam has been both multicultural and pluralist in theory and practice. The diverse Muslim cultures of Asia, Africa, and Europe are expected to tolerate one another's differences as well as those of the non-Muslims in their communities. Unfortunately, a more "centralist and narrow" view of the world, as defined by many minority social and political movements in Islamic societies, has often eclipsed this tolerant vision in the contemporary Muslim world (Kadi 1998).

Muslim scholars are still grappling with Islam's relationship to the ideas of tolerance and difference. For example, Farid Esack expresses skepticism in regard to diversity and its consequences for the Muslim community. He cautions against an automatic acceptance of all differences without discernment based on the logic of Islamic precepts and practices. He suggests that the primary theological challenge for Muslims resides in understanding where to set the limits on diversity and acceptance of changes (e.g., women leading Friday prayers). In essence, he argues that Western values and cultures underlie pluralism, which he views as an extension of Western hegemony over the so-called underdeveloped world. He proposes that the acceptance of diversity not be the mere willingness to entertain every novel idea and practice. Instead, it should be geared toward specific objectives, such as freeing humankind from injustice and servitude to other human beings, so that people are free to worship God in their own way (Esack 1998).

In peace building, diversity and tolerance of differences are core principles. Peace builders hope to bring people to the realization that they are different and that such differences should not constitute a basis for discrimination or bias. Moreover, it is harmful and unjust to deprive people of their rights because of their nation, race, religion, or creed. These values have been made integral parts of Islam since its inception. In short, for Muslims diversity and tolerance of differences are God's wish, since He created a diverse rather than a uniform human race.

Conclusion

The preceding assumptions and principles constitute only a portion of the bases for conflict resolution and nonviolence in Islam. All these precepts are well grounded in Islamic texts and traditions (Qur'an and Hadith). Satha-Anand reveals Islam's connectedness to nonviolence and peacemaking: "Islam itself is a fertile soil for nonviolence because of its potential for disobedience, strong discipline, sharing and social responsibility, perseverance and self-sacrifice, and the belief in the unity of the Muslim community and the oneness of mankind" (1993b, 14).

An Islamic peace-building framework, applied to a context of community socioeconomic development, can promote objectives such as an increase of solidarity among members of the community; bridging the gap of social and economic injustice; relieving the suffering of people and spare human lives; empowering people through participation and inclusivity; promoting equality among all members of the community; and encouraging the values of diversity and tolerance.

Initiatives for peace building, and social and economic development, in an Islamic community would benefit greatly if the above Islamic principles were integrated into the planning, implementation, and evaluation phases. At present these are ideals, not actual practices. The reality in most Muslim communities today is far from the realization of such principles. Contemporary Muslim scholars have often argued that many of today's Muslims seem not to follow them in their daily lives.[26] Nevertheless, these ideals persist and are being transmitted to successive generations through cultural and religious beliefs. In fact, much of the frustration among many Muslims stems from the failure to apply these values in their communities.

We have seen the significant gap between Islam's possibilities for nonviolent practice and its perception among Westerners as a warlike religion. This divide evinces the need for a stronger and more solid "community of interpreters" in studying Islam and peace building, as well as scholars who will attempt to contextualize Islamic religious and traditional values in the framework of peace building and nonviolence rather than war. The effort to reconstruct legitimate nonviolent alternatives—social, religious, and political—in resolving internal and external conflicts in Muslim societies is a starting point for socioeconomic strategies.

The evidence clearly shows that Islam as a religion is conducive to nonviolent and peace-building methods through its various rituals and traditions. For instance, the weekly Friday prayer is a natural place for gathering that has been used by many political leaders and movements (Satha-Anand 1998). Scholars such as Satha-Anand (1993a, b), Robert Johansen (1997), and Ralph Crow, Philip Grant, and Saad Ibrahim (1990) have begun examining Islamic traditions and religion to identify other rituals and traditions that can be an effective source for nonviolent actions, such as (1) fasting rituals, which are excellent training for hunger strikes; (2) ritualistic prayers, for the habituated formation of worshipers into parallel lines to prepare people for engagement in disciplined actions; and (3) religious chanting, which can become an outlet for peaceful marches, meetings, and sit-ins. These correspondences support the assumption that peace-building strategies, combined with economic and social development initiatives, can and should be based on local and indigenous traditions and beliefs.

Finally, two main challenges face Muslims today: identifying the obstacles that prevent their economic, social, and political development and designing and implementing effective strategies and intervention within the above framework of values and principles to overcome such obstacles. Having identified the principles and values of peace building in the Islamic tradition, the question of their mere existence becomes irrelevant. Thus, we can move on to an examination of the application of such principles in day-to-day contexts and identify the obstacles that prevent their application.

---

26. This notion of a gap between reality and the ideals of Islam has been discussed by Islamic scholars (see Sayyed Hussein Nasr, *Ideals and Realities of Islam*, 4th ed., Chicago: ABC International Group, 2000).

Bibliography

Abu Dawud Sulayman ibn al-Ash'ath al-Sijistani. 1998. Kitab al-Sunan: Sunan Abu Dawud. Jiddah: Reprinted by Dar al-Qiblah lil-Thaqafah al-Islamiyah.

Ahmad, Razi. 1993. "Islam, Nonviolence, and Global Transformation." *In Islam and Nonviolence*, ed. Glenn Paige, Chaiwat Satha-anand, and Sarah Gilliatt, 27–53. Honolulu: Center for Global Nonviolence Planning Project, Matsunaga Institute for Peace, University of Hawaii.

Ali, Abdullah Yusuf. 1991. The Meaning of the Holy Qur'an. Brentwood, MD.: Amana Corporation.

Ali, Muhammad. 1944. *A Manual of Hadith*. Lahore: Ahmadiyya Anjuman.

Ayoub, Mahmoud. 1996. "The Islamic Concept of Justice." In *Islamic Identity and the Struggle for Justice*, ed. Nimat Barazangi, M. Raquibuz Zaman, and Omar Afzal. Gainesville: University Press of Florida.

Al-Baladhuri, Ahmed ibn Yahya.1866. Futuh al-buldan (Conquest of countries). Ed. M.J. de Goeje. Leiden: E. J. Brill.

Al-Bukhari, Sahih. 1998. 8 vols. Beirut: Dar al-Kutub al-I'lmiya. (Arabic)

Burgess, Heidi and Guy Burgess. 1994. "Justice without Violence: A Theoretical Framework." In *Justice without Violence*, ed. Paul Wehr, Heidi Burgess, and Guy Burgess. Boulder: Lynne Rienner.

Commins, David. 1986. "Religious Reformers and Arabists in Damascus, 1885–1914." *International Journal of Middle Eastern Studies* 18.4: 405–25.

Crow, Ralph, Phillip Grant, and Saad Eddin Ibrahim, eds. 1990. *Arab Nonviolent Struggle in the Middle East*. Boulder: Lynne Rienner.

Esack, Farid. 1998. "Religion and Cultural Diversity: For What and with Whom?" Paper presented at the Islam and Cultural Diversity Conference, Center for Global Peace, American University, Washington D.C.

Esposito, John. 1988. *Islam: The Straight Path*. New York: Oxford University Press.

Galtung, Johan. 1969. "Peace Violence and Peace Research." *Journal of Peace Research* 6: 167–91.

Hourani, George. 1985. *Reason and Tradition in Islamic Ethics*. London: Cambridge Unviersity Press.

Howeidy, Fahmi. 1993. *Al-Islam wa al-Demugratiah* (Islam and democracy). Cairo: Cairo Center for Translation and Publication.

Ibn Hisham, 'Abd al-Malik. 1992. Al-sirah al-nabawaiyah. Beirut: Dar al-Fikr.

Ibrahim, Saad Eddin. 1990. "Why Nonviolent Political Struggle in the Middle East?" Introduction to *Arab Nonviolent Struggle in the Middle East*, ed. Ralph Crow, Phillip Grant and Saad Ibrahim. Boulder: Lynne Rienner.

Johansen, Robert. 1997. "Radical Islam and Nonviolence: A Case Study of Religious Empowerment and Constraint among Pashtuns." *Journal of Peace Research* 34:1: 53–71.

Kadi, Wadad. 1998. "Reflections on Islamic Perspectives on Cultural Diversity." Address to the Cultural Diversity and Islam Conference, Center for Global Peace, American University, Washington D.C.

Kelsay, John. 1993. *Islam and War: A Study in Comparative Ethics*. Louisville: Westminster/John Knox Press.

Khadduri, Majid. 1955. *War and Peace in the Law of Islam*. London: Oxford University Press.

———1984. *The Islamic Conception of Justice*. New York: Johns Hopkins University Press.

Laue, James, and Gerald Cormick. 1978. "The Ethics of Intervention in Community Disputes." In *The Ethics of Social Intervention*, ed. Gordon Bermant, Herbert Kelman, and Donald Warwick. New York: Halsted Press.

Naqvi, Syed Nawab Haider. 1994. *Islam, Economics, and Society*. New York: Kegan Paul International.

Sachedina, Abdulaziz. 1996. *The Islamic Roots of Democratic Pluralism*. New York: Oxford University Press.

———2000. *The Islamic Roots of Democratic Pluralism*. New York: Oxford University Press.

Satha-Anand, Chaiwat. 1993a. "Core Values for Peacemaking in Islam: The Prophet's Practice as Paradigm." In *Building Peace in the Middle East: Challenges for States and Civil Society*, ed. Elise Boulding. Boulder: Lynne Rienner.

———1993b. "The Nonviolent Crescent: Eight Theses on Muslim Nonviolent Actions." In *Islam and Nonviolence*, ed. Glenn Paige, Chaiwat Satha-Anand and Sarah Gilliatt, 7–26. Honolulu: Center for Global Nonviolence Planning Project, Matsunaga Institute for Peace, University of Hawaii.

Saiyidain, Khawaga Ghulam. 1976. *Islam, the Religion of Peace*. New Delhi: Islam and Modern Age Society.

———1994. *Islam, the Religion of Peace*. 2nd ed. New Delhi: Har-Anand.

Al-tirmidihi, Muhammad ibn Isa. 1965. *Jama I al-Tiridhi*. Beirut: n.p.

Voll, John and John, Esposito. 1994. "Islam's Democratic Essence." *Middle East Quarterly* 1.3:3–19.

Wahid, Abdurahman. 1993. "Islam and Nonviolence: National Transformation." In *Islam and Nonviolence*, ed. Glenn Paige, Chaiwat Satha-Anand and Sarah Gilliatt, 53–59. Honolulu: Center for Global Nonviolence Planning Project, Matsunaga Institute for Peace, University of Hawaii.

7

Applying Islamic Principles in the Twenty-first Century: Nigeria, Iran, and Indonesia[1]

David R. Smock

This report describes three projects that illustrate how Muslim scholars in three countries are addressing critical contemporary issues from an Islamic perspective. In Nigeria, more than 300 Muslim scholars and clerics engaged in a critical examination of shari'ah as it is being adopted and modified in Nigeria's northern states. In Iran, Iranian scholars, clerics, and others convened to address the relationship between Islam and democracy in that country. In Indonesia, a team of scholars has written a manual based on Islamic sources for religious schools on the topics of peace/violence, democracy, rule of law, conflict resolution, human rights, and pluralism.

The debates among scholars and clerics in these three countries, as in other Muslim countries, on issues such as shari'ah and ijtihad (scriptural interpretation) are spirited. Resistance to reform and liberalism is particularly strong in Iran, but also in Nigeria. Those adhering to literal interpretations of the texts challenge those adopting a more rational/interpretive approach. "Text proof" versus "rational proof" approaches divide the ulama in Iran and Nigeria into traditionalist and rationalist camps, with the majority leaning toward the former.

---

1. A priority of the Religion and Peacemaking program of the United States Institute of Peace has been to support Muslim efforts to reinterpret Islamic principles for the twenty-first century. The Initiative has organized workshops on Islamic perspectives on peace and violence, on Islam and democracy, and, most recently, on ijtihad (scriptural interpretation). This report describes Initiative-supported conferences in Nigeria and Iran to enable Muslim scholars to grapple with how faithful Muslims can respond to a range of contemporary issues. In Indonesia, a project yielded a peace-focused teaching tool based on Islamic principles. This report summarizes the three projects and offers salient points raised by some of the conference participants.

David R. Smock, "Applying Islamic Principles in the Twenty-first Century: Nigeria, Iran, and Indonesia," Special Report 150 (Washington, DC: USIP, 2005).

The projects in Nigeria and in Iran were cosponsored by the Center for the Study of Islam and Democracy (CSID), based in Washington, D.C. CSID arranged for scholars of Islam from the United States and elsewhere to make presentations at the two conferences. The Indonesian project was cosponsored by Nonviolence International.

Shari'ah, Justice, and Ijtihad in Nigeria

CSID, in collaboration with the Centre for Islamic Legal Studies in Zaria, Nigeria, and the London-based International Forum for Islamic Dialogue (IFID), organized a three-day conference in July 2004 titled "Implementation of the Shari'ah in a Democracy: The Nigerian Experience." The conference was funded by the United States Institute of Peace and the U.S. State Department. Three hundred Muslim scholars and leaders from inside and outside of Nigeria discussed how shari'ah can be interpreted through ijtihad to meet changing needs and provide justice in Nigeria.

Radwan Masmoudi, president of CSID, explained that, like the Hebrew Bible, the Holy Qur'an contains commandments that Muslims must follow and apply in their daily lives. These commandments address not only purely religious issues such as praying and fasting, but also political, economic, and social matters such as inheritance, interest, and economic justice, as well as punishments for crimes such as theft, adultery, and drinking alcohol. These Qur'anic teachings are supplemented by the tradition of the Prophet Mohammad (sunnah) and by the long history of scholars' interpretations. Throughout history, Muslim jurists and scholars have had divergent opinions about many issues, and the process of ijtihad has been essential to adapting Islamic jurisprudence (shari'ah) to changing needs and realities.

The Tension between Fundamental and Liberal Interpretations of Shari'ah

Traditionalists believe legal punishments (hudud) prescribed in the Qur'an—such as for stealing and adultery—must be applied literally (e.g., cutting off the hand of the thief) in order to obey God's commandments, said Masmoudi. Modernists believe that this interpretation does not represent the spirit of the Qur'anic teaching and, more important, that shari'ah has always been subject to multiple interpretations in light of the ever-changing needs of society. To address the changing needs of their societies, Muslim jurists and scholars have relied on a well-established process of innovation (ijtihad), which is based not only on the Qur'an and sunnah, but also on reason, deduction, and prioritization. Imam Abu Hamid al-Ghazzali, a renowned twelfth-century scholar and theologian in Sunni Islam, presented this guidance about the overarching purpose of Shari'ah: "The purpose of the law [shari'ah] for human beings is fivefold: the preservation for them of their religion, soul, intellect, offspring, and property."

Shari'ah has become a very divisive issue in Nigeria. Simmering discontent among the various segments of Nigerian society has resulted in violent outbursts—sometimes appearing as religious fervor and other times dressed in ethnic prejudice—but all underscoring the country's imperfect federal structure. Twelve northern states, under pressure from their populations, recently adopted or reintroduced the criminal component of shari'ah. While this step has enjoyed broad public support from the Muslim populations in these states, Christians living there and in other parts of the country have felt threatened.

Masmoudi concludes that objective examination of the relationship among shari'ah, justice, and sustainable plural democracy is essential. The need to bring together scholars and experts on Islam, politics, governance, and democracy to assess how to accommodate and harmonize the assertion of Islamic law within a plural democratic setting led him to convene the conference. This conference had the following objectives:

- Promote an interpretation of shari'ah that is modern and compatible with universal human rights, pluralism, and democracy, while remaining genuinely Islamic
- Discuss shari'ah's true meaning, its various forms, and its Islamic roots
- Encourage efforts at Islamic reformation (ijtihad) to solve the political, economic, and social problems of the Muslim world.

In addition, the conference discussed the broader subject of democracy and political pluralism, covering such topics as independence of the judiciary, women's participation, responsibility and freedom of the press, rights of minorities, good governance, freedom of worship, and social justice.

The Case of Amina Lawal

In Nigeria, the debate about shari'ah implementation reached a peak in 2002, when a shari'ah court sentenced a young woman, Amina Lawal, to death after she was convicted of adultery. The case generated great interest, and the court's decision met with international protest and condemnation.

Many Westerners saw death as an excessive punishment for an act that falls within the realm of private choice in most countries. Many Muslims also opposed the shari'ah court's ruling, and reputable Muslim scholars and jurists found many flaws in its judgment. The court did not, for instance, give sufficient attention to ensuring due process: among other issues, it accepted a forced confession the police took from the accused and it released the man, who denied having sexual relations with the woman, without any punishment. Although the decision was ultimately overturned by the court of appeals, the case generated fierce debate about the suitability of Islamic law in modern societies.

As Masmoudi points out, the challenge facing modern Muslim societies is how to reapply the principles of shari'ah in social, economic, and political contexts that are markedly different from those that existed during its original development. The question is debated in academic and intellectual circles in Muslim societies. But in the absence of an open political debate, little has been done to educate the public on these issues, or to determine the relevance of shari'ah to contemporary cultural and legal practices. In addition, there is a significant debate in academic and religious quarters about the historicity, and even the authenticity, of certain historical pronouncements of shari'ah laws. For example, some scholars contend that stoning and punishments for apostasy have no basis in the Qur'an, while other Muslim jurists claim that these interpretations of shari'ah were meant only for a particular time and place in Islamic history.

Morality vs. Legality

Many Muslims scholars and jurists are profoundly concerned about the literal and uncritical application of ancient shari'ah rules, as well as the lack of clear delineation between the moral and the legal in Islamic law. Which parts of shari'ah are moral—and hence fall within the realm of education and voluntary compliance—and which parts are legal and therefore must be enforced by society? Also, there are intense debates on the issue of state intrusion into individual privacy and on the extent to which the state should be allowed to police individual morality. Questions also arise about due process and rules of evidence in shari'ah courts. To what extent can courts rely on circumstantial evidence to convict a person of a crime?

At the conference's opening session, chaired by Nigerian Chief Justice Muhammad Lawal Uwais, the governors of the northern states of Kano, Bauchi, and Zamfara delivered keynote addresses. Other attendees included several prominent judges from Islamic courts, academicians, and government officials. In his address, the governor of Bauchi State posed several challenging questions:

- In the light of globalization, how do we determine the limits within which we will implement shari'ah so that non-Muslims are also accommodated?
- How do we evaluate the changes in shari'ah without losing our distinct identity as Muslims?
- Shari'ah does not only apply to the weak and the poor, while we turn a blind eye to the rich and powerful. How can we create a spiritual policeman or a spiritual judge?

Conference Presentations

Dr. Najah Kadhim of IFID observed that of the Qur'an's thousands of verses, only a handful deal with shari'ah, so there is considerable room for flexibility and interpretation. Professor Abdelaziz Sachedina of the University of Virginia reminded the audience that shari'ah was formulated in a transnational world and by a transnational people. Muslims have inherited a diverse tradition, which must be rethought if it is to work for the modern nation-state. "You and I have a responsibility as Muslims," he said, "to clarify what we mean by shari'ah."

Saudatu Mahdi presented a paper titled "Shari'ah and Women in Nigeria: The Expectations." Mahdi asserted that Nigerian women expect the Nigerian implementation process to draw from the broadest and most tolerant understanding of the Shari'ah's tenets. Moreover, she said, the entire Muslim world, as well as the world at large, is watching how Nigeria handles the implementation of shari'ah. Her presentation included both detailed recommendations, including the repeal or modification of specific laws, and a general discussion of women's rights in an Islamic state.

Does shari'ah as implemented meet the people's socioeconomic needs? This was the foremost question raised in Baffa Aliyu Umar's paper: chiefly, how shari'ah provides a basis for the social, political, and economic life of both Muslims and non-Muslims. Umar asserted that even the smallest of social programs, appropriately aimed at people's most pressing needs, improves the shari'ah system as a whole.

As the debate at the conference reveals, the scope of the contending perspectives is wide, particularly concerning how Islamic norms and heritage relate to modern society. Masmoudi asserts that the debate must continue, as openness and dialogue are the best guarantors that radical notions will not go unchallenged and that claims to exclusive authenticity by extreme voices will be addressed. Open debate and the freedom to put popular choices to the test of time (as long as they do not infringe on human rights and human dignity) have been crucial for the maturation of Western democracy. The maturation of Islamic democracy and law requires similar time and space, he said.

Recommendations

Many questions remained unanswered, underscoring the importance of organizing more international discussions of the variety of interpretations and the complexity of applying shari'ah in modern Muslim societies. The exchange between local and international Muslim scholars was particularly stimulating and should continue in follow-up meetings.

Western societies and policymakers, Masmoudi pointed out, should appreciate that Muslim societies and lawmakers have every right to reconcile their legal system with their moral values. Instead of voicing alarmist condemnations of shari'ah, Westerners should pay closer attention to the lively debate on law and morality within Muslim societies. While all human beings, regardless of nationality and religion, have the right to be critical of practices they deem immoral, inhumane, and degrading to human dignity, no culture or religion has the right to dismiss the capacity of another to develop its own moral and legal systems through an open process and dialogue.

Reflections on Islam and Democracy in Iran

In recent years, attempts to engage Iran in a productive dialogue regarding developing a constitutional democracy have been thwarted by internal Iranian politics and external negativism, particularly from the United States. For almost a decade, a number of American foundations have led delegations to meet with Iranian religious leaders and other political activists to discuss political reform. Such meetings became possible after the election of reformist president Muhammad Khatami. However, none of these foundations was seen as empathetic to the Iranian political intricacies by the Iranians themselves. Most were regarded as American agents intrinsically opposed to Islam and anything Islamic.

The Center for the Study of Islam and Democracy, with its mission to search for the compatibility between religion and democratic politics, took a special interest in the Iranian experiment. Then-chair of the CSID board Abdulaziz Sachedina was in Iran in the summer of 2002 when Radwan Masmoudi suggested that he submit a proposal to hold a conference at his alma mater, Ferdowsi University of Mashhad (FUM). The story of how this conference was planned and executed helps elucidate the complexities that surround debate about religious and political change in Iran.

The subject of democracy and religion has been controversial in the Islamic Republic of Iran since its establishment under the late Ayatollah Khomeini. The government has been divided on the exact nature of the Islamic state from its inception, dating to the 1978–79 constitutional debates. With the rise of anti-Americanism as a vehicle to keep the religious establishment in power, the Iranian academic establishment has become extremely sensitive about being seen as encouraging American interference in Iran's internal politics.

Confronting the Obstacles

FUM welcomed the opportunity to collaborate with CSID and took precautions to avoid potential problems. FUM applied for official permission to hold the conference in Mashhad; the request was approved at the highest level in Tehran. CSID was committed to including both proponents and opponents of constitutional democracy in Iran. It was relatively easy to enlist the participation of secularist-modernist academicians such as Dr. Abdol Karim Soroush and his group of Iranian thinkers. The critical task for CSID/FUM was to get the traditionalist ulama, who oppose democracy as a Western imperialist ploy, to participate. For that purpose, Dr. Hassan Jamshidi, who has excellent connections to the traditionalists, was appointed as a "shuttle diplomat" to get as many members of the conservative ulama on board as possible. Thanks to his efforts, the conference was able to enlist well-known figures whose views about the role of clergy and Islam in a modern nation-state were important to the debate.

There was constant risk that the conference would be derailed at the last minute, mainly because it was to be the first of its kind in the country. Twice, parliamentary elections—resulting in hard-liners' forming the majority—postponed the conference. They also served as a warning to CSID that antidemocratic forces connected with the religious establishment might pressure the university to cancel the event.

The final date of December 1–2, 2004, was mutually approved by CSID and FUM. During the last week of November, Dr. Ali Yousefi, the FUM-appointed conference director, informed Sachedina that Ansar-i Hizb Allah, an extremist group supporting clerical rule in Iran, had threatened to disrupt the proceedings. The university, in consultation with the government officials in Tehran, nevertheless decided to proceed with the conference.

As soon as the CSID delegation, made up of Masmoudi, Sachedina, and Antony Sullivan, arrived in Mashhad the morning of November 30, they learned that Ansar-i Hizb Allah had demanded that five prominent scholars, who formed the liberal group in support of democratic governance in Iran, be barred from participating. The group had also threatened the lives of these five scholars, including Soroush and Dr. Mohsin Kadivar, a liberal cleric.

The First Day of the Conference

CSID and FUM moved quickly to arrange for alternative programs in Mashhad and Tehran, where a number of key participants had been asked to stay until further instructions from the conference organizers. On December 1, the CSID delegation met with several faculty members in the Theology School and Faculty of Arts and Humanities. In the evening, some scholars who were already in Mashhad met for about three hours at FUM to present their views and discuss issues connected with democratization. The atmosphere was tense, but the discussions were open and critical of the role religion was playing in Iranian politics. The participants were unanimous in feeling that unchecked state religiosity could lead to a dangerous and tyrannical system of governance, as the events of the past few years had indicated.

In addition to Masmoudi and Sachedina, the Iranian group was led in discussion by Professor Mohammad Mojtahed Shabestari, a member of the clerical establishment; Professor Gholam Abbas Tavassoli, and Drs. Mohammad Reza Beheshti and Arjomand. They spoke about secularism and the problems posed by the fact that in modern democratic society, religion is privatized and its scope limited to spiritual and moral well-being. There were also interesting exchanges about critical conceptual clarity concerning the meaning and nature of democracy and its cultural relativity.

Dr. Beheshti's presentation raised important issues in the emerging intercultural dialogue among world religions. Peaceful coexistence among peoples of different religions depends on changing faith communities' attitudes that they have exclusive control of the truth. The unique aspect of this frank exchange among Iranian thinkers was the total absence of anti-American rhetoric. The entire discussion demonstrated sophisticated understanding of the issues related to developing democratic freedoms within the framework of a secular state that respects the wisdom of religion in both its internal and external policies.

The Second Day of the Conference

On December 2, the scholars who had been prevented from traveling to Mashhad met with twenty-five other participants at the Ministry of Higher Education and Scientific Research in Tehran to present their papers and discuss the compatibility of Islam and democracy in Iran. The Tehran meeting compensated for all that was lacking in the Mashhad meeting. The atmosphere was relaxed and the participants contributed extremely well in terms of quality and transparency. The issue that dominated the afternoon was not whether religion and democracy are compatible. That was taken as a given, as was recognition that religion in a country like Iran cannot be eliminated from the public square.

Soroush argued that Muslim sensibilities are offended when liberal democracy tolerates or encourages immoral social behavior. Iranians must search for political democracy; they need an accountable government that creates laws for individual Iranians as citizens, not as believers.

Dr. Reza Eslami contended that no true reform could ignore the critical need to make the official religion more inclusive in order to guarantee the human rights of all citizens, regardless of their faith. Dr. Forough Jahanbakhsh, the only woman participant in the session, underscored the paradigm shift in the Muslim modernist discourse on religion and democracy and the obstacles confronting the reformers advocating democratic governance for Iran. Dr. Mohsen Kadivar spoke about various twentieth-century readings of the Islamic tradition. In some important ways, Kadivar took

Mohammad Mojtahed Shabistari's relativism in the religious readings a step further by providing an alternative paradigm for democratic governance to become deeply ingrained in the Iranian political processes.

Dr. Ali Paya's model of democracy argued for an efficient political system responsive to the needs of modern citizens searching to implement the best in society. Islamic democracy can compare favorably with the best Western democracies if it represents the social, religious, political, economic, legal, educational, and human aspirations of Islamic societies. Yet Islamic democracy has to be based on a minimalist-rationalist reading of Islam.

Two of the papers submitted in writing that could not be presented in person—both by traditionalist scholars—deserve special mention. Ayatollah Mohamed Jannati questioned whether freedom and equality—the two pillars of human rights—are compatible with human nature and with "divine religions" in which human rights are based on natural law. He believes freedom is the sum of rights recognized for human beings, who are free to accept them. However, human freedom, having private and public dimensions, should not be exercised in a way that causes harm to others or threatens other people's moral values. In Islam, freedom is not absolute; it is delimited by the law that regulates mutual rights and duties to others.

Ayatollah Amid Zanjani's paper critically assessed the crisis over democracy in the Muslim world, which either totally rejects or conditionally accepts democratic governance. His prescription for democratic politics is to adopt a middle path: no people, including Iranians, should adopt alien systems of governance without ensuring their cultural and religious legitimacy.

Peace Education in Aceh, Indonesia

The Gate of Mecca

Aceh, on the northern tip of the island of Sumatra, was once known as the Gate of Mecca for its contribution to the development of Islamic spiritual scholarship and Indonesian-Malay civilization. Today, Aceh is still among Indonesia's most religiously conservative and observant provinces. The ulama have been the principal initiators of religious, academic, and cultural life, giving them a special place within Acehnese society. While they continue to play a dominant role as the guardians of faith and values, the contemporary ulama are facing a serious challenge. They must respond to the fast-changing global information age on the one hand and uphold the Prophet's legacy on the other hand. The tension between these two expectations puts tremendous pressure on the ulama and on the headmasters of the madrassas (Islamic schools) or, as they are known in Indonesia, pesantrens (private Islamic boarding schools).

The Peace Education Program

To address this challenge, a team of Acehnese scholars, ulama, and educators, led by Asna Husin, organized the Peace Education Program, supervised by the leaders of the Consultative Council of Ulama of Aceh. The international partners for this program are Nonviolence International, the United States Institute of Peace, and the Canadian International Development Agency. As one ulama put it, "Peace education is empowering our leadership." The ulama embrace this program because they view peace as inherent to Islam. Peace and security from that which negates human dignity are essential components of Islam, as the very name "Islam" (submission to the will of God) connotes. Promoting Islam and peace as well as maintaining security are central duties of every believer, and especially of the ulama. The ulama can claim to be "heirs of the prophets" only if they are equipped with knowledge and use it to benefit their communities. The ulama of Aceh seek to reinforce Islamic peace and promote communal good and justice.

A Province in Conflict

As Husin explains, Aceh's prolonged conflicts, rooted in communal violence and severe human rights abuses, compel the ulama to seek methods of resolving violence and conflict. They recognize that most Acehnese look to them for moral and practical guidance in the context of communal bloodshed and the growing political and social isolation of the Acehnese within Indonesian society. This is not an easy task, since the ulama are caught between the struggle of Free Aceh Movement (GAM) to achieve independence for Aceh, lawless gangs, and various police and military forces, in addition to suffering the demoralizing effects of corrupt political leadership. Finally, the tsunami of December 26, 2004, destroyed two-thirds of the provincial capital of Banda Aceh, sweeping away the coastal cities of Meulaboh and Calang and killing more than 245,000 inhabitants. The tragedy greatly intensified the challenges the ulama face and increased their awareness of their responsibilities.

The New Curriculum

The Peace Education Project, initiated in early 2003, is helping Aceh's ulama to address contemporary challenges and apply Islamic principles to contemporary realities. The project has had two phases: the creation of a peace education manual and its pilot implementation in selected pesantrens. By early 2005 the project had finished developing the peace manual, Kurikulum Pendidikan Damai: Perspektif Ulama Aceh (Peace Education Curriculum: Perspective of the Ulama of Aceh). This 385-page training book, which presents peace education from an Islamic and Acehnese perspective, is being used both to train ulama and as a resource for teaching in Aceh's pesantrens. It promotes a positive, comprehensive peace, encompassing peaceful relations with God the Creator, with oneself, with one's fellow humans, and with the environment. The curriculum teaches communal peace in accordance with a positive Islamic approach, namely the absence of war and discrimination, as well as the necessity for justice. It emphasizes that peace is neither subjugation to inequitable situations nor a passive acceptance of injustice, discrimination, and war.

This curriculum, according to Husin, takes advantage of the power of play in education and actively engages learners with a "playing for learning" methodology. It incorporates various game strategies, humorous teaching stories, and classical wisdom, along with drawings and illustrations. The "thinking for reviving" methodology is a cornerstone technique. This teaching/learning method is critical to ulama empowerment, because it permits the primordial values of Islam to be revitalized in a way that meets the challenges of contemporary global realities.

The manual is a product of serious research into the Islamic intellectual wellsprings, including the Qur'an, prophetic tradition, the history of Islam, and the work of the classical ulama and contemporary scholars—with the focus on peace, conflict, and violence. The study of non-Muslim sources is integral to the manual. It also incorporates Acehnese moral values and traditional wisdom, along with indigenous mechanisms for conflict management. In adopting such peace education principles as rights and responsibilities, this peace initiative is consistent with Islamic principles.

The manual covers a wide range of critical topics, including democracy, pluralism, human rights, conflict and neutralization of violence, emotion management, leadership, natural resources, and conflict resolution. That the project team has been able to address such important and potentially sensitive topics in a way that satisfies the ulama and also stretches their thinking is a credit to Husin and her team. Husin indicates that it is still too early to assess the impact of the project. Nevertheless, the manual has generated awareness among the ulama of the need for new approaches to contemporary realities while still maintaining their religious pride and scholarship. Many educational leaders from the pesantrens/dayahs have expressed their willingness to implement the curriculum in their institutions, once their teachers are properly trained.

The ulama have demonstrated a strong sense of ownership of this manual, both because a number of them were members of the curriculum team that helped review the draft and because its content fully accords with Islamic values and principles. This does not imply that no controversial issues are raised, but such topics as gender are dealt with from a solid religious foundation. More important, this curriculum helps the ulama take responsibility and leadership at a time when Aceh stands in great need of such guidance. They thereby become worthy heirs of the prophets. This manual has generated considerable interest both in other parts of Indonesia and in other Muslim countries. It is being translated into English and Arabic and will be disseminated for use in places that face similar challenges of interpreting Islamic principles to address rapidly changing global realities.

Conclusion

Northern Nigeria, Iran, and Aceh are typically characterized as places gripped by rigid religious ideologies and practices. Northern Nigerian states have adopted very conservative versions of shari'ah. Iran is governed by conservative clerics. Some movements in Aceh agitate for more thorough going Islamic forms of government. But the three projects described in this publication add another dimension to the picture:

- Nigerian jurists, scholars, and clerics are engaged in an ongoing dialogue among themselves, with the international Muslim community, and with Nigerian Christians about the appropriate scope of—and limitations on—shari'ah in northern Nigeria.
- Iranian clerics and scholars are grappling with the proper balance between Islam and democracy, as heard in the presentations at the CSID workshop and in other forums. Iran is still evolving, and liberal scholars and clerics, while sometimes silenced, speak out.
- The ulama in Aceh have enthusiastically supported a project to introduce peace studies in Achenese religious schools, emphasizing peace, democracy, and pluralism. The ulama have been supportive because the teaching materials are all based on Islamic texts.

In these projects in Nigeria, Iran, and Indonesia—as well as in Muslim communities worldwide—Islam and the application of Islamic principles to modern realities are under active review and subject to intense debate. This dialogue is also carried on internationally, as indicated by the involvement of Muslim scholars from the United States and other countries in the discussion of shari'ah in Nigeria and of Islam and democracy in Iran. The Institute has been pleased to be able to play a supportive role in these projects, as well as with comparable projects in other countries.

Part III

Fixing Politics? Power Sharing and Political Reform

8

Afghanistan's Post-Taliban Transition: State Building after War

Thomas H. Johnson

Is Afghanistan approaching unheralded success or tragic failure?[1] The answer depends upon whom one asks. Several years after an international coalition and U.S.-backed Afghan insurgents removed the ruling Islamic fundamentalist Taliban from power, experts differ as to Afghanistan's future: will it be stability and democracy or a return to its chaotic and turbulent past? On the one hand, after decades of fighting, this volatile state has been the site of watershed elections and significant rebuilding. Much work remains, but significant progress has been achieved in human rights, political and economic reform, and infrastructure development.

On the other hand, a number of extremely disturbing countervailing trends are evident. First, the state is extremely weak. The actual influence and control of the new, democratically elected government of Hamid Karzai extends only minimally beyond the outskirts of Kabul, an increasingly sophisticated insurgency threatens stability, and large areas of Afghanistan are still ruled by warlords and drug lords. Second, there are severe economic constraints: the country has become a narco-state, with opium crops and transport representing 60 percent of the licit GDP.[2] This reliance on a criminal, informal economy strengthens the powers of those resisting the imposition of state authority, thus creating a negative feedback loop. Finally

---

The views expressed in this chapter are the author's own and do not reflect the views or opinions of the U.S. government. A version of this chapter was previously published in *Central Asian Survey* 25, nos. 1/2 (2006): 1–26.

1. Gordon Cucullu and Paul Vallely, "Stabilizing Afghanistan: A Promising Template for Iraq," *Washington Times*, January 9, 2006; and John C. Bersia, "Moves Fall Short of What's Needed in Afghanistan," *Orlando Sentinel*, December 13, 2005.

2. United Nations Office on Drugs and Crime and the Government of Afghanistan's Counter Narcotics Directorate, "Afghanistan Opium Survey, 2004," November 2004, www.unodc.org/unodc/en/crop_monitoring.html.

Thomas H. Johnson, "Afghanistan's Post-Taliban Transition: State Building after War," in *Interim Governments: Institutional Bridges to Peace and Democracy* ed. Karen Guttieri and Jessica Piombo (Washington, DC: U.S. Institute of Peace Press), 287–317.

(and perhaps most troubling), ethnic fragmentation is on the rise and old patterns of identity politics continue to exist in the "new" Afghanistan.

This chapter assesses the effectiveness of the "post-conflict" political transitional process that created the Kabul regime upon Afghanistan's stabilization and good governance. I will review and critique the Bonn Agreement and process—the major driver for Afghanistan's post-conflict transition—assess the current situation in Afghanistan, and examine prospects for democratization, development, and stability. I will also identify the opportunities and obstacles generated from Afghanistan's transition for peace, stability, and nation building after three decades of state failure.

Political Reconstruction: The Bonn Agreement and Process

Since the fall of the Taliban in late 2001, the Agreement on Provisional Arrangements in Afghanistan Pending the Re-Establishment of Permanent Government Institutions, commonly referred to as the Bonn Agreement, has served as the Afghan political road map.[3] Once the imminent defeat of the Taliban became obvious, the United States pushed the United Nations to organize a conference to map out a future plan for Afghanistan. The United Nations complied by convening a conference in Bonn, Germany, on November 26, 2001, and after nine taxing days of meetings and deal making among various Afghan factions,[4] participants signed the Bonn Agreement. Heavily influenced by the desires of the United States, the agreement established the provisional arrangements for Afghanistan to create permanent governmental institutions.[5] The goal was to lay the groundwork for Afghanistan's future political processes and institutions of governance based on the commitment of "the right of the people of Afghanistan to freely determine their own political future in accordance with the principles of Islam, democracy, pluralism and social justice."[6]

Democracy was merely "an afterthought for the White House," according to James Dobbins, a former envoy to Afghanistan and a participant at the Bonn Conference, since the George W. Bush administration believed that democracy "had little application for Afghans." Rather, Bonn was

---

3. United Nations Security Council, Agreement on the Provincial Arrangements in Afghanistan Pending the Re-Establishment of Permanent Government Institutions, December 5, 2001, S/2001/1154. The text of the Bonn Agreement was endorsed by the United Nations Security Council on December 7, 2001.

4. Key factions at Bonn were the Northern Alliance (primarily Tajik), the Rome Group (representing the former king, Mohammed Zahir Shah), the Cyprus Group (allegedly Iranian backed), and the Peshawar Group (primarily Pashtun).

5. The Bonn Agreement was endorsed by UN Security Council Resolution 1385, and an international peacekeeping force was authorized by Security Council Resolution 1386.

6. UN Security Council, Agreement on the Provincial Arrangements, 2.

meant to establish international legitimacy for the Kabul government. It was the Iranian delegation, Dobbins says, who introduced the word "democracy." As a result, the agreement was, unfortunately, vague regarding how to achieve a democratic system.[7] The Bonn Agreement created a government but not a state.

The Bonn Agreement was also *not* a peace agreement to end the decade-long Afghan civil war or the conflict between the Taliban and the U.S.-led Northern Alliance, as Bonn brought together only the winners of the U.S.-led Operation Enduring Freedom (OEF), *not* the warring parties. Ironically, many of those "winners" were Afghan factions that were historically opposed to one another; indeed, many were direct opponents during the brutal civil war that began in earnest after the Soviets withdrew from Afghanistan in January 1989. The Bonn Agreement did not try to reconcile differences between the warring parties or attempt to draw members of the defeated group—the Taliban—into the process of government reestablishment or state creation. Bonn did create the agenda and the process for establishing permanent governance institutions, representing a new level of commitment and political will by both Afghans and major powers. However, it ignored many root problems, most notably the ethnic fragmentation and distrust that has plagued the country for decades, narcotics production, and regional "warlords."

The agreement, as critics noted, codified de facto power relations and disregarded certain actors' legitimacy or lack thereof.[8] In particular, Bonn gave control of key ministries to the Tajiks and the Northern Alliance, who at the time of the conference controlled Kabul.

The Bonn Agreement recognized the problem of the multiple armed forces operating in Afghanistan, even if scant resources were applied to address it. The text called for a single national army. Section V(1) states, "Upon the official transfer of power, all *mujahedin*, Afghan armed forces and armed groups in the country shall come under the command and control of the Interim Authority, and be reorganized according to the requirements of the new Afghan security and armed forces."[9] Bonn and UN Security Council Resolution 1386 (2001) left law and order responsibilities in the hands of the Afghans themselves, but they provided a role for outside help to create a new national force. The external military force provided

---

7. Quoted in Sidney Blumenthal, "Democracy Was Only an Afterthought," *Guardian*, July 21, 2005, www.guardian.co.uk/print/0,3858,5243844-103677,00.html.

8. See Barnett Rubin, "Afghanistan and Threats to Human Security" (essay adapted from a speech titled "Human Security and Terrorism—Diversifying Threats under Globalization—from Afghanistan to the Future of the World," delivered at the International Symposium on Human Security, Tokyo, December 15, 2001), www.ssrc.org/sept11/essays/rubin.htm.

9. The text of the Bonn Agreement is available from the Afghanistan Independent Human Rights Commission, http://www.aihrc.org.af/bonn_agreement.htm.

to address Afghanistan's security challenges initially included the five thousand troops, led by Great Britain, in the International Security Assistance Force (ISAF)—a Chapter VII UN authorized force—and the eight thousand U.S. and coalition troops in OEF.[10] This number of troops was significantly smaller than those provided for Bosnia, Kosovo, or Iraq. The troop-to-population ratio of less than one-half to one thousand in Afghanistan scarcely compares to the more than eighteen per thousand in Bosnia and twenty per thousand in Kosovo.[11] Moreover, of the total U.S. financial assistance to Afghanistan, two-thirds is devoted to supporting the U.S. troop presence there, with $3 billion of the remaining $5 billion per year devoted to supporting the Afghan National Army.[12]

The process spurred by the Bonn Agreement established an explicit time frame for the implementation of interim, transitional, and, finally, fully representative and elective governments. The Bonn Agreement likewise established deadlines and procedures for constitutional development and explicit elections and laid the groundwork for the following:

- the formation of *loya jirgas* (grand councils)—emergency and constitutional
- national elections
- the role of the United Nations in Afghan reconstruction
- the reorganization of Afghan military forces
- the establishment of an ISAF
- the discharge of humanitarian and reconstruction aid

Interim and Transitional Authorities

The Bonn Agreement called for the establishment of an interim governing structure and set a timetable for a transition to a more "broad-based gender-sensitive, multi-ethnic and fully representative" government.[13] The interim authority was to rule for six months until a traditional *loya jirga* convened to elect a transitional authority or government. The delegates at the Bonn

---

10. UN Security Council resolutions 1386, 1413, and 1444 authorized the International Security Assistance Force. The lead passed from the United Kingdom to Turkey and Germany before NATO took on the leadership, beginning in 2003. See www.afnorth.nato.int/ISAF/about/about_history.htm.

11. John G. McGinn, James Dobbins, Keith Crane, Seth G. Jones, Rollie Lal, Andrew Rathmell, Rachel Swanger, and Anga Timilsina, *America's Role in Nation-Building: From Germany to Iraq* (Santa Monica, Calif.: RAND, 2004), 136.

12. Hugh Riddell, John Ewers, Rebecca Linder and Craig Cohen, *In the Balance: Measuring Progress in Afghanistan* (Washington, DC: Center for Strategic and International Studies, July 2005), 16.

13. UN Security Council, Agreement on the Provincial Arrangements, 2.

Conference chose Pashtun tribal leader Hamid Karzai to serve as head of an interim power-sharing council, which took office in Kabul on December 22, 2001. Most of the remaining administrators or ministers were selected from the representatives at the Bonn meetings.[14]

The United States was unlikely to settle for any Afghan interim leader other than Karzai. After the Taliban's assassination of Abdul Haq on October 25, 2001,[15] Karzai was the one creditable Pashtun leader whom the United States knew well and, more important, trusted. The United States lobbied vigorously to secure Karzai's position as the leader of the Afghan interim government. A Durrani-Polpolzai Pashtun, Karzai was the son of a senator who had served in the government of former king Zahir Shah. After suspected Taliban elements assassinated Karzai's father in Quetta, Pakistan, in 1999, Karzai was named the Pashtun clan chief, positioning him for a high-level leadership role in post-Taliban Afghanistan. The United States' relationship with Karzai was to become a major factor in Afghanistan's post-Taliban transition.

Karzai's interim administration (cabinet of ministers), "entrusted with the day-to-day conduct of state," was significantly composed of victors in the war.[16] The three most powerful ministries of this cabinet went to Panjshiri Tajiks of the Northern Alliance who had controlled the militia in possession of Kabul since the Taliban's defeat. Yunus Qanooni, who led the Northern Alliance's Bonn delegation, was selected interior minister. General Mohammad Fahim, commander-in-chief of the Northern Alliance, was selected defense minister, and Dr. Abdullah Abdullah was selected as foreign secretary. The thirty-member interim cabinet included eleven Pashtuns, eight Tajiks, five Shi'a Hazara, and three Uzbeks, with the remainder drawn from other minorities.

The composition of this cabinet undermined both the interim and transitional regimes. Critics contended that neither Bonn nor the chosen government was very representative of the traditional power centers in Afghanistan. In particular, relatively few Pashtuns were given administrative or cabinet positions. Pashtuns expected this imbalance to be corrected in the emergency *loya jirga* (or ELJ, which was to select the transitional administration). Karzai was expected to shift the balance of power back to Pashtuns and give the former king a prominent national role. A transitional authority would then "lead Afghanistan until such time as a fully representative government can be elected," no later than two years from the

---

14. Some of this section is drawn from Thomas H. Johnson, "The Loya Jirga, Ethnic Rivalries and Future Afghan Stability," *Strategic Insights* 1, no. 6 (August 2002): 1–10.

15. "Desperate Call from the Valley of Death: Help Us," *Observer*, October 28, 2001, http://observer.guardian.co.uk/afghanistan/story/0,1501,582247,00.html.

16. UN Security Council, Agreement on the Provincial Arrangements, 5.

convening of the ELJ.[17] The ELJ would also select a head of state for the transitional administration.

It was no surprise that Hamid Karzai was selected as transitional president at the ELJ of June 2002. The major issues of the ELJ turned out to be the role of the former king—Zahir Shah—and the role of the Panjshiris. Once the former king gave his support for the election of fellow Pashtun Karzai as the Afghan head of state—after considerable pressure was applied by the United States—ethnic issues were temporally defused. (Before Zahir Shah made his decision to support Karzai, a petition, signed by more than half the *jirga* delegates, was being circulated calling for the return of the king to power.) Subjects such as religion, the role of parliament, stability, and economic development dominated the *loya jirga* debates. This easing of ethnic suspicions and rivalry, however, proved short-lived.

Karzai increased Pashtun representation in his new transitional administration. Pashtun membership rose from the eleven members in the interim administration to sixteen members, while representation of the remaining ethnic groups stayed fairly constant relative to their total representation in the transitional administration.[18] This increase in Pashtun representation was certainly an attempt by Karzai to shore up support with his Pashtun brethren and to respond to Lakhdar Brahimi, the special representative of the UN secretary-general, and others who suggested that the ELJ should correct the imbalances resulting from Bonn and more closely reflect the Afghan demographics. Nonetheless, many of the most important and powerful ministries remained with the Panjshiri Tajik Shura-e Nezar who were in control of the security apparatus dominating Kabul.

Karzai signaled his acceptance of the Panjshiris as necessary partners in his militarily weak government. He renamed as defense minister Mohammed Fahim, leader of the Northern Alliance forces based in the Panjshir Valley and boss of a private militia of ten thousand. He also strengthened Fahim's position in the transitional government by appointing him one of his three vice presidents.[19] This move indicated the power of the Tajiks and the Northern Alliance.

For all practical purposes only one key removal from the cabinet resulted from the ELJ—the departure of interior minister Qanooni. Qanooni, a senior figure in Jamiat-e Islami, had represented Northern Alliance interests at Bonn and played a key role in initially securing support for Karzai's candidacy

17. Ibid., 3.

18. Note that the total number of cabinet positions increased in the transitional government as compared to the interim administration.

19. Fahim controls a private militia of ten thousand, most of whom are loyal, well equipped, and well paid. In his Panjshir Valley base of operations, he controls a vast heavy-weapons arsenal, which includes BMPs (combat infantry vehicles), BTRs (another Soviet infantry ground vehicle), and Scud missiles.

among the powerful Tajik-led political and military coalition. But the relationship between Karzai and Qanooni had become contentious, which led to his controversial dismissal. Panjshiri soldiers and policemen in the ministry initially resisted the change, staging roadblocks and work stoppages. Karzai then appointed Qanooni as adviser for internal security, a newly created post, as well as minister of education.[20] At the time of the ELJ, Fahim, Qanooni, and Ahmad Zia Masoud[21] were all vying for the leadership of the Panjshiris (Shura-e Nezar), and relations among them reportedly became strained. Karzai was caught in the middle of this politicking among the Panjshiri clique.

The interim government did not hold a monopoly on the legitimate use of force in Afghanistan, as both ISAF and separate U.S. troops within the coalition forces continued operations throughout the country. Nor did the interim government control the use of force in general. One year after the agreement, Human Rights Watch noted that the problem of warlordism was not merely pervasive, it was seemingly permitted: "The U.S. and its coalition partners, as well as Iran and Pakistan, failed to back immediate efforts to centralize military authority. While the official policy of these countries was to work with President Karzai to help him strengthen his administration, the U.S., Iran, and Pakistan actively supported local warlords in various regions of the country."[22] The external powers that had pledged to support Karzai thus undermined his authority at the same time, given that he had stated an intention to reduce the influence of the warlords. Instead, Karzai continued to fight with them "for authority, money, and legitimacy."[23]

Loya Jirgas and Post-conflict Stability: Ethnic Dimensions

Questions of ethnicity are critical in assessing the implications of the *loya jirgas* to future Afghan political and social stability. Past attempts at modern state formation in Afghanistan that directly challenged local tribal and religious structures resulted in ethnic backlash and state failure. Critics argue that the former mujahideen parties manipulated the *loya jirga* and transi-

---

20. "Karzai Swears in the New Afghan Cabinet," *Washington Post Foreign Service,* June 24, 2002.

21. Ahmad Zia Masoud is the younger brother of the slain Northern Alliance leader and Afghan national hero, Ahmad Shah Masoud.

22. According to the report, this support includes cash, weapons, uniforms, and communications equipment from the United States as late as October 2002. Human Rights Watch, "Afghanistan's Bonn Agreement One Year Later: A Catalog of Missed Opportunities," December 5, 2002, www.hrw.org/backgrounder/asia/afghanistan/bonn1yr-bck.htm. See also Milan Vaishnav, "Afghanistan," in *Winning the Peace,* ed. Robert C. Orr et al. (Washington, DC: Center for Strategic and International Studies, 2004), 252.

23. Vaishnav, "Afghanistan," 252.

tional administration. As one International Crisis Group report stated, Karzai's failure to ensure transparent and accountable procedures meant a missed "opportunity to establish new constituencies and develop support for the peace-building process."[24]

Afghanistan's diverse ethnic composition makes democracy and even state building difficult. The present boundaries were created to serve as a buffer between British and Russian empires as Afghanistan confronted modernity through its forced integration into a Eurocentric state.[25] As is often the case in Asia, Africa, and the Middle East, Afghanistan's boundaries were not drawn along ethnic, linguistic, or religious lines. The externally imposed "state" comprises a complicated mix of people, most of whom live in small, kin-based communities outside of the limited urban areas. Some of these groups are ethnically and linguistically distinct, but they are not necessarily different in terms of culture.[26] However, Afghanistan's governments have been unable to create a sense of genuine national unity in times other than during crisis.[27]

Not only do Afghans lack a sense of national identity, they also do not agree on what form of state Afghanistan should have. Afghanistan's Pashtuns would like a strong Pashtun-run central state, Tajiks focus on power sharing in the central state, and Uzbeks and Hazaras desire recognition of their identities and mechanisms of local government.[28] Historically, the more populous Pashtun tribes of the south ruled Afghanistan, and therefore the early Pashtun dominance of Karzai's interim government created an atmosphere of tension between them and the remaining ethnic groups in Afghanistan. Unlike other ethnic groups, the Pashtuns emphasize tribal structures and codes at the expense of the state. Other ethnic groups did not truly establish themselves as a political and military force until the Soviet Union's invasion of Afghanistan in 1979. Before the Soviet incursion, fighting for control of the state had occurred primarily among Pashtun groups (for example, Durranis versus Ghilzais). As other ethnic groups rose in importance and sought to rule, civil war destroyed the Afghan state structure.

---

24. International Crisis Group, *Afghanistan's Flawed Constitutional Process,* ICG Asia Report no. 56 (June 12, 2003), 2.

25. Barnett R. Rubin, *The Fragmentation of Afghanistan* (New Haven and London: Yale University Press, 2002), 5.

26. The Pashtuns, representing 42 percent of the population, are the largest ethnic group in Afghanistan. Ethnic Tajiks represent 27 percent of the population. The Hazaras represent another 9 percent. Groups such as the Aimaks, Turkmen, Baluch, Uzbek, among others, comprise the remaining 22 percent. The country is almost totally Muslim, with the Sunnis representing 80 percent of the population and the Shi'as representing 19 percent. See "Afghanistan," *The World Factbook 2004* (Washington, D.C.: Central Intelligence Agency, 2004), www.cia.gov/cia/publications/factbook/geos/af.html.

27. John C. Griffiths, *Afghanistan: Key to a Continent* (Boulder, Colo.: Westview Press, 1981), 78.

28. Rubin, *The Fragmentation of Afghanistan,* 11.

Afghan rulers have commonly attempted to manipulate ethnic groups in their efforts to control the state. For example, as Barnett R. Rubin writes, "to weaken the Barakzais, Ahmad Shah Masoud, the 'father' of modern Afghanistan, appointed a separate khan for the Achakzais, making the clan into a separate tribe, a status that they retain today."[29] Successful Afghan ruling authorities have been artful in underscoring and exploiting the differences among groups, often encouraging conflict among them in order to maintain control. Further complicating the dynamics of Afghan society are the relationships among the tribes themselves and among the varying ethnic groups that compose the nation-state. Simply put, the relationships among tribes are generally marked by "competition and outright animosity."[30] Unfortunately, many past Afghan regimes have failed to bridge the gap among these competing groups and have played different groups against each other in order to consolidate their power.[31]

Karzai's choice of cabinet members for the transitional government did not favor a balanced and professional cabinet. Karzai had not been able to remove faction leaders and install members with professional qualifications, as the Pashtun community had anticipated, because the Northern Alliance was reluctant to cede the considerable power it received from the Bonn Conference. In his cabinet, Karzai recognized the importance of balance between the Pashtuns and the Tajiks. He also recognized the extremely difficult task of assembling an administration that would satisfy all major ethnic groups while meeting the country's desperate need for professional governance after years of ruinous conflict.

Although the United States and other international actors viewed the outcome of the ELJ as legitimate, fellow Pashtuns were skeptical about Karzai's transitional government. The continued power of the Tajiks alienated Karzai's Pashtun power base. Many Pashtuns were dismayed and angered that none of the king's aides had been given senior posts.[32] In July 2002, a *Washington Post* article titled "Pashtuns Losing Faith in Karzai" posited that the Pashtuns were "becoming rapidly disillusioned by a series of developments that have reinforced the power of rival ethnic Tajiks and militia leaders, left the former king politically sidelined and a Pashtun vice president assassinated, and subjected Pashtun villages to lethal U.S. air attacks."[33] Padsha Khan Zadran, a powerful Pashtun warlord who reportedly controlled the three southeastern provinces of Khost, Paktia, and Pak-

29. Ibid., 46.

30. Kenneth Christie, *Ethnic Conflict, Tribal Politics: A Global Perspective* (Richmond, Surrey, UK: Curzon Press, 1998), 5.

31. Rubin, *The Fragmentation of Afghanistan*, 47.

32. Pamela Constable, "Cabinet Is Sworn in; Intense Negotiations Yield Greater Ethnic, Political Balance," *Washington Post Foreign Service*, June 25, 2002.

33. "Pashtuns Losing Faith in Karzai," *Washington Post*, July 13, 2002.

tika, in the spring and summer of 2002 summed up the sentiments of many Pashtuns when he asked, "Why are they humiliating Pashtuns? We're the majority. They placed Hamid Karzai at the top as a representative of Pashtuns. But in reality he's no longer a Pashtun. He's sold himself out. He's a traitor. Pashtuns cannot sit around waiting. They will react and will claim their rights."[34]

The Constitution

While the constitution and the actual process employed for its ratification and adoption must be seen as positive steps for Afghanistan's future, the actual document and process surrounding it were not without flaws and have the potential to inhibit future stability. The Bonn Agreement called for a constitutional *loya jirga* (CLJ) to adopt a new Afghan constitution within eighteen months of the establishment of the transitional authority. In January 2003, Lakhdar Brahimi acknowledged at an open meeting of the UN Security Council that the "drafting and ratification of the new constitution . . . will also be a fundamental state building exercise." Brahimi stressed the need to "broaden the political base supporting the peace process" because "too many Afghans feel excluded from the government and political transformation which Afghanistan is undergoing."[35]

Brahimi's warnings were not heeded. The constitution was delayed and thus a rushed affair that provided few opportunities for participation by Afghan citizens. None of the bodies involved in the process of drafting, ratifying, and debating the constitution consulted or incorporated nonelites in the process. Three constitution-making organs—the Drafting Commission (DC), the Constitutional Review Commission (CRC), and the CLJ—played a role in the process.[36] Of the eighteen months originally envisaged in the Bonn Agreement for a constitution-making exercise, only thirteen remained when the DC began work—a limited amount of time in which to educate the Afghan people, who are largely illiterate, and to query them on subjects as complicated and foreign as many of those in the constitution.

The CRC, a thirty-five-member commission appointed by the president, also suffered delays. The jihadist group Shura-e Nezar dominated the commission, and therefore it was "never likely to yield individuals who could

34. "Warlord Pushes for Control of a Corner of Afghanistan," *New York Times,* August 6, 2002.

35. Open Meeting of the United Nations Security Council, Briefing of Special Representative of the Secretary-General Lakhdar Brahimi, January 31, 2003, www.un.org/News/dh/latest/afghan/brahimi31jan03.htm.

36. The United Nations (especially the UN Assistance Mission, UNAMA, and the UN Development Programme, UNDP) heavily supported these organs. See "The Constitution-Making Process in Afghanistan," report prepared by the Secretariat of the Constitutional Commission of Afghanistan, March 10, 2003.

be viewed as legitimate national figures capable of transcending narrow, sectarian interests. . . . several experienced politicians from *jihadi* groups have been included but respected moderate leaders and members of democratic groups are conspicuously absent."[37] Like the drafting commission, this review body constituted "primarily factional bargaining at the cabinet level without significant consideration of the public interest."[38]

The 502-person CLJ, which was selected in UN-run caucuses, met to deliberate on the draft constitution from December 13, 2003, to January 4, 2004. This body, which could include no militia commanders or government officials, was meant to confer legitimacy on the constitution through review and adoption.[39]

The final version of the constitution established a strong presidential system in which the president served as both head of state and head of government.[40] The president would be elected by a majority of the popular vote and would be eligible to serve two five-year terms.[41] A proposal sponsored by the Northern Alliance to establish a prime minister as a check on the presidency was removed, probably owing to Karzai supporters' concerns that a prime minister might emerge as a rival to the president.

The constitution established a bicameral legislature and a supreme court with high courts and appeals courts. It established no separate religious courts, but powerful Islamists presently are in or have influence in the emerging Afghan judiciary. The legislative body of the Wolesi Jirga (lower house or House of People) would promulgate laws, ratify treaties, and approve budgets. The Meshrano Jirga (upper house or House of Elders), with the authority to approve proposed laws and the budget, would consist of a mixture of appointed and elected members.[42] The constitution explicitly stipulated that 50 percent of the appointees to the Meshrano Jirga must be women, meaning that one-sixth of upper house members were to be women. In the elected lower house, at least sixty-eight of those elected (two per each of the thirty-four provinces) "should" be women.[43] That gave

---

37. International Crisis Group, *Afghanistan's Flawed Constitutional Process*, 16–17.

38. Ibid., 16.

39. Ibid. UNAMA coordinated international technical and financial support; UNDP provided financial management and administrative and operational support.

40. For the entire text of the constitution, see www.afghangovernment.com/2004constitution.htm.

41. Two vice presidents would run on the same election ticket as the president, and one would succeed him in the event of the president's death. Vice presidents were to serve a single five-year term. If no presidential candidate received at least 50 percent of the vote on election day, a run-off was to be held within two weeks.

42. One-third of the seats were to be appointed by the president, one-third were to be selected by Provincial Councils, and one-third were to be selected by District Councils.

43. This goal of female representation was to be met through election rules that would give the top two women vote getters in each province a seat in the Wolesi Jirga.

women about 25 percent of the seats in the Wolesi Jirga. Aside from these quotas, the precise nature of the electoral system was left to legislation rather than enshrined in the constitution. The constitution also gave the legislature the ability to impeach the president.

Map drawing in Afghanistan has always been contentious and related to issues of power alignment between Kabul and the hinterlands. In order to create multiethnic local government representation and to respond to long-held perceptions by minority ethnic groups that the primarily Pashtun-dominated provinces were biased against the non-Pashtun regions, the constitution called for two new non-Pashtun–dominated provinces. Therefore, on March 28, 2004, a Hazara-dominated province, Diakondi, within the northern section of Oruzgan Province, came into being, and on April 13, 2004, the government created a Tajik-dominated province, Panjshir, within Parvan Province. The thirty-four provinces, total, are governed by a provincial council whose members are to be popularly elected to four-year terms.

The constitution was vague about political parties. It allowed for them to be established so long as their charters "do not contradict the principles of Islam" and they do not have affiliations with foreign countries. The political parties law that was later enacted by the Karzai government provided the procedures for the legal registration of political parties in accordance with the constitution. This law prohibits political parties whose charters are "opposed to the principles of the holy religion Islam," which is problematic since Islamic principles are open to interpretation. Furthermore, this dynamic affords influential Islamist groups an instrument to block parties they deem politically unacceptable.[44]

Security Sector Reform

The security environment in Afghanistan suffered from reinforcing flaws: the accommodation of warlords, the availability of narcotics to fund nonstate forces, the slow development of the Afghan army, and the uneven footprint of external forces. In May 2005, the Afghan National Army, reported to have a strength of thirty thousand, was far from its authorized level of seventy thousand. A report by the Feinstein International Center identified three zones of perception among Afghans regarding external security forces: a "Kabul bubble," in which the ISAF are concentrated, "benign and well accepted"; a light footprint of ISAF Provincial Reconstruction Teams (PRTs) in the northeast, the north, and the west; and "menacing and aggressive" coalition forces in the remaining areas fighting residual Taliban and al-Qaeda elements, as well as coalition PRTs engaged in nation

---

44. International Crisis Group, *Political Parties in Afghanistan,* Asia Briefing no. 39 (June 2, 2005).

building.[45] The general lack of security made public consultation and organization for elections very difficult for the interim regime.

Efforts to reorganize the Afghan National Army were beset with problems, including recruitment shortages and infiltration issues. The domestic and international actors alike were many and inchoate. Disarmament, demobilization, and reintegration (DDR) of uniformed armies is challenging, and militias are even less easily brought into the fold. The lead nations assigned at Bonn to address these issues had overlapping duties. Japan took the lead in DDR, but the United States led the process of training the Afghan National Army. The American Coalition Joint Task Force Phoenix—composed mainly of National Guard units as well as other U.S. and coalition elements—held overall responsibility for the Afghan National Army to the level of creating the Ministry of Defense. U.S. Embedded Training Teams provided coaching and mentoring for Afghan forces.[46] British Gurkhas taught the course for noncommissioned officers, while the French taught the Officer Basic Course and the Command and General Staff Course for senior officers. Meanwhile, Germany led in training the police forces and the United Kingdom in the counternarcotics effort. If coherent education and training are vital to army cohesion, the Afghan program was not promising.

Afghan Elections

According to the Bonn Agreement, free and fair elections had to be held no later than two years from the date of the convening of the ELJ.[47] Concurrent elections for the presidency, the National Assembly, and Provincial Councils were scheduled for the spring of 2004, a timetable that was repeatedly changed. A series of events—including electoral infrastructure delays, accelerating instability, and the apparent reemergence of the Taliban—led to the postponement and separation of those three types of elections. The presidential elections were moved from June to September, then to October 2004. National Assembly and Provincial Council elections were eventually scheduled for September 2005.

On May 25, 2004, Karzai passed an electoral law by presidential decree.[48] This law made the following provisions:

---

45. Antonio Donini, Larry Minear, Ian Smillie, Ted van Baarda, and Anthony C. Welch, *Mapping the Security Environment* (Medford, Mass.: Tufts University/Feinstein International Center, 2005).

46. Coalition Joint Task Force Phoenix official Web site, www.globalsecurity.org/military/agency/dod/cjtf-phoenix.htm; and Lt. Col. Susan Meisner, "Command and General Staff College Graduates 4th Class" (Kabul: OMC-A Press Release, January 26, 2005).

47. UN Security Council, Agreement on the Provincial Arrangements, 3.

48. "New Afghan Election Law Endorsed," *Kabul Radio,* FBIS No. IAP20040527000095, May 27, 2004; and "Afghan Leader Karzai Endorses Election Law," *Kabul Hindokosh News Agency,* FBIS No. IAP20040527000099, May 27, 2004.

- The populace would vote for individual candidates rather than political parties in the parliamentary elections.
- Government officials, *except the president,* who sought office as candidates were required to resign from their government positions at least seventy-five days before the elections.
- To be eligible to run, presidential candidates were required to produce at least ten thousand copies of eligible voter registration cards as evidence of voters' support.

The months leading up to June 2004, the date originally set for the elections, saw a significant rise in violence throughout the country, especially toward election workers.[49] While some of this violence could be attributed to the reemergence of the Taliban, there was also a significant acceleration of an insurgency (especially in the east and west of the country) against the Karzai regime and U.S. forces. Voter registration soared in anticipation of free and fair elections, with most eligible voters registering even under the cloud of Taliban threats to kill registrants.[50] Although 9 million of the eligible 9.8 million eligible voters registered, the registration process was marked by blatant irregularities, including 140 percent voter-registration rates in thirteen provinces.[51] The Organization for Security and Cooperation in Europe (OSCE) refused to send election monitors to Afghanistan because it believed that "conditions in Afghanistan [were] significantly below the minimum regarded by OSCE . . . as necessary for credible election observation."[52]

In December 2003, with the encouragement of the United States, Karzai tried to undercut support for the Taliban by inviting "moderate supporters" of the Taliban (who also happened to be mostly ethnic Pashtuns) to join the political process in exchange for their agreement to cease fighting the government.[53] Tajik leaders viewed this move with suspicion, thinking Karzai sought to promote his fellow Pashtuns within his government. Karzai received de facto endorsement by the U.S. and European governments and took advantage of U.S. assets during his campaigning. It was alleged that much of Karzai's campaign financing came directly from foreign countries, in violation of Afghan election laws.[54] Concerning foreign support for Karzai, as M. Nazif Shahrani notes, it was suggested that

49. A total of 4,807 polling centers were eventually staffed by approximately 120,000 workers.

50. Craig Charney, "Afghan Success Story," *Washington Post,* July 30, 2004.

51. Scott Baldauf, "Afghans Vote, Ready or Not," *Christian Science Monitor,* October 8, 2004.

52. Ibid.

53. Nicholas Kralev, "U.S. Backs Intention to Work With Ex-Taliban," *Washington Times,* June 15, 2004.

54. See, for example, "Afghanistan: President Karzai Accused of Illegal Electioneering," FBIS No. IAP20040810000129, August 10, 2004.

> Karzai was . . . the only candidate who enjoyed access to US military aircraft for campaign travel as well as round-the-clock protection by a private US security firm. The Afghanistan Research and Evaluation Unit (AREU) report also found ambient suspicion that the US had allocated $30 million for the registration of Afghan refugees in Pakistan, who are primarily Pashtun, to enhance Karzai's chances for reelection. The appearance of favoritism in the ethnically charged climate of Afghan politics makes it seem that the goal of the campaign is to elect a president at any cost, especially in the eyes of the often ignored and abused non-Pashtun "minorities."[55]

Karzai needed to expand his influence beyond the city limits of Kabul. Therefore, as part of the election process, he took long-expected (and long-threatened) action to marginalize the warlords. On September 2004 Karzai removed Ismail Khan as governor of Herat Province.[56] A particularly bold move on July 26, 2004, was the dismissal of Mohammad Fahim, the powerful Tajik minister of defense and leader of the Northern Alliance, as one of his vice presidents. It is very interesting to note that July 26 was the last official date for the filing of presidential election candidacy forms, according to the rules adopted by Afghanistan's Joint Electoral Management Body.[57] It is reasonable to believe that Karzai waited to the very last moment before dumping Fahim because he probably expected that such a strategy would prohibit the Tajiks from regrouping and promoting a new candidate.

Karzai's strategy backfired; it provided the impetus for the emergence of overt ethnic politics. The Tajik and Northern Alliance leader Qanooni parted from Karzai to announce his own candidacy, taking the opportunity to suggest that Karzai's dismissal of Fahim had exacerbated "inter-ethnic tension."[58] On July 27, Karzai placed Kabul on a high security alert, probably because of rumors in the capital that armed forces loyal to Fahim might stage an uprising. In addition to being Afghanistan's defense minister, Fahim commanded the Afghan army's 8th Division, with an estimated five thousand loyal troops stationed in the Shomali Plain—the fertile land just north of Kabul—and in the capital itself. Fortunately, Fahim and his militia did not take any extralegal actions. Qanooni's candidacy soon garnered the support of Fahim, Foreign Minister Abdullah, and all the core leaders of the Tajik-dominated Northern Alliance. It seemed that the election was going to revert to a question of renewed interethnic strife.

---

55. M. Nazif Shahrani, "Afghanistan's Presidential Elections: Spreading Democracy or a Sham?" *Middle East Report Online,* October 8, 2004, www.merip.org/mero/mero100804.html.

56. "Administrative Reforms or Settling Accounts with Herat?" *Kabul Arman-e Melli* in Dari, FBIS No. IAP20040912000048, September 12, 2004.

57. "Afghan Election Body Urges Presidential Candidates to Register by 26 July," *Kabul Radio Afghanistan* in Pashto 1330 GMT, FBIS No. IAP20040725000113, July 25, 2004.

58. Camelia Entekhabi-Fard, "Afghan President Karzai May Rue Dumping Fahim—Presidential Rival," *Eurasia Insight,* July 28, 2004, www.eurasianet.org/departments/insight/articles/eav072804a.shtml.

The Presidential Elections

On October 9, 2004, the presidential election took place, with eighteen eligible candidates on the Afghan presidential ballot.[59] As expected, Hamid Karzai was elected with 55.4 percent of the vote, garnering three times more votes than any other candidate. Karzai's main opponents—Qanooni, Haji Mohammed Mohaqiq, and Abdul Rashid Dostum—received, respectively, 16.3 percent, 11.7 percent, and 10 percent. Twelve candidates received less than 1 percent of the vote. The lone female candidate, Masooda Jalal, finished sixth, with ninety-one thousand votes, or 1.1 percent. While there were complaints about voter intimidation (especially in the Pashtun south and east) and voting procedures, along with allegations of multiple voting and irregularities in counting in some areas, an impartial panel of election experts concluded that the outcome had not been affected.[60]

The presidential election was a watershed event, but what do the results represent? A statistical analysis suggests that the election clearly reified traditional ethnic splits in the country and that traditional ethnicity remains at the forefront of Afghan politics.[61] Afghans tended to vote along ethnic lines. Karzai was elected with a majority of the vote, but not with a majority of the vote from any ethnic group outside his own dominant Pashtun base. His claim to represent a truly national candidate with support across ethnic lines is not borne. Qanooni received most of the Tajik vote, while veteran strongman Dostum garnered the votes of his fellow Uzbeks in the north; Mohaqiq received the vote of the Shi'a Hazaras from his stronghold of central Afghanistan.

The challenge now is to unite the Afghan people: to bolster national identity while respecting ethnic traditions and norms. Unification will be extremely difficult because each ethnic group is attempting, often at the expense of other groups, to gain a foothold in government. The fragmentation will continue until either one dominant ethnic group controls all of the governmental power or ethnic politics makes way for increased internal conflict.[62]

The Legislative Elections

The Afghan legislative elections (including district elections), initially planned to be held simultaneously with the presidential elections, were

---

59. This section draws upon previous work. See Thomas H. Johnson, "Democratic Nation Building in the Arc of Crisis: The Case of the Presidential Election in Afghanistan," in *Critical Issues Facing the Middle East Security: Security, Politics, and Economics*, ed. James Russell (New York: Palgrave Macmillan, 2006), 125–146.

60. See International Crisis Group, "Political Parties" and "Final Report of the Impartial Panel Concerning Afghanistan Presidential Elections 2004," November 1, 2004, www.elections-afghanistan.org.af/.

61. Johnson, "Democratic Nation Building."

62. Ibid.

eventually rescheduled for September 18, 2005. These elections were expected to be a mandate concerning the political direction taken since the ouster of the Taliban and the subsequent Bonn Agreement. The Karzai administration had pushed vigorously for political reforms and governmental institutionalization, and the continuation of Karzai's agenda depended significantly on the government's ability to engender support of a National Assembly. These elections were also expected to establish political blocs that would eventually become actual political parties, a seemingly critical component for a lasting Afghan democracy. Finally, the voting patterns of these elections would "signal the extent to which influence [would] be based on common political ground—rather than strictly ethnic, religious, or provincial divisions."[63]

Approximately six thousand candidates sought approximately 390 parliamentary (Wolesi Jirga) positions and 217 Provincial Council positions through direct elections in multimember constituencies, using the single nontransferable vote (SNTV) system.[64] Under SNTV, candidates run as individuals rather than as a party bloc; multiple candidates run in each constituency; each voter casts one vote, and the candidates with the most votes win the seats. The Joint Electoral Management Board determined the number of seats for each province based on population figures provided by the Central Statistics Office and a formula established in the 2005 electoral law. At a minimum, each province was guaranteed two seats. Larger provinces such as Kabul, Herat, and Nangarhar received thirty-three, seventeen, and fourteen seats, respectively, in the Wolesi Jirga, while smaller provinces such as Nimrus, Nurestan, and Panjshir received the minimum of two seats. A similar, but more complicated, apportionment of seats was decided for Provincial Councils.[65]

Unlike the presidential election, which had suggested that Afghanistan remains deeply divided along multiple fault lines—ethnic, linguistic, and ideological—the legislative elections were thought to provide the opportunity for politics to move in a less factionalized direction. Unfortunately, the structure and procedures for these elections were typical of the more general personalistic political processes that have been employed since

63. For the official Afghan government views concerning the importance of these elections, see Afghanistan Votes, www.rferl.org/en/specials/elections/FAQs.asp.

64. Forty-five candidates were refused because of their connections with armed groups or for not giving up their government jobs, although an alleged 207 other militia leaders were legislative candidates. During March 2005 it was announced that the district elections were postponed until 2006 (exact date to be determined) because of complications in the determination of individual district boundaries. This postponement means that these District Councils cannot select their upper house representatives.

65. For complete election rules, see the Joint Electoral Board Management Body (JEMB), "Wolesi Jirga and Provincial Council Elections 2005: Background Briefing," September 15, 2005, www.jemb.org.

Bonn. In particular, the notion of political party development to articulate voter interests was thwarted in the early electoral sequence.

The electoral law severely weakened the new political parties because it prohibited them from running on the ballot, and candidates were not allowed to run under a party banner. Candidates could be independent—nominated or endorsed by a political party—but the actual political party symbols could not appear on the ballot. Meanwhile, "old *jihadi* networks continued to have access to power and resources."[66] So many candidates contended because the election rules played against political parties in favor of individuals. Moreover, this rule portended to favor candidates appealing to regional or ethnic biases rather than political ideologies and programs such as would have accompanied an election that encouraged political party participation, because forcing individuals to operate within the ideological frameworks of larger political organizations often moderates their appeals.

The fact that this electoral system disempowered political parties was entirely intentional. As suggested by the Afghan government itself, Karzai's electoral law chose the SNTV voting system precisely to limit the potential influence of political parties.[67] The rationale was that many Afghans are leery of political parties because parties such as the Communist People's Democratic Party (both the Khalq and Parcham factions), the Taliban, and various mujahideen parties wreaked havoc on the country over the past three decades.[68] Despite Karzai's efforts, at the time of the elections, seventy-two political parties were registered in Afghanistan.[69] Nevertheless, all political parties confront a hostile climate.[70]

Karzai's decision to adopt the SNTV system and to reject proposals for a proportional representation, party-list electoral system was made against the advice of UN and international advisers—with the exception of his most powerful backer, U.S. ambassador Zalmay Khalilzad.[71] The critics of SNTV have been harsh, arguing that in a context like that of Afghanistan, SNTV creates a legislative body that does not reflect the political preferences of the citizens. First, as Rubin argues, SNTV "virtually guarantees the formation of an unrepresentative parliament of local leaders with no incentive to cooperate with one another or the government. It places a

66. International Crisis Group, *Afghanistan Elections: Endgame or New Beginning?* Asia Report no. 101 (July 21, 2005): i.

67. Afghanistan Votes, www.rferl.org/en/specials/elections/FAQs.asp.

68. In fact many Afghans associate the words *hizb* (party), *harakat* (movement), and *tehrik* (way) with the violent histories of former leftist and Islamist parties. See International Crisis Group, *Political Parties in Afghanistan*, Asia Briefing no. 39 (June 2, 2005): 11.

69. See JEMB, www.jemb.org/.

70. International Crisis Group, *Afghanistan Elections*, 3.

71. Ibid., 10.

premium on vote buying and intimidation, since swinging even a small number of votes can easily affect the outcome."[72] Other experts argued that SNTV was particularly ill suited for Afghanistan precisely *because* the country lacks well-organized political parties. When SNTV operates in a context without strong political parties, voters will pool their votes behind a few strong candidates, leaving open room for many candidates without strong popular bases to win seats. When parties are strong, however, they can educate their supporters in each region as to how to apportion votes across candidates. A party could easily gain a very different number of parliamentary seats than its percentage of the vote might suggest it deserved.[73] In the Afghan context, this meant that those with the ability to discipline their supporters were large ethnic and regional parties, leading to the disproportionate representation of some of those parties or, conversely, resulting in a fragmented legislature.

Fifty-seven percent of the Afghan population registered and were eligible to vote in the legislative elections. Three provinces had more than 100 percent voter registration.[74] These data suggest voter fraud in the primarily Tajik home province of Karzai's major opponent, Qanooni, and in the primarily Pashtun province of Paktika. The latter also had significant over-registration in the presidential election and overwhelmingly voted for Karzai (88.4 percent). The over-registration did not lead to additional votes in Panjshir. Only 35 percent of Panjshiri "registered" voters actually voted in the election. This would seem to suggest that the registration process in this Tajik province was of questionable integrity, but the ultimate implications proved negligible.

The national election voter turnout—49.8 percent—was substantially lower than in the October 2004 presidential election. Turnout was highest in the north—generally greater than 60 percent—and lowest (below 30 percent) in some of the Pashtun-speaking southeastern areas where the Taliban insurgency is strongest. Oruzgan (23 percent) and Kandahar (25 percent) have been Taliban strongholds—the former being the home of Mullah Omar and the latter being the spiritual capital of the Taliban (as well as Karzai's home base)—where remnants of the Taliban pursued campaigns of intimidation against prospective voters. Surprisingly low turnout (34.5 percent) in Kabul is especially troubling considering that this urban

---

72. Barnett Rubin, "Afghanistan: The Wrong Voting System," *International Herald Tribune*, March 16, 2005.

73. Andrew Reynolds and Andrew Wilder, *Free, Fair or Flawed: Challenges for Legitimate Elections in Afghanistan* (Afghanistan Research and Evaluation Unit (AREU), September 2004), 12.

74. For the full electoral results, see JEMB, www.results.jemb.org/home.asp. Unless otherwise noted, all analyses of the electoral results are the author's own. For a more extended analysis of the results, see Thomas H. Johnson, "The Prospects for Post-Conflict Afghanistan: A Call of the Sirens to the Country's Troubled Past," *Strategic Insights* 5, no. 2 (February 2006), www.ccc.nps.navy.mil/si/2006/Feb/johnsonFeb06.asp.

populace is the best educated and most politically sophisticated in the country.

Electoral rules created confusion in many voters as to whom they were voting for. Moreover, the sheer number of candidates running under ballot banner icons, such as cups, beds, lions, rings, leaves, footballs, and cars, was extremely confusing. Candidates were not able to choose the icons themselves; instead, the electoral committee selected them. Such icons were reportedly used because a sizable percentage of the Afghan population is illiterate. Illiteracy and lack of voting experience also had other influences on the actual act of voting. The *Economist,* for example, found that some provinces required ballots up to forty pages long. The journal suggested that some voters were confused simply by the notion of turning the pages of those ballots.[75]

The final election results were delayed by accusations of fraud and were not declared until November 12, 2005. The results upheld the notion that the procedures used in this election would favor localized candidates and strong regional figures and groups. In particular, they represented a victory for Islamic conservatives and the mujahideen: nearly half the seats of Wolesi Jirga were captured by Islamist or conservative religious figures.[76] Most of the elected former mujahideen leaders, shut out of the Karzai administration, found their way into the legislature because they had electoral bases in ethnic groups and regions where they exercise considerable influence and control. Thus, the legislative elections gave the mujahideen an opportunity to reassert their influence.

The results represented a defeat for the Karzai government. While these results did not deliver a clear anti-Karzai parliamentary majority, neither did they represent a clear mandate for the Karzai administration.[77] The election results suggested that the 249-member Wolesi Jirga will consist of five broad, possibly overlapping groups: (1) former mujahideen, including approximately forty members of Hizb-e Islami;[78] (2) independents, technocrats, and those tribal or regional leaders who are not presently affiliated with any of the established Afghan political parties; (3) former communists and other leftists, many of whom have joined mujahideen parties or remnants of the Taliban; (4) former members of the Taliban establishment; and (5) former ministers and deputy ministers of the government, many of

75. "A Glass Half Full," *Economist,* September 15, 2005.

76. "A Place for Warlords to Meet," *Economist,* January 5, 2006.

77. A Congressional Research Service Report to Congress posited that "the new parliament . . . appears to have a slim majority of Karzai loyalists." Kenneth Katzman, *Afghanistan: Presidential and Parliamentary Elections,* CRS Report for Congress (Washington, D.C.: Congressional Research Service, November 16, 2005), 5.

78. The party was registered in August 2005 with the Justice Ministry by its new leader, Khaled Faruqi, a former commander of Hekmatyar. Faruqi won a seat in the *Wolesi Jirga.*

whom Karzai had dismissed as he attempted to consolidate power over the previous three years.[79]

Because of SNTV and the prohibition of meaningful political party participation, many candidates won almost by chance, and the legislature became populated with virtually unknown candidates. For example, in Wardak Province, where sixty-nine candidates competed for five Wolesi Jirga seats, the leading vote getter (Abdul Reza Rezaee) received 10 percent of the vote. The other winners, who included the former Taliban planning minister (Haji Mosa Hotak) and a Hizb-e Islami candidate (Roshanka Wardak), received from 6.6 percent to 3.9 percent of the votes, respectively. Numerous other provinces experienced the same kind of results, where candidates were elected by chance.

Kabul is the most populous province in the country, with more than 3 million people; 1,193,472 registered voters cast only 399,810 valid votes (35 percent). Mohaqeq received the highest percentage of votes of any candidate in Kabul—13.2 percent.[80] Qanooni and Dostum were the next two largest voting percentages, with 7.8 and 7.7 percent, respectively. The other thirty winning candidates received from 2.5 to 0.4 percent of the vote. That thirty of the thirty-three representatives elected to the parliament from the country's capital individually received less than 3 percent of their constituents' votes is amazing. Fifty-six percent of the Kabuli electorate voted for losing candidates; this would not be surprising if only two or three candidates where running, but for Kabul representation in the legislature there were 387 candidates. The aggregate nationwide votes collected by all Wolesi Jirga winners represented only 35.8 percent of the total vote.[81] Put another way, 64.2 percent of the Afghan voters supported losing candidates.

It is evident that the SNTV and the lack of political party participation helped to skew the election results and produce a Wolesi Jirga that will be highly fragmented and potentially gridlocked. If the legislative body proves ineffectual, then the odds of groups pursuing their own parochial interests by other means are greatly increased. This is a dangerous possibility considering that Afghanistan, an ethnically, linguistically, religiously diverse and extremely complex country with no democratic tradition, has been in continual violent conflict since the 1970s. Faith in the democratic process could quickly wane, and discontent could ignite the many elements in the country that are already interested in pursuing power via extralegal ways.

---

79. The most prominent member of the ousted Taliban regime, former foreign minister Mawlawi Wakil Ahmad Mutawakkil, fared very poorly in his candidacy in Kandahar Province. Abdul Rasul Sayyaf, an ethnic Pashtun and a Karzai supporter who is an extreme Islamist and alleged war criminal as well as terrorist supporter, also won a parliament seat from Kabul with a bare minimum of votes.

80. The author calculated these Kabul electoral results based on data presented by the JEMB.

81. The aggregated vote of all Wolesi Jirga winners was 2,225,068; 6,207,843 total votes were cast.

A legislative impasse in the Wolesi Jirga could also push Karzai to personalize the Afghan government to an even greater extent and, in the process, alienate his opponents.

The members of the legislature body were not elected with the support of the majority of Afghan citizens. Moreover, they comprise influential coalitions of former mujahideen and Taliban commanders, communists, tribal nationalists, royalists, warlords, and urban professionals who do not like one another. Two parliamentarians were murdered before the legislative body convened. Although Karzai backed Abdul Rasul Sayyaf, an Islamic extremist, for speaker in parliament, allegations about his war crimes hurt his candidacy, and Karzai's rival Yunus Qanooni won the post.[82]

Conclusion

There is little doubt that substantial, indeed historic, achievements have taken place in Afghanistan since the fall of the Taliban, and many of these achievements are directly attributable to the Bonn process. Nevertheless, serious flaws bode ill for Afghanistan's prospects to become a democratic, peaceful, and secure country.

In an interesting twist on the theme of international interventions in transitional governance that unites this volume, it is possible that Afghanistan's transition would not have taken place were it not for the al-Qaeda attack on the United States on September 11, 2001, and the subsequent U.S. attack on the Taliban government. That is, internal processes were previously insufficient to unseat the Taliban nor, after the fall of 2001, to unify the nation.[83] Yet, echoing Manning's analysis in this volume, regime change through foreign invasion has not been able to radically change the power elite in Afghanistan. Some Taliban remnants and local warlords gained power in the Wolesi Jirga, while others have regrouped and are presently engaged in an intensifying insurgency that is beginning to mimic those in Iraq. In retrospect, Bonn should have attempted to draw in moderate Taliban elements and include them in the government. Just wishing the movement will go away is not enough.

The failure of Bonn to address the problem of regional warlords was a monumental mistake that has undermined the ability of the fledgling central state to impose order on the country and to become the genuine ruler of Afghanistan. Without first demobilizing the regional power holders and mujahideen, the interim and transitional governments became dependent on them, and in the process of creating a permanent government, they earned themselves some measure of formal legitimacy. While Karzai even-

82. "A Place for Warlords to Meet."

83. Barnett R. Rubin, "(Re)Building Afghanistan: The Folly of Stateless Democracy," *Current History* 103, no. 672 (April 2004): 165–170.

tually moved, with considerable U.S. support, to co-opt these warlords, their power bases remain intact. The problem of regional militias and the influence of warlords, many fueled by lucrative drug production and trade, is a colossal one.

The Afghan constitution is an extremely important accomplishment of the Bonn process. But the lack of a full public debate before its ratification was a missed opportunity to address two divisive issues: the role of Islam and the specification of relations between Kabul and the regions. Divisions between the mujahideen and the central government could deepen factional conflict if improperly handled. Islam, in contrast, could become an umbrella issue that would facilitate a coalition among disparate regional commanders who are discontented with the Karzai administration or are searching for ways of expanding their territorial influence. Yet this is not a panacea: there is a long-term risk that the incorporation of Islam into the constitution will empower extremist groups, such as Ittehad-e Islami Afghanistan and factions within Jamiat-e Islami, and weaken new democratic groups, thereby undermining the foundations of civil liberties, particularly for women and the Shi'a minority.[84]

Karzai's election was a reification of long-held ethnic biases and conflicts. He was not able to engender significant support beyond his Pashtun base, and he has not proven to wield much influence beyond the city limits of Kabul. The legislative election results were even more disappointing. The election rules backfired on the Karzai administration: rather than disempowering organized political formations, as intended, and providing space for politics to coalesce around new lines, the election allowed elements that were already strong and organized to gain representation. Moreover, the voting results suggested that the Wolesi Jirga does not have public legitimacy, being elected by a minority of the electorate. The fact that so many candidates could be elected to this important legislative body with less than 5 percent of their respective electorates' support does not suggest that democracy is flourishing in Afghanistan. These elections were tragically flawed, and their results have the potential to derail the ordinary Afghan's faith in the legislative process.

Karzai's fear of a multiparty system was extremely counterproductive. The numerous parties that have been formed since Bonn should be encouraged to participate in public debate. Afghanistan is and will remain a fragmented society. But diversity of opinions need not be manifested in conflict dynamics. Interchange and a viable Afghan multiparty system should be encouraged, not discouraged.

Another problem facing Afghanistan and its transition to a stable democratic country is its narcotics production and transport. Afghanistan's

---

84. International Crisis Group, *Afghanistan's Flawed Constitutional Process*, 6.

economy has been captured by opium production and trafficking. Approximately 87 percent of the world's heroin is now produced in Afghanistan.[85] Current estimates posit that opium accounts for 45 to 60 percent of the national economy. Quite simply, Afghanistan is on the verge of becoming a narco-state, according to the United Nations, with drug barons, narco-terrorists, and corruption overwhelming the society.[86] As suggested by President Karzai, "poppy, its cultivation and drugs are Afghanistan's major enemy."[87]

The opium economy and the influx of narco-money have contributed to the spread of corruption into all spheres of government. Narco-associated corruption permeates Afghan society, especially in the judiciary and police, according to Ahmad Fahim Hakim, deputy chairman of the Afghan Independent Human Rights Commission.[88] Abdul Latif Pedram, an Afghan opposition politician, states, "There has never been so much corruption in the country. We have a mafia economy and a drug economy."[89] According to the *Washington Post*, "The drug trade in Afghanistan is growing more pervasive, powerful and organized, its corrupting reach extending to all aspects of society."[90] Ali Jalali, a former interior minister who quit the job last summer, explicitly points to the extent of the problem. According to *Newsweek*, he has stated that he has a "list of more than 100 high-ranking Afghan officials he suspects of involvement in the drug trade. A source close to him, fearful of being killed if identified, says Jalali's unpublished list includes at least 13 former and present provincial governors and four past or present cabinet ministers."[91] Jalali's supposition is supported by others.

Many of the underground industry's most important figures are said to be senior government officials in Kabul and the provinces. Amanullah Paiman, a newly elected member of Parliament from the far northern province of Badakhshan, has studied the country's drug problem and says Afghan government officials are involved in at least 70 percent of the traffic.

---

85. See United Nations Office on Drugs and Crime and the Government of Afghanistan's Counter Narcotics Directorate, *Afghanistan Opium Survey, 2005* (United Nations, November 2005).

86. United Nations Office on Drugs and Crime, *2006 World Drug Report* (New York: United Nations, 2006).

87. Yousuf Azmiy, "Karzai Says World Is Not Doing Enough on Afghan Drugs," ABC News International and Reuters, August 22, 2006, abcnews.go.com/International/wireStory?id=2341232.

88. Carlotta Gall, "Nation Faltering, Afghans' Leader Draws Criticism," *New York Times*, August 23, 2006.

89. Ibid.

90. PBS Online NewsHour, "Combating Poppy Production," www.pbs.org/newshour/bb/asia/afghanistan/aug03/drugs.html.

91. Ron Moreau and Sami Yousafzai, "A Harvest of Treachery," *Newsweek*, January 9, 2006.

"The chain of narco-dollars goes from the districts to the highest levels of government," he says.[92]

Ultimately, the problem of opium production and trafficking will have a major impact on the success or failure of democratic development in Afghanistan. The U.S. State Department has recently stated that an increase in the production of illicit drugs in Afghanistan is "a problem for the integrity" of the Afghan government.[93]

Ultimately, the success or failure of Bonn will depend on conditions particular to Afghanistan—a legal state, but one that has been in conflict for nearly three decades. The essential condition for a state is to have an effective monopoly over the means of violence, and there is no escaping the fact that Afghanistan suffers from inefficient, dysfunctional political institutions, including its security services. Heavy reliance on the international community—particularly the United States—to fill the gap in both functional political processes and security services has left Afghanistan without an effective revenue base and dependent on international donor aid for reconstruction. Bonn's results would likely be in question regardless, particularly due to the condition of the Afghan state and the underlying problems within the country, including extremist beliefs, patronage politics, highly available drug revenues, and tribal rivalries.

---

92. Ibid.

93. Tom Casey, "Daily Press Briefing," U.S. Department of State, August 17, 2006, www.state.gov/r/pa/prs/dpb/2006/70877.htm.

9

Iraq's Constitutional Process: An Opportunity Lost

Jonathan Morrow

On Sunday September 18, 2005, Iraq's Transitional National Assembly approved a draft constitution and submitted it to the United Nations Assistance Mission for Iraq, which was to be published throughout Iraq prior to the October 15 national referendum. The Independent Electoral Commission has now confirmed that the Iraqi people approved the constitution in conformity with Article 61(C) of Iraq's interim constitution, the Transitional Administrative Law (TAL). Large sections of Iraq's Sunni Arab community and other groups in Iraq, however, opposed the constitutional text. Notwithstanding the strong support for the text in Iraq as a whole, 96.96 percent and 81.75 percent of voters from Sunni Arab-dominated Anbar and Salahaddin governorates voted no. Though there is evidence for some Sunni Arab support for the constitution in Ninevah and Diyala governorates, where the "no" vote was as low as 55.01 percent and 48.73 percent respectively, it is clear that Sunni Arabs in Iraq generally voted against the constitution.

Even with the approval of Iraq's constitution in the October national referendum, the future of Iraq is uncertain. For Sunni Arab Iraqis, the constitutional text poses difficult questions. What are the consequences of the success of the draft at the referendum if it does not command the support of one large section of the Iraqi people?

This Special Report traces the events that led to the creation of the draft constitution, and identifies both the strengths and shortcomings of Iraq's constitution-making efforts. It argues that the refusal of the Iraq National Assembly to extend the constitution-drafting process by using the mechanism provided in Article 61(F) of the TAL was a mistake. Under U.S. Government pressure, the National Assembly insisted that the August 15 deadline be met, allowing the Constitution Committee, which included Sunni Arab

---

Jonathan Morrow, "Iraq's Constitutional Process II: An Opportunity Lost," Special Report 155 (Washington, DC: USIP, November 2005).

members, to operate for only one month—a plainly inadequate period of time. The truncation of the constitutional-drafting process:

- precluded the real possibility that the confidence of Sunni Arab Iraqis might have been built around the model of a federal Iraq;
- amplified imbalances in the technical competency of the respective negotiating camps;
- removed opportunities for international mediation, in particular the United Nations;
- increased U.S. visibility as an agent and participant in the Iraqi negotiations; and
- excluded meaningful Iraqi citizen participation in the constitution-making process.

This chapter identifies Iraq's constitutional process as a unique opportunity lost to build new institutional legitimacy, as well as inter-ethnic and inter-sectarian alliances. Further opportunities to include Sunni Arabs and other groups within a federal Iraq still exist and should not be ignored.

Background: Iraqi Constitutionalism

Participatory Constitutionalism

Since the March 2003 occupation, those in Iraqi political circles, the Iraqi media, the U.S. administration, and the United Nations have shared the assumption that a constitutional democracy would be the hallmark of success in post-Saddam Iraq. Well before Iraq's first national election on January 30, 2005, there was a real expectation that the completion of a permanent constitution would represent an important, perhaps critical, turning point in Iraq's fortunes.

Moreover, the TAL unequivocally signaled that a constitution on its own would not be sufficient. Also necessary would be a participatory, transparent, and well-ordered drafting process; a process that would display the virtues of democracy that the constitutional text itself was expected to embody. As one influential Iraqi civil society organization, the Iraq Prospect Organisation, put it in December 2003: "This process in itself will help root democratic values and set Iraq on a course to freedom." The TAL stipulated in some detail the means by which a permanent constitution would be prepared. TAL Article 60 states that the National Assembly should write the text, "in part by encouraging debate on the constitution through regular general public meetings in all parts of Iraq and through the media, and receiving proposals from the citizens of Iraq as it writes the constitution."

Security Council Resolution 1546 mandated the United Nations to "promote national dialogue and consensus-building on the drafting of a national constitution by the people of Iraq," as requested by the Iraqi government. To achieve this broad national dialogue, the TAL provided an ambitious timetable from the January 2005 election until August 15, 2005, with the option of a further six-month extension as stated in TAL Article 61(F).

Sources of Constitutionalism

Where, precisely, did these expectations of constitutionalism come from? Internal and external factors contributed to the desire and goal for a permanent constitution. In part, the desire was distinctly nationalist, including a popular Iraqi yearning for a level of stability and justice unknown in the Saddam period, a period characterised by conspicuously "interim" constitutions. A senior independent Shia intellectual and one of the deputy speakers of the National Assembly, Dr. Hussain Shahristani, recounts one of Saddam Hussain's favorite *bons mots*: "A constitution is written by men so that another man can tear it up." From 2003, this desire for a truly permanent constitution was compounded by a growing frustration with the operational shortcomings of the U.S.-led Coalition occupation and appointed interim government, for which an elected constitutional government seemed the obvious remedy.

A demand for constitutionalism within Iraq was consolidated by a survey of the international scene. In particular, there was an appreciation of the post-Cold War "new constitutionalism" and the symbolic significance of popular constitution-making in the democratization of countries as diverse as Poland, Hungary, and South Africa. It also arose in part from more recent post-conflict experience in Afghanistan and East Timor, where international programs supporting peacekeeping and governance culminated, almost triumphantly, in the entry into force of newly drafted constitutions. These comparative constitutional experiences are now well documented, and contain lessons for Iraq which USIP, among others, have identified. (See "Iraq's Constitutional Process: Shaping a Vision for the Country's Future," USIP Special Report 132, February 2005.)

Moreover, the overwhelming U.S. political and cultural influence in post-2003 Iraq brought to bear the specific U.S. vision of a constitution as the centerpiece of stability and democratic independence of post-Saddam Iraq. Constitutionalism is at the heart of the U.S. vision of its own democratic identity; thus, it may not be surprising that this vision was rhetorically projected onto the massive democratization project in Iraq. In a dynamic which is familiar to observers of transitional governments, over time the idea of permanent constitution for Iraq became more and more closely linked, in the U.S. imagination, with nation-building success and a plausible exit strategy.

Finally, and more pragmatically, many Iraqis—particularly, but not exclusively, Iraqi Kurds—perceived that in a multi-sectarian, regionalized country, a permanent constitution would be desirable, if not necessary, as a kind of an inter-communal peace treaty. This constitution-as-treaty would not be a principled discussion leading to the consolidation of Iraqi political identity: it would, more modestly, represent a *modus vivendi* to settle competing interests surrounding religious law, local self-governance, and resource management. As far as this last source of 'constitutionalism' was concerned, the relevant analogies were less to the United States or even Afghanistan and East Timor, and more to Bosnia-Herzegovina, Sri Lanka, and the Sudan.

Expectations of Citizen Involvement

Each of these intellectual origins for Iraqi constitutionalism—nationalist, "new constitutionalist," and pragmatist—were to some extent popular. That is, each derived from a demand from non-elite Iraqis for a new social contract. Each presupposed that the Iraqi citizenry would have some opportunity to directly influence the constitution-making process. As one young Baghdadi man put it in late 2004, "When we hear talk of a permanent constitution, our eyes light up." Early ambitions of the Coalition Provisional Authority for a constitution to be drafted by U.S. appointees quickly gave way to pressure from Shia religious leader Ayatollah Sistani for a constitution to be drafted by elected representatives. Even the minimalist, pragmatist approach was premised, for instance, on the importance of Kurdish popular opinion and a Kurdish popular desire for a large degree of autonomy, if not independence, from Baghdad.

This demand for citizen involvement in constitution-making was increased by the widespread criticism of the process by which the TAL had been drafted in early 2003 during the period in which the Coalition Provisional Authority exercised the rights of an occupying power. The TAL process, though it involved some senior Iraqi political figures, was notoriously, if unintentionally, hasty and secretive, and was heavily influenced by U.S. political interests. The build-up of popular constitutionalism in Iraq during the occupation added considerable significance to the task of the future elected National Assembly in writing the constitution by an initial deadline of August 15, 2005, or if the National Assembly considered that an extension using Article 61(F) was needed, by February 15, 2006. The National Democratic Institute (NDI) found that by April 2005 "almost every participant" in national focus group research "is of the opinion that the Iraqi citizens should be involved in the preparation of the constitution."

If transitional Iraq was always in need of a credible constitutional process, by late 2004 this need was made acute by Iraqi electoral politics and the dynamics of a predominantly Sunni Arab insurgency. In December

2004, it became clear that the January 2005 election outcome would be dictated by ethnic and sectarian politics, and that large sections of Iraq's Sunni Arab community would not participate.

The Process: Sunni Arab Exclusion

The Threat to Constitutionalism: January Election Boycott

Sunni Arabs, a minority that enjoyed favor in pre-2003 Iraqi governments and that had traditionally managed the state apparatus of unelected Iraqi governments, had least to gain from an election. Sunni Arabs supply the most promising recruiting ground for insurgents and terrorists, but they are also the most vulnerable to violence, which escalated during the campaign period leading up to the January 2005 elections. In November 2004, Sunni Arab leaders, including the umbrella Iraqi National Foundation Congress, rejected the election on the grounds that it was taking place under Coalition "occupation," and therefore illegitimate and likely, in the words of the Muslim Scholar's Association leader Harith al-Dhari, to be "faked." The more moderate Iraqi Islamic Party, led by Mohsen Abdul Hamid, also boycotted the election.

The Sunni Arabs' January 2005 election boycott and the simultaneous campaign of intimidation of Sunni Arab voters by the insurgency resulted in only seventeen Sunni Arabs elected to the 275-member Assembly—a very low number by reference to the proportion of Sunni Arabs in Iraq, conventionally estimated at 15 to 20 percent. By contrast, the Kurdistan Coalition List won seventy-five seats and the predominantly Shia United Iraqi Alliance won 140—an absolute majority that in theory, if not in fact, gave the Alliance the ability to write a constitution without the involvement of any other political grouping.

In practice, however, the strength of Iraqi Shia majoritarianism was doubtful in the context of a future Iraq constitution. Neither the Shia nor Kurdistan parties could afford to ignore the interests of Sunni Arabs completely. The Sunnis pointed to the TAL provision—Article 61(c)—that gave any three of Iraq's eighteen governorates the ability to veto any constitutional draft by a two-thirds majority. Sunni Arabs are believed to constitute a majority of residents in at least three Iraqi governorates: Anbar, Salahaddin, and Ninevah. It was always seen as at least possible that Sunni Arabs might have sufficient numbers and cohesion to invoke the Article 61(C) veto successfully. It is well known that Article 61(C) had been included in the TAL text as a last-minute modification of a demand from the Kurdish parties. Many commentators have remarked on the irony that it was now the Kurds, likely to do well in the constitutional negotiations, for whom Article 61(c) posed the greatest threat.

In these circumstances, the low Sunni Arab turnout at the January election raised the discomfiting spectre of a draft constitution that would explicitly exclude Sunni Arab views and that, in an already deteriorating security environment, would cement Sunni Arab opposition. This exclusion presented immediate problems: first, the possibility that the constitution would be blocked at the referendum; and secondly, in the event of the constitution's success at the referendum, a still more profound failure—the failure of Iraqi nationalist, "new constitutionalist" and pragmatist ambitions for a constitutional compact including all three of Iraq's major groups. The constitution might fail to deliver on the promise of true Iraqi consensus.

A Possible Solution: Constitutional Engagement

No doubt anticipating the problem, a number of Sunni Arab leaders publicly indicated in November 2004 that though they would likely boycott the election, they would be willing to engage in the post-election constitutional discussions. Statements of boycott often contained an implication that the future constitutional discussions for a democratic Iraq could be relatively free from coalition influence and, as a sovereign Iraqi process, could therefore be supported.

In the weeks before the election, Shia and Kurdish party leaders were reciprocating these Sunni Arab advances. Dr. Hussain Shahristani, charged with assembling the Shia Alliance, stated on January 23: "If the people of [any area of Iraq] are not represented in the elected National Assembly—and we hope and pray the issue will not be so—we will call for a national dialogue with the real representatives of all these areas. We will not write a constitution that does not satisfy all sectors of the Iraqi society." This rapprochement came with the clear encouragement of the centrist, nonsectarian parties, including the Iraqi List, the party of then Prime Minister Ayad Allawi. He stated on January 24: "We know that the [TAL] does not mean that only the ones who voted will write the constitution. It is possible for anyone to participate in writing the constitution." On January 27, Wamidh Nadhmi, a secular spokesman of the Iraq National Foundation Conference, echoed the views of the Muslim Scholars Association that notwithstanding the electoral boycott, "[i]f we were invited by respectable committees [in the National Assembly] I don't see why we wouldn't say what we think of the constitution."

Party leaders re-affirmed their rapprochement after the election results were announced in February. At that time, Iraqi lawyers and political advisers discussed the question of Sunni Arab inclusion in detail in a cross-factional working session, convened by USIP and the American Bar Association in Jordan. These discussions set the stage for a constitutional process that might rescue Iraq's transitional governments from the perception of illegitimacy among Sunni Arabs and other nationalists. The International Republican Institute's (IRI) polling conducted in April showed a large public desire across Iraq to include Sunni Arabs into the constitutional process.

Sunni Arab Opposition to Constitutional Draft

As events transpired since the January elections, however, the spectre of an exclusionary constitution has become real. The substantive criticisms of the draft by Sunni Arabs also included serious procedural complaints.

Elements of the Draft Constitution

The terms of the constitution itself are fairly familiar to Western eyes: a parliamentary, republican, asymmetrical federal democracy that posits a central government with certain enumerated exclusive powers, including foreign affairs, defence, and fiscal policy. Executive, legislative, and judicial powers are balanced, if not with great precision. The exclusive powers of the federal government are very limited and do not include, for instance, an explicit power of taxation; though, it seems clear that the central government has the power to legislate outside the list of enumerated powers. As for Iraq's all-important hydrocarbons, the constitution explicitly gives management control over existing petroleum production to the federal government "with" the producing regional government, and implicitly gives control over future petroleum production to the regional government, with revenues to be shared throughout Iraq. Regional governments enjoy wide residual powers, with regional law overriding non-exclusive federal law to the extent of any inconsistency between the two. The constitution gives recognition to Iraqi Kurdistan as a region, and allows for one or more governorates to come together as new federal regions in the future.

The constitution provides for a fairly modern bill of rights, but also provides for many of the rights to be elaborated through legislation, under which these constitutional rights could be reduced. Though the constitution purports to preserve the essence of these rights, conservative Islamic law can clearly qualify them. The constitution describes Islam as "a fundamental source of legislation," prohibits legislation which contradicts "the established provisions of Islam," and inscribes a role for "experts in Islamic jurisprudence"—generally understood as Islamic clerics—on the constitutional court. Perhaps less obvious is the large scope which the constitution allows regional legislatures to prevail over federal law in those areas in which Islamic jurisprudence conventionally holds sway, including family law and criminal law. A referendum by the end of 2007 will resolve the outstanding status of multi-ethnic Kirkuk.

Substantive Opposition to Draft Constitution

The draft constitution attracted criticism from a range of Iraqi groups and parties, and in particular Sunni Arab groups. After the National Assembly adopted the draft constitution on August 28, influential secular and religious Sunni Arab political groups, including the Iraq Islamic Party, the National Dialogue Council, and the Muslim Scholars Association, publicly indicated that they would oppose the draft at the national referendum.

The stated reasons for opposition were not uniform. For instance, secular and religious Sunni Arab groups were divided on the statement in the draft that Islam, "is a fundamental source of legislation." Secularists thought this was too much religion; clerics thought it was not enough. There were common themes, however. Typically, the Sunni Arabs objected to the regional federalist model for Iraq and, in particular, the prospect of a southern, predominantly Shia, federal region. In many cases, there was a specific rejection of regional control of petroleum production, a demand for a stronger statement of an Arab identity for Iraq, and an objection to provisions in the draft condemning Ba'athism. Later efforts to bring the August 28 text closer to the Sunni Arab position led, eventually, to a statement of support by the more moderate Iraq Islamic Party for the constitutional text. The majority of Sunni Arab representative groups, however, maintained these objections up to the date of the referendum.

Significantly, opposition to the text was not confined to Sunni Arab groups. Former Prime Minister Ayad Allawi had also publicly opposed the model of regional federalism in the constitutional draft. The influential Shia clerics Moqtada al-Sadr and Ayatollah Mohammed al-Yaqoubi indicated their opposition to the draft at referendum, for reasons that likely stem from hostility towards the Iranian ties of the Supreme Council for the Islamic Revolution in Iraq (SCIRI). SCIRI is the powerful Shia party and major proponent of constitutional provisions that facilitate a southern federal unit. Some women's groups and certain ethnic minorities also opposed the draft on grounds that the text insufficiently promoted and protected their interests.

The Problem: Time Pressures

These substantive Sunni Arab criticisms of the draft were also accompanied by procedural complaints. Sunni Arab representatives said that they were not sufficiently included in the constitutional negotiations.

The creation of the Committee was promising in some respects. In particular, Sunni Arab negotiators nominated fifteen new representatives to join the National Assembly's fifty-five-member Constitution Drafting Committee ("the Committee") in late June 2005, and the following weeks saw the participation by those representatives in the Committee's activities. (The enlarged body was notionally renamed a "Commission" [*hay'a 'ameh*] but was continually referred to as the "Committee" [*lajneh*], and this report follows the common practice.)

The Assembly had elected a SCIRI member Sheikh Humam Hamoudi to chair the Committee. He was not appointed until May 23, after negotiations over the formation of an Iraqi Cabinet extended to April 28, and the negotiations over Committee membership continued until May 11. Once appointed, Sheikh Hamoudi heard evidence from international experts from constitutional commissions in South Africa, Albania, Kenya, Afghanistan, East Timor, and elsewhere. He agreed to bring Sunni Arab members into the Committee structure and to take decisions by consensus. This principle of consensus was adopted to provide some assurance that Sunni Arab Committee members would not be sidelined in a Committee on which, because they were not elected to the Assembly, they had no vote. In finalizing the Committee composition in this way, the Assembly implicitly rejected earlier proposals in February suggesting that the constitution be drafted by a commission which would be independent of the Government and the Assembly. The Assembly also rejected the possibility that the drafting body contain, as members, Iraqi civil society representatives or constitutional experts. As a result, additional, unelected Committee members were limited to the Sunni Arab political leadership.

The extent to which the Committee was able to operate as a forum for the expression of Sunni Arab constitutional positions, however, was marginal at best. First, the period during which Sunni Arabs were able to take part in the Committee activities was very short. It was late June before the fifteen Sunni Arab members of the Committee had been invited onto the Committee; and it was later still, on July 8, before they attended their first meeting. Matters were tragically complicated on July 19 when a Sunni Arab Committee member, Mijbil Sheikh Issa, was assassinated in the Baghdad suburb of Karrada—presumably by Sunni Arab insurgents. As a result, some Sunni Arabs on the Committee suspended their membership until the government could assure them a higher level of security protection.

The Committee leadership, having made repeated public commitments that they would meet the default TAL constitutional deadline of August 15, remained under intense time pressure to produce a draft. Public and private statements of senior U.S. officials, including the Secretary of State, the Secretary of Defense and the President himself, dramatically increased this pressure. These officials made it clear that any move to extend the constitutional deadline beyond August 15 would earn the displeasure of the U.S. and U.K. Governments. The standard U.S. pronouncement was: "The [United States] supports the Iraqi people in their desire to complete a constitution by August 15," in circumstances where an expression of that desire was far from universal within Iraq, and did not precede the statement by the United States of its position.

Defunct Constitution Committee

As it turned out, however, the Committee was effectively scrapped, or rendered defunct, by the meeting of political party leaders that began in the Baghdad International Zone on August 8. Scrapping the Committee on August 8 meant that in effect the Sunni Arab Committee members, after no more than one month of trying to do the impossible—develop and asserting a coherent constitutional position—were retired *en masse*.

After August 8, constitutional negotiations took place in a series of private, ad hoc meetings between Kurdish and Shia party leaders—the "Leadership Council," as it was termed by the international press, or more informally by Committee members, "the kitchen" (*matbagh*). In its basic form, the Leadership Council consisted of SCIRI leader Abdul Aziz al-Hakim, Shia Dawa party leader Prime Minister Jaafari, Kurdish PUK party leader President Jalal Talabani, and Kurdish KDP party leader Masoud Barzani. These meetings took place at irregular intervals at a number of private residences and compounds in the International Zone. These were meetings to which the Sunni Committee members had no right of attendance, to which they frequently requested attendance, but were not often invited. The protocol was quite clear: the Shia and Kurdish parties would agree to a constitutional text, which would then be presented as a fait accompli to the Sunni Arabs, who would be asked to take it or leave it.

Timeline: A Better Process?

The question arises, then, as to whether before the Leadership Council began meeting on August 8, a more extended time period for constitutional deliberations within the Constitutional Committee would have produced a better result, and specifically would have created the conditions for Sunni Arab acceptance of a constitutional draft. The answer to this question has implications for any post-constitutional Iraq strategy.

Iraqi Support for 61(F) Extension

At the outset, it should be noted that many of those Iraqis closest to the negotiations clearly favored a more extended timeline, including the Chairman of the Committee himself. Under the terms of the TAL, if the provisions to extend the constitutional process were to be invoked, such action had to be taken by the Assembly before August 1, presumably on the advice of the Committee.

On July 31, Sheikh Hamoudi indicated to the Committee his wish to extend the process to September 15. In early June, he had sought independent advice from USIP consultants on timeline extension options; the work needed to reach true consensus weighed heavily on his mind. This preference for an extension was shared by Mahmoud Othman and other senior

Kurdish negotiators, international advisers to the Kurds, and senior Shia List officials on the Committee, including Abbas Bayati. This preference also had private support amongst senior independent Shia leaders in the Assembly, from Committee member and Chairman of the Council of Iraqi Minorities Dr. Hunain Al-Qaddo, and from Dr. Younadam Kanna, Committee member and leader of an independent Chaldo-Assyrian Christian party. The leaders of most, if not all, important civil society organizations expressed their desire for an extension. NDI focus group research in April 2005 revealed strong reservations across Iraq regarding the value of a hasty constitutional process. On August 1, Speaker of the Assembly Hajim Al-Hassani was expecting to receive a request from Sheikh Hamoudi for an extension. Some observers in the international community, including the International Crisis Group, had publicly doubted the possibility, and desirability, of meeting the August 15 deadline, and these views had been influential in the Iraqi political class.

The United States, however, maintained its policy. In the days prior to August 1, U.S. Ambassador Khalilzad convened meetings with political party leaders to impress upon them the importance of meeting the August 15 deadline. He issued similar messages to members of the international community. The U.S. Government's strong demarches stand out as the principal reason for the Assembly ultimately declining the TAL extension provision on August 1.

Committee Shortcomings

Given the shortcomings of the Committee, the proposition that an extension would have helped is, at first glance, doubtful. First, through June and July, the Committee lacked the ability to identify constitutional differences and reach common ground across factions. As one Iraqi observer put it: "These days, if someone wishes you good morning, you are suspicious." Committee drafting work was slow, and discussions at Committee meetings were frequently abstract and academic. The discussions were not characterised by the practical bargaining and trading clearly necessary to produce the consensus that the Committee had rightly established as its goal. Political party leaders did not provide their Committee representatives with clear mandates, inhibiting true consensus. Committee meeting minutes were not taken.

Second, the Committee did not implement a set of rules and work plan to clearly define, for all participants, the stages in the constitutional process. There was no protocol to address the fact that crucial offline bilateral negotiations between the three major political blocs of Shia Arabs, Kurds, and Sunni Arabs would be needed at each step of the way. In Iraq's difficult security environment, these constitutional discussions were always fated to take on the nature of peace treaty talks, as if among three sovereign governments. (Indeed, as late as June one senior Kurdish negotiator,

Dr. Saedi Barzinji, was insisting Kurdish autonomy be protected in the constitution by a set of international guarantees.) The life of the Committee was characterised by frequent resignations and walk-outs by Sunni Arab, Kurd, and other representatives. Also no protocol provided for Committee interaction with the Iraqi public. Occasional press conferences were held in the heavily guarded Convention Center to update the media on the Committee's drafting work, but these did not involve serious dialogue on constitutional issues.

Sunni Arab Committee members were continually criticized for being composed largely of the Baghdad political elite and insufficiently representing their constituency. Some also felt that Sunni Arab civil society leaders, including tribal leaders, had been largely overlooked to the peril of the final constitution. For example, in early June, Shia and Kurdish Committee members rejected a proposal to identify Sunni Arab constitutional drafters through a multi-week, regional caucus process. The Iraq Institute of Peace, a nongovernmental interfaith dialogue organization with strong Sunni Arab tribal connections, had tested the idea, but the Shia and Kurdish members thought the process would be too time-consuming.

Insurmountable Differences?

Even with all the time in the world, the gap between the Sunni Arab and Shia constitutional positions on federalism may not have been reconcilable. There was arguably little chance for the Sunni Arabs to reach an accommodation with SCIRI, which over the course of July had strongly pressed for a constitutional right to create a new southern federal unit to mirror that of the Kurdistan Region. The model of federalism the Kurdish and Shia "kitchen" finally offered to Sunni Arab negotiators would not only consolidate a large degree of autonomy to the Kurdistan Region, but would also allow for other future federal regions, including a southern, predominantly Shia, federal unit.

In rejecting this model, the Sunni Arabs took a stance that bluntly and fundamentally contradicted the bilateral Kurd-Shia agreement on the terms of federalism, in circumstances where that agreement was apparently not open to modification. The terms of that Kurd-Shia agreement give to one or more of Iraq's eighteen governorates the right to "organize into a region" following a referendum in the respective governorate(s). The central Sunni Arab objections as stated lay with the prospect that a southern federal unit would radically challenge a Sunni Arab conception of the integrity of the Iraqi nation, and that would (or so it is imagined) isolate Sunni Arab nationalists between two sectarian and strong provincial powers of Iraqi Kurdistan and a new Iraqi "Shiastan."

As constitutional positions hardened towards the end of August, adherents of the Kurdistan and Shia parties made private allegations that the

Sunni Arab negotiators had no intention of finding common ground. They stated a belief that the Sunni Arab negotiators had as primary objective a failure by the Assembly to meet the August 15 deadline. Under the relevant TAL provisions, a failure to meet—or extend—the August 15 deadline would automatically precipitate the dissolution of the Assembly and mandate new constituent elections for a new Assembly, to which more Sunni Arabs would be presumably be elected. In their darker moments, Kurdish and Shia negotiators ascribed this "nuclear option" to the ambition of the Sunni Arabs.

Reasons for Extension

Several indicators suggest, however, that Sunni Arab positions had not hardened against federalism, and were not as intractable as some have suggested. For several reasons, an extended constitutional process would have produced better results.

A Moderating Sunni Arab Position on Federalism

First, it is a fact that influential sections of the Sunni Arab community in June and July, in evolving discussions on the terms of Iraqi federalism, were beginning to produce more moderate constitutional positions. There were signs that some influential Sunni Arabs were coming to accept the possibility that federalism might work to their benefit. They were already accepting, for instance, a governorate based federalism that would imply self-government in Sunni Arab areas of Iraq. As one Sunni Arab lawyer put it: "When you ask a Sunni if they want Anbar to rule Najaf, they say no; if you ask if they want Najaf to rule Anbar, they say no. They want federalism without realising it." Moreover, at no point was there a strong statement by Sunni Arab negotiators against the existence of a relatively autonomous Kurdistan Region.

USIP was in close contact with some of these Sunni Arab opinion makers, who were working with their constituents to bring about credible and acceptable Sunni Arab positions. A large part of the problem within Sunni Arab elites was the fact that the Kurdish and Shia parties overlooked Sunni Arab technical constitutional expertise. Sunni Arab leaders pointed to a professional class of lawyers who had been kept away from the constitutional negotiations. The leaders often stated their ambition as no greater than to have these lawyers review the text negotiated between Kurdish and Shia parties. In this way, much Sunni Arab hostility to the terms of federalism as they were developed in the August negotiations was due to this sense of professional pride and a belief in constitution-making as a technical, not only political, exercise.

In the final days of August, leading Sunni Arab negotiators were privately sympathetic to some models of Iraqi regional federalism, but were unable to move because of their constituent institutions and populations. In Sunni Arab populations, evidence collected by NDI and others shows that hostility to the concept of federalism stems not from principle or an informed self-interest, but rather from a perception that "federalism" (*ittihadiyyah*) is code for Kurdish separation and, more generally, the partition of Iraq. There was little recognition in the Sunni Arab heartland that federalism is an internationally recognized way of structuring a state that can be neutral, or at least mutually beneficial, as to the respective interests of different regional and ethnic groups. Interviews conducted by the United Nations Office for Project Services in late July showed that of the Sunni Arabs in the interview group, 51.7 percent believed federalism would lead to a divided Iraq, and 46.8 percent believed it would lead to civil war. By way of contrast, a year earlier Shia popular opinion reflected a similarly limited understanding of federalism, including a belief that federalism simply meant Kurdish separation. Over several months of Shia strategising on constitutional matters, the position of popular Shia sentiment moved significantly—if not uniformly—towards an acceptance federal constitutional models. Similarly, if Sunni Arab constitutional negotiators were to accept the terms of a federal Iraq, their constituents would need to empower them to do so.

The deadline of August 15, however, did not allow this discussion to take place. To this extent, the Sunni Arab position as articulated in July and August was premature, hastily crafted, and without the benefit of an informed debate amongst the broader Sunni Arab population. While it is arguable that convening a party leaders' summit in early August was necessary, it was neither necessary nor desirable for the Constitution Committee to be disbanded at the same time.

Imbalanced Negotiating Capacity

The highly compressed timeline for constitutional discussions also amplified the imbalance between the respective competencies of the established Kurdistan and Shia parties on the one hand, and the Sunni Arab representatives on the other. The effective August 8 dissolution of the Committee apparatus and the beginning of a last-minute, unstructured three-way negotiation shifted great weight, very suddenly, onto the respective negotiating teams. The Sunni Arab team was by far the least organized.

By August 2005, the Kurdistan Region parties were well prepared for ad hoc negotiations. They had developed constitutional positions and even draft Iraqi constitutional texts which, over time, became increasingly ambitious and firm. Most recently, the Kurds had internally agreed on their non-negotiable "red line" positions, which Constitutional Committee members from the Kurdistan Coalition were not at liberty to modify. During the January election, the Kurdistan parties were able to orchestrate a regionwide poll that predictably showed a popular preference for independence over integration into Iraq. This result sent the message to non-Kurdish parties that the Kurdish leaders had little room to retreat from maximalist constitutional positions. Similarly, in late July, the Kurdistan National Parliament gave the Kurdistan parties a clear mandate on these red line positions, which were made public. Street demonstrations across the Kurdistan region on August 15 also showed support for the Kurdish parties. Lastly, the Kurdish parties were able to invite into the ad hoc meetings experienced non-Iraqi international negotiators and constitutional lawyers, including former U.S. diplomat Peter Galbraith and University of Maryland Professor Karol Soltan, to advance the Kurdish case.

The Shia parties, for their part, did not have clear mandates from their constituencies, and did not choose to deploy international negotiators. The Shia Alliance position during the final days of the Shia-Kurd negotiations was subject to radical changes and reversals, frequently wavering on the basic terms of federalism, petroleum management, and the constitutional status of Shia clergy. Somewhat surprisingly, no Shia party tabled a ready-made draft constitution for Iraq. (An earlier, very Islamist draft circulated in early 2005 by the Islamic Dawa Party of Iraq did not arrive at the negotiating table.) Strong factions within the Shia Alliance, however, clearly had resources to use as soon as their strategic interests became clear. In particular on August 11, in the final days of negotiations, the SCIRI leader Abdul Aziz al-Hakim was able to mobilize the well-organized SCIRI base to stage large public demonstrations in Najaf and other southern Iraqi cities in favor of the formation of a southern federal unit, a move which even the Kurds declared to be surprising. Anecdotal evidence suggests also that the government of Iran was channelling financial and in-kind support to SCIRI's position.

The Sunni Arab negotiators, though not without institutional affiliation and support, lacked the ability to rally constituents and resources around a coherent constitutional strategy. Iraq's Arab neighbours have little practical experience with constitutional matters and were of little practical help. Indeed, at least until August there was no clear Sunni Arab constitutional position of any sort. Again, Sunni Arab competence, negotiating mandates, and ability to organize their constituents could have coalesced with adequate time, but time was the resource least available to them.

This capacity imbalance further isolated and radicalized Sunni Arab positions. A definitive Sunni Arab denunciation of regional federalism came after, not before, the Committee dissolution. As the July and August discussions progressed, it became increasingly commonplace for Iraqi leaders to identify themselves and act according to ethnic and sectarian politics. The Sunni Arab participants, who typically saw themselves as nationalists, were not well versed in these practices and did not succeed in pressing a coherent constitutional position. As with any negotiation, all parties were likely disadvantaged by the relative lack of competency of one of the parties. Under these circumstances, it was always much more likely that Sunni Arab negotiators would quickly move away from the negotiating table and revert to a strategy hinging on threats of non-participation and opposition to the referendum.

Lack of International Mediation

The compressed time frame also forestalled the United Nations and independent international constitutional experts from mediating between the parties to the negotiations as well as providing options and alternatives for bridging factional divides.

Nicholas Haysom, who led the constitutional support team of the United Nations Assistance Mission in Iraq (UNAMI), arrived in Baghdad in May to begin the task of supporting the Constitutional Committee. UN Headquarters had been slow in starting to discharge its mandate under Security Council Resolution 1546, waiting to formalize its role with the Transitional Iraq Government, and taking time to assemble its constitutional team. As in East Timor and Afghanistan, the United Nations in Iraq suffered from the lack of a ready roster of experts for rapid deployment to the field in support of post-conflict constitution making.

The Iraqi Government did not issue a formal invitation to the United Nations until early June. Further, Sheikh Hamoudi was clearly sceptical of the value and propriety of any international involvement, however enlightened and unobtrusive, in the Iraq constitution. Even before this invitation had been issued, Haysom, a veteran of the South African constitutional negotiations, was working behind the scenes to help the Committee incorporate Sunni Arabs as members. He developed a consensus model of decision-making that would avoid the question of whether Sunni Arab appointees would have full voting rights. He later worked with the Committee in designing the arrangement of thematic and technical subcommittees. He also helped develop federal models that might be sufficiently flexible as to allow for future federal units, and to balance regional and national interests in natural resources. A paper he circulated on August 10 entitled, "A Framework for Decentralised Government in Iraq," was particularly influential in setting out a scheme of exclusive federal powers, a mechanism for the creation of new federal units and joint federal/regional oil management.

International experts brought to Iraq by the United Nations and USIP, including constitutionalist Professor Yash Ghai, worked directly with Sheikh Hamoudi from early June. They gave particular attention to the Sunni Arab Committee members, spending much time illustrating the value of federalism in multi-ethnic states. Specifically, Professor Ghai referred extensively to comparative constitutional models, explaining that federalism, far from precipitating the break-up of the state, in fact might hold Iraq together. "Iraq does not face a choice between unitary or federal/autonomous system," he advised, "but between federalism/autonomy and bitter civil war (and ultimately no Iraq)." During this time, Committee members paid a great deal of attention to the Spanish constitution. More than any other model, the Spanish constitution provided the conceptual basis for the gradual federalism negotiated in the final Iraq text.

These important colloquies with Sunni Arabs were broken, however, when the Committee dissolved in August. Where Haysom had quite properly formalized a role for UNAMI with the Committee, from August 8 that role became unclear and informal. Haysom and other UN officials were sometimes called on to speak to the party leaders and serve secretarial functions. The UN officials worked especially hard with Saleh Mutlaq of the National Dialogue Council, who had emerged as the leading Sunni Arab negotiator, to reconcile his views with those of the Kurdish and Shia leadership. By this stage, however, there was no longer a negotiating table to which the UN had a standing invitation. The UN's position was considerably weakened, especially by U.S. intervention in the negotiations. The UN position in the "kitchen" was never clarified or assured.

Increased U.S. Visibility

The compressed timetable allowed, and probably required, a much heavier and more visible involvement of U.S. officials at the negotiations than would otherwise have been the case. The visible involvement of a foreign power in something so uniquely sovereign as the writing of a constitution is probably always regrettable. Especially with Iraq, even moderate Sunni Arab nationalists would frequently express the fear that the Iraq constitution would be written in Washington, DC and, as one Baghdad University political science professor put it, only half-joking, "dropped from a helicopter onto Baghdad." Prior to August 8, the U.S. Embassy had kept some distance from the Committee, referring to the need for the Iraqi constitution to be settled with Iraqi, not American, solutions. It was apparently not possible, however, to maintain this distance and at the same time to insist, as a matter of U.S. policy, that the August 15 deadline be met. From the time the Leadership Council was formed, U.S. Ambassador Zalmay Khalilzad attended meetings regularly, and U.S. Embassy officials were engaged in less than subtle efforts to accelerate a final constitution. Several of the early meetings of the Leadership Council took place at the US Embassy. By August 10, the United States was strongly expressing its views on substantive constitutional issues to reach fast compromises that resembled the terms of the TAL. For example, the United States clearly favored an entirely centralized petroleum sector even where the UNAMI had, in its August 10 paper, identified shared regional and central control as the only way of reaching a compromise.

On August 12, in efforts to accelerate the drafting process, the U.S. Embassy circulated its own draft constitution in English. This took the form of a "track changes" version proposing amendments to the Committee's draft text, offering extensive U.S. views on the terms of federalism, the judiciary, human rights protections, de-Ba'athification, and other matters. It is somewhat ironic that the U.S. Government, having encouraged an early Shia-Kurd deal to the exclusion of Sunni Arabs, expended a great deal of effort in the final days of negotiations urging a speedy settlement of outstanding issues by pressing the Shia parties to accommodate Sunni Arab concerns. This effort included a telephone call from President Bush to SCIRI leader Abdul Aziz Al-Hakim on August 25. The American press and in the Baghdad-based *Al Sabah* newspaper reported this telephone call, raising the U.S. profile in Iraq to a point that might confirm Sunni Arab suspicions the constitution would be a U.S. product—without any observable softening of the SCIRI position. Ambassador Khalilzad took the unusual step of attending the meeting of the National Assembly on August 15 where the Assembly leadership moved for a seven-day extension, and again on August 22 when a further extension was sought. Domestic Iraqi television channels broadcasted his attendance in the Assembly, predictably attracting criticism from Iraqi nationalists and sections of the Arab media.

Charges of National Assembly Illegality

Finally, and perhaps most obviously, the unrealistic decision on August 1 not to extend the timetable beyond August 15 using Article 61(F) led to a series of ad hoc decisions by the Assembly after the deadline was missed on August 15. This exposed the Assembly to charges that it was operating illegally. Sections 61(E) and (G) of the TAL treat the eventuality of a missed August 15 deadline in the same way as a failed referendum. In both cases the TAL prescribes that, "the National Assembly shall be dissolved. Elections for a new National Assembly shall be held no later than 15 December 2005." Had the Assembly behaved lawfully, so the argument goes, it should have automatically dissolved and the Government would plan for new elections.

The precise nature of the Assembly's proceedings on the evening of August 15 are unclear; though, it seems arguable that the Assembly, by a show of hands that exceeded the necessary 75 percent majority, amended the TAL to change the deadline to August 22. In doing so, it seems that the Assembly acted lawfully, albeit in a way that the TAL drafters may have thought eccentric. It is less clear, however, if the Speaker's August 22 announcement stating three additional days were needed, or the August 25 press conference announcing that still more time was needed, conformed either with the letter or the spirit of the TAL. It seems that after August 15, the Assembly did not make any formal amendment of the TAL deadline; after August 1, formal amendment of the TAL deadline was the only legal mechanism by which to avoid the mandatory provisions of clauses 61(E) and (G). The Leadership Council was clearly unwilling to submit a series of rolling amendments of the TAL deadline to the Assembly, in circumstances where the negotiating text of the constitution was being withheld even from Assembly members.

Indeed, the Iraqi constitutional process was remarkable in the way in which the Assembly, though legally charged with responsibility for writing the draft, was not involved. Rank and file National Assembly members had no access to constitutional drafts from August 8 to August 22. The Assembly leadership denied requests by Assembly members to address constitutional issues on the floor. For their part, the U.S. and UK embassies had always been somewhat vague as to the legal consequences of a failure to meet the August 15 deadline, being unwilling to strategize around the probable scenario that the deadline would not be met. In any event, criticisms from the Sunni Arab community and elsewhere stating that the Assembly acted contrary to the interim constitution continued, and added some force to claims that the current Assembly, and the document it later produced, lack legitimacy. It is likely, of course, that had the United States allowed the Assembly to adopt a more realistic deadline—a deadline which the Assembly could reasonably meet—the Assembly would not be exposed to these claims.

Exclusion of Civil Society: Women, Minorities, and the Center

The breakdown of the process also worked against the interests of women, Iraqi ethnic, and religious minorities other than Sunni Kurds, as well as liberal and centrist political interests. From the time of the occupation, the continued rise of sectarian and ethnic political parties fragmented and marginalized these groups. It is doubtful whether any constitutional process would have delivered them the constitutional recognition which they sought, including strong statements of equality and human rights protections that were contested by the Shia Muslim religious conservatives, now clearly in the ascendancy. Smaller segments in Iraqi society had not had the chance to group together under strong civil society institutions.

Forgone Civil Society Influence

For that reason, some of the most promising initiatives in the post-election period came from civil society leaders who wanted to form umbrella organizations to represent civil society in constitutional discussions. From a centrist, more secular perspective, Dr. Ghassan Al-Atiyyah of the Iraq Foundation for Development and Democracy developed a proposal for an

Independent Constitution Commission (ICC). The stated purpose of the ICC would be to work alongside the "official" Constitution Committee, and to "bombard" it with civil society constitutional views—under the oversight of a board composed of senior political party members. The ICC membership would consist of a large number of the Iraqi nongovernmental organizations (NGOs) who were active in canvassing popular views on the constitution through 2005.

Similarly, the Thaqalayn Research Institute, an independent-minded, Shia religious NGO, started up a "Civil Constitutional Forum" of NGOs working on the constitution under the leadership of Dr. Sallama al-Khafaji and Sheikh Fateh al-Ghitta. The Forum was designed to educate religious Shia communities on the value of constitutionalism, the separation between church and state, and to bring consolidated civil society views to the Constitution Committee. Both the Iraq Foundation for Development and Democracy and the Thaqalayn Research Institute were, in the end, able to play a role in bringing civil society views to the Constitution Committee. Neither organisation, however, was able to realize its goal of creating the institutions necessary to strengthen civil society's influence on the draft. Both Ghassan Al-Atiyyah and Sheikh Fateh al-Ghitta pointed to the lack of time as the primary reason for failure.

Women's Groups Ignored

The truncated timeframe problem also affected women's groups. At meetings of women's groups in late July, many participants identified the unmet need for a greater level of coordination if they were to successfully represent women's views to the Constitution Committee, for instance proposing the creation of an Iraqi women's "Coordination Committee" to manage this relationship. Again, it was clear that lack of time was the major constraint. Hanaa Edwar, leader of one very active women's group the Iraqi Womens' Network, recounts her meeting with the Constitution Committee in late July: "We've expressed our worry about very short time behind the drafting committee to accomplish it's work in a close doors. We're still demanding for prolonging the dead line of writing the constitution in order to get the chance for Iraqi people to be involved actively in this very serious process. This will enhance peaceful dialogue and bridge trust on national reconciliation among all Iraqi society constituencies." Women's groups were particularly concerned at provisions in the draft that would apparently erode the secular basis of Iraqi family law.

Committee Participation

The Constitution Committee itself represented a way of partially correcting the lack of minority and women's participation. Some care had been taken by the Kurdish and Shia blocs to ensure that women were represented on the Constitution Committee—with a total of nine—as well as representatives of the Assyrian, Shabak, and Yazidi communities. One of the Committee members, Hunain Al-Qaddo, was also serving as Chairman of the Council of Iraqi Minorities, a body formally established on July 2, 2005, by eight ethnic minority groups to advocate their concerns in the constitutional discussions. One of the Deputy Chairmen of the Committee Adnan Al-Janabi was a representative of the centrist party of Ayad Allawi.

The demise of the Committee on August 8 dramatically reduced the ability of these groups to participate in negotiations. The ad hoc Leadership Council meetings included no women and no non-Kurdish minorities. Centrist party representatives, when they attended, played a minor role, having moved closer to a Sunni Arab scepticism. As a result, the constitutional provisions that these groups were seeking in the text were frequently removed from the Committee text, diluted, or modified in ways that bore little relationship to the views of the groups concerned. For example, the Council of Iraqi Minorities had been seeking a provision that would recognize several of Iraq's many ethnic and religious minorities by name. Such a provision was included in Article 3 of the Committee draft: "The Iraqi people is comprised of two major nationalities, Arabs and Kurds, and from basic nationalities: the Turkmen, the Chaldeans, the Assyrians, the Syriacs, the Armenians, the Shabak, the Yazidis, and the Mandean Sabeans, all of whom are equal in rights and citizenship obligations." This provision was removed from the draft after August 8 without consultation with the Council of Minorities or individual minority groups, and was replaced by different minorities language that does not, for instance, explicitly recognize the Shabak or Armenians.

Civil Society Need for International Support

The removal of the drafting responsibility from the Committee resulted in smaller groups, including Iraq's ethnic and religious minorities, turning immediately to international institutions for lobbying support and patronage, where previously they had been able to access Iraqi members of the Committee directly. Hoping to influence the draft after August 8, these groups had an incentive to seek the backing of the U.S. Embassy, and to a lesser extent the United Nations, since there were no longer accessible or sympathetic Iraqis close to the drafting action. The United States and the United Nations clearly welcomed this role. For instance the UN Special Representative, Ambassador Ashraf Ghazi, defined his own role as that of the protector of human rights and minority rights in the constitution. The press releases he issued in August reveal a series of meetings with Iraqi supplicants looking for UN help where apparently none was available elsewhere.

It is far from clear that the adopted roles of the United States and UNAMI as a human rights lobbyists were successful. There is no doubt that some of these Iraqi actors found the meetings with the U.S. Embassy and United Nations to be useful, if only so that they could determine the status of the latest drafts of the constitution. By August, it became very difficult even for participants to the negotiations to follow the drafting work, with at times two or even three different drafts being circulated by different negotiators as the "latest draft." Competing "authoritative" texts were variously held by Dr. Hajim Al-Hassani, the Speaker of the Assembly, Sheikh Humam Hamoudi, the U.S. Embassy, and the United Nations. Although on two occasions these drafts were leaked to the Iraqi press, none of these successive drafts were officially released to the Iraqi public for comment. Very few, if any, were released to members of the Constitution Committee or to the National Assembly.

United States and Civil Society Patronage

This absence of drafting and consultation protocols made it extremely difficult for non-expert Iraqis to follow the process. However, this background of confusion and the desire for patronage by smaller Iraqi interests led, in turn, to the U.S. Embassy gaining still greater public involvement in Iraqi constitutional politics. The Embassy also became the most obvious agent for a range of international lobbying and advocacy institutions based outside Iraq, including the U.S. Commission for International Religious Freedom, Freedom House, and a range of U.S.-based Iraqi expatriate and women's groups. Regardless of the value of these efforts to improve the constitution, the time pressure increased the likelihood that Iraqis would see foreigners as dominating their constitutional process, minimizing popular legitimacy of the text.

The Committee, Secretariat: Engaging the Iraqi Public

If relatively well-organized and well-connected women's and minority groups found it difficult to interact with the constitutional drafters, these difficulties were greater for ordinary Iraqi citizens. Every meeting of the Constitution Committee, the National Assembly, and the Leadership Council took place behind the blast walls, barbed wire, and gun turrets of Baghdad's International Zone. Iraqi citizens could gain entry to the International Zone only after time consuming and dangerous queuing and multiple body searches. The opportunity for Iraqis to communicate, either formally or informally, with their constituent representatives was practically nil. In one sense, the national dialogue and debate on constitutional matters were widespread, covered extensively in Iraqi media. However, notwithstanding the enormous efforts of the Committee staff, very little of this dialogue was formally presented to the Constitution Committee in time for it to influence the constitutional text.

Creation of the Outreach Unit

In early June, Chairman Sheikh Hamoudi established under the management of Dr. Adnan Ali, a skeleton Secretariat for the Constitution Committee. The Secretariat was to include an Outreach Unit, responsible for disseminating constitutional information to the public, and for receiving and analyzing the public response. The Outreach Unit structure and mandate were prepared with the assistance of UN and USIP experts, including Scott Carlson, who advised the successful Albanian Constitutional Commission.

There was great difficulty in starting the Outreach Unit, however. Prior to June, neither the United States nor the United Nations had taken steps to prepare office space for the Committee Secretariat. As a result, it was working in an ad hoc fashion out of a cramped space in the Convention Center through late July. Several weeks were lost in recruiting the Iraqi staff. At the end of July, the Outreach Unit issued a constitutional questionnaire with seven questions in total, which were designed to be disseminated throughout the country, and returned to the Outreach Unit for entry into a computer database. The UN, NDI, and USIP each provided practical support to the Outreach Unit, including funding and staffing. By late July, USIP visited the newly established Outreach Unit offices in downtown Baghdad. A staff of fifty was working around the clock in precarious security conditions to enter piles of public submissions into a computerized database and to prepare a report to the Committee.

Constraints: Time, Resources, and Security

Despite the professionalism and bravery of the Outreach Unit staff, the shortcomings of the process were striking. From its inception in early June, the Outreach Unit had no more than eight weeks to complete its work. The attempt to conduct a serious national constitutional dialogue in such a short space of time was probably unprecedented. By way of comparison, East Timorese and Afghan constitutional processes, widely regarded as overly hasty, took around six and fifteen months respectively. The effort in Iraq was all the more remarkable given the poor and deteriorating security situation, and the nationwide difficulties in delivering basic government services, including power and water. Therefore, it is not surprising that public participation did not work well.

In particular, there was no period of public education on constitutional issues, so that non-elite Iraqis had little chance to understand even the simple questionnaire. The Outreach Unit had no clear ability to receive substantial input from Sunni Arab and Kurdish regions of Iraq, arguably the most important in building true constitutional legitimacy. On July 28, the Outreach Unit had received only 20,300 submissions. On August 10, the Outreach Unit had received 126,000 submissions, with none from Kurdistan or the Sunni Arab regions. As of August 15, it had received around 150,000 submissions, of which only around 20,000 had been received from the Kurdistan Region and only around 10,000 from Sunni Arab regions—indeed, all 10,000 were from Fallujah.

Largely because of the SCIRI Chairmanship of the Committee, the staff of the Outreach Unit were drawn mainly from religious Shia social networks, and the networks put in place to receive submissions were biased towards Shia areas of Baghdad and other cities. It is unclear whether there were any Sunni Arabs on the Outreach Unit staff, though in early August the Unit did recruit some Iraqis from the smaller ethnic and religious minorities. Submission boxes were distributed by the Outreach Unit in government buildings in Baghdad to allow citizens to lodge completed questionnaires and written submissions for later collection by the Outreach Unit; however, the distribution of these boxes was uneven at best. There was no ability to enter non-questionnaire submissions into the database, obviously limiting the range of views that the public could express on constitutional issues. The results of the extensive constitutional awareness programs run throughout Iraq by international organisations, including NDI and IRI, either were not presented to the Outreach Unit, or were presented too late for those results to have an impact on the draft, or to strengthen the Outreach Unit's own analysis.

Little Review of Public Input

Most importantly, perhaps, the Outreach Unit did not have the ability to circulate a report to the Committee members before August 13. Interviews conducted with various Committee members in early August confirmed that they had not received reports from the Outreach Unit. This was hardly surprising given the time constraints. This meant that there was little or no chance for the views of the public, as expressed to the Committee, to be taken into account in the preparation of the constitution. By August 13, a mature negotiating draft had existed for some time with no political will within the political blocs to reopen settled agreements within that draft. In very precise terms, then, the National Assembly failed to meet the obligation imposed by Article 60 of the TAL of "receiving proposals from the citizens of Iraq as it writes the constitution."

Inadequate Public Outreach

In summary, the activities of the Outreach Unit further suggest that the finalization of Iraq's constitution was premature, and that another opportunity was lost. It was not until late July that the Outreach Unit was fully operational, with a multi-ethnic staff and adequate equipment, security, and reporting protocols. Had the process allowed them even just a few more weeks, the Committee might have been in position to take the views of the public, and in particular the views of Sunni Arabs, into account; and might have been *seen* to take them into account. Indeed, there is a danger that a widely advertised, but ultimately unsuccessful, constitutional participation campaign may have marginally worsened conditions in Iraq. Iraqis expected that their views would be taken into account, but clearly saw that they were not.

It is unlikely that a properly conducted public participation campaign in Iraq would, on its own, have bridged the large constitutional divides that now confront Iraq following the referendum. Public participation typically does, however, have the effect of moderating constitutional views, both in the general public and among the drafting elites. From NDI focus groups conducted in April 2005, it was clear that Iraqi citizens had not withdrawn their demands for transparency and participation in constitutional matters. The fact that these demands were not met almost certainly affected, in particular, Sunni Arab perceptions of the final constitution. Had the Iraqi Government and the international community worked harder and longer with Sunni Arab groups on issues surrounding federalism, and had Sunni Arabs been given a chance to express to the Constitution Committee their unmediated, individual views on constitutional issues, the results would almost certainly have been encouraging, perhaps surprisingly so.

Conclusions: The Referendum and Iraq's Constitutional Future

The merits and demerits of the constitutional text that resulted from this Iraqi process have been the subject of extensive Western press, academic, and policy commentary, particularly in respect of the provisions of the text which favor, or are seen to favor, the new conservative Shia establishment. The fact that the constitution also contemplates a fairly weak central government has also attracted much commentary and criticism. The arrival of this draft will no doubt encourage continued international policy discussions that revolve around competing conceptions of consociation and integration. Some commentators, including the International Crisis Group, catalogue the ambiguity of certain constitutional provisions, seeing in the ambiguity the "seeds of future discord." Others, including Professor Yash Ghai, have serious reservations as to "whether the constitution as it stands can be fully and effectively implemented without grave danger to state and society."

These criticisms have force; however, this constitutional text will be difficult to change. Given the mutually intersecting interests that now characterize Iraqi politics, it seems the major Shia and Kurdish political blocs will willingly revise very little in this constitutional text. Despite the very serious problems of constitutional process that have accompanied this text, the constitution as written may represent a reasonable approximation of a workable constitution for Iraq. It is certainly not the comprehensive constitutional document that some may have wanted, and given the Sunni Arab rejection of the text at the referendum, it probably does not satisfy even the modest goal for an Iraqi constitution-as-treaty. By way of comparison, however, the TAL was hardly more detailed. It is difficult to imagine a very different constitutional text for an Iraq which is already highly regionalized and in which, for better or worse, the majority of the citizens see a role for Islam in public decision-making. Like any treaty text, most of the ambiguities in the draft constitution are neither casual oversights nor the result of deliberate evasiveness. The text is silent because the parties could not agree. Significantly, it is difficult to see any substantive change to the text that would guarantee Sunni Arab support, and indeed the support of all women, secularists, and ethnic and religious minorities.

In the case of Iraq, it may be that it is the process, more than the substance, which has created the current predicament. The recent Iraqi constitutional experience illustrates all too clearly the practical importance of the distinction, usually made by comparative constitutional specialists and academics, between constitutional substance and constitutional process. It would be difficult to describe the process by which that text ultimately emerged from the National Assembly as meeting either the expectations of Iraqis, international standards, or the TAL itself. Specifically, it has been the dynamics of Sunni Arab opposition, more than mutually conflicting constitutional arguments, which has created Iraq's constitutional crisis. Even allowing for some intransigence on the part of Sunni Arab negotiators, the fact remains that Iraq's constitutional process was seen, with some justification, as an insult to Sunni Arab Iraqis.

Those familiar with recent post-conflict constitution-making processes, including East Timor and Afghanistan, are all too aware of the price—paid in stability, legitimacy, and the rule of law—when constitutional discussions are rushed. Unfortunately for Iraq, the consequences of a rushed constitutional process will not simply manifest themselves, as in so many other countries, by misunderstandings or legitimacy deficits in the medium- to long-term. Because of the peculiarly violent scene in contemporary Iraq and the polarization around the October constitutional referendum, it is reasonable to speculate that the deficiencies in constitutional process are already having an immediate and violent effect on the lives of Iraqis.

It was a mistake on the part of some in the Iraqi leadership and the U.S. Government, to insist on an adherence to the August 15 deadline. The constitutional discussions began much later than the framers of the TAL envisaged. The terms of the TAL itself clearly foresaw the possible need for a six-month extension. The pressure-cooker approach that the United States adopted may conceivably have been effective if the central problem was that Iraqi parliamentarians were simply being slow in moving to consolidate their Iraqi identity and shared vision of government in constitutional terms.

The problem, however, was more profound. Iraqi constitution-making always required a complex three-way negotiation in circumstances where nothing—not even a residual shared Iraqi identity—could be taken for granted. Conventional wisdom presented Iraq as a centralized state undergoing a form of decentralization, when the reality was almost diametrically opposite. Regional powers were, in effect, negotiating the terms of a possible delegation of powers to the center. The three major negotiating blocs—Shia Arab, Kurd, and Sunni Arab—derived their authority from de facto regional interests, and the power of central government during the negotiating phase was marginal at best. For each of the three major blocs, the attractions of a constitution were not necessarily greater than living with no constitution at all, a fact which made the process even more delicate. The complexity of the negotiations and the backdrop of increasingly sectarian violence in Iraq meant that the meetings increasingly resembled peace talks, where peace was clearly elusive. The insurgency timed its mortar and car bomb attacks in Baghdad to coincide with National Assembly sessions. It was probably no coincidence either that the final stages of the negotiations were interrupted by violent intra-Shia clashes between loyalists to the Iranian-backed SCIRI and the nationalist followers of Moqtada al-Sadr.

Sadly, there is no obvious policy solution to Iraq's constitutional predicament. The challenge is no longer the building of governmental and institutional legitimacy so much as it is a challenge of conflict management. The finalization of the constitution coincided with a statement plausibly attributed to insurgent leader Musab al-Zarqawi that he had "declared war against all Shiites in Iraq," and with a significant rise in Sunni-Shia violence. We should confront the reality that Sunni Arab opposition to the constitution that emerged during the negotiations will continue, and that a national "yes" vote may have consolidated Sunni Arab isolation and moved Sunni Arabs still further towards an unrealistic insistence on a centralised state. This leaves only a medium- to long-term hope that Sunni Arab moderates might learn to embrace their federal constitution, and that in the meantime Shia and Kurdish political leaders might implement the constitution in a way that does not work to Sunni Arabs' disadvantage.

Efforts to bridge the Sunni-Shia divide by tinkering with the constitutional text are unlikely to be fruitful, and a pre-referendum agreement to consider amending the text after the December 2005 election may well prove to be hollow. It is not clear that a constitutional consensus could be attained that is different from the terms of the current constitutional draft. In particular, there is no evidence from the Kurdish or Shia camps that new electoral politics would soften their core demands that apparently cause so much offense in Sunni Arab Iraq. Even with active Sunni Arab participation in a new election, Shia and Kurdish factions will likely still command a large enough majority in a new National Assembly to force through their positions. Additional time for constitutional negotiations would have been useful before the current draft hardened Sunni Arab positions; but now, the prospect of continued "reaching out" to Sunni Arabs and continued constitutional negotiations is a fairly arid one. The fact is that Sunni Arabs' alienation has been amplified by procedural problems in July and August. The damage has already been done; continued constitutional negotiations will simply confirm the existing divisions. This has been shown already in the continued eleventh hour negotiations in September, which made some minor adjustments to the "final" text, stating that Iraq is "a founding and active member of the Arab League," moderating the language treating the Ba'ath party, confirming the "unity" of Iraq, and adjusting provisions relating to international covenants and water resources. It is apparent from the referendum results that these efforts, however well intentioned, did not significantly mollify Sunni Arab opposition to the text.

Back to the Grass Roots

In the absence of an obvious immediate solution to Iraq's constitutional crisis, what should Iraqis do? How can the international community help? How can Iraqi expectations of constitutionalism possibly be met? The answer may be simply to redouble efforts on the less glamorous, grass-roots work that so many Iraqis —and so many international organizations—have begun. This work includes bringing the political elites in closer contact with their constituents, enlarging the circle of constitutional debate, and finding new ways of cultivating cross-ethnic and cross-sectarian coalitions on constitutional issues and new forms of Iraqi identity.

Certainly there is much technical work to be done in order to resolve the many ambiguities and silences in the constitutional text. Implementing legislation is needed, in particular, to ensure human rights protections, and protocols are needed for inter-governmental relations within the federal system. The central problem remains, however, with Sunni Arab alienation. Working with Sunni Arab elites and local communities to strategize within the terms of an inevitably federal Iraq—including the possible establishment of a new federal region in the Sunni Arab areas of Iraq—may yet pay dividends. Given the heightened levels of inter-communal tension and violence in Iraq, these conversations will increasingly take on the nature of reconciliation talks, and such important initiatives have begun. It is this work which has some chance of producing results in years to come. Out of this work, a nationwide popular commitment to democratic federalism may emerge, not as a reaction to a rushed Kurdish-Shia negotiation, but as a genuine and pragmatic expression of the peoples of Iraq.

Recommendations

- **Public education:** the Iraqi Government, National Assembly, and the international community should make all efforts to educate the Iraqi people, particularly those in the Sunni Arab areas, on the contents of the constitution and the next stages of the transition.
- **International mediation:** the United States, the United Nations, and the international community should support initiatives for reconciliation and understanding among Iraqi communities on constitutional issues.
- **Sunni Arab strategies:** the United States, the United Nations, and the international community should help Sunni Arab communities strategize within a federal framework, and in particular to encourage moderate and progressive Sunni Arabs to consider creating federal units and political alliances with other moderate and progressive Iraqi political forces.
- **UN office of constitutional expertise:** the United Nations should establish a permanent office of constitutional advice and support within the Secretariat, analogous to the Electoral Assistance Division.
- **Constitutional implementation:** the Iraq Government, National Assembly, and the international community should develop a strategy for constitutional implementation that focuses on inter-governmental relations and the enforceability by the Iraqi citizens of their constitutional rights.
- **Non-partisanship:** the international community, in assisting the Iraq Government on constitutional implementation, should not engage in the selection of political favorites, recognizing that any initiative must have broad political support.
- **Equal representation:** the institutional vehicles for constitutional implementation should visibly include Sunni Arabs, women, and members of ethnic and religious minorities.
- **Public views report:** the Outreach Unit of the Constitution Committee needs support in preparing a final report on Iraqi views on the constitution to form part of the public record.
- **Permanent Center for Constitutional Dialogue and Research:** the Iraqi Government, with the support of the international community, should transform the Outreach Unit of the Constitution Committee

into an independent Center for Constitutional Dialogue and Research established by national legislation.

- **Benchmarks:** the Iraqi leadership and the United States should adopt a strategy for Iraq's transition that prioritizes constitutional reconciliation, rule of law, and democracy-building benchmarks instead of adherence to TAL or other timetables.

10

Political Progress in Iraq During the Surge

Rend Al-Rahim Francke

The military surge under way since February 2007 was prompted by the rationale that reducing sectarian violence in and around Baghdad and curtailing insurgency and terrorist attacks would create a breathing space for political and social groups to engage in national reconciliation and agree on common principles and policies. The U.S. administration expected to see a binary relationship emerge between military and political achievement that would lead to stable conditions and permit U.S. troop reduction. Does such a binary relationship exist? Has the expanded military presence with its new operating strategies increased security, reduced sectarian violence, and controlled insurgent and terrorist attacks? If violence has decreased, have government and political forces found a respite to engage in the necessary trust building measures and dialogue for reconciliation? What are Iraq's political prospects as the surge continues?

By the end of summer 2007 the security situation had improved in Baghdad and its environs but still in flux, and the political process lagged far behind the military effort. During this period impassioned debate about Iraq took place in Washington, but it was almost exclusively confined to discussion regarding the timing and pace of U.S. troop withdrawal. Very little, if any, debate concerned the steps necessary to bring about political conditions in Iraq conducive to troop reduction and eventual withdrawal. Although the consensus in Washington is that political stability in Iraq serves the interests of the United States and constitutes the best exit strategy, policymakers in Washington risk losing sight of the political dimension of the relationship between military and political achievement. From now until March 2008, when General Petraeus is due to give his second report to Congress, the United States needs to assess the political situation in Iraq and undertake intensive efforts to promote Iraq's political stability.

Rend Al-Rahim Francke, "Political Progress in Iraq During the Surge," Special Report 196 (Washington, DC: USIP, 2007).

This report is based on conversations held with Iraqis in Iraq in July 2007 and in Beirut, Lebanon, and Amman, Jordan, in October–November 2007. These included Iraqi political leaders and senior government officials, members of Parliament from the major parliamentary groups, as well as a wide range of Iraqi citizens from Baghdad and the provinces. The author met in Baghdad with senior political leaders, notably the president of Iraq, the prime minister, the vice presidents, and several ministers, as well as members of Parliament from the Shia United Iraqi Alliance, the Sunni Tawafuq bloc, and the pan-Iraqi secular Iraqia bloc. In addition, the author spoke with residents of Basra, Najaf, Diwaniya, Anbar, and Salah Eddin governorates. The report is based on personal accounts and exchanges and private and public reports.

Security in Baghdad

By late July 2007, people who live in the city's red zone reported having mixed experiences of the security situation.[1] Residents of some "hot" neighborhoods say that the presence of American troops has a deterrent effect on militias, gangs, and snipers—and thus gives comfort to citizens. They complain that Iraqi forces, including the police, army units, and the Kurdish paramilitary forces called *pesh merga* sent down from Kurdistan, do little to confront troublemakers. For example, some neighborhoods in the Amiriya district have benefited from increased U.S. military presence and patrols, while others, such as Furat and Jihad, are still in conflict because U.S. forces have not intervened. In these places Iraqi police and army do a poor job of stopping violence and intimidation.

A decline in the number of suicide bombings and a decrease in mass sectarian killings and kidnappings in the city are also attributed to the higher U.S. profile. Another factor contributing to a sense of greater safety in Baghdad is the success of U.S.-Iraqi initiatives south of Baghdad (the so-called "Triangle of Death"), where Sunni tribes have recently cooperated with U.S. forces. Residents of some neighborhoods said that for the first time in more than a year they had been able to shop in their area in relative peace and stay out after dark.

Other residents said that the surge had done little to improve security in their area, citing continuing sectarian purges, assassinations, and mortar attacks that afflicted their immediate neighborhoods. They complained that the "clear" operations were not followed by the necessary "hold" operations because the Iraqi army did not have the capacity to hold. The "build"

1. The red zone of Baghdad comprises all the areas of the city outside the green zone (now officially the International Zone), which is a heavily guarded and walled enclave that houses the U.S. and other embassies, the Iraqi Parliament, and senior government officials.

was nowhere in sight.[2] The army is not sufficiently capable, is not motivated, is afraid, or is simply not there. Residents of Baghdad regard the Iraqi police with extreme suspicion; two Sunnis, one a government official and the other a citizen, said that the Ministry of the Interior should be disbanded and rebuilt.

Many Baghdadis interviewed in July felt that the security situation was marginally better than it had been at the beginning of the year, but they believed the gains were precarious and fragile. Many complained that when U.S. forces cleared an area and handed it over to Iraqi forces to hold, the neighborhood returned to lawlessness. Snipers have emerged as a relatively new and deadly danger in residential neighborhoods. Sniper murders are especially unnerving to residents because although they look targeted, they may in fact be random. Because of fear of snipers, residents of some neighborhoods (particularly women) have had to give up their jobs and stay at home.

But Baghdad is full of anomalies. A predominantly Sunni area in the northeast has a sizable Shia population, and the two communities continue to live peacefully, albeit under the protection of an "enlightened" group of the Mahdi Army militia. The militia not only provides the residents (Sunni and Shia) with protection but also mans checkpoints and controls entry into the neighborhood, distributes gas and kerosene, regulates the supply of electricity from private generators, and offers other services to the population. Zayyuna, an upper-middle-class neighborhood that houses many former Iraqi army officers, is still mixed and peaceful. Al-Atayfiya is a predominantly Shia area with a sizable Sunni population. It has stayed quiet in the shadow of the influential Baratha mosque and under the wing of the mosque's powerful imam, Sheikh Jalal Eddin Al-Saghir, who is also Member of Parliament for the Islamic Supreme Council of Iraq (ISCI, formerly SCIRI). The militia that protects the mosque also protects the area's inhabitants, both Sunni and Shia.

The reality of Sunni-Shia fighting that Baghdad and other mixed areas witnessed in 2006–07 is far murkier than Western press reports convey. Sectarian fighting is not restricted to politically motivated militias, and labeling perpetrators of violence as either "Sunni terrorists or insurgents" or "Jaish al-Mahdi" militias oversimplifies and masks the complex facts on the ground. The lawless conditions originally triggered by terrorist attacks (presumed to be Sunni), counterattacks by militias (presumed to be Shia), and the impotence of Iraqi security forces in effect paved the way to other forms of violence cloaked in sectarian garb.

---

2. "Clear, hold, and build" is a policy articulated by Secretary of State Condoleezza Rice in her remarks before the Senate Foreign Relations Committee on October 19, 2005. See www.state.gov/secretary/rm/2005/55303.htm. "Clear" refers to clearing areas of terrorists and insurgents; "hold" refers to sustaining control over cleared areas; and "build" refers to the reconstruction and economic revival of cleared and held areas.

Violence in neighborhoods now includes family vendettas avenging former murders and assassinations or revenge killing of former Baathists accused of criminality under the previous regime. The skein of violence is further tangled by the proliferation of gangs that are mini-mafias masquerading as sectarian or political militias. These are actually only interested in profit, and they engage in the lucrative trade of killing or evicting residents, looting their homes, and renting the houses to new residents. In the absence of law enforcement, the competition among rival mafias expands the range of targeted violence.

To the distress of the Sunnis Baghdad is increasingly a Shia city, either because Sunnis are being pushed out or are choosing to leave. The geographic area of the capital in which Sunnis are now a majority and feel safe is shrinking. For example, Sunni parts of Saydiya, a fierce battleground between Sunni and Shia militias, are now Shia-controlled. Shia political parties and militias have taken over large sections of the city. Although this control reduces sectarian killing, it is a source of extreme anxiety to Sunni political groups, who fear above all the loss of the capital.

In the past year Sunnis who left Baghdad increasingly were escaping to Jordan rather than moving to safer Sunni areas of Iraq. Their exodus is causing consternation to the leaders of the community, who see their numbers, political position, and leverage shrinking. A major Sunni demand now is not only to halt sectarian cleansing, but also to create the conditions in which refugees and displaced persons can return to their original homes and restore the former sectarian composition of the city.

In addition to increased U.S.-Iraqi troop presence in the capital's neighborhoods, two further developments have contributed to improvement in security. First the sectarian battles in many areas have been settled in favor of one side or another (usually the Shia militias), providing a respite in some districts after eighteen months of fighting. Second the military operations around the Baghdad periphery to the south, in Mahmudiya and Yousifiya, and in the north (Diyala) and west (Anbar) have helped curtail the activities of insurgents and terrorists.

Terrorists being squeezed in these peripheral areas apparently are moving to Kirkuk, and the incidence of suicide and car bombings in that governorate has risen dramatically. Iraqi government officials are concerned that Mosul (Naynawah governorate), so far relatively quiet, may be the next frontier for terrorists. In any event, increased security in the capital has been bought at a high price. Neighborhoods are less mixed, although reports of complete sectarian homogeneity in neighborhoods are exaggerated. Moving between neighborhoods is more difficult because of barriers and checkpoints. Where U.S. and Iraqi forces are not present, militias of one stripe or another exercise control. Even where physical barriers are not evident, Baghdadis think of neighborhoods somewhat as cantonments.

Iraqi security officials are optimistic that security will improve, and they believe that the surge has already shown results. During meetings in July, a senior Iraqi official affirmed that of the 446 neighborhoods in Baghdad only 5 percent were classified as "insecure" in June, compared to 10 percent earlier in the year. Iraqi officials also cite the increased competence, readiness, and intelligence capacities of Iraqi military forces, which have led in recent months to the foiling of terrorist attacks and the capture of terrorists. In July, both Iraqi officials and citizens expressed their belief that the surge, including the increased U.S. troop deployment in neighborhoods and the establishment of the Provincial Reconstruction Teams (PRTs), required more time to be fully effective.

In a statement that many respondents considered unfortunate, the Iraqi PM declared on July 14, 2007, that the Iraqi forces were ready and able to assume responsibility for the security of the country.[3] This was patently unrealistic, as Maliki aides acknowledged, and even Maliki himself had to backtrack. It is doubtful whether Iraqi forces on their own can professionally and competently maintain the security of the International Zone (IZ), formerly the green zone.

In late October 2007, Iraqis who spoke with the author in Beirut and Amman confirmed that the security in Baghdad had improved significantly. Neighborhoods that had been shuttered re-opened for business, circulation within and across neighborhoods was easier and safer, and there was a new sense of confidence that the security crisis and the sectarian fighting were under control. However, most of them were concerned about the sustainability of this improvement, and the Sunnis still felt vulnerable in Baghdad and worried about the changed demographics of the capital. Meanwhile, Iraqis from the southern governorates reported that increased tensions between rival militias presented security risks for the population and affected the delivery of services and economic recovery.

Many Iraqis do not want to see U.S. forces leave anytime soon. Harith Al-Dhari, the radical Sunni leader of the Association of Muslim Scholars, declared on July 17 that the association did not favor an immediate and precipitate withdrawal but only wanted a schedule. The Sadris, the one Shia group that had been vocal against the American presence, have moderated their position. In private conversations, moderate Sadri parliamentarians have strongly opposed any troop drawdown in the near future. Even publicly Muqtada Al-Sadr (following his long and mysterious absence in spring 2007) declared that his movement wanted a gradual troop drawdown linked to the increasing capacity of Iraqi forces. Although in April 2007 the Sadr bloc in Parliament launched a petition calling for the United States to schedule

---

3. Richard A. Oppel Jr., "Iraq Chief Says His Forces Are Able to Secure Country," *New York Times*, July 15, 2007, www.nytimes.com/2007/07/15/world/middleeast/15iraq.html?_r=1&oref=slogin.

troop withdrawal and obtained the signatures of 144 MPs, the Sadris have not highlighted this issue. Their withdrawal from Parliament in May was not over the presence of U.S. troops but was prompted instead by the second bombing of the shrine in Samarra and the failure of the government to protect it, investigate the bombings, and rebuild it.[4]

National Dialogue and Reconciliation

The gravest problem in Iraq now concerns the power relations between Sunni and Shia political groups. Arab-Kurdish relations, while always sensitive, are on the margin of this central question, at least for the moment. But Sunni, Shia, and Kurdish political leaders have failed to forge a common vision for the state.[5] They have not articulated common national objectives or reached acceptable power-sharing agreements. Any serious effort at national reconciliation must address these fundamental questions. In discussing political progress in Iraq, this report focuses exclusively on Arab-Arab relations in Iraq, and does not address any of the outstanding issues that involve Iraqi Kurds, such as the status of Kirkuk.

The national reconciliation initiative, launched by Prime Minister Maliki in June 2006 as part of his government's program, has been stalled by the lack of political will, conflicting interests, and the absence of thoroughgoing, sustained negotiations. The legislative items in the initiative, such as the de-Baathification law, have languished at different points along the path to approval. Disarming the militias, another pillar of the reconciliation initiative, is unrealistic, given the absence of political will, economic weakness, the absence of Iraqi forces able and willing to confront the militias and fill the security vacuum, and many other factors.

The national reconciliation gatherings held in fall 2006, which included meetings with tribal figures, former army officers, religious leaders, and civil society organizations, were about form rather than substance. These fleeting media events did nothing to address deep-seated fears and distrust regarding sensitive topics such as de-Baathification. The committee charged with reviewing the constitution submitted its work to Parliament in June.

---

4. Edward Wong, "Shiite Cleric Has Six Quit Cabinet in Iraq Shake-Up," *New York Times*, April 17, 2007, www.nytimes.com/2007/04/17/world/middleeast/17iraq.html; Kirk Semple, "Majority of Iraq Lawmakers Seek Timetable of U.S. Exit," *New York Times*, May 12, 2007, www.nytimes.com/2007/05/12/world/middleeast/12iraq.html.

5. The discussion in the CRC regarding the preamble to the constitution reveals the absence of a common national vision among the leaders who drafted the document. The preamble depicts Iraqi society as a collection of ethnic and religious fragments, recounts the history of persecution suffered by each community but primarily by the Kurds and the Shia, gives religious leaders a prominent role in the process of political change, and appeals repeatedly to the (Shia) imams and *marjis* for inspiration. Efforts to change the preamble by eliminating some language were unsuccessful. Only additions to the preamble were accepted and included in the draft sent to Parliament.

By October none of its recommendations had been debated in Parliament, as many of the issues are of a sensitive political nature and the political parties expect the debates to be contentious. A number of constitutional issues, including Article 140 of the Constitution regarding the status of Kirkuk and the powers of the presidency, were left out of the committee's deliberations.[6]

Both Shia and Sunnis recognize that the difficulties in passing the legislative agenda related to national reconciliation, including the laws on de-Baathification and amnesty, are symptoms rather than causes of deeper political divisions among the political groups. Nevertheless, according to a prominent Sunni politician, no real political dialogue has taken place among the political parties in the governing coalition. The Political Council for National Security, composed of nineteen political party leaders and designed to discuss and resolve political and strategic issues, is practically moribund. The Council of Ministers (cabinet) is not a suitable forum for dialogue because ministers are rarely decision makers in their own parties, and the cabinet as a whole does not have authority over political issues. Parliament is too fragmented, indecisive, and fraught with personality clashes, although a committee has formed to follow up on national reconciliation issues. According to members of the Political Council, debate of politically sensitive topics among senior officials is usually superficial and inconclusive. Efforts at serious discussion within the council degenerate into mutual accusations and verbal fights.

A complicating factor for national dialogue among Sunnis and Shia is the growing importance of the Sunni tribes in Anbar, Diyala, and south of Baghdad. As late as October 2007 these tribes were not formally part of the national political process and were not represented by any organized party. Although the government welcomes their efforts at fighting al Qaeda, Shia parties in government perceive them as groups that at best have had strong links to the insurgency and may have been part of Saddam Hussein's Baathist apparatus. Prime Minister Maliki has held talks with these groups, but neither Maliki nor other Shia religious parties have a strategy for dealing with them politically or incorporating them in state institutions.[7]

At the popular level, among the "red zone Iraqis," the squabbles between political parties acquire reality only insofar as they affect their daily lives and physical security. Political disagreements over the appointment of ministers have resulted in poor social services; the rivalry between Shia militias

---

6. The committee's recommendations do not cover the powers of the presidency, the preamble, or Article 140, which deals with Kirkuk, de-Baathification, and other constitutional items.

7. References to Shia parties or Shia politicians refer to the Shia religious groups in Parliament, including ISCI, Dawa, the Sadris, and Fadhila, who in 2005 formed the United Iraqi Alliance bloc. It does not refer to secular Shia who may belong to other groups, such as Iraqia.

in Basra, Karbala, and other cities in the south has cost the lives of scores of civilians. Thus the political turmoil contributes to the suffering and deprivation of Iraqi citizens in very tangible ways, and ordinary people are helpless and feel victimized by politics. They recognize that the power conflicts are playing out at the highest political levels, which they cannot hope to influence, in Baghdad, in the provinces, and with Iraq's neighbors. The reactions of Iraqis from all walks of life to the political stalemate range from bewilderment and incomprehension to anger, condemnation, and suspicions of deep conspiracy.

The Shia Position

Shia leaders face the dilemma of reconciling two opposites. On the one hand they are eager to assert fully their demographic dominance in politics: in this sense, demography *is* democracy. On the other hand they need to engage with the Sunnis to build the state. Shia hard-liners favor what is called the "80 percent option"—that is, a Shia-Kurdish ruling alliance—arguing that such an alliance can run the country without the Sunnis. Even Humam Hammudi, senior MP from ISCI and head of the Constitutional Review Committee, whom many view as a moderate and conciliatory figure, can be hawkish. He did not see the usefulness of reconciliation: "What is there to reconcile? Sunnis are unwilling to acknowledge their minority status and act accordingly."[8] As far as he and many Shia are concerned, democracy entitles the Shia to rule as the majority, and reconciliation is another word for Shia concessions.

Nevertheless, Shia politicians have told the author that they are willing to forgo the rewards of strict democracy by making concessions to the Sunnis (and Kurds) in the interest of national coexistence. Since the formation of the Iraqi Governing Council in 2003, the Shia parties have been willing to accept the principle of consensus in decision making (*ijma* in Islamic jurisprudence) as the necessary counterbalance to democracy; but this has meant giving veto power to the Kurds and Sunnis over certain issues (such as the ratification of he constitution) and renders decision making cumbersome and often impossible. The Shia say they are trying to find a middle ground but claim that the Sunnis do not cooperate and resort to obstructionist tactics such as boycotting parliamentary sessions or cabinet meetings. In practice the 80 percent option is not a real choice at present because of the disarray within the Shia bloc, as described below.

Several Shia leaders complained that the difficulty in talking to the Sunnis stems from Sunni reluctance to understand and accept the new political order: They cannot accept the fact that they are no longer in control and

8. Meeting with the author in Baghdad, July 9, 2007.

that the Shia have the upper hand in the political process. Consequently, willfully or subconsciously, they thwart political progress. The Shia political parties believe that virtually all Sunnis are "hidden" sectarians who support Sunni supremacy, and Sunni demands for a nonsectarian state conceal their desire to restore Sunni power.

At a visceral level Shia leaders affiliated with the religious parties find it hard to disassociate "Sunni" from "Baath," pointing to past oppression by the Baath regime and alleged Sunni support for an insurgency with strong Baathist roots. Therefore the Shia existentially fear the return of the Sunnis, whom they believe will be a vehicle for the return of the Baath. In such a scenario, not only would they lose all their gains, but they would be subjected to renewed persecution. Many Shia suspect a Baathist or terrorist conspiracy to eliminate Shia leadership and cite the assassinations of Sayed Baqir Al-Hakim, Izzeddin Selim, Ali Al-Adhadh, and others as validation of their suspicions.

Along with this fear, in conversations with the author Shia party leaders expressed a sense of entitlement: They believe that after centuries of oppression, it is their turn to rule. Senior leaders in ISCI and Dawa tend to define democracy as the rule of the (demographic) majority—therefore the rule of the Shia. In turn they convey these fears and ambitions in numerous explicit and implicit ways to the Shia population at large. Although these Shia leaders concede that not all Sunnis are Saddamis or Baathis, they maintain that all Sunnis benefited from Saddam's regime.

A contributing factor to Shia anxieties is the reappearance of Baathist groups in Iraq and their revitalization outside Iraq. After a couple of years of silence, Baathis recovered after 2005 and began to form cells around the country, including in southern cities. Baath pamphlets, press releases, and propaganda circulated under new names such as the "Awdah" party (the Return), but eventually explicitly under the Baath banner. To the great fear and distrust of the Shia, a few Sunni members of Parliament have been arguing for legalizing the Baath party and allowing it to reenter the political arena in Iraq.[9]

The Shia in government and Parliament fear the Sunnis they work with every day. They consider them at best tolerators of the insurgency or at worst collaborators with it. In March 2007 Nassir Al-Janabi, an MP from the Sunni Tawafuq, was accused by the government of working with Sunni assassination groups. After initial reluctance, the Tawafuq expelled him from their parliamentary ranks. Janabi is now a fugitive in Syria. Shia officials claim to have evidence incriminating other Sunni leaders in insurgent

---

9. The Baath party has splintered into at least two factions, one led by Izzet al-Douri, reputed to be in Yemen, and another by Younes Ahmed, in Syria. There were efforts in Damascus in summer 2007 to reconcile the two groups. See Maad Fayad, "Return of the Baathists?" *Asharq Alawsat*, February 13, 2007, www.asharq-e.com/news.asp?section=3&id=7990.

activities. Shia asked about this in the summer expressed a widely held view that some prominent Sunni MPs from the Tawafuq bloc in Parliament were associated with insurgent groups such as the Twenties Revolution Brigades and the Army of Muhammad. The government has also accused household staff and guards of Sunni leaders of aiding terrorist groups and possessing illegal weapons. The suicide bomber who detonated himself in Parliament in April 2007, killing Mohammed Awadh, a Sunni MP, allegedly belonged to the retinue of a Sunni parliamentarian. As a result of these fears Shia officials are reluctant to share security information with their Sunni colleagues. Thus when Salam Al-Zawbai, the deputy prime minister, complained that he was not informed of security arrangements and strategies, Ali Al-Adib, a senior MP with the United Iraqi Alliance (UIA) reportedly confirmed his complaint, saying it was only natural since Zawbai could not be trusted with security information.[10]

Members of ISCI and Dawa blame Iraq's neighbors and, more recently, the United States for aiding and abetting Sunni intransigence. In ranking the causes of problems in Iraq, the Shia place the meddling of Arab states at the top of their list. The prime culprits are Saudi Arabia, the United Arab Emirates, Syria, and Jordan. They believe that these countries are relentlessly hostile to Shia rule in Iraq, will go a long way to thwart it, and therefore turn a blind eye to the flow of money, arms, and volunteers to the insurgency. They also accuse Arab neighbors of encouraging Sunni political groups that have joined the political process to harden their positions and hold out for unreasonable demands. According to this interpretation Shia leaders worry that the Tawafuq group is not interested in reconciliation because it expects to gain a larger share of power in Iraq by being intransigent and getting support from Iraq's Arab neighbors.

More recently the same Shia groups have started to blame the United States for what they believe to be excessive support for the Sunnis, thereby encouraging them to adopt unyielding positions. They charge that the United States had made unwarranted concessions to bring Sunnis into the political fold through elections and the constitutional referendum and continues to send signals that it is listening to Sunni demands and yielding to Sunni pressure.

The influence of Saudi Arabia on the United States is a major problem for Shia religious parties, since the United States shares Saudi (and Iraqi Sunni) fears of Iranian interference and could use Sunni empowerment to counter Iran's influence. Thus the Shia religious groups see United States support for Sunni tribes in Anbar, and the prospect of incorporating elements from these tribes into the Iraqi army, through the lens of these fears.

---

10. Ernesto Londono, "For Eminent Sunni, Lessons in Weakness," *Washington Post*, February 10, 2007, www.washingtonpost.com/wp-dyn/content/article/2007/02/09/AR2007020902344.html.

The Shia are concerned that the United States is fostering and backing Sunni militias that can challenge Shia authority and is building an army that may, at a future date, stage a coup against a Shia-dominated government.

At its extreme, this fear becomes a paranoid projection of a U.S. conspiracy to bring Sunni Baathists back to power. Many Shia who spoke to the author, both those active in politics and ordinary citizens, harbor a fear that the U.S. is complicit in trying to restore Sunnis to power. The insistence of the Islamic Supreme Council in Iraq on forming a federated region south of Baghdad may be partly a precautionary measure against a U.S.-assisted restoration of the Sunnis.

The Sunni Position

Sunni concerns are the other side of the same coin. The Sunnis have an existential fear of Shia rule. They cannot accept the reality that they are no longer the ruling elite. In Parliament Adnan Al-Dulaimi, the head of the Tawafuq bloc, accused the Shia of "killing Sunnis everywhere" and demanded that the Shia "respect our existence."[11] Even Sunnis who were not associated with Saddam Hussein's regime or opposed it because they were Islamists, communists, or non-Baath Arab nationalists feel their loss of power as the social elite. Whereas the Shia accuse the Sunnis of hidden sectarianism, the Sunnis accuse the Shia of overt and avowed sectarianism and of using democracy and democratic tools to justify a sectarian agenda.

The Shia political position is straightforward and simple—majority rule using democratic tools—but the Sunni position is ambiguous. Publicly they reject the model of a state built on sectarian quotas, although in a self-contradictory way some Sunnis maintain that they constitute at least half the population of Iraq, if not a majority. Others are resigned to the system of sectarian quotas but want a larger share and role. Despite their misgivings some Sunnis now regard a sectarian quota system as their insurance policy for participating in the state.

The progressive loss of mixed neighborhoods in Baghdad to the Shia is particularly painful to Sunni politicians, clergy, and professionals. Irrespective of demographics, they felt that the capital—not Fallujah or Tikrit, which are provincial backwaters—was their domain. Under Saddam Hussein's rule, the intellectual elite concentrated in Baghdad and relied on the patronage and privileges provided by the Sunni government. In an undeclared class system, Sadr City (established as Revolution City in the late 1950s and changed to Saddam City in the 1970s), Shula, and Shaab, all strongholds of the capital's poor Shia population, were not really part of Baghdad but of the distant slums around the capital.

---

11. "UIA and Tawafuq Exchange Accusations in Parliament of Inciting Sectarianism," *Asharq Alawsat*, November 22, 2006.

The Sunnis fear a Shia hegemony in which they are relegated to second-class status, dependent on what the Shia agree to grant them. With loss of power there would be a loss of resources, less access to jobs, education, and commerce. Sunni parliamentarians claimed that Sunni academics were being assassinated in greater numbers than Shia, that Sunni university professors were being thrown out of their jobs or denied promotion, and that Sunni students were kept out of the top colleges and university programs, even if their academic performance exceeded that of Shia students. Sunni residents of Baghdad continue to complain of the role of Shia militias in the police force and the inherent bias of the police against the Sunnis, while Sunni politicians cite the exclusion of former army officers from service and the denial of financial resources to the Sunni governorates, even for projects approved by the government. In sum Sunnis see a pattern of persistent neglect of Sunni interests and demands by what they characterize as a Shia government and a Shia power elite.

According to the leaders of the Iraqi Islamic Party, the Sunnis want to be full and equal partners in government, not 20 percent junior partners. They argue that they are excluded from policy making and not consulted on major decisions concerning security or foreign policy. They believe that the government of Prime Minister Maliki confines its decision making to a narrow coterie and does not consult with the Sunnis in what is billed as a government of national unity.

The Sunnis have to play a delicate game with a weak hand. They believe their rhetoric has to be harsh to extract concessions from the Shia, and they cling to the armed groups as their defenders. But if they overdo either posture they increase the suspicions of the dominant Shia. They must also show their constituency that they can deliver benefits. Thus Vice President Tariq Al-Hashimi, head of the Iraqi Islamic Party (IIP), often comes across as a hard-liner because he is aware that his constituency is watching him and weighing his accomplishments on their behalf against the achievements of the insurgent groups. The Sunnis find themselves in a dangerous position: an over-reliance on the armed groups makes them hostage to these groups and reduces their credibility with the government (and with the United States). Distancing themselves from the armed groups leaves them exposed and diminishes their credibility within the Sunni community, especially if they do not succeed in delivering protection and benefits to the Sunni population.

Because of their complex position, the Sunni struggle with disagreements in their own camp. Within the Twafuq bloc, members of IIP, the largest component of the parliamentary bloc, privately regard Adnan Duleimi (leader of Ahl Al-Iraq) and Khalaf Al-Ulayan (leader of the Front for National Dialogue), both partners of IIP in Tawafuq, as impediments to Sunni political progress because of their crude political approach and their willingness to act as a cover for insurgent groups. For example, Uleyan has repeatedly threatened to resort to "armed resistance" if Sunni demands are not met.[12] According to Sunnis in Parliament Duleimi has openly declared that he is sectarian. Outside Tawafuq and Parliament, Harith Al-Thari, the head of the Muslim Scholars' Association, represents the radical extreme, and Tawafuq openly accuses him of supporting al Qaeda and extreme factions of the insurgency.[13] To everyone's relief (especially the Sunnis'), he has left Iraq.

The rising profile of the Sunni tribal leaders in Anbar, Diyala, and the so-called Triangle of Death south of Baghdad adds a new factor that is both useful and threatening. The tribal elders portray themselves as homegrown champions of the populations in these governorates, delivering real benefits by saving the people from the tyranny of al Qaeda, bringing in reconstruction funds and securing thousands of jobs in the police force.[14] They are playing an important role in combating al Qaeda and improving the security situation in their region, thereby forging close ties with the U.S. military. This places the tribes in a position of both political and military strength in their own communities and vis-à-vis the national government in Baghdad, enabling them to drive harder bargains with the Shia and forcing other Sunni leaders to be at least equally demanding. The invigorated tribes that have allied themselves with the United States may increase the clout of the Sunnis as a whole, but their rise may diminish the importance of the Sunnis currently in Parliament and government. In addition, the success of the Sunni tribal chiefs in combating al Qaeda may reduce the danger of international terrorism in Iraq but will make bargaining even tougher over power sharing and other divisive issues.

Recognizing the necessity to engage in serious political dialogue and the fact that existing efforts and frameworks have reached a stalemate, some Shia and Sunnis favor international sponsorship and mediation of a national reconciliation process. It should be noted, however, that the Shia are less inclined to involve outsiders in internal reconciliation efforts and view any external involvement, whether by the United States, regional countries, or the international community, as detrimental to their current position of power.

---

12. Maad Fayad, "Iraqi Sunni Leaders Threaten 'Civil War,'" *Asharq Alawsat*, December 26, 2005, www.asharqalawsat.com/english/pring.asp?artid=id3184; "Leader of Tawafuq Coalition: We Will Resort to Armed Resistance if the Government Does Not Obey Our Demands," *Asharq Alawsat*, July 17, 2007, www.asharqalawsat.com/details.asp?section=4&issue=10444&article=426336&state=true.

13. "Tawafuq Bloc Attacks 'Ambiguous Stand' of Al-Dhari Towards Al-Qaeda," *Asharq Alawsat*, October 10, 2007.

14. "Bomb Kills a Key Sunni Ally of U.S.," www.washingtonpost.com, September 1, 2007, and "Abu Risha in an Interview Weeks before His Assassination," *Asharq Alawsat*, September 15, 2007.

Political Dynamics

Four years after liberation, two elections, and a constitution followed by a referendum, the Iraqi political leaders and the United States have not succeeded in building state institutions that are viable, functional, or credible to Iraqi citizens.

The political situation is in stalemate. The executive branch is unproductive, with seventeen of thirty-six ministers either withdrawn from their ministries altogether or boycotting cabinet meetings (and one minister is jailed on a murder charge). Parliament rarely reaches a quorum. When it does it can reach decisions only about its internal affairs (salaries for MPs, pension plans, recess, and so on). Services are virtually nonexistent. Oil production is down to 1.95 million barrels per day, far below the prewar high of 2.4 mbd.[15] Political leaders across the board are acutely aware of the stagnation and failure of state institutions to meet the needs of the country but seem mired in helplessness. They disagree about the causes of the paralysis and poor performance and cannot agree on remedies.

A number of factors contribute to the failure of the state to function as a state. Although there are many leaders of political groups and factions in Iraq, no strong national leaders with broad national appeal have emerged in the post-Saddam era. The major political groups and their leaders are identified with a limited ethnic, sectarian, religious, or even regional constituency. The fragmentation of politics is exemplified by the most-used word in the Iraqi political lexicon, *mukawwinat*, constituent parts, as in "the constituent parts of Iraq society," which has replaced the expression "Iraqis." Sectarian groups follow their own narrow interests and build positions for self-defense. The most senior Shia and Sunni leaders in Iraq acknowledged in conversations that the political groups are driven more by fear than by any national vision. One of the consequences of the narrow agendas is the cabinet's failure to act cohesively in implementing a unified program for reconstruction and social and economic service delivery.

The absence of unified and uncontested leadership in both the Shia and the Sunni camps (in contrast to the Kurdish bloc) hinders deal making and agreement on important political issues. Combined with the absence of strong leadership, the disarray within the UIA and the Tawafuq parliamentary blocs makes internal parliamentary decisions, including voting on crucial laws, difficult. Many of these laws are political in nature and affect the power relations of the parties in the country. Thus they require either a negotiated deal, which is unfeasible without strong and unified leadership, or a majority vote in Parliament, which is not achievable on critical

15. Peter Grier, "Iraq's Oil Production Falls Short of Goals," *Christian Science Monitor*, May 7, 2007, www.csmonitor.com/2007/0507/p01s02-wome.html.

issues because of the divergent interests of these groups, even within the same bloc.

The most hopeful indicator is the recognition by senior politicians of all parties that successive Iraqi governments have failed to restore normalcy and stability and to deliver what the people need, although they cannot agree about the causes of failure. There is universal frustration and exasperation with the stalemate among the political class and citizens alike. Although leaders of the different parties acknowledge that political solutions are needed, they do not agree on what these solutions might be. At the same time intricate Byzantine political activity goes on in Baghdad. According to many politicians the negotiations, bargaining, deal making and deal breaking are the most hectic since the government's formation in spring 2006. Political dramas continue to occupy the political elite, but so far there is a great deal of motion without obvious progress.

Political Alliances

Shifts and fractures in political blocs have affected both the Shia United Iraqi Alliance (UIA) and the Sunni Tawafuq. These fractures affect the larger political context in Baghdad as well as conditions in the regions.

The Fadhila was the first party to withdraw from the UIA in March 2007.[16] The Sadris, who withdrew their ministers from the cabinet in April and temporarily suspended their participation in Parliament in June 2007, are by no means bound by the UIA, in or out of Parliament.[17] The Dawa is divided into the Maliki camp, the Jafari camp, and the Tandhim Al-Iraq, none of which feel particularly bound by UIA discipline; but they are likely to stick with the UIA mainstream. Some of the twenty-five independents within the UIA parliamentary bloc have formed the secular-leaning "Arab National Group," headed by Qassem Daoud. Thus only ISCI and the Dawa (in its varying manifestations) remain committed to a combined UIA platform.

Outside Baghdad and the national Parliament the UIA is even more fractured. In Basra, Diwaniya, Nasriya, Samawa, and Amara, political differences and rivalries have erupted in armed confrontations and deadly clashes among the groups that comprise the UIA coalition, resulting in many deaths on all sides, disruption of the provincial economies and services, and rampant corruption. It is an open question whether lack of cohesion at the top in Baghdad leads to warfare in the provinces, or whether the competition for power and resources in the provinces is so powerful

16. Ernesto Londono, "At Least 146 Shiites Killed Across Iraq," *Washington Post*, March 8, 2007, www.washingtonpost.com/wp-dyn/content/article/2007/03/07/AR2007030700357_3.html.

17. The United States encouraged formation of an alliance of "moderates" as early as December 2006; press conference by President George W. Bush, December 20, 2006, Office of the Press Secretary, www.whitehouse.gov/news/releases/2006/12/pring/20061220-1.html.

that it impedes political agreements at the top. Either way, it is no longer possible to see the UIA as the united Shia coalition Ayatollah Sistani so adamantly called for before the elections of January and December 2005.

A similar though less overt divergence of interests has occurred within the Tawafuq. Its voting has been more predictable and uniform than the voting of the UIA. IIP takes political positions to bolster its status with the Sunni public (partly in anticipation of provincial elections) and in the political power structure. Although IIP has hawks as well as moderates and often acts in ways that Shia consider obstructionist, it remains the most flexible party in the Tawafuq bloc and the most open to dialogue and deal making. With the accusation that Nassir Al-Janabi was involved in insurgency activities, the April suicide bombing in Parliament, the discovery of weapons caches in the houses of some Sunni leaders, and the infiltration of their guards by would-be terrorists, pragmatists in IIP are beginning to view people like Adnan Dulaimi (Ahl Al-Iraq) and Khalaf Al-Ulayan as a burden whose only value is to provide voting strength in Parliament and possibly connections with the more dogmatic elements of the Sunni community.

A new factor in the Sunni political game is the emergence of the tribes in Anbar, and increasingly in Diyala and south of Baghdad, as a vital and menacing force. The tribes pose a medium-term political threat to both the Sunni Tawafuq and the Shia. Because they have provided security, funds and jobs, they are gaining credibility within their communities and with the United States, thereby challenging Sunni politicians now in Parliament, and are eager for provincial elections to take place in Anbar to demonstrate their strength. The question now confronting the Tawafuq partners is how to deal with the new Sunni actors, and specifically how to take advantage of increased Sunni national visibility and leverage provided by the Anbar tribes in negotiation with the Shia and Kurds without losing out to them politically.

With the possibility of provincial elections in 2008 and national elections in December 2009, the balance of power between the tribal forces in Anbar, Diyala, and Salaheddin, on the one hand, and the Tawafuq group, especially the IIP, on the other, may shift in favor of the tribes in these regions. The current Sunni alliance could fracture, leading to fragmentation or the formation of new alliances. The Sunni parties already in the political process are faced with the difficult choice of becoming the allies of these tribes or their rivals. Reshuffling to address these new factors may mean the end of Tawafuq and the emergence of new Sunni alliances.

The tribal forces present a different problem for the Shia parties. According to his close advisers Prime Minister Maliki met with some of the tribal leaders as early as fall 2006 but did not develop a strategy to bring them into the political fold, and the government is still ambiguous about its support for the tribes. Shia leaders fear that U.S. support for these groups will create legitimized, U.S.-supported Sunni militias that might eventually challenge the government. Disputes have arisen between the Anbar tribes and the government about the appropriate size and level of funding of a police force in the province. In the short term, the Shia parties controlling the government may find ways of exploiting the tribes against their Sunni partners in government, such as Adnan Al-Duleimi and Al-Uleyan or even the IIP. Indeed the prime minister's office has floated trial balloons occasionally to test the possibility of appointing ministers nominated by the Anbar tribes, particularly after the withdrawal of the Tawafuq ministers from government in early August.

In the medium term, the empowerment of the tribes, through money, arms, and local support, will strengthen the bargaining power of the Sunnis as a whole. In the long term, the Shia fear that the inclusion of resurgent Sunni tribal elements in the Iraqi armed forces will bring back Baathis to the army and to the government. The Shia parties that dominate the government therefore have the delicate task of wooing the tribes without turning them into a threat, balancing the influence of the tribes within the Sunni community against the influence of the Tawafuq parties and maneuvering to prevent the emergence of a unified and powerful Sunni front.

Recognizing that the political process is at a standstill and other state functions (legislation, services, economic improvement) are paralyzed, since May 2007 the political parties and blocs have been exploring new political alliances, some to support the government, others to form a new government. In May 2007 the Fadhila party, the Sadris, the Iraqia group, and the small (Sunni) Hewar group headed by Salih Mutlaq met to discuss the possibility of forming a new front opposed to the Maliki government. Some favored declaring a formal opposition and withdrawing from government en masse, but others were reluctant. In the end neither the IIP nor the Sadris, deemed essential components of an opposition front, were prepared to join; the project was put on hold.

More significantly, ISCI and the Kurds, whose strategic alliance antedates the war of 2003, have sought to build a broader alliance that can produce a majority in Parliament and give the government bargaining strength. With Fadhila's walkout from the UIA and the strained relations between ISCI and the Sadr movement, ISCI was left with only Dawa as a reliable partner within the UIA, in addition to some of the twenty-five independents within the bloc. The strategy therefore involved forming an alliance of moderates, including ISCI, Dawa, the KDP and PUK, and the IIP.[18] An agreement between the two Shia parties and the Kurdish parties was relatively straightforward and was reached in July 2007. Persuading IIP to join

---

18. "Sadr Bloc Boycotts Parliament after Shrine Bombing," *Khaleej Times*, www.khaleejtimes.com/DisplayArticleNew.aspxfile=data/focusoniraq/2007/June/fpcispmoraq_June54.xml&section=focusoniraq.

the alliance has involved tough and sometimes acrimonious discussions. Frustrated and hoping to force the issue on the reluctant Sunnis, on August 16, 2007, the two Shia parties and the Kurdish parties formally signed an agreement for a moderate alliance without the IIP.

The four parties stress than any alliance will be open to all who wish to support the government and the political process. Nevertheless, an alliance of moderates implies that those outside it are extreme in some sense or at least excluded. Other groups may be spurred to join or may intensify their efforts to form a counter-alliance.

State Institutions

Nearly half the cabinet seats have been either vacant or nonoperational since August, with the withdrawal or resignation of Sadri and Iraqia ministers and the boycott of Tawafuq ministers in August. This shortfall does not seem to make a difference in a government that even with a full house was unable to discharge its executive responsibilities and had little control over the tools of governance. According to government officials the prime minister, who is commander in chief, has only limited authority over the army. The police in the provinces are under the control of the party that controls each governorate, while the national police are only tenuously controlled by the interior ministry. In areas like Basra, Amara, and Dhi Qar, where coalition forces have either withdrawn or reduced their troop numbers, the government has not been able either to maintain law and order or to contain internecine fighting between Shia militias.

Oil is only tenuously in the hands of the government. The militias in the south fight over control of the oil sector and oil smuggling. Tolls collected by militias at every stage of the operation—from fees on overland transport to sale of smuggled crude and import of refined products—provide enormous revenues and drive the wars of the militias in cities like Basra. Indeed control over oil facilities and the oil sector in the south is a major cause of intra-Shia fighting in the governorate of Basra and the struggle over political control of the provincial council.[19]

The government's record of service delivery has been poor. Fuel shortages create long gas lines that snake around city blocks, as well as a thriving black market in oil products, largely controlled by militias and mafias, although residents complain that even black-market fuel is in short supply. The scarcity of fuel exacerbates the electricity shortage, since owners of private generators frequently cannot find fuel to operate them. The health sector suffers from a severe shortage of supplies and equipment at a time of rising demand as a result of endemic violence. Physicians, who have

19. International Crisis Group, "Where Is Iraq Heading? Lessons From Basra," *Middle East Report*, 67–25 (June 2007).

been especially targeted by terrorists, are fleeing the country, creating a crisis that recently prompted the government to try to ban their travel. Services are only somewhat better in the southern provinces than they are in Baghdad and the central area, although accurate comparative data on fuel availability and the health sector are hard to obtain.

The most promising new development, designed to end the deadlock of the executive branch, was the decision in mid-July to create "quartet rule" by the prime minister and a three-man presidential council: Jalal Talabani, Adel Abdel Mahdi, and Tariq al-Hashimi. This arrangement was to achieve a number of objectives. Members of the presidential council believed that Prime Minister Maliki was taking decisions without consulting sufficiently with the partners in the national coalition. The quartet would lead to more consultation in decision making and ensure Shia, Kurdish and Sunni input and endorsement. In addition, Hashimi and the Sunnis complained that the government took strategic and security decisions without consulting the Sunnis, and the Sunnis had little say in governance. Quartet rule gives Hashimi, on behalf of the Tawafuq, equal input. Ideally the quartet will overcome the impediment of a fractured cabinet by providing consensus among the major political blocs.

Parliament has also been mired in problems. The top political leaders rarely attend meetings and the legislative process is often paralyzed by the absence of a quorum. Factional bickering is intense, and the crisis precipitated by the removal of Mahmoud Mashhadani as speaker and his subsequent reinstatement is symptomatic of the distrust between the Shia and Sunni factions. In addition to these problems, Parliament in reality has little power because the most important legislative issues it faces have political dimensions that require negotiations between the leaders of the political groups. Parliament can vote on such legislative matters only after leaders make political agreements and decisions, and the parliamentary vote is a tool to ratify these agreements. Thus the hydrocarbon law, the revenue-sharing law, the law on de-Baathification, and the law regulating the authorities of the provincial councils, among others, are stalled in Parliament for lack of decisions by the leadership of the parliamentary groups. At times lack of a quorum masks lack of agreement on sensitive legislation.

The Southern Governates

The withdrawal of coalition troops from southern governorates has led to intensified confrontations between rival militias, especially Badr, the military arm of ISCI, and Jaish Al-Mahdi, the military wing of the Sadr movement. Weak government institutions and law enforcement capability have also given rise to new militias and cults, such as the *Sarkhis* and *Jund Assamaa,* quasi-mystical, armed groups that operate on the periphery of the political order. Ordinary residents of the south who wish to carry on quiet lives must negotiate their way through dangerous political crosscurrents.

Elections for provincial councils in the south took place in January 2005, and governors were elected by the new provincial councils. At the time the Sadr movement formally boycotted the elections, although individual Sadris did run. Predictably elections did not spell an end to political problems. In Basra the governor from the Fadhila party is bitterly opposed by ISCI and Dawa council members, who have tried hard to remove him from office. The economic stakes are high in Basra, and the city is reportedly overrun by militias whose primary concern is control of the city's oil economy. According to residents political assassinations of rivals and revenge killings of Baathis are rampant and underreported by local authorities and the national government. The small Sunni community in the governorate has come under severe pressure, and Sunni mosques have been systematically burned down. Residents claim that the political, military, and economic influence of Iran in Basra is higher than anywhere else in the south.

In Diwaniya, Nasriya, and Simawa, ISCI controls the provincial councils but, as a resident of Diwaniya asserted, the Mahdi army controls the streets. The police in these governorates belong to Badr and ISCI, but they are constantly challenged by the Mahdi army and often threatened in their own homes. Deadly clashes between the army and the ISCI-affiliated police in these governorates have spiked, necessitating intervention by the Iraqi army.

The Karbela provincial council is split among Dawa, ISCI, Sadris, and the Islamic Action Party. The governorate maintains a precarious political balance, but because it shares a border with Anbar and is adjacent to the Triangle of Death southwest of Baghdad, the city of Karbela has been the target of suicide bombers and car explosions. As a result security at the entry points to the city and in the city is very tight. Maysan (Amara) is the only southern governorate directly controlled by Sadris and the Mahdi army, although clashes with the local police and Iraq army are frequent. In Amara the Sadris are said to control both the legal and the illicit traffic of goods from Iran.

Only Najaf appears to be quiet and prospering. ISCI fully controls the city, and despite the recent assassination of an aide to Sistani there is no serious challenge to ISCI's authority at present. As a result of the stability, Najaf's economy is in better shape than other governorates in the south. In addition to control of governorate institutions, Ammar Al-Hakim, the son of ISCI founder Abdel Aziz Al-Hakim, founded and presides over a huge and expanding charitable organization called *Shaheed Al-Mihrab*, which has established four private schools and a string of summer schools, helps orphans throughout the south, deliveries assistance to displaced families, runs women's organizations and women's education programs, and provides countless other social services that neither the state nor the governorate is providing. Some residents worry that the present calm will not endure because the Sadris will not cede Najaf so easily and will at some point contest ISCI's control.

Residents of the southern governorates believed that if elections for provincial councils took place in their governorates soon, the Sadris would make considerable gains. Because the Sadr movement boycotted the elections of January 2005, the present provincial councils do not reflect its true strength. The weak performance since the 2005 elections of the national government and the provincial governments, both dominated by ISCI and Dawa, has probably increased support for the movement. In conversations in summer 2007 residents of the southern provinces also expressed the belief that provincial elections would intensify the fighting among the Shia militias in their regions. Some southern residents expressed growing dissatisfaction with all religious parties, which, they felt, have failed to respond to the needs of citizens, tolerated corruption, and engaged in violent competition.

Federation and Regional Autonomies

According to its Constitution, Iraq is currently a federated country composed of two regions: Kurdistan and the rest. The Constitution grants the governorates the right to form additional federated regions. In March 2007 a law presented by ISCI, regulating the formation of new federated regions, passed by a slim majority in Parliament with minimal debate. The law does not address the crucial issues of the relationship between the regional government and the national government, or the competencies and authority of the regional government vis-à-vis the national government. Although the Constitution addressed these points, they are nevertheless the subject of continuing and intense debate in Iraq and constitute some of the thorniest questions tackled by the Constitutional Review Committee.

Federalism in the South

ISCI has led the calls to extend federalism to other parts of Iraq, but other Shia groups do not share its enthusiasm. The Sadr movement opposes federalism as a matter of principle, only grudgingly accepting Kurdish federalism; Fadhila and other Shia groups (both religious and secular) oppose the specific formula proposed by ISCI. Some political leaders and scholars have suggested alternative ideas for federalism or decentralization. The position of the Dawa party is more ambiguous, as it is now inclined to view ISCI as a senior partner and go along with the ISCI platform.

ISCI is actively seeking the creation of a single federated state covering the entire region south of Baghdad, presumably with Najaf as its capital—what some detractors call "Shiistan." Because a referendum is required to form a federation, ISCI is expending considerable financial resources to promote the concept among Iraqis in the south at every social level and among numerous social groups. The Shahid Al-Mihrab Institute, an ISCI-affiliated NGO headed by Ammar Al-Hakim, the son of ISCI leader Abdul Aziz Al-Hakim, regularly holds women's meetings to educate women about the advantages of a southern federation. On the assumption that this southern super-federation is achievable and ISCI will control it, ISCI, like the Kurds, will want to see maximum authority given to the federated regions.

However, the situation in southern Iraq is politically quite different from that in Kurdistan, where the two major parties, at times violent rivals, have arrived at a power-sharing agreement that allows for unification of the region. Far from a power-sharing agreement, ISCI and the Sadr movement are locked in a bloody power struggle in the south. Basra, Diwaniya, Nasriya, Samawa, and other cities have witnessed armed conflict, assassinations, and bombings attributable to the rivalry between the two factions.

Provincial elections in the south are likely to precipitate more violence and lead to a stronger showing by the Sadr movement. Other, smaller groups may also merge in the competition. Under the circumstances, and if its control of the councils is less certain, ISCI could lose its enthusiasm for a greater Shia federated region, and it might look to other forms of federation that are more easily managed.

In addition, the tribes of southern Iraq are at best divided over the idea of a grand southern federation. Although ISCI has wooed tribes in the south-central area, their endorsement is not certain, and the tribes of the far south have agitated against the idea. In a recent and striking challenge to the grand southern federation, tribal leaders from Basra, Nasriya, Simawa, Diwaniya, and Amara met in August 2007 and declared the establishment of a single self-governing (but not federated) region comprising their five governorates. The declaration explicitly rejected federalism but was otherwise vague about the relationship of this self-governing region and the national government.

Traditionally Iraq south of Baghdad has been organized around two distinct cultural and economic regions. The mid-Euphrates, centered in Najaf and including Karbela and Hilla, is a predominantly urban region organized around the Shia holy sites; the population is predominantly of the clerical and merchant classes. Its economy heavily depends on pilgrimage from the entire Muslim world to the holy shrines and on the revenue generated by the presence of senior Shia *marjis* (religious authorities) and the *hawza,* seminaries that attract students from around the Muslim world. Najaf and Karbela have always had a more cosmopolitan Muslim complexion than most cities in Iraq.

The second region is the far south, encompassing Basra, Amara, Nasriya, is tribal and clustered around the historic marshes. Semawa and Diwaniya, with their strong tribal presence, share more characteristics with this region than with the mid-Euphrates. The economy heavily depends on agriculture, animal husbandry, and fisheries. The local culture tends to be less cosmopolitan and less oriented toward religion than that prevailing in the shrine cities; tribal folklore is prominent and colorful, and the population continues to be attuned to Arab tribal traditions.

In sum intense political rivalries that include armed conflict, historical variables, and cultural and economic differences make the creation of a single super-federation in the south a considerable challenge.

Federalism in the West?

The Sunnis have accepted the principle of federalism for the Kurds but find it hard to reconcile themselves to an overall federated Iraq. At the same time several concerns have driven the Sunnis to think about the merits of self-governance and decentralization. A primary issue is the composition of the security forces, encompassing the national police and the army, both of which are heavily Shia. Efforts by the central government to introduce Iraqi army units in Anbar province have been unsuccessful because of the distrust between the population and Shia troops. A locally recruited and managed police force answering to the provincial government is a preferable solution, although its relationship to the interior ministry is ambiguous (as is the relationship of locally raised police forces in other governorates, notably in the south).

Allocation of revenue is another item of concern to the Sunnis. Sunni leaders from the Tawafuq alliance and the Anbar tribes complain that reliance on national ministries often dominated by Shia parties to approve projects and allocate and disburse funds has so far been an unproductive experience. They say they need to control their own finances. The undercurrent of Sunni thinking is that if Iraq's national government is going to be based on sectarian quotas, therefore giving the Sunnis minority status, then Sunnis need autonomous control over certain issues in areas where they are a majority. At present the precarious security situation and fluctuating balance of political forces in the majority Sunni governorates, as well as the different conditions in Shia governorates, make a clear policy on this issue difficult to achieve.

Conclusions and Recommendations

By October 2007 many Iraqi officials and Baghdad residents were willing to state that the stepped-up military effort had succeeded in reducing sectarian violence in the capital and squeezing al Qaeda out of traditional strongholds. Yet despite broad recognition that the success of the military effort can be sustained only by a political settlement, neither the United States nor the Iraqis have matched the military escalation with a comparable political acceleration. Iraqis have not used the opportunity provided by the slowdown of sectarian killings to engage more effectively in a national dialogue and reach accommodations. Notwithstanding its demands for the Iraqi government to meet benchmarks, the United States has not made the political process in Iraq its highest priority. Washington has not mobilized its considerable political and diplomatic capabilities to confront what is undoubtedly the most critical problem endangering regional stability.

The next report from General Petraeus and Ambassador Crocker is expected in March 2008, and the intervening period should be a time for U.S. policymakers and Iraqis to devote their energies to addressing political and governance problems. Iraqi, U.S., and regional constraints on the ability to shape political dynamics in Iraq should not lead to inaction. With the prospect of U.S. troop reductions and redeployment, it is crucial over the next year for the United States and the international community to confirm their political engagement with Iraq and their commitment to helping Iraqis establish a viable state. Otherwise the intensified military effort will have been wasted and U.S. troop presence may be prolonged.

Three principal initiatives can benefit from U.S. and international engagement and support.

1. International Mediation. President Bush and General Petraeus have both referred to the success of "bottom-up" approaches to reconciliation and security.[20] The security achievements in Anbar, south Baghdad, and other "hotspots" will translate into durable political success once the tribes in these regions integrate into the Iraqi state at a political level, not only as members of a local police force or national army. Although local efforts are important as building blocks, they do not preclude or diminish the necessity for agreements and accommodations at the top political levels, if only because senior politicians can scuttle or sabotage local successes.

Forums, such as the one for Iraq and its neighbors or the International Compact for Iraq, are useful for engaging the region and the international community, but they do not address the heart of the matter, that political leaders need to engage in candid, serious negotiations and accept unpalatable compromises. Sectarian entrenchment, fueled by killings and purges, has engendered distrust and discouraged candor, making it unlikely that leaders can undertake this painful process on their own.

---

20. Presidential radio address on Iraq's Anbar Province, September 8, 2007; "Transcript: Gen. David Petraeus on 'Fox News Sunday,'" June 17, 2007, www.foxnews.com/story/0,2933,283553,00.html.

Iraq urgently needs international mediation to bring the parties together at the highest decision-making level to forge a national compact. The negotiations should establish a sustained, continuous dialogue and reach agreements on power sharing, the nature of the Iraqi state, and compromises on specific national issues such as the Constitution. Iraq's neighbors must be brought into the process to endorse and uphold agreements struck by the Iraqi leadership. Once agreements are in place, compliance must be monitored by international observers. Although the United States must provide the motivation and impetus for such mediation, the process itself should be anchored in an international framework, with a UN Security Council resolution and mediators appointed by the Security Council. Resolution 1770, which gives the UN a larger role in Iraq, is a starting point for the Security Council to do more, but it does not go far enough.

2. Developing National Politics. Since 2003 Iraq has suffered from the polarization of sectarian politics, with the inevitable result that all negotiations are zero-sum games. Policy choices and decisions are measured by the yardstick of group interest rather than national interest. The state has been built on a sectarian premise with a mentality of cronyism and divvying up the spoils, making compromise and accommodation among the groups hard to reach. It is essential for Iraq to move away from the cycles of identity politics and develop national platforms and national institutions. Mechanisms have to be established within state institutions to reinforce their national mission, particularly in the armed forces, the national police, the judiciary, and institutions that handle the country's revenues.

Recent developments in Iraq provide a better opportunity than earlier to redefine Iraqi politics in terms of cross-sectarianism and national platforms. The breakdown of the UIA and the incipient disagreements within Taqafuq open a path to new cross-sectarian, cross-ethnic alliances that can develop issues-based rather than sect-based agendas. The rise of the Sunni tribes in Anbar and elsewhere against al Qaeda provides an opportunity to reduce distrust and reshape Sunni-Shia dialogue. Countrywide tribal forums that bring together Shia and Sunni tribal leaders can provide alternative political structures that transcend sectarianism. Social and professional structures that draw on the urban middle class can provide the social underpinnings for development of cross-sectarian and cross-ethnic common interests. A further important step in directing Iraq away from sectarianism and encouraging national politics lies in changing the current electoral custom of closed lists and adopting single candidate-single district elections.

3. Enabling Government. Along with changing the political model, the national government must acquire the ability and the tools to govern. As discussed earlier, the problems of government are systemic, caused by favoring quotas instead of competence, cronyism, lack of accountability except to the party, and corruption. If the executive branch hopes to improve performance, this underlying system must change in favor of better standards of competence and a traditional cabinet structure. More effort is necessary to professionalize and train the civil service and ensure the continuity of experience and knowledge in government agencies.

The argument that the national government should remain weak while provincial governments should be strengthened is unrealistic. A state that is vulnerable to internal threats from terrorism and unruly militias and external challenges from neighbors requires competent security institutions, and these can only be provided and managed by the national government. The national government is still, and will continue to be, responsible for the armed forces, distribution of revenue, and nationwide infrastructure projects. Outside Kurdistan, Iraqis still look to the national government to provide basic services and protection. At present the incapacity of the national government is not compensated for by strong provincial governments. Quite the opposite. The ills that bedevil the national government in Baghdad are mirrored in equal, if not greater, measure in the provinces.

Ultimately Iraqis have to make the hard decisions about the shape of the national compact, a political settlement, and necessary agreements to build a functioning and stable state. Nevertheless, what the United States does (or fails to do) will also be important in influencing political directions and outcomes.

The United States can play a significant role as a catalyst by providing support and assistance strategically and at the operational level and by persuading the international community to engage more vigorously and meaningfully in facilitating Iraqi dialogue and settlements. It would be dangerous for the United States to allow the debate in Washington over the military to obscure the fact that a political solution is the only feasible endgame in Iraq.

11

Promoting Middle East Democracy II: Arab Initiatives

Mona Yacoubian

In the aftermath of 9/11, international and regional interest has focused intensely on the Middle East's urgent need for reform. The region's stagnation dates back decades, yet, until the 2001 attacks, these long-standing ills received scant attention from governments in the region and their global counterparts. The 9/11 attacks and subsequent terrorist operations (Casablanca, Riyadh, Istanbul, Madrid) shattered the conventional wisdom that the region's stability—anchored by its authoritarian governments—could endure indefinitely and would come at little cost to U.S. interests. Precisely the opposite conclusion has become apparent: Middle East reform is critical for long-term stability and regional security. Absent change, the status quo will only breed greater popular disaffection and provide fertile ground for the continued growth of extremism.

Given the linkage between Middle East reform and the region's long-term stability, the United States and its European allies have accelerated calls for reform in the region.

Entering its second term, the Bush administration has signaled its continued emphasis on Middle East reform as a top priority in its foreign policy agenda. Indeed, President George W. Bush repeatedly underscored his administration's pledge to support democratic movements in the Middle East during both his second inaugural speech and State of the Union address.

While the United States has engaged more directly over the past few years to promote reform through the Middle East Partnership Initiative launched in December 2002 and the Broader Middle East and North Africa Initiative unveiled at the June 2004 G-8 summit, its efforts have been directed primarily toward a relatively narrow constituency of liberal, secular, pro-Western elites who do not represent the region's grassroots majority.

Mona Yacoubian, "Promoting Middle East Democracy II: Arab Initiatives," Special Report 136 (Washington, DC: USIP, 2005).

However, numerous Arab reform advocates—from Islamists to businessmen—have proposed a rich array of reform initiatives that merit U.S. policymakers' attention. Indeed, U.S. policymakers largely have ignored moderate Islamist voices for reform, even though Islamists retain a strong, populist following in various countries throughout the region. Ultimately, successful Arab reform efforts must bridge secular and Islamist demands for change. In its quest to promote reform in the region, the United States will need to work with moderate Islamists and ruling regimes in the region. It must sell both on the notion that sustainable reform should be implemented via a gradual process of change that creates transparent and accountable institutions and respects the rule of law.

Certainly, the need for democratic change in the region has been well-documented. In July 2002, a UN-sponsored Arab Human Development Report, authored by a well respected group of Arab scholars, found that Arab countries have the lowest level of political freedom of any region in the world. Specifically, the report states that critical deficits in freedom, women's empowerment, and knowledge plague the region. The study concludes with an impassioned plea for transforming the region through comprehensive political, economic, and social reform.

Yet the Arab world's democracy deficit should not be misinterpreted as a rejection by its citizens of greater opening and reform. Indeed, surveys and polling conducted in the Arab world reveal an intense desire for democratic freedoms. For example, a 2002 poll conducted by U.S. pollster James Zogby, head of the Arab American Institute, surveyed 3,200 people in eight Arab countries. Between 90 and 96 percent of respondents rated "civil and personal rights" as their highest priority among a list of potential concerns that included personal economic conditions, health care, and moral standards.

The intense international interest directed at the need for Middle East reform has helped to initiate an unprecedented dialogue about reform in the region. From Morocco to Saudi Arabia and beyond, governments, nongovernmental groups (both secular and Islamist), the media, and others have joined an often freewheeling discussion about the need for change. Further, the debate has penetrated popular discourse from television call-in shows to Internet chat rooms and weblogs, injecting a populist element into the dialogue.

This Special Report examines the numerous reform initiatives emanating from the Arab world. Specifically, it reviews reform platforms at the nongovernmental, national, and multilateral levels and assesses their potential for promoting positive change in the region. The report concludes by providing some recommendations as to how the U.S. government should respond to these Arab world reform proposals.

Defining the Challenge: The Arab Human Development Report

In July 2002, less than a year after the 9/11 attacks, a UN-commissioned panel of thirty Arab experts from a variety of disciplines issued the first Arab Human Development Report (AHDR) (http://www.undp.org/rbas/ahdr/english2002.html). The report offers a grim study on the state of the Arab world. Although planning for the report predated 9/11, the attacks imbued the document with a greater sense of urgency. The report, published in Arabic, English, and French, laid the groundwork for many of the Arab-initiated reform proposals that succeeded it by articulating the political, economic, social, and demographic challenges facing the region.

In blunt language, the AHDR issues a probing, self-critical look at what has gone wrong in the Arab world. Because of its Arab authorship, the study had great resonance, providing an instance of introspection that many outside the region complained had been lacking. While noting achievements such as an increase in life expectancy and a reduction of abject poverty, the report also points to ominous "warning signals." For example, it states that only sub-Saharan Africa had lower per capita income growth over the past twenty years. It also highlights low and declining labor productivity. With 38 percent of its population under the age of fourteen, the region's demographic pressures, spurred by demands for jobs and housing, will only intensify. The sense of hopelessness among Arab youths is underscored by the team's finding that 51 percent of older adolescents wanted to emigrate from the region.

The report qualifies poverty in the region as "poverty of capabilities and poverty of opportunities." Ultimately, it finds that the Arab world's ills are rooted in deficits of freedom, women's empowerment, and knowledge and that the region's shortcomings in these three areas impede the Arab world from reaching its true potential, effectively isolating it from the rest of the world.

The report dissects each of the three key gaps in detail. Regarding political freedom, the Arab world is noted as having the lowest level of political freedom of any region in the world. Using a variety of indicators that measure political participation, civil liberties, political rights, and civil society, the region falls short, indicating a lack of "voice and accountability." On women's empowerment, the AHDR highlights Arab women's lack of political and economic participation; women occupied only 3.5 percent of parliamentary seats as compared to 11 percent in sub-Saharan Africa and 12.9 percent in Latin America. Finally, the report chronicles the region's "knowledge deficit," noting, among other statistics, that the Arab world has the lowest level of information and communication technology access of any region in the world, that only 0.6 percent of the population uses the Internet, and that only 1.2 percent own personal computers. The report also notes the dearth of scientific research and innovative thinking originating from the region. In addition, the entire Arab world translates about 330 books annually, one-fifth of the total number translated by Greece. (A subsequent 2003 Arab Human Development Report is devoted to this knowledge gap; see http://www.undp.org/rbas/ahdr/english2003.html.)

The report concludes with a clarion call for reform, saying the Arab world is at a "crossroads," casting the region's choices in stark terms: its governments can either continue with the status quo, producing ineffective policies that will not meet the region's challenges, or they can strive for an "Arab renaissance, anchored in human development that will be actively pursued." The report also urges "free, honest, efficient and regular elections" and the right for opposition parties to exist. It advocates greater checks on executive power by assigning oversight responsibilities to the legislative branch, as well as the need for an independent judiciary. It recommends the empowerment of civil society through the lifting of administrative obstacles and restrictions. It calls for the rule of law and guarantees for basic citizens' rights, particularly freedom of expression and freedom of association. It also encourages the fostering of free and responsible media. Finally, it recommends the removal of gender bias in the labor market and greater emphasis on research and development in the "knowledge sciences."

The Arab Human Development Report is not a reform initiative per se. Rather, it seeks to establish the parameters for a reform dialogue, both within the region and internationally. Indeed, the AHDR played a key role in triggering the ongoing debate in the region on reform. The 170-page report defines the challenge from an Arab vantage point, sketching the key areas for reform in painful detail. It has provided U.S. and European policymakers with an important grounding for their own reform proposals and an Arab "voice" to reference when designing reform promotion policies. For example, then-Secretary of State Colin Powell, in his speech announcing the Middle East Partnership Initiative, quoted from the report, emphasizing that the words "[are] not my words . . . they have come from Arab experts who have looked deeply into these issues." And, not insignificantly, the report and subsequent Arab reform initiatives provide some cover against charges that the United States is attempting to impose reform on the region from the outside.

While the report's candid self-assessment provides a critical baseline, it suffers from two major drawbacks. First, the report largely evades a key issue, the role of Islam in Arab politics and society, and offers an implicit criticism of the role of Islamists through its references to an intolerant social environment. This explicit omission likely was intentional, as religion's role in politics constitutes a lightning rod in the debate over reform. However,

Islamists constitute perhaps the single most influential grassroots force in the region. As a result, the report does not establish the basis for a clear dialogue for reform that reaches across the secular-Islamist divide.

Second, the report fails to resonate with the Arab "street." Its authors principally hail from the Arab world's Westernized, liberal elite, a group with limited influence at the popular level. Indeed, the report engendered a hostile reaction from many in the Arab world, as opposed to the glowing response it received from the West. Yet, grassroots sentiment in the region is not inherently antidemocratic; many key themes articulated by reformers, such as the need for transparency and accountability, are echoed in Islamist discourse. However, in a somewhat predictable circle-the-wagons response, negative reaction in the Arabic-language press often stemmed from assertions that the report was overly gloomy in its assessment of the Arab world and that the West would exploit the report to impose its will on the region.

Underlying the popular rejection of the report resides a deeper issue, namely the ability of democratic reformers to connect with the broader Arab public. Liberal-minded, secular reformers often articulate a vision of reform that comports with Western ideals of democratic change. Yet, this view typically gets lost in the anti-Western diatribe that has come to dominate Arabic-language media and other popular outlets of expression. To some extent, the concepts of reform and democracy have become sullied by their association with U.S. foreign policy in the region. During the June 2004 Doha Conference (see below), for example, one participant bemoaned "the fact that the language of democratic reform in the Arab world has become the stock-in-trade of one of the most globally despised U.S. governments in history."

As such, Arab reform initiatives risk losing all popular credibility as long as they are associated with deeply controversial U.S. policies toward Iraq and the Palestinians. Indeed, the region's Westernized liberals form an elite minority, often estranged from the grassroots and viewed by many as pawns of the West. To the extent that it is identified with this relatively small Westernized intelligentsia, the Arab Human Development Report's long-term impact on Arab public opinion may be somewhat limited. Certainly, without a mass following demanding attention to the problems highlighted in the document, Arab governments have managed largely to ignore the report.

"People Power": Nongovernmental Reform Initiatives

The boldest and most detailed reform proposals originating in the Arab world have emerged from nongovernmental organizations (NGOs). While NGO-sponsored conferences on democratic reform date back twenty years, when a group of seventy-one Arab intellectuals met in Cyprus—no Arab country would host them—and established the Arab Organization for Human Rights at a conference entitled "The Arab World's Democratic Crisis," the past eighteen months have witnessed a significant surge in discussion and conferences devoted to democratic reform in the region.

Indeed, beginning in January 2004, a diverse array of groups ranging from the Arab Business Council to the Egyptian Muslim Brotherhood has published a variety of reform initiatives. The platforms vary, at times significantly, in degree of specificity, scope, seriousness, and independence. Some have been published in partnership with government, whereas in other cases the host government's role is less visible; others are fully independent. Most significantly, many of these reform initiatives have advocated forcefully for political reform. A number of these initiatives are examined here, in order of their relative significance (determined by content and degree of independence), beginning with those that hold the most promise for pushing the reform agenda forward.

Arab NGOs Beirut Summit Letter, March 19–22, 2004

The Arab NGO summit, also known as the Civil Forum, is among the most compelling non-governmental reform initiatives. The forum comprised fifty-two Arab NGOs from thirteen countries and was timed to precede the Arab League summit devoted to the question of political reform. Banned from holding their conference in Tunis, where the Arab League summit was scheduled to take place, the four-day forum was held in Beirut. (Due to squabbling among Arab governments, the summit was ultimately postponed until May 2004.)

Asserting its independence from any Arab government, the forum issued its final communiqué as a letter addressed to Arab kings and presidents. The fourteen-page letter underscores the importance of political and constitutional reform for the region's future, lamenting that in the eyes of many in the world, the Middle East has become little more than a haven for terrorism and violence. The forum determined that the Arab world's internal problems—regardless of external pressure—demand that the region embark on a path of reform or risk facing long-term instability and chaos.

The letter then lists several "general demands" for political reform. These include repealing emergency laws, abolishing exceptional courts, releasing political prisoners, ending torture, lifting restrictions on forming NGOs, and ensuring basic freedoms. The letter also raises the need for constitutional reform and calls for devolving more power away from the executive branch to legislative sources of power, specifically to municipal councils.

Most significantly, the letter highlights the importance of initiating a religious dialogue within the Muslim Arab community. The document calls on governments to review both religious and nonreligious educational curricula in order to inject more innovative thinking. By the same token, it appeals to Islamic scholars (ulama) and thinkers to debate the theological underpinnings of terrorism, extremism, and violence. The document also urges those in academe and the media to examine and open forums for discussion of the work of "religious innovators" (mujaddadun diniyun) in Arab society.

The Civil Forum letter is significant in several respects. First, the document is comprehensive and detailed, covering nearly every aspect of reform. While some of the demands are somewhat vague—for example, "take prompt measures toward administrative and financial reform"—many are quite specific. Further, the letter situates these demands within a broader framework of basic principles including respect for human rights and fundamental freedoms, acceptance of pluralism, and the renunciation of the use of violence.

Second, unlike many other reform initiatives, the Civil Forum letter directly addresses the role of Islam within the region and offers constructive suggestions for promoting dialogue on this critical matter. The initiative appears to make an important distinction between radicals and moderates. Its recommendations look to marginalize violent, extremist elements while allowing for the participation of peaceful moderates. In its preamble, the letter warns against adhering to dated interpretations of Islam—an implicit reference to the growing popularity of the salafist trend in Islam that calls for a return to the practice of Islam as it was during the time of the Prophet Muhammad. At the same time, it underscores the right of political participation for all citizens, regardless of national, religious, or linguistic "inclinations," thereby offering an opening for moderate Islamist political participation.

Later, the forum devotes an entire section to the renewal of religious discourse. Rather than signaling the total exclusion of the Islamist political strain, it demonstrates in the letter a wish to reach an understanding among the Islamists who eschew violence. The forum seeks to embark on a dialogue to renew (reform) Islam with the full participation of all its adherents: clerics, scholars, imams, Muslim thinkers, journalists, and academics. The letter highlights the important role debate and dialogue will play in addressing critical issues related to violence, extremism, and terrorism.

Third, the groups composing the Civil Forum reflect regionwide viewpoints, as well as the interests of human rights organizations, women's groups, and press freedom organizations. Collectively, they appear to be truly independent of any government in the region. As such, they represent a genuine alternative to government representatives and could be well-placed to promote popular aspirations for change, a critical element in any reform equation.

Fourth, the Civil Forum has identified an important follow-up mechanism, namely, the holding of parallel NGO conferences to coincide with Arab League summits. Pegging their conference to the Arab League meetings will help to ensure both continued follow-up and broader public attention to their reform proposals.

Doha Declaration for Democracy and Reform, June 3–4, 2004

(www.npwj.org)

The Doha Declaration for Democracy and Reform, although not as detailed or comprehensive as the Civil Forum letter, offers a bold formula for reforming the Arab world. The declaration was issued at the end of a two-day conference conceived by Egyptian reformer Saad Ed-Din Ibrahim and hosted by Qatar University's Gulf Studies Center. The Qatari government also supported the conference. More than one hundred participants from across the Arab world, representing a broad spectrum of journalists, activists, and politicians, signed the declaration.

The Doha Declaration opens by stating that "democratic change has become a non-negotiable choice which cannot be postponed." The statement asserts that no inherent contradictions exist between Arab culture, Islam, and democracy, noting that two-thirds of the world's 1.4 billion Muslims already live in democracies. It also admonishes against "hiding behind the necessity to resolve the Palestinian question before implementing political reform." It later calls on Arab governments to cease their exploitation of the Iraq and Palestine questions to postpone political reform.

The proposal's key demands include calls for constitutional reforms that will transform absolute monarchies into constitutional monarchies and circumscribe presidential powers in republics. The declaration also calls for free and fair elections; the abolition of emergency laws, special courts, and extrajudicial procedures; an independent judiciary; guarantees for the freedom of expression and association; greater political participation for women; and unrestricted freedom to form political parties. The proposal also demands the withdrawal of Arab militaries from politics, underscoring the need for civil-military transition. The initiative's follow-up mechanisms include the slated establishment of an Arab Democracy Watch based in Qatar. The group will monitor and follow-up on Doha Declaration proposals as well as other Arab reform initiatives such as those of Beirut (see above), Alexandria, and Sana'a (see below).

The initiative is notable for two key innovations that, if implemented successfully, may make significant contributions toward Arab reform promotion. First, the Doha Declaration calls for the creation of "national pacts" that would delineate the principles of political participation, establishing rules of engagement for the political arena. Fear that Islamist opposition groups will exploit any genuine political opening to seize power via elections and to implement antidemocratic measures (e.g., shari'a law) constitutes a key obstacle to moving forward with serious political reform. Essentially, these charters or pacts could lay out the "rules of the game" and establish an agreed-upon set of values and guarantees endorsed across the political spectrum, thereby opening the way for freer political participation within the confines of these universal guarantees. Equally important, these pacts could help consolidate and strengthen reform advocates, bridging the divide between secular and moderate Islamist reformers. By rallying these disparate pro-reform elements, the region's inchoate reform movement could gain important momentum. While the national pact concept is still quite vague and in need of further development, it nonetheless offers an innovative approach to a key challenge for reformers.

Second, the declaration provides an important opening for addressing the issue of civil-military transition, a pivotal question for many of the region's governments as they embark on the path of reform. In many Arab countries, particularly those with military-backed governments, the role of the army as defined by their respective constitutions has been kept purposefully vague. In countries such as Algeria or Syria, the military and its related security services typically serve the narrowly defined interests of the regime in power. The army is often used to ensure against the rise of a powerful domestic opposition rather than to safeguard national sovereignty against foreign threats. By raising the issue of the military's role in the political arena, the Doha Declaration could help to initiate a much-needed dialogue within countries on defining the future role of the military.

Finally, the Doha conference's participants included a number of representatives reflecting a broad range of political views and issues. Women's groups, media organizations, human rights groups, and a variety of political parties and other civil society organizations attended the conference. The conference also placed particular emphasis on the participation of both women and youth, two key constituent groups who will be critical to the success of any reform effort in the region.

Alexandria Charter, March 12–14 2004

(http://www.bibalex.org/ARF/en/index.html)

The Alexandria Charter—perhaps the most publicized of Arab reform efforts—was drafted by a group of 150 Arab intellectuals, former diplomats, and businessmen (100 Egyptians plus 50 from other Arab countries) at the Alexandria Library in March 2004. The Alexandria Charter adopts a multidisciplinary approach, addressing political, economic, social, and cultural reform. This quasi-governmental conference was opened by Egyptian President Hosni Mubarak, and over three days the group hammered out a comprehensive—albeit politically timid—reform proposal.

Its political reform proposals reference the need for a transfer of power, free elections, and term limits. It calls for the abolition of emergency laws, explaining that regular laws can adequately address all offenses. The charter endorses the freedom to form political parties within the framework of existing laws and the constitution, as well as the need for a free press via the laws regulating the publication of newspapers. Finally, the document encourages the amendment of restrictive laws governing the establishment of civil society institutions.

The Alexandria Charter is notable for its broad scope and its regionwide representation. It also promotes some bold political reforms such as free elections and the lifting of emergency laws. The charter also includes provisions for follow-up, including the establishment of an Arab Reform Forum, based at the Alexandria Library, that would facilitate ongoing dialogue. Additionally, the charter recommends holding national reform conferences in individual countries. A second multinational conference slated for spring 2005 will focus on sharing best practices, drawing on reform success stories from across the region.

However, the charter falls short in key areas. Less daring than the Beirut or Doha Declarations, the Alexandria Charter offers a "lite" version of reform. The participants signed the document as individuals rather than as representatives of specific organizations, leading some to question exactly whom the charter represents or how much weight it carries. Further, the document offers caveats to its recommendations by insisting that they fall within the purview of existing laws—many of which are restrictive and contribute to the region's closed political atmosphere. The resulting proposals are fairly dilute. As noted above, its proposal to lift restrictions on political parties is qualified by asserting that these parties must be within the confines of existing laws and the constitution. In Egypt, like many countries in the region, religious-based parties are banned, effectively sidelining some of the most potent political forces. Similarly, the charter advocates the need for a free press, but qualifies the proposal by endorsing the continuation of a press code regulating the media.

More generally, the document largely avoids the question of Islam, sidestepping another key issue that the region must confront. Indeed, Islamists, as well as other civil society groups, were largely excluded from the conference. Of the 150 participants, only one or two were considered to represent an Islamist viewpoint. Some have suggested that religion was purposefully excluded in order to define political legitimacy by citizenship rather than religion. The charter's cultural reform section touches on the role of religion, calling for the "eradication" (qada'a) of any form of religious extremism in school curricula, mosques, and the media. The stark language used appears to signal an unwillingness to reach out to more moderate Islamist elements.

Ultimately, the Alexandria Charter falters due to its lack of independence. The Egyptian government's influence is clearly discernible. Some Egyptian observers charge the conference was essentially hijacked by the Egyptian government, which wanted to control its outcome and ensure against any proposals that would be viewed as a threat to the Egyptian state. In any event, Mubarak's speech opening the conference conveyed a strong symbolic message—the conference was organized with the blessing of the Egyptian government. Participants, therefore, could not easily rock the boat.

The Sana'a Declaration, January 10–12, 2004

(http://www.caabu.org/press/)

The Sana'a Declaration emerged from a conference of 820 participants representing fifty-two countries and included representatives from governments as well as a variety of civil society organizations and political parties. Cosponsored by the Yemeni government, the declaration, although vague, calls for elected legislatures, an independent judiciary, respect for the rule of law, women's empowerment, and a free and independent media. The document also underscores the important role to be played by the private sector as a key partner in any reform effort.

The most salient aspect of the Sana'a Declaration is its emphasis on the need to strengthen the partnership between government and civil society. While such a partnership risks leading to the co-option of nongovernmental organizations by strong governments, some element of partnership and dialogue is necessary for the successful promotion of reform in the region. The conference offered government officials and civil society activists an important opportunity to exchange views. As part of its follow-up, the conference established an Arab Democratic Dialogue Forum as an instrument to promote dialogue between "diverse [public and nongovernmental] actors."

As one of the first Arab reform initiatives following the publication of the Arab Human Development Report, the Sana'a Declaration marked an important first step. However, subsequent initiatives, such as the Civil Forum letter and the Doha Declaration, offer more detailed and substantive recommendations. The Sana'a Declaration's proposals lack specificity, often relying on vague generalities, rather than concrete policy recommendations. Finally, the declaration's reference to the Palestinian question serves to dilute the document by digressing from reform and raising an issue often exploited by Arab governments to distract public attention away from the need for political change.

Constituent-Based Reform Initiatives

In addition to the numerous nongovernmental reform initiatives, some more narrowly defined constituencies have put forward their own vision of reform for the region. These initiatives are not as comprehensive and do not target as broad an audience as other reform proposals. However, their significance derives from their connection to reform proponents who hail from diverse sectors of Arab society. Two specific constituencies—the business sector and the Islamists—will be highlighted briefly in this report.

The Arab Business Council Declaration, January 2004

(http://www.weforum.org/en/index.htm)

Established in June 2003 as part of the World Economic Forum, the Arab Business Council focuses primarily on global competitiveness issues, seeking to elevate the Arab private sector in order for it to compete at a global level. The council's January 2004 document, therefore, is directed at economic-reform priorities in the Arab world. The declaration underscores the need for good governance as a critical element in enhancing competitiveness.

Specifically, the Arab Business Council Declaration calls for respecting the rule of law and enhancing transparency and accountability. The document also highlights the need to address corruption and to ensure an independent judiciary and calls for the establishment of a public-private partnership, fostering the role of civil society in the reform process.

While limited in scope, the Arab Business Council Declaration is significant in that it represents another important constituency for reform. Although collaboration on reform between the business sector and civil society has been minimal to date, private-sector interests intersect with those of the nongovernmental sector with regard to promoting good governance. (However, deeply entrenched business elites are often vested in the status quo and may be averse to reform measures.) The council's declaration does not offer recommendations for follow-up mechanisms. Nonetheless, it remains an important statement for the record, placing Arab business interests squarely on the side of reform promotion.

Egyptian Muslim Brotherhood Reform Initiative, March 13, 2004

The Egyptian Muslim Brotherhood (MB), Egypt's most powerful opposition force, issued its own comprehensive reform platform in March 2004. The MB's reform initiative is fairly detailed, addressing several types of reform, including political, electoral, judicial, economic, social, educational, and religious. The platform also features a section devoted to the status of women.

In a preamble to the proposal, the MB's general guide, Muhammad Mahdi Akef, rails against foreign intervention, decrying the "persistent and continuing attempts to impose change on the region from outside," specifically accusing the United States of trying to impose its hegemony on the region. He also characterizes the "small doses of reform" by the Egyptian government as too little and too gradual.

Regarding political reform, the eleven-page document asserts the MB's adherence to a "democratic and constitutional parliamentary republic within the realm of Islamic principles." It then calls on all political parties to agree to a national charter (mithaq watani) that would guarantee basic freedoms, as well as the unfettered transfer of power through free elections. (Clearly, this is a response to charges that if elected, Islamists would institute a theocracy resulting in "one man, one vote, one time.") It also calls for universal suffrage, presidential term limits, the right of both men and women to serve in parliament, and the withdrawal of the military from political life. It demands the abolition of emergency laws, the release of political detainees, and an end to torture.

The reform initiative seems to signal the MB's commitment to democratic principles (including equal rights for women) and appears to diminish the importance of the more controversial elements of its Islamization program. However, many important questions remain unanswered. Principally, how will the group reconcile its position on the implementation of shari'a law with its professed commitment to democratic reform? The Brotherhood's current position on shari'a law remains purposefully vague in the document. Additionally, is the Brotherhood's reform initiative a tactical maneuver designed to exploit the region's current focus on reform, or does it represent a genuine shift in thinking? Given the movement's illiberal tendencies, a strong dose of skepticism is warranted.

Despite these key questions, the MB initiative is a significant document that could represent an important opening for bringing moderate Islamists into the dialogue on reform. Specifically, the Brotherhood's proposal for a national charter agreed on by all political parties has merit. It offers a key opportunity to engage all elements of the political spectrum in a dialogue to determine a set of shared democratic values and principles to which all parties can adhere. Establishment of such a charter would constitute a significant first step on the path toward reform.

Indeed, credible reform must be inclusive. Although the MB platform is Egypt-specific, it raises the bigger issue of the Islamist role in reform promotion. Islamists represent perhaps the most powerful populist force in the Arab world today and are usually best poised to exploit political openings. However, while reform is often viewed as a potent antidote to extremism, the prospect of moderate Islamists in politics is colored by fears that Islamists coming to power via free elections would overturn a democratic system. The alternative notion of a peaceful evolution of Islamist politics that results in Islamists working within a system has not been fully considered. (Here, the case of the Justice and Development Party in Turkey is instructive.) The MB platform, if genuine, could offer a useful model for other Islamist groups in the region who seek to play a constructive role in the reform process.

The Word from on High: Government Reform Initiatives

Reform initiatives have been proposed not only by Arab nongovernmental initiatives but also by the region's governments. Following the international outcry over Islamist terrorism in the wake of the 9/11 attacks, many Arab states have promoted some type of political reform package. Indeed, governments ranging from the religiously conservative absolute monarchy in Saudi Arabia to Syria's staunchly secular regime appear to be jumping on the reform bandwagon.

The government-sponsored initiatives vary significantly in scope and intent from country to country. An emerging tension between antiterrorism measures implemented by governments in the region and calls for reform is also evident. Often, government reform efforts are largely cosmetic, designed to relieve pressure for change bubbling from below without implementing substantial and deep-rooted reforms. In some instances, government reform policies have translated into an expansion of political space, allowing an outlet for the expression of opposition. In fewer cases, government promises of reform have led to relatively free and fair elections. In nearly every case, political openings have been tenuous and fragile, subject to the whims of those in power. However, even if government calls for reform are superficial rather than genuine, they offer a potential entry point for the promotion of genuine change.

The following section offers a brief sampling of the reform efforts from each of the Arab world's subregions: North Africa, the Levant, and the Gulf, as well as Egypt. The examples chosen reflect either the significance of the reform initiatives (Morocco and Jordan) or the pivotal importance of the states promoting the reform package (Egypt and Saudi Arabia).

Morocco

Considered by many observers to be among the most open of Arab countries (despite the king's near-absolute authority), Morocco has implemented some important political reforms over the past few years. In 2003, the Moroccan parliament approved changes to Morocco's family code, yielding one of the most progressive laws on women's rights in the Arab world. In addition, the 2002 legislative elections were widely considered to be free and fair. The Moroccan parliament boasts a diverse group of members: female MPs make up more than 10 percent of the body and the opposition Islamist Justice and Development Party represents the third-largest bloc.

The 2003 municipal elections were also considered to be largely transparent, despite isolated reports of fraud.

The government has also held a series of hearings on its past human rights violations, generating significant popular interest. Established in January 2004, the Equity and Reconciliation Commission is investigating government human rights violations committed between 1956 and 1999, earning praise from numerous human rights groups. In addition, the Moroccan media are considered relatively open and have a variety of outlets. Morocco also holds claim to a vibrant NGO sector, and the Berber language, once outlawed, is now taught in schools.

However, controversial antiterrorism legislation, passed in May 2003 following terrorist attacks in Casablanca, may signal a rollback of Morocco's nascent political opening. (Indeed, an October 2004 Human Rights Watch report warned that "important elements of progress [on human rights] may now be endangered" following the Moroccan authorities' response to the attack.) The law allows police the right to hold suspects for up to twelve days without charging them or allowing them access to a lawyer. It also allows authorities to intercept phone, mail, and Internet communications and to search homes and businesses without a warrant. The Moroccan press has also been increasingly subject to greater restrictions, somewhat compromising its relatively open status. Meanwhile, Amnesty International reported a sharp increase in reported cases of torture, while Moroccan human rights groups have questioned the fairness of a number of terrorism trials held in the wake of the Casablanca attacks.

The Moroccan government's reform agenda appears to be in a holding pattern, if not in a backslide. Security concerns now trump demands for continued political opening. As a result, the kingdom's policies weigh in favor of antiterrorism measures and are presented as Morocco's contribution to the global war on terror.

Jordan

Wedged between the turmoil in Iraq and the bloody Palestinian-Israeli conflict, Jordan has emerged as a relatively tolerant country. Over the past two years, Jordan's reform plan has comprised several components, including parliamentary and municipal elections, the creation of a ministry for political development, and the establishment of a new Human Rights Center. However, more recently the Jordanian government has shifted away from allowing greater political freedoms and has focused instead on less-threatening administrative reform. Indeed, the kingdom's reform efforts are captive to popular sentiment over Iraq and Israel and seem somewhat tenuous, serving essentially as a pressure reliever. Therefore, any genuine political opening in Jordan remains vulnerable to a change in government policy.

After an electoral hiatus, the kingdom held parliamentary and municipal elections in 2003. The elections were deemed to be largely fair, with no significant reports of fraud. However, government gerrymandering favored tribal candidates who support the monarchy. Even so, the parliament includes some opposition elements, including the Islamic Action Front. Jordanians are also still contending with the impact of more than two hundred temporary royal decrees that were passed between 2001 and 2003, when parliament was dissolved. The decrees have dampened freedoms of expression, the press, and assembly and have been used to quash dissent. In a crackdown on September 9, 2004, thirty-eight Islamic leaders and activists were rounded up for violating a decree that prohibits political commentary inside mosques.

Despite its claim that political reform is a key priority, the Jordanian government's future political reform plans were thrown into question following an October 2004 cabinet reshuffle. The cabinet change was accompanied by a government announcement that administrative reform, namely streamlining the bureaucracy, would become a top priority. This new emphasis on largely technical administrative issues could signal a troubling shift away from more meaningful reform measures. Indeed, as part of this administrative reform plan, King Abdullah unveiled in January 2005 a plan to establish elected local councils to oversee the development and budget of local public services. However, this initiative toward decentralization may be a diversion from real, deep-rooted political reform that would allow for a genuine shift in political power.

Egypt

Typically, reform proposals in Egypt, largely channeled through the ruling National Democratic Party (NDP), have been somewhat cosmetic and often motivated by the Egyptian government's desire to appear responsive to external (largely U.S.) pressure to reform. However, President Mubarak's surprise announcement in late February calling for multicandidate presidential elections is significant. While additional steps are needed to ensure a fair vote—slated for fall 2005—the announcement could herald a historic move toward democracy in Egypt. Other Egyptian government measures are also noteworthy, even if they are not always long-lived. For example, in October 2004, the government licensed the opposition Al-Ghad (Tomorrow) party after having earlier rejected its application three times. This secular party boasts a pro-reform platform that seeks to balance presidential power by bolstering the legislative branch. In addition, two new daily newspapers with liberal leanings were given permission to publish. However, these gains dissipated in early 2005 when authorities arrested Ayman Nour, the Al-Ghad party's founder, and temporarily banned the party's newspaper.

Indeed, despite a lot of talk about the need for reform in various conferences and meetings, significant obstacles to deep-rooted political opening remain. The September 2003 NDP conference gave lip service to the need for democratic reform, publicizing its "new thinking" and offering vague proposals for reform. Meanwhile, the 2004 NDP conference introduced several minor reform measures, but the party endorsed an unprecedented fifth term for President Mubarak. NDP leaders also refused to consider opposition calls for lifting the twenty-three-year-old emergency laws and for implementing presidential term limits. In addition, this past May witnessed a major crackdown on Islamist opposition activists, resulting in fifty arrests and the shutdown of the Muslim Brotherhood's website. As a result of mounting government harassment, opposition forces representing a wide spectrum of political views have uniformly greeted the government's reform proposals with deep skepticism.

Ultimately, the Egyptian government's flirtation with political reform will be balanced by concerns over leadership succession and how to shape post-Mubarak Egypt. The government's dialogue on reform has thus been characterized by its reluctance to implement several key elements of any meaningful reform package, such as annulling the emergency laws and lifting restrictions on political parties. In addition, any multicandidate presidential election will likely be highly managed by the Egyptian government to ensure its total control over the process. In light of deep uncertainty about the post-Mubarak era and continuing instability in Iraq, more deeply-rooted reform is not likely in the near term.

Saudi Arabia

Soon after 9/11, many in the West turned a sharply critical eye toward Saudi Arabia, which produced fifteen of the nineteen hijackers. The Saudi government's initial reaction was defensive; key Saudi leaders refused to acknowledge the role played by their deeply conservative society—anchored in puritanical Wahhabi Islam—and closed political system. However, since 2003 the Saudis have embarked on a reform program that has included the first nationwide municipal elections in decades and a series of "National Dialogues." At the same time, a spate of terrorist attacks beginning in May 2003 has shattered the kingdom's sense of security, once again putting Saudi officials on the defensive and threatening to derail the kingdom's embryonic reforms.

The government held municipal elections on February 10, 2005, drawing an estimated 82 percent voter turnout. While tightly controlled—women could not run or even vote, and the government approved all candidates—the vote represents a significant milestone on the path toward greater political opening. The kingdom has also relaxed press restrictions, established a human rights organization, set up a committee to review school curricula, and enhanced the powers of the appointed consultative council by allowing it to propose legislation.

In addition, three National Dialogues on various areas of reform were held over a yearlong period. The first discussion took place in June 2003 in Riyadh and focused on religion, bringing together representatives of the religious establishment, opposition preachers, Shiite elements, and Sufis. The second dialogue, in December 2003, occurred in Mecca and explored the rise of Islamic militancy and related social issues; the third session, which was held in June 2004 in Medina, examined the role of women.

At the same time, the Saudi government's reform gestures have been marred by the arrest and harassment of reformers and other measures that ensure that the regime retains full control over the reform process. Therefore, the government's longer-term intentions remain unclear. While the greater openness in Saudi society is notable, questions about the government's seriousness as well as Saudi society's capacity to absorb change remain at the forefront of concerns. However, should the reform initiative in the kingdom—a bastion of extremist Islam—meet with success, its impact would reverberate across the Muslim world.

Multilateral Initiatives: The Tunis Declaration

(http://www.arabsummit.tn/en/tunis-declaration.htm)

Judged by its content, the Tunis Declaration, issued by Arab governments following the May 2004 Arab League summit, holds the least promise of all reform initiatives. Compelled to develop a unified response to the G-8's Broader Middle East Initiative, the Arab League signed the thirteen-point Tunis Declaration, calling in vague terms for a wide range of reforms. However, the document represents the first multilateral Arab call for reform and offers an important entry point for Western governments as they confer with their Arab counterparts on the need for reform.

While the Tunis Declaration is symbolically important, the document suffers from several key flaws. First, the declaration reflects the least common denominator with respect to reform proposals, offering nothing new or innovative. Second, the declaration lacks specificity, instead relying on a series of vague endorsements of reform in principle without committing to anything more substantive. For example, it calls for "consolidating the democratic practice by enlarging participation in political and public life," but it does not propose any real steps, such as lifting restrictions on NGOs. Third, the Arab League made no attempt to reach out to civil society activists and take their views into consideration.

Indeed, the document was roundly criticized by Arab NGOs, claiming the declaration made rhetorical promises but offered no concrete programs or policies. Therefore, the Tunis Declaration's significance lies not in its substance but in the cover it provides for those who seek to engage Arab governments on the question of reform. While the prospects of constructive multilateral Arab engagement on the question of reform remain slim, the Tunis Declaration offers a key point of reference. At a minimum, Western governments can refer to the document, calling Arab governments on their promise to move toward greater reform. Ultimately, disagreements among Arab countries regarding the pace and direction of reform, as well as the differing internal dynamics of each country, suggest that successful Arab reform initiatives are unlikely to emerge from multilateral Arab venues.

Conclusions and U.S. Policy Recommendations

Several conclusions can be made about Arab reform initiatives from which important U.S. policy recommendations can be drawn.

The Nature of Arab Reform Efforts

- As Arab governments stand to become net losers in any real reform effort, most government-sponsored initiatives are motivated by self-preservation and a desire to maintain the status quo rather than a wish to implement genuine change. Therefore, the boldest and most detailed Arab reform initiatives will generally originate from independent nongovernmental entities.
- All Arab reform initiatives share key common demands. These include calls for free and fair elections; constitutional reforms that feature a diminishing of executive power and a commensurate increase in legislative and judicial powers; the repeal of emergency laws and the abolishment of exceptional courts; an end to the practice of torture; and the lifting of restrictions on civil society, NGOs, and the media.
- Successful reform in the region must be inclusive; all nonviolent elements of the political spectrum, from Marxists to Islamists, need to be consulted and their viewpoints weighed and negotiated in any process designed to arrive at a comprehensive reform plan. To date, Islamists—perhaps the most influential grassroots opposition element—have been largely excluded from both government and nongovernmental initiatives. Greater effort to engage moderate Islamists in a reform dialogue is necessary. Bridging the divide between Islamists and secularists will be a critical component of successful reform efforts.
- The creation of national pacts to generate a set of common values and goals for reform stands as one of the most promising recommendations to date. By bringing together secular and Islamist reformers, these pacts could unify key reform advocates, accelerating the momentum for change. Unlike previous pacts (e.g., Jordan's 1991

National Charter) devised by governments to co-opt opposition elements, these agreements would allow government and opposition elements to work together to construct a mutually agreed-on set of values, such as those relating to the role of Islam in politics and the "road map" for reform. If constructed in good faith, such pacts could go a long way toward clarifying a number of worrisome ambiguities for both government and civil society.

- Nearly all of the reform initiatives, from nongovernmental to multilateral, suffer—to varying degrees—from a lack of specificity. Even the best-conceived nongovernmental efforts reflect broader region-wide concerns rather than country-specific priorities. Further, the initiatives offer little in the way of specifying how their proposals should be implemented. All of the proposals would benefit from more specific detail on the means of accomplishing the reform objectives.
- Nongovernmental reform initiatives that hold the greatest promise, such as the Beirut Letter and the Doha Declaration, need further thought and development. Specifically, these initiatives should be translated into country-specific action plans that identify and prioritize key reforms and then elaborate on specific steps for achieving these goals.

U.S. Policy Recommendations

- Bolstering U.S. credibility in the region stands as a key priority for policymakers. However, given the United States' faltering credibility in the Arab world, U.S. policymakers should steer clear of publicly endorsing any particular initiative. While the Beirut Letter and the Doha Declaration hold the greatest promise, any direct U.S. endorsement of these efforts could doom them. With a few exceptions, Arab reformers repeatedly suggest that any public association with the United States would dramatically diminish their credibility at home.
- Instead, U.S. policymakers should raise the urgent need for reform, as emphasized by Arab reformers, at the bilateral level. Consistent yet quiet diplomatic pressure, coupled with financial enticements for positive movement on reform (see below), offers the greatest chance of success. Both Washington and diplomats in the field need to signal that reform is a key objective by repeatedly pressing for the release of imprisoned reformers, an end to press censorship, and the cessation of repressive emergency laws.
- Engagement with moderate Islamist reformers is essential. Given the Islamists' strong popular appeal, the United States can no longer afford to call for democratic change in the region while ignoring one of its most powerful political forces. The United States should underscore the commonalities among the demands of secular and Is-

lamist reformers, leveraging the overlap between them to inject greater momentum toward broad reform in the region.

- Positive conditionality, which involves offering financial and other incentives for forward movement on reform, deserves further exploration. Specifically, U.S. policymakers should work to identify key "benchmarks" that adequately measure the progress of political reform. In particular, the creation of bulleted "action plans"—that is, laying out specific reform-oriented goals, a model favored by the European Union—might offer a useful format for the United States and its Arab counterparts. Incentives such as increased aid or enhanced market access could then be tied to the completion of specific action items, offering a stepped, benefit-based approach to reform.
- Greater cooperation and coordination with the United States' European allies could also improve the prospects for successful Arab reform efforts. The United States and its European allies can undertake several key measures to help move Arab reform forward. These include enhancing the transatlantic policy dialogue on Middle East reform; identifying shared transatlantic interests and objectives; coordinating more closely public statements on key reform-related events, such as elections; and synchronizing reform incentives. (For further elaboration on these and other recommendations, see "Transatlantic Cooperation on Democracy Promotion in the Middle East: Ten Recommendations for Enhanced Cooperation," http://www.usip.org/research/reports/usipfride.pdf.)
- In addition, the United States should consider establishing a quasi-public, privately run Middle East foundation as the key mechanism for administering political-reform promotion projects. A Middle East foundation would provide the necessary "arm's length" from the U.S. government, creating an important buffer for sensitive political-reform projects. Indeed, U.S. policymakers should resist the urge to publicly promote U.S. aid in the region, as U.S. credibility there will be enhanced through solid progress on reform than through flashy public rollouts and prominent U.S. branding of projects. A Middle East foundation would also provide an instrument for addressing policy interests that, by nature, are extremely long term and go beyond the purview of the traditional policymaking apparatus.
- U.S. policymakers should think ahead and anticipate potential reform-promoting opportunities. Specifically, they should look for milestone events, such as elections or succession scenarios, and devise policy options that exploit these potential openings for reform when they occur. For example, the Egyptian government will be holding presidential elections in the fall of 2005. The United States should strongly urge the Egyptian government to ensure that elections are

free and fair and to allow international observers. Furthermore, both Egypt and Saudi Arabia, pivotal states in the region, will undergo leadership successions in the near to medium term. U.S. policymakers should explore options for ensuring that these transitions—to the extent possible—result in more open political systems.

- Finally, at a strategic level, U.S. policymakers need to reconcile U.S. counterterrorism policies with the goals of democracy promotion in the region. To date, regimes in the region are sent mixed messages. They are both asked to reform and to cooperate in the war on terror. A successful U.S. policy for promoting reform in the region must answer the vexing question of how to nurture civil society while guarding against extremism. In this regard, a comprehensive Helsinki-type process (the early inspiration for the Broader Middle East Initiative) in which political, economic, and security issues are linked and addressed in a coordinated fashion may offer a promising approach.

12

Morocco: Betting on a Truth and Reconciliation Commission

Pierre Hazan

After forty-four years as a French protectorate, Morocco gained its independence in 1956 under King Mohammed V. In 1961 Hassan II succeeded to the throne and ruled until his death in 1999. He was the main architect of the "executive monarchy" that still rules Morocco today. Under the constitution promulgated by Hassan II in 1962, the king has nearly unlimited powers. Article 23 of the constitution states, "The king is inviolable and sacred." He holds sole executive power. He appoints and fires the prime minister. He can suspend the constitution or dissolve the assemblies and is chief of the armed forces. As Commander of the Faithful (as Hassan II styled himself in the constitution), he exercises spiritual power over Moroccan Muslims.

Context: The Progressive Process of Liberalization

Hassan II's reign spanned two distinct periods. The "Years of the Iron Fist" (known in Morocco as "les années de plomb," or years of lead) began in 1961 and lasted until the end of the Cold War in 1989. A climate of intimidation characterized this period. The security services were responsible for the "disappearance" of hundreds of political opponents and the torture of thousands. After 1989 Hassan II oversaw a period of liberalization prompted by the new international environment and intense external pressures.

After his father's death, Mohammed VI succeeded to the throne in July 1999 and immediately accelerated the process of political liberalization. In 2002 he allowed the freest organization of legislative elections the country had ever seen. The new king also authorized the return of political exiles, allowed somewhat more freedom of the press, reformed the penal code in 2003, and adopted a code (*moudawana*) guaranteeing the equality of women

---

Pierre Hazan, "Morocco: Betting on a Truth and Reconciliation Commission," Special Report 165 (Washington, DC: USIP, 2006).

in 2004. King Mohammed VI also pushed for the creation of a TRC, established later as l'Instance Equité et Réconciliation (IER).

This process of reform and democratization had its limits. Justice remained susceptible to executive pressure. The media were prohibited from questioning Moroccan sovereignty over the Western Sahara and from attacking the monarchy. Social questions were dealt with very timidly.

The IER was an important part of the king's political reforms. It had manifold purposes: to build a new social pact between Moroccan subjects and their institutions, close the dark chapter of decades of repression, solidify the image of a new, young, and modern monarchy, and project to the world the image of a dynamic, democratic Morocco. It was also a response to growing pressure from society for change.

Both radical and more moderate Islamist movements were becoming increasingly popular. They expressed the frustrations of many Moroccans facing a social crisis fueled by the high level of unemployment among young people, including college graduates; the absolute poverty that forced some 20 percent of the population to live on less than a dollar a day; an illiteracy rate of more than 50 percent; and rampant corruption. Transparency International's corruption perceptions index shows that Moroccans think the level of corruption is much worse now than a few years ago. (On its list of perceived less-corrupt countries, Morocco slid from forty-fifth in 1999 to seventy-eighth in 2005.) All these factors reinforced the appeal of the Islamist movements, which capitalized on their image of honesty and their social work. They also benefited from the fact that a significant segment of the Moroccan population was hostile to the U.S.-led military interventions in Afghanistan and Iraq, Israel's policy toward the Palestinians, and the king's close political ties with the West.

Tolerated as a social movement but not recognized as a political party, the (Islamist) Movement for Charity and Justice, led by Sheik Yacine, a staunch critic of the monarchy and the corruption of the regime, gained strong popular support. In 2002 the Justice and Democracy Party (PJD), a moderate but very heterogeneous Islamist party, became the third largest political group in parliament. Its gains would have been greater, but the PJD had decided not to run in many municipalities, fearing that its growing popularity could trigger a bloody confrontation with the military.

Last but not least, radical groups affiliated with al-Qaeda were the authors of the Casablanca bombings of May 16, 2003, which resulted in forty-five deaths, including those of the twelve bombers. Another al-Qaeda group composed mostly of Moroccans hit Madrid in 2004, leaving 200 people dead and 1,000 wounded. The "Zacarias Moussaoui syndrome"—named after the man convicted of involvement in the conspiracy that resulted in the September 11, 2001, attacks on the United States—stoked fear that European citizens of Moroccan descent could be attracted to terrorist networks and carry out actions in the West and their country of origin. By striking such targets and seeking to destabilize the monarchy, these bombers sent a shock wave through Morocco's ruling class.

Genesis of the IER

King Mohammed VI announced the establishment of the IER in a speech on January 7, 2004. Created by royal decree, the commission reported to him. This peculiar genesis structured and influenced the IER's work. Political parties were largely excluded from its establishment. Instead, the IER came about through lengthy consultations between the throne and certain elements in civil society, including former political prisoners. All these actors saw the IER as a tool to carry out their specific interests.

The idea for a TRC in Morocco came from Driss Benzekri, a former Marxist-Leninist imprisoned for seventeen years between 1974 and 1991. Following his release he became a human rights activist. He and a group of former detainees offered a "deal of historic importance" to the monarchy: They would collaborate with the regime and even support an amnesty of their former torturers and their superiors on the condition that the throne would strongly pursue democratization. They saw the TRC as a tool to give new impetus to democratization by publicly denouncing past systemic violations of human rights and recommending broad institutional reforms. They believed the domestic system could be reformed from within and wanted to use a TRC as a lever for democratic change.

They supported a "strategic amnesty," basing their arguments on two premises. One was that like the rest of the Arab world, Morocco was in a profound crisis whose resolution required swift democratization. The other was that a historic opportunity existed to have as an interlocutor a modern sovereign, willing to democratize the political system to a certain extent and improve the efficiency of state institutions.

Regarding the first point, Driss el Yazami, who would become a prominent figure in the IER, called attention to the somber state of affairs described in a 2004 United Nations Development Program report on the Arab world. He reiterated the UNDP's findings: "The Arab states are actually less developed than they were fifty years ago. There are fewer Internet connections in the whole of the Arab world than in the state of Israel alone. More than 20 percent of the Moroccan population is malnourished, and the majority of Moroccans are illiterate."

Driss Benzekri, Salah El-Oudie, and Driss el Yazami, the future leaders of the IER, agreed with the UNDP analysis, but they believed Moroccan society had the chance to rise to the challenge of development. Strategically, that implied a pragmatic alliance with the "young guard" surrounding King Mohammed VI. These human rights activists were influenced by the examples of Solidarity in Poland and Gorbachev in the former Soviet Union. They dreamed of being in Solidarity's position, and they hoped for an interlocutor like Gorbachev, not General Jaruzelski, Poland's former communist president. They wagered that they could reform the system from within with the support of the modern elites close to the king. For them, the clarification of past crimes, democratization, and the establishment of the rule of law were preconditions of social and economic development. Given the considerable powers he enjoyed through the constitution, the king was their indispensable partner.

They accepted the price to be paid: the absence of punishment for those who had committed human rights abuses. For these human rights activists, renouncing justice was easier to accept because "the conditions for an impartial process for the perpetrators and those that gave the orders are not feasible due to the lack of a proper judicial system," as Driss el Yazami told the author during an interview in Rabat on January 25, 2005. They also believed that without an alliance with the palace, no way existed to pursue democratization.

For the IER commissioners, its political functions differed from those of its predecessors elsewhere. The Moroccan TRC did not emerge out of political upheaval, as South Africa's did, but was intended to accelerate democratic change. The commissioners aimed to revitalize civil society and political debate, expand the democratic space, and give the king additional support to pursue reforms. Through the participation of victims who publicly testified about the tortures they had endured, and through denunciation of state organs that had violated human rights, the commission wanted to "push the envelope" of acceptable discourse in Moroccan society.

King Mohammed VI's support for the IER can be explained by a combination of factors. The king viewed the IER as serving his interests by disarming criticism, improving his image as a modern and democratic ruler, and countering the growing force of the Islamists. He also expressed his desire to modernize Morocco and state institutions, based on the assumption that it was necessary to restore trust between the state and citizens to "liberate energies" and turn toward the challenges of economic and social development.

The monarchy has used human rights to create political legitimacy for the king. Public opinion views most of the political parties, except the Islamist organizations, as co-opted by the monarchy. The king's alliance with NGO representatives, some of whom are ideologically distant from the monarchy and have long years of imprisonment to prove it, shelters him from suspicion that the IER is simply a pawn of the palace. Politically, this alliance with personalities on the left (which has been weakening in the past few years) counterbalanced the most conservative elements of the Makhzen, the system of formal and informal power that controls the state, which were intent on slowing political and economic liberalization to maintain the status quo. The alliance was also beneficial for the modernizing elite, which was positioned to profit from privatization and the enhancement of institutional functionality.

This strategy of equilibrium also countered the rising power of the Islamists. The alliance was presented as an embodiment of the "Moroccan voice," an alternative to Islamist theocracy and part of the soft war against radical Islamist networks.

The selection of the IER's seventeen commissioners reflected the alliance between elements of civil society and the throne. The king chose nine of the commissioners from members of the Consultative Council on Human Rights (CCHR); the others were civil-society members, such as the heads of NGOs, a political scientist, and a medical doctor. Six of the IER commissioners were former political prisoners and former far-left activists, some of whom had been forced into exile for years. The activists have abandoned their revolutionary ideologies and invested themselves in human rights organizations.

The four most prominent commissioners, beginning with the IER president, Driss Benzekri, are former Marxist-Leninist activists. Salah El Ouadie was sentenced to twenty years but paroled after ten. Driss el Yazami was forced into exile, and Latifa Jbadba, the only female commissioner, was first sent to prison at age fifteen. Mbarek Bouderka was sentenced to death in absentia and pardoned much later.

Not a single religious figure is included among the commissioners. Nor are any Islamists, who represent the main political force in the country today. This is partly because the initiative to establish the IER came from members of the left, who paid the highest price during decades of repression. In addition, the inauguration of the IER came shortly after the Casablanca bombing, and the throne wanted to keep some distance from even moderate Islamists.

The king gave a triple mandate to the IER: to shed light on all the cases of "forced disappearance and arbitrary detention," oversee "payment of reparations," and "ensure that the reparations compensated for all of the material and moral damage done to the victims." Finally, the IER was charged with "publishing a report . . . composed of an analysis of human rights violations . . . as well as recommendations and propositions, not only to preserve the memory of these past violations, but also to guarantee a definitive break with the former practices that had brought about the suffering of these victims, re-establishing and strengthening confidence in a state of law and the respect for human rights." (The IER's complete mandate may be found at www.ier.ma.)

No TRC had ever covered such a long period; its mandate encompassed a total of forty-three years, from independence in 1956 until the death of King Hassan II in 1999. Officially, the end of the IER's mandate coincided with the establishment of an independent arbitration commission to pay indemnities to victims of "disappearance" and torture, foreshadowing the IER. But 1999 also was the year of King Hassan's death, and the cut-off date of the IER's mandate may be seen as a clear line of demarcation between the new king and his father.

The IER's mandate was constrained by numerous limitations. It forbade mentioning the names of those who had ordered the human rights violations or those who had carried them out. Thus, these persons were sheltered not only from criminal prosecution, but also from public stigmatization. Before they could testify publicly, the victims had to sign a form agreeing not to mention the names of the perpetrators. This prohibition was an essential part of the deal between the palace and Driss Benzekri that led to the IER's establishment. The monarchy did not want to undermine the security organs or overtly criticize King Hassan's reign.

These limitations prevented the commissioners from lifting the veil from past crimes. The commission was not given the power of subpoena. Therefore, security service agents could decide for themselves if they would cooperate with the IER, and to what extent. Finally, the commission could present only recommendations for political and institutional change. It had no real teeth, except in the domain of reparations.

The IER at Work

Public hearings played an essential role in the work of the commission. Influenced by the South African TRC, before which 20,000 victims and hundreds of perpetrators had testified in highly dramatic proceedings, the Moroccan commissioners wanted to use public hearings to define the new narrative of decades of repression and unleash a social dynamic that would influence all of society, literate or not. They saw hearings as an effective tool to convey a political message, because not only words but also deep emotions and old scars would be revealed.

The commissioners obtained permission from the royal cabinet to broadcast the hearings on national television and radio. Because most of the populace was illiterate, TV and radio were the most effective vehicles of communication, with the potential to reach millions of people, in contrast to the daily press, whose total circulation is only 300,000 to 400,000.

The IER originally decided to hold twenty public hearings in every region of the country. The number later was reduced to seven (two in Rabat, one each in Errachidia, Figuig, Khénifra, El Houcéma, and Marrakech), because the commission worried about trivializing them and because of the huge amount of resources each one required.

As a result of the strict limitations on its mandate, the IER's position during the hearings was delicate. Its goal was to signify the beginning of a new era with the opening of the democracy desired by Mohammed VI. But the break with the past had to be made with great care. The reign of King Hassan II, under which almost all the human rights violations had taken place, could not be criticized.

Since naming the torturers and their superiors was not allowed, the "truth" the witnesses expressed was limited to victimization, not accusation. They could mention only the locations of their suffering (Tazmanart, Agdez, or Derb Moulay Chérif, for example) and the agencies (army, police, security services) that had mistreated them. Because no perpetrator was present or could be named and no one asked them any questions, the victims were the main characters on the stage. The dramatic intensity of the hearings depended solely on their accounts.

The commissioners' aim was to break the silence about the decades of repression. These hearings were a subtle exercise in indirect criticism of Hassan's reign and an all-powerful monarchy. From the commissioners' perspective, the emotional impact of the testimonies was greater when the victims themselves were shaken by their own accounts of tortures and rapes, especially if they were unengaged politically. Sometimes their only "fault" was their blood relationship to a political opponent. They projected an image of innocence disfigured by an arbitrary and cruel system, although that was never said explicitly. The message was nonetheless clear: "Never again."

The TRC encountered a mixed reception from human rights movements. Although some applauded the idea, others harshly criticized its limitations. The Moroccan Human Rights Association (AMDH), a number of former victims, human rights activists, Islamists, and most of the victims from Western Sahara complained that the IER had granted impunity to the torturers and their superiors. They accused the IER of distorting transitional justice mechanisms to protect those responsible for the repressive system—if not whitewashing their past, then sparing them any punishment. For the critics, installing the rule of law meant exacting justice for past crimes.

The human rights activists also charged that the IER mandate did not cover current human rights violations—in particular, those against nearly 3,000 Islamists after the bombings in Casablanca, under an antiterrorist law passed during an emotionally charged emergency.

The AMDH disagreed with the IER's careful approach. The association decided to organize parallel public hearings, an unprecedented step in the history of transitional justice. Called the "Completely Free Testimonies for Truth," these hearings took place in some of the same cities chosen by the IER: Rabat, Khénifra, El-Hocéma, and Marrakech, as well as Paris. They publicly announced the torturers' names and denounced human rights abuses committed against Islamists after 1999, the period not addressed under the IER mandate.

Ironically, the establishment of the IER enabled these public hearings to take place, creating a space for expression that surpassed the limits of the official truth commission. These unofficial hearings revealed the ambiguity and arbitrariness of the authorities' decision on criticism of the regime. Since the mid-1990s, NGOs, the press, activists, authors, and numerous ex-prisoners have broken the silence about the identity of the torturers. There has been no retaliation against those making the denunciations, but also no judicial consequences for the perpetrators.

The IER's seven official hearings took place between December 2004 and May 2005. Another was scheduled in the Western Sahara in May 2005, then postponed to July before being cancelled for political and security reasons. This hearing was of special significance and the toughest test for the commission. By holding a public hearing there as it did in other regions of the country, the Moroccan state would have demonstrated that the situation in Western Sahara had been normalized.

To this day the Western Sahara conflict has not been resolved. Moroccan authorities consider the region an integral part of the kingdom and have occupied it since the Green March in 1975. The independence movement of the Saharawis, Polisario (Popular Front for the Liberation of Saguia el Hamra and Gold River), supported by Algeria, claims their right to self-determination.

In 1975 the International Court of Justice recommended holding a referendum, which never took place. The most recent plan for peace, in 2003, came from James Baker, former U.S. Secretary of State, but Morocco rejected it. Today no international solution is in sight. In November 2005 the U.S. Congress held a public hearing on the issue. Supporters of self-determination for the "last African colony" clashed with Congress members sympathetic to Morocco, who asserted it was "absurd" to create a state in a sprawling territory with no more than 300,000 inhabitants, which moreover would be a haven for terrorists.

The commission faced a real challenge: How could a transitional justice mechanism be successful while the key question of sovereignty was not yet resolved? The IER did not rise to the challenge. The task might have exceeded its capacity: A commission established by Morocco's king would have had difficulty appearing neutral in the disputed region. Confidence between the IER and the Saharawi victims was hardly the rule. Only one of the seventeen commissioners was Saharawi, and he was from an old local family with ties to the Moroccan elite.

Nevertheless, four to five thousand men and women, almost a quarter of the people who identified themselves as victims to the IER, were originally from Western Sahara. Despite their doubts about the commission's neutrality, they agreed to collaborate for a variety of reasons: Some perceived the commission as a rare platform for denouncing human rights abuses; others hoped to obtain information about the circumstances of deceased victims who had been close to them and, above all, the location of their graves. Living in destitution, they also wanted compensation for their suffering.

Lahcen Moutik, a leading human rights activist in Layoune, explained to the author in an interview on December 3, 2005: "For the first time, we had a chance to speak to the Moroccan people about a reality that has been hidden from them. In addition, by collaborating with the IER, we can honor the memory of the disappeared and receive individual and collective reparations."

But riots denouncing "thirty years of Moroccan occupation" erupted in spring 2005, and the Moroccan flag was burned. Polisario sympathizers were determined to prevent the hearing from taking place in Western Sahara because they did not want any Moroccan institution to have a shred of credibility in this region. These activists believed that questions surrounding arbitrary arrests, disappearances, and inequitable legal proceedings could be resolved only by "the end of Moroccan occupation." They viewed independence as a prerequisite for the improvement of human rights.

Faced with the radical independence movement and the ill will of the local authorities who were to provide security, the IER postponed the scheduled date of the hearings and finally cancelled them altogether. Both the security forces and the radical militants thus achieved their goal of preventing the public hearings from taking place.

Regrettably, in the IER's summary report, not one word was devoted to Western Sahara, the area that undoubtedly had been hardest hit by repression. Nor did it confront the Moroccan agencies that had carried out the "disappearances" of dozens of Saharawis, tortured hundreds, and inflicted collective punishments whose numbers are still controversial but nonetheless significant.

Analysis of the IER

The IER is based on two ambiguities. The first is the legacy of Hassan II to his son, Mohammed VI. The second concerns the IER's political purpose. Both strongly affected the commission's work and are likely to affect its impact.

King Mohammed VI is caught between his proclaimed loyalty to his father and his need to put some distance between himself and his father's reign. His ambiguous attitude toward Hassan II is striking. The IER's mandate could have terminated in 1990, with the beginning of liberalization, or with the general amnesty of 1994. Instead, Mohammed VI decided to end it in 1999, the very year he came to power. Therefore, IER's mandate marks the boundary between the past and present sovereign. However,

Mohammed VI's distance from his father is countered by the fact that he justifies the establishment of the IER in the name of his father, who started the liberalization process. Addressing some of the victims of Hassan's repression, he spoke about the "immaculate soul of Hassan II."

Not once does Mohammed VI assign responsibility for the decades of repression. He never questions his father's repressive regime, nor does he accuse the groups that advocated armed struggle to overthrow the monarchy. Instead, he often has emphasized the need for "Moroccans to reconcile themselves to their past" and exhorted citizens "not to be prisoners of the negative past." The IER denounces the manifestations of repression—torture, disappearances carried out by state agents, secret prisons, and arbitrary detention—but never the system that created the repression. And the state remains silent.

During the seven public audiences organized by the IER, portraits of Hassan II were sometimes present, sometimes absent. Whenever they were there, they were in a position equal or inferior to the present king's. The ambiguity about the previous king was never elucidated: Was Hassan II the builder of modern and democratic Morocco or the primary architect of decades of repression? And if he was both, how is it possible to separate the two aspects? The right to list the pros and cons seems to be forbidden up to the present day, as the IER's final report shows. A torture victim from the reign of Hassan II explained the rationalization he had to make while testifying between portraits of the current king and his father: "I imagined that the left portrait [Mohammed VI] was defending me against the right portrait [Hassan II]."

This first ambiguity in the legacy of Hassan II leads to the second. What is the goal of the IER? What is the final destination of this process of democratization? Some IER commissioners and the monarchy disagree about these questions.

Driss Benzekri wagers that the work of the truth commission will create a dynamic for institutional reform, leading to a parliamentary monarchy in the near future. In a speech in Washington before the National Endowment for Democracy on January 19, 2006, he said such reform would mean "a limitation on executive powers, strengthening the role of the parliament, and a strict separation between the branches of power, with real independence of the judiciary."

King Mohammed VI never has fully explained his political objectives. In the speech establishing the IER in January 2004, he affirmed his desire "to complete the democratization process and to install the rule of law" and "to build a modern, democratic society, where all citizens can exercise their rights and comply with their obligations, with liberty and responsibility." But what political future does he envisage? Does he accept Benzekri's idea of establishing a parliamentary monarchy in the near future? In a recent interview, the sovereign refuted the idea that Morocco would be transformed into a constitutional monarchy with himself as a new Juan Carlos. "We cannot transport the European model of constitutional monarchy. We have our specific needs and obligations that direct us on the road we pursue" ("The Objective of the Public Hearings Is to 'Reconcile Morocco with its Past,'" *El Pais*, January 24, 2006). Is King Mohammed ready to renounce the almost unlimited powers the constitution gives him?

Moroccan authorities emphasized time and again that establishment of a TRC in the Arab Islamic world was unprecedented. In fact, thirty or so other commissions have been established in Christian or African societies, some of which include sizable Muslim minorities. The absence of TRCs in Islamic countries does raise a number of questions. Are truth commissions truly universal instruments, or does the lack of democratic regimes explain their absence in this part of the world? Does Islamic exceptionalism block the concept of forgiveness, and has Morocco succeeded in breaking through it? Or are westerners and Africans exaggerating the importance of their own cultures in establishing TRCs?

The Moroccan example shows that the way these questions are being framed is part of a political debate. The king stresses the importance of religion and the search for national unity in achieving reconciliation through forgiveness. On the other hand, the commissioners want to use the TRC to democratize institutions and are ready to grant political amnesty to the torturers and their superiors to achieve this objective. The result is practically the same: Both advocate a nonjudicial approach, but the terms used—forgiveness vs. amnesty—reveal differing strategies and goals. By using the term amnesty (which can be rescinded), the commissioners are trying to keep the process in the realm of politics. Meanwhile the king depoliticizes impunity by justifying it spiritually as forgiveness.

The king finds it appropriate to invoke Islam because one of his titles and roles is "Commander of the Faithful." Unlike other Arab regimes, Moroccan royal power is exercised in the religious arena, and the sovereign holds spiritual power. In a speech on January 6, 2006, the king invoked God to legitimate the lack of punishment of human rights violators: "The sincere work of reconciliation that we have achieved . . . is in keeping with the divine injunction which says: 'So overlook human frailty with gracious forgiveness. . . .' This is a gracious act of collective forgiveness." Another cultural argument favorable to the monarchy asserts, "Moroccan culture does not practice revenge." Punishment of a criminal act is presented as an act of vengeance. The meaning of the words is elided to remove any value from punishment. (King Mohammed's speech, marking the conclusion of the IER's work, may be found on www.ier.ma.)

Another argument the king put forth in favor of pardoning perpetrators of human rights abuses is simultaneously cultural, political, and developmental. From this perspective, forgiveness is a precondition of reconciliation "between Moroccans and their past," to free energies to build a new Morocco. This argument is essentialist (reflecting the supposed essence of the Moroccan nation), political (searching for national unity), and developmental (liberating productive energies).

The IER commissioners are reluctant to use religious and cultural arguments to justify amnesty. They accept "strategic" forgiveness, nothing more, elaborating an ethic of responsibility, assessing that the political and social benefits of establishing the rule of law outweigh punishing the authors of the repression and past crimes. In his 2005 interview with the author, Salah El-Ouadie explained: "I do not want only certain individuals to pay for the state's responsibilities. The individualization of the punishments would have relieved the state of its responsibilities, and that is exactly what we wanted to avoid. Those who stake out an extremist position are mistaken."

According to this line of reasoning, putting the perpetrators on trial would create a false sense of good conscience, because it is the system that is really responsible. Salah El-Ouadie believes that to "purify" the society, the individual authors of state crimes should not be punished; rather, the criminal system should be proscribed. It is as if the agents of the repressive apparatus did not matter.

For the IER commissioners, forgiveness—or rather amnesty—is purely a political act, and it is essential that society understand it as such. In an interview with the author on February 4, 2005, IER commissioner Abdelhay Moudden opposed cultural justification of the IER because "the commission has been thought of, conceived, and defined as a means to achieve a political objective, that of democratization." To transform the amnesty into "cultural forgiveness" would give it some local color but would depoliticize it and damage its potential to foster social mobilization.

The IER cannot be understood outside the political and security context in which it was created. At each stage of the commission, the "war against terrorism"—in particular the Casablanca and Madrid bombings—played a major role. It affected the commission's establishment, mandate, functions, perception by the public, and effects. Some state organs also used the rhetoric of "the war against terrorism" to justify their refusal to cooperate with the IER.

The king established the IER about seven months after the Casablanca bombings of May 16, 2003. At that time Morocco had become one of the theatres of the "war against terrorism" announced by the Bush administration eighteen months before. Morocco's association with terrorism intensified with the Madrid bombings (March 11, 2004), perpetrated mostly by Moroccan nationals.

Some Moroccan officials in the interior ministry wanted to use the TRC in psychological warfare. "The IER is a weapon in the antiterrorist struggle.

We are taking this war to two fronts. One, the hard war, includes the repressive aspects of dismantling terrorist cells; the other, the soft war, is to bring the population to our side. The IER is an element of this soft war," a high interior ministry official stressed during an interview with the author on December 3, 2005. By winning the confidence of the population, the IER could dry up the support essential for the hard-core "terrorists" to reach their goals.

In practice, however, making the IER an instrument of antiterrorism led to considerable difficulties and created a contradiction between the agendas of security and democracy. The authorities believed they had to reassure the repressive organs that were dismantling Islamist networks. Therefore the monarchy guaranteed those organs impunity and the option of refusing to cooperate with the IER, and they took advantage of those prerogatives. But to what degree can society adhere to a process that sheds light on the Years of the Iron Fist if the highest state officials refuse to cooperate with a commission created by the king? How can society subscribe to democratization, supposedly exemplified by the IER, if, in the name of the struggle against terrorism, the security services continue to make massive arrests marked by mistreatment and extremely flawed police work?

Abdelhay Moudden noted in an interview with the author on December 8, 2005: "People ask us, how can you investigate the past while the human rights abuses still go on, even if they don't compare with the past? How can these abuses continue like that and even be encouraged by our American allies?" There is little doubt that the way the Moroccan state organs conducted the war against terrorism weakened the IER.

The IER Report

After twenty-three months' work, the IER published its conclusions, including a thirty-page summary in French and a report of almost seven-hundred pages in Arabic, available at www.ier.ma. The IER report is one of the commission's main accomplishments. It presents a new historical narrative as it interprets a period marked by massive human rights violations and asserts the value of spotlighting them in the present. It also assigns responsibility and recommends institutional and political reforms to prevent repetition of past crimes. In his speech of January 6, 2006, the king announced his decision to make the report public.

The report's three sections deal with historical clarification, the question of reparations, and proposals for institutional reforms. In the historical section, the most sensitive part of the report, the commission sheds light on a number of cases, including 742 forced "disappearances." It documents the practice of arbitrary detention and describes "the systematic use of physical and moral torture," which led to the deaths of some detainees. The report also describes police's excessive use of force to suppress protests.

While writing the report's historical clarification, the commissioners came under pressure from two sides. Many victims, human rights activists, and leaders of large international NGOs wanted the IER to go as far as possible to highlight the violations and reveal which institution was responsible (since the IER's mandate prohibited placing blame on individuals). On the other hand, the palace and the political parties from left to right, not to mention the security services, had strong reservations about being criticized in a report that would become part of the historical record. It was this pressure group that proved the most effective.

In establishing the facts, the IER thoroughly investigated the forced disappearances. The report concludes that it cannot properly elucidate sixty-six other cases and recommends that the state pursue the investigations the commission already had begun. These cases are the most politically sensitive. The IER fails, for instance, to shed any new light on the fate of the famous leftist and Third World leader Mehdi Ben Barka, although it is public knowledge that the Moroccan secret services played a major role in his "disappearance" in 1965.

At times, the report criticizes the obstacles state agents and agencies created, hindering the commission's work. "The state of the archives is deplorable, if they exist at all, cooperation by the security apparatus was erratic, the testimony of those responsible was sometimes vague, and others refused to cooperate at all to establish the truth," it complains. (See the summary in French on http://www.ier.ma/_rapport_fr.php.) According to some Moroccan journalists, the army was united in refusing to cooperate with the IER.

The report also documents the practice of arbitrary detention and states that "the systematic resort to physical and moral torture" inflicted upon the detainees often led "to psychological and permanent physical disability or even death." The report notes that the moral and psychological torture of detainees consisted of "threats of death or rape, insults and other attacks on their dignity, torture, or the threat to torture a close family member." It notes that "women were subjected to other, specific forms of abuse," such as rape or the threat of rape.

The report documents "excessive and disproportionate use of public force" to suppress demonstrations, resulting in unknown numbers of victims at these events. The commission wanted "to stress that a number of children, some less than ten years old, were among the dead."

The report admits that as a result of lack of cooperation by state agents, certain events are still unclear. It recommends follow-up and clarification of these events within the following six months.

The report is silent on the hierarchical structure of the repression. Who gave the orders? What was the chain of command? The repression was presumably not the product of isolated acts committed by state agents on their own initiative, but rather came from a hierarchical system reaching the state's highest level. The report could have gone much further in explaining the methods of the state organs. After completing the report, Driss Benzekri sent a message to King Mohammed VI with the names of military and government functionaries who were responsible for human rights violations. How and when, if ever, this information will be used or made public depends solely on the will of the king.

The last aspect of historical clarification is the most delicate and important: to deliver to society an interpretation of the political and ideological causes of human rights violations. Since the IER's establishment, interpretation of those decades has aroused intense debate in society. What were the reasons for the repression? What were the respective roles of ideology, King Hassan II, and the armed groups that tried to overthrow the monarchy? The report provides no context—to the satisfaction of both the monarchy and the political parties, each of which feared that the IER would become a "historical tribunal." The monarchy did not want any accusations raised against King Hassan II. And the Union of Popular Socialist Forces (USFP) did not want the left to be blamed for having justified armed struggle in the past. But how can "Moroccans reconcile themselves with the past," to use the official phraseology, if historical clarification does not lead to analysis of decades of repression and violence?

The IER's mandate included completing the unfinished work of the 1999 arbitration commission. Accordingly, it has promised financial reparations totaling fifty to seventy million dollars to nearly ten thousand victims. Each victim will receive an average of five to seven thousand dollars.

These payments are intended to compensate victims of forced disappearance and arbitrary detention (with or without due process) that resulted in death or injury, as well as those subjected to arbitrary detention stemming from urban demonstrations or riots, forced exile, and sexual violence. The IER used six criteria to determine reparations: deprivation of liberty, forced disappearance, detention conditions, use of torture and other cruel, degrading, and inhuman treatment; the aftermath of physical and psychological abuse; and the loss of opportunity and potential income. In addition to financial reparations, some victims will regain public office or receive other administrative or professional reparations.

The IER also recommends adopting and supporting socioeconomic and cultural development plans for a number of cities (such as Casablanca), women, and regions such as Rif, Figuig, Agdez-Zagora, Tazmamart, and the Middle Atlas that were hard hit by the repression.

Originally, the TRC's goal was to give impetus to the pursuit of democratization. This was the objective of the "historic deal" between Driss Benzekri and the monarchy. Once the IER had completed its mandate,

Benzekri declared in his speech at the National Endowment for Democracy that he favored the establishment of "some type of parliamentary monarchy in Morocco in the not-too-distant future." The recommendations in the IER report present a road map to that goal.

The IER recommends constitutional reforms to guarantee human rights—especially inclusion of the primary principles of international human rights law, such as the presumption of innocence and the right to due process, in domestic law. The report proposes that the constitution explicitly state that rights and liberties such as the freedom to travel, freedom of expression, demonstration, association, the right to strike, the right to private correspondence, inviolability of the home, and respect for privacy are fundamental. The report also recommends reinforcing the separation of powers, strengthening independent judicial and legislative branches, and adopting national measures against impunity, as well as improving government oversight of the security apparatus.

The commission asked the prime minister (not the king) to assume responsibility for past human rights violations in the name of the Moroccan state and to ask forgiveness from the nation.

Conclusion

Internationally, the establishment of the IER helped Morocco improve its human rights image, projecting it as a model of a modern state in the Arab Islamic world. This image is politically and economically important for a regime with close ties to the West, especially at a time of tension between parts of the Muslim world and the United States.

The IER has demonstrated that religious and cultural factors are secondary in choosing between punishment and amnesty for massive human rights violations. These factors might come into play at a later stage, to legitimate political decisions. In this regard the Moroccan case is particularly revealing. The semantic battle over the king's use of the word "forgiveness" and the commissioners' use of the word "amnesty" shows differing intentions and goals. By employing a spiritual term, the king sought to make a nonjudicial approach to the perpetrators more acceptable and less political. On the other hand, the commissioners sought to keep restorative justice in the political arena. They used political and judicial terms in hopes that society would pressure the state to undertake fundamental reforms.

The framing of the TRC is itself part of a wider debate about the country's political future. It also underlines the fact that TRCs are flexible instruments. They can be used even without regime change, and each state can extract what it wants from its culture and religion to justify a symbolic policy of forgiveness, in line with its political objectives.

However, the "war against terrorism" created permanent obstacles for the TRC. The "antiterrorist struggle" has superseded the defense of human rights in many official circles in Morocco and elsewhere. In practice, a truth commission cannot be an effective instrument in the soft war against terrorism. The tension is too strong between the interests of repressive agencies that want to operate with fewer restrictions and the TRC's need to shed light on these agencies' actions.

Although it would be difficult to confirm this speculation, the IER's existence and establishment by the king may have prevented further human rights abuses by state organs. The king's personal involvement with the IER gave legitimacy to human rights discourse inside the state apparatus. It also may have increased the perception that future abuses would be prosecuted.

One of the striking peculiarities of Morocco is the absence of dramatic regime change. Without it, the TRC aimed to foster democratization. Has it worked? Did the commissioners have reason to put their faith in the "historic deal" they struck with the monarchy? This is the decisive question. Fulfilling the commission's recommendations would involve a substantial change in the structure of power in Morocco, as Prince Moulay Icham, fourth in line to the throne, stressed: "Democracy and the sacredness of the king are not reconcilable. That is the systemic problem in Morocco. It is a question that we touch upon all the time. . . . The question now is how to disassociate the monarchy from the caliphate system, or to transform the monarchy. Reforming the monarchy is the only way to perpetuate it" (as quoted in *Tel Quel*, December 25, 2004).

Although the current king has broken with his father's autocratic regime, he paradoxically claims continuity with that regime. Before a group of victims he said: "Praise be to Almighty God that as the loyal successor of my venerable father, I have seen to it that this mission has been successfully carried out. On behalf of the entire Moroccan people, I send these glad tidings to his blessed soul to bring joy to his heart, as well as to the hearts of all victims, sufferers who were harmed and their grieving families, about whom I care so deeply" (www.ier.ma). Should this speech be read as empty rhetoric? Or is it, rather, a pledge to the "old guard" who remain at their posts? This persistent ambiguity in the consideration of the legacy of King Hassan II raises uncertainty about Morocco's political development.

Nonetheless, the IER has given legitimacy to the words of the victims. It has proposed reforms that would transform Morocco into a parliamentary monarchy if they were implemented. The IER has offered a road map for political and institutional change that could lead to the establishment of the rule of law. No one knows yet how the security forces will react to this proposition, especially while they engage in a "war against terrorism." Nor can one predict how the economic actors who have a direct stake in the status quo will react. What is the king's margin for maneuver, especially when confronted with opposing pressures from Moroccan society?

Recommendations

1. **Reform the system of governance.** Although it initially made the security apparatus nervous, the platform of reforms advocated by the IER will contribute to strengthening the democratic option, the most conducive to long-term stability. Likewise, as the IER suggested, a public apology by the prime minister or the king to victims of past abuses and the nation would constitute official recognition that the violations were the product of an organized, structural, hierarchical system that reached all the way to the pinnacle of the state.
2. **Lustration.** Even if the Moroccan authorities remain determined not to punish judicially those responsible for repression during the Years of the Iron Fist, they nevertheless could drive those responsible from public office. This measure would strengthen the credibility of the state. If state organs cooperated in revealing the circumstances and fate of the "disappeared," their credibility also would be enhanced. Without their help, the IER has proven to be incapable of accomplishing this objective.
3. **Providing technical support.** Western governments could help the Moroccan government reform its judicial system and offer technical support in training police forces, judges, and prosecutors, thus reinforcing respect for human rights.
4. **Resolving the situation in Western Sahara.** In coordination with its European allies, the United States would be well advised to start a diplomatic initiative to help settle the Western Sahara conflict, which has lasted since 1975. This conflict remains the principal barrier to normalization of relations between the two most important countries in North Africa, Morocco and Algeria, both of which play a key role in the stability of this strategic region.

No one knows yet if or how the Moroccan monarchy and political class will use the IER's recommendations. If the recommendations do take hold, Morocco will have demonstrated that transitional justice mechanisms can free new political space and rebuild confidence between state and society. This would constitute a stimulating and hopeful precedent in the Arab Islamic world. If the IER commissioners lose their wager to renovate the Moroccan system, that will only reinforce the frustration of those who will feel duped. Thus the IER could have the unintended consequence of playing into the hands of extremist Islamists, who believe that violence is the only way to bring about real change.

13

Islamists at the Ballot Box: Findings from Egypt, Jordan, Kuwait, and Turkey[1]

Judy Barsalou

In an era when much attention has focused on how to promote democracy in Middle Eastern countries with centralized, semiauthoritarian governments, the inclusion of Islamist political parties in electoral politics has been a subject of vigorous debate. How does their inclusion affect the political systems of which they are a part? Does electoral participation by Islamist political parties engender moderation in their politics? If so, is moderation on sensitive political issues a temporary expedient to gain political advantage or is it expressive of changes in core values? Is there evidence that Islamist parties have cooperated or collaborated with secular political parties and other groups to promote political goals of mutual interest, and what happens when they do? Under what circumstances does such cooperation come about, and how extensive is it? When, if at all, does such cooperation induce conservative Islamist political parties to moderate their views and political values? How do Islamist parties relate to centralized political authority in their societies, and what happens when an Islamist party comes into power?

These are among the questions investigated by Professors Janine Astrid Clark, Sultan Tepe, and Carrie Rosefsky Wickham in their work on the role of Islamist parties in the Middle East. Their research, which was based on

1. On April 12, 2005, the United States Institute of Peace's Grant Program organized a roundtable discussion featuring three Institute grantees who had conducted research in the Middle East on the role and impact of Islamist parties. This report summarizes their presentations. The three grantees—Professor Janine Astrid Clark (University of Guelph, Ontario), Professor Sultan Tepe (University of Illinois, Chicago), and Professor Carrie Rosefsky Wickham (Emory University, Atlanta)—were joined at the roundtable by discussant Daniel Brumberg, a professor at Georgetown University and special consultant to the Institute's Muslim World Initiative. Judy Barsalou, the Institute's vice president for Grants, moderated the discussion and prepared this report.

Judy Barsalou, "Islamists at the Ballot Box: Findings from Egypt, Jordan, Kuwait, and Turkey," Special Report 144 (Washington, DC: USIP, 2005).

extensive fieldwork in Turkey (Tepe), Jordan (Clark and Wickham), and Egypt and Kuwait (Wickham), clearly revealed that in each country Islamist parties have eagerly participated in electoral politics. But this participation has had mixed results—both with respect to the impact of participation on the parties' own politics and the parties' impact on the political systems of which they are a part. This report summarizes the professors' findings, which they presented at a recent roundtable discussion organized by the United States Institute of Peace's Grant Program.

Shortcomings in the Scholarly Literature

Professor Wickham argued that much of the existing literature on Islamist parties is problematic on three accounts. First, it tends to equate the notion of "moderation" with "growing support for democracy" on the part of Islamist parties. Wickham indicated that, as a consequence, the literature largely "fails to acknowledge the possibility that Islamist opposition leaders might come to embrace certain aspects of democracy while continuing to reject others." Clark concurred with Wickham that the existing literature has limitations in this respect because it refers principally to "moderate" Islamists as persons who accept the procedural elements of participating in elections—without regard to their vision of what shape a future Islamic state might take—as opposed to "radical" Islamists who reject participation in secular political systems.

According to Wickham, an undifferentiated approach to Islamist parties is reflected in a second problem in most of the literature on the subject, namely the tendency by many scholars to treat moderate Islamist parties as "monolithic entities supportive of a single interpretation of Islam and committed to a single set of political objectives." Instead, Wickham argued, Islamist parties represent a wide array of positions on strategic political issues as well as on "end goals." In this regard, she said that "while the leaders of Islamist opposition groups in Egypt, Jordan, and Kuwait remain committed to the establishment of a political system based on Islamic law, or shari'a, they differ among themselves on the question of how much of the 'historical shari'a'—that is, the corpus of traditional Islamic legal rulings inherited from the past—can and should be revised." Clark believed that much of the literature that argues that participation in elections and cooperation with non-Islamic groups leads to moderation in political positions and views does so without examining the nature of cooperation—that is, what exactly cooperation entails and whether the conditions of cooperation do, in fact, foster moderation.

The third major problem with the existing literature on Islamist parties, according to Wickham, is that it fails to establish clearly whether they moderate their politics because they actually have come to embrace new positions on "core beliefs and values," or whether they simply take these positions, perhaps on a temporary basis, to gain political advantage. In this connection, Wickham asked, "If Islamist moderation is in fact driven, at least in part, by a deeper process of what we might call 'democratic learning,' what types of participation are likely to trigger it, and why are some Islamist leaders more predisposed to such learning than others?"

Motivations for Participation

Wickham looked for an answer to this question through her research, which has focused on the three main Islamist political organizations in three countries—the Muslim Brotherhood (MB) in Egypt, the Islamic Action Front (IAF) in Jordan, and the Islamic Constitutional Movement (ICM) in Kuwait. Additionally, she examined the behavior of two relatively new Islamist parties, the Wasat (Center) Party in Jordan and the Wasat Party in Egypt, which have split from the IAF and the MB, respectively.

After studying what she described as the "reformist or islahi trend within the nonviolent mainstream of the 'revivalist' Islamist movement" in these three countries, Wickham arrived at three main conclusions. First, these parties have pushed for participation in their respective political systems "even when these systems fall short of Islamic ideals." Second, within these groups, Wickham discovered a drive both to promote "greater transparency and internal democracy" within their organizations and a commitment to work with secular parties to achieve shared goals. Third, among these groups, Wickham pointed to what she called "a call for change in the end goals of the Islamic movement, including calls for a revision of historic conceptions of shari'a rule." Wickham immediately cautioned, however, that reality is "more complex." The leaders of these parties have differing levels of commitment to the above three variables. She indicated that "while near consensus has been reached on the value of participation in democratic elections, the question of how much, and what type, of organizational and ideological reforms should accompany it remain a subject of heated internal debate [within the various parties]."

Regarding the first variable—a commitment by Islamist parties to participate in electoral politics—Wickham suggested that it is difficult to ascertain precisely how much electoral support Islamist parties have developed. This is because the semiauthoritarian governments of the countries in which these parties operate place limitations on free communication and on fair districting and voting practices. It seems clear, however, that Islamist parties have an advantage over secular political parties because, according to Wickham, the latter lack "anything equivalent to the vast network of mosques through which Islamists can mobilize support." Wickham suggested that a major reason why Islamist political party leaders have actively engaged in electoral politics and are "some of the most outspoken advocates of democratic elections in the Arab world" is because they assume that "they would be the first to benefit from an expansion of democratic freedoms, at least in the short term." They have justified their participation in electoral politics in relation to the Islamic concept of shura, or consultation. In this connection, Wickham added, "Some leaders have even gone so far as to equate shura and democracy, in a sharp break from earlier statements depicting calls for democracy as an assault on Islam, and despite the stigma historically attached to democracy as a secular political system rooted in the West."

Embracing New Values?

Wickham examined the evidence on whether the main Islamist parties in Egypt, Jordan, and Kuwait have substantially moderated their views on key social and political issues as a result of their participation in electoral politics. She concluded, first of all, that groups in all three countries have embraced democracy "as a set of procedural rules." The record on their willingness to support "the full range of civil and political rights guaranteed to citizens of democracies in the West," however, is mixed. For example, some leaders of the ICM in Kuwait remain opposed to women's participation in electoral politics as voters and office seekers, but there has been some evolution in the ICMfs position on this issue in recent months after prolonged internal debate. IAF leaders in Jordan opposed a temporary law permitting women the right of uncontested divorce. Further, MB leaders in Egypt, like their IAF counterparts, support the right of women to participate in political life. But, according to Wickham, "[they] insist that such participation not lead to any violation of ethical rules laid down by the shari'a." In sum, Wickham noted that, "in defense of the religious character of society, and the primacy of the family—rather than the individual—as its basic social unit, leaders of the Brotherhood, IAF, and ICM reject the liberal ethos which informs the secular legal codes of the West." The current views of these three parties regarding Islamic rule, if translated into public policy, pose risks to equal citizenship not only for women but also for minorities and secular and observant Muslims with dissenting views.

That is not the whole story, however. Wickham found evidence of what she called "deepening Islamic auto-reform," particularly among the Wasat Parties in Jordan and Egypt. In what she described as "a progression from strategic participation in elections to calls for changes in . . . end goals," Wickham pointed to growing support among some Islamist leaders for ijtihad, the reinterpretation of Islamic sacred texts in relation to current circumstances. In this connection, she indicated that "a small but growing number of Islamist leaders are invoking the principle of ijtihad to challenge the validity of traditional shari'a rulings inherited from the past, and to articulate new positions on such sensitive issues as the proper scope for intellectual and political pluralism and the rights of women, minorities, and nonobservant Muslims in a modern Islamic state." Wasat Party platforms in Egypt and Jordan give clearest expression to this trend, particularly on the issues of financial and organizational transparency, the role of women and non-Muslims, and cooperation with secular parties and NGOs promoting democratic reforms.

Referring to findings presented by Clark in her presentation, Wickham indicated that some might conclude that her findings regarding the moderating effects of cross-party interaction contradict those of Clark. Clark's case study of the Higher Committee for the Coordination of National Opposition Parties found no evidence that IAF compromised its core political positions through cooperation with secular parties. Wickham emphasized, however, that there is good evidence that the Wasat Parties in Jordan and Egypt have moderated their positions on important issues through sustained dialogue and coalition building with secular parties.

The Relationship between Participation and Value Change

Wickham argued that there is evidence that participation in electoral politics can lead to changes in core values and beliefs among some Islamists, particularly by "middle-generation Islamists who spearheaded the movement's entry into electoral contests for political power." She suggested, moreover, that "some types of participation were more likely to trigger value change than others," particularly when Islamists have the "incentive and opportunity to break out of the insular networks of movement politics and engage in sustained cooperation with secular groups in pursuit of democratic reform." This tendency among the MB, IAF, and ICM, however, is limited by "intragroup dynamics," and conservative old guard leaders in all three groups are "generally resistant to any redefinition of the group's historic mission." The social conservatism of the base constituencies of the ICM and the IAF, in particular—especially in rural, tribal areas—has also limited or blocked the political evolution in these parties on key issues. Wickham noted that in Egypt and Jordan the Islamist leaders most likely to embrace changes in core values have left the mainstream Islamic organizations and formed their own groups or remained independent. "The result," according to Wickham, "is that revisionist opinion is hemmed in by more conservative voices in the leading political organizations of the Islamic movement, while new parties with a more explicit revisionist agenda have a very limited mass base."

Given these realities, Wickham concluded that mere participation in elections is insufficient to motivate parties to liberalize their party platforms and agendas. She argued that the extent to which parties do embrace change in core values has to do with four variables: (1) whether parties can "go it alone without changing their agendas" or must engage in coalition building with other parties or forces, including parties with different positions on important issues; (2) whether such cross-party interaction "enhances party leaders' receptivity to new ideas"; (3) whether new ideas can be "justified in movement-valid terms"; and (4) whether circumstances permit "auto-reformers" to "marginalize internal critics and build a constituency for change within their own movement."

Policy Implications for the West

Wickham cautioned that "there is no way that democratic reform in the Arab world can succeed if the region's largest, best organized, and most popular opposition groups"—the Islamist groups she studied—"are excluded from it." Considering how best to incorporate such groups into democratic transitions in the region, she argued for an approach that "falls somewhere between exclusion and inclusion, a path we might call "inclusion with conditions" to reduce the possibility of takeover by a "popular but illiberal" group.

According to Wickham, strategies to promote democratic reform involving Islamists should include the following: (1) encouragement for Islamist leaders to "participate in national, cross-partisan efforts to establish a common framework for reform"; (2) a strengthening of secular democratic parties "so they can eventually serve as an effective counterweight to the Islamic trend"; and (3) in the absence of strong secular democratic parties, development of "procedural mechanisms to prevent any one group from monopolizing political power." Such measures could include "construction of heterogeneous electoral districts, the devolution of power from national to subnational governments, rules which promote coalition building and compromise across partisan lines, and the granting of veto power to an unelected but prodemocratic body, such as a constitutional court."

Delving Deeper: A Case Study in Jordan

In an effort to understand precisely what happens when an Islamist party coordinates with non-Islamist political groups to create political change, Professor Janine Astrid Clark focused her research on a particular political coalition in Jordan—the Higher Committee for the Coordination of National Opposition Parties (HC). The size and composition of this group has changed over time but currently encompasses thirteen opposition parties, including the IAF, the most dominant party in the HC, two Bafathist parties, the Communist Party, and several other leftist parties. Its members meet regularly and frequently. The spokesperson for the HC—a position that rotates among the parties every three months—manages the meetings, while a permanent, non-rotating leadership committee composed of six members from the six biggest and most powerful parties, including the IAF, sets the HCfs agenda. According to Clark, the HC has "cooperated successfully on joint actions, such as sending memorandums to the king and/or statements to the press." She added that "the IAF is very proud of the HC and claims that it is a democratic model for the Arab world."

The Islamic Action Front

Licensed as an umbrella political party in 1992 representing primarily the political wing of the Muslim Brotherhood as well as a limited number of independent Islamists, the IAF first came into existence following the 1989 elections. In that election, members of the MB and independent Islamists collectively won 40 percent of the seats in Jordan's lower house of parliament. But implementation of the new law that governed the 1993 elections resulted in a decline of seats won by Islamists by about one-third—even though their share of the total vote was about the same in the two elections—around 16 percent. According to Clark, "While under the old system, voters could cast as many ballots as there were seats in his/her constituency, the new law—still in enforcement today—gives each voter one vote regardless of the number of seats in his/her district (which could vary from two to nine). The new law had a dramatic effect as it forced voters to choose between tribal loyalties and other political leanings, such as Communist or Islamist." Moreover, said Clark, the new law also favored rural, tribal areas and small towns—both traditionally supportive of the monarchy—as opposed to larger urban areas that form the base of Islamist support.

Clark indicated that the IAF chose to sit out the 1997 elections to protest press restrictions and the one-person, one-vote system. When elections were next held in 2003, IAF participation led it to receive more votes than any other political party (winning 17 seats out of 110), although the majority were won by pro-regime candidates. Given these developments, the IAF had significant incentives to participate in the HC as a means of gaining leverage vis-à-vis the regime. Clark argued, "Frozen out of power and faced with declining political liberties and democratic freedoms, the cost of noncooperation [by the IAF] was simply very low."

Compromise on Sensitive Issues?

Clark examined the interactions between the IAF and the HC on three particularly sensitive political issues: the amendment of the honor crimes law (Law 340) in Jordan; the personal status law giving women greater rights to divorce; and the quota promoting women's participation in parliament. Clark argued that the conditions of participation in the HC require very little actual cooperation or compromise from its members. By tracking the positions of the IAF on these issues and its interactions with other HC members in relation to them, she further revealed significant limitations in IAF willingness to bring sensitive issues, particularly those related to shari'a law, to the HC for potential discussion, raising doubts about the relationship between cross-party cooperation and IAF moderation.

- *Honor Crimes.* According to Clark, four different laws address a man's right to "cleanse" his family's honor by killing or injuring a female relative and her partner engaged in "unlawful" sexual transgressions. Legislative efforts to overturn these laws were defeated four times by Jordan's elected lower house of parliament after being approved by the appointed upper house, although the cabinet approved a temporary amendment to one of the laws—Law 340—in December 2001 when parliament was suspended. Clark noted that while the IAF opposed honor crimes as "un-Islamic," they also opposed the amendment to Law 340 introducing tougher punishments for adulterers because clear penalties for adultery are specified in shari'a law. Even though the IAF had concerns about various aspects of the four laws regulating honor crimes that were similar to views held by some secular lawyers and human rights activists, Clark argued that the IAF was not interested in engaging with others opposed to the amendment because the IAF's views were based on religious objections while other opponents' concerns were of a secular nature.
- *Divorce Law.* The second case cited by Clark addressed an amendment in divorce law—namely, the right of women to ask for divorce on demand without evidence of maltreatment, abandonment, etc. It was passed by the cabinet as a temporary law in 2001 after parliament was suspended. Clark noted that, similar to the amendment to the honor crime law, it was twice defeated in the lower house of parliament with the help of the IAF, despite the fact that it was supported by Chief Islamic Justice Sheikh Tamimi, the king's adviser on Islamic affairs. Clark indicated that the IAF, in fact, supported women's right to divorce but opposed the divorce procedures as "un-Islamic" because the new law removed the role of the judge.
- *Quota for Women.* The third case cited by Clark dealt with the quota for women in parliament, which arose out of a context in which women won no seats in the first elections in 1989, 1 seat in the 1993 elections, and none in the 1997 elections. Clark indicated that in 2003 the cabinet passed a temporary law granting women 6 out of 110 seats in parliament—alongside quotas for Christians (9 seats), Circassians and Chechens (3 seats), and Bedouins (6 seats). The IAF opposed the quota for women arguing, said Clark, "that women are not a minority [and] the quota was unconstitutional as the constitution gives equality between women and men."

What Clark found interesting about the three cases is that while the IAF opposed all three amendments and would have found support for its position among certain members of the HC, they cooperated with the HC only on one—the quota for women. She argued that "of the three cases, the quota stands out in that there is no specific religious injunction regarding quotas. And it is precisely because of this that the quota was the only issue discussed by the HC for possible cooperation." Clark asked, "Why did other members of the Higher Committee also not raise the issue of honor crimes or khula [divorce on demand] for possible discussion?" She concluded that "the Higher Committee simply does not discuss controversial issues upon which members recognize there will be dissent."

In short, Clark indicated that her study of the HC suggests that "cross-ideological interactions per se cannot be said to lead to the increased tolerance and moderation of Islamist parties and, as a result, a deepening of the democratization process." "Cooperation, as practiced by the Higher Committee," she concluded, "is largely a matter of coordination between parties over issues on which there are established, shared interests. It is not a cooperation that involves compromise or the 'give and take' inherent to the spirit of tolerance." While cooperation between the IAF and other members of the HC extended over a wide array of issues, it did not occur on issues with a "direct bearing upon shari'a [law]." Moreover, because the IAF is by far the largest party in the HC, issues which the IAF was unwilling to discuss with other members simply were not raised. Clark noted that "Rarely is a memo of protest sent [by the HC] to the government if the IAF is not a signatory." She added, "Higher Committee members avoid issues related to sharifa, recognizing their inability to find a common ground between the Islamists and the secularists."

In response to a question about why the IAF should bother to participate in the HC and coordinate or compromise with other HC members when real power resides in the regime, Clark indicated that the IAF leaders have indicated a desire to join their voices to those of other political parties—even very weak ones—to show that "all parties are in this together against the state."

The Turkish Case: A "Pro-Islamic" Party in Power

The role of Islam in politics looks very different in Turkey. The "pro-Islamic" Justice and Development Party (JDP) came to power in the 2002 elections on the heels of an economic crisis and without significant opposition. Professor Sultan Tepe presented material on the ideology and performance of the JDP, which she characterized as having the "task of defining the terms of new Islamic politics in Turkey."

The JDP's Three Dilemmas

Tepe argued that the JDP faces three central dilemmas, the first of which relates to defining its identity. Although observers outside Turkey commonly refer to the JDP as an "Islamist" party, that term does not fully explain the complexity of the JDP's identity or distinguish it adequately from Islamist parties in Egypt, Kuwait, Jordan, and elsewhere.

Tepe pointed out that political apathy, electoral rules, and the demise of secular parties play an important role in the success of Islamist parties. Three factors need to be taken into account in the assessment of the JDP's electoral success: (1) the increasing apathy of the Turkish electorate (in the 2002 election 20 percent of eligible voters did not cast ballots); (2) the 10 percent national threshold rule in Turkey that leaves supporters of small parties garnering less than 10 percent of the vote unrepresented in parliament (more than 40 percent of the votes cast in the 2002 election); and (3) the leadership and ideological conflicts marking the secular parties of the left and the right, which mired these parties in controversy in the 2002 election and left the JDP without meaningful or effective political opposition.

According to Tepe, the JDP's leadership maintains that its primary goal is to "limit the gap between the state and the public and integrate the common values of Turkish society into the policies of the Turkish state." Tepe noted that "Islam is explicitly mentioned in Conservative Democracy, the party's statement of ideology, only in the section that discusses whether Islam and democracy are compatible with each other. Conservative Democracy concludes that they are not in conflict." It specifically states, "Although religion is sacred, religious ideas are not sacred, and there can be more than one idea in the public sphere. Therefore pluralism is acceptable. Experiments, and trial and error learning, are acceptable not only in the natural sciences but also in the social sciences. Therefore these social inventions are acceptable to religion."

Tepe argued that "while the JDP's roots are that of a pro-Islamic party, it tries to distance itself from the Islamists and goes to the other extreme, presenting itself as an almost un-Islamic party. Instead of bringing Islamic ideas into the marketplace of ideas the party either subsumes them under the 'common values label' or shows that democratic principles can be deduced from them." In coining its ideology "conservative democracy," the JDP presents this largely undefined concept as the "ideological anchor" for its policies. According to Tepe, this ideological elusiveness may prevent the party's successful development.

The JDP's second dilemma, Tepe argued, "results from its commitment to introduce institutional reforms swiftly, as a way to limit the state's role, decentralize political power, and improve the free market economy." Indeed, the party's legislative record is impressive; according to Tepe, under the JDP the government has enacted a "record high number of bills (553) . . . preparing the way for entry into the EU." The dilemma, however, is that most of these radical reforms have been adopted rapidly with little or no public debate, even though many provisions raise important questions. For instance, some reforms were meant to limit the role of the state, yet, according to Tepe, they have the potential of "actually strengthening it even further." Paradoxically, said Tepe, "While the JDP aggressively seeks to transform Turkey's centralized state structure into 'administrative federalism,' it has adopted a policy of centralization in its party organization, and is excluding dissenters and civil society from the policymaking process." The mode of politics adopted by the party brings to mind Ghassan Salamefs phrase (and book title), "democracy without democrats." Tepe said, "The party seeks to secure the institutional foundation of a democratic society without permitting individuals in its party and outside of it to play an active role in this transformation."

The JDP's third dilemma, according to Tepe, "concerns the party's conviction that selective reforms will create a domino effect that will resolve controversial issues automatically." The party believes that important issues pertaining to the public role of Islam can be addressed more effectively after the reforms have curbed the power of the state and removed the restrictions on Turkey's public sphere. Tepe cited the controversial ban on Islamic headscarves (turbans) in public institutions—such as parliament and schools—a policy that predates the JDP's rise to power. One might assume that the JDP would be interested in addressing this issue directly, which it has not done. Instead, Tepe argued, the JDP has relied on civil-society organizations and international institutions for the solution of controversial issues. In the case of headscarves, Tepe said that the "European Court of Human Rights recently decided to endorse Turkey's current headscarf policy. Contrary to the belief of the JDP elite that the court would revoke the ban on turbans, the court concluded: 'Measures taken in universities to prevent certain fundamentalist religious movements from pressuring students who do not practice the religion in question, or those belonging to another religion, can be justified.'" Tepe argued that "the decision shattered one of the major components of the JDP's approach to the turban issue."

This gap between the party's rhetorical commitment and actual practice also manifests itself in the party's failure to promote the participation of women in political life. Tepe noted that in the 2004 local elections, "only sixteen of the JDP's 3,184 candidates for local leadership positions were female and only one woman won office." This failure, Tepe suggested, grew out of the party's "election driven approach, based on a multilayered selection process (including local popularity pools, references from the party organization, and interviews by the party center). The overall process reinforces the power of popular, traditional leaders, which, in effect, blocks the advance of female candidates."

Fear of weakening the JDP's power and its exhaustive reform agenda has silenced the debate on headscarves and other controversial issues that existed among Islamists before the JDP came to power. According to Tepe, "The fear that outspoken women's groups will undermine the JDP's power generates a form of self-censorship among female supporters." The result, Tepe, suggested, is "a process of politics without politics and politics of Islam without Islam"—that is to say, a policymaking process without the competition of ideas, negotiations, or compromises in which Islamic issues are treated as derivative of other issues.

The ability of the JDP to forge a novel pro-Islamic and democratic platform, according to Tepe, will depend on whether the party successfully "articulates a clear ideology without being elusive; translates its commitment to the procedures and ideals of democracy to the actual practice of liberal democracy; questions its reductionist approach which sees the root of all problems, including those derived from the public role of Islam, in the ineffective state structure and weak liberal economy; constructs policy solutions to controversial issues by addressing differences and incorporating views of competing social groups." If it does not accomplish these tasks, Tepe concluded, "the JDP will [just] be another center right party that failed in its attempts to include Islam in Turkey's public sphere and serve as a model for other Islamist parties."

Considering the Cases Altogether

Professor Brumberg proposed three responses to the presentations. First, the inclusion of Islamist parties in democratic political change remains a tremendous challenge because their agendas are fundamentally different from those of secular political parties. In the Arab world, the way this challenge has been handled by semiauthoritarian regimes is to allow political liberalization without democracy. Political parties, including Islamist parties, seek patrons within the state, and "participation" in politics resembles lobbying more than it does direct representation of political interests. In such systems of state-managed political liberalization, according to Brumberg, "nobody wins and nobody loses." For that reason, it is difficult to measure Islamist party commitment to democratic values because no party is ever really allowed to exercise real political authority. The extraordinary paradox of politics in the Arab Middle East, he said, is that state monopolization of political power prevents the development of democratic systems in which Islamist parties, such as the IAF, could win control through elections and impose their agendas without regard to the rights of others.

Brumberg's second observation was that preoccupation, especially in the West, with how to update, reform, or "fix" Islam misses a more fundamental need. What counts most in regulating the behavior of Islamist parties, he argued, are the constraints and opportunities operating on those parties. In the Arab world, Islamist parties are vying for power in systems in which non-Islamic parties—other than those controlled by the regime—have no significant presence or voice. This lack of serious secular political-party alternatives to Islamist parties suggests that Islamist parties will have fewer incentives to moderate their politics.

A third and related point made by Brumberg focused on the advantages and disadvantages inherent in the Turkish case, in which non-Islamic political forces have enjoyed organized support for many years. Islamists in Turkey know that secular political parties present the electorate with serious non-Islamic alternatives. The JDP feels the pressure, moreover, of an export-oriented Turkish bourgeoisie, including members of the JDP itself, which has a keen interest in the development of Turkish democracy and its linkage to Turkey's accession to the European Union. The existence of this interest in Turkey generates deep contradictions within the JDP, whose more religiously conservative supporters feel it is insufficiently "Islamic." The Turkish example of a relatively moderate Islamist party—the JDP—that operates within a competitive political system provides a useful example for the Arab world, Brumberg argued. The main challenge for Arab societies, he concluded, is to create political arenas in which Islamists participate but are constrained by the need to compete with secular political parties and thus moderate their positions in order to maintain their popularity.

Conclusions and Recommendations

Islamist political parties in the Middle East are diverse in nature, as are the systems in which they operate.

- Much of the existing literature equates the notion of "moderation" with "growing support for democracy" by Islamist parties. In fact, there is good evidence that the more conservative Islamist parties embrace procedural aspects of democracy while rejecting the liberal values that go with it.
- To better assess whether Islamist parties endorse democracy or not depends, in part, on whether the definition of democracy goes beyond the minimalist interpretation of democracy as participation in elections. When the definition includes protection of individual rights and liberties, it becomes clear that some Islamist parties do not support democracy because they endorse a reduced version of political

freedom—namely, freedom from the state at the expense of the exercise of broader liberties within civil society.

- Mere participation in elections is insufficient to motivate parties to liberalize their party platforms and agendas. Moreover, conservative Islamist parties in Egypt and Jordan cooperate and sometimes have joined forces with secular and even progressive political forces and parties to voice joint opposition to government policies. But there is little evidence that participation in elections or interaction between the secular parties and mainstream conservative Islamist parties in Egypt, Jordan, and Kuwait (the MB, the IAF, and the ICM, respectively) has caused the Islamist parties to compromise on issues that have direct bearing on sharifa law.
- If these conservative Islamist parties were to come to power tomorrow, the translation of their current views into public policy would pose risks to equal citizenship not only for women but also for minorities and secular Muslims with dissenting views.
- In contrast, new, breakaway Islamist parties—such as the Wasat Parties in Jordan and Egypt—have a more liberal orientation and are more inclined to promote ijtihad (reinterpretation of Islamic law in relation to current circumstances). Unlike the more conservative Islamist parties, which sometimes cooperate with secular parties to express opposition to government policies, the more liberal Islamist parties have modified their positions on shari'a law issues in a process aided by interaction with secular parties and forces.
- The structural circumstances in which Islamist parties compete for support significantly affect outcomes. Electoral systems in the Arab region have been designed by semiauthoritarian regimes to permit political liberalization but prevent the emergence of fully democratic governments. The ability of secular as well as religious parties to mobilize support has been affected by these constraints. Generally speaking, however, the organizational power and outreach of the secular parties does not compare favorably to that of the Islamist parties, which can draw upon vast networks of religious institutions.
- The situation is different in Turkey, where an Islamist party—the JDP—is in power but is mindful of competition from well-established secular political parties. In an effort to appeal to a broader constituency and to promote the accession of Turkey to the European Union—a matter of paramount importance to Turkey's export-oriented bourgeoisie—the JDP has declined to take strong positions on sensitive political issues of importance to its core constituency, such as the wearing of Islamic head-scarves.
- The absence of strong secular political parties in Egypt, Jordan, and Kuwait means that conservative Islamist parties are less likely to

modify their positions on core issues than they would if they were forced to compete with strong, more liberal secular parties, as they do in Turkey.

- A central paradox of the politics of the Arab Middle East is that state monopolization of political power prevents the development of democratic systems in which conservative Islamist parties could win control through elections and impose their agendas without regard to the rights of others. The main challenge for the region is to create political arenas in which Islamists are able to participate but are also constrained by the need to compete with secular political parties, compelling them to moderate their positions to maintain their popularity.

14

Islamists and Non-Islamists in the Egyptian Opposition

Dina Shehata

In the 1970s the regime of late Egyptian president Anwar Sadat moved away from the more hegemonic or closed form of authoritarianism adopted under former president Gamal Abdel Nasser and toward a more pluralistic semiauthoritarian political formula. Sadat oversaw the creation of a number of opposition parties, allowed the Muslim Brotherhood to resume its activities, and extended greater freedoms to the media and to civil society organizations. However, the ruling party remained firmly in control of the real levers of power, restricting political contestation to the outer limits of the political system and thus insulating the core power elite from any serious political challenge or competition.

Over the past three decades, Sadat's semiauthoritarian formula has remained largely intact. President Hosni Mubarak's regime has institutionalized and consolidated semiauthoritarianism by continuing to extend a limited margin of political freedom to opposition parties and movements, while keeping in place a battery of laws and procedures that allows the regime to limit the autonomy and effectiveness of the opposition. Moreover, the Mubarak regime has relied extensively on emergency laws and procedures to suppress serious opposition to the regime, which have been in force continuously since the assassination of Sadat in 1981. These emergency measures have allowed the Mubarak regime to create parallel legal and judicial structures, and thus, to override many of the rights and freedoms guaranteed by the constitution and the normal judicial system. Such legal dualism has given the regime expansive powers while enabling it to maintain a thin veneer of democracy.

The resilience of semiauthoritarianism in Egypt has belied earlier claims that political liberalization is by definition an unstable equilibrium that must eventually give way either to full-fledged democratization or to a reversion to more repressive forms of authoritarianism. This claim was born out of the belief that, once authoritarian regimes open up, mass mobilization occurs on a wide scale and authoritarian regimes are forced either to democratize or to crack down.[1] However, Egypt's experiences with political liberalization indicate that it does not always lead to the resurrection of civil society and that, in some instances, political liberalization may in fact discourage further democratic mobilization. This tends to be the case in countries where opposition movements are divided along foundational, social, and economic issues and where a transition to full fledged democracy is perceived as a zero-sum game that could lead to the permanent exclusion of one or more of the main forces in the opposition.[2] In such situations, some groups in the opposition may prefer a semiauthoritarian formula, under which their interests are at least partially represented, to a complete transition to democracy where they may be permanently excluded.[3]

I contend that, in the Egyptian context, divisions between Islamists and non-Islamists have discouraged broad-based mobilization against the regime and have driven many democrats and would-be democrats to align themselves with the authoritarian regime against Islamist forces in the opposition. As a result, democratic mobilization in Egypt has been weak even during periods of relative political openness or regime crisis; the regime has thus been able to maintain a semiauthoritarian equilibrium for over three decades.

This research project examines how divisions among the different forces in the Egyptian opposition, particularly between Islamists and non-Islamists, have affected the capacity of the Egyptian opposition to challenge the authoritarian regime successfully. The project also examines how the regime has, in its turn, manipulated and perpetuated divisions within the opposition to reproduce its power even as its legitimacy and ability to govern effectively continue to decline.

I begin by considering efforts to build alliances in three arenas: parliamentary elections, issue-based movements and committees, and professional syndicates. As we shall see, the record suggests that successful alliance building has been a function of two distinct clusters of variables: those that are internal to the opposition and those that are imposed by the regime. Internal variables include the level of ideological convergence and polarization between Islamists and non-Islamists and the balance of power among different actors in the opposition. External variables include the degrees of political liberalization and repression as well as divide-and-rule tactics that the regime has employed to inhibit alliance building. The paper concludes by exploring the potential effects of presidential succession and

1. Adam Przeworski, *Democracy and the Market: Political and Economic Reforms in Eastern Europe and Latin America* (New York: Cambridge University Press, 1991).

2. Daniel Brumberg, "The Trap of Liberalized Autocracy," *Journal of Democracy*, vol. 13, no. 4 (2002), pp. 56–68.

3. Brumberg, "The Trap."

generational replacement—in both the regime and the opposition—on the prospects of alliance building between Islamists and non-Islamists in the opposition, and proposes a number of different scenarios for the future.

Alliance Building between Islamists and Non-Islamists in the Opposition

Electoral Alliances

The regime in Egypt regularly manipulates parliamentary elections to ensure the ruling party's continued hold on the two-thirds majority necessary to amend the constitution. Nonetheless, despite their controlled nature, parliamentary elections are an important political event for opposition forces. Since the transition to limited political pluralism in the mid-1970s, the ruling party has allowed opposition parties and movements a limited degree of representation in parliament. Though such representation has never exceeded one-third of the seats, parliamentary representation nonetheless remains one of the few avenues available to political parties and movements to make their presence felt, to communicate with a broader public, and to break the isolation that the regime imposes on them.

Moreover, despite widespread rigging and fraud by the regime, parliamentary elections provide the various political forces with one of the few opportunities, in an otherwise opaque political system, to test their popularity and the size of their support, at least compared to other forces in the opposition. Opposition parties and movements have thus attempted to maximize their gains in parliamentary elections, either by forging alliances with other forces in the opposition or by making deals with the regime—often at the expense of other actors in the opposition.

During the 1980s, a favorable political and institutional environment encouraged electoral alliance building between Islamists and non-Islamists in the opposition. For the 1984 elections, the newly reconstituted liberal Wafd party and the Muslim Brotherhood joined forces and ran a single list of candidates. The Wafd/Brotherhood list won fifty-eight seats, constituting the largest opposition bloc in parliament. Similarly, during the 1987 elections, the Socialist Labor Party, the Liberal Party, and the Muslim Brotherhood formed the Islamic Alliance, which won sixty seats and constituted the largest opposition bloc in the 1987 parliament.

During the 1990s, a more repressive political environment, growing polarization and asymmetry between Islamists and non-Islamists, and a new electoral system discouraged electoral alliances of the kind that occurred during the 1980s. Except for a flawed electoral boycott during the 1990 elections, there was a marked lack of coordination among the various opposition actors during the 1995 and 2000 elections.

After a decade of political deliberalization and polarization that inhibited successful cooperation between Islamists and non-Islamists in the opposition, the 2000–05 period experienced a renewed cycle of political liberalization. The relaxation of political controls during that period created conditions conducive to greater cooperation among different actors in the opposition. The crackdown on the Brotherhood during the second half of the 1990s drove the movement to moderate its discourse and seek alliances with other opposition actors, and the outbreak of the intifada and the first U.S. invasion of Iraq helped unify the various segments of the opposition after deep divisions over foreign policy issues during the 1990s. Furthermore, external pressures on the regime to democratize created a political opening that drove secularists and Islamists to converge around a fixed set of demands for political and constitutional reforms and provided them with an opportunity to mobilize more effectively against the regime.

The 2005 parliamentary elections acquired special importance because they occurred in an environment of heightened domestic mobilization around issues of democratization and unprecedented external pressure on the regime to democratize. Observers expected the elections to be freer and fairer than previous elections, given the international scrutiny, judicial supervision, and election monitoring by civil society associations. Opposition parties and movements hoped that these favorable conditions would allow them to end the long-standing two-thirds majority of the National Democratic Party (NDP). Attempts were made to build a grand coalition that united all actors in the opposition, but despite the favorable conditions, the efforts to unify failed. The Muslim Brotherhood, which felt empowered by the successes of Islamists elsewhere in the region and by external pressures on the regime to democratize, refused to join the National Front and decided to contest the elections independently. The other forces in the opposition succeeded in forming an electoral alliance, agreed on a joint program, and fielded a joint list of candidates. This was the first time that secularists and semisecularists in the opposition succeeded in forming an electoral alliance.

Popular Committees and Issue-Based Movements

Since the late 1970s, alliances between opposition parties and movements often have assumed the form of ad hoc committees created in response to international and domestic developments. These committees bring together organizations and individuals from the different segments of the opposition that share a common position toward a particular event or development. They tend to be issue specific and organized on an informal, decentralized, and nonhierarchical basis. The first such committee, the Egyptian Committee for the Defense of Freedoms (ECDF), was created by the Egyptian opposition shortly after the bread riots of 1977. The ECDF included representatives from the Progressive Unionist Party (PUP), the Socialist Labor Party (SLP), the Liberal Party (LP), the Wafd Party, the Muslim Brotherhood, Marxists, and Nasserists, in addition to representatives from the Lawyers Syndicate, the Journalists Syndicate, human rights organizations, and independent public figures. The committee aimed to provide legal aid and support to activists who had been persecuted for their beliefs and political positions and to raise public awareness about freedom issues through publications, conferences, and partnerships with local and international organizations.[4]

The ECDF format became typical of subsequent committees that the opposition created. During the late 1970s and 1980s, a number of similar committees were created that centered primarily on foreign policy and democracy issues. After Egypt signed its peace treaty with Israel, which most forces in the opposition rejected, a number of committees were formed to oppose normalization with Israel and to protest Israeli policies in the region. These committees included the Egyptian Committee for the Defense of National Culture; a number of antinormalization and boycott committees; the National Committee for Supporting the Palestinian and Lebanese Peoples, which was formed in the wake of the Israeli invasion of Lebanon; and the Egyptian National Committee for supporting the Palestinian intifada, which was formed in January 1988, shortly after the outbreak of the first intifada.[5]

Other committees were created during that same period to address issues of political rights and democracy: in addition to the ECDF, the Alliance of Egyptians was formed after the fraudulent 1979 elections. The Alliance aimed to bring together a broad coalition of actors that included a large number of independent public figures in addition to representatives from political parties and movements. In 1983, the National Committee for the Defense of Democracy (NCDD) was formed to promote fairer electoral procedures, an end to the state of emergency, and comprehensive political reforms.

Committees formed during the 1970s and 1980s tended to be fairly inclusive and broad based, given the high level of convergence that existed between actors in the opposition over foreign policy and democracy issues. During the 1980s, these committees were fairly successful at influencing the policy orientations of the regime. Committees focused on foreign policy issues helped create a public opinion antagonistic to Israel and resistant to any attempts to normalize relations with the Jewish state. For its part, the Mubarak regime responded by cooling relations with Israel and adopting a strategy of cold peace that did not promote economic or cultural exchange. Similarly, committees created around democracy issues helped reinforce the atmosphere of greater political openness that existed during the 1980s.

4. Abdel Ghafar Shukr, *Political Alliances in Egypt, 1976–1993* (Cairo: Al-Ahaly Books, 1994), p. 65.

5. Shukr, *Political Alliances*, p. 78.

Even though the regime never relinquished its control over the real levers of power, it significantly expanded the margin of political freedoms available to the opposition and responded to some of the opposition's demands to change the electoral system.

During the 1990s, as political parties began to fragment and atrophy—and as divisions between the various segments of the opposition over foreign policy, socioeconomic, and identity issues deepened—efforts to create broad-based committees were largely unsuccessful. The issue-based committees that were created in the 1990s tended to be more narrow, including only a fragment of the opposition rather than all the principal actors. Committees that were created to oppose privatization and the new land tenancy laws only included leftist forces from the opposition. Liberals and Islamists, who largely favored the privatization and land measures, did not join the committees.[6] Similarly, committees that were formed during the 1990s to oppose the peace process and regional cooperation schemes were not as inclusive as those of the 1980s, as some segments of the opposition supported these initiatives. The committees of the 1990s reflected the internal divisions that afflicted political parties and movements at that time, as a new generation of activists increasingly broke off from existing parties and movements and began to operate through the vehicle of these informal committees and movements.

Democratization issues, upon which opposition actors converged during the 1980s, proved to be a source of controversy during the 1990s. The National Consensus Project, initiated by activists from the 1970s generation in 1994 in an effort to arrest the growing polarization among the different opposition actors, failed because of divisions between secularists and Islamists on one hand and socialists and liberals on the other. Similarly, the Committee for the Defense of Democracy, created in 1999 to oppose a new restrictive non-governmental organization law and which comprised the major political parties and human rights organizations, did not include the Muslim Brotherhood, as the Brotherhood had supported the law.[7]

The Committee for the Coordination among Political Parties and Forces was the only successful attempt to create a broad-based committee during the 1990s. The committee was created shortly after the 1995 elections, which were the most fraudulent and violent since Mubarak assumed power. The marginalization of Islamists and non-Islamists alike during those elections forced them closer together. Moreover, the Brotherhood's greater moderation—a result of government repression during the 1990s—allowed the committee's creation.

International and domestic developments in the 2000–05 period once again helped create conditions conducive to broad-based committees

6. Personal interview with Hamdeen Sabahi, September 30, 2003.

7. Personal interview with Hussein Abdel Razek, March 20, 2006.

focused on foreign policy and democracy issues. However, in contrast to the committees created during the late 1970s and 1980s, which were driven by the leaders of the principal political parties and movements, the issue-based committees created during the 2000–05 period were largely created by 1970s-generation activists who had split off from these parties and movements during the 1990s. As a result, the involvement of political parties and movements in these committees tended to be largely symbolic; often the older opposition movements perceived the new committees as competitors and attempted to undermine them.

After the polarization caused by the first Gulf War and the peace process during the 1990s, the outbreak of the Palestinian intifada in September 2000 and the second invasion of Iraq in 2003 helped unite the opposition around a common foreign policy agenda. Shortly after the outbreak of the Palestinian intifada, 1970s-generation activists created the Egyptian Popular Committee for the Support of the Palestinian Intifada (EPCSPI). The Popular Committee succeeded in gaining the support of the various segments and forces that make up the opposition. However, unlike earlier committees, EPCSPI membership was open to all activists in their individual rather than institutional capacities. Thus, even though activists from all the major opposition parties and movements joined the committee, the committee was not, formally speaking, an alliance between political parties and movements. This format proved to be a successful mechanism for allowing a measure of cooperation between 1970s-generation activists and the parties and movements they broke with in the 1990s, and many of the opposition committees created afterward in the 2000–05 period adopted it.

The period that followed the second invasion of Iraq witnessed a renewed interest in issues of political reform and democracy, driven in large measure by growing external, particularly U.S. pressures on the regime to democratize. In 2004–05, a number of issue-based movements and committees advocating long-standing demands for political and constitutional reforms came into being. The Egyptian Movement for Change (Kifaya) was created by some of the same founders of EPCSPI and it adopted the same organizational model. Though activists from all the main parties and movements joined Kifaya in their individual capacities, the movement was in large part representative of 1970s-generation activists from the leftist, Islamist, and liberal opposition.

Kifaya's success in generating domestic momentum for reform and attracting global attention drove some of the older movements and parties to establish competing movements and committees. During that same period, eight formal political parties formed the National Accord for Political Reform, which advanced some of the same demands advocated by Kifaya and which entered into a national dialogue with the ruling NDP. The dialogue was intended to pull the rug out from under movements such as Kifaya and to rechannel the political debate into the state-sanctioned pluralist order. The Muslim Brotherhood, which was shunned by the parties of the National Accord, also sought to create the National Alliance for Reform, which included some fringe Marxists who had refused to join Kifaya because of its soft attitude toward the United States. A number of public figures and former government ministers also decided to step into the debate by forming the National Union for Change, which focused on the question of constitutional reform and positioned itself as a movement of elders that sought to unite the various segments of the opposition and infuse moderation and wisdom into the debate on political reform.

In addition to the various movements and committees, the 2004–05 period also witnessed the emergence of more specialized issue-based movements and committees that sought to advance the long-standing demands of discreet social groups. These included the 9th of March Movement for the Independence of the Universities, formed by university professors to free Egyptian universities from the administrative and financial control of the regime and end the ubiquitous presence of state security forces on Egyptian university campuses.[8] Professors' clubs, dominated by the Muslim Brotherhood, perceived the 9th of March Movement as a challenger. However, the movement's visibility and activism on university campuses in 2004–05 drove professors' clubs to mobilize around some of the same issues that the movement raised.[9] Other movements that emerged during that same period included Artists for Change, Journalists for Change, Youth for Change, and Doctors for Change. Most of these movements gathered under Kifaya's umbrella and sought to advance both Kifaya's general demands and also demands particular to their own group or sector.[10]

That said, as mentioned above, the committees created from 2000 to 2005 tended to reflect the generational divide that had begun to characterize the Egyptian opposition starting in the 1990s. Even though most committees created during that period included activists from different ideological orientations, they were nonetheless largely representative of 1970s-generation activists who had broken off from the principal parties and movements of the opposition during the 1990s. The older parties and movements, for their part, tried to reassert their primacy by establishing parallel movements and committees; even as these various committees converged around a common set of demands, their fragmentation allowed the regime to pit the groups against one another and thus prevent the emergence of a broad-based coalition able to challenge the NDP's long-standing hegemony effectively.

---

8. Personal interview with Mohamed Abul Ghar, June 12, 2006.

9. Personal interview with Mohamed Abul Ghar.

10. Shaimaa Abdel Hady, "The Informal Opposition in Egypt: Kifaya and Its Sisters," *Ahwal Masriyya*, vol. 8, no. 31 (Winter 2006), pp. 99–111 (in Arabic).

Most of the movements and committees that emerged in 2000–05 became inactive or lost momentum in the wake of the 2005 elections, which revived the polarization between Islamists and non-Islamists in the opposition. The successes of the Brotherhood during the 2005 elections and the parallel defeat of the non-Islamist opposition reduced external pressures on the regime to democratize and raised fears among some secularists that their activism helped pave the way for the Brotherhood's ascendance. In subsequent months, the regime proceeded to crack down, not only on the Brotherhood, but also on some of the movements that led the democratic activism of the 2004–05 period, such as Kifaya.

Professional Syndicates

During the 1980s, professional syndicates became an important arena for conflict and cooperation between Islamists and non-Islamists in the opposition. Islamists began to penetrate professional syndicates during the 1980s, when many syndicates suffered serious internal divisions and high levels of financial mismanagement and corruption. The feuding between syndicate leaders affiliated with the regime and the secular opposition—and their mismanagement of syndicate resources, which were often considerable—created a high sense of disenchantment among the syndicate members.[11] This was particularly the case among young graduates who entered syndicates in large numbers during the 1970s and 1980s, who felt that syndicate leaders were oblivious to their needs and demands at a time of high unemployment and economic retrenchment. Islamists capitalized on this disenchantment by addressing the needs of these young graduates and distancing themselves from the infighting among the syndicate leaders. When Islamist activists began to contest syndicate elections during the 1980s, many Islamists and non-Islamists in professional syndicates supported them and saw them as a clean alternative to the corruption and factionalism of the old leaders.

However, during the late 1980s and early 1990s, as Brotherhood activists began to dominate the boards of a number of syndicates and adopt an exclusive attitude toward other political forces, non-Islamists began to turn against them.[12] During the 1990s, many non-Islamists—some of whom had previously supported the Brotherhood—tacitly supported the regime's measures, such as Law 100 in 1993, to reverse the ascendance of Islamists within professional syndicates. In fact, in a number of syndicates, such as the lawyers' and engineers' syndicates, non-Islamists used the provisions

11. *The Arab Strategic Report 1999* (Cairo: Al Ahram Center for Political and Strategic Studies, 2000), pp. 296–304.

12. Ahmed Hussein Hasan, *The Political Rise of Islamists within Professional Syndicates: A Case Study of the Egyptian Engineers Syndicate* (Cairo: Al Dar Al Thaqafiyya Publishing, 2000), p. 52 (in Arabic).

of Law 100 to call for the dissolution of the elected boards of their syndicates and the appointment of judicial committees in their stead. Moreover, some non-Islamists in these syndicates cooperated with the regime in its efforts to postpone elections indefinitely by contesting the integrity of the membership rosters of these syndicates. As a result of these divisions, most of those syndicates that had fallen under the control of the Brotherhood during the late 1980s and early 1990s were placed under the control of state-appointed judicial committees and most have been unable to hold elections for over a decade.

During the 2000–05 period, Islamist and non-Islamist activists joined forces in a number of professional syndicates to end continued state control and convene new elections. In the lawyers' syndicate, such cooperation was made possible by the emergence of an implicit and often tenuous power-sharing arrangement between Islamists and non-Islamists on the board of the syndicate. In the engineers' syndicate, Islamists and non-Islamists formed Engineers Against State Control, which, since 2003, has been attempting to pressure the regime to end judicial control and allow for the convocation of new elections. However, despite these efforts, most of the syndicates that fell under the control of the Brotherhood during the late 1980s and early 1990s continue to be controlled by a state-appointed judicial committee. The regime and some non-Islamists within these syndicates have resisted efforts to convene new elections, fearing that the Brotherhood will once again assume control.

External and Internal Obstacles to Successful Alliance Building between Islamists and Non-Islamists

The various instances of alliance building and cooperation between Islamists and non-Islamists in the opposition reviewed in the previous section indicate that successful alliance building is a function of two distinct clusters of variables: those that are internal to the opposition and those that are imposed by the regime. Internal variables include the level of ideological convergence or polarization between Islamists and non-Islamists and the balance of power between Islamist and non-Islamists. External variables include the degree of political liberalization or repression and divide-and-rule tactics employed by the regime. And even though, in reality, these variables are closely intertwined and often mutually constitutive, it is nonetheless useful, for analytical purposes, to consider them independently.

Internal Factors

Ideological Convergence and Polarization: Successful instances of cooperation and alliance building between Islamists and non-Islamists have been more likely during periods of ideological convergence and less likely during periods of ideological polarization. During the 1980s, as the regime adopted less divisive foreign and domestic policies and the secular opposition increasingly began to Islamize its discourse, the ideological gap between Islamists and non-Islamists began to narrow and cooperation was made more possible. During that period, Islamists and non-Islamists in the opposition converged on a common agenda for political reform and shared common positions regarding the principal foreign policy issues of the day.[13] This convergence allowed for a number of successful alliances between Islamists and non-Islamists in parliamentary elections, issue-based movements, and some professional syndicates during the 1980s.

Similarly, during the 2000–05 period, support for the Palestinian intifada and opposition to the war in Iraq helped unite the opposition behind a common foreign policy agenda. External pressure on the Egyptian regime to democratize helped focus the attention of Islamists and non-Islamists alike on issues of political and constitutional reform and away from some of the more divisive social and economic issues. During those five years, Islamists and non-Islamists mobilized separately and jointly around foreign policy and democracy issues and converged on a fixed set of demands. This convergence allowed for greater cooperation between Islamists and non-Islamists in movements, such as EPCSPI and Kifaya, and in a number of syndicates, including the lawyers', journalists', and engineers' syndicates.

In contrast, polarization during the 1990s over questions such as sharia, the peace process, and economic reform inhibited cooperation and alliance building between Islamists and non-Islamists, on one hand, and liberals and socialists, on the other. During the 1990s, the division between secularists and Islamists became the principal fault line in the Egyptian polity and many non-Islamists aligned themselves with the regime in its attempts to crack down on both radical and moderate Islamists. Except for the Committee for the Coordination between Political Parties and Forces, most attempts at coalition building during the 1990s were largely unsuccessful.

Though ideological convergence seems to create conditions conducive to cooperation between Islamists and non-Islamists, it does not necessarily ensure that such cooperation occurs. This was amply demonstrated during the 2005 elections: Despite the high level of programmatic convergence between Islamists and non-Islamists on foreign policy and democracy issues during the 2000–05 period, Islamists refused to enter an alliance with other forces in the opposition and decided to contest these elections independently.

Balance of Power between Islamists and Non-Islamists: Alliance building and cooperation between Islamists and non-Islamists proved to be more likely

13. Noha El Mikawy, *The Building of Consensus in Egypt's Transition Process* (Cairo: American University Press, 1999).

when there existed some parity between the two sides and less likely when there existed a large imbalance between them. During the 1980s, the Wafd party was a strong secular counterweight to the Muslim Brotherhood; it was the biggest winner in the 1984 elections, winning fifty seats compared to the eight seats won by the Brotherhood. However, in the late 1980s and early 1990s, as Islamists began to realize a series of electoral successes in both Egypt and other Arab countries and to push non-Islamists from spaces they had previously dominated, relations between Islamists and non-Islamists deteriorated significantly and cooperation declined visibly. During the 1990s, secularists aligned themselves with the regime, reasserted their commitment to a secular state and to the principles of pluralism and equal citizenship, and became less willing to appease the Brotherhood on issues of sharia, as they had done in the 1980s.

During the late 1990s, after suffering a series of blows at the hands of the regime, a humbled Brotherhood showed greater willingness to moderate its discourse and cooperate with the secular opposition. During the 2000–05 period, Brotherhood activists cooperated with non-Islamists on foreign policy and democracy issues and Brotherhood activists joined movements such as EPCSPI, the Popular Campaign, and Kifaya. However, as these movements tended to be dominated by 1970s-generation activists, some of whom had split off from the Brotherhood during the 1990s, the participation of the Brotherhood tended to be largely symbolic. During that period, Brotherhood activists also cooperated with non-Islamists in a number of professional syndicates.

In 2005 the Brotherhood began to abandon its accommodating and cooperative attitude toward other opposition actors in favor of a more competitive and exclusive approach. Foreign pressure on the regime to democratize placed the regime on the defensive and emboldened the opposition, including the Brotherhood. Moreover, signals sent by the United States and Europe that they were willing to cooperate with moderate Islamists, coupled with the electoral successes of Islamists in Iraq and Palestine, emboldened the Brotherhood. Feeling strengthened, the Brotherhood began to shun cooperation with other forces in the opposition and refused proposals to form a grand coalition with the other forces in the opposition for the 2005 elections. The Brotherhood contested these elections separately and won 20 percent of the votes compared to the 2 percent won by the non-Islamist opposition. The large gap between the performance of the Brotherhood and that of non-Islamists reinforced divisions within the opposition and created a situation akin to that which existed in the early 1990s, giving the regime the excuse it needed to usher in another episode of political deliberalization, which negatively affected Islamists and non-Islamists alike.

External Factors and the Prospects for Cooperation

Levels of Repression or Toleration: Cooperation and alliance building have been more likely during periods of relative political liberalization and less likely during periods of political closure or deliberalization. In the 1980s and in the 2000–05 period, the regime tolerated efforts at alliance building between Islamists and non-Islamists in the opposition. In the 1980s, and despite an electoral law that restricted independents and nonparty actors from running for parliament, the regime allowed Brotherhood candidates to run on the slates of officially recognized political parties. As a result, the Wafd party and the Brotherhood formed electoral alliances in 1984, and the SLP, the LP, and the Brotherhood formed the Islamic Alliance in 1987. Similarly, during the 2000–05 period, the regime tolerated cooperation between Islamists and non-Islamists within the context of issue-based movements that focused on foreign policy and democracy issues.

In contrast, during the 1990s, as the regime began to crack down on the Islamist opposition, it significantly raised the costs of cooperation with Islamists. The regime made it clear that it no longer tolerated the long-standing alliance between the SLP and the MB. As a result, the Islamic Alliance was formally dissolved and the SLP, the LP, and the MB had to contest the 1995 election separately. When the SLP continued to cooperate with the Brotherhood and to provide its activists with a formal platform through which to operate, the regime retaliated by suspending the SLP and its newspaper. The regime similarly suspended the activities of a smaller and less-known political party, the National Accord Party, whose leader had approached the Brotherhood and proposed an alliance.[14] And even though the regime was willing at times to use blunt tactics to prevent cooperation between Islamists and non-Islamists, more often than not, the regime relied on less direct divide-and-rule strategies to prevent the emergence of a broad-based coalition among actors in the opposition.

Divide-and-Rule Tactics: The regime has been extremely adept at using a variety of divide-and-rule tactics to break the ranks of the opposition and prevent sustainable alliance building between Islamists and non-Islamists. The extension of selective incentives to individual groups in the opposition and the convocation of national dialogues with a chosen group of opposition parties have been favorite tactics. The regime has also often preempted joint mobilization in the opposition by making partial concessions to the opposition and rechanneling the political debate back into the state-sanctioned pluralist order. In the 1980s, as joint mobilization by the opposition focused on the question of electoral reform, the regime preempted this mobilization by making frequent cosmetic amendments to the election law, dissolving

14. Amr Rabie Hashem, ed., *Small Political Parties and the Party System in Egypt* (Cairo: Al Ahram Center for Political and Strategic Studies, 2003) (in Arabic).

parliament, and calling for early elections. Thus the regime diverted the opposition's attention away from joint mobilization and toward electoral competition. Moreover, the regime prevented the opposition from forming a grand coalition by promising seats in parliament to parties that refused to join alliances with other opposition actors.

In 1994, in its attempts to gain the support of secular opposition forces, the regime invited officially recognized political parties to a national dialogue, from which the Brotherhood was excluded, demarcating the emergence of a new fault line between secularists in the regime and the opposition on one hand and radical and moderate Islamists on the other. In the course of this dialogue, the regime secured from opposition parties a strong condemnation of terrorism; in return, the regime made some nominal concessions.[15] Similarly, in 2005, as mobilization around issues of reform and democratization was coming to a head, the regime, in an attempt to divide the opposition and isolate both the Brotherhood and new secular movements such as Kifaya, invited officially recognized political parties to yet another national dialogue. In the course of this dialogue, the regime managed to convince political parties to postpone demands for constitutional reform until after the parliamentary elections. However, just a few weeks later, the president embarrassed opposition parties by proposing a constitutional amendment to allow for competitive presidential elections. Aware of the weakness and fragmentation in the secular opposition, the regime has not felt the need to pay a high price to reward secular forces that have cooperated with it against the Brotherhood. Opposition parties have repeatedly demonstrated that they can be coopted for a very low price.

Succession, Generational Replacement, and Breaking the Vicious Cycle

Over the past quarter-century, government-opposition and opposition-opposition relations in Egypt have fallen into a cyclical pattern, or a vicious cycle, that has inhibited progress toward greater political liberalization and a full-fledged transition to democracy. On a number of occasions, domestic or external crises have driven the regime to liberalize the political sphere. Liberalization measures, in turn, have encouraged opposition forces to mobilize against the regime and demand further liberalization. Elections are held and Islamists, who command greater mobilizational and organizational skills, can overpower other opposition forces and polarization ensues. Strengthened by the growing divide between actors in the opposition, the regime cracks down on Islamists and proceeds to deliberalize

15. *The Arab Strategic Report 1994* (Cairo: Al Ahram Center for Political and Strategic Studies, 1994), p. 37; Mona Makram Ebeid, "Democratization in Egypt: The 'Algeria Complex,'" *Middle East Policy*, vol. 3, no. 3 (1994), pp. 119–124.

the political sphere. This pattern occurred during the second half of the 1970s, again during the late 1990s, and most recently in the wake of the 2005 elections.

Islamists and non-Islamists often have cooperated during the early stages of mobilization. However, once it becomes apparent that Islamists alone reap the benefits of such mobilization, both sides begin to shun cooperation. Islamists feel that, as the stronger party, they should not be forced to make concessions and share power with other opposition forces. Non-Islamists fear being overpowered and ultimately excluded by Islamists, and because they cannot compete electorally with Islamists, they often have aligned themselves with the regime, which they perceive as the lesser of two evils. As a result, non-Islamists often have tacitly supported measures to deliberalize the political sphere and arrest Islamist ascendance, even though such measures tend also to undermine the secular opposition. This vicious cycle has inhibited sustainable cooperation between Islamists and non-Islamists and has prevented the emergence of a broad coalition able to challenge the long-standing hegemony of the ruling NDP effectively.

Given the continued weakness and fragmentation of the secular opposition and the Brotherhood's continued ambivalence regarding questions of citizenship and equality, it is conceivable that this cyclical pattern will continue to repeat itself into the foreseeable future, allowing the regime to reproduce its power even as its legitimacy and ability to govern continues to decline. However, given that both the Egyptian regime and the opposition are undergoing processes of generational replacement, it is also conceivable that this cyclical dynamic could be broken in the medium or long term.

After the NDP's poor performance in the 2000 elections, the ruling party began a process of elite recruitment to revamp its base of support and rehabilitate its public image. This process was led by President Mubarak's son, Gamal, who is a former banker with close ties to the Egyptian business community and good relations with Western governments. Positioning himself as a reformer with a neoliberal economic vision and pro-Western orientation, the young Mubarak began to recruit businessmen, technocrats, and liberal intellectuals into the NDP's newly created High Council of Policies as well as the Policies Secretariat, which he presided over. The new recruits oversaw the redrafting of the party's basic principles to emphasize the party's commitment to economic liberalism, citizenship rights, civil society, the empowerment of women, and the peace process.[16] Moreover, reformers within the NDP oversaw the adoption of a number of largely cosmetic political reforms, which were nonetheless the first to be adopted after nearly a decade of political deliberalization. These included the creation

16. Amr Rabie Hashem, *The National Democratic Party* (Cairo: Al Ahram Center for Political and Strategic Studies, 2004), p. 40 (in Arabic).

of the National Human Rights Council, the dissolution of state security courts, and some minor amendments to the political parties and political participation laws.

In 2002–05, there was much talk in the Egyptian polity about an internal struggle within the ruling party, between a reformist new guard and a conservative old guard, which had dominated the party since its inception in 1979. During that period, many leading figures from the old guard were removed from positions of influence within both the party and the government and were replaced by individuals associated with the new guard. However, in the wake of the 2005 elections, as foreign pressures on the regime began to subside and as preparations for the prospective process of presidential succession got underway, reformers abandoned many of their reformist claims and the old guard and the new guard joined forces to set the stage for the process of succession. This convergence was reflected in the manner in which the constitution was amended in the spring of 2007 to give the NDP total control over the process of nominating presidential candidates in forthcoming presidential elections. Other amendments were also carefully drafted to tighten the regime's control over the political sphere, to preclude competition from the Muslim Brotherhood, and to limit judicial oversight over the electoral process.

However, despite growing convergence among the old and new guard within the NDP, it is conceivable that Gamal Mubarak and his supporters will feel the need to seek allies outside the regime to ensure a smooth process of succession. Unlike his father, whose legitimacy rests on his military background, his role in the 1973 war, and his previous position as vice president, Gamal Mubarak has no claim to legitimacy and a weak basis of support independent of his father. To consolidate his position, first and foremost, Gamal Mubarak will have to secure the support of the Egyptian security establishment, but he might also seek to gain the endorsement of actors in the opposition to imbue his accession to the presidency with a modicum of legitimacy. This could potentially pave the way for pactmaking between actors in the regime and in the opposition, creating opportunities to transcend an increasingly unsatisfactory status quo.

For its part, the opposition is undergoing a process of generational replacement that could create opportunities to break the vicious cycle that has characterized Egyptian politics since the mid-1970s. The changing face of the Egyptian opposition became apparent during the 2000–05 period, when 1970s-generation activists began to assume a leading role in mobilizing opposition, overshadowing, at least temporarily, some of the older parties and movements of the opposition. The rise of Wasat-generation activists to leading positions within the opposition could enable greater cooperation and increase the prospects for effective alliance building, particularly because 1970s-generation activists have, for the most part, demonstrated a greater propensity for pragmatism and compromise, despite their varying ideological commitments.

The political outlook of the 1970s generation of activists was deeply affected by Egypt's 1967 defeat at Israel's hands, which they attributed to the repressive and undemocratic features of the Nasser regime. Democracy became a priority for an important segment of this generation, the activists of which led the 1969 and 1971–72 student demonstrations that demanded, among other things, the restoration of political rights and freedoms. During the 1980s and 1990s, Wasat-generation activists were important in Egyptian public life. Leftist activists from the 1970s generation were largely responsible for creating the Egyptian human rights movements. They also were important in professional syndicates, particularly in the journalists' syndicates and in the media; some of them rose to become leading journalists, writers, and artists.

Islamist activists from the Wasat generation have also been important during the 1980s and 1990s. Some of the more radical elements formed militant Islamist groups and engaged in a violent confrontation with the regime for most of those two decades. However, the more moderate elements joined the Brotherhood in the late 1970s and were largely responsible for the electoral successes of the movement in student unions, professional syndicates, professors' clubs, and in parliament. Moreover, Wasat-generation activists tried to push the Brotherhood toward greater ideological moderation and were responsible for producing statements and declarations that affirmed the movement's commitment to pluralism and democracy.

During the 2000–05 period, Islamist and non-Islamist activists from the Wasat generation assumed a leading role in mobilizations around domestic and foreign policy issues. These activists oversaw the creation of new parties and movements, such as al Ghad, al Karama, al Wasat, EPCSPI, and Kifaya, and succeeded in injecting new dynamism into the Egyptian political sphere after a decade of political polarization and stagnation. Moreover, Wasat-generation activists made serious attempts to transcend the dichotomies that have polarized the Egyptian polity over the past quarter century and take their respective movements beyond ideology and toward greater moderation and pragmatism. This was demonstrated by the more pluralist and inclusive discourse that al Ghad, al Wasat, and al Karama adopted, and also by the successful cooperation between the various segments of the Wasat generation in the context of professional syndicates and issue-based social movements. However, despite the importance of Wasat-generation activists in Egyptian public life, over the past quarter century, their ability to rejuvenate the Egyptian opposition and transcend the dichotomies of the past has been limited by the efforts of both the regime and opposition old guards to isolate them. Yet, given the biological inevitability of generational replacement, these efforts are bound to fail; many of the older parties and movements are already experiencing the pangs of change. Soon the divide between the old and the new guard within the Egyptian opposition is bound to disappear, giving way to new dynamics that could lead to a fundamental change in the rules of the political game.

15

The JMP Alliance: New Political Pragmatism in Yemen?

Iris Glosemeyer and *Hesham Sallam*

The experience of Yemen's Joint Meetings Parties (JMP) between 1996 and 2006 offers some useful answers to the question of what strengthens and weakens opposition cooperation across the divide between Islamists and non-Islamists.[1] The JMP, an alliance encompassing an ideologically diverse group of opposition political parties, is a rare example of long-term strategic cooperation among opposition groups in the Arab world. The case of the JMP both puzzlingly and pleasantly deviates from theoretical expectations about the difficulty of launching and maintaining strategic alliances among ideologically diverse political groups. The strengths and shortcomings of this experience contain valuable insights that could both enhance our understanding of cross-ideological cooperation among political opposition groups and provide useful lessons for fragmented opposition communities throughout the Arab region. This analysis proceeds on the assumption that intraopposition cohesion is essential to any serious democratization process under hybrid authoritarian regimes, broadly defined as political systems that combine authoritarian rule and formal elements of democracy, such as multiparty elections.[2]

This essay presents an account of the founding of the JMP and its development; analyzes the factors and motives that gave way to its creation,

---

1. Fieldwork for this paper was completed in July 2006.

2. This assumption reflects a growing consensus in the field. As Larry Diamond writes, "While an opposition victory is not impossible in a hybrid regime, it requires a level of opposition mobilization, unity, skill, and heroism far beyond what would normally be required for victory in a democracy." See Larry Diamond, "Thinking about Hybrid Regimes," *Journal of Democracy*, vol. 13, no. 2 (April 2002), pp. 24. Observing a significant correlation between opposition cohesion and liberalizing electoral outcomes under competitive authoritarian systems, Howard and Roessler state: "What is important in competitive authoritarian regimes is how opposition leaders and civil society groups choose to organize in the electoral arena and their ability to create strategic coalitions that are resilient in the face of government force and fraud." See Marc Morjé Howard and Philip G. Roessler, "Liberalizing Electoral Outcomes in Competitive Authoritarian Regimes," *American Journal of Political Science*, vol. 50, no. 2 (April 2006), p. 371.

strengths, and weaknesses; and evaluates its overall impact on Yemeni politics, specifically the process of political reform.

Yemeni Politics on the Eve of the JMP

The Civil War and the Shaping of the Yemeni Political Arena

Except for a few brief periods, Yemen has never been ruled as a single unified state since the early eighteenth century. Immediately before the unification of 1990, what is known today as the Republic of Yemen (RoY) encompassed two separate states, namely the Yemen Arab Republic (YAR, North Yemen) and the People's Democratic Republic of Yemen (PDRY, South Yemen). After decades of unity talks and several wars, on November 30, 1989 the two governments finally signed an agreement outlining a roadmap for unifying their countries. The agreement, commonly known as the Aden Agreement, provided for a referendum on a new constitution and parliamentary elections before formal unification. However, faced with unexpected opposition to the unity project, the two governments decided to skip these measures and speed up the process of unification, postponing the referendum and elections until after unification. In April 1990, they signed the Sanaa Agreement, which set May 22, 1990, as the date for unification. The RoY established political pluralism and ensured the survival of the two former ruling political organizations: the General People's Congress (GPC), which dominated the politics in the YAR, and the Yemen Socialist Party (YSP), the PDRY's ruling and only party. Initially, the government of the RoY was based on power sharing between the former leaderships of the YAR and PDRY. This formula unified their legislatures and established a five-member presidential council, which comprised figures from the two republics and was headed by former YAR president Ali Abdallah Salih.

Between 1990 and 1994, Yemen witnessed a period of genuine political openness, made possible by competition among members of the ruling coalition, which consisted at the time of the GPC, YSP, and, after the 1993 elections, the Yemeni Congregation for Reform, also known as the Islah Party, a conservative-Islamist party. Competition among the ruling parties ensured that no single party fully controlled the political process and made room for smaller parties, non-governmental organizations (NGOs), and a vibrant press.[3]

By 1993 a power struggle between the northern leadership and the YSP reached a hazardous level, as the former began abandoning the informal commitments it had made prior to unification. As the power struggle intensified, political violence rose. By the end of 1993 the YSP alleged that

---

3. Sheila Carapico, *Civil Society in Yemen: The Political Economy of Activism in Modern Arabia* (Cambridge: Cambridge University Press, 1998), p. 136.

militant Islamists tied to Islah's ideologues and President Salih's security apparatus murdered 150 of its members.[4] Efforts to negotiate an exit strategy from this crisis failed, and by May 1994 the power struggle turned into open warfare between the government of the RoY, dominated by GPC and Islah, and a separatist government led by the YSP.

By the time hostilities ended on July 8, 1994, the southern leadership had fled to exile and YSP's property had been confiscated. National unity was preserved, but for a price: The democratization achieved during 1990–94 suffered a setback as the victorious northern elite tried to revive the more closed political system of the YAR. After the war, any criticism of the regime was quickly condemned as a threat to Yemeni unity, and critics of the government were often defamed as separatist. Yet, unwilling to destroy its reputation as a prodemocratic government and risk the loss of international support, the state leadership maintained party pluralism.

Even after excluding the YSP, conflict within the ruling coalition did not disappear entirely. Competition between the two remaining parties in the ruling coalition, GPC and Islah, intensified in 1996 as President Salih tried to concentrate power in the hands of his own GPC. In what later proved to be a critical turning point, Islah's leadership began searching for partners among the opposition; a search that, as explained below, ultimately ended in the creation of the JMP.

Yemeni Opposition Alliances before the JMP

The JMP is by no means the first intraopposition alliance in Yemen's modern political history. Such alliances date back to the first half of the twentieth century. However, during the brief period of genuine political competition described above (1990–94), a number of new political alliances emerged. In August 1993, when the threat of civil war seemed imminent, five small parties, which were politically closer to the YSP than the GPC, formed the National Opposition Bloc. A few weeks later, a group of smaller parties loyal to the GPC formed a similar bloc under the name National Democratic Alliance of the Opposition (NDAO). The formation of NDAO was seen as an attempt by the GPC to undermine its opponents, especially the YSP, which was still formally a partner in the government coalition.

By the mid-1990s the National Opposition Bloc developed into the Supreme Coordination Council of Opposition Parties (SCCOP), which later formed the basis for the JMP. By then SCCOP was comprised of six parties, including the remnants of the YSP,[5] and showed some promising signs of coordination among its members.

---

4. Iris Glosemeyer, *Liberalisierung und Demokratisierung in der Republik Jemen, 1990–1994, Einführung und Dokumente,* Aktueller Informationsdienst Moderner Orient, Sondernummer 14 (Hamburg: Deutsches Orient-Institut, 1995), p. 31f.

5. The Unionist Nasserist Popular Organization, YSP, Arab Socialist Ba'th, Truth Party, Union of Popular Forces, and Liberal Constitutional Party.

JMP: Founding and Development

Deteriorating relations between the conservative-Islamist Islah Party and its dominant coalition partner, the GPC, instigated talks between the former and the rest of the opposition about possible cooperation. In mid-1996 it dawned on the Islah leadership that the GPC would not cooperate with them in the 1997 parliamentary elections under acceptable terms. According to a leading Islah functionary, the GPC was planning to allocate seventeen seats to Islah in the 1997 parliament, the same number as before unification.[6]

To Islah's leaders, it became clear that the GPC was striving for a comfortable majority at the marginalization of Islah and that the GPC would not treat their party as an equal partner if they were to participate in government. Thus, Islah decided to entertain the option of cooperating with all other political parties, including their former foe, the YSP. Finding themselves gradually but irrevocably excluded from any meaningful government participation,[7] Islah leaders approached the YSP-dominated SCCOP to initiate a dialogue over issues of mutual concern. On August 27, 1996, the parties issued their first joint statement.[8] However, it was only in the 2003 parliamentary race that they launched their first serious attempt at electoral coordination. In 2005, the JMP parties issued a joint platform, and in the 2006 presidential election, the parties agreed to endorse a joint candidate to challenge the incumbent president. By then, this alliance officially comprised six opposition parties: Islah, YSP, Unionist Nasserists, Truth Party, Union of Popular Forces, and one of the two registered Ba'th parties. The Ba'th, however, while not having officially left the alliance, stopped signing the alliance's documents.

Asked who started the JMP initiative, YSP's former secretary-general, Salih 'Ubbad Muqbil, answered in a newspaper interview:

> It knocked at our door. We asked: who is there? They said: al-Islah. We said: what do you want? They said: we want to reach mutual understanding. We said: welcome, come in.[9]

---

6. Interview by Iris Glosemeyer, Sanaa, April 30, 2006.

7. See also Jillian Schwedler, "The Yemeni Islah Party: Political Opportunities and Coalition Building in a Transitional Polity," in Quintan Wiktorowicz, ed., *Islamist Activism: A Social Movement Theory Approach* (Bloomington: Indiana University Press, 2004), p. 218.

8. The communique is called *"al-barnâmaj al-tanfîdhî lil-liqâ' al-mushtarak baina al-tajammu´ al-yamanî lil-Islâh wa majlis al-tansîq al-a´lâ lil-mu´âradha."* It was signed by Muhammad Qahtan (Islah), Jarallah 'Umar (YSP), and representatives of the Truth Party, Union of Popular Forces, Unionist Nasserist Popular Organization, Ba'th, and the Constitutional Liberal Party. Copy with the author. See also Schwedler, "The Yemeni Islah Party," p. 220.

9. Quote cited by Muhammad Qahtan. Unable to locate the original citation; the reference here is to Muhammad Qahtan's narrative (interview by Iris Glosemeyer, Sanaa, April 29, 2006). Unfortunately the humor of this anecdote does not translate very well.

Actually, before Islah knocked on YSP's front door, there had been some neighborly chats over the garden fence. It seems that cooperation between the two former deadly opponents was at least facilitated, if not made possible, by personal links among members of the two parties. It is ironic that personal relations and regional identities, two factors that have traditionally hindered political development in Yemen and still hamper opposition coordination to some extent, built bridges of cooperation inside the opposition. That Islah has intensified its activities over the last decade, specifically in the territories of the former PDRY, might have had another unexpected positive effect on cooperation between Islamists and socialists. Currently, many of Islah's rank and file come from the former stronghold of the YSP, live under similar conditions as YSP members, and share common grievances about the dominance of the tribal north, as personified in President Salih.

However, launching the alliance was not without hurdles. During the late 1990s many Islahis opposed any cooperation with the YSP, as ideological differences exaggerated by the Cold War were still pronounced and the political arena at the time was still overshadowed by the civil war of 1994.[10] A facilitating factor that might have helped overcome this obstacle is that Islah's official dealings with its former adversary, the YSP, were not direct, but occurred through SCCOP. In this sense one could argue that the smaller parties' participation in the alliance was important even though the public following they brought to the alliance is fairly insignificant.

Other sources of tension were Islah's endorsement of incumbent Ali Abdallah Salih in the 1999 presidential election and its support of the 2001 constitutional amendments that further strengthened the executive vis-à-vis the parliament, both of which the YSP adamantly opposed. These two moves greatly strained YSP-Islah relations. As it took the JMP parties some years to overcome this setback, there was a considerable gap between the release of their first joint communiqué in August 1996 and the beginning of serious coordination efforts in the early 2000s. However, during this period, it became apparent that differences between Islah and YSP were to be found on the level of realpolitik rather than ideology. Both Islah and YSP officials credit the integrating role of former YSP vice-secretary-general Jarallah 'Umar, particularly during the early years of the alliance. If it were not for 'Umar, many observers acknowledge, the first JMP meeting might have failed.[11] However, the seeming success of the JMP initiative provoked a violent reaction. 'Umar was shot and killed in the meeting hall minutes

---

10. This view was expressed by Islahis during Iris Glosemeyer's interviews in 2006.

11. For Jarallah 'Umar's biography, see Sheila Carapico, Lisa Wedeen, and Anna Wuerth, "The Death and Life of Jarallah Omar," *MERIP Press Information Note 115*, December 31, 2002, and www.al-bab.com.

after he had delivered a speech to 5,000 Islah functionaries at Islah's third conference in December 2002. According to Islah's head of the political section, 'Umar's speech is remembered as one that went "straight to the hearts."[12] In retrospect, his assassination, which some speculators attribute at least partly to the ruling regime, was a catalyst for Islah-YSP cooperation, which entered a new phase in December 2002. However, at that point it was too late for the parties to begin efficient electoral coordination for the 2003 parliamentary race.

There is no doubt that the parties' decision to join forces was made by their leaders in Sanaa, not by the grassroots. However, cooperation between alliance members began trickling down to the constituency shortly thereafter, as Islah, YSP, and Nasserists supported one another's candidates in some districts during 2003 parliamentary elections.[13] Today some YSP and Islah leaders are convinced that they might have achieved greater gains in the 2003 elections had they begun their coordination efforts earlier. During the runup to the presidential and local election in 2006, cooperation intensified again, and in November 2005 the JMP released a joint program and held widely publicized joint press conferences to present their goals and critique government policies. In April 2006 the JMP managed to get one of their major conferences broadcast on the pan-Arab news network al-Jazeera.

Although some of the member parties still showed a certain degree of uneasiness with the JMP initiative, this resistance did not threaten the immediate future of the alliance. Moreover, party leaders tried to strengthen cooperation at the province level.[14] Party functionaries from the provinces met with their leaderships in Sanaa and agreed to extend coordination efforts down to the local level. However, coordination at that level remained difficult in some regions due to persistent conflicts over issues such as land and water among the supporters of JMP parties, many of whom viewed their party membership as no more than a convenient link to powerful networks. Despite these caveats, it is clear that opposition parties have come a long way in building serious strategic partnerships considering the extreme—and sometimes deadly—antagonism between the two most important JMP members, Islah and YSP, during the first half of the 1990s. In other words, "the opposition has learned," as one Yemeni observer put it.[15]

12. Interview by Iris Glosemeyer, Sanaa, April 29, 2006.

13. See also Sheila Carapico, "How Yemen's Ruling Party Secured an Electoral Landslide," *Middle East Report Online*, May 16, 2003.

14. The author joined a symposium in Mukalla that had been organized by the JMP—obviously dominated by Islah—at the province level.

15. Interview by Iris Glosemeyer with a Yemeni member of National Democratic Institute (NDI), Sanaa, April 28, 2006.

JMP: Shared Concerns and Agenda

One issue on which all Yemeni political forces—including members of the ruling party—agree is the rejection of U.S. policy in the Middle East, particularly since the beginning of the Iraq war in 2003. Although the Yemeni government often proclaims its support for the Palestinian and Iraqi peoples, it cannot claim to have achieved much. Hence, all political actors believe that their government, having declared its unlimited allegiance to Washington, is part of the problem rather than the solution.

Nonetheless, Yemen's foreign policy is by no means the sole interest that opposition parties share. The rules for political participation constitute a major point of contention between government and opposition. The bylaws of the party law, the electoral system, the composition of the Supreme Committee for Elections and Referendum (SCER), voter registration, and the drawing of electoral districts are only some examples of such concerns.

A comparison of the JMP's 2005 platform and pre-1994 opposition documents shows that current JMP demands for the reform of the electoral system, further decentralization, and a bicameral parliament are very much in line with Yemeni opposition demands since the prewar period.[16] The platform also criticizes the centralization of power in the hands of the president and calls for a parliamentary instead of a presidential system. This proposal, however, might be difficult to sell to Yemenis, who after nearly thirty years under the rule of Ali Abdallah Salih have become quite used to the strongman executive often found in the Arab world. If implemented, the JMP's demands—particularly the call for a stronger parliament—would strip the executive of the financial resources that support the president's patronage network. Before 2008, strengthening parliament would have yielded greater political power for the Al-Ahmar family, as Sheikh Abdallah Al-Ahmar, former Islah chair, headed the parliament until his death in December 2007.

The program's emphasis on decentralization by direct elections of governors and autonomy for local governments also can be traced back to YSP demands, publicized as an eighteen-point catalog in 1993. Although initially proposed by the YSP, calls for decentralization resonated early on with Islah's tribal-wing members, who support decentralization for their own interests.[17]

All the same, none of the above means that the ideological foundations of Islah and YSP were miraculously fused. Contentious issues, including the position of women and the role of sharia in legislation, have been given

16. See the eighteen points of the YSP and the sixteen points of the Union of National Forces, released in 1993, and the Document of Pledge and Accord of 1994.

17. See Glosemeyer, *Liberalisierung und Demokratisierung* (including copies of the documents). The term *wing* is used for the different currents within Islah to simplify a more complex situation.

scant attention, at least in the JMP platform. The text discusses women's rights in reference to the constitution, which has become a lot less supportive of women's rights since 1991.[18] While the introductory and closing chapters of the platform contain some citations from the Quran, the text itself does not refer to the Quran or Sunna—or to any socialist project.[19] As a member of the YSP politburo explained, the two parties decided to set "ideology aside and go about it in a pragmatic way."[20]

It is obvious that much of the JMP agenda has been set—to a large extent indirectly and with delay—by its junior partners, and not by Islah, its biggest and most influential member. According to a member of the YSP politburo, Islah submitted the first draft of the joint platform, which was later amended. However, the platform's resemblance to the YSP's eighteen points is evident. Asked about this resemblance, a YSP member remarked not without bitterness: "Yes. And in the 1990s they [the Islah] called us infisali [separatist] because of these demands."[21]

JMP: Motivation, Common Ground, and Potential Weaknesses

Although the partnership between JMP's largest parties, YSP and Islah, still looks rather fragile, collaboration between the two sides is anything but new. As partners in the same coalition government along with the GPC in 1993 and 1994, their higher-ranking members sat together at the same table. There is no doubt, however, that the JMP is a marriage of convenience, in which each party hopes to benefit from the other's political capital, and this strategic alliance is not meant to last forever.

Cooperation between Islamists and leftists is neither unique nor unprecedented outside Yemen.[22] Nevertheless, one may wonder why a wealthy and comparatively powerful Islamist opposition party would join ranks with socialists. Despite the differences between them, however, both parties oppose the GPC's political dominance and virtual monopoly over the state and its resources; both also share admiration for the state of law and institutions, something that the YSP claims has existed in the PDRY and that many Islahis, especially in the political wing, have been keen to establish since

18. See *"mashrû´ al-liqâ' al-mushtarak lil-islâh al-siyâsî wa-l-watanî"* (The Joint Meeting Parties program for political and national reform), Sanaa (November 2005).

19. Such religious references are not entirely alien to the YSP. Islam had been the official state religion of the PDRY. Unlike the YAR and RoY constitution, however, the PDRY constitution guaranteed religious liberty. See Article 47 of the PDRY constitution (1978).

20. Interview by Iris Glosemeyer, Sanaa, April 9, 2006. Members of Islah's leadership confirmed this statement.

21. Interview by Iris Glosemeyer, Sanaa, April 9, 2006.

22. Fred Halliday, "The Left and the Jihad," *Qantara,* September 19, 2006, available at http://qantara.de/.

their party was founded. The allegedly firm application of law and effective functioning of institutions in the former PDRY makes the YSP attractive for Islah members who are on difficult terms with the tribal wing of their own party and neopatrimonial structures in general. Moreover, the majority of Islah members might look for ways to marginalize the radicals and thus seek allies outside its own party. The need to close ranks with other opposition parties definitely has strengthened Islah's political wing.

Moreover, by 2006 the ideological gap between Islah and YSP had decreased. Islah is a moderate Islamist party, though by no means homogeneous, and in some respects it is more conservative than Islamist. Its more radical elements have lost influence in recent years. The YSP had already lost many members of its more dogmatic leadership in the civil wars of 1986 and 1994. Not least, over the course of the last decade, the YSP has embarked on developing into a social democratic party.

Unlike in the early 1990s, when the relationship between YSP and Islah was one of ideological antagonism, by 2006 major sections of the two parties had found a common ground and developed personal and institutional relations that make long-term cooperation between YSP and Islah a realistic option. Even if the JMP disintegrates, its activities have contributed to reconciling the major political currents in the opposition.

Being composed of several parties with different ideologies and histories is a liability to the JMP. Nevertheless, these differences could be turned into an advantage, as each party enjoys a regional stronghold and appeals to specific groups in society. The 2006 elections demonstrated that the JMP has not yet made full use of its potential because important segments of Islah threw in their weight with the incumbent president and not enough attention was paid to the electorate. Whether the JMP realizes its full potential in mobilizing electoral support remains to be seen in the parliamentary elections scheduled for April 2009.

The JMP clearly undermines the government's divide-and-rule strategy. Both the YSP and Islah believe that the regime has used them in the past, and this common grievance brings the two sides together. Feeling threatened by regime members—whom both YSP and Islah members believe are associated with militant Islamists—is another integrating factor. However, negotiating jointly with the government has been one of their major points of weakness. As observed in the pre-2006 election period, the JMP acts as if it were the stronger party in such negotiations, while in fact it is weaker.

In-house opposition to the JMP initiative is not limited to Islah; some YSP members have yet to lend their full support to the alliance. Opponents usually raise the question of what remains of YSP's original identity and principles if it is to cooperate with parties that do not share its core values.[23]

23. See question 14 in the online chat with the YSP secretary-general published in *ath-Thauri*, July 13, 2006.

According to the YSP's head of the Executive Section, everybody is free to voice his or her opinion, but majority decisions have to be respected by all party members.[24] Yet it seems that at least some YSP members do not always respect the so-called majority decisions. After the party had decided to back the JMP candidate during the 2006 presidential elections, a YSP member ran for the same office, defying his party's position.[25]

Another challenge facing the JMP is that its support comes mainly from urban middle-class party functionaries, who do not possess the power to recruit a public following because three-quarters of the population live in rural areas. Tribal sheikhs and preachers, who hold most of the keys to unlocking the support of the masses during elections, are often at odds with the decisions that party leaders in Sanaa make.

Given the history of antagonism between the two parties, cooperation between the YSP and Islah is not without risks. The alliance gives the regime the opportunity to demonstrate to the public that opposition parties are willing to go to any lengths to oust Ali Abdallah Salih—even if that entails striking a deal with their worst enemies. Who would want to be ruled by people who will strike a deal with the devil just to come to power? So the regime's argument goes.

The gap between the demands of the opposition and the basic needs of the population is not insignificant. The general public does not easily comprehend many of JMP's demands, particularly those related to technical issues about electoral reform. Additionally, many of the demands are focused on building stronger political institutions—an idea that may not appeal to the Yemeni voter, whose experience with institutions is either negative or nonexistent given the heavy reliance on patronage structures. Similarly, the proposal to limit the power of the executive is hard to sell to most Yemenis, who doubt that a political system with a weaker leader could keep military and paramilitary forces in check.

Finally, it is unclear whether the JMP would survive if the regime decided to make an expensive offer to one of its major parties. What would become of the JMP if the regime offered the YSP compensation for its confiscated assets, or if it promised Islah a significant percentage of parliamentary seats in return for political acquiescence? The potential for regime cooptation could turn out to be a deadly blow to any opposition cooperation in Yemen in the coming years.

That said, the record thus far shows some promising prospects for future cooperation. By 2006 the opposition had demonstrated a remarkable ability to find compromises acceptable to the majority of all JMP member parties. The selection of a joint candidate for the 2006 presidential race is a case in

24. Interview by Iris Glosemeyer, Sanaa, April 29, 2006.

25. See, e.g., *Yemen Times*, September 7, 2006.

point. It seems that the JMP initially had faced some difficulty in selecting a candidate acceptable to all JMP members and the electorate. The JMP finally agreed on Faisal bin Shamlan.[26] However, given that the religious and tribal wings of Islah were not overly supportive of bin Shamlan's candidacy during the 2006 elections—and that Islah chair Sheikh al-Ahmar, one of the major symbols of tribal power in Yemen, endorsed the incumbent president—it comes as no surprise that Faisal bin Shamlan received only 22 percent of the votes.

JMP: Strategies for Change

The JMP strategy is defined by three main factors, namely, the international community, relations with the regime, and domestic public opinion. As the 2006 presidential and local elections illustrate, the JMP usually gives greater attention to the first two elements than to the third, and this is probably one of the prime weaknesses of the alliance.

The JMP devotes careful attention to relevant external actors and their attitudes toward Yemen. To undermine the international standing of the regime, the opposition refers with relish to statistics that document the poor performance of the Yemeni government.[27] The opposition is very much aware of the importance of elections for the regime as it tries to portray itself as democratic, or at least democratizing, to the outside world. The JMP threatened more than once to boycott either SCER or the elections altogether. The boycott of JMP members in the presidential and local elections in 2006 would have rendered the elections meaningless in the eyes of the international community, on which the current regime depends to finance its patronage network.

At the same time, the opposition tends to overstate its leverage and power. In anticipation of the local and presidential elections in September 2006, the JMP demanded the expansion of the GPC-dominated SCER and a larger share in its subcommittees. When the president declined their demands, the JMP withdrew altogether from the SCER and refused to provide staff for the registration committees. Thus, in effect, the JMP ceded control of voter registration committees to the ruling party that hastily recruited mostly untrained staff for the committees. In the election's aftermath, the JMP complained about irregularities, many of which could have been avoided had the opposition not abandoned SCER completely and helped staff the committees with more competent personnel. Monitoring of the registration process was mainly left to NGOs, who were drawn into the

26. For biographical data on the candidates, see e.g., *Yemen Times*, September 7, 2006, and *al-Hayat*, July 1, 2006 (translation by Mideastwire.com, July 3, 2007).

27. See, e.g., *mashrû´*, 2005, p. 7.

parties' conflict even more deeply. While voter registration went on for fifteen days, opposition parties were hardly seen encouraging their supporters to register. Rather, they were preoccupied with negotiations with the president and later tried to explain to the public why they had turned down his offer for an informal agreement. The JMP was caught in a dilemma: Should they participate in elections they considered unfair, thus legitimizing them, or should they boycott, thus risking the loss of any influence on the institutional level?[28]

Only on June 18, 2006, well after the voter registration, did the opposition and the regime reach an agreement.[29] Among other things, the deal provided for a committee of GPC and JMP members to review the voters' registers. According to the opposition, the GPC protracted the committee's work and its achievements are debatable.[30] Having committed the opposition to participate in the elections, less than a week after the agreement had been signed, President Salih announced that he would run for reelection.

Moreover, the negative attacks that characterized the later stages of the campaign put off many voters.[31] Mutual accusations of supporting terrorism and corruption brought back memories of civil war to Yemeni voters, who thus preferred to follow Shaikh Abdallah al-Ahmar's advice to vote for Salih, or as he put it "vote for a *jinn* [demon] that you know [rather] than a human you don't know."[32]

Regime Responses to Opposition Coordination

Initially the ruling party did not oppose the rapprochement between Islah and the YSP. Irregularities during the voter registration period in 1996 had led the YSP, smaller opposition parties, and even Islah to discuss a boycott of the elections.[33] In late 1996 and early 1997, the YSP had yet to make a

---

28. Interviews in Sanaa, April 2006.

29. *Sahwanet*, June 27, 2006, and *Yemen Times*, June 26, 2006.

30. According to the *Yemen Times*, 63,000 cases were referred to the courts. See *Yemen Times*, July 27, 2006. According to the preliminary statement of the European Union Election Observation Mission, a "review of the voter register . . . led to the deletion of over 200,000 names but was undertaken in a nontransparent way . . . and prevented proper opportunities . . . to verify its accuracy." See also European Union Election Observation Mission, "Yemen 2006, Final Report, Presidential and Local Elections—20 September 2006," p. 17, available at http://ec.europa.eu/external_relations/human_rights/eu_election_ass_observ/yemen/final_report_2006_en.pdf.

31. See European Union, "Yemen 2006," pp. 2, 20; April Longley, "The High Water Mark of Islamist Politics? The Case of Yemen," *Middle East Journal*, vol. 61, no. 2 (Spring 2007), p. 247.

32. Interview in *al-Quds al-Arabi*, November 14, 2006 (translation by Mideastwire.com).

33. For details on the 1997 elections, see Iris Glosemeyer, "Parliamentary Elections in Yemen," in Bertelsmann Stiftung/Forschungsgruppe Europa, ed., *Working Papers: Elections in the Middle East and North Africa* (Munich: Guetersloh, 1998), pp. 35–47.

final decision on this issue. Because the regime was eager to use the elections as proof of its commitment to democratic reform, a boycott would have tainted its image. It is not completely unlikely that Islah was sent out to convince the YSP to participate in the elections, as some observers suspect. Nevertheless, the YSP and several smaller parties finally decided to boycott the 1997 elections, and if the regime really sent its friends to bring the YSP back into the realm of controlled opposition, the strategy not only failed, but also facilitated the creation of an opposition alliance.

Since the YSP's assets were confiscated and redistributed in 1994 and Islah is the only JMP party formally entitled to government subsidies, there is little that the GPC can do to impose further legal or economic constraints against the JMP. Thus, the regime often resorts to informal means to weaken the alliance. Not surprisingly, one of the regime reactions to coordination efforts among the opposition was to create loyal opposition councils—bodies made up of so-called opposition political parties that were in fact loyal to the regime. Similarly, since the early 1990s, the regime has created a network of loyal newspapers, NGOs, and parties as a counterweight to the opposition. Although this strategy might make it hard for international observers to identify credible opposition, it cannot deceive politically engaged Yemenis, and therefore, the effect of the approach on the opposition is probably negligible. Nonetheless, the regime has not abandoned the game. During the presidential election in 2006, a loyal opposition bloc nominated a candidate by the name Yasin 'Abduh Sa'id Nu'man, who could easily be confused with a leading JMP figure, YSP secretary-general Yasin Sa'id Nu'man.

The president's order to release a number of extremists from prison after negotiations with the JMP failed in the spring of 2006 has been interpreted as a warning to YSP and Islah.[34] In some areas, particularly on the issue of socialist-Islamist cooperation, the interests of the militants and the regime coincide, which makes engaging in opposition activity a life-threatening endeavor. The strongest reaction against cooperation between the YSP and Islah came from militant extremists, culminating in the murder of then-YSP vice-secretary-general Jarallah 'Umar in December 2002. The opposition believes that the murder was planned by people who felt threatened by the increasingly dynamic opposition coordination. Some members of the opposition even hint directly at militants who are said to have ties to the regime. However, as explained above, the events had the opposite effect of what JMP members believe the regime intended. Instead of going to war with each other, opposition members' common fear of militants has brought the parties closer together.

34. Interview by Iris Glosemeyer with the vice-secretary-general of one of the smaller JMP parties, Sanaa, April 28, 2006.

Balance Sheet and Implications for the Political System

The overall balance sheet for JMP impact on democratization in Yemen is mixed. On one hand the effect of interopposition cooperation on the political system appears to be limited so far, with no significant changes occurring to the balance of power between the ruling party and the opposition. The regime's continued control over an elaborate patronage network allows it to maintain the support of powerful actors, including the military and relevant tribal forces. Moreover, the regime's strong relations with influential forces within the religious and tribal wings of Islah have limited the JMP's ability to realize its full potential, as illustrated by the 2006 presidential election.

On the other hand, the alliance arguably has prevented the political system from sliding further toward a full-blown authoritarian system. In assessing the impact of the JMP, one must also note that the alliance is rather new. Due to several setbacks, cooperation only began to take concrete form after the assassination of Jarallah 'Umar in December 2002.

Almost a decade after the first real talks between the YSP and Islah, the JMP can be considered a strategic alliance, not merely a tactical one. JMP members have more than one motive to act together. Apart from the feeling of having been cheated and even threatened by the regime, they share interests in limiting presidential power and having a say in the future distribution of power, particularly as it relates to presidential succession. However, some segments of the opposition—most of the YSP and Islah's political wing—also share long-term interests in building the state and ending neopatrimonial rule.

The most remarkable aspect of the JMP is that its two major opposition parties do not share tribal links, a common history—except perhaps a violent one—or an ideology, but they have managed to develop a long-term working relationship. They produced a joint platform and a common strategy, all while maintaining their respective independence and without falling into the trap of merging their party structures. The JMP has been officially declared a strategic alliance based on common interests and there are no efforts to hide that it serves the interests of its members, who will start competing with each other once its goals have been achieved. Over a period of ten years, the JMP has grown without dissolving itself, despite numerous challenges, including the history of antagonism among its member parties and the generally cooperative attitude of Islah's leadership toward the GPC. In recent years the JMP has reached an organizational degree never seen in the history of political alliances in Yemen.

The alliance has greatly limited one of the regime's core survival strategies, divide and rule, as the regime finds it increasingly difficult to exploit the chasm between Islamists and socialists; its measures are clumsy and old-fashioned. Yet the JMP has not helped the parties overcome some important weaknesses. Not all members of the two main parties fully support the alliance. Additionally, the neglect of the concerns of the electorate poses some serious challenges. The JMP tends to overemphasize the need for specific political reforms while the electorate is much more concerned with issues that are directly related to its basic needs, such as poverty and unemployment. While JMP leaders believe that such political reforms are essential to solving the country's economic troubles, which are in part the result of regime corruption and weak government institutions, for Yemenis, the link between the JMP's agenda and the needs of voters remains unclear.

Moreover, the JMP faces the same dilemmas as individual opposition parties, one of them being the boycott dilemma. On one hand, working within the system means condoning, and thus legitimizing, the transgressions of the ruling regime. On the other hand, boycotting elections and state institutions deprives the opposition of access to state institutions and the electorate. A second dilemma might be called the conflict dilemma. What stops the opposition, especially Islah, from openly challenging the government is fear of a return to civil war or the deployment of security forces and international military intervention. Islah leaders cite Somalia, Lebanon, and other countries in the region as examples of their worst fears. In their view, conceding to the regime every now and again is not an expression of loyalty, but responsibility. Nevertheless, sometimes the dividing line between loyal and responsible opposition is very thin and hard to see.

Part IV

Engaging Peoples and Polities

16

Building Interreligious Trust in a Climate of Fear: An Abrahamic Trialogue

David R. Smock

Conflicts among faith communities trouble those communities in many parts of the world. For Americans the most important relationships are those among Christians, Muslims, and Jews, and this includes relationships with the wider Muslim world. The events of 9/11 and after have made painfully clear the need for improved understanding among Christians, Muslims, and Jews. Misconceptions and misunderstandings abound. Little effective communication occurs. Extremists on both sides would like to see a clash of religiously defined civilizations. And the more that extremists define conflict in those terms, the more it will turn out to become a true clash of civilizations, thus becoming a self-fulfilling prophecy.

To forestall such a clash, dialogue is essential at various levels. First, there must be dialogue among political leaders from the West and from the Muslim world. Equally important is dialogue among people of faith, among religious leaders, among scholars, and among lay people. The fact that Muslims, Christians, and Jews all consider Abraham to be their spiritual ancestor and progenitor provides a natural basis for dialogue and religious communication. The sacred texts of the three traditions are also interrelated with each other.

Despite the genuine differences that exist among the three Abrahamic traditions, they all put forward visions of peace. We need to consider how the enduring virtues of these three great faiths can be used to build a shared community in terms of mutual respect, openness, trust, dignity, and responsibility. These three monotheistic religions need not meet as rivals, but can meet as partners and moral equals in building a shared future. In know-

---

David R. Smock, "Building Interreligious Trust in a Climate of Fear: An Abrahamic Trialogue," Special Report 99 (Washington, DC: USIP, 2003).

ing each other, they can give the best of their traditions and values to creating a genuinely peaceful interfaith community.

Cultural contact between Islam and the West has been marred by historically unequal power relations, leaving the West often arrogant and insensitive and the Muslim world frequently defensive and insecure. But active engagement with one another, through sustained dialogue and interaction, permits each to understand the deeper meanings, associations, and history of the other. Active engagement permits us to understand the authentic, life-affirming expressions of human religiosity in each of the other faiths. Above all, we seek a paradigmatic shift in how we see, understand, and relate to one another. Our awareness can and must be expanded beyond existing limitations, as we develop a greater sense of belonging to the family of humankind.

There are sections of all three faith communities that are not prepared to engage in dialogue or accept responsibility for the conflicts generated within their own traditions. But all three communities also have members and leaders who cherish the opportunity to become better informed, who welcome the opportunity to hear and acknowledge the pain that each may feel in relation to the other, and who are prepared to collaboratively work toward a more enlightened and peaceful future. And in doing so they recognize that there are serious issues that divide them and that these issues are often as much political as theological.

The overarching question is how to develop interfaith trust in the prevailing atmosphere of fear and mutual suspicion. In situations of trauma, as experienced continuously in the Middle East and as experienced in the West since 9/11, people are likely to turn inward. Accordingly, they have great difficulty in reaching out to the religious "Other." The prevailing attitude is often that no one's suffering can be compared to our own suffering. In this climate of victimhood, the Other—whether nation, ethnic group, or religious community—is often labeled simplistically and unhelpfully as either good or evil.

Agenda for This Trialogue

The Religion and Peacemaking Initiative of the U.S. Institute of Peace organized two two-day Abrahamic trialogue meetings in 2002 to address these concerns and issues. Muslim, Christian, and Jewish leaders were convened in Washington to consider these questions:

- How can relations among the three religious communities be improved and how can mutual recrimination be avoided?

- How can the three communities increase their mutual understanding and respect for each other?
- How can the three communities strengthen their commitments to reconciliation and peaceful coexistence?

A total of twenty-one religious leaders from the three communities participated in these sessions. The Christians and Jews were generally Americans; the Muslims came from the United States, Europe, and primarily Muslim countries. (The names of the participants are listed at the end of this report.)

This report summarizes the conclusions drawn by the participants in the two meetings. For the most part these are consensus conclusions, but when no consensus existed, that fact is indicated. The recommendations for action are grouped under the following topics:

- How to make dialogue/trialogue more effective.
- Action required by religious communities.
- Action required from nations and governments.
- What the media need to do.
- What the educational sector needs to do.

Promoting Greater Mutual Understanding

Religion and faith are increasingly influential forces in many parts of the world. Reza Sheikholeslami, one of the trialogue participants, said: "From Latin America to Algeria, Palestine, and Israel, to Indonesia and the Philippines there is a revival of articulation of resentment, opposition to factual or fictional suppression, and recognition of oneself in solidarity with others on religious terms. 'Religion,' as Rabbi Jonathan Sacks points out, 'is the sigh of the oppressed creature, the feeling of a heartless world, the soul of soulless conditions.' The liberal democracies are increasingly becoming managerial and procedural and lack vision to deal with the common good. Market forces are devoid of moral content. The prevailing order is increasingly and systematically depriving many of dignity and even minimal respect.

"As our political systems are incapable and far too short-sighted to address the basic moral questions, which have significant impact on world political stability and prosperity, it is the duty of religion to fill the dangerous chasm. If religious leaders fail to lead the moral crusade for justice and human dignity, if they fail to enunciate the essentially humane roots of religion, the oppressed, the deprived, the humiliated, and the dispossessed will flock to others who have chosen to forget the humaneness of religion, but will use its language and the solidarity it entails for violence. If religion does not become part of the solution, it will motivate hate."

But the increased salience of religion also carries liabilities. Many participants were concerned about widespread stereotyping of Islam and misunderstanding about the nature of the Islamic faith. This has been particularly troublesome since 9/11. According to Abdul Aziz Said, "The shared cultural roots joining Islam with the West are forgotten far too often. Although recently voiced opinions regarding a 'clash of civilizations' posit that Islam falls outside the Judeo-Christian and Hellenic cultural continuum, the reverse is in fact the case. Classical Islamic civilization was constructed out of Arab, Biblicist, and Hellenic cultures but cast a wider net by integrating Persian, Central Asian, and Indian components within its cultural synthesis. Historically, Islam is the true bridge between West and East.

"With respect to Islam, one distinction that many observers fail to make concerns the difference between revivalism and fundamentalism. Islamic revivalism is a broad-based social and political movement directed toward internal renewal. First and foremost, it is a response to a widely felt malaise that has left Muslim societies weak and unable to meet the modern world on its own terms. Although its manifestations are remarkably widespread, Islamic revivalism is not a monolithic movement, nor is it equivalent to the militant fundamentalism that arose as a reaction to foreign incursions and perceived threats to identity and security and that captures the attention of the media. Islam and the West today are dangerously out of touch with one another, and misperceptions and mistrust have led to an ever-deepening estrangement. But there is the prospect of a cooperative nonadversarial relationship between Islamic and Western civilizations. Such a relationship would be premised not on ideas of cultural triumphalism, but on mutual respect and openness to cultural eclecticism."

Sheikholeslami asserted that as a small step in changing public opinion, Muslims themselves should become reintroduced to some of the early conceptions which were essential to the Islamic faith: acceptance of the other, the divinity of social/communal differentiation, equality before God, and the dismissal of any superiority of one community over others. "I believe that the Christian and Jewish communities should become familiar with the essential message of Islam, which I think to be that of peace and tolerance. It is important if we want to live with each other to recognize the humanity and humaneness of the other. Many examples can be cited from the Quran of the non-confrontational dimension of Islam."

In an effort to overcome some of the confusion that Christians and Muslims often exhibit in relation to Jews, Robert Eisen said, "What I believe is frequently misunderstood by Christians and Muslims is the ambiguity and complexity of Jewish identity in the modern period. The Christians and Muslims with whom I have spoken tend to think of Judaism as a religion and of Jews as a people who adhere to that religion. What is underestimated is the extent to which Jewish identity is as much defined by a host of other factors such as nationality, ethnicity, and culture. Often religion plays an important role in combination with these other factors in the formulation of an individual's Jewish identity, but there are any number of Jews for whom religion is of less importance than these other factors—or of no importance at all. Jews with a historical or cultural identity may simply not be as interested in dialogue with Christians and Muslims as Jews who have a more purely religious identity. A Jew who has a strong sense of Jewish identity that is not predicated on religion may find it difficult to relate to devout Christians or Muslims."

An obstacle to improved interfaith relationships is fear surrounding "supersecessionism," particularly on the part of Jews in relation to Christianity and Islam. In so far as these faiths proclaim themselves to supercede and to be the "perfection of a new version" of Judaism (by Christianity and Islam) and Christianity (by Islam), this denigrates the older traditions. But Christians pointed out that supersecessionism is only accepted by some branches of Christianity, and Muslim participants identified a number of statements in the Quran that assert that it is God's will to have diversity and that God has ordained three distinct Abrahamic paths to the Holy.

Mutual understanding is frequently deterred by the rigidity of fundamentalism. Participants agreed that fundamentalism exists within each of the three traditions. Fundamentalism is often accompanied by an inclination to see the world sharply divided into good and evil forces. An inclination toward religious zealotry is often reinforced by the unquestioning adherence to rigid religious dogmas and submission to religious authorities.

Interfaith Dialogue or Trialogue

Participants advocated that interfaith dialogue be conducted at all levels of religious hierarchies and across all segments of religious communities. Said articulated the consensus view in stating: "Together we can explore and conceptualize a shared vision of peace that has depth and integrated meaning, that integrates our understandings, experiences, needs, hopes, and fears. A vision of total peace, achieved through dialogue, permits us to know one another not as rivals, but as partners exchanging the very best that each other has to offer."

Dialogue can explore common values, challenges (such as structural inequalities, terrorism, peacebuilding), adversaries, prejudices, and mistaken assumptions. All these can be surfaced and mutually explored. Participants then may be able to identify interfaith partners and connect their communities with shared societal concerns and joint action projects. New models and ways of relating to the Other can emerge through the dialogic process of listening, sharing, learning, and emphathizing.

But participants shared two reservations about how interreligious dialogue is normally conducted. First, dialogue generally places too much emphasis on talk; the greatest impact comes from undertaking activities together. Engaging in joint activities and projects is generally a more effective means of building trust and mutual understanding than is discussion or debate.

Second, participants in interreligious dialogue tend to be like-minded moderates who are already committed to dialogue and have considerable understanding of the other two faiths. They may be marginal to their communities and not reflect the majority view of their co-religionists. Often interfaith elites who serve as the "official representatives" of their faith communities are eager to preserve their positions, when they actually have little credibility within their own communities. In turn, they are unlikely to be accountable to or responsible for their communities. It is primarily extremists or separatists who create interfaith conflict but they are rarely willing to engage in dialogue. Their encounters with the other communities are more likely to be confrontational. Even if extremists cannot be successfully engaged with dialogue, those individuals who are invited to participate should carry weight in their own communities and be able to influence the thinking of significant portions of these communities.

Donald Shriver suggested fruitful topics for dialogic exploration. The three religions, especially Christianity and Islam, make certain exclusive claims of authority. On what particular internal bases (for example, scripture and theology) would each of them call for social-political orders that legally mandate religious tolerance? What internal standards make it difficult for tolerance to emerge unambiguously from each religion? What sorts of help would each faith provide for the maintenance of religious neutrality in government, that is, how does faith itself undergird the very concept of "secular"? How, on the contrary, does it hinder or contradict a secular definition of the functions of government? What is the difference between mutual tolerance and mutual affirmation? What would each of us most regret if we looked back on our respective religious histories? What are the times and places in each of our faith-histories that function as sources of pride?

It has been observed that each community tends to promote the best in its own tradition while criticizing the worst in others. This tendency seems especially common in our respective uses of our own scriptures. All of this raises the question of what authority we assign to these scriptures. Are each of us permitted by our own traditions to be selective in the use of scripture? Is every word authoritative, or are some themes and texts more authoritative than others? Are there illustrations from each tradition of themes and texts that, in our time, we consider more "weighty" than others, especially for the purposes of dialogue? What does each of us admire in the traditions of the other two? What does each of us fear in the other two?

It can be enormously valuable for persons of each religious community to hear members of the other communities confess the problems and shortcomings that that community is experiencing. Communication of humility and self-criticism can go a long way toward healing, understanding, and mutual respect.

The principal goal must be to build trust. This can be achieved through coming to know and understand the Other. Those engaged in these efforts must be prepared to take risks and confront the possibility of offending or alienating both members of one's own community and of the other communities. But over time and through creative efforts, misunderstandings can be overcome and trust will hopefully follow. At the very core of any trust-building program must be empathy. Authentic trust cannot be built without convincing demonstration of empathy emanating from both sides.

Other recommendations for effective dialogue include the following:

- More thought needs to be given to how to engender trust among the three faith communities and particularly how to promote intra-community awareness of the suffering of the Other. Each community needs to be convinced that the other communities genuinely feel its pain.
- There is a need to develop programs for interfaith reading of sacred texts to educate, inform, and deepen our understanding of one another. This also builds awareness of textual linkages that exist among the three Abrahamic traditions and expands opportunities for cultivating a greater interfaith Abrahamic identity. Similarly, devotional practices can be developed together. Particularly valuable would be shared study of Islamic, Judaic, and Christian texts on acknowledgment, empathy, confession, repentance, and forgiveness.
- The three traditions need to share with each other their understanding of peace and spirituality, and they need to broaden their understanding of peace collaboratively.
- There is a need to develop shared mourning processes surrounding death, destruction, and injustice, particularly in relation to terrorism and acts of governmental oppression. More thought needs to be given to how to promote acts that express repentance and facilitate reconciliation and mutual forgiveness.
- Through dialogue each community can articulate what it needs from the other two communities. For instance, Jews express the need to hear Muslims and Christians condemn all forms of terrorism, including suicide bombers in Israel. Muslims express the need to hear from Jews and Christians that they truly comprehend the suffering experienced by Palestinians at the hands of Israeli authorities.

- Through dialogue each community can work to see itself as others see it.
- A severe problem in many dialogues, particularly in the Middle East, is asymmetry of power. In the Middle East, most dialogues are initiated and dominated by Jews and held in Jewish locations, which tends to alienate Muslims. More dialogues should be held in neutral locations.
- Dialogue must not be confined to clerics. Dialogue must be multifaceted; different dialogue efforts should involve different constituencies and strive to achieve different ends. The most promising participants are those with the potential to develop a commitment to peaceful coexistence and mutual enlightenment. The role of women as potential religious peacemakers must be recognized.
- It would be helpful to develop handbooks to guide local congregations on how to engage in productive dialogue with congregations of other faiths. Many local congregations experiment with dialogue but they could benefit from the prior experience of other congregations.
- Similarly, handbooks could be developed for particular regions of the world. One of the trialogue participants has started writing a handbook on how to conduct interfaith dialogue in the Middle East, particularly Egypt, Jordan, Lebanon, the Palestinian Authority, and Israel.

Need for Action by Religious Communities

Participants expressed deep concern over the problems confronting their own communities today. Much of the hard work to promote peaceful coexistence must be done internally by each community. The religious peacemakers must take on the defamers and mythologizers within their own communities who are demonizing the Other. Religious peacemakers within each community have essential roles to play in countering the hostile and distorted statements made by their co-religionists toward the other religious communities.

But participants lamented that internal critics of the defamers are often not listened to, so they remain marginalized and ultimately ignored by their own communities. These critics are often the chief advocates of pluralism, peaceful coexistence, and dialogue with the Other. In the end, the voices of hard-liners and those espousing intolerant views end up being the ones generally heard, in part due to the media's tendency to focus on negative news, and in part due to the ease with which political leaders manipulate deep sensitivities and in turn generate fear and outrage. Finding ways to support the views of internal critics advocating pluralism, within and across communities, emerges as one of the most important challenges confronting religious peacemakers.

One of the biggest challenges to creating a pluralistic framework is how to react to co-religionists who have adopted separatist mindsets. These exclusivist perspectives, often forged in isolation, entail the exclusion or denial of the equal rights of others and thus form some of the greatest obstacles to the legitimacy of religious pluralism. One of the main challenges for peacemakers is bolstering moderates while exploring the views of, and making room for, separatists as well.

Cultivating an ethic of self-criticism emerged as one of the central concerns of participants. Self-criticism in two respects—accountability to and responsibility for the highest values of one's own community, and as a path for building trust and security with other religious communities. Self-criticism within a religious tradition reflects the belief that each tradition has the obligation to reflect deeply on the practices and principles governing its own religious system. Internal self-criticism involves an awareness that leads to accountability, to the need and ability to correct actions and thoughts inconsistent with religious ideals. On the other hand, participants were deeply concerned over whether internal self-criticism is possible or desirable for any community that feels weak, defensive, or under attack.

Self-criticism is implicit in the freedom to interpret, which invites other communities to respond in kind. In relation to others, self-reflection and interpretive freedom are essential confidence-building measures that have the potential to establish the sense of trust and hope for peaceful coexistence. But the practical application of self-criticism entails costs and risks for religious peacemakers. Critics have been censured, kicked out of religious houses of worship, and even had their lives threatened and their offices targeted for speaking out critically.

Several participants emphasized the need to recognize the fear and sense of vulnerability that Muslims in this country feel. They do not feel as free as other groups. Wire tapping, religious profiling, problems confronted at immigration, government statements that whoever is not with us is against us—these all create hypersensitivity and a predisposition to pull back from interfaith interaction. Jewish participants also pointed out the sense of vulnerability that many Jewish families in this country feel.

Recommendations for action by religious communities included the following:

- Religious peacemakers in each community need to inform religious peacemakers in other communities about those with whom they can work, that is, those who share their commitment to peaceful coexistence and mutual understanding. Each community needs to know who its potential partners might be in the other two communities.

- Peaceful coexistence can be most effectively advanced by having activists in the three communities develop a common program of action to facilitate joint commitments across lines of religious division. Examples include developing a justice agenda or a project to help humanize globalization from an Abrahamic perspective. A powerful illustration occurred when Rabbis for Human Rights in Israel organized delegations of Christian, Muslim, and Jewish clerics to jointly visit both Palestinian and Israeli casualties in hospitals. This compassionate act received good media attention and had a public impact in both Israel and the Palestinian Authority.
- The three communities should explore and promote the option of nonviolence in such zones of conflict as the Middle East. The three communities can also work to discourage the use of religious justifications for violence and hateful actions or policies.
- It is essential to recognize that there are narratives in all three religions that are pluralistic and peaceful, but that there are also exclusive narratives in each of these faith traditions as well.
- Muslim participants pointed out the effect of mutuality. For instance, if Christians and Jews can acknowledge the evil of Israeli oppression of Palestinians, then Muslims will be more prepared to condemn Palestinian suicide bombers.
- Religious actors might take a civility pledge, if not formally at least personally, to guide their manner of communicating on interfaith matters, to make sure that they do not demonize the Other or make ad hominem attacks.
- "Boundary leaders"—those who operate on the borders of their communities and are ready to reach out to other communities—need support from each other. Their work is psychologically and spiritually taxing. Boundary leaders are primarily experts at empathy, and this can be threatening to the separatists. Support networks would be particularly valuable for boundary leaders who are under attack.
- It would be helpful for boundary leaders to share with the wider communities stories of their "conversion" experiences that led them to the boundaries, ready to reach out to other faith communities.
- Religious leaders should be urged to utilize their skills as empathizers and conflict resolvers not to reinforce boundaries but to reach out to other religious communities. Clergy often protect boundaries rather than reaching across them.
- We should provide training for seminary students and military chaplains about the other two faiths. Clergy who are well trained in

interfaith relations can have an enormous impact on the level of intercommunity understanding.

- Sermonic aids and ideas for sermons relating to interfaith issues could be made available to preachers in the three traditions to promote mutual understanding. A Web site could be developed for this purpose. Model sermons on interfaith topics could also be posted to give guidance.
- It might be possible to form facilitation teams composed of representatives from the three faith traditions to enter situations of conflict and tension. Multifaith media teams might also be created to jointly author essays and articles on religious, particularly interfaith, issues.
- Greater publicity needs to be given to examples of religious peacemaking and interfaith collaboration. Such examples can provide models for others to replicate. Little press attention is given to these activities because goodness is generally not considered newsworthy.

The Interface between Religion and Politics or Diplomacy

"One area where work is greatly needed in the United States is to promote more awareness of how the United States and its actions are viewed around the world," noted Susan Thistlethwaite. "Even from a Just War perspective, it is critical for the security of peoples and nations that they understand clearly how others regard them and their actions. We need to look at how our religious traditions can be used to promote the virtue of empathy. Dualistic understandings of good and evil promote violence. All evil is projected onto the other; the theological category that remains for oneself is that of goodness and innocence. The sense of American innocence has been extended to include an almost complete deadness to the understanding, interests, and perspectives of the other side, which would contribute to the work of empathy. One of the functions of terrorism is to deaden empathy and make the work of peace and reconciliation more difficult, if not impossible. The evil-doer deserves punishment and because the evil-doer is the embodiment of all evil, no punishment is too extreme. This generates a descending spiral of violence and hatred. Vengeance is the companion of unresolved anger, lack of acknowledgment of wrongs, and a dualistic understanding of good and evil. It is our duty as religious peacemakers to be critical of our governments, when appropriate, in the name of religion, spirituality, and citizenship."

She then quoted Alan Geyer, who wrote, "Peacemaking, whether in personal, group, or international relations, requires a variety of capacities for self-transcendence: transcendence of one's own interests and perspectives for the sake of understanding the interests and perspectives of the other side, which calls for the virtue of empathy; transcendence of one's pride and defensiveness, which inhibit the acknowledgment of injuries done to others—a capacity for repentance and perhaps restitution; transcendence of one's own grievances and desire for vengeance over injuries inflicted by others—a capacity for forgiveness" (Glen Stassen, ed., *Just Peacemaking: Ten Practices for Abolishing War,* Pilgrim Press, Cleveland, 1998).

Participants asserted that diplomats need to recognize that religious peacemakers can be their allies in the promotion of peace and reconciliation. Many observers believe that the public response to the Oslo process in the Arab-Israeli conflict could have been more positive if religious leaders had been drawn in and had been associated with the process. The negotiators insisted that the Oslo process remain exclusively secular. The involvement of religious actors could have helped avoid the alienation that key members of the respective religious communities felt toward Oslo. To leave the language of faith out of peacemaking is a serious deficiency. This language is powerful. It motivates people. The language of faith needs to be central.

Interfaith teams need to seek out government officials to help them understand the intersection between faith and policy. A network of interfaith organizations should be created to provide a national voice for interfaith harmony and for the shared justice concerns of faith groups engaged with each other.

Interfaith delegations should be sent to Capitol Hill, to testify on the state of interfaith relations and the need for dialogue, and on the issues that are important to religious peacemakers. An interfaith delegation could be helpful both on Capitol Hill and at the White House to answers such questions as "Why do they hate us?"

Several participants asserted that trust and peaceful coexistence do not come so much from mutual learning and sharing through dialogue as from action on the ground and policy change, particularly in relation to the Middle East. These participants said that dialogue should focus on the promotion of justice rather than on spirituality. They also pointed out that there is a general failure in the United States to appreciate the impact of American policy toward the Middle East and the extent to which the American bias in favor of Israel is deeply resented by the Muslim world. One participant stated that any interfaith initiative that does not relate to the justice issues in the Middle East is comparable to "grinding water"; interfaith dialogue in the United States should focus on U.S. policy toward the Middle East. Unfortunately, he asserted, traditional interfaith dialogue tends to avoid divisive justice issues and policy.

Some participants suggested that commemorations of the second anniversary of 9/11 would provide opportunities for greater self-reflection, more openness to accepting some responsibility for some of the forces that cause hardship and suffering in the world, and a greater empathy for persons in other parts of the world who have died unjustly at the hand of a variety of malevolent forces. This would reflect a greater acknowledgement of the victimhood, not only of Americans, but of the Other as well. This would provide an opportunity to mourn all those who have died innocently around the world.

The Impact of the Media on Interfaith Relations

Many participants expressed strong views about the negative impact that the media has on interfaith relations. News accounts generally focus on religion as a source of conflict. The separatists and extremists are given the most prominence, which means that the fundamentalists are the most visible representatives of each tradition. The excessive emphasis on the negative side of religion and actions of religious extremists generates interfaith fear and hostility. Those with pluralist and inclusive perspectives usually have great difficulty conveying their messages. The media often highlight and glamorize radical perspectives and behavior to the detriment of peace.

Both Muslims and Jewish participants stated that most of their coreligionists feel that they are not understood by the media or given a fair hearing. Muslims believe the U.S. media have a serious anti-Muslim bias. This bias contributes to anti-Muslim prejudice and exacerbates tension with the other two faith communities. Similarly, many Jews are concerned about what they view as a growing anti-Israel bias on the part of key U.S. media.

Greater media attention needs to be given to actions taken post 9/11 to reach out across religious boundaries. On an unprecedented scale, Christian congregations have visited mosques, synagogues have invited Muslim leaders to speak, and mosques have reached out to the other two communities. National Public Radio could productively broadcast a series of programs on local Abrahamic interfaith activities. Reports on interfaith initiatives of this kind in the United States can have important spill-over impact in places like the Middle East.

Religious leaders have an obligation to try to sensitize the media to the two-dimensional character of most current news stories on religion and interfaith relations, particularly in relation to Muslims.

The Role of Education and Culture

Efforts should be made to develop teaching materials about the three faith traditions for use at various levels in the educational structure. For example, an anthology on the three Abrahamic traditions could be developed for use in high schools. And teaching materials on Islam need to be developed for use in Christian and Jewish seminaries, and vice versa. A common curriculum could be developed for religious schools that focuses on shared values among the three religions. A study should be undertaken of the depiction of the three religious traditions in textbooks in use in schools in the United States and internationally, to correct biases and distortions.

Courses need to be developed on Abrahamic peacemaking, teaching how the three faith traditions understand and promote peace. Guidance needs to be given to college student leaders on how to handle interfaith relations. Some campuses are exploding, with the atmosphere filled with mutual recriminations. Student religious organizations on campuses should be encouraged to have regular exchanges.

Interfaith camps for high school students, built on the model of Seeds of Peace, can be effective, both domestically in the United States and internationally. Interfaith camp experiences should focus on building mutual trust. Often the most effective form of interfaith sharing and mutual appreciation comes from sharing of cultural materials, such as films, novels, and music.

Conclusion

Building interfaith trust in a climate of fear is both a challenging and urgent task. Principal responsibility for taking up this challenge rests with the respective religious communities. Unfortunately, not all religious leaders wish to assume this responsibility and some religious leaders promote religious triumphalism at the expense of interfaith amity, and this only compounds the levels of fear and mutual hostility. Those within these communities who are committed to pluralism and peaceful coexistence must step forward and take the initiative. While the responsibility rests primarily with people of faith, governments, educational institutions, and the media can play critical roles in either exacerbating the problem or contributing to the solution. This report has enumerated steps that each of these actors can play to contribute to religious peace and the reduction of religious tensions.

Participants

Prof. Mohammed Abu-Nimer, American University
Prof. Leila Ahmed, Harvard University
Prof. Azizah Y. Al-Hibri, University of Richmond
Rabbi Robert Carroll, Edah
Dr. Drew Christiansen, S.J., Woodstock Theological Center
Rabbi Rachel Cowan, Nathan Cummings Foundation
Rabbi Dr. Robert Eisen, George Washington University

Rabbi Dr. Marc Gopin, Fletcher School, Tufts University
Rabbi Irving Greenberg, Jewish Life Network
Alma Abdul-Hadi Jadallah, Institute for Conflict Analysis and Resolution, George Mason University
Yehezkel Landau, Open House Center for Jewish-Arab Coexistence
Prof. Ali Mazrui, Binghamton University, SUNY
Prof. Sulayman Nyang, Howard University
Prof. Ayub Khan Ommaya, George Washington University Medical Center
Prof. Tariq Ramadan, University of Fribourg
Prof. Abdul Aziz Said, American University
Prof. Adam Seligman, Boston University
Prof. Reza Sheikholeslami, Oxford University
Rev. Dr. Donald Shriver, Union Theological Seminary

17

The Diversity of Muslims in the United States: Views as Americans

Qamar-ul Huda

With recent attention on European Muslims in France, Belgium, Germany as well as with the London bombings of July 7, 2005, there is a focus on how Western Muslims integrate, assimilate, and contribute to society. This Special Report examines how American Muslims have expressed themselves as Americans in a post 9/11 world of suspicion. In doing so, this study analyzes different, major American Muslim organizations' activities and their distinguishing views on violence, terrorism, and conflict resolution. The objective of this Special Report is to identify key trends in American Muslim organizations; their major religious and secular activities, as well as understand the ways in which American Muslims are carving out a distinct American identity as citizens. This report demonstrates that unlike Muslims in Europe, American Muslims do not feel marginalized, isolated, or locked out of political participation. Social-economic mobility is far more obtainable. For the most part, American Muslims have successfully created professional, cultural, human rights, civil rights, educational, and political organizations as an expression of feeling included in the larger spectrum of American society and liberal democracy. The analysis presented here illustrates that American Muslims' contribution to the United States is a product of not only of their own diversity, but also of the diversity of views in understanding themselves as Americans.

American Muslims face a range of challenges to which Muslim organizations are responding. After 9/11, American Muslims have had to confront widespread suspicion, challenges to civil liberties, and a Muslim-specific response to Muslim radicalism (domestically and internationally) and the war on terrorism. In doing so, Muslim and Arab Americans have created a variety of new organizations and invigorated existing ones. The material in this report describes and analyzes the programmatic responses of key

---

Qamar-ul Huda, "The Diversity of Muslims in the United States: Views as Americans," Special Report 159 (Washington, DC: USIP, 2006).

American Muslim organizations to these challenges. In addressing these challenges, these organizations walk a fine line between reassuring the American public about Muslims and Islam, while not alienating their constituents on issues important to them.

Overview of American Muslim Nongovernmental Organizations

The American Muslim community consists of a wide range of ethnic, racial, cultural, and professional groups, all of which contribute immensely diverse opinions on contemporary issues, such as conflict and peacemaking. With the war in Iraq and Afghanistan as well as the implementation of the Patriot Act, American Muslims no longer play an undefined role in American policy; rather, many political analysts and congressional representatives are seeking them out as sources of information. In the aftermath of 9/11, American Muslim organizations became critical consultants for U.S. foreign policies toward Afghanistan and Iraq. In addition to offering policy analysis, several American Muslim organizations have made it a priority to work with law enforcement agencies in identifying intolerant attitudes within the Muslim community. Some American Muslim organizations created in the wake of 9/11 have a stated mission to support the armed forces unconditionally in order to defeat the global threat of terrorism. Other organizations have devised alternative strategies, such as fostering interfaith dialogue and examining ways to reconcile Islam with democracy in Muslim societies as a means of dealing with violence and promoting peacemaking.

The rich diversity of the American Muslim community illustrates that there is no single response or approach to confronting contemporary issues, such as civil and human rights violations, religious intolerance, and domestic violence. There are several religious organizations—both Sunni and Shia—dedicated to the spiritual development and religious life of American Muslims. Some prominent national civil rights groups based in Washington, D.C., are committed to the protection of American Muslim civil rights and interests. Several American Muslim legal organizations are also working toward increasing Muslims' legal knowledge and expertise to help them develop greater awareness of the American judicial system and the opportunities with democratic institutions. There are human rights and feminist organizations devoted to improving the lives of women by battling domestic violence in the United States and abroad. Several, recent American Muslim organizations are devoted to combining education and activism in order foster identity, promote social justice, achieve gender equality, and create a more meaningful interpretation of their Islamic beliefs. Some recently-formed groups believe that interfaith dialogue with Christians and Jews on both local and national levels is critical to understanding their religion within a monotheistic tradition. Some organizations believe that for Muslims to be truly Americans, they must be active partners in U.S. efforts to eliminate global terrorism and radicalism, including anti-Semitism, Islamophobia, and all forms of bigotry.

The Pew Research Center for the People conducted a survey immediately following the London bombings that indicated that 55 percent of Americans had favorable opinions of American Muslims, an increase from 45 percent in March 2001. The report showed that there was considerably less hostility toward Muslims in the United States and Europe than four years previously. Simultaneously, the survey showed that in predominantly Muslim societies, support for acts of terrorism in defense of Islam had vastly declined.

Shortly after the London bombings, the National Fiqh Council of North America, an American Muslim group concerned with Islamic jurisprudence, issued an extraordinary *fatwa* (a nonbinding legal opinion) condemning all forms of extremism, terrorism, and any destruction of property or human life, and it specifically called the perpetrators "criminals." The *fatwa* stated that it is forbidden for any Muslim to cooperate with individuals or groups involved with violence, and it is Muslims' civic and religious duty to support law enforcement efforts to protect the lives of all civilians.

The American Muslim community faces a complex set of challenges and debates after the 9/11 attacks. Even during a climate of Muslim suspicion, most American Muslims favor political involvement and are open to being involved in civil society institutions. While the community cannot be categorized as conservative or liberal, there is increasing participation in the local activities, such as school boards, parent-teacher associations, interfaith programs, city councils, and chambers of commerce, compared to a decade ago. Also with the Patriot Act, stricter immigration regulations, greater surveillance over their religious and charitable institutions, and the Christian religious right discriminatory statements against Islam, created instant challenges for American Muslims to develop coalitions and partnerships with law enforcement, politicians, and other organizations.

A decade ago, most studies on American Muslims simplistically categorized American Muslims into two groups: immigrants and converts. It was common for these studies to classify the American Muslims as a community in "diaspora"—referring to their non-indigenous and foreign origins. However, American Muslims are far more complex than the essential ethnic categories of Arab-American, African-American, or Turkish-American. These ethnic categories may capture a certain aspect of ethnic origins, but they miss the trend of American Muslims using alternative identities to express themselves. Over the past decade, or more, the emergence of Islamic centers, Islamic schools, community-based groups, social service and charitable organizations, public advocacy associations, political parties, professional associations, and research organizations have all contributed to multiple identities that go beyond a one dimensional ethnic identity. American Muslims, like many Americans, have an amalgamation of identities—some have religious meaning; while others are linked to the variety of activities in which they are involved.

The diversity of American Muslim organizations demonstrates an interesting mosaic of perspectives on, opinions about, and approaches to being an American and the roles of Muslims in conflict prevention and resolution. National umbrella organizations have endeavored to integrate all the ethnic and racial Muslim communities as a way to bring all groups together based on common issues. There is an overwhelming consensus within American Muslim organizations to promote mutual understanding through interfaith dialogue, political participation, education, activism, charity, public diplomacy, and an awareness of civil rights. American Muslim organizations, both religious and secular, contribute a distinctive voice to the national conversation on conflict prevention and terrorism.

Pew Research Study on Islamic Extremism

Conducted between July 7, 2005, (the day of the first terrorist attacks in London) and July 17, 2005, the Pew Research Center for the People survey, *Islamic Extremism: Common Concern for Muslim and Western Publics,* reported that the number of Americans who believe Islam is more likely than other religions to encourage violence fell noticeably, from 44 percent in 2003 to 36 percent in 2005. A majority of Americans (55 percent) said they have a favorable opinion of American Muslims. That figure is significantly higher than the 45 percent holding favorable views in March 2001, prior to the 9/11 terrorist attacks.

The Pew Global Attitudes Project, a seventeen-nation, 17,000-respondent global attitudes survey, found that the majority of Muslims believe radicalism poses a threat to the stability of their respective countries. There is very little agreement among Muslims on the causes of extremism; however, 38 percent of survey participants in Pakistan and 39 percent in Morocco pointed to poverty, severe economic disparities, and joblessness; 35 percent in Indonesia thought immorality was the primary cause; and 34 percent in Turkey attributed extremism to lack of education. However, in the more pluralistic nations of Jordan and Lebanon, respectively 38 percent and 40 percent cited U.S. policies as the primary cause of Islamic extremism.

The most important part of the Pew study shows that support for acts of terrorism in defense of Islam has declined immensely among Muslims overseas. In the past three years, support for terrorism fell in Lebanon from 73 percent to 39 percent, in Indonesia from 27 percent to 15 percent, and in Pakistan from 33 percent to 25 percent. In just the past year in Morocco, it declined from 40 percent to 13 percent.

Even in a post 9/11 world and with the uncertainties in the war against terrorism, there are favorable views of Muslims in most countries in Europe and North America. Hostility toward Muslims is actually much lower in the United States and in Canada than in Great Britain and other Western countries surveyed. Some have argued that rather than being isolated, both Sunni and Shia American Muslim organizations have facilitated an understanding with other Americans through active participation in the political arena with a coalition of grassroots community organizations.

National Fatwa Condemning Terrorism

The Fiqh Council of North America: U.S. Muslim Religious Council Fatwa Against Terrorism (religious/Islamic law)

As noted, on July 27, 2005, the Fiqh Council of North America, an American Muslim group concerned with Islamic jurisprudence, issued a historic *fatwa*, a nonbinding legal opinion, that condemned terrorism and religious extremism. The *fatwa* stated,

> Islam strictly condemns religious extremism and the use of violence against innocent lives. There is no justification in Islam for extremism or terrorism. Targeting civilians' life and property through suicide bombings or any other method of attack is forbidden—and those who commit these barbaric acts are criminals, not martyrs.

The sixteen-member panel of the Fiqh Council is composed of mainly Sunni scholars who traditionally comment on religious and secular life. The *fatwa* quoted the famous Koranic passage 5:32, which states, "Whoever kills a person unjustly, it is as though he has killed all of humanity. And whoever saves a life, it is as though he has saved all of humanity."

Almost two weeks after the London bombings of July 7, 2005, and an astonishing number of suicide bombings around the same time in Iraq, the U.S. *fatwa* asserted concisely that (1) all acts of terrorism targeting civilians are forbidden in Islam; (2) it is forbidden for a Muslim to cooperate with any individual or group involved in any act of terrorism or violence; and (3) it is the civic and religious duty of Muslims to cooperate with law enforcement authorities to protect the lives of all civilians.

A scholar of jurisprudence usually writes and issues a *fatwa* to respond to contemporary disputed issues and the related legal challenges. The scholar must be grounded in the classical legal systems of thinking and be cognizant of the legal histories surrounding the issues. Unlike papal edicts from the Roman Catholic Church, a *fatwa* does not commit Muslims to the scholar's legal opinion; rather, it can be viewed as a dialogue between the scholar and the American Muslim community at large. The social and political function of the American *fatwa* means these legal-religious and societal issues are not only critical for the community, but in this instance leading American Muslim scholars are asserting their authority on the topic of conflict and terrorism. This articulated declaration is a demonstration that American Muslims are defining and affirming an unambiguous position on conflict prevention and terrorism—a position carefully constructed in a post 9/11 atmosphere. Two hundred American Muslim organizations and mosques supported the historic *fatwa* of July 2005, the first of its kind to assemble a consensus on such a grand scale. It concluded by affirming,

> We issue this *fatwa* following the guidance of our scripture, the Qur'an [sic], and the teachings of our Prophet Muhammad—peace be upon him. We urge all people to resolve all conflicts in just and peaceful manners. We pray for the defeat of extremism and terrorism. We pray for the safety and security of our country, the United States, and its people. We pray for the safety and security of all inhabitants of our planet. We pray that interfaith harmony and cooperation prevail both in the United States and all around the globe.

Although the *fatwa* urged the importance of the illegality and nontraditional nature of terrorism and extremism in Islam, some American Muslim critics felt it did not go far enough in identifying Osama bin Laden and his associates as terrorists. Muslim critics argued the *fatwa* was merely a symbol to demonstrate publicly the Fiqh Council's positions on the issues of violence and terrorism. Further, they wished the *fatwa* had used fewer scriptural references and shown a more contemporary global understanding of terrorism and the sociopolitical context of violence. Instead of issuing such statements as, "God mandates moderation in faith and in all aspects of life," many American Muslim critics said the Fiqh Council needed to address specifically issues of discrimination, injustice, and social and political inequality, and to express ideas that actually touch people's daily lives. This *fatwa*, like all legal opinions, was written to respond to a particular concern, but it also produced a vibrant debate within the American Muslim community.

Religious and Interfaith Organizations

Islamic Society of North America (religious)

The Islamic Society of North America (ISNA) is the national Sunni association of Muslim organizations that provides a common platform for presenting Islam, supporting Muslim communities, and developing educational, social, and outreach programs, such as interfaith dialogue. ISNA's headquarters is located in Plainfield, Indiana, where they feel a comfortable fit in rural America. The combination of interfaith activities and charitable activities has made ISNA successful in integrating Muslims in the heart of American social fabric. A major supporter of the *fatwa* issued in late July 2005 and one of the primary religious Islamic organizations in the United

States, ISNA objectives include providing leadership and religious training to religious leaders (imams), developing community programs, educating young Muslims in religion, and expanding interfaith programs.

The annual ISNA Convention, convened during Labor Day weekend, is the largest gathering of Muslims in North America. This convention brings together more than 40,000 attendees, including individuals, families, businesses, scholars, nonprofit organizations, dignitaries, and people of other faiths. The attendee demographics encompass a wide spectrum of professions and backgrounds. The convention provides an opportunity to listen to and interact with eminent Muslim scholars and leaders and to meet and exchange views with Muslims and people of other faiths. In addition, ISNA holds regional conferences in different cities throughout the United States and Canada on subjects such as, "The Islamic Education Forum," "Muslims Against Domestic Violence," "Muslims on the Information-Highway," and "Islam in America."

Viewed as the mainstream Sunni Islam group, ISNA was one of the leading American Muslim groups to voice criticism against Massachusetts Governor Mitt Romney when he suggested in September 2005 that there be a national surveillance program of mosques instituted in the United States. American Muslim critics have repeatedly stated that ISNA's focus on religious and interreligious programs isolates them from critical issues like civil rights, public policy, immigration enforcement, and the war on terrorism. ISNA's deliberate refusal to engage in these areas has led to serious criticisms of their overall leadership role in the American Muslim community.

Shiite Islam in America

Overall, the American Shia community is a minority within the Muslim community, and it has experienced major transformations over the past two decades. Often faced with religious stereotypes and misunderstanding of Shiite Islam, the American Muslim Shia community consists of a diverse group from East Africa, the Middle East, South Asia, and Europe. Shia Muslim Americans form small centers called *jamaats* where religious services and educational programs are conducted.

The North American Shia Ithna-Asheri Muslim Communities (religious)

The largest umbrella group for Shia Muslims is called the North American Shia Ithna-Asheri Muslim Communities (NASIMCO) and is an example of creating a central authority. NASIMCO formed the Islamic Education Board in order to have standardized books for religious schools. They also publish resources on Shia history and theology. The organization's Web site provides a database for research and maintains a calendar for Shia events. In 1994, the

Council of Shia Muslim Scholars in North America was created as a central body of Shia American Muslim religious leaders, also known as imams.

Another important American Shia Muslim institution is the Imam Al-Khoei Foundation in New York, named after the famous Iraqi Shia philanthropist and scholar. In the United States, the Al-Khoei Foundation is a leading Shia Muslim institution that has a full-time accredited school from kindergarten through twelfth grades, and it conducts all religious rituals relating to Shiism in Urdu, Persian, Arabic, and English.

Both NASIMCO and the Al-Khoei Foundation maintain that violence, terrorism against noncombatants, and all types of extremist attitudes are illegal in Islamic law. With a hierarchical clerical class, trained jurists can only decide legal reinterpretations of war. NASIMCO, the Al-Khoei Foundation and other Shia organizations feel that there is a gross misunderstanding of Shia Islamic beliefs and practices, and global politics more often eschew the essential teachings of their faith.

Zaytuna Institute *(religious/Islamic law)*

Zaytuna Institute was founded in 1996 by Hamza Yusuf and Hesham Alalusi and incorporated in 1998 in Hayward, California. Zaytuna Institute is an educational organization established to revive classical training in Islamic jurisprudence and in Koranic studies in order create a new generation of American Muslims to build upon the intellectual history of Islam. Zaytuna Institute adheres to the idea that American Muslims need to reconnect with the heritage of Islam in order to gain a holistic and comprehensive understanding of the world. The Institute believes that Muslims will become enlightened citizens through engagement with and critical study of Islamic texts. According to Zaytuna Institute's beliefs, one of the many illnesses in American society is disillusionment with the relativism, nihilism, and materialism of modern life that have created spiritually empty lives for many people. The Institute hopes education will fulfill the lives of American Muslims.

Hamza Yusuf was one of the many American Muslim leaders the White House consulted after 9/11 as a way of fostering tolerance and dispelling the fears of American Muslims about the rising backlash. Zaytuna Institute has aggressively condemned terrorism and sectarian violence in the Middle East and around the globe. It believes terrorism arises from individuals who have very little or no knowledge of Islamic ethics and religious principles and are misusing the religion for their own political agendas.

Zaytuna Institute believes the appropriate way for American Muslims to combat extremist ideologies is to recognize the level of ignorance that dominates their understanding of faith and the world. For the Zaytuna Institute, the struggle is to study, to examine oneself, and to connect with the diversity of religious ethics as guidance. Knowledge in itself is not the goal; instead, the purpose is to obtain wisdom from sacred scriptures and to learn from past and present eminent scholars. Their understanding of terrorism differs from typical political, social, economical, and ideological analysis; whereby, they view terrorism as a belief of ignorant nihilism as better than life. For them the best way to counter terrorism is to restore order with enlightened, broad-based, pluralistic, and tolerant education in order to cultivate values of citizenship. Major issues, such as economic injustice, racism, the oppression of women, classism, totalitarianism, and the lack of freedom of expression are all part of manipulating the natural order. The Institute believes human illnesses can be treated only through healing the hearts of humanity with spiritual truths and an understanding of the true purpose of existence. Zaytuna Institute's mission is to establish a leading educational institution for the cultivation of intelligent, open-minded individuals who are grounded in the Islamic tradition in their response to terrorism and all types of injustice.

American Society for Muslim Advancement *(religious/interfaith)*

American Society for Muslim Advancement (ASMA's) mission is to build bridges with the Muslim and non-Muslim community through workshops, conferences, interfaith dialogues, and the arts. ASMA believes that American Muslim youth need to be empowered with a faith that is tolerant, forward-thinking and develops a distinct American Muslim identity. Feisal Abdul Rauf, a prominent New York City imam, is founder of the ASMA and author of *What's Right with Islam: A New Vision for Muslims and the West* (San Francisco: HarperSanFrancisco, 2004). He has worked in the area of interfaith dialogue not only nationally but also with interreligious organizations in Europe, the Middle East, Asia, and Australia. According to Imam Feisal: "Dialogue between the religions offers the opportunity for uncovering the common ground of shared values and goals that resonate in each of our faiths, even as we clarify real differences. Dialogue within a religion offers the opportunity for its adherents to be amazed at real differences that can arise from shared theology and ritual."

Since 9/11, Imam Feisal has been one of the most visible American Muslim leaders in speaking against terrorism and the misuse of religion to defend extremist ideologies. He called the London terrorist attacks "crimes against humanity" and said, "We cry out against such violence and seek to console those who have suffered from it."

In December 2004, Imam Feisal spoke at a seminar entitled "Confronting Islamophobia: Education for Tolerance and Understanding" hosted by Shashi Tharoor, under-secretary-general for communications and public information of the United Nations. Imam Feisal reiterated a famous *hadith*, or saying of the Prophet Muhammad, that the diversity of opinions is a blessing in his community, and explained how this saying not only advocates tolerance, but also mandates that Muslims understand traditions other than their own. He added that there need to be interlocutors in the American Muslim community to work with other religious traditions to communicate Muslims' fears, hopes, and aspirations in order to engage each other in peaceful ways. Imam Feisal said that Islamophobia is an awful experience to live with; however, there is an opportunity to learn from Jewish and Catholic communities that have handled severe prejudices in the last century.

Cordoba Initiative *(religious/interfaith)*

The Cordoba Initiative is a unique multifaith organization and an affiliate of ASMA that strives toward healing the relationship between the Islamic World and the United States. Named after the great medieval Spanish city known for its pluralism and religious tolerance, members of the Cordoba Initiative believe intercultural understanding and sincere educational programs will stimulate creative thinking on peace in the Middle East. The Cordoba Initiative has cooperated with Christian and Jewish religious leaders to examine the underlying roots of cultural intolerance and violence. Moving beyond descriptive analysis of political violence, the Initiative aspires to make an impact on religious self-understanding, identity, and the treatment of others.

Daisy Khan of the Cordoba Initiative stated that there is a real need for Muslims in America to accept their enormous responsibility to forge new creative thinking about religion, peace, and violence. She asserted that the freedom of thought and expression lacking in most predominantly Muslim cultures means there is a greater burden on American Muslims to work toward reforming these oppressive societies. In a short time, the Cordoba Initiative has been successful in bringing together younger Muslim scholars, activists, businesspersons, artists, physicians, and others from around the world to engage in serious scrutiny of their Islamic identity and tradition. Khan believes that freedom of expression allows American Muslims an incredible amount of space in which to be creative with their religious self-understanding, and this process is connected to helping Muslims self-discover their own meaning.

International Islamic Conference on True Islam and Its Role in Modern Society

In July 2005, both Imam Feisal's and Khan's groups attended the historic "International Islamic Conference on True Islam and Its Role in Modern Society" in Amman, Jordan, held by His Majesty King Abdullah II. The conference produced a final declaration of more than 180 scholars representing forty-five countries—supported by *fatwas* garnered beforehand from seventeen of the world's major Islamic scholars, including Shaykh

Al-Azhar, Grand Ayatollah al-Sistani, and Sheikh Yusef Al-Qaradawi. The scholars unanimously condemned the practice known as *takfir*, calling others "apostates," which extremists use to justify violence. The Amman meeting also recognized the legitimacy of all eight of the traditional schools of Islamic religious law from the Sunni, Shi'i and Ibadi branches of Islam, and identified their common theologies, ethics, principles, and beliefs. It defined the necessary qualifications and conditions for issuing *fatwas*, thereby exposing the illegitimacy of the so-called ones that justify terrorism and are in clear violation of Islam's core principles.

The Amman conference was successful in bringing both Sunni and Shiite leaders from around the globe to cooperate against the rising tide of extremism. The King of Jordan will sponsor a subsequent conference titled, "The Iraqi Islamic Reconciliation Summit," which will engage Grand Ayatollah al-Sistani and major Iraqi Sunni scholars in discussing sectarian violence and intra-faith dialogue in Islam. This is an example of American Muslim leaders' gradual involvement with the affairs of the larger Muslim world and view that their work can go beyond local and national issues. The significance of American Muslims engaging in the religious, political, and social affairs of global Muslim politics demonstrates aspirations to contribute to global affairs and to express a distinct position and identity from the global Muslim community.

American Muslims Intent on Learning and Activism
(religious, social activism)

American Muslims Intent on Learning and Activism (AMILA, which means "to work" or "to act" in Arabic) is a well-known, California-based organization that builds community through activism, Islamic education, spirituality, and networking with other groups. AMILA's goals are to develop a community that helps each member to grow spiritually, to foster brotherhood and sisterhood, and to cultivate a greater divine consciousness. Recognized by many American Muslim leaders as one of the nation's most dynamic Muslim organizations, AMILA is entering its second decade as an influential voice among young American Muslims.

Founded by second-generation American Muslims born and raised in the San Francisco Bay Area of northern California, AMILA has an introspective and undogmatic approach to religion. AMILA provides its members an array of events and groups, such as inviting Muslim and non-Muslim intellectuals to their lecture series, study groups, book clubs, and annual Ramadan spiritual retreats. AMILA's constitution has remarkably cultivated over five new cycles of elected leaders, both men and women. AMILA's inclusive message has bridged the differences between Muslims of different ethnic and ideological backgrounds by including Sunnis, Shiites, Sufis, African-Americans, and converts.

The organization stands adamantly against any and all acts of terrorism and any use of violence. AMILA views the outer conflict of terrorism as a mirror reflection of the complex social and political inequities that exist in Muslim societies. One critical response to eliminating terrorism is to focus on education and activism that will aid in bringing spiritual awareness and harmony to others. The lifelong process of learning and activism binds the members to one another, thereby helping them develop a strong sense of community.

Relying on the skills of its members with computer expertise, AMILA uses cyberspace and the media for coalition building with non-Muslim organizations, both secular and religious. AMILA has collaborated with groups on a "Walk for Remembrance and Peace," promoted a cultural and philanthropic program regarding Islamic art fairs, sponsored a multifaith event called "Eid Festival for Everyone," and sponsored a biannual gift drive for hundreds of children in the Bay Area for the Muslim holidays. AMILA is at the forefront of forging an American Muslim identity that begins with communal faith building and fosters respect for the diversity of beliefs both within Islam and from other traditions. Increasing spirituality and Islamic knowledge has been a major emphasis in AMILA. Besides inviting speakers for monthly meetings, AMILA has sponsored intensive study groups on topics, such as "Ṭhe Science of the Qur'an" and "The Concept of Worship in Islam."

Civic and Political Organizations

Muslim Public Affairs Council *(civic/political)*

One of the supporters of the *fatwa* was the Muslim Public Affairs Council (MPAC), which, since 1988, has been working for the civil rights of American Muslims and a constructive relationship between American Muslims and their political representatives. MPAC promotes an American Muslim identity by fostering grassroots activities and by training a future generation of Muslim activists in the political process. MPAC is committed to the understanding that empowering the community requires educating individuals with the skills necessary for them to be effective American citizens. In addition, MPAC tries to encourage an accurate portrayal of Muslims and of Islam in mass media and popular culture by educating the American public about diversity within the tradition.

MPAC initiated a "National Grassroots Campaign to Fight Terrorism" that consists of the endorsement and participation of over 600 mosques and Muslim institutions across the country. MPAC's "National Grassroots Campaign to Fight Terrorism" has three essential components: (1) enlighten religious awareness and education within the American Muslim community, stressing a zero-tolerance policy on terrorism or the suicidal destruction of human life or property; (2) protect mosques and Muslim institutions from external forces that wish to exploit them; and (3) train community members on the necessary skills to detect potential criminal activities and work with local and federal law enforcement agencies. The campaign training manual states, "It is our duty as American Muslims to protect our country and to contribute to its betterment . . . Muslims should be at the forefront of preventing [terrorist] attacks from happening." MPAC has seen a visible change with its "Campaign to Fight Terrorism," particularly by holding regular town meetings and training sessions in American Muslim communities.

In November 2002, MPAC testified before the Senate Judiciary Committee on "An Assessment of Tools Needed to Fight the Financing of Terrorism." As part of its ongoing efforts to protect the civil liberties of American Muslims, MPAC sponsored a variety of forums on topics that included the following:

- America's Image in the Muslim World,
- Religious Freedom in the Muslim World,
- Nuclear Disarmament, and
- The Islamic Stand Against Terrorism.

In the aftermath of 9/11, MPAC was flooded with reports of hate crimes and discrimination, which prompted creating a department specializing in victim assistance. By December 2001, MPAC had officially established its Hate Crimes Prevention Department and had partnered with Los Angeles County's Hate Crime Victim Assistance and Advocacy Initiative to aid in victim assistance and hate crime prevention. MPAC's unambiguous position on terrorism, suicide bombings, and other illegal attacks on civilians and noncombatants has been its primary message to community leaders, the media, policymakers, and law enforcement officials. The organization aims to elucidate that global terrorism repulses American Muslims, and that they could be active players in preventing attacks. As an important integral group in American pluralism and democracy, MPAC believes American Muslims must take on more civic duties to increase their presence in local and national discussions.

In March 2005, MPAC held a "Muslim Policy Forum to Enhance Government-Muslim Dialogue" with members from national Muslim organizations and the Justice Department, including assistant attorney general—Division for Civil Rights, and the Treasury Department. Stressing the need for Muslim charitable institutions to become more diligent in identifying funding sources, Salam Al-Marayati, executive director of MPAC, said, "The creation of [a] National Council is a historic step in the coordination of activities and responsibilities within the American Muslim nonprofit sector." In response to the London attacks that year, MPAC organized young Muslim leaders across the country, including members of the national Muslim Students Association, to announce that they "condemn all acts of terrorism and the ideology of hatred that fuels them."

Council on American Islamic Relations (civic/political)

The Council on American-Islamic Relations (CAIR) is the nation's largest Muslim civil rights and advocacy group, with regional offices nationwide and in Canada. The national headquarters, established in 1994, is located on Capitol Hill in Washington, D.C. After the 1991 Persian Gulf War and before CAIR became a formalized organization, the founding members met informally to promote a positive image of Islam and Muslims in America by providing the media with accurate information on Islamic beliefs, practices, and cultures. It naturally progressed to work toward education and advocacy on behalf of the American Muslim community. In addition to promoting Muslim representation in politics, the media, and domestic policymaking groups, CAIR encourages American Muslims to be politically active and to take their civic duties seriously in American society.

Since its inception, CAIR has been aggressive in condemning all acts of violence against civilians by any individual, group, or state. After the 9/11 attacks, CAIR was one of the leading American Muslim organizations to collaborate with the White House on issues of safety and foreign policy. CAIR devised a plan on domestic policies that studied the problems of limiting civil rights, permitting racial, ethnic, or religious profiling, infringing on due process, and preventing American Muslims and others from participating fully in American civic life. For over three years, CAIR has been running a public service announcement called "Not in the Name of Islam," which explicitly denounces Muslim extremism and advocates dialogue between faith communities both in Am erica and worldwide. In response to the London bombings, CAIR's urgent announcement stated, "We condemned the barbaric bombings and [we] join Americans of all faiths, and all people of conscience worldwide, in condemning these barbaric crimes that can never be justified or excused."

CAIR has been a critical player in asking Congress to conduct civil liberties oversight hearings on the implementation of the Patriot Act and to ensure that activities truly target terrorism—not civil liberties. In December 2001, CAIR appeared before the U.S. Commission on Civil Rights to testify on 115 cases of employment discrimination following the 9/11 attacks. In January 2002, CAIR went before the Judiciary Committee in the House of Representatives to testify on the serious problems of racial and religious profiling faced by American Muslims, and it reported nearly 1,700 complaints from community members.

Mohamed Nimer, the research director for CAIR and author of *The North American Muslim Resource Guide*, published a policy bulletin entitled "Islam, Democracy and American Muslims" that discusses the diversity of the American Muslim community in terms of ethnicity, religious observance, race, and socioeconomic class. The report noted that democratic practices in Muslim institutions are evident in their formal membership, the inclusion of women in leadership, the election of a board, the terms of leadership, the thoroughness of their constitutions, and their visionary statement for the community. The policy bulletin highlights how American Muslims have established faith-based and ethnic-based organizations; some promote educational and social organizations and businesses, while others, namely Islamic centers across the country, function on a multidimensional level. According to Nimr, "American Muslims embrace democratic change and value pluralism as principles consistent with Islamic teachings," which are crucial ideas because "the blending of Islamic values with the American democratic experience can provide a solid bridge of understanding between America and the Muslim world."

CAIR's work in defending the civil rights of American Muslims has not come without criticism. Some advocacy groups believe CAIR's criticism of American foreign policy, particularly on the Israel/Palestine conflict, is excessively one-sided. CAIR has been criticized as being too soft on Palestinian suicide bombers or hypercritical of Israel. Some critics are American Muslims themselves who disagree with CAIR's positions on domestic and foreign policy issues and advocate an open exchange of ideas in the American Muslim community. Within academia, several American Muslim scholars have asserted that CAIR's vision of Islam is essentialist, and their statements on Islamic beliefs are presented often as simplistic and dogmatic. In midst of all types of criticism, CAIR maintains that their primary mission is to protect the civil rights of American Muslims and to provide accurate information on Islam.

American Muslim Alliance *(civic/political)*

The American Muslim Alliance (AMA) is a national civic organization determined to transform the American Muslim community by training and supporting Muslims in the U.S. political system. The organization is working toward three goals: (1) identifying Muslims who are capable of running for office in the U.S. Congress or a state's legislature; (2) supporting qualified American Muslims elected as delegates to the Democratic and Republican state and national conventions; and (3) producing leaders for American mainstream politics. AMA views itself as taking active responsibility for U.S. homeland security, while simultaneously building coalitions with fellow Americans on a wide variety of social, political, economic, and moral issues.

AMA is committed to the idea that political power is a result of a community's efforts in areas of initiative, innovation, and determination.

AMA believes the frustration of some American Muslims concerning U.S. foreign and domestic policy can be resolved in meaningful ways, such as by participating in a grassroots political process that relies on its citizens to articulate policy concerns. AMA supports workshops on volunteering with the office of a local representative, city council member, or state senator. AMA concentrates on political education, leadership training, campaign and issue analysis, developing political strategies, and gaining insight on policymaking decisions. As an organization, AMA issues endorsements and election advisories to educate Muslims about the candidates and the issues of concern.

On the topics of terrorism and senseless violence, AMA has consistently condemned these actions as baseless and horrific. AMA believes transforming present frustration and anger into constructive and meaningful action will empower the American Muslim community and will ultimately encourage its members to be more responsible citizens. One way of achieving this goal is to move beyond attempting to influence candidates and elected officials by actively participating in the American political system. At this time, AMA has ninety-eight chapters in thirty-one states and aspires to organize chapters in all fifty states and in each of the 435 congressional districts.

Center for the Study of Islam and Democracy (political/research)

The Center for the Study of Islam and Democracy (CSID) is a nonprofit organization, based in Washington, D.C., dedicated to studying Islamic and democratic political thought and to merging these two streams into a modern Islamic democratic discourse. Founded in 1999, CSID consists of a diverse group of academics, professionals, and activists from all around the world who examine how democratic reform and liberal democracy can be institutionalized in the Muslim world.

CSID's primary objective is to conduct rigorous research on the principles of Western democracy and on Islamic principles of governance and law. CSID sponsors conferences, workshops, and training sessions in the Muslim world and holds its annual meeting in Washington, D.C. In 2005, the sixth annual conference had distinguished keynote speakers, such as Andrew Natsios, administrator of the United States Agency for International Development; Carl Gershman at the National Endowment for Democracy; Lorne Craner at the International Republican Institute; Michael Kozak at the Department of State; and Anwar Ibrahim, former prime-minister of Malaysia and named CSID's Muslim Democrat of the Year.

CSID has been proactive in denouncing all forms of terrorism and acts of violence. In response to the London bombings, CSID's statement said,

"These senseless acts are in complete violation of the basic moral and ethical principles of Islam and of other faith traditions, we maintain that there is absolutely no justification for them on any grounds." Asma Afsaruddin, chair of CSID's board and associate professor of Arabic and Islamic Studies at Notre Dame University, said, "CSID's primary mission is to promote democratic, pluralistic societies in the Islamic world based on the teachings and intellectual heritage of Islam itself. It is absolutely crucial that we continue to investigate nonviolent means of neutralizing the rhetoric of the militants and seek solutions to some of the festering political problems that breed extremism."

Through its special reports and newsletter, titled *The Muslim Democrat*, CSID is active in conducting seminars and conferences in Muslim countries on the topics of human rights, democratic governance, Islamic law and democracy, women's rights, and citizenship. CSID believes the best response to global terrorism is to transform authoritarian, closed societies—where there is no or very little freedom of expression, assembly, or representation—into open, mature, democratic, pluralistic institutions.

Free Muslims Coalition *(political)*

The Free Muslims Coalition (FMC) consists of American Muslims and Arab Americans who agree that the Muslim community needs to reject religious violence and terrorism. FMC was created after 9/11 to promote secular democratic institutions in the Middle East and in the Muslim world by supporting Islamic reformation efforts. For FMC, reformation entails a modern secular interpretation of religion that encourages peace, democracy, and the acceptance of other faith traditions, and in particular, an agreement that no single religious tradition should dominate the judicial, executive, and legislature branches of government.

FMC clearly states that terrorism is a global threat and countering terrorism committed by Muslims is an ideological battle that cannot be won without the help of Muslims. According to FMC, "fundamentalist Islamic terror represents one of the most lethal threats to the stability of the civilized world. The existence of Islamic terrorists is the existence of threats to democracy. There is no room for terrorism in the modern world and the U.S. should take a no-tolerance stance on terrorism to avoid another tragedy."

Kamal Nawash, the president of FMC, has publicly supported the U.S. government's efforts in fighting global terror, including the wars in Afghanistan and Iraq. Nawash said, "Our goal is to defeat and discredit the ideology that leads to extremism and support for terrorism."

FMC has been severely criticized by other American Muslim organizations as aligning itself too closely with the U.S. administration and their aims in fighting global terrorism. FMC repudiates these criticisms and stands firm on eliminating what its members understand to be the global terrorist threat. In addition to its fervent antiterrorism message, FMC's open statements call for an elimination of anti-Semitism. The organization feels it is the responsibility of all to speak out against intolerance and hatred.

Muslims against Terrorism (civic)

Immediately after 9/11, young American Muslim professionals formed Muslims Against Terrorism (MAT) in New York City. Horrified by the terrorist attacks and unimpressed by the attempts of local religious institutions to respond, MAT members initially focused their energies on working with the media with respect to American Muslim perspectives on violence, conflict, terrorism, and peacemaking. Their niche was in strengthening interfaith dialogues among New York City churches, synagogues, and temples. MAT's outreach efforts extended to the New York City Public School system, major corporations on Wall Street, and local activist groups.

MAT contends that any and all terrorism, whether conducted by individuals or state actors, is immoral, and that there is no place for it in a civilized world. MAT members felt it was necessary to go beyond condemnations of terrorism to working with local, national, and international Muslim organizations on the complete intolerance of terrorism. As a relatively young and professional organization, MAT's strength lay in highlighting the humanistic aspirations of all people and the need to understand the commonalties that unite all people. They wanted to counteract the fear that the 9/11 terrorist attacks had implicated all American Muslims, the Islamic religion in the heinous crimes, and, even worse, that there was scriptural evidence for legitimizing violence. In response to such attitudes, MAT worked toward outreach activities by talking about common American values.

MAT's primary mission was initially fundraising to provide assistance to the victims of terrorism. Its high-profile presence after 9/11 was intended to demonstrate its civic commitment to the United States and to play an active part in healing and reconciliation. The organization is interested in ensuring that younger American Muslims continue to be active in fighting terrorism.

American Islamic Forum for Democracy (political)

A physician, Dr. M. Zuhdi Jasser, and several Muslim professionals in the Phoenix Valley of Arizona formed the American Islamic Forum for Democracy (AIFD) in March of 2003. With the increased attention on the Muslim world and on the war against terrorism, Dr. Jasser felt American Muslims needed to act aggressively in fighting terrorism by building an anti-terror ethos in the Muslim community and by publicly denouncing religious leaders who preach intolerance. AIFD's principal goals are to cultivate moderate, mainstream American Muslim voices on topics, such as the separation of religion and state, which it believes is not contradictory to the ideals of

Islam. Dr. Jasser is a former U.S. Navy Lieutenant Commander who served as a medical officer from 1988 to 1999.

Dr. Jasser believes that Muslims around the globe need to have a public debate on hate, violence, terrorism, radicalism, and such fundamentalist ideologies as Wahhabism. Identifying Muslim terrorists as Islamo-fascists, AIFD believes at the "core of terror is simply a barbaric evil tactic in a war of ideologies and it is only the Muslims who hold the keys to the flood gates that can drown the militants."

As Americans, AIFD members unconditionally support the armed forces. As citizens, they support their absolute pledge to the nation and to all of its national interests domestically and overseas. AIFD is committed to educating the public on the special relationship among Judaism, Christianity, and Islam.

AIFD's central goal is to defeat radicals who exploit the Muslim religion through militancy. AIFD views its goals as serving as a bridge between the West and the Muslim world by fighting terrorism and preventing the growth of radicalism. For many American Muslim critics, AIFD is too closely aligned with current foreign policies on fighting terrorism, and the organization has not seriously differentiated between the complexities of post-colonial Muslim societies and their various histories and economies that generate Islamic political activities. American Muslim critics believe AIFD is using the post 9/11 climate of Muslim suspicion as an entry into politics and positioning itself with the Bush administration.

The Muslim Peace Fellowship *(peace and justice)*

The Muslim Peace Fellowship (MPF) has existed for more than twelve years and is based in Nyack, New York. MPF is committed to cultivating peace and justice in American society. MPF was founded on religious principles of resolving conflict by nonviolence, a focus it believes is grounded in Islamic ethics and scripture. MPF's main concern is to teach the values of integrity and kindness that are based on Islamic teachings, a message it believes reveals the presence of the divine in all things.

In resolving conflict and establishing peace, MPF's position is that there are no quick fixes that have lasting results; rather, the focus should be on the long-term goals of transforming the inner chaos of the individual toward true peace. MPF believes that both pious and nonobservant Muslims are obligated to address violence and terrorism on the individual level by asking, "What can I do to establish peace?" According to MPF, the work of building peace and preventing conflict should not be left up to experts or nongovernmental organizations. Instead, individuals need to reflect upon their personal responsibilities for creating a harmonious society. This demands concrete steps in one's family and local community.

MPF's goals in combating violence extend from the personal to the larger human family; ultimately, the injustice in each person and in their relationships tears apart communities around the globe. MPF believes that a deeper understanding of nonviolence teachings and ethics in Islam will enrich the lives of Muslims and their communities. Eradicating global terrorism is part of a larger struggle to eliminate the daily violence existing in each person. Violence and terrorism are manifestations of several inner layers of discontent, and it is these myriad levels of hostility that need to be understood before an earnest effort at reconciliation can begin. MPF believes its efforts to work on these issues with the American Muslim community and the larger American society will enhance mutual understanding and respect.

Legal Organizations

National Association of Muslim Lawyers

(secular, professional, legal)

The aim of the National Association of Muslim Lawyers (NAML) is to serve American Muslims, the general public, and the legal profession by promoting justice for all peoples as well as improvements in American laws and the American system of justice.

NAML believes a sustained involvement in American executive, legislative, and judicial decision-making processes is essential to the long-term prosperity and assimilation of Muslims into American society. The organization affirms that the community's interests are best protected by those with an understanding of and respect for the law, legal processes, and the role of the legal profession in developing, enforcing, and changing the law. NAML promotes legal representation for Muslims and thereby promotes Muslims' full, fair, and equal participation in American society overall. NAML also disseminates information on employment discrimination, harassment, gender, and civil rights, as well as religious, ethnic, and racial biases in the workplace.

Since 9/11, NAML has been overextended with discrimination cases and racial incidents. In addition, the organization has created the Transparency Project, an initiative to encourage Muslim charitable institutions to implement operational guidelines and procedures that ensure compliance with law and increased transparency. The Transparency Project also assures donors that charitable institutions are in fact abiding by the law and adhering to their missions as charitable organizations. NAML believes expanding legal knowledge and expertise will increase civic responsibility in the United States. The opportunity for people to participate in politics, and in their own destiny, will diminish any extremist tendency.

KARAMAH: Muslim Women Lawyers for Human Rights
(feminist, legal, advocacy)

Muslim Women Lawyers for Human Rights (KARAMAH) works to protect the human rights of Muslims in the United States and in Muslim societies. KARAMAH, meaning "dignity" in Arabic, aims to provide support through education, grassroots advocacy, and activism. Since 1993, the organization has been committed to dialogue, peaceful conflict resolution, and democratic institutions. The organization's objectives are to transform misconceived ideas about women's status within Islamic communities. KARAMAH works to improve the treatment of women and to ensure that Muslim women take an active part in governing their lives and seeking leadership positions. It believes active involvement can counter the destructive effects of ignorance, silence, and prejudices against women.

KARAMAH is one of the few American Muslim organizations that openly proposes an Islamic perspective on issues of human rights, and members of the organization regularly publish their work in international law journals. KARAMAH's board of directors includes American Muslim women lawyers, experts in mediation and conflict resolution, and experts in Islamic jurisprudence. KARAMAH has worked vigorously to educate the general public about the role of human rights in Islam. In September 1995 the organization participated at the United Nations Fourth World Conference on Women in Beijing, China. KARAMAH spoke against the Taliban's edict on religious minorities and published papers on educational rights of Muslim schoolgirls in France. KARAMAH views its activities as a way to bridge American Muslim women with women in the Muslim world and to simultaneously build coalitions with Muslim women non-governmental organizations.

The organization has developed new programs, such as confronting domestic violence and advancing Muslim women's human rights globally. KARAMAH is an important resource for American Muslim women who seek advice on civil rights, spousal abuse, and employment accommodation on religious practices. KARAMAH members see themselves as partners with other civil rights groups advocating the protection of civil liberties in the United States.

Particularly since 9/11, KARAMAH has provided legal services and sponsored educational programs to women's groups, both nationally and internationally. It strives to educate a new generation of American Muslim women who can serve as experts in both American and Islamic law. KARAMAH's board member Amr Abdalla, a George Washington University professor, currently directs KARAMAH's Conflict Resolution Project with the goal of creating new thinking and awareness about conflict prevention and nonviolent measures to resolving conflicts.

Views of American Muslim Scholars

Efforts to avert violence and promote conflict resolution and peacemaking have developed into a richly diverse and intellectual field among American Muslim scholars with different methodologies and perspectives. Ingrid Matson, vice-president of ISNA and professor of Islamic Studies at Hartford Seminary, stated that American Muslims have a special obligation to stop violence: "Who has the greatest duty to stop violence committed by Muslims against innocent non-Muslims in the name of Islam? The answer, obviously, is Muslims." For other scholars, the primary issue lies in the narrow fundamentalist interpretations of Islam and in the way fundamentalists project themselves as the sole guardians of the religion. Professor Ali Minai, of the University of Cincinnati, remarked, "the interpretation of Islam can no longer be left to the most regressive segment of Muslim society. Muslims who believe that their faith is compatible with progressive humanist ideals will express themselves—not as apologists of Islam to the West but as proponents of new possibilities for Muslims."

One leading scholar who has examined the juristic history of war and violence in Islam is Professor Khaled Abou El Fadl, law professor at UCLA and author of *Islam and the Challenge of Democracy: The Place of Tolerance in Islam,* and *Rebellion and Violence in Islamic Law*. According to El Fadl, the world of the terrorists is tied to a puritanical theology that is responding to powerlessness and a crisis of identities. The major issues are that "there are profound feelings of defeatism, alienation, frustration, and arrogance. It is a theology that is alienated not only from the institutions of power in the modern world, but also from its own heritage and [Islamic] tradition." Contrary to many analogies of terrorism to an infectious disease, El Fadl believes, "terrorism is an aberration, an extreme manifestation of underlying social and ideological currents in a particular culture. Terrorism is not a virus that suddenly infects the brain of a person; rather, it is the result of long-standing and cumulative cultural and rhetorical dynamics. In Islamic law terrorism (*hirabah*) is considered cowardly, predatory, and a grand sin punishable by death."

Professor Muqtedar Khan, assistant professor in the Department of Political Science and International Relations at the University of Delaware and author of *American Muslims: Bridging Faith and Freedom*, operates an online column and Web site titled, *Ijtihad,* to help Muslims rationally reflect on their faith and contemporary issues. Critical of U.S. foreign policy and of the erosion of civil rights domestically, Khan believes that American Muslims need to move from their difficult positions and be active in democratic processes. Khan stated,

> Democracy is not a function of numbers, but of participation. The [American Muslim] community needs to find a new way of thinking

> about its future in America. They have to transcend the Islam vs. the West, which still shapes their leaders' politics. They need to listen more to the intellectuals and scholars who are seeking to chart a new path for the community.

Professor Khan thinks it is vitally important that every American Muslim contribute to the interpretative process of the Islamic tradition. According to Khan, when each person's interpretation is viewed as an equal voice among experts, democracy has a greater role in Muslim lives.

Professor Asma Afsaruddin of Notre Dame University recalls the historical lessons of early Islam. Even though dynastic rule became the norm, accountable, consultative government remained the ideal; despotism was denounced as un-Islamic and unjust. She said, "modern democracies are fully consonant with Islamic values and in fact, principles of good governance were developed and practiced in early Islam. Democratic governments in vibrant civil societies are able to mediate internal conflicts and are answerable to their peoples through regular elections." Afsaruddin believes that the existence of autocratic governments in the Muslim world and the lack of basic political and civic freedoms for most of the citizenry are the real root causes of violence. The most effective way of reducing conflict and terrorism solution is to work toward democratic reform and the strengthening of civil society.

Conclusion: Multipronged Conflict Prevention

The American Muslim community is diverse in every conceivable way. There are numerous national and regional organizations dedicated to important civic, religious, cultural, educational, political, and social issues. On the subject of terrorism and conflict resolution, clearly all American Muslim groups have denounced it emphatically, while some have gone beyond words by becoming involved with foreign policy, lobbying efforts, and mobilizing grassroots campaigns in the community.

The Fiqh Council of North America *fatwa* is an example of American Muslims taking proactive positions on global terrorism, while practicing zero tolerance of violence and religious extremism. Their positions have examined conflict and peacemaking in Islam and have advocated the explicit need for American Muslims to cooperate with law enforcement.

National American Muslim organizations like MPAC, CAIR, ISNA, and AMA have focused on violence and religious extremism as critical issues with local and international strategies. MPAC's "National Grassroots Campaign to Fight Terrorism" and CAIR's "Not in the Name of Islam" efforts are examples American Muslims' innovative programs to raise awareness on issues of radical ideologies. The coordination of their efforts with those of law enforcement agencies demonstrates mutual recognition of the roles each group plays in conflict prevention.

Organizations like CSID, FMC, MAT, and AIFD exhibit new types of thinking in the American Muslim community by fostering, cultivating, and institutionalizing democratic reform in the Muslim world as the primary answer to extremism. Their own experiences in the United States confirm that Islamic values and democracy are compatible, and it is vitally important to institutionalize democracy in order to reform despotic totalitarian societies. Their activities display a conscious effort to make for themselves in American society, while contributing as bridge builders to the Muslim world. Their activities have already established a definite American Muslim model of inclusion and participation that differs from Muslim communities in Europe where Muslim communities are less involved in law enforcement and civic participation.

The participation of American Muslims in mainstream politics is to empower the community in many different levels of public life. American Muslim advocacy groups have tackled stereotyping of Muslims as a matter of public debate, and they have aggressively worked toward resolving incidents of discrimination and civil rights abuses. These achievements have shifted political attitudes that have enabled American Muslims to integrate in American political institutions.

Another strategy in the American Muslim community is to focus on human rights, gender inequality, and interfaith dialogue, and to increase the Muslim presence in the American legal system. KARAMAH, NAML, and ASMA represent specialized groups whose members believe that injustices can be overcome by addressing the various legal, socioeconomic, political, and religious systems involved. ASMA's interfaith dialogue programs in the United States and around the world reflect the desire for reconciliation and humanizing of all people. Each of these groups recognizes that mutual respect is tied to taking real steps toward tolerance and is part of alleviating suffering.

Some organizations are concerned with improving the condition of all human beings through education and spiritual awareness, not terrorism. Other groups believe their particular expertise is not conflict resolution, but rather a focus on cultural, social, professional, artistic, democratic, and human rights issues. With such immense diversity in the American Muslim community, it is difficult to reduce it to a single voice. Instead, there needs to be greater appreciation for the efforts and contributions of Muslims in areas of conflict resolution, interfaith dialogue, peace building, education, political activities, civic work, human rights and women's rights advocacy, legal expertise, and humanitarian efforts. The immense contributions and growing involvement of American Muslims in the public square clearly reflects that Muslims in the United States are situating themselves within civic, governmental, and political structures of the nation. Each organization has its own vision for its members as Americans and for their contributions to contemporary issues of conflict and peacemaking.

Sources

Carl S. Dudley and David A. Roozen, *Faith Communities Today: A Report on Religion in the United States Today* (Hartford Seminary, 2001)

Khaled Abou El Fadl, *Islam and The Challenge of Democracy* (Princeton: Princeton University Press, 2004)

Yvonne Haddad, ed., *Muslims in the West: From Sojourners to Citizens* (Oxford; New York: Oxford University Press, 2002)

Yvonne Haddad and Jane Smith, eds., *Muslim Communities in North America* (Albany: State University of New York Press, 1994)

Muqtedar Khan, *American Muslims: Bridging Faith and Freedom* (Beltsville: Amana Publications, 2002)

Kathleen M. Moore, *Al-Mughtaribun: American Law and the Transformation of Muslim Life in the United States* (Albany: State University of New York Press, 1995)

Muslim Public Affairs Council, "MPAC Offers Ten Tips to Enhance Partnership Against Terrorism," press release, May 28, 2003

Mohamed Nimer, *The North American Muslim Resource Guide: Muslim Community Life in the United States and Canada* (New York: Routledge, 2002)

Sulayman Nyang, *Islam in the United States of America* (Chicago: ABC International Group, Inc., 1999)

Mustafa al-Qazwini, *Inquiries about Shia Islam* (Islamic Educational Center of Orange County, CA, n.d.)

Fariyal Ross-Sheriff, "Immigrant Muslim Women in the United States: Adaptation to American Society," *Journal of Social Work Research* (2001), pp. 283–294

Jane Smith, *Islam in America* (New York: Columbia University Press, 1999)

Zogby International and Project MAPS: Muslims in American Public Square, "American Muslim Poll (Nov/Dec 2001)" December 19, 2001

Web Links

1. Fiqh Council of North America, www.fiqhcouncil.org/
2. Muslim Public Affairs Council, www.mpac.org
3. Council on American Islamic Relations, www.cair-net.org
4. Islamic Society of North America, www.isna.net
5. The North American Shia Ithna-Asheri Muslim Communities, www.nasimco.org
6. American Muslim Alliance, www.amaweb.org

7. Center for the Study of Islam and Democracy, www.islam-democracy.org
8. Free Muslims Coalition Against Terrorism, www.freemuslims.org
9. Muslims Against Terrorism, www.m-a-t.org
10. American Islamic Forum for Democracy, www.aifdemocracy.org
11. The Muslim Peace Fellowship, www.mpfweb.org/
12. American Muslims Intent on Learning and Activism, www.amila.org
13. Zaytuna Institute, www.zaytuna.org
14. National Association of Muslim Lawyers, www.namlnet.org
15. Karamah: Muslim Women Lawyers for Human Rights, www.karamah.org
16. American Society for Muslim Advancement, www.asmasociety.org
17. *Ijtihad*, www.ijtihad.org

Part V

Engaging Parties and Movements:
Beyond Islam

18

Between Realism and Wilsonianism: The U.S. and the Muslim World after Iraq

Daniel Brumberg

Nowhere do the tensions and contradictions that animate American foreign policy display themselves more decisively than in the Muslim world. Barely four years after the Bush administration inaugurated its "Freedom Agenda," democracy activists have been demoralized by Washington's support for some of the Muslim world's least freedom-loving regimes. It is possible that the administration's initially sharp criticism of President Musharraf's November 2007 crackdown on the democratic opposition signals the high water mark of a democracy backlash that was provoked in 2005, when civil war in Iraq and Islamist electoral successes in Palestine and Egypt sent shock waves throughout the American foreign policy establishment. Still, Pakistan's increasingly isolated general has good reason to hope that the escalation struggle against Islamist extremism will continue to swell the tides of a revived *realpolitik*, one that finds growing favor in the American foreign policy establishment, not to mention in the palaces and presidential mansions of several of Washington's closest Muslim allies.[1]

While the mercurial nature of its foreign relations was vividly displayed by America's response to the horrors of September 11, Washington's long-studied foreign policy dualism has deep historical roots. Since its very

1. While President Bush initially suggested that Musharraf's actions "would undermine democracy" he subsequently asserted that the general "truly is somebody who believes in democracy." Such inconsistencies are bound to reassure Pakistan's leaders. See Michael Abramowitz and Robin Wright, "Bush More Emphatic in Backing Musharraf," *Washington Post*, 21 November 2007, p. A01.

Daniel Brumberg, "Between Realism and Wilsonianism: The U.S. and the Muslim World after Iraq," in *The Challenge of Islamists for EU and US Policies: Conflict, Stability, and Reform,* eds. Muriel Asseburg and Daniel Brumberg, 9–14 (Research Paper no. 12, Stiftung Wissenchaft und Politik German Institute for International and Security Affairs, Berlin, 2007). Reprinted with permission.

inception, American diplomacy has alternated between bouts of isolationism backed by the occasional use of force and selective intervention, and high minded efforts to engage the world in the name of a universal creed that the U.S. is thought to embody.

The end of the Cold War seemed to open up space to forge a more consistent foreign policy. The disappearance of Washington's chief rival and ensuing democratization of Central Europe lowered the geostrategic risks of democracy, a development that was conceptually reinforced by the optimistic vision spelled out in the "end of history" and the "democratic peace" literatures. The political and ideological shift was crucial because it narrowed the ideological fault lines that had fractured the foreign policy establishment. The resulting consensus called for prioritizing democracy as long as doing so did not dramatically increase the risks of damaging American security interests. While not satisfying the most ardent human rights activists, this formula facilitated cooperation between foreign policy elites who had previously remained in fairly fixed ideological camps. Yet less than a decade later, the invasion of Iraq and escalation of U.S. military involvement re-polarized the foreign policy establishment in ways that echo the bad old days of the Vietnam War.

From Limited War to "Shock and Awe"

This development was hardly on the horizon when the US first responded to the attacks in New York and Washington. Indeed, the US intervention in Afghanistan echoed the traditional as well as realist impulses, i.e., to distance the US from foreign entanglements and to only use force when circumstances are seen to justify such action. The war in Afghanistan was first and foremost about defeating an enemy, not promoting democracy.

But it did not take very long for the other more expansive foreign policy impulse to manifest itself in what President Bush proclaimed was at a sea change in US relations with the Muslim world. This approach was animated by a desire to reach out to that world, to understand and engage it on behalf of what many believe to be universal aspirations. More philosophical than analytical, this neo-Wilsonian impulse was tied to the simplistic axiom that Islamist radicalism is a pathology resulting from a developmental disease. Treated with a healthy dose of democratic reforms, Muslim feelings of resentment and despair would subside, thus preparing the ground of a new era of freedom and prosperity throughout the Middle East. This theory was then tested in Iraq in the hope that toppling a dictator would eventually create an Arab polity that, while keeping with local cultural and religious traditions, reflected a universal desire for freedom.

It would be simplistic to attribute the invasion of Iraq to the influence of this or that foreign policy cabal or to the so-called "neo-conservatives." Such reductionism misses the *revolutionary* dynamic that produced the Iraq invasion. As with most revolutions, this one gathered steam as different interests, motives, and players converged on a single agenda. Some of these players were genuinely committed to the principles of neo-Wilsonianism while others merely manipulated these ideals to camouflage a *realpolitik* agenda, one whose chief concern was the prospects for proliferation of unconventional weapons in the hands of state and non-state actors. This convergence of motives and actors may have helped bring Saddam Hussein's regime down, but it could not be sustained as the human, political, and financial costs of occupying Iraq multiplied. By 2005, a revolutionary foreign policy that brought "shock and awe" had all but dissipated. In its wake was a divided foreign policy establishment that pitted an inchoate and weakened neo-conservative constituency against an ascendant group of realists who applauded signs of a more pragmatic approach within the Bush administration.

The Vagaries of US Policy after Iraq

Paradoxically, the resulting backlash against democracy promotion owes much to Washington's missteps in Iraq and beyond.[2] By exacerbating a range of domestic and regional security challenges, these mistakes reinforced the leverage of actors at home and abroad who asserted that political reform undermines the "war on terror."[3] Still, several critical points have been lost in the rush to a new realism. These include the fact that in Palestine, Iraq, and Lebanon, escalating security problems may have less to do with the intrinsic risks of democracy than with the minutiae of bad policy innovation and implementation. Even more so, critics fail to realize that the growing threat of radical Islamism in Pakistan may be due to the *failure* to support democracy. Thus, some of the hubris, wishful thinking, and analytical sloppiness that sent the American foreign policy pendulum careening in a messianic direction after September 11 could now be swinging it back with equally unreflective zeal.

While such a debilitating swing towards a foreign policy completely dominated by *realpolitik* logic cannot be ruled out, it is too early to sound the death knell of US democracy promotion in the Muslim world. What can be said with a fair decree of certainty is that the brief interlude of democracy as a matter of high policy has ended. Henceforth, American policy will be guided by two related principles. First, the intensity of commitment to democracy promotion—and in particular the readiness to engage with

2. See Carl Gershman, "Surviving the Democracy Backlash, 25 Years Later, Ronald Reagan's Visionary Address Meets a Hard Historical Moment," *Washington Post*, 8 June 2007, p. 19.

3. For an analysis of how missteps in promoting political reform and democracy aggravated Washington's security challenges in Lebanon and Palestine, see Daniel Brumberg, "Democracy and Security in the Middle East," *Democracy and Society*, vol. 4, no. 2, Spring 2007, p. 1.

Islamists—will vary in inverse proportion to the security threats that Washington faces. Second, where and when such security challenges intensify, existing democracy promotion programs will probably endure, but they will also receive less and less political protection from our highest officials.

The following brief tour of the complex horizons of US policies in the Muslim world illustrates the above two axioms. In the Middle East, Turkey is the only Muslim country for which American support for democracy not only endures but is likely to thrive as a matter of high foreign policy. The AK Party's moderate policies, as well as Turkey's enduring and very stable geostrategic relations with the US—relations that are of course a top concern of the Turkish military—have enhanced Washington's support for integrating Muslim parties and movements into Turkey's democratic experiment.

Further to the east, the Bush administration's early hopes that it would forge a similar relationship with Islamist forces in a post-Saddam Hussein Iraq have been dashed. Indeed, ethnoreligious civil war and the bloody Sunni insurgency make it very unlikely that Washington will sustain the political will or the military means to transform Iraq's precarious and flawed power sharing government into a functioning democracy.

Washington's dream of a transformed Iran has been similarly deflated. Buoyed in 2003 by what it perceived to be a quick and sustainable victory in Iraq, policy makers within or close to the Bush administration suggested that Saddam Hussein's downfall would set the stage for a democratic revolution in Iraq. But Iran's (much ignored) efforts at developing nuclear technology, disarray within the reformist camp and the resulting electoral victory of Maimed Ahmadinejad—all of which unfolded against the backdrop of Tehran's enhanced political and strategic leverage in Iraq—took the winds from the Bush administration's neo-Wilsonian vision. In its wake remains an Iran policy driven by a *realpolitik* calculation that probably will endure even if Washington takes the still unlikely step of bombing Iran's nuclear facilities.

However, central to the administration's grand vision of a post-Saddam Middle East, the case of Iraq and Iran are exceptional. Rather than pushing for regime change in the wider Middle East, Washington continues to fund more conventional democracy promotion programs in Kuwait, Jordan, Yemen, Algeria, and Morocco. In all five countries American democracy promoters have worked with secular and Islamist political parties. Indeed, in the case of Yemen, the National Democratic Institute (NDI) played a key role in promoting a formal alliance between the Islah Party and the Yemeni Socialist Party (YSP).[4] This engagement strategy saw its high point in 2003–04, a brief but hopeful period during which President Bush proclaimed

4. See Mona Yacoubian, "Engaging Islamists and Promoting Democracy: A Preliminary Assessment," USIP Special Report 190 (Washington, DC: United States Institute of Peace, September 2007).

his support for democracy in the Arab world. Still, even during the resulting "Arab Spring," there was always a gap between Washington's bold rhetoric and the actual strategic focus of its political reform programs. The latter largely consisted of demand-driven civil society projects that had little effect on the readiness of Arab governments to supply substantive political reform. Indeed, well before the escalation of civil conflict in Iraq and the electoral successes of Islamists in Palestine and Egypt in 2005, Washington did not press Arab governments to move beyond state-controlled political liberalization. Thus, the political cover that Washington gave American groups such as NDI and IRI—as well as their Arab partners—began to shrink when the security challenges facing the US and key strategic Arab allies intensified in 2005–06. As a result, most of Washington's current democracy programs have not so much been downsized as downgraded.

The prioritization of security over democracy concerns is especially manifest in those countries or regions considered of pivotal importance to US geostrategic interests. Thus Washington works with mainstream Islamists in far-away Morocco, colorful Yemen, forgotten Algeria, and little Kuwait, but not in geostrategically important Saudi Arabia or Egypt. In the former case, Washington has no democracy promotion programs, while in the latter, Washington has avoided engaging the Muslim Brethren and has repeatedly failed to criticize Cairo's repression of democracy activists. For similar reasons, Washington backs autocratic Uzbekistan and will probably maintain a similar line in Pakistan, while it has virtually ignored democracy issues in its relations with Malaysia and Tunisia, two countries whose relatively successful efforts at export-oriented industrialization have magnified the perceived risk of promoting political reform.

By contrast, in Indonesia—home to the world's single largest Muslim population—the US assists a range of Islamic parties and movements. Despite a growing climate of anti-Americanism that several prominent leaders have manipulated to substantially strengthen their support base, Washington maintains its indirect funding of powerful mass-based Muslim organizations such as the 30 million strong *Mohammadiya*. In Indonesia, the slow but forward moving consolidation of democracy has complicated—rather than undercut—the security interests of Jakarta and Washington. Thus the US can pursue a more balanced foreign policy in a region where the struggle against local affiliates of Al Qaeda constitutes a "second front" in the war on terror, but where nevertheless the geostrategic stakes are not as high as compared to those in the Middle East.

What Is to Be Done?

Although the securitization of American policy has undercut Washington's support for democratic reform, efforts to engage the Muslim world and to promote reform, pluralism, and inclusion are unlikely to disappear. Where the perceived risks of pursuing both security and reform are seen to be small, engagement with Muslim leaders, political parties, and associations will survive and sometimes even thrive. Where those risks are viewed as high, democracy promotion will remain, at best, a matter of low rather than high policy. Thus the dualist nature of American foreign policy, deeply embedded in American history and manifest in the institutional missions and identities of an array of competing official and non-governmental organizations, will continue to both animate and hobble the US approach to the Muslim world.

While neo-realists applaud the downgrading of democracy and neo-Wilsonianists decry it, Washington's critics within and beyond the Muslim world cling to the belief that American foreign policy suffers from a terminal case of double standards. But no country, especially a superpower, can afford to base its relations on one single standard or objective. Thus the challenge for the US, for its allies in Europe, and for genuine political reformers in the Muslim world, is to map a strategy by which power and principle can be more closely and consistently aligned. Although the dire security challenges born of the Iraq gambit will complicate this challenge, they should also serve as an incentive for transcending the conflicts and antagonisms that have divided Europe and the United States. There is simply too much at stake to avoid the task of designing a more coherent approach, especially towards the Middle East.

Doing so will require paying close attention to the particular problems of prioritization and sequencing presented by different countries and regions. For example, in South Asia, and in Pakistan in particular, had Musharraf chosen a more democratic approach early on, he might have enhanced his government's struggle to tackle radical Islamist forces. As it happened, an opportunity to confront security interests democratically may have been lost. But in the Middle East, the regional context requires a different prioritization of security and democracy. As the record shows, by implying that democratization in Iraq would have required engaging rather than antagonizing Iran and Syria. Similarly, Washington's eight year failure to push hard and consistently for Palestinian-Israeli peace helped fragment Fatah and thus set the stage for a Hamas victory. In short, while the domestic and regional architecture of peace and security in the Middle East should not be used as an excuse for avoiding political reform, neither should it be ignored, de-prioritized, or mishandled in ways that undermine the long term prospects for real democratic change.

19

The Challenge of Political Islam: Understanding the U.S. Debate

Steven Heydemann

Islamist politics pose what might well be seen as the most significant and complex set of foreign policy challenges that the US has faced in the post–Cold War era. At the same time, these challenges have been exceptionally resistant to efforts to impose coherence on US responses to Islamists, to the often-intense frustration of those who prefer to cast the world in black-and-white terms, or to force policy into simplistic containers such as the global "war on terror." Instead, it is the complexity and fluidity of the challenges associated with political Islam that have dominated US policy debates. Formulas proliferate for engaging or confronting militant Islam and political Islam more broadly. Tension and uncertainty about whether and how to engage Islamist challenges continue to roil the policy system. Along the Northeast corridor linking Cambridge, New York, and Washington, the punditocracy remains deeply divided, belligerently strutting its differences whenever and wherever the opportunity presents itself.

Thus, almost 30 years after the Iranian revolution, and more than six years since the terrorist attacks of September 11, no overarching architecture for managing US responses to political Islam has taken hold. Despite the effort of policy academics such as Samuel Huntington to promote the notion of a "clash of civilizations" as the organizing principle for American's grand strategy in a post-containment world, US policy toward Islamist politics remains profoundly disorganized. What those seeking coherence may not recognize, however, is that such a goal may be neither feasible nor desirable. The complexity of the challenges posed by Islamist politics does not lend itself to a sound bite approach to policy making. Nor is it appropriately addressed through rigid ideological prescriptions or one-size-fits-

---

Steven Heydemann, "The Challenge of Political Islam: Understanding the US Debate," in *The Challenge of Islamists for EU and US Policies: Conflict, Stability, and Reform,* eds. Muriel Asseburg and Daniel Brumberg, 15–19 (Research Paper no. 12, Stiftung Wissenchaft und Politik German Institute for International and Security Affairs, Berlin, 2007). Reprinted with permission.

all strategies. What is more important, in my view, is to understand the sources of the complexity, how US policy debates around the challenges of Islamist politics are organized, and what we can learn from this about where the major fault lines in US policy debates are to be found.

Complex Challenges of Islamist Politics

Political Islam resists simplification for at least four reasons. The first is simply a matter of scale. Though the scope of the phenomenon is well known, it is worth reminding ourselves of the truly global scale on which the challenges of Islamist politics present themselves. They dominate or heavily influence policy agendas ranging from Iraq, Afghanistan, Pakistan, Iran, Lebanon, and Palestine—the large epicenter of US overseas commitments at the moment—to the rest of the Middle East, Turkey, and South Asia. They extend in tangible and influential ways into our relationships across much of East Asia, a large part of Africa, the Balkans, and even to our European partners.

Second, Islamist challenges have enormous spillover effects on US diplomatic endeavors in other domains, notably democracy promotion. For almost two decades, the US commitment to democracy promotion in the Arab and Muslim worlds has been tightly linked to—and in many respects been contingent on—concern about what would happen if Islamists came to power. The threat of "one person, one vote, one time" has had a substantial dampening effect on US efforts to promote political reform in some of the world's most resilient authoritarian regimes. Experiences of Islamist rule in Iran and recent Islamist violence in Palestine have done little to mitigate these concerns. Today, only four years after President Bush swept aside Republican reservations about nation building to embrace regime change with his so-called "Freedom Agenda," the Administration has largely retreated from the Agenda's adventurism and returned to a cautious, risk-averse approach to political change in Muslim majority states. Ironically, this retrenchment comes just at the moment when some fifteen years of US effort to support moderate Islamist movements seemed to be paying off, with Islamist political parties and independent politicians actively participating in elections in Jordan, Morocco, Yemen, and Egypt.

Third, Islamist challenges also spill over into the domestic politics of the US, driving debates about homeland security, the future of military budgeting and force structure, the future of multiculturalism, and the relationship between domestic security and civil liberties that all figure prominently in American politics, and will continue to do so in the run up to the 2008 presidential elections. For all of these reasons, expressions of Islamist politics intersect with a wider range of relationships and interests, foreign and domestic, than almost any other challenge the US confronts.

Fourth, the challenge of responding to the rise of Islamist politics has been so daunting for the US policy system because of the difficulty of defining precisely what these challenges are. What does it mean, for example, to talk about an Islamist challenge in Saudi Arabia? Does it mean the challenge of reforming the regime, or protecting it? What does an Islamist challenge mean in a case like Morocco, where Islamist movements like the Party of Justice and Development (PJD) and its competitors are themselves divided about how to confront a regime that is, itself, anchored in its Islamic identity and religious claims to legitimacy and the right to rule? What are the Islamist challenges the US faces in Iraq, Afghanistan, or Pakistan, where the threads of Islamist politics are so tightly and intricately woven into every strand of US relations with these countries that untangling them may well be impossible?

In virtually every Muslim society in which American interests are at stake, similar complexities confront the US. They are central for understanding why, as my colleague Daniel Brumberg points out, US policies toward Islamist challenges so often seem to be at odds with themselves, and are so often inconsistent in ways that leave the US exposed to charges of hypocrisy in its relations with Muslim societies and Islamist movements. They are also central for understanding why what is often referred to be ideologues, such as "*the* Islamist challenge," or concepts such as Huntington's "clash of civilizations," are inadequate starting points for understanding the dynamic of US debates and the struggle to shape policy responses to the challenges of Islamist politics.

Elements of US Policies Toward the Muslim World

Instead, I would argue that it is more useful to think about policy debates in terms of six distinct elements and to understand how the interplay of these elements defines the organization of US policies in various settings where the US confronts the challenges of political Islam. The six elements are by no means unique to the challenges of Islamist politics, yet they are all visible in especially significant ways in this broad and diffuse domain. These six elements are

1. **Engagement**, represented by a range of policy instruments that encompass Track 1 and Track 2 dialogue with key allies and extend to public diplomacy efforts, attention to issues of interfaith dialog, and other related strategies. These approaches have been prominent in US relations with governments in Jordan and Morocco, but have been widely deployed in US policies toward the Muslim world. Engagement tends to be diffuse, has thus far not been terribly effective in changing the attitudes of Islamist actors toward the US, and has been

subordinated to other policy elements when it comes to Islamist groups and parties identified by the US as terrorist organizations.

2. **Accommodations**, which tend to prevail in settings where security and economic interests are felt to be centrally at stake in US relations with the governments of Muslim majority states. This element is evident in US relations with Arab Gulf states in particular, which have not been subjected to the pressures for reform directed at regimes that are less central to US strategic concerns.
3. **Negotiation,** figures more prominently in cases where the US perceives a benefit in seeking the realignment of local actors as a way of responding to Islamist pressures, as seen in recent efforts to encourage regimes to open space for moderate Islamist parties to participate in elections in Jordan and Egypt.
4. **Containment or isolation**, which have emerged as a central instrument of US policy over the past several years, notably in response to the electoral victory of Hamas in Palestine, the perceived threat of Iran's nuclear program, and in efforts to contain Hezbollah's role in Lebanon and internationally.
5. **Confrontation**, which continues to define US policy toward extremist groups and terrorist networks such as Al Qaeda, the Taliban, and extremist movements operating in Iraq.
6. **Coordination**, an element of US policy that includes efforts to develop joint approaches toward Islamist actors with governments in the Arab worlds, South Asia, and Africa, as well as the increasing interest of the Bush administration in reviving multilateral strategies for responding to the challenges of Islamist politics with European and other allies.

Listing these elements is not intended to suggest that they constitute stand-alone policy frameworks—quite the contrary. Typically, all six of these elements are present in a variety of combinations and forms throughout US policies in the Muslim world, overlapping and interacting in distinctive ways in specific contexts. Moreover, the preference for one element over another is not only context-sensitive, but also time-sensitive. Over time, policies that rest heavily on confrontation and containment have gained preference over those favoring accommodation and engagement in US policy debates.

Keeping Policy Options Open

What is universally the case, however, is that US policy debates about how to respond to the challenges of Islamist politics play out in terms of disagreements and tensions, both publicly and within the policy community, over which *particular blend of these elements* should define US policy toward a specific Islamist challenge. Since September 11, and even more so since the electoral victory of Hamas and the rise of Iranian influence in the Arab Middle East, US debates have been dominated by distinct political factions that seek to define an Islamist group, government, or network as extremist in order to make confrontation a policy option when it might not otherwise have been seen as a viable course of action. This is most visible at the moment in debates about the future US course of action toward Iran, but is also evident in policy debates concerning Hamas, Hezbollah, and various Islamist parties across the Middle East.

There is, moreover, a characteristic dynamic to policy debates about Islamist challenges, with ideologues pressing to reduce the legitimate components of US policy to those elements anchored only in confrontation, isolation, and containment. Realists and pragmatists, on the other hand, are less likely to view Islamist challenges in terms of one-size-fits-all policy responses. Instead, they work to preserve access to a wider range of instruments, seek strategies for incorporating them flexibly into frameworks that permit moving in a more accommodating or more confrontational direction in response to the level of threat in a given context.

Viewing these six elements as a kind of a matrix—and recognizing that the components of this matrix often overlap—offers insights into policy debates in the US about how to respond to the challenges of militant Islam. These debates are organized around reasonably predictable efforts by identifiable elements of the policy elite to determine which elements from this matrix should be deployed in any given case; how they should be sequenced; what would trigger a move from the engagement-accommodation-negotiation side of the matrix toward the isolation-containment-confrontation side (e.g., the effort to establish benchmarks for judging Iran's compliance with UN Security Council directives); but also about which agencies within the policy system, notably the State Department or the Pentagon, will take the lead in defining and executing policy in any given instance.

To be sure, this conception of how US policy debates are organized is not intended to imply that the policy making process is either coherent or effective. Indeed, viewing policy as a fluid combination of these six components, and of ongoing bureaucratic and political debate, underscores the enormous demands that the management of Islamist challenges places on the US foreign policy system. Yet understanding how debates are structured helps to clarify why US policies in the Muslim world are themselves both complex and dynamic, shifting over time as conditions change, and as political weight within the US policy system shifts from one locus to another. US responses to the challenges of Islamists contain far too broad a mix of elements to be viewed through any framework that privileges confrontation and containment over the other components of the policy matrix. The central challenge for an American administration is to turn this flexibility and responsiveness into a policy asset rather than a source of confusion, mixed signals, and flawed implementation.

20

Islam and Symbolic Politics in Somalia

Annette Weber

In the winter of 2007, the current civil war in Somalia is entering its second year.[1] However, the collapse of public order and the evaporation of the rule of law in the war-torn society started even before the fall of the last Somali president, Siad Barre, in 1991. For most of the seventeen stateless years since then, warlords have controlled the territory and economy of Somalia. Militia factions have only provided clan security locally. Basic state functions have been nonexistent or privatized in the hands of sub-clan militias. In mid-2006, the Union of Islamic Courts (UIC) took control in Somalia. By December 2006, however, they were ousted in a military intervention launched by neighboring Ethiopia to secure the stability of Somalia's Transitional Federal Government (TFG). Since the intervention, more than 400,000 people have fled the capital due to heavy fighting and deteriorating security. The intervention has led to polarization between clans. Those that feel excluded from power, such as the Hawiye clan, have joined insurgents fighting both Ethiopian forces and the weak Somali government.

The conflict in Somalia is multileveled. The domestic causes of conflict lie in the disastrous fragmentation of warlord fiefdoms, the absence of a state; the mushrooming of criminal networks; and repression of the population by warlords, factions of the Islamic Courts movement, and the TFG. None of the parties, including neither the TFG nor the UIC, have presented a political program for creating a functioning government. Beyond Somalia,

1. Somalia here refers to the southwest, without Somaliland or Puntland. Somaliland declared itself an independent state after the fall of Siad Barre in 1991, but has not been recognized by any other country. Puntland declared its autonomous status in 1998.

Annette Weber, "Islam and Symbolic Politics in Somalia," in *The Challenge of Islamists for EU and U.S. Policies: Conflict, Stability, and Reform,* eds. Muriel Asseburg and Daniel Brumberg, 37–43 (Research Paper no. 12, Stiftung Wissenchaft und Politik German Institute for International and Security Affairs, Berlin, 2007). Reprinted with permission.

a main factor in the war is the power struggle between Ethiopia and Eritrea. The absence of a legitimate government in Somalia facilitates this proxy war. Regional interests—economic, political, and ideological—are played out in Somalia, relatively unhindered by a functional Somali state or other international actors. The civil war in Somalia thus increases the extant polarization in the Horn of Africa. This has regional implications far beyond Somalia. The states that identify as Christian in the region, such as Uganda, Kenya, Ethiopia, and Southern Sudan's autonomous government, stand on the side of the TFG and receive support and military backing from the US. In turn, Sudan and Eritrea, along with Egypt and other Muslim majority states in the region, support the UIC.

Surprisingly, the conflict has been framed as having a religious component by Ethiopia, the TFG, and the UIC. Islam, although not a decisive political factor in Somalia so far, has become part of a larger game of symbolic politics. There has been a significant increase in Islamist rhetoric with less of an emphasis on problems specific to Somalia. For both sides, appeals to Islam have become a unifying and mobilizing force. The UIC rallies behind Islam as a legitimizing force to engage in a jihad against infidels and occupying forces, while the TFG uses it to legitimize its intervention and stabilize its position vis-à-vis "the Islamists" by framing Somalia's conflict in terms of the war on terror.

In order to deescalate the conflict in Somalia and beyond, it is necessary to promote a rights-based approach that is inclusive and secures public space for political actors, civil society, and ordinary citizens alike to voice their positions. Local governance needs to be strengthened and moderate members of the UIC should be engaged in building an inclusive and representative government. At the same time, building state institutions to provide a framework for governance is imperative. However, conflict transformation processes have to be owned by the people of Somalia in order to be sustainable.

The Use and Abuse of Islam

Somalia is a religiously homogeneous country, with a population that is 98 percent Muslim. Sufi practices and worldly Sunni rituals dominate Islam in Somalia. Religion was traditionally a framework to seek guidance and spiritual enlightenment. However, historically, Islam did also play a role in the political field. Dervish movements and Sufi brotherhoods were sources of resistance against various colonial regimes. Since the collapse of the state, there has been a massive influx of Wahhabi charities. Radical elements in the Islamic Courts have found an interested audience in the otherwise neglected and desperate population. Now there are more and more Quranic recitation schools (madrassas) and public health services provided by religious entities. Yet the warlord system has been based on oligopolies of violence that disregard religion, and Islamist movements have never managed to overrule the tight grasp of the warlords over the past 17 years. One earlier group with an Islamist agenda, the Al Ittihad al Islamiya (AIAI, or Islamic Union), founded in the mid-1980s, became a strong force with links to Sudan's chief Islamist, Hassan al Turabi, and to the Arab World in general. AIAI was officially defeated in a battle with forces under the command of the current president, Abdullahi Yussuf, in the mid-1990s. But one of the strongmen of AIAI, Sheikh Hassan Dahir Aweys, became a rising star with the Islamic Courts as speaker and leader of its radical wing. Both the organization and its leader Sheikh Aweys appear on the terrorist list of the US State Department.

There is evidence of Al Qaeda members operating in Somalia. Attacks on the US embassies in Nairobi and Dar es Salaam in 1998, and on a hotel and airline frequented by Israeli visitors in Mombassa in 2002, were undertaken after preparation in Somalia. However, there is no evidence of continuously functional Al Qaeda cells and networks. Due to the tightly knit clan network, clandestine operations are almost impossible. Lately, using Ethiopia's occupation as a mobilizing factor, various Al Qaeda members have used Web sites to rally jihadis to come fight in Somalia.[2] As the polarization and the abuse of religion by all actors involved in Somalia gains momentum, there is a high possibility that Al Qaeda will take advantage of the jihadist agenda of the Shabab, the UIC's zealous armed wing fighting Ethiopian force. The use and abuse of Islam by political actors, domestically, regionally, and internationally, became most apparent during 2006, which witnessed the UIC's victory over the CIA-sponsored Alliance for the Restoration of Peace and Counter Terrorism (ARPCT). In the perception of Ethiopia and many western states, the UIC followed an Islamist, irredentist, and jihadist agenda. In contrast, for a substantial proportion of the Somali population, the courts were the first movement to bring a modicum of order to the war-torn country. Nonetheless, some court leaders alienated the Somali population by enforcing Islamic modes of behavior, e.g., by prohibiting Bollywood movies, public screenings of the World Cup matches, chewing qat, and wearing dresses rather than hijabs.

In the course of 2006, radicals in the court, such as Sheik Aweys, the head of AIAI, and Aden Ayro, the leader of the military wing, Shabab, became dominant within the movement and acted as the spokespersons for what was in reality a heterogeneous assemblage of courts. The split in the UIC between radicals and moderates, and between jihadists and nationalists, became even more apparent after the Ethiopian invasion. Radical court

---

2. Zawahiri calls for attacks on Ethiopian forces in Somalia (www.globalsecurity.org/security/profiles/zawahiri_calls_for_attacks_on_ethiopian_forces_in_somalia.htm). Accessed on October 20, 2007.

members fled the country and found refuge in Eritrea and Yemen while the majority of the court leaders simply merged back into local clan structures, showing how tightly knit the links are between the clans and the courts.

Prior to the invasion, and in its aftermath, there has been little evidence that the TFG is committed to the population that it claims to govern. On October 29, 2007, Prime Minister Gedi, the only Hawiye clan member in a higher political position, resigned after being accused of incompetence and blamed for the deterioration of security in Mogadishu. However, using Gedi, a close Ethiopian ally, as the scapegoat for what goes wrong in Somalia will not solve the problems facing the TFG. Following his resignation, violence in Mogadishu escalated and another 80,000 people fled the capital in the last week of October 2007.

Ostracizing the courts as well as the Hawiye, a powerful clan, creates a mobilization factor for jihadists not yet seen in Somalia. A new alliance, the Alliance for the Re-Liberation of Somalia (ARS), which combines dissident TFG ministers, the Somali Diaspora, politicians, and intellectuals, might provide new momentum and a broader basis for what remains of the UIC. Whereas part of the ARS aims to become a political movement presenting the international community with a broader alternative to the hapless TFG or the radical Shabab, another branch, connected to Sheikh Hassan Aweys, plans to "re-liberate" Somalia from Ethiopian occupation. In early October 2007, Islamic Court militias captured the town of Bu'aale in southern Somalia, close to the Kenyan border. According to media information, one of Al Qaeda's Eastern Africa members, Abu Taha al Sudani, was involved in the fighting.

The International Response

For the last 17 years, Somalia has been a juridical entity without a functional government. There have been fourteen attempts to solve the political crisis, mainly by the regional organization Intergovernmental Authority on Development (IGAD). In 2004, the TFG was formed in Kenya. It remained there until pushed by Kenyan authorities to relocate to Baidoa, Somalia, in 2005, waiting until security conditions improved in Mogadishu. On 14 June 2006, the UIC took control after toppling the CIA-supported grouping of warlords, the ARPCT. In December 2006, the TFG called on the Ethiopian government to help them against the UIC, which by then controlled most of the country and moved to attack Baidoa, the seat of the TFG. With the political and military backing of the US, Ethiopian troops overran UIC positions in a matter of days. Insurgents, whose ranks consist of UIC members and Hawiye clan militia, have since waged a guerrilla war against Ethiopian forces and the weak military forces of the interim government.

The formation of the TFG has been fully supported, financed, and facilitated by the international community, including the EU. All EU statements therefore refer to the TFG as the legitimate government, as do UN Security Council resolutions, African Union (AU) communiqués, and IGAD position papers. On 20 February 2007, the UN Security Council unanimously adopted Resolution 1744, authorizing a six-month African Union Mission to Somalia (AMISOM) to support the TFG. Eight thousand troops were envisioned, but only 1,600 Ugandan troops were on the ground in fall 2007. But survival rather than peacekeeping seems to be the main aim of the Ugandan soldiers, who control only the harbor and part of the airport. The General Secretary of the United Nations, Ban Ki Moon, gave a gloomy evaluation of the impact of the mission and the future situation when calling for a "Coalition of the Willing" for Somalia. He said a UN peacekeeping mission would be neither realistic nor viable given the security situation in Somalia and observed that neither the AU mission nor the heavy Ethiopian presence could stabilize the situation.

One mechanism for mediating the conflicts in Somalia was the Somalia Contact Group, established in June 2006.[3] Whereas there is a unified position in the EU on the need to have an inclusive government in Somalia, there are vast policy differences on these issues with the US administration. The Contact Group supported a reconciliation conference in which the TFG was expected to include moderate court members and Hawiye clan representatives. Only some Hawiye were included, but not those with political influence, and no UIC members joined the conference. The reconciliation conference took place from 15 July to 30 August 2007 in Mogadishu and ended with no tangible result. Insurgent attacks increased during the conference despite a truce with some Hawiye elders, as the TFG was accused of being exclusive.

International Confusion

Somalia is placed at a geostrategically important position between the Horn of Africa and the Arab peninsula. Historically this needle eye meant good trade connections and relative prosperity. For the last decade or so Somalia was known as a chaotic warlord-run state, feared for its pirates. Smugglers of drugs, electronics, and weapons use the ports and airports in Somalia, controlled by warlord businessmen who practice clan-feudalism, bound by neither national taxation nor international law.

The failure of the international community during the US and UN interventions from 1992 to 1995 became a decisive factor in the subsequent reluctance to intervene in Africa. This failure has had multiple sources. Though humanitarian agencies were relatively successful in distributing

3. The International Somalia Contact Group includes the EU (Presidency and European Commission), Italy, Kenya, Norway, Sweden, Tanzania, United Kingdom, and the US, with the AU, IGAD, the League of Arab States, and the United Nations.

aid and alleviating widespread famine, military forces cooperated selectively with warlord factions and came to be seen by local actors as an occupation force. The missions have left Somalia in the lawless state of warlord rule. The Somalia experience, and the "Black Hawk Down" incident in particular, left the US traumatized. The consequences of this humiliating failure led the US government to abjure intervention in African countries, ultimately leading to the horrific failure to deal with genocide in Rwanda in 1994.

Since September 11, Somalia has ranked high on the list of countries where the US sees the imperative to fight the "war on terror." For the US government, Somalia's statelessness and the absence of rule of law pose threats reminiscent of Al Qaeda's Afghanistan sanctuary. At the same time, the lack of a real state allows the US military to directly target Somalia's territory without fear of reprisal or international condemnation. Operation Enduring Freedom—Horn of Africa (OEF-HOA), part of the US military's response to the attacks of September 11, is based in neighboring Djibouti. From the perspective of OEF's military leaders, Somalia is seen as a breeding ground for Al Qaeda operatives. The US thus supports Ethiopia through the exchange of military intelligence as well as in its broader competition with Eritrea. Currently the US administration threatens to list Eritrea as a state sponsor of terrorism due to the supply of weapons and training for UIC militias, including the Shabab. Whereas Ethiopia enjoys the full support of the US, including military training in spite of human rights atrocities committed by the Ethiopian forces in Somalia and Ethiopia's Ogaden, the US is categorical in its condemnation of Eritrea.

These policies lack the support of other international actors, namely the EU, AU, and the Arab League. European actors do not share a common agenda with the US regarding Somalia. There are diverse relations and interests informing EU member state policies. In the absence of a comprehensive European policy, the EU has failed to engage the US government in a critical dialogue. While the EU appears to be united behind a more proactive engagement with Eritrea to counter its isolation by the US, there is no outspoken criticism of Ethiopia. Human rights abuses and atrocities committed by Ethiopian troops in Somalia and the Ogaden are not condemned, leaving the impression that the West is obliged to keep quiet because it is thankful for Ethiopia's military presence in Somalia. Cases of rendition by Ethiopian and CIA personnel are documented; however, no international or European reaction has been registered. The continuation of a culture of impunity does not give hope for positive developments in Somalia.

Stabilizing Somalia

A common interest of the US and the EU is the stabilization of the Horn of Africa. Somalia—as a center of gravity in regional conflicts—cannot be sidelined and needs a political settlement to its conflicts. Somalia needs multileveled support to reconcile social groups and to build a framework for state functions that allows the Somali people to negotiate their political differences. The policy of the US, the EU, and its member state governments should be based on universal rights, not on cultural and religious preferences. The US policy of focusing on a military solution in Somalia is not sustainable. Somalia's domestic power dynamics need to be considered as much as Somalia's role in the proxy war between Ethiopia and Eritrea, and the broader "war on terror." Indeed, the tendency to confuse Islam, terror, and Islamism has impeded the formulation of a response to Somalia's complex crisis.

The international community, including the UN, the AU, and the Arab League, should continue to call for inclusive negotiations, including those Islamists who refrain from violence, as well as clan representatives sidelined because of their proximity to radical courts. The AU and the Arab League could and should play a proactive role in facilitating negotiations with moderate members of the UIC. Meanwhile, the donor community should encourage institution and state building efforts along with a system of transparent benchmarks based on good governance and human rights. Benchmarks would provide a transitional government with a framework for action and allow the donor community to harmonize efforts to improve security in the short-term and build institutions over the long term. It is also of utmost importance to rebuild a judiciary and to support mechanisms of transitional justice to end the culture of impunity.

Because the conflict in Somalia has such enormous regional implications, it is essential to tackle it with a regional approach. Somalia will not be stabilized without a change in policy vis-à-vis Ethiopia and Eritrea. Germany, with no former colonial history in this region, is respected by many regional governments and could therefore seek a more proactive role in bridging contested EU positions and communicating them as a united EU position vis-à-vis governments in the region. Germany could play a role as an intermediary in the region, using Germany's access to the Arab League, the AU, and IGAD countries to facilitate talks between the warring parties.

21

The Conflicts in Sudan: American and European Policies

Dorina A. Bekoe

Insurgencies have arisen in three main regions of Sudan: Southern Sudan, Darfur, and Eastern Sudan. While the specific causes of war for each region differ, there are important commonalities that show a pattern of political, economic, and social marginalization in Sudan. The roots of Sudan's conflicts stretch back several hundred years and lie in the domination of the north, namely the government in Khartoum, over other non-Arab groups; in poor governance and administration; and in identity issues. These patterns of interaction persist today and have transformed themselves into religious and cultural fissures in the country. US and European Union policies have only dealt with Sudan's conflicts in recent times. For the US in particular, Sudan policy has mostly reflected efforts to stop the spread of communism during the Cold War and the spread of religious extremism following the September 11 attacks. When Sudan's wars have been addressed, the root causes have oftentimes been simplified or glossed over, overlooking the mutually reinforcing nature of the grievances. This contribution reviews the major conflicts in Sudan and the foreign policy responses of the US and EU to both the government of Sudan and its conflicts.

Southern Sudan

The modern conflict between Khartoum and Southern Sudan is usually considered to have begun shortly before independence with a mutiny by southern soldiers against the north in 1955, but the sources of the conflict date back at least to the 1820s. The Egyptian conquest of Sudan encouraged

---

Dorina A. Bekoe, "The Conflicts in Sudan: American and European Policies," in *The Challenge of Islamists for EU and US Policies: Conflict, Stability, and Reform*, eds. Muriel Asseburg and Daniel Brumberg, 44–49 (Research Paper no. 12, Stiftung Wissenchaft und Politik German Institute for International and Security Affairs, Berlin, 2007). Reprinted with permission.

the exploitation of the south by the northern regions in order to promote commerce and sustain the Egyptian empire. Northern and Southern Sudan had effectively been ruled and developed as two separate entities, divided by religion, wealth, and resources. Islam and Arab culture came to dominate Sudan through the trading relationships between Arabs and northern Sudanese, and the British Empire's policy of investing disproportionately more in the north.

As such, the Sudanese government's central goal at independence was national unity. The uncertainty rested on what the unifying factors would be. While the north saw Islam as a unifying attribute, the south felt that the imposition of Islam would not differ much from the imposition of colonialism.[1] Forced Arabization and resistance to Islam thus became the defining features of north-south relations after independence. In 1969, Jaafar Muhammed Numeiri's coup sought to reverse the policies of Arabization, which led to a peace agreement with southern rebels in 1972. However, Numeiri's increasingly conservative Islam resulted in the unraveling of the Addis Ababa Agreement and a resumption of hostilities in 1983. Numeiri's overthrow in 1985 did not improve relations between the north and south. Finally in 1989, a military coup brought Omar Hassan Ahmed El-Bashir and Hassan al Turabi's National Islamic Front (NIF) to power, resulting in an attempt to impose Islam more aggressively throughout the country. The new drive to unify the country under Islam and Arab culture entrenched rifts between the two regions, which had by then transformed the conflict to include racial and cultural divisions between not only the north and south, but between the north and the other regions as well.

The Comprehensive Peace Agreement (CPA), signed in January 2005, calls for greater wealth and power distribution between the north and south and provides a measure of autonomy for the south. The CPA ushered in the Government of National Unity (GNU), comprising the ruling National Congress Party and the Sudan People's Liberation Movement (SPLM), and permits the government of Southern Sudan to administer the south. In 2011, according to the timetable of the CPA, southerners are supposed to vote in a referendum on independence. Presently, however, the CPA remains largely unimplemented. Although the CPA deals explicitly with the grievances of Southern Sudan, its broad framework of wealth and power sharing, and inclusion of minority cultures, serves as a viable approach to address the sources of conflict in Sudan's other regions. Thus, the lag in implementation of the CPA is also a strike against the credibility of the government's commitments to abide by agreements it signs with rebel groups in Darfur and eastern Sudan.

---

1. Francis M. Deng, *War of Visions: Conflict of Identities in the Sudan* (Washington, DC, The Brookings Institution, 1994), p. 21.

Darfur

Since it was defeated and incorporated into the British Empire in 1916, Darfur has been marginal to Sudan. Under the British, Darfur did not enjoy the same level of economic and political investment as other regions; the British administration was mostly concerned with pacifying the region. After independence, Darfur did not fare much better under the Sudanese government, suffering continued political and economic neglect. The severe droughts of the 1970s and 1980s exacerbated the region's underdevelopment. Darfur became caught up in the Islamization and Arabization of Sudan when Khartoum began to favor groups of Arab-descent over Africans—in particular after the NIF, led by Hassan al Turabi, came to power. For example, a reorganization of Darfur into three states in the mid-1990s—North Darfur, West Darfur, and South Darfur—resulted in making the non-Arab Fur, also the largest ethnic group, minorities in each of these states.[2] Arabs almost exclusively staffed the new administrative posts in the three Darfurian states, marking a concerted effort by the NIF to Arabize and Islamicize the country. The disenfranchisement of non-Arab groups added to tensions that were already simmering after the severe drought of 1985–86 pitted nomadic pastoralists (frequently Arabs) against farmers (frequently non-Arabs) in the competition for resources. To clamp down on the growing armed resistance of non-Arabs, the government of Sudan armed local militia groups. By 2003, when the world came to know of Darfur, these groups had transformed into the infamous *Janjaweed*.

However, the grievances in Darfur do not simply suggest animosity between Arabs and Africans. Indeed, the first rebel attack of the modern conflict in Darfur was staged by a Fur-Zaghawa alliance.[3] The Zaghawa, who had previously formed an alliance with the Arabs, agreed to an alliance with the Fur because of their disappointment with government services and support to Darfur and a commitment to fight Arab domination. The Zaghawa-Fur alliance thus reveals the complexity of the conflict in Darfur. While there is an element of Arab-African conflict, the grievances reflect a deeper reality of political marginalization.

Since 2003, experts estimate that more than 200,000 people have died in the fighting in Darfur and two million have been displaced. In May 2006, the armed factions in Darfur were brought to Abuja to negotiate a peace agreement. Only one group, the Minni Minawi faction of the Sudan Liberation Movement, signed the Darfur Peace Agreement (DPA). Since then, Darfur's rebels have splintered into approximately twelve new groups and the

---

2. Julie Flint and Alex de Waal, *Darfur: A Short History of a Long War* (New York: Zed Books, 2005), p. 57f.

3. Flint and de Waal, *Darfur*, p. 73.

DPA remains unimplemented. The latest attempt to negotiate a peace agreement between the rebels and the government of Sudan has faltered, as the main rebel groups refused to attend peace talks in Sirte, Libya. Continuing instability in Darfur will delay the start of the census, which in turn may affect the date of the general elections, currently scheduled for July 2009.

Eastern Sudan

Eastern Sudan, which comprises the three states of Gedarif, Kassala, and Red Sea, is home to the Beja, the majority ethnic group, along with the Rashaida, and other smaller groups from Darfur and West Africa. Sudan's only port is located in Eastern Sudan, making the region strategic for Sudan's oil economy. Inhabitants of Eastern Sudan have long suffered from political, economic and cultural marginalization. The Beja Congress, formed in 1958, sought redress for these issues through political means at first, but turned to armed conflict in 1993 when they were effectively shut out of the political process by the NIF's 1989 ban on political parties. In 2004, the Beja Congress joined with the Rashaida Free Lions, which was established in 1999 to protest political disenfranchisement, to form the Eastern Front (EF). The conflict in the east has always been one of low intensity, though there were significant events, such as the killing of 22 protestors by government security forces at Port Sudan.

In October 2006, the East Sudan Peace Agreement (ESPA) was signed. Modeled after the CPA, it promised increased wealth and power sharing, and importantly, a US$600 million development fund for the east. More than one year later, the ESPA has made progress in demobilizing the EF and with a number of political appointments, but key aspects remained unfulfilled. In particular, the development fund has not received its first transfer of US$100 million and a reconciliation conference has yet to be scheduled.

These three major armed conflicts are linked by the politics of exclusion practiced by Khartoum. In each case, inhabitants of the regions have been marginalized through religious exclusion, economic neglect, or ethnic domination. The CPA explicitly addresses these grievances and thus holds the key to peace and reconciliation in Sudan. However, stability in Sudan is threatened by the inadequate implementation of the CPA, weakening the prospects of the other agreements to be fulfilled. The international community, in its efforts to seek a negotiated solution to the conflicts in Sudan, must acknowledge that stability will only be attained when the peripheral regions, and both non-Arab and non-Muslim groups, can participate more meaningfully in national politics and economic policy.

US and EU Policy Toward Sudan

US policy toward Sudan is characterized by both continuity and change. Since the beginning of the Cold War, Sudan has been both an ally and a pariah state in US foreign policy. During the Cold War, the US supported Numeiri, who tried to cultivate a strong relationship with the US by portraying his government as anti-communist. From the US perspective, Sudan stood as a bulwark against the effects of Ethiopia's 1974 Marxist revolution. As a US ally in the Cold War, Sudan received significant amounts of economic and military aid. US policy collided with developments in the Sudanese domestic realm, where Numeiri was being challenged by hard-line Islamists who wanted to review the 1972 Addis Ababa Agreement, institute a more aggressive policy of Islamization, and impose *sharia* law. The conservative Sadiq al Mahdi overthrew Numeiri in 1985, and then Sadiq al Mahdi himself was deposed in the 1989 coup that brought Omar al Bashir to power.

The end of the Numeiri regime also marked the beginning of changes in the US relationship with Sudan. Bashir's administration adopted *sharia* and moved closer to Libya and Iran. The US worried that the introduction of *sharia* in Sudan would destabilize the region and harm US interests. Thereafter, relations between the two countries deteriorated steadily. Sudan's support of Iraq's invasion of Kuwait and the UN's citation of Sudan as a violator of human rights served as the key factors that altered US-Sudan relations. In 1993, the US designated Sudan as a state sponsor of terrorism. This designation made Sudan ineligible for most American economic and military assistance, although it continued to receive humanitarian aid. Air and other diplomatic sanctions were imposed in 1996 following the attempted assassination of Hosni Mubarak in Addis Ababa; the alleged murderers were suspected of being harbored by the Sudanese government.[4] In 1997, Sudan was included in the Antiterrorism Act, which prohibits trade between US companies and states designated as supporters of terrorism. Finally, after the 1998 US embassy bombings in Nairobi and Dar es Salaam were alleged to have links to a pharmaceutical firm in Khartoum, the US launched air strikes that destroyed the facility. The passage of the Congressional International Religious Freedom Act (CIRF) in 1999 brought the religious element of the conflict into sharper focus. The conflict in Sudan, having attracted the interest of US religious organizations, began to be described in religious terms, with warnings that the Islamic government was dominating and enslaving Christian southerners. With the passage of the CIRF, the Sudanese government began to be cited as a gross violator of human rights.

4. Human Rights Watch, *Sudan, Oil, and Human Rights* (Washington, DC: Human Rights Watch, 2003), p. 479f.

Despite the fact that the EU did not impose the same range of sanctions on Sudan as the US (only arms trading was banned), the EU broke off formal relations with Sudan in 1990, citing the country's poor human rights record. It was about the same time that US-Sudan relations began to sour. But in 1999, the EU sought to normalize commercial relations through the African-Caribbean-Pacific-EU negotiations. This shift in EU policy clashed with pressure by European civil society to prohibit oil companies from doing business in Sudan.

US engagement with Sudan began to change again at the turn of the millennium, as Sudan began to cooperate with US counterterrorism efforts. However, the September 11 attacks altered US and EU policy toward Sudan very quickly—especially given that Osama bin Laden had lived in Sudan for a number of years before departing for Afghanistan in 1996. Sudan became at once a focal point and ally in the war on terror. After September 11, Sudan began to provide information on Al Qaeda to the US government. There was also increased pressure on Sudan to end the war with the South. In 2002, the EU pegged continued relations with Sudan to progress in securing a peace agreement with the South. After the CPA was signed, Sudan received €400 million in EU development support.

In the meantime, little attention was paid to the developing crisis in Darfur. Some claim that the US failure to address Darfur in 2003, when reports of atrocities first emerged, reflected the new complicated relationship between the US and Sudan: with Sudan providing information in the war on terror and a peace agreement imminent in the south, the US feared that addressing the conflict in Darfur would harm both objectives.[5] The ongoing war in Darfur has brought US and EU policies toward Sudan closer, with combined pressure from both to end the violence. In light of the failed Darfur Peace Agreement, both the US and the EU support the implementation of a 26,000-strong UN hybrid force in Darfur combining UN and African Union forces. While it is scheduled to begin deploying in early 2008, Khartoum has imposed several conditions on the force's composition and mandate. Moreover, on both continents, civil society organizations have mounted large campaigns to shed light on the atrocities in Darfur and force stronger action by their governments. In contrast, the civil war in the East has not received much attention. Instead, Eritrea was the major external power that mediated the peace talks between the EF and the Sudanese government.

Alternate Concepts of the Conflict

Neither the US nor the EU focused on ending Sudan's wars until relatively recently. When the US and EU did focus on ending the wars, the initial

5. Michael Abramowitz, "US Promises on Darfur Don't Match Actions," *Washington Post*, 29 October 2007.

simplistic framing of the conflict as north versus south, Muslim versus Christian, and Arab versus non-Arab ignored wider questions around the unequal distribution of wealth and power. Moreover, it obfuscated a more general pattern of Khartoum's marginalization of the regions in the hinterland—grievances that require political, not military, solutions. Belatedly, these relationships are surfacing, as negotiators in Eastern Sudan and Darfur have adopted the wealth and power sharing frameworks of the CPA.

In recasting the conflicts in Sudan as part of similar center-periphery relations, attention must also turn to how land-use policy—such as the construction of the 200 kilometer long Merowe Dam in the Nile Valley of Northern Sudan—fuels conflict and disenfranchises communities; how implementing peace agreements causes conflict and re-orders relationships between ethnic groups—as is occurring in Eastern Sudan; and how to increase decentralization and transparency in policy decisions. In short, policies supporting peace efforts in Sudan must take account of the enormous complexity of the political and economic relationships in the country and the need for a renegotiation of the social contract between the state and its citizens. More concretely, policymaking should be more consultative, reflect the religious and ethnic diversity of Sudan, live up to democratic ideals of pluralism and transparency, and ensure a more equitable distribution of the country's wealth.

22

Engaging Islamists and Promoting Democracy: A Preliminary Assessment

Mona Yacoubian

Deeming democratic change to be a long-term antidote to Islamist extremism, the Bush administration coupled its military interventions in Afghanistan and Iraq with intensified efforts to promote democracy in the Arab world, underscoring the need for free and fair elections. To date, parliamentary elections of varying openness have taken place across the region, from Morocco to Kuwait. However, the elections ushered in a wave of Islamist victories, dubbed by many as an "Islamist tsunami."[1]

The Islamists' successes stem from their effectiveness as vehicles for popular opposition. As liberal, secular opposition parties remain largely detached from much of the population, Islamists have developed vast and easily mobilized grassroots networks through charitable organizations and mosques. The leadership is often younger and more dynamic, with strong ties to the community, and the party organizations brim with energy and ideas, attracting those who are seeking change.

The U.S. government has quietly engaged a number of moderate and legal Islamist parties across the region for several years, sometimes through normal diplomatic activity, sometimes through government-funded grants to U.S. organizations. This Special Report examines U.S.-funded engagement with legal, nonviolent Islamist parties through the National Democratic Institute (NDI) and the International Republican Institute (IRI), which have the most extensive experience engaging with Islamists in the region,

1. For the purposes of this paper, Islamists are defined as those who believe that systems of governance should be rooted in Islamic beliefs and practices. Significant differences exist among Islamists with respect to how and to what degree Islam should affect governance. Some advocate nothing short of the full implementation of *sharia*. Others have more flexible interpretations.

Mona Yacoubian, "Engaging Islamists and Promoting Democracy: A Preliminary Assessment," Special Report 190 (Washington, DC: USIP, 2007).

and focuses on Morocco, Jordan, and Yemen, because of their relative political openness and the strength and vibrancy of their Islamist political opposition.

Successful Strategy. A successful Islamist engagement strategy both empowers individuals and strengthens institutions to yield greater transparency, more accountability, and shifts toward moderation. Training and empowering individuals cultivates moderates within the parties and enhances their political sophistication and influence. Meanwhile, as regimes in the Arab world resist or manipulate political reforms, strengthening democracy's infrastructure is as important as supporting individuals. Independent electoral procedures and monitoring establish transparent, independent, and accountable electoral laws. Institution building ensures appropriate checks on executive power and a strong rule of law. Strengthening parliaments is especially crucial, as Islamists participate primarily in legislatures.

In assessing whether Islamist parties have moderated in response to U.S. engagement, it is difficult if not impossible to quantify or measure shifts that may themselves be relative and subjective. Directly linking greater moderation to specific U.S. engagement activities is also highly problematic. At best, this engagement should be considered a contributing factor. Nevertheless, the tentative results in Morocco, Jordan, and Yemen are promising enough that continued engagement with moderate Islamists should be encouraged, albeit with greater emphasis on institution building and a eye on the broader context of the ideological battle in the Muslim world between extremism and moderation.

The Case Studies: Morocco, Jordan, and Yemen

Morocco

Path to Reform. Of the three countries examined in this assessment, Morocco's political opening has been the most significant. The NDI termed it "one of the most compelling examples of democratic reform in the Middle East and North Africa."[2] As the Islamist Party of Justice and Development (PJD) has benefited from Morocco's democratic reforms, the kingdom offers perhaps the most dynamic case of Islamist integration into the political arena, and could be a model for other Arab countries. However, the kingdom's democratic openness remains limited. The king retains ultimate power with no real constraints; he can block or withdraw reforms at will, dissolve the parliament, and declare a state of emergency. A vast system of patronage backing the king functions as an informal bureaucracy.

2. National Democratic Institute for International Affairs, "Morocco: The Edge of Promise," briefing paper, Washington, DC, April 7, 2005, p. 6.

A Potent Islamist Force. The PJD is Morocco's most powerful opposition force, holding the third-largest bloc in the country's parliament (42 out of 325 seats).[3] An IRI poll conducted in late 2005 showed the PJD polling 47 percent of the vote for the September 2007 parliamentary elections, far more votes than other parties. A 2006 poll supported this result, suggesting that the PJD continues to be the front runner.

The PJD was formally established in 1998 when the monarchy authorized political participation by Islamist groups. The party's roots lay in the Unification and Reform Movement (MUR), a grassroots Islamist organization that had cultivated a significant popular following. The MUR merged with the Popular Constitutional Democratic Movement (MCPD), an inconsequential political party with Islamist leanings, and ran in the November 1997 parliamentary elections, winning nine seats. The party had loose connections to the palace. The PJD emerged from the MUR as a formal political party in 1998 but maintains strong ties to the movement, which supplies a vast grassroots network of support.

The PJD is noted for its strong, clear vision: It stresses Islamic values as a key point of reference for principles of governance. At the same time, the PJD endorses the king's title as commander of the faithful and insists on maintaining the monarchy's supremacy. It does not call for systemic change, but rather seeks to be an opposition party within the status quo. The party is known for internal transparency and effective grassroots outreach. The NDI has described it as having "a strong service ethic that provides needed resources to the community, a decentralized party structure that allows for greater flexibility and more opportunities for multiple leaders, a young leadership, and perhaps most importantly, internal democracy."[4] In this sense, the party starkly contrasts with its secular counterparts, which are largely governed by aging leaderships with autocratic ruling structures and limited popular support.

Plying its image as clean and accountable, the PJD campaigns on criticizing government corruption and cronyism, pledging governance that responds to the people. The party touts its superior attendance record in parliament, distinguishing it from other parties that appear detached and unaccountable. The PJD parliamentary delegation usually submits the largest number of questions to the government and denounces government delays in answering them.

The PJD's well-developed grassroots network is largely young and urban, with strong pockets of support in city slums and among university

---

3. The author wishes to acknowledge Andrew Mandelbaum for his research on the background of the PJD.

4. "Morocco: The Edge of Promise," p. 10.

graduates, whose unemployment rate is estimated at 40 percent.[5] IRI polling suggests that jobs and unemployment are by far the largest voter concerns. The PJD has worked hard to attract this disgruntled segment of the population by campaigning on socioeconomic issues, and consequently, it has also drawn in technocrats with no background in Islamic activism who are eager to work on such problems. The PJD is the only Moroccan party that has constituent offices in Europe and actively courts Moroccan communities there.

However, the PJD is by no means monolithic, but encompasses a spectrum of views. Moderates typically push for democratic reforms, a broader role for women, and greater engagement with the West. Some maintain close ties to the palace. Party hardliners call for a stricter interpretation of Islamic law (*sharia*) and generally hold more socially conservative views. They are far less comfortable with any sort of co-optation by the palace, more suspicious of democracy advocates, and oppose wider engagement with the West and the United States in particular.

NDI and IRI Programming. The NDI launched its first survey mission to Morocco in 1993, establishing a field office in 2001. NDI programming expanded markedly as political reforms accelerated. The NDI currently runs programs in political-party building, parliamentary strengthening, women's participation, and media training. It also operates a focus group center[6] and has trained election monitors. The organization's work in Morocco has been directed largely at the national level.

The IRI has conducted programming in Morocco since 1997, but did not establish a field office until 2004. IRI programming focuses largely on public-opinion polling and political-party training. The institute has worked with municipal councils on local governance issues, though these projects are being phased out. The IRI is also working to increase the presence of women within political-party structures.

NDI Engagement with Islamists. The NDI works exclusively with the PJD and its related non-governmental organizations (NGOs). The decision to work closely with the PJD is grounded in a broader strategy to seek out activist parties with deep grassroots support. As one staffer explained, "We were going to be the right kind of democrats. We weren't going to operate in an exclusive manner, as others had, because they were Islamists."[7]

---

5. The party wields significantly less influence in rural areas, which generally maintain greater allegiance to traditional government-affiliated parties.

6. Established in 2003, the People's Mirror has conducted more than 150 focus groups on topics ranging from public perceptions of the parliament and political parties to women in public life and attitudes on freedom of expression.

7. Telephone interview, June 29, 2006.

The NDI typically deals with those in the PJD who are reform-minded and moderate, rather than hardline conservatives. For their part, moderate reformers within the party actively seek out NDI assistance and expertise; hardline elements remain adamantly opposed to any engagement with U.S. democracy promoters.

NDI program implementers described PJD participation in institute activities as enthusiastic and engaged, characterizing the party as "well ahead" of other political parties and a "model" participant in trainings and workshops. Other implementers underscore the party's discipline, noting that it attracts people who are very serious, committed to their work, and maintain a strong degree of party loyalty.

IRI Engagement with Islamists. The IRI has had more limited contact with the PJD; the PJD has cited its opposition to regional U.S. policy to explain its relative lack of interest in working with the IRI, which it associates more closely with the Bush administration. The institute first contacted the PJD only in 2004. Despite these difficulties, the IRI's chief representative meets regularly with the PJD secretary general.

The PJD has not participated in IRI political-party trainings, but it has been very interested in IRI polling activities, and the party was among the Moroccan political parties to be briefed privately on IRI polling. The institute has sought to engage parties at earlier stages of its public-opinion polling programs by showing them how polls are constructed and soliciting their advice when designing survey instruments.

Results of Engagement. It is difficult if not impossible to draw direct linkages between U.S.-funded engagement with the PJD, either in the party's evolution toward greater moderation or in supporting moderates within the party. Other areas, such as the degree to which U.S. efforts have facilitated greater cooperation between Islamist and secular groups, may be slightly easier to measure. Indicators of the PJD's evolution toward moderation include party statements and interviews with senior leaders, the degree of internal transparency, the PJD's actions in the parliament, and its willingness to work with secular parties.

Tracking the PJD's Evolution. As mentioned above, the PJD has always held a relatively moderate position in Moroccan politics, acknowledging the ultimate authority of the monarchy and calling for nonviolent, democratic change. It has had longstanding ties to the palace, but with a boost in confidence just after the 2002 parliamentary elections, the party began to strike a more strident tone. Hardliners who favored a more conservative social agenda and minimal contact with outsiders had significant influence.

The May 16, 2003, suicide attacks in Casablanca were a turning point in the PJD's political evolution. The PJD was not implicated in the attack, but popular sentiment shifted against the Islamist party, and the PJD defended itself from calls for its dissolution and judgment from political elites that it was morally responsible for the attacks. As one NDI staffer noted, "Prior to May 2003, PJD moderation may have been more questionable. Their platform was more conservative, hewing closely to traditional demands for *sharia*. Things changed after Casablanca."[8] The party purged hardliners from leadership posts[9] and reversed its position on two key pieces of legislation: the reform of the Family Code (the Moudawana) and new antiterrorism legislation. In 2000, the PJD had staunchly opposed the Family Code reforms, deeming them anti-Islamic. However, the party supported the king's renewed calls for Family Code reform in October 2003 and voted for the revised code in January 2004. In a number of press interviews, PJD leader Saad Eddine al Othmani justified his party's support of the Family Code by explaining that the PJD's previous opposition was based on the government's lack of consultation with political parties, the absence of a religious point of reference in the code, and the initial draft's failure to address concerns of the family as a whole. Broadened consultations and new revisions to the draft satisfied party concerns. He noted that the PJD had participated in the debate and discussion leading up to the code's passage and that the law was democratically enacted.[10] The PJD also voted in favor of a controversial antiterrorism law that it had initially opposed; the law was passed after the Casablanca attacks. The shift in position has been described as a politically shrewd, pragmatic decision. Human rights groups have criticized the law for its wide-ranging measures, which have been used to arrest and detain scores of terrorist suspects.

The PJD's moderation continued when it elected Othmani to be its new leader at the party's 2004 congress. Garnering 80 percent of the vote, Othmani embodies the moderate trend within the PJD. He has strongly supported democratic reforms, comparing the PJD to the Christian Democratic parties in Europe. A psychiatrist by training, the charismatic leader stresses that the PJD is not an Islamist party, but a party with an "Islamic reference point." Othmani differentiates between religion and politics, emphasizing that political authority comes from citizens and that those in power should answer to them. He has also argued that *sharia* has evolved over the centuries and encompasses broad themes of equality, justice, and social

---

8. Telephone interview, June 30, 2006.

9. These included Mustapha Ramid, who was forced to resign as head of the PJD's parliamentary bloc, and Ahmed Reisouni, president of the Unity and Reform Movement, which has close ties to the PJD. Reisouni had challenged the king's title as commander of the faithful, placing the supremacy of his religious authority under question.

10. "Secretary-General of Morocco's Islamist PJD Party Interviewed," *Jeune Afrique*, April 2, 2006; "Interview with Saad Eddine al-Othmani," conducted by Amr Hamzawy, *Arab Reform Bulletin* vol. 3, no. 10 (December 2005), available at www.carnegieendowment.org.

development. Othmani has promoted engagement with the West, traveling and lecturing throughout Europe and the United States.

Despite the party's apparent ideological shifts, however, its newspaper, *at-Tajdid,* continues to reflect more extreme views. Some have suggested that the dichotomy is intentional: *At-Tajdid* ensures the support of the PJD's base while the party leadership becomes more moderate to assuage the concerns of the palace and elites. The paper regularly runs articles that rail against the United States and Israel, and it has a decidedly hardline stance on social issues. An editorial in the paper during the 2004 tsunami described the event as divine punishment that could befall Morocco for its moral debauchery. *At-Tajdid* has also strongly criticized music festivals and spearheaded a campaign against the film *Marock,* directed by a Moroccan woman.

Degree of Internal Democracy and Transparency. Democracy promoters consistently applaud the PJD for its internal democracy: considered the most democratically structured of all of Morocco's parties, it is also the most decentralized. Leaders are transparently elected on a regular basis rather than holding positions of authority indefinitely. Regional and district offices are filled through elections and conferences with all members present. Internal debates and votes are held on key policy issues. The party's budget and financing are also relatively transparent, with no suggestion of internal corruption. The party also works to ensure an active role for women through an internal quota system. The party's leader claims that the PJD has more women as members than does any other party in Morocco, and the PJD has more women serving in local councils than does any other party.[11]

The PJD in Parliament. The PJD has been perhaps the most active party in the parliament, especially since the 2002 elections, when the party tripled its representation. It has focused on battling government corruption and increasing transparency. In addition, the PJD has a strong attendance record, unlike other political parties. The PJD emphasizes the value of the parliament, as it both represents the populace and checks executive power. The party requires its members of parliament (MPs) to attend general assembly and committee sessions, publishing attendance lists and demanding explanations for absences or tardiness. As a result, PJD delegates have the lowest rate of absenteeism of any party.

The PJD holds internal strategy sessions before any hearing questioning a government minister. It requires its deputies to draft at least one oral question per week, one written question per month, and to propose one bill per legislative session. As a result, PJD deputies submitted more written questions to the government than any other party. The party also requires

11. Speech by Saad Eddine al-Othmani, Carnegie Endowment for International Peace, Washington, DC, May 8, 2006.

its MPs to remit a minimum of 22 percent of their salaries to the party, both to bolster party financing and to counter any possible image of individual profiting from public office.[12]

NDI focus groups show that the PJD's appeal stems from its anticorruption stance and its ability to assist with the provision of basic services, such as health care, through well-organized grassroots networks. The two key planks of the party's 2007 campaign platform are battling corruption and achieving 8 percent economic growth. The PJD has also sought to use its parliamentary position to broaden its public appeal by promoting good governance; the PJD's parliamentary delegation is extremely active in demanding government transparency, often questioning government budget allocations and demanding audits.

In the parliament, the PJD deemphasizes its moral agenda, adopting a more pragmatic and sophisticated approach to a number of moral issues. Tourism is a key source of jobs and foreign exchange earnings, but conservative Islamists strongly oppose the gambling and prostitution that often accompany foreign tourism. In response, the PJD has pushed to develop Morocco's infrastructure and establish retirement communities for European retirees. The project both capitalizes on the opportunities inherent in Europe's aging population and preserves the conservative social mores that are important to many Islamists.

Cooperation with Secular Parties. NDI multiparty training sessions have facilitated contact and perhaps cooperation between the PJD and secular opposition parties, particularly on reform-related issues. The trainings offer opportunities for networking and future collaboration. In its quarterly reporting, the NDI noted that the PJD continued consultations with other parties after NDI programming. Upon completing a group facilitation training, a PJD member remarked, "By bringing all these political parties together in the same workshops, NDI is in fact gathering the un-gatherable."[13] The NDI has also organized study missions abroad that bring together different political parties, including the PJD.

The PJD may be closer ideologically to some parties than others, but it has managed to cooperate quietly with the secular Socialist Union of Popular Forces (USFP), its ideological rival on certain questions. Some cooperation stems from the typical give-and-take of politics, but the parties also share genuine common ground on electoral and constitutional reforms. Both parties have pushed for constitutional amendments that reduce the power of the monarchy and enhance the independence of the parliament

12. Eva Wegner, "Morocco: PJD Works at Being New and Different," *Arab Reform Bulletin* vol. 4, no. 3 (April 2006).

13. "Morocco Party Strengthening and Parliamentary Reform," CEPPS/NDI Quarterly Report, July 1–September 20, 2005, Washington, DC, p. 7.

and prime minister. In preparing for the September 2007 parliamentary elections, the PJD has been more open about its contact with the USFP. If expectations become reality, the PJD will gain a plurality in parliament and could be asked to form a coalition government with the USFP as a potential partner.

Conclusions. The PJD has moved clearly toward greater moderation over the past five years. Still, the depth of the moderation and whether it constitutes a normative shift in the party's outlook remains open to question. Certainly, the Casablanca bombings and the resulting fallout caused the party to moderate its ideological stance. However, several indicators suggest that the party's ideological and policy positions might be rooted in more than short-term pragmatism.

The extent to which the NDI and IRI have facilitated the PJD's moderation is also unclear. The institutes have fostered Islamist-secular cooperation and building technical capacity. Both organizations have established strong working relationships with the PJD, meeting with its leadership regularly and including the PJD in numerous workshops, conferences, and trainings. The NDI retained open lines of communication even during periods of official PJD boycott of U.S. organizations, though as of mid-2007, the PJD has refused to work with any U.S.-funded organization, including the NDI, to protest U.S. foreign policy in the region. The Islamist party could exploit widespread anti-United States sentiment to strengthen its position in the 2007 elections.

The connection between the PJD's ideological evolution and its engagement with the U.S. political party institutes is even more tenuous. The PJD's moderate trajectory could originate from within the party, or be due to external pressure from the government. Democracy promoters themselves have suggested that the Ministry of Interior contributed to the PJD's moderation, pointing to a government strategy to divide the Islamists by ostracizing extremists and co-opting moderates. One NDI staffer admitted that the "Moroccan Ministry of Interior had a much more powerful impact on forcing the PJD to evolve than NDI ever could."[14]

Neither the NDI nor the IRI appear to have any illusions about the extent of their ability to transform the Islamist party. However, distinct differences in approach were evident. IRI representatives stated that they were "not targeting the PJD to moderate it." Their approach takes the Islamist party "at face value and at how *they* define themselves."[15] The NDI sees itself as helping to reinforce the PJD's move toward moderation. As such, the institute contributes to legitimizing moderates in the party and building a

14. Telephone interview, June 30, 2006.

15. Interview, July 6, 2006.

relationship based on mutual trust. The NDI's strategy is to work with reformists within the movement and strengthen their position in the PJD; NDI staffers have underscored that ostracizing the PJD is unthinkable. As one implementer explained, "Refusing to work with the PJD because they are Islamist would be equivalent to concluding that any Islamist party, however moderate, should not participate in politics. It is equivalent to contending that every Islamist party is by definition too radical to respect democratic values and civil liberties. Rather, it would have the consequence of favoring Islamic radicalism more than marginalizing it."[16]

Jordan

Path to Reform. Jordan's political opening dates to 1989, when growing popular disaffection prompted the government to launch a substantial political-reform program featuring heightened civil liberties, legalized political parties, and relatively free elections. Throughout the 1990s, however, Jordan's reform process seesawed between limited progress and significant setbacks. When King Abdullah II ascended the throne in 1999, Jordan's reform program stalled due to continued economic troubles and rising political tensions. In 2003, despite continued domestic instability, King Abdullah restored some political freedoms, holding moderately free municipal and parliamentary elections. However, Jordan's limited political opening has yet to be anchored in the rule of law and remains hostage to shifts in the security environment and regional instability emanating from Iraq or the Palestinian territories. Ultimately, political reform depends on the king, who retains nearly total control. He can dissolve the parliament and dismiss the prime minister and cabinet at will.

Islamist Parties. Founded in 1992, the Islamic Action Front (IAF), the political branch of Jordan's Muslim Brotherhood, is considered to be the most credible political party in Jordan. The Islamist party is well organized with a high degree of internal transparency, promotes a coherent platform, and most important, claims broad-based popular support. It benefits substantially from the electoral support of a deeply entrenched grassroots network of mosques, schools, and charitable organizations run by the Muslim Brothers.

In the June 2003 parliamentary elections, the IAF won 17 out of 110 seats, the largest number of any party (most MPs are independents, not affiliated with any particular party). The party is a vocal critic of the government, chastising it for widespread corruption and calling for comprehensive reforms, such as democratic elections, an independent parliament, and greater press freedoms. However, the IAF insists on Islam as the only source of

16. Telephone interview, June 30, 2006.

legislation. Its leadership is considered to be hardline and rigid, and the more doctrinaire faction of the party maintains the upper hand, though, like other Islamist parties, the IAF contains a spectrum of political views. Some mid-level party officials are more moderate and can be more forward-thinking and pragmatic.

Although the Islamists have been vocal opponents of government policies, the Muslim Brotherhood's relations with the palace are several decades old. During King Hussein's reign, the government reportedly promoted Islamists as a counterweight to leftist opposition groups, who were deemed a greater threat. The Islamist opposition has not called for systemic change and recognizes the monarchy's legitimacy.

However, buoyed by Hamas's landslide victory in January 2006, the leader of the IAF parliamentary bloc boasted that the Islamists were ready to take power like their "brothers in Palestine."[17] IAF members claim that their party would win 40 to 50 percent of the seats in a free and fair vote. The IAF also has become increasingly outspoken against government repression and corruption, accusing the government of cracking down harshly on its members following the Hamas victory. The IAF has criticized political-party reforms that would ban parties based on religion and demanded a new electoral law that would remove the government's gerrymandered districts.

More socially conservative than the PJD in Morocco, the IAF explicitly calls to implement *sharia* in Jordan, supporting segregated classrooms, mandatory head covering, and a ban on nightclubs and alcohol. It has also opposed calls for a 20 percent quota for women in the parliament, saying that it is unconstitutional and underestimates women's abilities. However, with the November 2007 parliamentary elections approaching, the party has moved corruption and good governance issues to the top of its agenda, playing down its conservative social posture. The IAF is also deeply opposed to Jordan's peace treaty with Israel and remains a staunch critic of U.S. policies in the region.

The IAF is not Jordan's only Islamist party: The more moderate al-Wasat party—the name means "center"—was founded in 2001 as a breakaway faction of the IAF. The party has a number of independent Islamists among its estimated 400 members, including some women. Compared with the IAF, however, al-Wasat is a minor party with very limited influence. It currently holds no seats in the parliament, although two to three independent legislators maintain a nominal affiliation. Al-Wasat is preparing intensively for the November 2007 elections, through which it hopes to establish a formal party presence in the lower house.

---

17. Thanassis Cambanis, "Jordan's Islamists See a Path to Political Power," *The Boston Globe*, March 21, 2006.

Al-Wasat occupies a moderate middle ground between more traditional Islamist parties such as the IAF and secular, reform-minded parties. Like the Moroccan PJD, al-Wasat's platform refers to itself as one of an "Islamic reference." The party nods to its historic roots in Jordan's Islamist movement, but believes that it is a modern version of the earlier movement, arguing that the values of *sharia* are dynamic, not static. Al-Wasat strongly emphasizes the need for democratic reforms and political pluralism, and has called for a balance of power in government and broader civil liberties.

Party leaders stress that their pro-reform positions are not tactical, but reflect the deeper values of the Islamist centrist (*wasatiyyah*) movement. Al-Wasat party is very open to engaging with the West and working with U.S. organizations. Finally, in public interviews, its party leaders have strongly condemned violent extremism, including attacks in the West, as rooted in an "erroneous understanding of Islam," calling instead for "disproving their ideas . . . through the emergence of an enlightened ideological trend that truly understands Islam."[18]

Despite observers who suggest that the Jordanian government created al-Wasat as a counterweight to the IAF, one democracy promoter described the party's organization as "impressive" despite its youth; it "appears to be gaining grassroots support."[19] The party also maintains good ties with the Jordanian government. But it will be a long time before al-Wasat party can challenge the IAF: it is still quite small and does not represent a significant segment of Jordanian society. One democracy promoter opined that it "will take years for the party to get to the point of being a serious political party."[20]

NDI and IRI Programming. The NDI began working in Jordan in 1993 and opened its Amman field office in 2004. Current programming consists of parliamentary strengthening and political-party training. The NDI also has opened a focus group center modeled after Morocco's program. In general, the NDI promotes a more representative multiparty system and strengthening of women's political participation. Through workshops and trainings, NDI works with both political parties and parliamentary blocs in constituency outreach, platform development, and media relations.

The IRI has been working in Jordan since 2002; it opened its field office in late 2004. The IRI's Jordan strategy is based on its assessment that political-party development is premature given the weakness of Jordan's political parties. Instead, current programming focuses on increasing citizen participation and developing leadership skills among emerging community

18. Quote from Fayiz al-Rabi, member of al-Wasat's political bureau, in *al-Ghad*, October 5, 2005.

19. Telephone interview, June 29, 2006.

20. Telephone interview, September 11, 2006.

leaders. The institute's strategy has been to build on the potential for political leadership from the grassroots, working on advocacy skills and issue engagement as a step to running for elected office. The IRI also conducts regular public-opinion polling. The institute has sponsored three national-level polls and two municipal polls in Jordan.

Engagement with Islamists. Both the NDI and IRI have had limited contact with the IAF, which has maintained a tacit boycott of all U.S. organizations to protest U.S. policies in the region. The IAF also forbids its members from traveling to the United States, precluding them from study missions there.

By contrast, al-Wasat has participated actively in both NDI and IRI programming. The NDI's engagement has been continuous, contacting al-Wasat leaders and members on a biweekly basis. Al-Wasat maintained its engagement with the NDI even under increased tension during the Israel-Lebanon war in the summer of 2006. The IRI has also included al-Wasat in some of its trainings, though the party temporarily suspended its participation to protest the Israel-Lebanon war, as it saw the IRI as more closely connected to the Bush administration. Trainings with IRI resumed in September 2006 when al-Wasat participated in a seminar on platform and membership development.

NDI and al-Wasat. NDI engagement with Islamists in Jordan has been conducted largely through its interaction with al-Wasat, focusing on political-party training. Since 2004 the party has participated in numerous trainings and sessions, and the NDI works with the party at both the national and regional levels. Trainings have included strategic planning, recruitment, constituent outreach, and message development. In anticipation of the 2007 parliamentary elections, the NDI has intensified its activities with al-Wasat, helping the party to identify areas in which NDI can be of assistance.

IRI and al-Wasat. As mentioned above, the IRI Jordan programming takes a long-term approach to political-party development. Most of the IRI programming in Jordan has not directly targeted Islamists or political parties in general. Nonetheless, the institute has undertaken some training with al-Wasat in the belief that the party has the long-term potential to develop as a centrist political party with Islamic leanings.

IRI activities with al-Wasat have focused on platform development. Its training sessions help the party to identify what it stands for and how to project its core values, relying on the IRI's public-opinion polling. The institute helped al-Wasat to analyze the results and shape the party's strategy. Additional activities include broader message development, candidate recruitment—particularly important because 98 percent of candidates in municipalities run as independents—and constituent outreach at the municipal level.

Limited Engagement with the IAF. The IAF maintains some distance from both of the U.S. democracy-promotion institutes, often boycotting them implicitly if not explicitly. Nonetheless, the NDI meets periodically with the IAF, although to date, it has had only limited engagement with the party through its programming. With the 2007 parliamentary elections, the NDI is trying to improve its contact with the IAF, particularly with women and moderates in the party.

The IRI has had some communication and dialogue with the IAF, but the party is not a target for IRI assistance. Meetings with the IAF typically do not get beyond statements of protest against U.S. policy in the region.[21] However, two prominent IAF members were present at an IRI-sponsored poll briefing, and the IAF has discussed the poll at length with the IRI's Jordanian partners. IAF MPs have also approached the institute's local polling partner to analyze IRI polling results.

Results of Engagement. Given both U.S. institutes' relatively short periods of programming as well as their limited dealings with the IAF, the results of NDI and IRI engagement with moderate Islamists are difficult to track and modest at best. The most comprehensive Islamist engagement consists of NDI activities with al-Wasat. Al-Wasat's potential for moderation and evolution into a key democratic actor is viewed through its level of interaction with democracy promoters, the party's internal transparency, and its potential for working with secular parties, as these elements of engagement can be measured more easily.

Level of Interaction. As noted above, both the NDI and the IRI appear to have established good working relations with the party. The IRI has undertaken some trainings with al-Wasat and the NDI meets with the party regularly. However, it is difficult to measure the effect of these working relationships on the ideological or programmatic emphases of the party.

Degree of Internal Democracy and Transparency. NDI has suggested marked improvements in al-Wasat's degree of internal democracy and transparency. When the institute began working with al-Wasat, the leadership was not democratically elected, nor was there an ethic of working for the common good; the party operated to serve the individuals who headed it. The party's former leader reportedly used the party as a political tool to promote his own self-interest. The NDI engaged with mid-level activists

21. Telephone interview, September 11, 2006.

extensively and with some elements of the leadership, and the party participated in numerous party-strengthening activities, covering party structure and transparency, message development, and outreach. Last year, the party elected as its leader Muhammad al-Qudah, one of the NDI's most active participants in many of their trainings. However, other analysts argue that al-Wasat continues to suffer from a high degree of corruption and still lacks transparency. Some have noted that the party continues to fall prey to personality-driven conflicts.[22]

The NDI also worked closely with a number of women in al-Wasat. Nawal Faouri, one of their most frequent trainees, was elected in May 2006 to the party's political bureau, a senior leadership position. A party moderate, she has made a strong connection between her training and her enhanced political skills and electoral victory. Faouri has also taken moderate public positions, calling on Muslim clerics to allow women to participate in public decision making. She presented a paper on the issue to the International Islamic Conference held in Amman in July 2006.[23]

Bridging with Secular Parties. Al-Wasat is both capable of and interested in cooperating with secular parties, particularly on reform issues. Party members were cordial and cooperative with other parties during NDI-sponsored multiparty training sessions. Al-Wasat is a member of the National Movement, a coalition of nine centrist opposition parties, both Islamist and secularist. The coalition has exerted only minimal influence to date, but it could effectively lobby for reform in the future.

Conclusions. U.S. engagement with Islamists in Jordan has not been as lengthy or rich as in the Moroccan case. First, Jordan's democratic reforms have been more fragile, with periods of opening followed by significant and sometimes abrupt reversals. The November 2005 hotel bombings, called Jordan's September 11, further dampened efforts at political liberalization, as security matters trumped political openness.

Second, Islamist politics in Jordan are influenced more deeply by international events, particularly the war in Iraq and the Hamas victory in the Palestinian territories. Protesting U.S. policies in these countries, the IAF has eschewed significant contact with U.S. democracy promoters, one of whom emphasized that "claiming engagement would be difficult given the IAF's protests over U.S. policies."[24]

---

22. Janine Clark, "Political Opposition in the Arab World: The Case Study of Jordan," forthcoming from United States Institute of Peace.

23. Mahmoud al Abed, "Muslim Scholars Debate Role of Women in Islam," *Jordan Times*, July 6, 2006.

24. Telephone interview, September 11, 2006.

Third, Jordan's political system is difficult to liberalize. The parliament remains extremely weak and political parties—excepting the IAF—are poorly developed, with little ability to represent popular aspirations and little integration into Jordan's political culture. Dominated by their leaders' personalities, the parties are typically devoid of any unifying ideology or specific policy-oriented platforms. As one democracy promoter described them, "At best, they are intellectual clubs with an Amman address. Essentially there is the government and the Islamists, and a desert in between."[25] Promoters thus must help to create key democratic building blocks from scratch to develop political alternatives to the IAF.

Political apathy in Jordan is also quite high. As one analyst explained, "The regime's Achilles heel is the feeble bond of trust between most of the citizens and state."[26] In a September 2005 IRI public-opinion poll, more than 90 percent of those surveyed did not believe that current political parties represented their aspirations.[27] Instead, politics is driven largely by tribal affiliations.

Nonetheless, NDI has developed a meaningful working relationship with al-Wasat, and as indicators above suggest, albeit vaguely, al-Wasat appears to have benefited from the interaction. It appears to have greater potential to develop a grassroots network as well as an enhanced capacity to cooperate with secular parties.

The 2007 parliamentary elections will test al-Wasat's political development. Democracy promoters are hoping that the party will win parliamentary seats, a clear indicator of success. Perhaps more important, however, al-Wasat may be able to counter the jihadist Islam that continues to threaten Jordan's political development by offering a moderate counter-ideology to violent extremism. The party is already a foil to the IAF's staunch social conservatism and opposition to the government. Still, more time and assistance will be needed for the party to grow and mature.

Yemen

Path to Reform. Yemen's path to reform has been dogged by widespread poverty, high illiteracy rates, and endemic corruption. Significant democratic reforms were implemented in the 1990 unification of North and South Yemen, including the legalization of opposition parties, creation of an independent electoral system, and expanded press freedoms. Parliamentary elections were held in 1993. However, Yemen's democratic opening was marred by numerous setbacks, capped in 2001 by a presidential consolida-

---

25. Telephone interview, September 11, 2006.

26. International Crisis Group, "The Challenge of Political Reform: Jordanian Democratization and Regional Instability," Middle East Briefing no. 10, October 8, 2003, p. 2.

27. Public Opinion Poll Unit, *Democracy in Jordan* (Amman: Center for Strategic Studies, 2005), p. 10.

tion of power that amended the constitution to extend both parliamentary and presidential terms. The president also gained new powers to dissolve the parliament and extended his control over the legislature by enlarging the president-appointed upper house.

In September 2006, in an election questioned by observers, Ali Abdullah Saleh remained as president, lengthening his rule to nearly three decades. Yemen's short-term prospects for democratic reform remain dim, but democracy advocates still view the presidential race—which featured a genuine opposition candidate backed by a secular-Islamist pro-reform coalition—as a potential step toward greater political opening. Observers are now focusing on whether the opposition, particularly the powerful Islah party, with its strong grassroots base, can be a political counterweight to the regime and agitator for democratic reform.

Islah: Yemen's Principal Islamist Party. The Yemeni Assembly for Reform, known popularly as Islah, was founded in 1990. Its roots and spiritual core lie in Yemen's Muslim Brotherhood, which was established in the early 1960s. Led by one of Yemen's most influential tribal leaders, Sheikh Abdullah Hussein al-Ahmar, the Islah party is more of a loose coalition of tribal and religious elements than a political party. Its membership includes people associated with the Muslim Brotherhood, pious conservatives attached to Yemen's religious institutes, and key segments of the tribal population. Islah's base, considered the fastest growing in Yemen, is young and angry with the status quo. As 40 percent of Yemenis live below the poverty line, the party mobilizes its popular support by opposing widespread government corruption and the lack of basic public services.

Islah initially was allied with the government and still has tribal ties to the president. However, beginning in the late 1990s, it spearheaded opposition to the government's encroachment on Yemen's nascent democratic reforms. During the 2003 parliamentary elections—marred by widespread irregularities—the ruling General Popular Congress (GPC) gained 225 of 301 seats while Islah won only 46 seats. Nonetheless, the Islamist party had the greatest number of seats among opposition parties. The Yemeni Socialist Party (YSP), the other principal opposition group, won only 7 seats.

Islah's platform is socially conservative, seeking "social reform in all fields of life on the basis of Islam,"[28] and the party emphasizes that its commitment to reform and democratic governance is bound by Islamic laws. However, Islah's approach to reform is modern, calling for enhanced political pluralism, an independent judiciary, and the peaceful transfer of power.

---

28. Ahmed A. Hazam al-Yemeni, *The Dynamic of Democratisation—Political Parties in Yemen* (Bonn: Friedrich Ebert Stiftung, 2003), p. 45.

Today, Islah is the only opposition party with broad grassroots appeal. It has an extremely sophisticated organizational structure, with a strong presence at the national, provincial, and local levels. To advocate for democratic reforms, it has joined forces with secular parties, principally the YSP; in November 2005, Islah presented a comprehensive reform platform as part of the Joint Meeting Parties (JMP), a coalition of six opposition parties. The program calls for a parliamentary system with diminished executive powers, an independent judiciary, improved electoral laws, and the depoliticization of the military. It is an important milestone for cross-party cooperation, though skeptics point to differences among the parties as an inherent weakness in Yemen's reform movement.[29]

Islah's members break down generally into reformers and hardliners. The reform faction occupies the party's middle and upper echelons of leadership and exerts the most influence on Islah's policy positions. Reformers in the party typically hail from Yemen's intelligentsia; they are editors, journalists, or technocrats in government and business.

Among hardliners, Sheikh Abd al-Majid al Zindani has been considered by some Islah's spiritual guide. He is the president of al-Iman University and, until February 2007, headed Islah's Shura Council. Zindani's more doctrinaire approach appeals to Islah's conservative base, though he is reportedly marginal to the inner workings of the party. Zindani is deeply opposed to engagement with the West and often criticizes moderates within the party for their ties to Western organizations. He represents Islah's hardline membership, many of them veterans of the Afghan war of the 1980s; some analysts argue that without Islah, the veterans might have continued on the path of violent extremism.[30] Concerned by Zindani's radicalism and possible links to al-Qaeda, the U.S. government labeled Zindani a "specially designated global terrorist" in February 2004 and has pressured the Yemeni government to extradite him to the United States.[31] Islah party members voted Zindani off the Shura Council in February 2007, but also urged the Yemeni government to pressure Washington to remove him from its list of global terrorists.

Yemen has a deeply rooted tradition of Islamist extremism, but an International Crisis Group report asserts that Islah itself "plays a mediating role between the state and the country's more conservative elements." The report also describes Sheikh Abdullah as "far more a traditional tribal leader and republican hero than Islamist ideologue" and asserts that there

29. Ana Echague, "Yemen," in *Strategies for Democratic Change: Assessing the Global Response*, eds. Ted Piccone and Richard Youngs, pp. 151–176 (Washington, DC: The Democracy Project, 2006).

30. Echague, "Yemen," p. 9.

31. Gregory Johnsen, "Profile of Sheikh Abd al-Majid Zindani," *Terrorism Monitor* vol. 4, no. 7 (April 6, 2006), available at www.jamestown.org.

are two principal streams of Yemeni Islamism: "members of Islah who opt to participate in the system and the radical groups that oppose the Yemeni state as well as the West."[32]

NDI Programming. The IRI does not conduct programming in Yemen. The NDI began working in Yemen in 1993 and opened its field office in 1997. NDI programming centers on political-party development, parliamentary strengthening, and women's participation. The institute also provides election-monitoring training and support and operates a tribal conflict–resolution program. The NDI's political-party training focuses on message development, recruitment, and constituent outreach. Its parliamentary-strengthening component seeks to identify reform-minded members of the parliament and strengthen their core skills. The women's programming aims to increase national and political-party support for women candidates and provide them with campaigning skills.

Engagement with Islah. The NDI has engaged with Islah through all three of its programming components and in elections preparations and monitoring. The institute works exclusively with moderates in the party, as Islah hardliners remain adamantly opposed to the party's ties to Western organizations. The NDI's chief representative in Sanaa meets regularly with Islah's secretary general, deputy, and other leaders. NDI staff also meets regularly with mid-level party officials. NDI staff in Yemen underscored "the endless phone calls and meetings that overall make a real difference. Trainings simply open the door for contact. A tremendous amount of follow-up, advice, and strategizing goes on beyond the formal training programs. It is here that we may in fact have the greatest impact."[33] NDI representatives noted that, compared with other political parties participating in their trainings, Islah was better organized and had a greater capacity to affect the reform movement.

Cross-Party Cooperation. A crucial part of the NDI's work centers on building relations between opposition party leaders and fostering secular-Islamist cooperation on reform. The NDI uses interparty dialogue to advance the reform agenda, actively supporting the aforementioned JMP, a group of six opposition parties including Islah that has pushed for greater democratic reform and political opening. Founded in 2002, the JMP is essentially a collaborative effort between Islah and the YSP, an ardently secular party. The parties have worked together on a number of process-related issues, such as electoral law reform. The NDI helped to bring the parties

32. Johnsen, "Profile," p. 9.

33. Telephone interview, July 3, 2006.

together and has hosted numerous JMP meetings and sponsored Islah and YSP delegates on a number of trips abroad. The NDI asserts that the parties can more easily forge important bonds by meeting outside of Yemen.

Results of Engagement. Islah has worked closely with the NDI for several years, and certain areas, such as encouraging women's political participation and cross-party cooperation, have yielded tangible results. However, NDI's parliamentary work with Islah does not appear to have had a significant effect. NDI's limited success with regard to parliamentary programs could reflect the parliament's relative weakness. Similarly, it is difficult to measure the effect of engaging Islah by the party's performance at the local level where municipal councils are weak. The local councils were only established in 2001. They have little revenue and councilors have minimal training. Gauging Islah's response to NDI efforts, therefore, may best be accomplished through examining its capacity for Islamist-secular cooperation, level of such interaction, and potential for greater moderation.

Islamist-Secular Cooperation. The JMP is perhaps the most resounding success of the NDI's work in Yemen. The Islamist-secular reform coalition began as a weak and ineffectual alliance, wracked by division. It has become a serious advocate for reform that might be an effective counterweight to the government. The JMP's two primary members, Islah and the YSP realized that cooperation was essential to opposing the government's power. As Abdul Wahab al-Anisi, Deputy Secretary General of Islah explained, "We subordinated our ideological agendas to the one thing we all had in common, which was a realization that political reform was a necessity if we were to save democracy in Yemen and stop the country's descent into endemic corruption."[34]

The JMP members' reform platform serves as a model for bridging the gap between secularists and Islamists throughout the Arab world. The JMP also pressured the government to amend electoral procedures before the September 2006 elections and agreed on a joint presidential candidate whose campaign offered Yemenis a genuine reform alternative to President Saleh and the country's first true multicandidate presidential election.

The NDI did not create the JMP, but members of both Islah and the YSP have commend NDI for its advice and training, noting the institute's important contributions to their joint efforts. In particular, the NDI has focused on promoting the coalition's reform platform. In early 2006, soon after the platform's publication, the NDI met with several JMP representatives to translate elements of the program into a concrete election platform. In addition, the institute provided training on message development and

34. Faiza Saleh Ambah, "Technocrat Recasts Yemen's Presidential Race, Political Future," *Washington Post*, September 20, 2006.

communication methods that JMP members could use in local election campaigns.

Level of Interaction. The NDI appears to have established excellent working relations with Islah. NDI staff meet regularly with Islah members at all levels, which seems to have fostered a well-established sense of trust between moderate Islah reformers and the institute. Again, directly linking a strong working relationship to the ideological and programmatic emphases of Islah's leaders is difficult, but the progress toward democratic reforms—however tentative at times—likely owes something to the depth and professionalism of Islah's relationship with the NDI and the party's openness to trainings and other activities. The effect of face-to-face meetings and regular personal contact should not be underestimated even though it is difficult to quantify.

Potential for Evolution. Here the record is mixed. Certainly, several of Islah's policy positions can be taken as evidence of moderation. The party voted to oust Sheikh Zindani from its Shura Council and Islah's help in drafting the JMP reform platform, which calls for substantive democratic reforms, suggests that the party's moderate wing may have gained the upper hand. The reform platform's demands include: the peaceful rotation of power, popular empowerment, and an end to corruption. NDI representatives believe that Islah's reform positions are not merely tactical directives to bring the party to power, but a potential shift in the party's ideological perspective.

At the same time, radical hardliners in the party, led by Zindani, continue to rail against the party's reformers and refuse to engage with Western organizations. NDI implementers acknowledge that Islah is clearly still an ideological religious party and caution that observers should not romanticize it. Concerns about Islah's ultimate intentions may be legitimate, and it remains to be seen whether the party's moderate or hardline faction will ultimately prevail. But in the short term, Islah offers the only real alternative to an increasingly authoritarian government.

Conclusions. NDI engagement with Islah has yielded important results, most notably in Islamist-secular cooperation on reform. The Yemen case study is an unparalleled success in this area. None of the other cases feature similar levels of cooperation between Islamists and secular parties. Given Yemen's precarious path toward reform, the JMP is critical to ensuring that sustained democratic opening remains on the agenda, and despite the government's attempts to sow dissent within the coalition, the opposition force already has begun to demonstrate its ability to oppose the government more coherently and forward its reform agenda. The Islamist-secular coalition appears to embody precisely the type of cooperation on reform that many observers deem necessary throughout the Arab world.

The NDI's continued engagement with Islah could also strengthen moderates within the Islamist party. As described by one U.S. democracy advocate, "The worst thing we can do is isolate the ideological roots of these movements so that they end up merely supporting and promoting the same ideals with no outside influence, no influx of fresh ideas. It is essential to introduce a new way of thinking."[35] Islah's moderation is by no means insured, but the party appears to offer a nonviolent, potentially democratic alternative to the radical Islamic extremism that is deeply embedded in Yemen's history and traditions. One democracy promoter noted that September 11 was a defining moment for Islah, as the party distanced itself from the terrorist attacks, calling them extreme and not representative of Islah's vision of Islam. Nonetheless, Yemen's tribalism and radicalism are serious challenges for moderates within Islah. Certainly, NDI assistance has helped moderates in their task, but the end result is by no means assured.

Final Conclusions

A number of broad strategic conclusions emerge from this examination of U.S. engagement with moderate Islamists in Morocco, Jordan, and Yemen. Not surprisingly, engagement has been most effective in countries where democratic reform is most deeply rooted and where government leadership has demonstrated genuine commitment to political opening. Opposition parties, both secular and Islamist, benefit from an open political space, especially a relatively independent parliament. Successful engagement also appears to correlate with the degree of the Islamist party's political sophistication and development, popular credibility, and openness to working with a U.S. organization.

In every case, U.S.-funded efforts to engage moderate Islamists resulted in strong working relationships, featuring regular contact between democracy promoters and Islamist-party partners and a strong reservoir of trust. Often, Islamist parties demonstrated great enthusiasm for and interest in democracy-promotion programs, though in nearly every case, anger over U.S. policies in the region—particularly regarding Iraq or the Palestinians—led to boycotts and disrupted engagement. Even during boycotts, however, informal ties and dialogue continued in most cases.

Of the three countries considered, Morocco appears to hold the greatest promise for U.S. engagement with moderate Islamists. A unique blend of factors, from the kingdom's steady reform trajectory to the PJD's sophistication, popular credibility, openness to working with U.S. organizations

35. Telephone interview, July 3, 2006.

combined to yield an interesting test case of Islamist moderation. Of course, it is difficult to determine the extent to which other factors affected the PJD's moderation, such as the May 2003 Casablanca terrorist attacks and pressure from the Ministry of Interior.

Meanwhile, Jordan and Yemen offer important though limited instances of success. In Yemen, the NDI's fostering of the JMP is laudable. Analysts and observers argue for the importance of such Islamist-secular alliances to engender moderation and pressure recalcitrant regimes to reform, and the Yemen case offers important insights to be emulated elsewhere.

As for Jordan, despite the disadvantage from the IAF's boycott of U.S. organizations, efforts to engage with al-Wasat are commendable. The party's recent arrival on the political scene and Jordan's tenuous political opening suggest slow progress at best, but U.S. efforts to strengthen the party may pay off in the long term. As the Arab world struggles with the larger battle of ideas being waged between violent extremism and moderation, an ideological compromise may have its roots in such an Islamist centrist movement.

Two final conclusions bear consideration. First, moderate Islamist parties are crucial to the U.S. strategy to promote democracy in the Arab world. The parties have proven their popular strength, ability to win free elections, and capacity to moderate. Such evolution requires close scrutiny, but fears of Islamist parties run amok and a repeat of an Iranian-style revolution elsewhere appear to be exaggerated. Instead, we should ask whether we could have democracy in the Arab world without Islamists. The arguments for engaging with them are powerful, as meaningful political participation appears to exert a moderating influence on Islamist parties. As one democracy advocate explained, "We will get nowhere with the Islamists by screaming at them from the outside. It is essential to work with them, train them, include women party members, strategize and engage in discussion. It is critical to expand their worldview."[36]

Second, U.S. engagement of moderate Islamists must be understood within a broader political context. The Arab world—and the larger Muslim world—is in the throes of an ideological battle to define the role of Islam in public life, and the threat of Islamist extremism has pervaded each of the three countries to varying degrees. Morocco and Jordan each suffered terrorist attacks, in which several innocent Muslim civilians perished. Meanwhile, Yemen—the ancestral homeland of Osama bin Laden—has been a crucible of Islamist militancy, with a number of violent extremist cells operating within the country. Moderate Islamist parties that reject violence and practice democratic ideals are an important counterweight to these forces, and could be crucial to developing an indigenous, forward-looking

36. Telephone interview, July 3, 2006.

counter-ideology that seeks to bring the Arab world into the twenty-first century, albeit on their own terms.

Policy Implications

- **Better analytical instruments to measure Islamist parties' transparency and ideological evolution—and the effectiveness of U.S.-funded training—must be developed.** Measuring moderation is inherently difficult, but a more rigorous approach to evaluating Islamist engagement programs is possible. Certainly, more intensive empirical research on the Islamist parties, their internal transparency, party platforms, policy positions, and public statements is in order. As Islamist parties gain offices at the local and national levels, discrete studies of their political behavior and policies while in office could gauge political tendencies and better measure the effectiveness of programming.
- **Political-party strengthening should be accompanied by institution building, particularly of national parliaments and municipal councils. Strengthening the rule of law is essential to any Islamist engagement strategy.** Parliaments and municipal councils are the arenas most frequently open to Islamist participation. Emasculated parliaments that are rubber stamps for ruling regimes are far less likely to promote political maturity and moderation among Islamist parties. Fears that Islamists could exploit political openness to gain power and overturn democratic change should be assuaged through establishing the rule of law and a system of checks and balances.
- **Islamist engagement activities should be expanded to professional syndicates and religious charitable organizations.** Islamist engagement strategies should look beyond focusing solely on political parties and seek to provide the same types of training to professional syndicates and NGOs, including Islamist charities. Professional syndicates are an important venue for political aspirations, often claiming membership in the tens of thousands. Over time, such associations have taken on increasingly political overtones and could be influential actors in the political arena. Yet many of these organizations suffer from opacity, corruption, and other problems. Broadening engagement of moderate Islamists to include professional syndicates, possibly even Islamist charities, is an untapped opportunity that deserves further exploration.

Conclusion:
Security, Reform, and Diplomacy Challenges Ahead

23

Islamist Political Power in Turkey: Challenges for Brussels and Washington

Steven A. Cook

Turkey is undergoing profound change. In the last two decades, Turkish society has become more complex and differentiated as a new class of politicians, entrepreneurs, and activists has emerged and accumulated political power. The *Adalet ve Kalkınma Parti* (Justice and Development Party, AKP), which was founded after a historic split within Turkey's Islamist movement in 2000, represents this new elite. Since 2002 the party has held an overwhelming majority in Turkey's legislature, the Grand National Assembly. With the end of President Ahmet Necdet Sezer's term in office in the spring of 2007, the AKP succeeded in electing one of its own, Abdullah Gül, president. For a party that did not even exist in 2000, it was impressive that by the end of 2007, AKP was firmly in control of the executive and legislative branches of government. There are elements of the Turkish government, notably the Turkish General Staff and the judiciary, that are deeply suspicious of the party and its intentions. The expression and success of Islamist power that AKP represents is nothing less than extraordinary in Turkey's officially secular political order.

The emergence of AKP as the most important nonmilitary actor in the Turkish political arena has generated an often heated national debate over, among other issues, the relationship between religion and state, the continued relevance of Kemalism, and the direction of Turkish foreign policy. The acceleration of Turkey's transition to democracy has been the most surprising development since AKP came to power in 2002. This is not to

---

Steven A. Cook, "Islamist Political Power in Turkey: Challenges for Brussels and Washington," in *The Challenge of Islamists for EU and US Policies: Conflict, Stability, and Reform,* eds. Muriel Asseburg and Daniel Brumberg, 23–28 (Research Paper no. 12, Stiftung Wissenchaft und Politik German Institute for International and Security Affairs, Berlin, 2007). Reprinted with permission.

suggest that the party harbors an antidemocratic agenda. Hardly the Islamists of Hamas, Hezbollah, or even the Muslim Brotherhood, AKP's platform reveals that one of its primary goals is to forge a more democratic, modern, and pluralist Turkey. Indeed, at the time the party gained control of the parliament, the Turkish political system featured a range of authoritarian institutions and an influential military establishment intent on protecting the political order that Mustafa Kemal founded in 1924. In the 47 years since it first seized control of the country from a democratically elected government, the military undertook three additional *coups d'état*. Indeed, the combination of the structure of Turkish politics and the historical record indicated that AKP should have had difficulty pursuing its professed goals of political and economic reform.

Yet there was a new factor in Turkish politics that provided both an impetus for change and a favorable environment for AKP to embark on a wide-ranging project of reform in relative safety from the predatory politics of the General Staff: the European Union (EU). To be sure, Turkey has been an associate member of what was the European Economic Community since signing the Ankara agreement in 1963. Yet when combined with the AKP's objectives, the EU's 1999 invitation to Turkey to become a candidate for full membership had a dynamic effect on Turkish politics. The incentive of EU membership altered the interests of Turkey's Islamists—who had traditionally been wary of and at times hostile to Turkey's Western vocation—and constrained the ability of the military to act. As a result, AKP was able to lead a coalition of conservative Muslims, big business, urban elites, and average Turks who, for a variety of interests, all supported the EU membership process. Between early 2003 and late 2004, the AKP-controlled parliament undertook seven reform packages—including measures that make it more difficult to close down political parties, enhance personal and political freedoms, and rein in (albeit incompletely) the General Staff—intended to bring Turkey's political system in line with European norms and standards.

Obstacles and problems remain before Turkey's democratic transition is complete. Still, there is no denying that Turkey is a different country from what it was five, ten, and fifteen years ago. To be sure, not all of the achievements are linked to the Justice and Development Party. For example, Turkey's impressive economic growth since 2002 has everything to do with the economic reform project that Kemal Derviş, Minister of Economic Affairs in the Ecevit government, guided before AKP came to power. It is important to note, however, that the impressive array of political changes since 2003 have been the work of the AKP. The party is responsible for forging a more democratic, more modern, more pluralist Turkey, thereby moving the country closer to the European Union and within reach of Atatürk's dream of "raising Turkey to the level of civilization." As positive as these changes are, they nevertheless present both Europe and the United States with critical, yet different policy challenges.

Europe: Confronting the Unexpected

It is fair to say that at the 1999 meeting of the European Council in Helsinki, none of the Europeans actually expected Turkey to be able to pursue far-reaching institutional change in such a short period of time. Now that Turkey and the EU are involved in formally negotiating Ankara's membership, Europe is confronted with the vexing question of whether it wants to integrate a country of 74 million people who are overwhelmingly Muslim and, on average, significantly poorer than most EU citizens.

Although the European Commission recommended that Europe formally begin negotiating Turkey's entry into the Union in October 2004, Ankara's transition is not complete. The Europeans are correct to point to a series of economic, foreign policy, and domestic political issues that raise important questions about Turkey's candidacy. On the economic front, beyond the well-developed and westernized cities of the Aegean coast and the capital Ankara, Turkey is a largely rural, agrarian, undeveloped country.[1] The Europeans fear that Turkish membership will lead to mass migration of Turks into other EU member states.

On the foreign policy front, the continuing conflict in Cyprus is a primary source of friction between Ankara and Brussels. Since AKP came to power, it has consistently sought to take a more flexible position regarding the conflict than previous governments. Prime Minister Recep Tayyip Erdogan and then-Foreign Minister Abdullah Gül counseled Turkish Cypriots and their leaders to accept the so-called Annan Plan when it was put to a referendum in the spring of 2004. In the event, 66 percent of Turkish Cypriots voted for the plan whereas three quarters of Greek Cypriots voted "no." From the perspective of Ankara, since then the EU has failed to live up to commitments made to Turkish Cypriots that would have helped them break their international isolation. This has thus led to a hardening of the Turkish position on Cyprus. As a result, Ankara refuses to fulfill its own commitments to the EU by barring Greek Cypriot air and sea traffic from Turkish ports.

On domestic politics, Europe maintains serious reservations about what Brussels perceives to be institutional shortcomings that compromise the quality of Turkey's democratic practices. For example, Article 301 of the penal code limits freedom of expression and has been used to target those who question long-held orthodoxies related to Turkey's Kurdish minority and Turkish culpability for the killing of 1.5 million Armenians in Anatolia during the collapse of the Ottoman Empire. Well-known figures such as

1. Turkey's GDP per capita in 2006 was US$5,400 as opposed to US$29,000 per capita CDP for EU countries.

Turkish Nobel laureate Orhan Pamuk and the French-Turkish writer Elif Şafak have been prosecuted for "insulting Turkishness" under the provisions of Article 301. In addition, Europeans are concerned about the continuing human rights abuses in Turkish police stations and prisons.

There is also the matter of Kurdish cultural rights. In 2004, Turkey formally lifted its ban on radio and television broadcasts in Kurdish dialects as well as its prohibition on education in Kurdish. While Kurds have access to an array of television programs in their language, including on state-run Turkish Radio and Television, problems remain in access to Kurdish education. State education bureaucrats have used a sudden meticulous adherence to legal measures, such as fire code violations, in an effort to shut down schools providing instruction about Kurdish culture in Kurdish language, thereby achieving political ends by alternative means.

Finally, the EU continues to criticize the role of the military establishment in Turkey's political system. The Turks deserve credit for making significant changes that provide parliament with greater oversight over the military budget and downgrade the influence of the once seemingly all-powerful military-dominated *Milli Güvenlik Kurulu* (National Security Council). Yet, the Turkish General Staff retains the capacity to influence politics and maintains its self-endowed right to intervene directly in the political arena should the officers deem it necessary. Continuing problems in civil-military relations were on full display in April 2007 when the military interfered in Turkey's scheduled presidential election. The General Staff, who issued a public ultimatum to the AKP government stating that there would be consequences should its candidate Abdullah Gül be elected, precipitated a constitutional crisis and intensified the perennial *kulturkampf* between Turkey's secularists and Islamists. Gül was ultimately elected president after a four-month delay and a demonstration of AKP's political power when it scored 47 percent of the vote in parliamentary elections held in July. Nevertheless, the military's actions in April raised real concerns about backsliding in Turkey's reform drive.

All of these concerns are valid, yet at the same time there are plausible resolutions to each of these issues. The greater problem, and the one left largely unsaid or to be communicated only indirectly, is the issue of faith. The central challenge for the EU is answering the first-order question: Is Europe a Christian club or is it a union of countries that share common values, norms, and principles? To date, Europeans have not been able to agree upon an answer to this question. Nevertheless, it seems that most people within the EU, as well as the leaders of some of its most influential states (France's Nicolas Sarkozy and Germany's Angela Merkel, in particular), believe that there is no place for an overwhelmingly Muslim country in Europe.

There is no polling data suggesting that Europeans oppose Turkey's entry into the EU on outright religious grounds, though there are a variety of proxy indicators to conclude (as many Turks have done) that this is the case. For example, France plans to hold a referendum on Turkey's accession when the time comes for Ankara to sign an Accession Treaty—a measure that does not apply to any other EU applicant. In addition, a number of former members of the Soviet bloc, such as Slovakia, Romania, and Bulgaria, whose economic development lags Turkey and whose democratic traditions are suspect, have jumped ahead of Turkey in line to become members of Europe. Finally, the failed 2005 referendums in France and the Netherlands on the proposed EU constitutional treaty were largely regarded as a way of voicing the public's opposition to Turkey's membership.

There are three clear consequences of what seems to be Europe's rejection of Turkey on religious grounds. First, for the larger Muslim world, but particularly the Arab world, Turkey is a test case for how the West deals with the accumulation of Islamist political power in a Muslim society. If Turkey is left literally at the gates of Vienna, people and governments in the Middle East will perceive this as yet additional evidence that the West is hostile to Islam and Muslims. Second, the EU has been the anchor of Turkish reform. Given the structure of the Turkish political system, it is unlikely that the Turks could have undertaken significant reforms beginning in 2003 on their own. Indeed, Turkish leaders were very clear that they were pushing successive reform packages through the Grand National Assembly in order to meet European requirements. Without the incentives for change that the EU provides, the necessary widening and deepening of Turkish democracy may not occur. Finally, it is likely that Turkey's failure to join the EU will produce an angry, insular, and nationalist society. This is not to suggest that Ankara will break its historic ties with NATO, but that it will be increasingly difficult for Europe (and the US) to achieve its interests in the Balkans, Caucuses, Middle East, and Central Asia without a Turkey that believes it is a full partner with the West.

The United States: Failing to Perceive Change

The challenge for Washington emerging from Turkey is of an altogether different sort than the issues that Brussels confronts. Turkish foreign policy is changing, though it is less a function of the AKP and its ostensible Islamist agenda than three critical developments in and around Turkey and the international system over the last 15 years: first, the US invasion of Iraq has fundamentally altered the geostrategic environment in Turkey's region; second, the increasing recognition that most of Europe does not want Turkey within the EU has led Turks to think either about strategic alternatives or to place emphasis on Turkey as a great power itself; and finally, with the disappearance of the Soviet threat, the primary issue that bound Turkey and the US together during the Cold War no longer exists. These structural changes, combined with the promises of greater policymaking transparency that AKP made when it came to office, have resulted in a more "normal" Turkish foreign policy.

Not only does public opinion matter more in Turkish foreign policy, Turkey's interests will also no longer necessarily coincide with those of the US. To be sure, Ankara and Washington share broad common goals in the stability of Iraq, Middle East peace, reconciliation in the Balkans, and energy policy. At the same time, however, the "normalization" of Turkish foreign policy will result in policies that the United States does not like. For example, just as Washington is seeking to isolate Tehran and Damascus, Ankara is developing ties with both countries. Indeed, the impetus that regime change in Iraq provided to Kurdish nationalism—an existential threat from Ankara's perspective—is driving the development of relations between Ankara and two previously troublesome neighbors, Tehran and Damascus, both of whom are also worried about a possible independent Kurdistan in northern Iraq. A more immediate challenge to all three countries is the problem of Kurdish terrorism. Turkey is under the most acute threat as the Kurdistan Workers' Party (PKK) has increased the intensity of its attacks against Turkish forces along Turkey's border with Iraq. Both Syria and Iran have expressed solidarity with Turkey should Ankara decide to pursue PKK terrorists into Iraqi territory. The possibility of a Turkish military incursion is a grave concern for Washington, which fears a Turkish operation could undermine the relative stability of northern Iraq.

There is a tendency among some observers to attribute changes in Ankara's foreign policy to AKP's roots in Turkey's Islamist movement, specifically the *Milli Görüş* (National Outlook) movement, which sought closer Turkish relations with the Muslim world at the expense of Turkey's Western orientation. This analysis prejudices the ostensible Islamism of the AKP. Given the structural changes in international politics that coincide roughly with the two wars against Iraq, it is clear that any Turkish government would be pursuing policies similar to those of the AKP. Moreover, if AKP were pursuing an Islamist agenda, it would not be seeking Turkey's entry into the EU.

Ultimately, Turkey's foreign policy is coming more into line with Atatürk's maxim of "Peace at home, peace in the world," which seeks good relations with all of its neighbors regardless of the character of their regimes. The great challenge for Washington is appreciating why this change in Turkish foreign policy is taking place while crafting a policy that takes advantage of the areas where the US shares interests with Turkey. Ankara literally sits at the geographic center of many of Washington's pressing foreign policy concerns. Turkey can play an important role in helping Washington achieve its interests, but only if the United States recognizes that as Turkey comes into its own as a political, economic, and diplomatic player, there will be differences between the two allies.

24

Thwarting Afghanistan's Insurgency: A Pragmatic Approach Toward Peace and Reconciliation

Mohammad Masoom Stanekzai

Afghanistan is at a crucial stage of transition. The Taliban, with sanctuaries and a support base in Pakistan's Federally Administered Tribal Areas (FATA), has grown stronger, relying on a wide network of foreign fighters and Pakistani extremists who operate freely across the Afghan-Pakistani border. As a result, violence in Afghanistan has been escalating for the past two years. More than 14,500 people, including hundreds of foreign troops, have been killed there since the Taliban began its comeback in 2006. Recent statistics suggest that the situation is only getting worse. June 2008 represented the deadliest month for foreign troops in Afghanistan since the 2001 fall of the Taliban and the second month in which casualties exceeded those in Iraq.

Complicating matters, the insurgency is not a pure, genuine national insurgency that is simply fighting against occupying forces or the government, and the Taliban is not the only source of violence and unrest. Other groups, including Hizb-i Islami, armed criminals, and drug networks linked closely with illegal armed groups, as well as corrupt elements inside and outside the government, contribute to the country's security concerns. Additionally, a record increase in opium production provides up to 40 percent of the Taliban's total financial support and contributes dramatically to corruption. If the current levels of violence and poppy production are not contained, both the government and international security forces will lose further support among the people, providing more space for the insurgents and terrorist groups to operate (see figures 1 and 2).

To date, the Afghanistan government and the international community have typically responded to the violence by being reactive rather than

---

Mohammad Masoom Stanekzai, "Thwarting Afghanistan's Insurgency: A Pragmatic Approach toward Peace and Reconciliation," Special Report 212 (Washington, DC: USIP, 2008).

Figure 1. Average number of violent incidents per month, 2003–2008

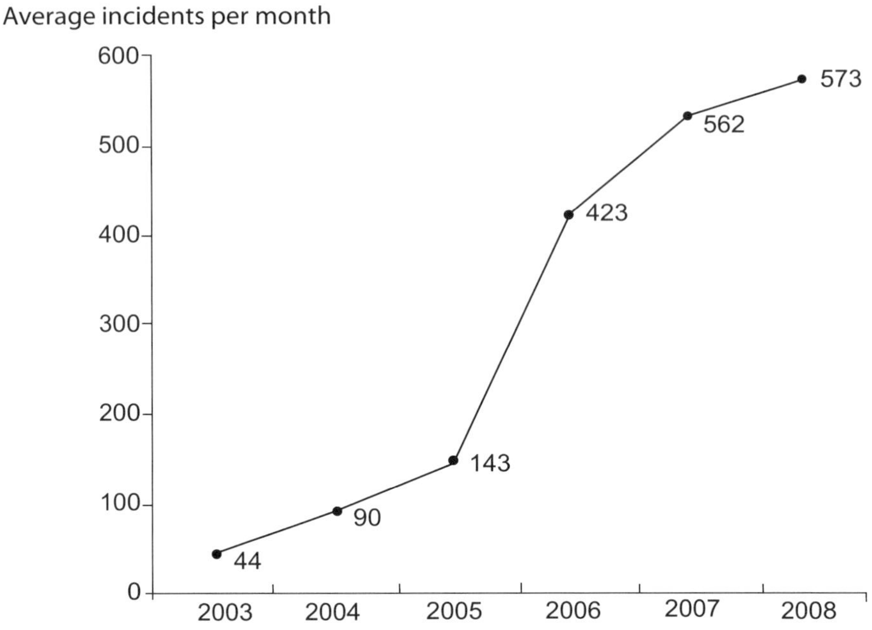

Sources: Afghanistan's Ministries of Defense and Interior, the National Directorate of Security, and the UN Department of Safety and Security.

Figure 2. Opium poppy cultivation and production levels, 2002–2007

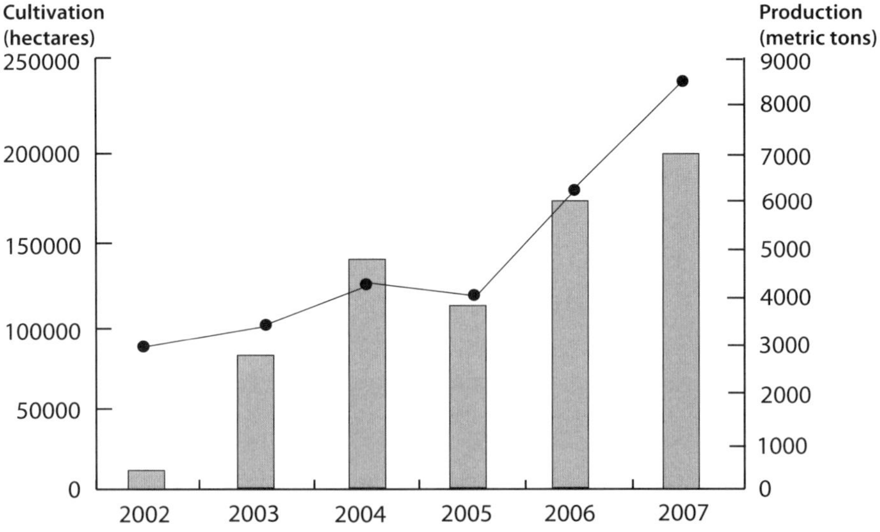

Sources: UN Office of Drugs and Crime and Afghanistan's Ministry of Counter Narcotics.

proactive, as evidenced by the gradual increase of the International Security Assistance Force (ISAF) in Afghanistan in response to rising security threats and a general lack of contingency planning. Although military and peacekeeping operations are absolutely vital for creating a secure environment conducive to state building and reconstruction, present trends raise serious doubts about whether military solutions alone will be able to defeat the insurgency and stem the expansion of terrorism. In short, reconciliation must also be a key element of stabilization operations in Afghanistan.

Although the danger that Afghanistan could once again become a failed state is real, the chance to stabilize Afghanistan is not lost: broad support is emerging for an effective national reconciliation and negotiation program that will end the bloodshed. But what might such a program look like, and how might it succeed when past attempts have failed? This report represents an attempt to answer these important questions and to provide an approach for encouraging reconciliation among Afghans in the name of stabilization and peace. It begins by arguing that an opportunity exists for reconciliation and then explores the various challenges to reconciliation, including Afghanistan's unique sources of conflict and wide spectrum of insurgent, terrorist, and criminal groups. Next, it briefly examines the government's past attempts at reconciliation with the Taliban and then offers a pragmatic framework for overcoming the country's various sources of conflict and promoting reconciliation among the conflict's key actors. The report concludes with a series of recommendations for the Afghan government and its international partners acting in support of the country's peace and reconciliation.

An Opportunity for Reconciliation

Although Afghanistan's insurgents have proved adept at exploiting local fissures, creating horror, and attacking high-value targets, Afghanistan has witnessed positive progress on numerous fronts since 2002. At present, multiple factors suggest that the time is ripe for a reconciliatory process to begin (see table 1).

First, Afghans are tired of long years of conflict and the majority are willing to support a peace process, but they are uncertain and afraid due to past experience. If reassured and mobilized, they will stand firmly and support the current democratic process as they did when the Taliban was first ousted. Indeed, Afghans prefer the current democratic process over Taliban rule, but they are frustrated by the government's corruption and incompetence in delivering basic services, especially security, jobs, and justice.

Second, the Taliban is not enjoying the same level of support that it enjoyed when it first emerged as a political and military power. This is partly because of the Taliban's increasing indifference to civilian casualties

Table 1. Progress achieved in Afghanistan, 2002–2008

S/No	Description	2002	2008	Notes
1	Afghan National Army	1700 (estimate)	70,000	Field strength of 50,000
2	Afghan National Police	50,000 (estimate)	79,910	In 2002, none were properly trained, equipped, or paid. At present, 20,000 are properly trained and paid, and are better equipped but still lagging behind the army
3	Afghan Military Forces	100,000	Decommissioned	64,000 ex-combatants reintegrated
4	International Security Forces and Provincial Reconstruction Teams	1 PRT 4,900 ISAF troops	52,700 ISAF troops 26 PRTs	Deployment has been expanded to all regions with 26 PRTs now covering all 34 provinces
5	Illegal Armed Groups	1,800 groups (estimate)	342 groups disbanded	64,000 weapons and 27,000 tons of ammunition have been collected.
6	Access to Health Care	9%	85%	Percentage of the population covered by basic services
7	Education	3.7 million children enrolled	5.7 million enrolled	In 2005 there were almost 11.8 million children under the age of 15
8	Rural Development	0	32,000	Number of villages that have benefited from development projects
9	Infrastructure development	Mostly destroyed	13,150 km	Combined length of roads that have been rehabilitated, improved, or built
10	Natural Resources Management	13% and 8%	23% and 12%	Percentage of population with access to safe drinking water and adequate sanitation facilities, respectively. Three million citizens have benefited from rural water and sanitation projects. Sanitation facilities in urban areas are provided by connections to public sewers or by household systems. In rural areas, pit privies, pour-flush latrines, septic tanks, and communal toilets are considered adequate.
11	Economy and Trade		70%	Percentage increase in income per capita
12	Media and Telecom	5%	75%	Percentage of the population that has access to communication

Sources:

1. UNAMA, "International Conference in Support of Afghanistan: Paris, 24 May, 4 June, 12 June 2008," www.unama-afg.org/news/_londonconf/_factsheet/paris-con-factsheet.pdf.
2. Ibid.
3. *Afghanistan: Getting Disarmament Back on Track*, Asia Briefing No. 35 (Kabul/Brussels: International Crisis Group, February 23, 2005), www.crisisgroup.org/home/index.cfm?id=3290.
4. U.S. Department of State, "Afghanistan: Provincial Reconstruction Teams," January 27, 2006, www.state.gov/p/sca/rls/fs/2006/60031.htm; NATO, "ISAF Regional Commands and PRT Locations," June 20, 2008, www.nato.int/isaf/docu/epub/pdf/isaf_placemat.pdf; and Kenneth Katzman, *Afghanistan: Current Issues and U.S. Policy*, Rep.No. RL30588 (Washington, DC: Congressional Research Service, December 3, 2002), available at http://digital.library.unt.edu/govdocs/crs/.
5. UN News Centre, "Afghanistan: More Illegal Armed Groups Disbanded with UN Help," July 24, 2008, www.un.org/apps/news/story.asp?newsid=27472&cr=afghanistan&cr1=.
6. U.S. Agency for International Development, "USAID Assistance to Afghanistan, 2002–2008," March 27, 2008, www.usaid.gov/press/factsheets/2008/fs080327.html.
7. UNAMA, www.unama-afg.org/news/_londonconf/_factsheet/paris-con-factsheet.pdf; and UN Development Programme (UNDP), *Afghanistan: National Human Development Report 2004—Security With a Human Face. Centre for Policy and Human Development (UNDP, 2005)*, available at www.cphd.af/nhdr/nhdr04/nhdr04.html.
8. UNAMA, www.unama-afg.org/news/_londonconf/_factsheet/paris-con-factsheet.pdf.
9. Ibid.
10. UN Children's Fund (UNICEF), "Annex 3: Progress on Access to Clean Drinking Water, 2002), www.unicef.org/media/files/progesscleanwater.doc; UNAMA, www.unama-afg.org/news/_londonconf/_factsheet/paris-con-factsheet.pdf; Worldwater.org, "Table 4. Access to Sanitation by Country, 1970 to 2002," www.worldwater.org/data20062007/Table4.pdf; UNICEF, "UNICEF Humanitarian Action Update Afghanistan, 17 January 2008," available at www.reliefweb.int/rw/rwfiles2008.nsf/filesbyrwdocunidfilename/ammf-7-axh7n-full_report.pdf/$file/full_report.pdf.
11. UNAMA. www.unama-afg.org/news/_londonconf/_factsheet/paris-con-factsheet.pdf.
12. Ibid.

Figure 3. Annual economic growth rate, 2002–2008 (in percentages)

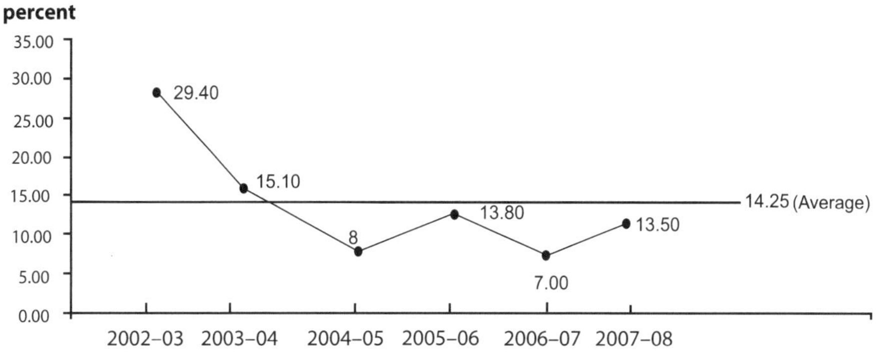

Sources: Afghanistan's Ministry of Finance, Afghanistan National Development Strategy, and World Bank.

and partly because Afghans are once again getting frustrated with its free-market approach to war in which it enlists criminals to conduct operations in its name.

Third, Afghan national institutions, especially the Afghan National Army (ANA), are gaining in strength and slowly becoming trusted. If further strengthened, the army has the potential to gradually replace ISAF. Such a strategy will put an end to widespread speculation about a long-term Western occupation that insurgents presently use to advantage in their propaganda.

Fourth, for more than six years Afghanistan's average annual economic growth rate has been above the ten-year annual target of nine percent recommended in the report Securing Afghanistan's Future, which was presented at the 2004 Berlin Conference on Afghanistan (see figure 3). This is welcome news given that more than 60 percent of the Afghan population is below twenty years old, comprising a generation that lost virtually all opportunity for education and risks suffering from massive unemployment.

Fifth, growing regional fears about the threat posed by extremist militants means it may now be possible to develop a region-wide consensus for dealing with the threat: China is worried about the Uighurs; Uzbekistan about the Islamic Movement of Uzbekistan (headed by Namangani); Russia about Chechen rebel groups (all linked with al Qaeda); Iran about the Taliban and al Qaeda; and Pakistan about the expansion of criminality and insecurity and the further loss of control over its border areas.

Sixth, although members of Pakistan's Directorate for Inter-Services Intelligence (ISI) and military continue to support the Taliban and al Qaeda, Pakistan's recent election represented a vote of no confidence in extremist groups. Indeed, if Pakistan does not help stabilize Afghanistan by taming groups in FATA, a collection of seven agencies and six "frontier districts" that share 250 miles of mountainous border with Afghanistan, it may ultimately face the same situation that Afghanistan suffers from today. Both Afghanistan and Pakistan are increasingly burdened with security challenges that divert significant resources and energy from much-needed services and economic development initiatives.

Seventh, it was recently announced that United Front opposition leader and former Afghan president Burhanuddin Rabani was in contact with the Taliban and wanted to negotiate with it. In the past, United Front leaders were equivocally against any negotiation with insurgents. This announcement demonstrates a growing consensus among Afghans to reach out to groups that engage in political violence against the state.

Eighth, the NATO Summit in Bucharest in April 2008 and the Paris donor conference in June 2008 highlighted the strong commitment of the international community to peace and stability in Afghanistan, sending positive signals and boosting confidence and morale inside Afghanistan.

Challenges to Reconciliation

Despite the favorable developments that may make the present an opportune moment for reconciliation, the various sources of conflict and the multitude of insurgent and terrorist groups within Afghanistan will present formidable challenges to any reconciliation process.

Principal Sources of Conflict

Conflict in Afghanistan springs from several sources and can be classified into two broad categories, the first of which can be broken down along real-world geographical lines—regional, national, and local—and the second along the more abstract lines of religion, ethnicity, and family.

Regional Sources of Conflict. Afghanistan is at the center of numerous regional disputes, including its territorial dispute with Pakistan over the Durand Line, Pakistan and India's territorial dispute over Kashmir, and potential future water-related disputes with neighboring countries. In this complex regional environment, many of Afghanistan's neighbors are trying to increase their influence in Afghanistan to promote their own security and economic interests. In the process, they have abused Afghanistan's ethnic and religious diversity by supporting one group over another for their own ends. Pakistan, for example, has used and continues to use the Taliban and the militias in FATA as a strategic asset to secure its strategic interests in Afghanistan, to help it reestablish its position as the key regional player, and to receive more aid from the United States. Similarly, Iran has supported Shia groups in Afghanistan to further its influence there.

National Sources of Conflict. Throughout Afghanistan's modern history, the conflict between modernizers—principally urban, educated elites—and conservatives—principally rural, illiterate villagers led by ulema and tribal leaders—has continually led to revolts against the state. In 1929, King Ammanullah was overthrown after embarking on a rapid modernization program based on the Turkish model. In 1979, the modernizing reforms of Communists provoked widespread revolt, ultimately leading to the overthrow of the central authority and collapse of the Communist regime in 1992. And now, today, the fundamentalist Taliban, with support from al Qaeda, is revolting against the current moderate democratic process and attempts at modernization and development.

Over the past three decades, separate power bases have emerged in Afghanistan in the form of political-military parties and networks of commanders and their followers. Fed by the illicit economy and supported by foreign powers, these parties and networks have access to vast human support and financial resources, much of which is generated by drug trafficking, illegal taxation, and customs fees, and are thus able to maintain power outside the state.

Local Sources of Conflict. Many local disputes in Afghanistan are related to conflicts over land and access to water. Such disputes are mainly between displaced persons who returned from refugee camps to their places of origin and those who either stayed in the area or returned at any earlier period. In some cases, local commanders have claimed the lands of those who were displaced; in other cases, local commanders belonging to one majority ethnic group have forced villagers belonging to a minority group to flee only to redistribute the abandoned land to the remaining population. Such cases have mainly been registered in the northern provinces of Takhar, Mazar, and Fariba. Land has also been acquired unjustly or sold illegally through the use of fake documents or the abuse of government positions.

The destruction of water distribution systems has also led to violent conflict, as have disputes over the ownership and use of public property, such as forests and pasturages, especially between nomads (Kochies) and other tribes (mainly the Hazara residents of the central highlands). In each of the past two years, for example, fighting erupted during the seasonal movement of Kochies and their herds toward the central highlands. Fighting was over land ownership and grazing rights. Several people were injured, while others were killed. Additionally, homes were burned, and herds were taken by force. Spoilers on both sides, principally Kochie and Hazara political leaders, have exaggerated the dispute.

Religion-Based Sources of Conflict. Islam is the predominant religion in Afghanistan and is mixed with Afghan culture, making it difficult for the majority of illiterate people to make distinctions between certain aspects of Islam and their own indigenous traditions. Although moderate Islam, in particular, has deep roots in Afghan society and is the most important part of belief in the day-to-day life of Afghans, Afghans can be deeply angered by incidents that are perceived as contradictory to their Islamic belief.

An overwhelming majority of Afghans reject the radical version of Islam practiced by the Taliban not only because it has caused social strife but also because it contradicts their principle understanding of Islam.

Promoting moderate Islam in Afghanistan will have a significant positive impact on the peacebuilding process and help unify and heal the country. The rule of the mullahs (traditional clergy) is dominant, particularly in the rural areas of Afghanistan. Their network is loose but pervasive throughout the country, and their decisions, in many cases, determine people's decisions and actions. Reaching out to them and using their potential for peacebuilding will be an important step that can help offset the extremists' appropriation of mosques in their propaganda campaign against the government.

Ethnic Sources of Conflict. Although Afghanistan is not ethnically homogenous and its national culture is not uniform, there is a strong collective sense of identity within the country. Most ordinary Afghans broadly believe that they will be prosperous only if they are united and live in peace with one another under a lawful and just system where they equally benefit from services. As Louis Dupree wrote in his book Afghanistan, "In Afghanistan, only distinctive tribal and ethnic clothing, language, religion and other cultural impediments make the difference. But like the United States, and for a much longer period, Afghanistan had been a cultural, as well as physical, melting-pot . . . the influences of many empires rose, fell and blended."[1]

The ethnic divisions within Afghanistan were deepened during the initial years of resistance against the Soviet invasion, when leaders organized jihadi parties and militia groups around networks of close friends and relatives, creating new ethnocentric power structures. As a result, militia groups on all sides were dominated by geographical location and tribal and ethnic affiliations. When these groups were threatened by a common foreign enemy, they joined together, but when the time came to share power, they fought one another with all the means at their disposal and played the "ethnic card" to mobilize support and retain power and access to resources.

The individualistic approach of these groups created an environment in which each group put its own interests over national interests. During the civil war in Kabul, for example, these groups banned the movement of ordinary Afghans and contact between Afghans belonging to different ethnic groups. They also tortured members of other groups to create hate

1. Louis Dupree, Afghanistan (Princeton: Princeton University Press, 1980), 55.

and dependency and to force people to follow them out of fear. None of the ordinary Afghans interviewed by me during the past ten years approved of what their respective leaders and commanders had done in the name of ethnicity. Hence, Afghans did not necessarily follow the leaders and militia commanders because of their inherent ethnic interests or loyalties; rather, they were forced to because of fear and a need to protect themselves and their families.

Familial Sources of Conflict. Family disputes and feuds are an additional cause of conflict in Afghanistan and mostly involve issues of marriage and shared property. In some cases, ISAF has been intentionally misled by locally hired individuals in the middle of a personal or familial dispute. For example, such individuals have been known to falsely accuse their rivals of having links with al Qaeda, knowing that their homes will be searched or that they will be arrested. Such circumstances in which innocent parties are treated unjustly or unfairly have the unintended effect of damaging the image of the international forces and government in the eyes of Afghans and creating further space for the insurgents.

Insurgent, Terrorist, and Criminal Groups

Although the nature and composition of the country's insurgent and terrorist groups change frequently and require continued assessment, the following groups are the ones that will likely present a key challenge in any reconciliation process.

The Afghan Taliban. The Afghan Taliban is currently led by two main shuras (councils): the Quetta Shura and the Peshawar Shura. The Quetta Shura, also known as the Leadership Council, is headed by Mullah Omar and dominated by those from Kandahar, Uruzgan, and Helmand. Most council members come from the old leadership of the Taliban. The Peshawar Shura, which is headquartered in Pakistan's North-West Frontier Province (NWFP), is composed of smaller tribes but lacks a leader with Mullah Omar's overall authority and legitimacy. There are additional differences between the Quetta Shura and the Peshawar Shura with regard to status and resources.

As a whole, the Taliban operates in small groups—from three to thirty individuals, most of whom are between the ages of seventeen and twenty-six (except for the commanders and secret operatives). Although these groups are composed of core madrassa-trained Taliban and local recruits, they also include mercenaries—criminals hired for special tasks. Each group also generally has foreign fighters and advisers, many of whom are in command positions. Support for these groups comes from the drug mafia, which not only provides financial resources but also information, linkages, and help in penetrating high-value-target areas that are under effective government control.

Of the numerous Taliban groups, one of the strongest and most active is led by Jala-ludin Haqani, a member of the Taliban's Leadership Council and an experienced Afghan rebel commander from the Zadran district in southeast Afghanistan. Once trusted by the CIA, Haqani was the first Afghan leader to sponsor Arab fighters during the last years of the anti-Soviet war, establishing very close relations with wealthy Arab sheikhs and Pakistan's ISI.[2] Assisted by his son Sarajudin, he is once again proving himself to be a capable organizer, operating as a middleman between al Qaeda and the ISI from his base in Waziristan. Sarajudin has recently called for a change in the Quetta Shura leadership, arguing that a lack of leadership has led to the killings of some of the Taliban's most senior commanders.

The Hekmatyar Group (Hizb-i Islami). Based mostly in the Dir District of Pakistan's Bajaur Agency along the Afghanistan border (near Kunar and Nuristan), Hizb-i Islami is led by Gulbuddin Hekmatyar, a controversial figure who lost much of the credibility among Afghans that he had gained during the initial years of the anti-Soviet war. This was largely due to his continued rocket attacks on Kabul after the fall of the Communist regime in 1992, causing serious damage to ordinary Afghans and the new mujahidin government. As a result, his group has not been able to mobilize new recruits and instead relies on a network of former commanders and followers (some of whom maintain close links with their old ISI friends). Many members have already left him, with some joining the government in senior positions. Although they have broken off from the group and separated themselves from its current policy of fighting coalition forces, they represent potentially important points of contact between the government and Hekmatyar. Indeed, there is a growing possibility that Hekmatyar's group could, at some point, join a reconciliation process at the leadership level, although such a scenario would be very complicated because of Hekmatyar's past actions and because Hekmatyar and his group are on the UN Security Council's terrorist designation list.

Contractors and Criminals. Large networks of illegal armed groups involved with poppy production and drug trafficking exist in Afghanistan. Many young unemployed Afghans, particularly some of those who were forcibly returned from Iran, have joined their ranks as criminals and addicts. This represents another major threat to security and the rule of law and only serves to strengthen the insurgency.

---

2. Steve Coll, *Ghost Wars: The Secret History of the CIA, Afghanistan, and Bin Laden, from the Soviet Invasion to September 10, 2001* (Boston: Penguin, 2004), 201.

Afghan criminal groups engage in a range of money-generating activities, whether its robbing and killing traders, or kidnapping children and foreign aid workers for ransom. They are also often contracted by the Taliban to carry out specific acts in return for payment or to provide protection during smuggling or kidnapping operations. Corruption in the police force has only added to the problem, further contributing to the country's instability and hurting the government's image.

Tehrik-i-Taliban Pakistan. Following the launch of Operation Enduring Freedom in 2001, the Taliban and al Qaeda fled to Pakistan. They found sanctuary in FATA, a region ruled by old tribal customs that has been the site of major guerrilla and terrorist training camps since the Soviet invasion of Afghanistan in the 1980s (many of which were established with U.S. and Saudi money under the direct supervision of the ISI). Far from Islamabad's reach, FATA currently serves as a launching pad for terrorist and cross-border attacks on Afghan and international security forces.

Established as an umbrella organization by a shura of forty senior Taliban leaders, the Tehrik-I-Taliban Pakistan (PTT) quickly and effectively established itself in FATA, killing more than 300 tribal elders. Militia leader Baitullah Mehsud, who once operated under Sarajiden Haqani, was appointed as the group's amir (leader) in 2007, while Mulana Hafiz Gul Bahaddur of North Waziristan and Mulana Faqir Muhammad of Bajaur Agency were appointed as the second and third in command.

As a syndicate, the PTT is composed not only of Taliban but also of groups such as Lashkar-e-Taiba (LET), Tehreek-Maram-Shariya Mohammadyah (TNSM), the Harkatul Mujahideen al-Aalmi (HMAA), the Harkatul Ansaar (HA), the Harkat-i-Jehad-I Islami (HJI), the Ansaru Sunnah (AS), and the Ansarul Muslimoon (AM). These groups have concentrated their human and material resources in Waziristan in preparation for renewed attacks on international and Afghan security forces. Most of these groups were formed in the late 1990s by the ISI as a proxy force of jihadists to fight the Indian government in Kashmir. Each of these organizations has independent weapons stockpiles, millions of dollars in funds, and hundreds of fighters.

Foreign Fighters and al Qaeda. With its ability to mobilize foreign fighters and its access to financial resources, al Qaeda represents one of the most sophisticated networks of terrorists capable of attacking targets on a global level. It has played a central role in spreading militancy in the region, providing the insurgency with strategic communication and planning, financing, and networking opportunities. In addition, it brings recruits to Afghanistan not only from Arab countries but also from Chechnya, Uzbekistan, and China's Xinjiang province.

Relations among al Qaeda, the Taliban, and other extremist groups are very complicated. They can be direct or indirect and are characterized by a combination of hostility and friendship. They need one another for survival, but sometimes they have conflicts of interests. What is clear is that the Taliban and extremist groups need al Qaeda's money, brains, and experienced fighters, while al Qaeda needs safe havens from which it can operate worldwide.

With multiple sources of conflict and numerous destabilizing forces in Afghanistan, it is clear that developing a successful reconciliation program and building durable peace will not be an easy task. But before a framework to address the problem can be designed, past and present attempts at reconciliation must be examined and their shortcomings understood.

Past Attempts at Reconciliation

Following the Taliban's removal from power by the United States, the Bonn Agreement provided an opportunity to not only recreate the State of Afghanistan but also to end conflict there by developing a road map for peace. It recognized the need to ensure broad representation in the interim arrangement and to include those groups that have not been adequately represented at the UN-sponsored talks on Afghanistan. Although the Taliban had been defeated, was seeking amnesty and personal safety, and had no significant political ambitions, the political environment at the time made it difficult to accommodate them, leaving an opportune moment for reconciliation to be lost. As 10 Lakhdar Brahimi, the United Nations special representative of the secretary-general, publicly stated, "The Bonn talks were dominated by one group and at that time nobody was ready to consider the partly defeated side of the conflict; therefore, the Taliban were left by themselves, which gave an opportunity to spoilers to regroup."

President Hamid Karzai first announced plans for a reconciliation policy in a speech before a gathering of ulema in Kabul in April 2003. He stated that "a clear line has to be drawn between the ordinary Taliban who are real and honest sons of this country, and those who still use the Taliban cover to disturb peace and security in the country. No one has the right to harass/persecute any one under the name of Taliban." He added that all those who were active within the ranks of the Taliban—and who were not among those known to have committed crimes against the Afghan people—could begin living as normal citizens of Afghanistan by denouncing violence.

In early 2005, the government established the Independent Peace and Reconciliation Commission (PTS) to facilitate the reconciliation process. Shortly thereafter, commission chairman Hazrat Sebghatullah Mojaddedi announced that the amnesty offer from Karzai was being extended to all Taliban leaders, including the regime's former head Mullah Omar. Although the U.S. military supported the Afghan government's general reconciliation policy and the commission, it stated unequivocally that those guilty of terrorism or other serious crimes would not be allowed to join the amnesty. Resistance to such an idea came not just from the United States: Mojaddedi's announcement was in direct contradiction of two UN Security Council Resolutions (UNSCR 1267 [1999] and 1735 [2006]) that sanctioned those very leaders.

On December 12, 2005, the Afghan Cabinet formally adopted the Action Plan on Peace, Justice, and Reconciliation in Afghanistan. The action plan focused mostly on the past and not on how to end the current violence. Then, on January 31, 2007, the lower house of the Afghanistan National Assembly approved a controversial draft amnesty bill that would provide amnesty to war criminals of the past three decades (from 1979 to 2001). An amended version, which was approved in March 2008, notes specifically that, "the law does not include those who are wanted for internal and external charges against the security of the country." It further adds that "[the bill] will not cover those who do not accept the constitution of Afghanistan and the present government." Although the bill also recognizes the right of direct victims to appeal for justice, it states that in the interest of "stability and peace," those who fought against one another for the independence of Afghanistan would be granted amnesty.

Aside from these broad national initiatives at reconciliation with the Taliban, attempts at outreach and reconciliation on a more local level have been initiated with modest success by a number of actors—namely, the Afghan government, nongovernmental organizations, and the international community.

The Afghan Government

Although the Afghan government's primary focus has been on reaching out to individual members of the insurgency and to midlevel leaders, the Independent Department of Local Governance (IDLG) recently began to reach out to community leaders, commanders, and mullahs. It is trying to engage and encourage them to actively improve security in their districts. These initiatives are not well coordinated, however, and there is a gap between strategic focus and tactical approaches. Further, local insurgent leaders occasionally engage with the government to gain its trust and receive compensation only to continue with their illicit and antigovernment activities. Making such attempts at reconciliation more difficult still is the sheer number of Afghan governmental departments either directly or indirectly involved in outreach and reconciliation initiatives:

- the Office of National Security Adviser to the President

- the National Department of Security
- the Independent Peace and Reconciliation Commission (PTS), which has nine offices in the most violent provinces of the south, southeast, and west of the country
- the Independent Commission of Human Rights
- the Ministry of Interior Departments of Intelligence
- the Ministry of Defense Department of Intelligence
- the newly established Independent Department of Local Governance
- individual members of parliament, provincial councils, and provincial governors

Nongovernmental Organizations

Recently initiated by the IDLG and the Ministry of Rural Rehabilitation and Development (MRRD), the Community Based Development Councils are created through the National Solidarity Program and tasked with directly supervising and managing the implementation of rural development projects together with the district councils. Their mission is to mobilize communities for active participation in local security and stabilization and in the disbandment and demobilization of illegal armed groups.

The Afghan Civil Society Forum and a number of national and international nongovernmental organizations, such as Oxfam, the Tribal Liaison Office, and the Cooperation for Peace and Unity in Afghanistan, are also engaged in peacebuilding and conflict resolution training and initiatives at community levels. The Afghan National Solidarity Plan (NSP), created in 2003 to develop the ability of Afghan communities to identify, plan, manage, and monitor their own development projects, provides a unique opportunity for reconciliation at the community level through its wide network of more than 21,000 village development councils. However, this capacity is not yet fully utilized at the local level.

Supported by the Ministry of Religious Affairs, the Ulema Shura (Council of Islamic Scholars) meets on a bimonthly basis with the president to exchange views and advise the government on religious matters, but unfortunately the insurgents' outreach to the mullahs is currently more robust than that of the government.

The International Community

The United Nations Assistance Mission Afghanistan (UNAMA) is engaged in political outreach and supports the reconciliation efforts of the PTS and the Afghanistan Independent Human Rights Commission (AIHRC). Its mandate is to "provide good offices to support, if requested by the Afghan Government, the implementation of Afghan-led reconciliation programs, within the framework of the Afghan Constitution and with full respect of the implementation of measures introduced by the Security Council in its resolution 1267 (1999), and other relevant resolutions of the SC." With eight regional offices and ten provincial offices, UNAMA has significant capacity at the field level, but this capacity needs to be more effectively and strategically utilized in support of government-led initiatives.

Diplomatic missions, mostly through the development agencies of major donor and troop-contributing countries, generally focus on areas where troops are deployed and on supporting PTS, civil society organizations, and AIHRC through financial and technical assistance at the local level. Some missions even have their preferred local tribal and warlord contacts and use their network to reach out to local members of the insurgency to negotiate deals or at least reduce pressures on their military outposts. All forty-seven troop-contributing countries have their own small cells of outreach and intelligence.

Provincial Reconstruction Teams (PRT), set up by the U.S. military and NATO coalition forces, reach out to Afghans through the provision of development projects. In cases where they work closely with provincial governors, they make better contributions and help in improving the reach of local governors.

Through the combined efforts of the government and its partners, especially the PTS, some progress has been made to date, but the results have been modest. Due to organizational weakness and the general political climate, the process has never been able to get sufficient political or financial support, nor has it been able to make any headway toward breaking the insurgency and generating momentum for sustained peace and stability.

A full review of past efforts at reconciliation with the Taliban reveals that the process has lacked consistency. The government and its international partners offer conflicting messages, and no agreed-upon policy framework exists to pursue reconciliation in a cohesive manner. Additionally, an incomplete understanding of the Taliban and other groups engaged in violence further contributes to a lack of serious progress. Nevertheless, although attempts at talks have not been successful, experience shows that the Taliban can be engaged and, in fact, are willing to engage in negotiations. Experience also shows that when the government negotiates from a position of strength and has something to offer (e.g., security and economic development), negotiations are more likely to lead to a successful outcome. Based on this knowledge and the preceding analyses, one can begin to construct a pragmatic framework for peace and reconciliation in Afghanistan.

A Framework for Reconciliation

The goal of reconciliation in Afghanistan must be to achieve peace and long-term stability under the Afghan Constitution with full respect for the rule of law, social justice, and human rights. To successfully meet this goal, Afghanistan's reconciliation program needs to be carefully targeted and guided by a clear set of principles.

The Targets of Reconciliation

To be all inclusive and comprehensive, reconciliation in Afghanistan must take place on the national, community, and individual levels.

The National Level. Reconciliation efforts on the national level should focus on building trust with neighboring countries through active diplomacy and on ending sanctuaries and support to the insurgency leadership. They should also focus on providing senior-level rebel commanders with an alternative way out of the violence by offering them opportunities to participate in the political system and by guaranteeing them and their families safety from harassment by the Taliban and coalition forces and safety from national and international prosecution. These efforts will require clarity and dedicated government leadership and must be attempted from a position of strength to make them credible.

They will also require the support of the international community and an active role from the United States (under the lead of the Afghan government) and the United Nations in fostering regional cooperation, implementing Security Council resolutions, and helping end the Taliban sanctuaries in Pakistan.

The Community Level. Promoting community-based peacebuilding initiatives and tapping their full potential will be key components of encouraging reconciliation from the ground up. Organized communities have a demonstrated ability to pressure insurgents into joining a peace process and have already proven to be instrumental in weapons collection at the district level and in providing security during elections. For example, district councils successfully helped pressure commanders of illegal armed groups to cooperate in the disarmament process. This generated positive momentum in more than seventy-one districts and resulted in the collection of thousands of weapons and tons of ammunition.

There is great potential for further initiatives on the community level, but it is thus far largely untapped. The NSP of the MRRD, the IDLG, nongovernmental organizations, development agencies, members of Afghanistan's parliament, provincial councils, the Ulema Shura, the private sector, women's groups, and other civil society organizations are all involved on the community level but not in a structured and coherent way. They lack effective strategic communications and require a framework of support and interaction. Thus, positive results are not visible at large. Initiatives at the community level will be most effective if they are well connected with initiatives on the national and individual level through an effective support and monitoring mechanism.

The Individual Level. Reconciliatory efforts in the form of covert negotiations and invitations to join the peace process are currently focused on individual and midlevel commanders, particularly those who do not want to be part of the neo-Taliban movement but who otherwise fear arrest or harassment. Efforts have also been made by U.S. and coalition forces to release certain prisoners so that they can rejoin their families and communities. They are provided with amnesty letters by the chairman of the PTS. In return, community and tribal elders guarantee that these newly released individuals will no longer engage in violence. Included among these released prisoners are some former high-ranking Taliban officials: Mullah Zaief, Mullavai Wakil Ahamad Mutawakel (the foreign minister under the Taliban), the director of Radio Sharia, and Mullah Abdul Salaam (the current governor of Mossa Qala). Although this initiative represents visible cooperation between the PTS and a number of national and international partners, the program requires a full review and redesign and needs to be partnered with broader stabilization initiatives. To make it fully effective, greater focus is needed on the political level to better guide the process.

Principles of Engagement

Based on the analysis herein and work already being done by members of the Policy Action Group (PAG) in Kabul, a group of senior Afghan government officials and representatives from the international community, the following series of principles should guide Afghanistan's reconciliation program:

Fundamental Principles

Afghan ownership. All reconciliation initiatives must be led by Afghan government mechanisms and institutions.

- The Afghan government may ask the United Nations and other international actors to provide support to Afghan-led reconciliation programs.
- International military forces, including ISAF, should respond expeditiously to any Afghan government request to suspend military action against specific individuals or groups identified as prospective insurgent "reconcilees" for the duration of any future reconciliation talks and against those individuals or groups whom the Afghan government identifies as reconciled.

- The international community should coordinate its efforts and avoid actions that discredit the Afghan government in the eyes of its people and damage the process of reconciliation.
- International military forces, including ISAF, and the Afghan government should notify each other, at the earliest possible opportunity, of talks by their representatives or agents with prospective insurgent "reconcilees" to avoid any damage to reconciliation proceedings and to link the talks with broader initiatives.

Compliance with national and international law. Reconciliation efforts will be guided by (and should be in compliance with) the Afghan Constitution, sharia law, and UNSCR 1267 (1999), 1735 (2006), and 1820 (2008). The Afghan government will seek international agreement for measures that may contradict certain resolutions but have significant promise for stabilization and reconciliation.

Control over territory. The Afghan state is one and reconciliation initiatives should not allow discussions that call for concessions with regard to control over territory.

Flexibility. The reconciliation process should be tailored to allow some level of flexibility to facilitate reconciliation on a case-by-case basis.

Renunciation of violence. Reconciliation with individual insurgents or insurgent groups contributes to the goal of long-term stability only if prospective interlocutors comply with constitutional disarmament requirements and renounce violence.

Rights of individuals. The rights of individuals who suffered as a direct result of atrocities and criminal acts should be recognized. The existing legal framework, including sharia law, provides provisions on the rights of individuals to register criminal cases against those who have committed crimes. Although no one has the right of forgiveness (Haquall Abde) except the victims, all reconciled individuals should enjoy the full rights and protections of citizens of Afghanistan as ensured by law.

Process-Related Principles

Confidentiality. The details of negotiations between the government and insurgents should be accessible only to a limited number of responsible people. There should not be a release of information too early in the process.

Monitoring and accountability. A mechanism of individual accountability should be put in place that allows room to maneuver when prompting reconciliation, but not at the cost of the rights of individual victims who may wish to take future legal actions. The reconciliation program and reconciled individuals should be carefully monitored to (1) verify that the behavior of individuals who are protected by their reconciled status is in line with the Afghan Constitution and the agreed-upon legal framework and (2) ensure that reconciled individuals are not harassed by government or international security forces without a genuine legal reason and are being fully reintegrated.

Power sharing. Decisions on power sharing should be made on the basis of the constitution and in accordance with the democratic process.

Organizational and Institutional Principles

Organizational arrangement. Based on an initial review of the structure of PTS, the following is needed:

- a senior focal point with a small secretariat who presides over a small committee of authorized professionals, including senior representatives of the international community, that helps coordinate the range of actors and activities at the highest levels of the government and international community;
- new PTS members with strong and respected personalities, skills, and talents and credible influence in the local politics of areas under the control of the insurgents;
- reorganized PTS operational, managerial, and financial systems.

Strategic coordination. A direct channel of communication should be maintained at all times between those engaged in reconciliation and those providing security services. The government should also coordinate with all organizations authorized to engage prospec-tive reconcilees. The senior focal point should be responsible for the strategic coordination of reconciliation efforts. This individual should report directly to the president. The senior focal point should also be responsible for coordinating between reconciliation processing offices and Afghanistan National Security Forces (ANSF) and international military forces and for ensuring that the Afghan government and international community avoid any contradictory statements that could destroy dialogue or the credibility of the reconciliation process.

The senior focal point should also seek verifiable confirmation that reconciled individuals are contributing to peacebuilding and adhering to the Afghan Constitution. Additionally, this individual should also be notified of all reconciliation efforts, including those by members of parliament, Afghan national security organizations, the PTS, and international partners. This will help avoid confusion and ensure that no individuals or organizations engage in any kind of political negotiation with insurgents on behalf of the government without proper authorization.

Strengthen local capacity. The government should support community-based peacebuilding initiatives and strengthen capacity at the subnational level to promote and support reconciliation at the local level, especially to prevent violent conflict over land and pasturage disputes and to gain commitments for full disarmament.

Outreach-Related Principles

Generate public support. A robust public relations campaign should be implemented that works in concert with Afghanistan's civil-society organizations, ulema, tribal leaders, and political groups to establish contacts and mobilize people in support of peace and stability. The role of political parties and non-governmental actors at the community level will be cru-cial. Community-based organizations, elders, mullahs, the private sector, and women should be effectively utilized and their positive role in promoting reconciliation and strengthening democratic principles should be supported.

Outreach. Efforts must be made to communicate with and involve individuals and groups engaged in political violence against the state.

Support reconciled individuals. The experience and resources of the Disarmament and Reintegration Commission and Afghanistan's New Beginnings Program are invaluable and should be drawn on in developing reintegration and support networks for reconciled individuals.

First Steps. While most key actors in Afghanistan would welcome reconciliation, much skepticism exists. Some critical questions need to be answered and clarified before moving full speed toward reconciliation. Specific questions remain about who should negotiate with whom and under what conditions negotiations should occur. First steps should be geared toward addressing this skepticism and answering these outstanding questions.

To this end, an advisory team composed of experienced, senior-level international and Afghan diplomats and experts should be established with UNAMA support to help the government and the Special Representative of the United Nations Secretary-General develop a precise program document, which would include details on reorganization, outreach, reintegration implementation, monitoring, and management support. Such a team would undoubtedly be invaluable in devising a strategy geared toward building regional consensus, putting an end to the Taliban sanctuaries, promoting reconciliation, and developing trust at the national level. It would require not only the support of the Afghan government and the

United Nations but also the full support of NATO, major donor countries, and the United States. The program document itself must outline a clear division of labor among the key parties and be agreed to by the principles in Kabul. The United States Institute of Peace, with its links to Afghanistan and expertise in post-conflict stabilization and peacebuilding, could help in the design, training, and mentorship of such an initiative.

Conclusions and Recommendations

In order to move forward in Afghanistan, a comprehensive and coordinated political reconciliation process must be started. At the same time, significant progress must be made on the security front and on the international (regional) front. Without security, stability, and cooperation from Afghanistan's neighbors, reconciliation will not occur. This report outlined the contours of a reconciliation process, but a number of actions will be critical to creating an environment conducive to reconciliation.

First, ISAF/NATO should temporarily increase the level of troops, which is justifiable since preparation for next year's election should start now. In the absence of such a surge, the cost of security over the long term will be intolerably high. The United States and other NATO member countries should act now.

Second, the Afghan government should accelerate security-sector reform, paying particular attention to the Ministry of Interior and police. It should also increase the ceiling of the ANA up to at least 220,000. This increase should be in the form of reserve or National Guard so that they can replace the international troops after the troop surge is over. As soon as the security threats are reduced to a manageable level, the number can be brought back to the original ceiling to ensure the sustainability of ANA.

Third, in order to prevent social unrest, political and military measures need to be complemented with substantive efforts to accelerate reconstruction, generate good governance, and overcome the food crises.

Fourth, the time has come for the United Nations and the international community to enter into serious discussions with Pakistan about cooperative measures to end Taliban sanctuaries and the cross-border insurgency. The UN Security Council should start immediate discussions on improving the implementation of its resolutions and decide on additional measures against those who continue to support the Taliban, harbor its leadership, or provide it with logistical, training, and planning support. The leadership of both Afghanistan and Pakistan should be helped and pressured to put their differences aside and cooperate seriously and sincerely with mutual respect for each other's territorial integrity and sovereignty and to work toward improving security for both countries. This engagement should build upon the concrete steps agreed to in the Peace Jirgah, which was organized jointly by Afghanistan and Pakistan in 2007 to build peace along their common border areas.

Fifth, India, Pakistan, and Afghanistan should engage in a direct dialogue with the United States as mediator in an attempt to end the use of Afghanistan soil as a proxy Indo-Pakistani battleground. Although such a dialogue has never been tried before, building confidence and providing security guarantees would reduce tensions and help stabilize Afghanistan.

Sixth, the Afghan government and the international community must invest in a state that is functional and able to provide basic services so that the Afghans themselves can take charge without relying on others. Investment in education, media, and civil society is the only way to help overcome extremism. Promoting moderate Islam is a key unifying factor. The positive role of Islam in promoting peace and reconciliation must be recognized. Copying models from the outside will not work in Afghanistan. Building functional state institutions and ensuring equal social and economic opportunities as well as justice are fundamental to building national unity. Such an approach will help transform ethnic diversity from threat to asset.

Seventh, the government should intensify its fight against corruption and drug trafficking. Continuation of the status quo will not help rebuild public confidence.

Eighth, the Reconstruction Opportunity Zones initiative of the United States and the decision of the G-8 in Japan to invest in tribal areas on both sides of the Afghan-Pakistani border represent important steps toward stability in the region. Resources must be made available in a timely manner and spent effectively in order to generate results that promote peace. This requires a comprehensive program for investment that should be developed by a joint team of Afghan, Pakistani, and international experts.

Ninth, the current reactive approach toward the stabilization of Afghanistan has not proven productive. Further, hesitation by NATO and other troop-contributing countries to address the needs of international field commanders in Afghanistan and restrictions on troop deployment undermines the struggle against terrorism, prolongs the mission, and ultimately weakens the Afghan government's position in any reconciliation effort. It is very important that ISAF works to lower civilian casualties and avoids any incidents in which religious and traditional Afghan values are demeaned. In addition, the international community must now deliver on the commitments it made at the Bucharest and Paris conferences.

25

Negotiating with the Islamic Republic of Iran: Fifteen Points to Remember

John W. Limbert

The Baghdad meetings between Ambassadors Ryan Crocker and Hassan Kazemi-Qomi in May and July of 2007 marked the first official bilateral American-Iranian contacts since relations were formally broken during the U.S. embassy hostage crisis in April 1980. Previous contacts, productive or not, had been indirect, clandestine, or part of some multilateral framework. Earlier attempts to establish official dialogue had foundered on pervading suspicions and the view that "now is not the time" and "if they want to talk, then they must be up to something."

Like adolescents dealing with a prom invitation, when one side came forward, the other pulled back. In 1998–99, for example, Tehran—politically hobbled by internal disputes—rejected Secretary of State Madeleine Albright's offer to discuss, without preconditions, a "roadmap to better relations." In 2003, the United States ignored an Iranian proposal—transmitted through the Swiss embassy in Tehran—to open discussions on all outstanding issues, including a broader Middle East settlement. It is ironic that the United States ignored such an approach after it had insisted, in the aftermath of the 1986 Iran-Contra fiasco, that it would talk to Iran only through the "official" channel of the Swiss protecting power. By all accounts, that 2003 decision came from the illusory euphoria of an easy military victory in Iraq and the view, popular with some in Washington at the time, that "real men go to Tehran [in tanks]."

Talking to Iran may be difficult and perhaps unpleasant. There are, however, some points that are worth remembering and that might help avoid some of the missteps that have doomed previous attempts to hold conver-

John W. Limbert, "Negotiating with the Islamic Republic of Iran: Raising the Chances for Success—Fifteen Points to Remember," Special Report 199 (Washington, DC: USIP, 2008).

sations. Many of these points will be obvious to those with experience in negotiation and to those who have dealt with the Middle East in general and Iran in particular. In the case of Iran, however, the U.S. government has lost its cadre of expertise. Through the 1980s and 1990s it did not train Persian speakers, and eventually those with language and country experience aged and retired, leaving a gap that, with the best will in the world, will take at least a decade to fill. Ambassador Crocker, for example, must be among the last active-duty American diplomats who served in Iran.

Creating such a well-prepared cadre will take time. Training someone to a level of professional speaking and reading proficiency in Persian—a process that experts believe requires at least nine months of full-time study—is just the beginning of the process. Understanding nuances, historical references, cultural and class views, and other subtleties will take much longer, ideally through personal immersion in an Iranian social context. Yet without at least some understanding of these facets of the Iranian mindset, the American negotiator's task will be much harder.

On the other side, few Iranian counterparts are likely to have much understanding of the United States. Iran's cadre of U.S.-educated technocrats has aged and a new generation of Iranians from a different social background has come to occupy key posts. Even those Iranians who lived and studied in the United States often did so at a fairly advanced age (most were graduate students) and lived—like many American expatriates in Iran—in an environment unaffected by and remote from the main currents of American life. Although the Islamic Revolution and the subsequent turmoil brought hundreds of thousands of Iranians to the United States, there are fewer and fewer people inside Iran who have had any direct contact with America and Americans.

Many in power in Iran today have gained their positions by riding waves of anti-American sentiment. Many leaders of the Islamic Republic see the power of American popular culture as a direct threat to the austere strictures of the dominant ideology and, as such, a threat to the current leaders' control of the state. Ayatollah Khomeini once said that he did not fear America's ships and armies; America's most terrifying weapon, he asserted, was its popular culture, with its power to mislead Iran's young people and to turn them away from the true path of religion and revolution. The earlier flows of students, tourists, business visitors, and others from Iran to the United States have become a trickle. Iranians' views of the United States are likely to be highly distorted either by the Islamic Republic's official hate machine or by an idealized picture coming from Iranians' dislike for their own government. According to this latter view, "if this government says America is the root of all evil, then America must be the source of all that is beneficent."

Following the suggestions listed below will help, but will not guarantee the success of a negotiation. Expertise and a few helpful hints by themselves will not always overcome the formidable barriers to that success. Festering resentments, perceived grievances, and suspicions run deep on both sides, so that negotiations by the most skilled and experienced parties may still fail—or at least not achieve what is hoped for. The key to progress is keeping expectations realistic. One or two negotiating sessions are not going to make people forget the real or imagined humiliations of the past. For in the near term, the American side is no more likely to overlook the wounds of the 1979–81 hostage crisis than is the Iranian side likely to put aside the memories of the 1953 CIA-sponsored coup against the Mossadegh regime.

Some of the points listed below are basic negotiation techniques and would apply in negotiations with almost any state counterpart, not just the Islamic Republic. Such principles, however, deserve special emphasis in the Iranian case, because of the deep and mutual mistrust that has existed between the two countries since 1979. In the case of Iran, there is no reservoir of good will that a negotiator can tap to overcome difficulties of process or substance. Since relations were formally broken in 1980, there has been an almost complete lack of official, bilateral contact. That estrangement has deprived Americans of face-to-face negotiating experience and has left the field mostly to the speculators, the professional pundits, and those pursuing personal or political agendas. Lacking that firsthand knowledge and serious analysis, we are often left with distorted stereotypes about Iranians' basic "irrationality and egoism" and with sweeping statements such as "Iranians hate negotiations."[1]

Of course, today the setting for American-Iranian negotiations is unpromising and the chances of success are uncertain. Yet if there is mutual interest in coming to the table—as there was in 2001–02 about Afghanistan and there should be today about Iraq, then the recommendations below may just raise the chances of a productive negotiating encounter from none to at least slim.

Fifteen Points to Remember

1. Negotiating with Iran—hard as it may be—is worth doing.

Some American observers argue that, after twenty-eight years of uninterrupted Iranian-American hostility, the Iranian regime is so evil, so irrational, and so mendacious that there is nothing to gain from negotiations except more sterile rhetoric, absurd accusations, and blatant untruths. In this view, if the Islamic Republic today is, as some are arguing, the equivalent of Nazi Germany in 1938, then negotiating with such a regime ignores

1. See David Ignatius, "Countering Iran's Distrust," *Washington Post*, May 27, 2007, B7.

its true nature and will only give it a legitimacy it does not deserve.[2] These observers claim that this member of the axis of evil is only a worthy target for regime change, or that, at a minimum, Iran must "change its behavior"—that is, do all that we demand of it—before any kind of discourse can begin. In this analysis, the regime in Tehran is beyond the pale. It is so brutal, benighted, and paranoid that there is no point in opening a dialogue unless its only subject is the terms of Iran's surrender.

The problem with this Manichean view—regarding Iran as a manifestation of pure evil—is that it is likely to become a self-fulfilling prophecy. When we approach the Iranians (or any counterpart in a negotiation) as though they are the malevolent beings described above, they will quickly perceive how we look at them and adapt their tactics accordingly. Approach Iranians as irrational, dissimulating cheats, and they are quite likely to fulfill those expectations. This dark view of Iran and Iranians also ignores the possibility that negotiating could be one method of changing what has been a twenty-eight-year destructive U.S.-Iranian relationship of mutual grievance, hostility, and suspicion into something more productive. During that period, mutual recrimination, name-calling, finger-pointing, posturing, and sermonizing have had few results. The Islamic Republic still exists, remains hostile and suspicious, and has recently reminded us of its antagonism by the high-profile arrests of Iranian-Americans whose mission was to encourage Iranian-American dialogue and scholarly research. The United States, for its part, has imposed more and more sanctions, encouraged others to do likewise, and issued barely veiled threats of military action.

The point is that the United States should be talking to the Islamic Republic not because doing so is easy or even likely to produce immediate and positive results, but because both sides might find significant common interests in doing so. Talking, hard and disagreeable as it might be, is likely to be more productive than continuing twenty-eight years of noisy and sometimes violent confrontation. We should have no illusions. Discussions with the Islamic Republic are unlikely to produce in the short run the kind of productive outcomes we might wish for. Iran is not going to "change its behavior" immediately and stop all of its misdeeds in the areas of terrorism, Middle East peace, human rights, and nuclear development. Yet serious negotiations may elicit areas of common interest that lurk behind walls of hostility and distrust.

2. Establish objective criteria free of legalisms.

Closely reasoned legal arguments may have their place in a negotiation, but for the most part they will not impress the Iranian side. This feature of Iranian negotiating style long predates the Islamic Republic. In February

2. Such is the view of Norman Podhoretz, as expressed on PBS's *News Hour*, October 29, 2007.

1946, for example, Iranian prime minister Ahmad Qavam, meeting with Stalin on the sensitive issue of Soviet military units remaining on Iranian soil after World War II, deliberately avoided arguing the legalisms of the 1921 Soviet-Iranian friendship treaty, which gave the USSR the right to intervene in Iran under certain conditions, and referred to Soviet withdrawal as a matter of equity and friendship between the two countries.

The Islamic Republic has had a contentious relationship with the law and legal issues. In its earliest years, the new authorities took drastic steps to eradicate the European-based legal system it had inherited from the Pahlavi era (1925–79) and attempted to replace it with something the new rulers believed was in accordance with Shia religious law. The new regime also undertook a wholesale purge of judges, lawyers, and prosecutors—especially women—and replaced them with clerics who were supposed to establish an "Islamic" and "revolutionary" legal system. The regime also sacked many members of the Iranian Foreign Service, who traditionally had brought strong legal qualifications to their work.

In such a setting, it is vital—although sometimes difficult—to establish what experts call "objective criteria" in a negotiation. The Islamic Republic, particularly in its most revolutionary and ideological moods, has often regarded what others call "international law" as a pretext for foreigners to cheat Iranians out of their rights. One expert, writing of "the historical distrust Iranians had for Western legalism," asks rhetorically, "Had treaty after treaty not proved that international law was simply a political device to ensure Western control?"[3] The test of an action, therefore, is not whether it conforms to some abstract notion of legality, but whether it can be presented as a victory for Islam and for Iran. Such criteria, of course, are subjective and ambiguous, and one group's victory is often presented as another group's betrayal.

The negotiator, therefore, should look for unambiguous, mutually agreeable standards that avoid legal jargon and technicalities. Legal arguments will often carry less weight with Iranians than with Americans. For the American side in a transaction, maintaining the integrity of the *process*—grounded on legal principles—is often crucial. For the Iranian side, that process is seen only as a means or an obstacle to achieving an all-important result. An Iranian visa applicant, for example, will probably have little interest in upholding the integrity of American immigration law. He or she will show genuine confusion if a visa officer protests indignantly ("You lied to me!") on discovering that the applicant lied.

There is an important distinction here. A lack of interest in points of law may at first suggest that the Iranian side is taking an emotional, subjective view of an issue while ignoring logic and objective factors. The reality is

3. See Ali Ansari, *Confronting Iran: The Failure of American Foreign Policy and the Next Great Crisis in the Middle East* (New York: Basic, 2006), 203.

not so simple. The emotional factors may be important, but the true motives of the Iranian side in a negotiation will sometimes be difficult to comprehend. Those motives may include a mixture of the political, personal, financial, and ideological. The outsider, lacking clear insight into these motivations, should be wary of taking refuge in the oversimplified and time-honored view of Iranians as emotional and incomprehensible (as opposed to "rational" Westerners). In so doing, one risks creating a self-fulfilling prophecy. Treated as irrational, the Iranian side in a negotiation is likely to become so.

3. The past matters: be aware of Iran's historical greatness, its recent weakness, and its grievances from decades or centuries earlier.
Iranians know well that in pre-Islamic times their country was a world power, ruled a large empire, and on several occasions defeated even the mighty armies of Rome. The Iranian plateau is covered with reminders of Iran's ancient glory, even if popular memory now associates those pre-Islamic monuments with mythological heroes such as Jamshid and Rostam rather than long-forgotten historical kings such as Cyrus and Darius. In more recent times—until the eighteenth century—Iran rivaled the neighboring Ottoman and Mogul Empires and could deal with the West on equal terms.

Beginning in the 1700s, however, Iran lost its great power status. It progressively surrendered territory and influence to outsiders, notably to Britain, Russia, and (later) the United States. The nineteenth century saw multiple humiliations for Iran: bankruptcy, military defeats, and losses of territory and authority in Afghanistan, Central Asia, and Transcaucasia. Foreigners gained control of Iran's finances and oil resources and even its security forces. Iran avoided overt colonial status only because British-Russian rivalry kept the country feeble but nominally independent. In the twentieth century, foreign powers formally divided Iran into spheres of influence (in the Anglo-Russian treaty of 1907), occupied the country (during both world wars), backed provincial separatist movements (in 1945–46), and frustrated Iranians' attempts to gain control of their own destiny by suppressing the Constitutional Movement (in 1906–11) and by overthrowing Prime Minister Mohammad Mossadegh's nationalist government (in 1953).

History, or at least some version of it, will be very much alive for Iranian counterparts. Iranians, like all of us, are captives of their history. In their case, however, that history is a very long and tragic one. What Iranians remember is likely to be some disastrous event that in the retelling has grown and transformed itself into near mythology. With such memories, suggesting that the Iranian interlocutor "forget the past," or "move on" is unlikely to meet with much success or response beyond puzzlement or hostility.

The Iranian side may never mention history explicitly (unlike Israeli prime minister Menachem Begin, whose one-hour meetings famously began with thirty minutes of Old Testament and twenty minutes of Holocaust, or Yasir Arafat, who loved to dwell on past injustices to the Palestinians to the exclusion of anything else). Depending on the Iranian negotiator's cultural orientation, however, one or more of the following events will have shaped his approach to the issue under discussion:

- the civil wars of early Islamic history, climaxing in the martyrdom of the prophet's grandson, Imam Hossein b. Ali, at Karbala in 680 CE;
- the Arab invasion and defeat of Iran's pre-Islamic Sassanian Empire in the seventh century CE;
- the constitutional revolution and its failure, 1906–11;
- the tripartite Allied (British, Soviet, and American) occupation of Iran, 1941–45;
- the foreign-backed separatist movements in Azerbaijan and Kurdistan, 1945–46;
- the overthrow of Prime Minister Mossadegh and the restoration of the Shah, 1953;
- the Islamic Revolution of 1978–79 and its bloody aftermath, including the Iran-Iraq War of 1980–88;
- the United States and others siding with Iraq during the Iran-Iraq War, and the downing of an Iranian civilian airliner by the USS *Vincennes* in July 1988.

Most of these events ended badly for Iranians (or at least for some Iranians) and have created a profound sense of national victimization and grievance that can still pollute the Iranian political atmosphere. Even where the events, in the view of some individuals, did not end badly, the lesson that Iranians often draw from their history is one of "us alone against a hostile world." As a result, Iranian counterparts may come to a negotiation with a view of their nation's history that has too often featured defeat, tragedy, victimization, and betrayal.

Can Iranian negotiators ever bury the past? Of course they can, if doing so serves some larger interest. As one observer recently noted, the Iranians, in an effort to mend fences with their Arab neighbors, appear willing to overlook the fact that Saudi Arabia and most of the Persian Gulf states were strong financial and logistical backers of Saddam Hussein's Iraq throughout the course of the bloody 1980–88 war. The Iranian side could always bring up that history again, but for the moment the need to normalize relations with those Arab states dictates putting aside (if not forgetting) historical grievances.

4. Choose intermediaries with great care.

In any negotiation, and especially in the absence of formal American-Iranian diplomatic relations, a trusted and skilled intermediary can be very useful. The Algerians—to whom each side could talk without making an apparent concession to the other—played such a positive role in the 1980–81 negotiations between the United States and Iran to end the U.S. embassy hostage crisis.

In contrast to such official, respectable intermediaries, the last twenty-eight years of American-Iranian contact have featured numerous self-appointed individuals and groups who will act on their own initiative from more questionable motives. As long as there are no official bilateral U.S.-Iranian relations, there will be no shortage of persons volunteering their services as channels to this or that influential person within the murky Iranian political universe. Everything about such persons and their claims, however, should be suspect: their contacts, their motives, their veracity, and their ability to deliver.

Such would-be intermediaries, however, know they have an American audience and often exploit it skillfully. They can play on the absence of official contact and on the known political leanings of their American listeners, tell them what they want to hear, and attempt to convince them, for example, that

- Iranians are seething with discontent and are ready to make a new revolution with outside support (especially financial) and encouragement.
- A particular ethnic group (e.g., Kurds or Azeris) or region (e.g., Baluchistan) is ready, with outside support, to make trouble for the central government.
- Most Iranians would welcome American efforts to overthrow the Islamic Republic, even by force if necessary.
- The leaders of the Islamic Republic are ready to moderate their policies and require only a "gesture" from the United States to show support for policies of some (imaginary) moderate Iranian faction.

U.S.-Iranian relations are littered with the wreckage of ill-judged attempts to use such intermediaries. The lawyers Christian Bourguet and Hector Villalon were doing a profitable business with Iran when they, offered their services as intermediaries during the 1979–81 hostage crisis. Eventually their efforts led nowhere because their Iranian contacts had no power beyond the doors of their own offices. The notorious wheeler-dealer Manouchehr Ghorbanifarr—teamed up with NSC staffer Oliver North—almost brought down an American president (Ronald Reagan) by manipulating and misrepresenting the views of all sides during the notorious arms-for-hostages deal of 1985. Despite Ghorbanifarr's well-documented shortcomings as an intermediary, some American officials continued to deal with him as late as 2002.

Such persons should be dealt with warily, if at all. They can and will drag their American contacts into the middle of Iranian political swamps and use them to gain respectability and further their own political and financial fortunes. We should be especially wary if such intermediaries claim disinterested or humanitarian motives and declare, "Of course I want nothing for myself. I just want to be of service to both countries." Any variation of the above statement is a clear warning to stay away.

5. Talk to the right people.

The unique and opaque structure of the Islamic Republic—with duplicating and conflicting authorities in a world of contentious and arcane internal politics—can make it very difficult to understand exactly who has authority and responsibility to reach agreements in any given area. The conventional wisdom, in dealing with the Islamic Republic, is "Everyone is in charge; no one is in charge." Rarely will the other side in any negotiation, however, announce that he or she is not authorized to make an agreement or does not have the power to carry out a commitment. That unpleasant news usually arrives only after one believes he has reached a deal.

The tempting explanation for such a breakdown may be "Oriental duplicity," but the reality is that one has probably been negotiating with the wrong people. The American negotiator should remember that there are parallel and sometimes competing governing structures within the Islamic Republic. There is a "republican" system, with a written constitution, a presidency, ministers, a parliament, and popular elections. Such a system is familiar to us, and resembles, at least in appearance, parliamentary and presidential systems in other countries. In this system, titles more or less reflect responsibilities, and fundamental laws will limit terms of office and establish mechanisms for accountability. The Iranian parliament, for example, must confirm nominated ministers, and can also dismiss them by votes of no-confidence.

Alongside this republican system, however, there exists a second "revolutionary," or "theocratic," structure that operates very differently and with substantial independence from the formal governmental structure. Controlling this system is a group of about twenty-five individuals, members of an elite inner circle who, with varying titles, have held the reins of power in the Islamic Republic since its beginnings in 1979.[4] This system evolved from the chaotic events of 1979–80, when the existing civil administration,

4. For further discussion of this elite, see John Limbert, *Iran: At War with History* (Boulder, Colo.: Westview Press), 145–149.

police, and military had collapsed and the new regime found itself in a struggle for power with ethnic separatists, armed militias, and dissidents from across the political spectrum. Distrusting those civil and military institutions it inherited from the monarchy, the victors of the revolution created new structures, such as the Revolutionary Guards (Iranian Revolutionary Guard Corps [IRGC]) as a private security force, the revolutionary courts to administer summary justice, and the *Ansar-e-Hezbollah* (literally, "the supporters of the Party of God") to be the enforcers and goon squads assigned to intimidate opponents and fight the vicious street battles of the time against nationalists, Marxists, and the hated liberals.

In the provinces, governors (employees of the Interior Ministry) found themselves overshadowed by the local "imam's representative" and Friday prayer leader (who was often the same person). During the Iran-Iraq War, the IRGC, established in 1979 as an internal security force and palace guard, was organized into major front-line units, eclipsing the role of the regular military. In the March–April 2007 crisis over detained British military personnel, it was clear that the IRGC's maritime units—not the Iranian navy—were the forces involved. Throughout this crisis, the role of the "official" Iranian government remained ambiguous.

6. Understand that the Islamic Republic's priority is survival.

Rightly or wrongly, Iran's leaders see themselves surrounded by enemies seeking the Islamic Republic's overthrow. They see American military forces in Afghanistan, Iraq, Turkey, and the Persian Gulf; they see hostile Sunnis in Saudi Arabia, Afghanistan, Pakistan, and elsewhere; they see hostile Arabs to the south and west; they see hostile Turkic peoples to the west and north; they see nuclear-armed states in India, Pakistan, and Israel; and they see hostile Azeri irredentists to the north and Kurdish separatists to the west. When these leaders hear terms like "regime change" and "axis of evil," such rhetoric confirms what they already suspect: that the United States is determined to overthrow the Islamic Republic, using subversion if possible and force if necessary.

Under these conditions, the leaders of Iran will do what they believe they must do to ensure their regime's survival. With survival at stake, they will vacillate between extremes of concession and brutality. Near the end of the Iran-Iraq War, in June 1988, for example, they suddenly executed hundreds of political prisoners—some of whom had already served their sentences—for reasons still unclear. Although willing to sacrifice thousands of their country's young men in the swamps of Khuzestan and southern Iraq during the 1980–88 war, Iran's leaders were not ready to sacrifice themselves and their positions. In August 1988 they thus accepted a humiliating peace deal with Iraq when they realized further fighting threatened to bring down the entire Islamic Republic. They will make alliances with the non-Islamic

(Armenia), anti-Islamic (Russia), and godless (North Korea) at the expense of their fellow Muslims in Azerbaijan and Chechnya. They allied themselves with Libya's Muammar Qaddafi and overlooked his role in eliminating Lebanese Shia leader Imam Musa Sadr. They will support terrorist groups and operations to eliminate dissidents abroad. Believing Iran vulnerable to a Czech-style "Velvet Revolution," they will lash out and arrest, imprison, harass, and murder domestic opponents, including women, harmless dissidents, and intellectuals whom they somehow see as a threat. Then, when driven to the wall, they will make sudden reversals of policy, as they did when, despite their earlier defiant statements, they accepted a cease-fire with Iraq in 1988.

Facing this suspicious view of the world from his Iranian counterpart, the American negotiator has both a problem and an opportunity. On the negative side, the American negotiator will encounter a wall of suspicion and mistrust from an Iranian counterpart who assumes that America's ultimate purpose in dealing with Iran is to destroy the Islamic Republic. On the positive side, a negotiation can progress well if one can convince or reassure the Iranian side that its agreement to an action will not destabilize the Islamic Republic and may, in fact, help it survive. Tehran's cooperation with the United States during the 2001–02 negotiations on Afghanistan is a case in point. At that time, the Iranians knew very well how they would benefit from the downfall of the Taliban and from their replacement by a government that did not subscribe to a radical anti-Shia and anti-Iranian ideology. Similar considerations should apply in the case of Iraq, where the Islamic Republic, in the interest of its own survival, shares the American aversion to a divided Iraq, a Iraq dominated by Sunni extremists, or an Iraq under a new version of Saddam Hussein.

7. Let the Iranians define what is in their national interest.

Iranians do not appreciate hearing lectures from others on what is logical and what is in *their* (i.e., Iranians') self-interest. Misreading Iranian interests has led to serious problems in the past, when, for example, American policymakers in 1979 assumed that Iran's basic economic and security interests would limit the new regime's anti-American actions to rhetoric and symbolism. Such an analysis may have been correct as far as it went, but it failed to consider the interests of subgroups and factions in provoking a confrontation and sabotaging any possibility of a normal relationship between the United States and the new government in Tehran. In 1979–80, such groups ridiculed the whole idea of "national interest" and, by creating an atmosphere of hysteria and fear, ensured the ultimate victory of radical, absolutist religious factions in the revolutionary coalition over their nationalist and leftist rivals.

The Iranian representative in a negotiation knows very well what serves his national, partisan, family, and personal interests. Such interests may differ—and may even contradict—what an outsider, largely unaware of the factional infighting in progress, decides is in Iran's "national interest," a concept that has been enormously suspect since the 1979 revolution.[5]

The same consideration applies to logic and illogic. An American negotiator should be wary of seeing himself or herself as the only logical side at the table and of dismissing the Iranian as the illogical and emotional party. As noted earlier, viewing the Iranian side as irrational can become a self-fulfilling prophecy. In many cases, however, the Iranian side is using a logic that the American side cannot penetrate—a logic perhaps dictated by an instinct for personal survival and by political and social forces poorly understood by outsiders.

8. Understand the Iranian BATNA: Expect actions that may appear (to you) self-destructive.

American negotiators should never convince themselves, "The Iranians will never be so foolish as to do *x*." In the past, that statement has often been a guarantee that they will do precisely *x*, driven not by foolishness, but, as noted above, by a logic that the outside observer does not understand. In commercial dealings, for example, informants often report that Iranians are willing to sabotage an entire deal rather than make some minor concession. Some experts say that Iran's refusal to negotiate seriously with foreign partners on oil and natural gas contracts has stopped crucial investments and has damaged that sector's ability to maintain long-term supply and revenues.

In negotiation with Iranians, as in all negotiations, it is vital to be aware of the other side's best alternative to a negotiated agreement, or BATNA,[6] as well as one's own. The Iranian BATNA may be difficult to predict. In some cases, the Iranian counterpart may be afraid to make *any* agreement lest he come under criticism from political adversaries at home for "selling out" to the foreigner. Some historians, for example, argue that Prime Minister Mossadegh rejected compromise settlements of the 1951–53 Anglo-Iranian oil nationalization dispute out of fear that his domestic political opponents would accuse him of surrendering to foreign interests. Such an analysis maintains, in effect, that Iranian domestic politics forced Mossadegh into taking self-destructive actions.

---

5. Iranian opponents of President Ahmadinezhad, for example, criticize him for goading the Western countries in a way that does not serve Iran's national interests. For his part, Ahmadinezhad might compare his rhetoric to earlier statements by Imam Khomeini in which he subordinated national interest to pan-Islamic ideals.

6. The term was coined by Roger Fisher and William Ury in *Getting to Yes: Negotiating Agreement without Giving In* (Boston: Houghton Mifflin, 1981).

In other cases, the Iranian negotiator may not have the power to make any reasonable agreement, and the negotiation may itself become an exercise in futility. He may also, in a commercial negotiation for example, be seeking a bribe, either for himself or on behalf of a patron, to close the deal. Finally, he may be what the Iranians call *mard-e-rendi*, someone who outsmarts himself though pursuing short-term gain with a single-mindedness that blinds him to larger issues at stake. Although Iranians have a term for this kind of negotiator, they often impute it to others on whom they look down. Asked about this trait, a senior Iranian official complained to me that being *mard-e-rendi* (sometimes made stronger and called *khar* [donkey] *mard-e-rendi*) was an annoying characteristic of Indians and Pakistanis!

9. Give your Iranian counterparts credit for intelligence.

Iranians have a long history of being treated as simple-minded and as incapable of drawing obvious conclusions from available evidence. When Britain and Russia, for example, signed the treaty that divided Persia into spheres of influence in 1907, the preamble to their agreement stated that both parties pledged to respect Persian independence and territorial integrity. As one contemporary British observer put it, "Such statements are a sure sign that a country is about to lose both its territorial integrity and its independence." In October 1979 the American administration thought it could somehow placate Iranian public opinion by announcing that the United States was admitting the deposed Shah for medical treatment and for purely humanitarian reasons. The American administration may have accepted such a statement. Given the history of Iranian-American relations, however, no Iranian cognizant of that history would have believed it. The statement, rather than reassure its Iranian audience, insulted its intelligence and seemed to confirm what many, in the highly-charged atmosphere of late 1979, already suspected: that the United States was plotting against the revolution and was looking to restage the events of 1953.

In a similar way, most Iranians were perceptive enough to see the reality behind Mohammad Reza Shah's pretensions to power. They saw the regime's flashy parades, expensive military hardware, uniforms, statues, and ceremonies for what they were—the ornate exterior of a hollow shell. They understood the empty reality behind the monarchy's showy exterior, and understood the profound insecurity lying just below the surface.

Although the Shah was skilled at deceiving outsiders, he found it difficult to deceive his own people, who knew he owed his position to foreign backing and that he depended on continued foreign support to stay in power. The extent of that dependence became obvious in 1964, when the United States pressured the Shah and his submissive parliament into accepting changes in the existing American-Iranian Status of Forces Agreement (SOFA), expanding the number of resident American military advisers (and their family members) enjoying immunity from Iranian legal jurisdiction. At the time, the United States presented the change as no more than a "technical adjustment" to the existing agreement. To most Iranians, however, the new agreement was just further evidence of their country's degradation and of the Shah's complete subjugation of Iranian pride and sovereignty to the will of the Americans. Even the obedient parliament had great difficulty swallowing this particular humiliation.[7]

10. Expect a case based on vague and uncertain claims.
Lacking in diplomatic expertise and a well-trained cadre of support staff, rarely will the Iranian side be equipped with facts, figures, maps, and precedents to make its case. It is likely to rely on ill-defined historical claims or on appeals to "justice" (see point 13 below). Although some observers have noted the Iranian elite's ability to reproduce itself despite political turmoil, the Islamic Republic has yet to recover from the policies and purges of its early years. At that time, the new regime openly distrusted its experts, who it saw as insufficiently ideological (*maktabi*), and deliberately encouraged much of the country's intelligentsia—unable to adapt to the nation's new and harsh social realities under a theocratic system—to emigrate. What remained were slogans, a cultural revolution, and a lingering mistrust of intellectuals and technocrats as representing alien, decadent, and "non-Islamic" values.

The Islamic Republic associated technical expertise with the old regime. In October 1979, for example, one heard the cry at rallies, "As for those carping intellectuals, we will break their pens!" (or their legs, depending on the translation of the Persian *qalam*). The new, revolutionary regime preferred to put ideologues in charge of ministries, where true belief in the new theocracy outweighed training and qualifications. The result was a social and cultural revolution in which a generation of inexperienced "new men" took positions of influence and marginalized those tainted by travel, foreign education, and association with the old regime. The Islamic Republic quickly purged the foreign ministry, for example, of its experienced professionals, and replaced it by inexperienced radicals, including those who had learned their diplomacy by capturing and holding the staff of the U.S. embassy in 1979–81.

11. Expect grandstanding, political theater, and flamboyant gestures.
Much of what happens in Iran's political life includes a large element of theater. During the 1980–88 Iran-Iraq War, for example, the media would show ordinary citizens donating jewelry and other valuables for the war and mothers saying how happy they were to have their sons martyred for

7. Ayatollah Khomeini established his nationalist credentials with Iranians by his outspoken opposition to this agreement. His blunt criticism of the SOFA led to the Shah's sending him into exile, where he remained until early 1979.

the cause. During political conflict partisans will parade purportedly martyred bodies through the streets in noisy processions in order to stir up pride and anger. The mourning ceremonies marking the holiest days of Shia Islam often feature music, chanting, costumes, animals, and elaborate displays. When students seized the U.S. embassy in November 1979, they saw themselves making a "gesture" against the United States without much thought about consequences or what came next. When President Ahmadinezhad announced the release of the British military captives in April 2007, he described the action as a "gesture of friendship" to the British people.

In such a setting, the appearance and the grand gesture can replace substance, and the American negotiator needs to sort out which is which. The equivalent of bumper stickers can replace policy. Iran's political discourse often features fiery rhetoric, slogans, and words like "never," "to the death," and "not one inch." Even the feeble and bankrupt Qajar monarchs of the nineteenth century, while presiding over their country's collapse, portrayed themselves as mighty conquerors and heirs to the great Iranian kings of history and mythology with titles such as "he to whom the world directs its prayers" (*qebleh-ye-alam*). During the conflicts of the early twentieth century, fiery telegrams and petitions flew around the country as citizens pledged to defend the new Iranian constitution to the death. When matters got difficult, however, the thousands of would-be defenders of the constitution weighed their options and made themselves scarce, joining what Iranians call the "party of the winds" (*hezb-e-baad*).

Khomeini himself was a master of defiant rhetoric. During the 1979–81 hostage crisis, his memorable statement "America can't do a damn thing" (a polite translation of a much cruder Persian original) immediately appeared on hundreds of walls and banners throughout the country. In 1981, in a fit of anti-British pique, the Iranians renamed Churchill Avenue near the British embassy for martyr Bobby Sands, the IRA operative who had starved himself to death in a British prison. In an ironic sequel to that incident, a British reporter in Tehran in 2007 describes having a meal at the "Bobby Sands Snack Bar" near the British embassy.

Such rhetorical gestures and flourishes can sometimes become policy and lock the Iranians into uncomfortable and even self-destructive positions. The slogan "War, war, until victory" meant that thousands of Iranians became victims of their leaders' rhetoric, and died pursuing a pointless conflict with Iraq after Tehran rejected the opportunity for a favorable settlement in 1982. In the late-1980s, as revolutionary fervor cooled, the reminder, "Don't forget 'Death of America' " would appear on Tehran walls, a tacit admission of the end of revolutionary enthusiasm. The Islamic Republic spent years untangling itself from the effects of Khomeini's 1989 famous ruling ordering the death of the British writer Salman Rushdie for the heretical views expressed in his novel *The Satanic Verses*.

12. Remember that power is respected, weakness despised.
Iranians may fear Aesop's merciless King Stork, but they detest quiescent King Log. A recurring theme of Iranian history is the respect accorded strong leaders—even bloodthirsty ones—who are able to check the powerful centrifugal forces in the society. Public order has always been very precarious in Iran, and a powerful ruler is seen as the only safeguard against the anarchy that is always lurking in the wings. Iran has seen recurring social and economic collapse when there is no strong ruler in charge. Tribes, ethnic groups, the clergy, urban mobs, external enemies, and opportunistic politicians are always ready to challenge current authorities. The pious, weak, and ineffective last ruler of the Safavid dynasty (1500–1722), Shah Sultan Hussein (1694–1722), is still Iranians' proverbial King Log, the feeble leader who brings the country to ruin and collapse. The contrast is the seventh-century Caliph Omar, who, although hated by Shia Muslims as a usurper, earns grudging admiration as a strong, harsh, decisive, and effective ruler. Both of these rulers' names have entered the common language as symbols of weak and strong leadership.

Connected to the above is another recurring theme of Iranian history: leadership is always personal and always charismatic. Ayatollah Khomeini drew a huge personal following when he was seen as a savior of Iran and Islam. Although some convinced themselves he would withdraw to his mosque to teach and study after the victory of the revolutionary forces in February 1979, the realities of Iran's political culture meant that he could never leave to others the business of governing. As long as he was alive, he remained the final authority, and no one—not a president, a prime minister, or anyone else—could exercise any meaningful power. In such an environment, American attempts in 1979 to deal with revolutionary Iran through the nationalist technocrats of the Provisional Government were doomed to failure when it became obvious that the real power Iran did not lie with officials carrying ministerial titles.

Similarly, after the moderate and scholarly Mohammad Khatami became president of Iran in 1997, many Iranians saw him as their country's savior after the years of postrevolutionary austerity and violence. When President Khatami proved unable to fulfill those high expectations, his prestige plummeted as Iranians felt that they had been deceived into electing a new version of Shah Sultan Hussein. By the end of his second term in 2005, many Iranians dismissed not only Khatami but the entire reform movement as a collection of feckless, squabbling intellectuals who were no match for those tough ideologues who had cut their teeth in the street battles, political infighting, and gang warfare of the 1980s and 1990s.

The Iranian respect for power does not mean that an American negotiator can rely on threats and intimidation to make his or her case. That respect means only that the Iranian side will well understand the multiple pressures—internal and external—that impel them to accept or reject a particular offer. In response to an American proposal, the Iranian side will calculate—rightly or wrongly—how much pressure (of all kinds) lies behind the proposal, and that degree of pressure will become part of the calculation of response.[8]

13. Understand that justice, often in a harsh version, in the abstract is extremely important.

From ancient times Iranian history has abounded in references to *dād* and *adl*, two words for "justice," both closely associated with *din* (religion). Shia Islam even adds divine justice (*adl*), along with the imamate, to the three fundamental elements of religion—divine unity, prophethood, and resurrection—that it shares with Sunni Islam.

In a negotiation, the Iranian side may therefore frame its demands, not in specific, or quantitative terms, but in terms that claim, "All we are seeking is justice," or "We want our rights." For Ayatollah Khomeini, for example, such justice meant assigning blame and punishing the guilty party in a dispute. In this spirit, he once told a visiting Non-Aligned Movement team seeking to mediate a settlement to the Iran-Iraq War that its true "mediation" mission was to visit both Iran and Iraq, examine what had happened, and determine which of the warring parties had right and justice on its side. "If we are wrong, then condemn us. But if they are wrong, then condemn them. *Justice demands you do this*" (author's emphasis).[9]

Justice in the Iranian context can be harsh and not always tempered by mercy. The Persian proverb says, *Zolm bessaviyeh adl ast*, "Injustice equally applied equals justice." With a fragile society, a violent history, and foreign and domestic enemies always ready to take advantage of weakness, many Iranians believe that justice should be quick, decisive, and visible. After the victory of the 1979 revolution, for example, there was little interest among the victors in long and carefully prepared trials for the vanquished. Despite an international outcry against the rapid verdicts and procedural shortcuts of the revolutionary courts, "justice"—in that context—demanded swift and visible punishment of the guilty (or even the innocent). A nationalist minister in the Iranian provisional government of 1979 rejected the American chargé's argument that the summary justice and verdicts of the revolutionary courts were harming Iran's image. The minister replied, "If we had had faster trials and more executions in 1953, then maybe the CIA couldn't have overthrown Mossadegh."[10]

---

8. There is a often-quoted statement (of uncertain origin) that says, "Iranians will never give in to pressure. They will give in only to a lot of pressure."

9. Cited in Limbert, *Iran: At War with History*, 141.

10. Author's memory of Laingen-Foruhar meeting, Tehran, October 1979.

14. Remember that conspiracy theories have great currency—and are sometimes true.

Iranians seem unable to accept simple and straightforward explanations of events. The complex account is preferred, if only because it is more interesting and creative. Behind the surface of events, Iranians often see hidden hands pulling strings and manipulating the world to some subtle and malevolent purpose. To some royalist Iranians, for example, Iran's 1978–79 Islamic Revolution was the product of foreign conspiracies to remove a Shah who had become too powerful and too independent-minded for the taste of his Western friends. According to one version of this theory, President Carter and his allies no longer saw the Shah as a reliable buffer against Soviet expansion, and sought to replace him with a "green belt" of Islamic regimes, which could better resist the godless Communists.

While some of the conspiracy theories may appear absurd, behind them lies a deeper reality. Iranians have often been subject to historical forces out of their control or comprehension, whether from the brutal Mongols in the thirteenth century or the manipulating British and Russians in the nineteenth and twentieth. These forces were never benevolent, and were willing to use violence, terror, bribery, and subversion—including recruiting Iranian agents—in pursuit of their ends and in destroying Iranians' attempts to control their own destiny.

The model of modern conspiracies turned out to be true. The CIA *did* manipulate and bribe Iranians to bring about the downfall of the nationalist Prime Minister Mossadegh in August 1953. Although historians still argue about the details of what happened during those events, no one disputes that the CIA played a central role in toppling the popular prime minister and restoring the weakened Pahlavi monarch. Given that history, it was hardly surprising that twenty-six years later Iranians found it hard to accept the American explanation that in October 1979 the exiled Mohammad Reza Shah was coming to the United States "only for medical treatment." In the hysterical postrevolutionary atmosphere of 1979 and in the prevailing chaos inside Iran, those Iranians predisposed to see conspiracies could easily find signs of a new U.S.-sponsored plot to create instability, restage the events of 1953, and undo the revolution.

15. Expect hands to be overplayed.

The Iranian side may push a small or momentary advantage to a point beyond calculations of gain and loss. Many Iranians attach a negative connotation to the adjective "calculating" (*hesabgar*), which implies that someone is willing to sacrifice principles, friendships, or feelings for material gain. At times of political stress, Iranians can appear to discard calculation of advantage and disadvantage and become captives of unrealistic, rigid positions and extremist rhetoric.

During the 1979–81 hostage crisis, for example, the Islamic Republic felt that possession of the American embassy staff gave it an advantage over a U.S. government determined to destroy the revolutionary regime and replace it with either a restored monarchy or something else more friendly to American interests. Rather than calculate their country's long-term interests—which would have demanded a quick end to the crisis and would have reinforced the international credentials of the new Islamic Republic—the country's leaders, bolstered by mass demonstrations of support for the students' action, felt themselves able (or perhaps compelled) to defy the world. Many of the former hostage-takers have since said that they lost control over events and have justified their action as a product of the "revolutionary fury" that gripped Iran in those days. It is worth noting, however, that during the anti-Shah disturbances of 1978–79, the revolutionaries were usually very careful to avoid targeting foreigners. At that time, at least, they knew the value of favorable press in Europe and the United States—a press that could enlist world opinion on their side.

After capturing American personnel, Iran pushed its temporary advantage to an extent that eventually cost hundreds of thousands of Iranian lives and almost destroyed the country. When Saddam Hussein's Iraqi forces attacked Iran in September 1980, Tehran found itself, thanks to having overplayed its hand and alienated potential supporters, with very few friends willing to admit that, in all fairness, Iran was in this case the victim and Iraq the aggressor. In 1982, after Iranian forces won a major victory and expelled the Iraqis from the port at Khorramshahr, Saddam offered Iran a peace based on the *status quo ante*. Urged on by Imam Khomeini's rhetoric, however, the Iranian side felt it could press its momentary advantage (under the slogan "war, war, until victory") to bring about the final defeat of its enemy. The results were six more years of carnage, poison gas warfare, and, finally, a humiliating acceptance of a U.N.-brokered cease-fire in 1988.

In such a setting it is crucial for the American negotiator to be patient, remain focused on the issues under discussion, and not be drawn into debating dead-ends. If one sees the other side is overplaying its hand, the best response is to ask, "Please explain why are you demanding this?" "On what basis are you asking for that?" "How did you come to that figure?" In such a setting, establishing objective criteria that both sides can accept will be vital. Sometimes mediation or arbitration by an impartial body (such as the Hague Tribunal for adjudicating financial claims) can be a useful mechanism to counter what may appear to be unreasonable demands. In late 1980, when Deputy Secretary of State Warren Christopher received a message from the Iranians that tripled their monetary demands for the release of the American hostages to $24 billion, he persevered in the negotiations and eventually those demands were dropped.[11]

11. Warren Christopher, "Welcome to the Bazaar," *Los Angeles Times*, June 13, 2006.

No Sure Thing

What works in any negotiation—being prepared, building relationships, exercising patience, knowing both one's own and the other side's BATNA, understanding the other side's real interests, among other things—can work in negotiations with the Islamic Republic. Such was the experience of Americans and Iranians in 2001–02 during negotiations over Afghanistan following the fall of the Taliban. Both sides have described the other as professional, businesslike, and, most important, free of the negative preconceptions that have sabotaged so many attempts at dialogue.

The negotiators who apply the above principles *can* reach an agreement—but they may not. Even the above guidelines are no guarantee of productive contacts.[12] As noted, both Americans and Iranians too often arrive at the negotiating table burdened with preconceptions, grievances, ignorance, resentment, and the opinion—based on a special reading of history—that the other side is deceptive, infinitely crafty, and will, in the end, reveal its true nature in hostility, treachery, and lies.

The first thing to do is to define carefully what is "successful" and "productive" in a negotiation. Of course the American side would like to see the Islamic Republic end its suspicious nuclear program, cease supporting terrorist movements, announce its backing for a negotiated Middle East peace settlement, end its supply of deadly weapons to Iraqi militias, and treat its own people, particularly its women, with decency. For the Iranian side, the ideal outcome is that the United States lifts economic sanctions, stops supporting Iranian dissidents, ends talk of "regime change," and removes the Islamic Republic from the American government's list of state sponsors of terrorism.

Such happy outcomes, however, will not be the result of at least the first, second, or even third meetings. Expectations for productive results in these initial meetings should be more modest: recognition of potential common interest—in Iraq or Afghanistan, for example, and that it is worthwhile to sit at the table for discussions free of accumulated rancor and rhetoric. Given the unfortunate history of the U.S.-Iranian relationship for the past twenty-eight years, such discussions would represent a major step forward. In the current climate, it would be more than fair to describe such negotiations, whatever their immediate outcome, as productive.

---

12. Even that master of negotiation Professor Roger Fisher (the author of *Getting to Yes*) admitted to his Harvard Law School class in January 1991 that his contacts with Iranian senior officials during the crisis were fruitless.

About the Editors

Daniel Brumberg is acting director of USIP's Muslim World Initiative, associate professor of government at Georgetown University, and codirector of Georgetown's Democracy and Governance Studies program. He has written extensively about issues of political, social, and economic change in Muslim polities, and has pursued research in Egypt, Morocco, Jordan, Algeria, Kuwait, Saudi Arabia, and Indonesia. He is author of *Reinventing Khomeini: The Struggle for Reform Iran* and coeditor (with Larry Diamond and Marc Plattner) of *Islam and Democracy in the Middle East*. He is also author of the *Washington Post/Newsweek* weekly blog, Islam and the West.

Dina Shehata is a senior researcher at Al Ahram Center for Political and Strategic Studies. She previously worked as a special adviser for USIP's Muslim World Initiative.

Contributors

Mohammed Abu-Nimer was a 2007–08 Jennings Randolph fellow.

Judy Barsalou was the director of the USIP Grant program and vice president of the Grants and Fellowships program from 2000 to 2007.

Dorina A. Bekoe is a senior program officer in USIP's Center for Conflict Analysis and Prevention.

Steven A. Cook was a contributor to Muriel Asseburg and Daniel Brumberg (eds.), *The Challenge of Islamists for EU and US Policies: Conflict, Stability, and Reform*, a joint publication of the German Institute for International and Security Affairs (SWP) and USIP.

Rend Al-Rahim Francke is a 2008–09 Jennings Randolph Iraq fellow.

Iris Glosemeyer was a senior researcher for the Arab Political Oppositions Project of USIP's Muslim World Initiative from 2005 to 2007.

Pierre Hazan was a 2005–06 Jennings Randolph fellow.

Steven Heydemann is the vice president of USIP's Grant and Fellowships program and is a special adviser to the Muslim World Initiative.

Qamar-ul Huda is a senior program officer in USIP's Religion and Peacemaking program.

Thomas H. Johnson was a contributor to the USIP Press book *Interim Governments: Institutional Bridges to Peace and Democracy?* edited by Karen Guttieri and Jessica Piombo.

John W. Limbert is author of the USIP Press book *Negotiating with Iran: Wrestling the Ghosts of History*.

Abdeslam M. Maghraoui was director of USIP's Muslim World Initiative from 2004 to 2007.

Jonathan Morrow was senior adviser to USIP's Rule of Law program from 2004 to 2006.

Ahmad S. Moussalli was a recipient of a USIP research grant.

Hesham Sallam is a program specialist in USIP's Center for Conflict Analysis and Prevention.

David R. Smock is the vice president of the Center for Mediation and Conflict Resolution and associate vice president of the Religion and Peacemaking program at USIP.

Mohammad Masoom Stanekzai was a 2007–08 Jennings Randolph fellow.

Annette Weber was a contributor to Muriel Asseburg and Daniel Brumberg (eds.), *The Challenge of Islamists for EU and US Policies: Conflict, Stability, and Reform*, a joint publication of SWP and USIP.

Mona Yacoubian is a special adviser to USIP's Muslim World Initiative.

Board of Directors